DAVID GRANICK

Enterprise Guidance in Eastern Europe

A Comparison of

Four Socialist Economies

Princeton University Press

Princeton, New Jersey

Library of Congress Cataloging in Publication Data will
be found on the last printed page of this book

This book has been composed in Linotype Times Roman

Printed in the United States of America
by Princeton University Press, Princeton, New Jersey

To my parents, Harry and Ray,
who tried to teach me to combine
empathy and objectivity

CONTENTS

ROMANIA

G.D.R.

HUNGARY

YUGOSLAVIA

MANAGERS

LIST OF FIGURES

ROMANIA

G.D.R.

THIS book is a result of field research carried out during 1970-71 in eastern Europe. The support of many institutions, and the aid of innumerable individuals, was essential to the carrying out of this research.

Primary financial support was provided by the International Development Research Center of Indiana University. I am indebted to the two chairmen of the Center, George Stolnitz and William Siffin, as well as to Paul Marer, for their support throughout the study.

Interviews in Romania and Hungary were carried out under the auspices of an exchange agreement between the American International Research and Exchanges Board (IREX) and the Romanian National Council for Scientific Research and the Hungarian Institute for Cultural Relations. The Romanian Council and the Hungarian Institute also acted as my immediate hosts in their own countries, going to a great deal of trouble to arrange interviews with people in industry. Financial support was provided by all three agencies.

My host agency in the German Democratic Republic was the Economic Research Institute of the State Planning Commission; in Yugoslavia it was the Ljubljana Chamber of Commerce. I am especially indebted to these organizations for making possible my research in their countries, since neither was operating under an exchange agreement or other exchange relationship. The generosity of the Economic Research Institute of the East German State Planning Commission should be particularly noted, in view of the absence at that time of diplomatic relations between our two countries.

The Romanian Management Development Center (then known as CEPECA) allowed me to attend classes for senior industrial managers, and provided autobiographic vitae on all of the students in its top management classes of 1970. These vitae have been an invaluable source of information as to the backgrounds of Romanian upper managers in industry.

The Österreichisches Institut für Wirtschaftsforschung, its director Professor Franz Nemschak, and the relevant subunit's directors Peter Knirsch and Kazimierz Laski, provided me with a most useful and enjoyable base in central Europe during my European stay.

Supplementary financial aid for this study was provided by the American Philosophical Society, the Business School of Indiana University, the Graduate School of the University of Wisconsin from special funds voted by the State Legislature, and by the University of Wisconsin's International Studies and Programs Division.

Jacob Naor was my research assistant for one year, and aided significantly in the preparation of materials. The secretarial pool of my own Department has been most helpful in typing the first draft of the manuscript. The Netherlands Institute for Advanced Study in the Humanities and Social Sciences provided me with time for the final stages of preparing the manuscript for publication. Delight Ansley prepared the Index.

While it is impossible to acknowledge the help of all individuals who have advised me regarding this book, the counsel of Ichak Adizes, Frederic Pryor, and Josip Županov can and deserve to be mentioned. Of course, neither they nor any other of the commentators on my drafts bear any responsibility for the facts or interpretations reported here. In particular, it would be quite unwarranted to assume that readers of my draft who are natives of the socialist countries studied necessarily agree with those points regarding which they did not raise specific objections.

I am grateful to the following journals for permission to use materials which they originally published in articles of mine:

"La planification centrale de l'industrie en Roumanie," *Revue de l'Est* (of the Centre National de la Recherche Scientifique), iv, 2 (April 1973).

"The Hungarian Economic Reform," *World Politics*, xxv, 3 (April 1973).

"The Orthodox Model of the Socialist Enterprise in the Light of Romanian Experience," *Soviet Studies*, xxvi, 2 (April 1974).

My principal acknowledgment has been reserved for last. The willingness of senior and middle industrial managers in all four of the countries I have studied to provide me with endless hours of interviews in the midst of very busy work schedules, and their patience with my questions, with my inadequate use of a language often foreign both to interviewer and interviewee, and with the difficulties inherent in the use of interpreters, went far and beyond the call of duty. I hope that they will find this study to have warranted their efforts; the open-mindedness displayed by most of them leads me to believe that they will not reject it simply on ideological grounds or because of criticisms which I make of their countries' economic systems.

ENTERPRISE GUIDANCE IN

EASTERN EUROPE

LIST OF ABBREVIATIONS
OF SECONDARY SOURCES

ABSEES *Soviet and East European Abstracts Series* (National Association for Soviet and East European Studies: University of Glasgow)

JPS United States Government, *Joint Publications Service*, Translations on Eastern Europe, Economic and Industrial Affairs

JTS *Joint Translation Service* (Bulletin of the United States and United Kingdom embassies: Belgrade)

RFE *Radio Free Europe Research*

SYSTEM OF REFERENCE TO SOURCES

The first reference in the footnotes *within each chapter* to a given source is made in complete form. The same holds true for the first reference in the tables *within each chapter*.

THIS book is a comparative study of the contemporary management of industry in four socialist countries: Romania, the German Democratic Republic (G.D.R.), Hungary, and Yugoslavia. It is essentially ahistorical and gives no systematic attention to the evolution of the management systems of these countries.

Management of industry is defined here as consisting of the methods used throughout all levels of the national management apparatus, from the Council of Ministers to the individual factory, to achieve stated objectives. Starting from the view that, in all of these socialist economies except Yugoslavia, industry as a whole may be viewed as though it were administered as a single organization, national variations in the degree of concentration of authority at the center are treated as differences in management methods: i.e., in planning and control techniques. A similar perspective is adopted with regard to incentives, whether these take the form of bonuses or of career opportunities.

The objectives of top national management are excluded from the study, being taken as givens which the existing managerial system is intended to realize. Thus, for example, no interest will be shown in decisions as to the rate of total industrial investment or the relative growth rates of different sectors of industry. Similarly, since the emphasis is upon interactions of decisions of management at different levels of the national organizations, there will be no treatment of techniques which are restricted to a single level of the organization. Therefore integration of financial and physical planning on a national level will be ignored, as will also the various forms of input-output techniques intended to guide central decision makers in determining the output programs for different industrial sectors.

The three countries belonging to the Council for Mutual Economic Assistance or Comecon (hereafter called CMEA) share the common ingredient of central national planning. In all three, basic economic decision making is carried out at a single national center. This is not, however, the case in Yugoslavia, where genuine autonomy exists at the enterprise level. The binding economic dogmas of Yugoslavia are self-management and workers' management, and these create a unique set of conditions for the coordination of industry.

The focus of the study consists of the variations in management (as defined above) which have resulted from the three different kinds of economic reforms introduced in the G.D.R., Hungary, and Yugoslavia during the second half of the 1960's. How have the reforms worked out in the actual operation of industry? What is the significance of the G.D.R.'s devolution of central authority, of Hungary's attempt to exercise central control through financial mechanisms rather than through direct instructions to enterprises, and of Yugoslavia's almost total renunciation of the national government's authority to direct the economy? How do all three compare with Romania, where the level of centralization seems much greater than that ever attained in the Soviet Union?

In all four countries, the enterprise will generally be the lowest organizational unit of analysis. This means that little will be said as to the control exercised over individual factories by the enterprise, or over individual shops by the factory; similarly, efforts by organizational subunits within the enterprise to act in their own self-interest will normally not be treated. In the G.D.R. and Romania, larger units—the *Kombinat* and the *centrala* respectively—will often be taken as the lowest level of organization; this is because of the tendency in both countries to eliminate the legal independence formerly given to enterprises now consolidated within these organizational bodies. This does not mean, however, that relationships among decision makers within the enterprise will be totally ignored; these relationships will be given particular attention in Yugoslavia where the significance of workers' management will be a major focus of analysis.

The prime source for the book consists of what is probably a unique experience: eleven months of interviewing (between February 1970 and July 1971), the overwhelming majority of which was spent with people holding managerial posts in the four countries. I believe that these interviews provide a base for realism of analysis which is impossible to derive solely from the literature of the countries concerned. In addition to these interviews, the available literature and statistical handbooks have also been used extensively; these have been followed through 1972, and major changes from the situation in 1970-71 are noted in the course of the study. National statistics are mostly cited through 1970 or 1971, the precise date depending upon the latest year for which figures were available at the time of writing. Where extension to a later date (through 1973) was deemed likely to change the results, this was done.

The eleven months of interviews were concentrated primarily at the level of the enterprise (including here the *Kombinat* and the *centrala*). In Romania and the G.D.R., and to a minimal extent in Hungary, interviews were also conducted in bodies which supervise the enterprises examined; in this way, the same problems and actions were seen from the vantage point of different organizational levels. Interviews were also arranged in the State Planning Commissions, banks, customer organizations such as the Ministries of Domestic and Foreign Trade, and among academics.

In each enterprise studied, an effort was made to speak with the Communist Party and trade union secretaries as well as with managerial personnel. This effort was most successful in Yugoslavia and Romania, least so in Hungary. Some discussions were also held with Party and trade union leaders at regional and national levels; only in Hungary was I totally unsuccessful in arranging these. Nevertheless, it cannot be claimed that my study is particularly illuminating concerning the influence of Party and trade union officials on managerial behavior.

In all countries, enterprises from both consumer and producer goods' industries were selected, and in all countries these firms represented a reasonably wide spectrum of priority in the eyes of the national leadership. The people choosing the enterprises to be studied promised to be guided by my criterion that they should not choose either the best- or the worst-managed firms; my impression is that in fact they respected this criterion, although doubtless I saw a better-than-average sample. In Romania, I was to a very large extent able to pick the specific firms which I wished to visit. This was not possible in the G.D.R. or Hungary, and did not seem desirable in Yugoslavia.

The number of firms visited in each country differed substantially, from Yugoslavia (eleven) and Romania (nine) to Hungary (five) and the G.D.R. (four). My prime objective was intensive interviewing in each firm rather than covering a large number of organizations. With some exceptions in Yugoslavia and Romania and one exception in the G.D.R., I was given sixteen to forty hours of managerial interviews in each enterprise covered.

Managerial interviews in enterprises were normally conducted with members of the enterprise top staff and with a representative of one important shop or factory within the enterprise. Typically, I talked with the enterprise director and/or his deputy and with a representative from each of the departments of marketing, economics, controllership, personnel, and production or engineering. The departmental representative was usually the head or his deputy.

Interviews in an enterprise usually began with a group session attended by a number of the managers concerned with the issues to be discussed. But the time constraints on managers generally resulted in my follow-up interviews being primarily with single individuals or at most with two people. Thus it was feasible to explore the same situation in an enterprise with different individuals at different times, and to uncover varying viewpoints as to the same set of events. Enterprise managers, as well as my hosts in the various countries, were quite aware that I was using this interview technique and only occasionally tried to frustrate it.

Reliability of interview results was promoted by focusing the questions narrowly on the recent and current activities of the organization in which the interviewee worked, rather than allowing him to generalize about his branch of industry or region. Specific cases of behavior were elucidated wherever possible, and these were often checked independently with other managers. Both my prior knowledge as to the working of Soviet industry, and my experience in interviewing middle and upper managers in west European and American firms were important in establishing rapport; in this kind of interviewing in any country, it is critical to convince one's partners early that one is not a novice and that shallow or thoughtless remarks will be challenged and will have to be defended.

Although I was able to interview in the national language only in the G.D.R., communication problems were much less severe than might have been expected. In Romania, French is widely spoken except in Transylvania, and there German is a good working language. In Yugoslavia, I found German (with English a good second) most useful in Slovenia, and French (again with English a good second) in the enterprises of Serbia. In Hungarian enterprises, German, French, and English—in that order—were spoken. Interpreters were provided by the enterprises themselves in Yugoslavia and Romania; the advantage of this was that they were familiar with the technical vocabulary relevant to the specific industry. In Hungary, my host organization provided the interpreters and so this advantage was lost; but these interpreters were very good. All in all, I would estimate that I was able to converse directly with about one-fourth of the people interviewed in enterprises outside of the G.D.R., and with about half of those interviewed in organizations other than enterprises. Curiously, it was only very rarely that I found someone competent and willing to discuss in Russian.

The language problem is much more serious in limiting my access to the relevant literature in three of the four countries studied. Of course, I have used the secondary foreign literature, the national statistical handbooks, English-language journals published within the respective countries, and abstracts published both in Hungary and in the West; I have also had a few particularly important articles translated. Nevertheless, the problem of linguistic access to the literature remains. I believe that the generally high quality of the interviews makes this less of a limitation upon reliability of results than might have been expected.

The selection of countries studied was made on the following basis: First, restricting a comparative study of socialist countries to those in

Europe offered the advantage of providing a degree of cultural homogeneity which would otherwise have been lost and would have constituted a troublesome disturbing variable. Second, the Soviet Union was omitted because the size of its economy makes it incomparable to the other countries with respect to decentralization problems and to the significance of foreign trade in the economy. Aside from Albania, an effort was made to interview in the remaining seven countries.

From the beginning, the Bulgarian government refused to permit me interviews at the enterprise level. A preliminary visit to Czechoslovakia in 1970 made it clear that this would have been an inopportune time for such a study in that country. Two months were spent in Poland in the spring of 1971; here, some top-level permissions for interviews were given, but the nonacademic interviews granted proved rather barren and I myself terminated my stay. My strong impression was that the resistance in Poland came from those interviewed much more than from the higher authorities. The remaining four countries are all included in this book.

A word should now be said as to the regional coverage in the four countries studied. The Romanian production units (*centrale* and enterprises) which I observed were spread throughout the entire country. In Hungary, on the other hand, four of the five enterprises visited were in Budapest or its suburbs. In the G.D.R., about two-thirds of my interviews in industrial enterprises, *Kombinate*, and VVBS were in Berlin. Clearly, this distribution raises the issue of lack of regional representativeness, but I do not believe that it is a serious limitation for the sorts of problems which interested me.

In the case of Yugoslavia, on the other hand, the regional nature of the sample has considerable importance. Because of the widely disparate economic and cultural levels of the various Yugoslav republics, I felt that my time would be best employed by investigating a single republic. Thus virtually all the enterprises studied were located in Slovenia: a small republic quite distinctive for its high standard of living and low unemployment rate. Only two Serbian enterprises were visited, and this was done so as to study specific problems which could not be readily examined in Slovenia. In many respects, it would be appropriate to say that this book represents a comparison of Slovenia, rather than of all Yugoslavia, with the three CMEA nations.

In all countries, the possible identification of specific enterprises poses a problem of confidentiality. Just as was the case in previous interviews I have conducted in the United States and in western Europe, east European enterprise managers eagerly welcomed my assurance that I would not identify their firms. Often they were willing to provide detailed statistics as to specific aspects of their operations on the basis that only thus could I really understand the policies they were following and the effects of these policies; but they quite properly insisted that the detailed figures not be revealed. In one country, the same was true on the level of an entire industrial branch.

The requirement of confidentiality explains why enterprises will be unnamed in this study, and why their industrial branches will be described only in rather broad terms. Similarly, manufacturing processes cannot be categorized in detail. I do not believe that this restriction presents a major obstacle to proper interpretation and evaluation.

Three features of the study deserve special mention here since they do not relate specifically to the enterprises.

Coordination among the central organizations (especially the branch ministries of industry) was explored in detail only in Romania. Extensive interviews in both the State Committee for Planning and in seven branch ministries constitute the basis for this analysis.

Particularly for Romania, but also to a lesser degree for the G.D.R., estimates have been made as to the proportion of experienced engineering and managerial manpower in industry which is concentrated at levels above the enterprise, *centrala*, and *Kombinat*. These estimates are based upon interview materials. They are one indication of the gross manpower costs involved in a system of centralized planning.

Finally, detailed data were assembled on the backgrounds and careers of some six hundred managers in the four countries. These people are at all hierarchical levels, primarily in the enterprises but also in the ministries. While data were noted as to age, education, Party status, and the like, the prime contribution of this material is to trace the career development of the executives concerned. Here we can see the changes in work organization, the changes in work function, and the length of time in each job. The only comparable materials which exist for any other country were those collected for a sample of large industrial corporations in the United States.[1] The nature of the collection process suggests that these data constitute a fairly representative sample in each of the four countries, particularly in Romania and Slovenia where the samples were the largest.

The organization of this book is along country rather than subject lines. The justification for this approach is my belief that a managerial system must be viewed as a whole; thus, four-country comparisons of foreign trade administration (to take an example) cannot be properly

---

[1] See D. Granick, *Managerial Comparisons of Four Developed Countries: France, Britain, United States, and Russia* (The M.I.T. Press, Cambridge, Mass. and London: 1972), chapters 7 and 8.

interpreted without understanding other features of the various national systems. Realizing that this system of organization places a burden upon the reader, I have tried to lighten this burden somewhat by making occasional comparisons with the other three countries at relevant portions of the individual country studies, as well as by pointing to the more interesting differences in the conclusion. The reader, however, should not infer from this organization that the book is simply a framework for assembling four separate studies: it is intended to be a comparative study.

The first chapter within each country section is primarily a description of the broad framework of the country's economy and economic organization. It should therefore not be taken as representative of the level of generality employed in the remaining chapters.

The first chapter of the book presents an analytic framework for the remainder of the study. It points to the key organizational factors which will be examined in each country section, and attempts to justify the choice of these factors. It also points to some critical political constraints affecting the different countries, and relates these to their economic behavior. The main emphasis of the chapter is on presenting a common managerial framework for analyzing the economies of the three CMEA countries; this is a different framework than that used in the study of Yugoslavia.

This chapter is followed by the four country sections, arranged in order of the degree of centralization of the national economy. The last section compares the backgrounds, career patterns, and relative monetary earnings of managers at all levels of industry in the four countries.

A FINAL word is necessary as to the terminology used to describe members of top management. In all four countries, for all organizations below the level of ministry, the term "general director" is used to refer to the unit's chief executive officer. Immediately below him in the managerial hierarchy is a small group of functional directors: production director, commercial director, financial director, and the like. The third level of management consists of nondirector members of middle management, usually department heads; depending on the organization, some of these report directly to the general director, and these or other managers may be in charge of individual functions which are considered as of insufficient importance to warrant a director as their head. I have employed the titles used within each individual organization to distinguish between directors and department heads.

CHAPTER 1

The Analytic Framework

O NE WAY of viewing the four countries treated in this book is that they represent a continuum with regard to detailed, centralized decision making in industry, ranging from Romania to the G.D.R. to Hungary to Yugoslavia. The difficulty with this perspective, however, is that a major discontinuity exists between the three CMEA countries on the one hand, and Yugoslavia on the other.

The three CMEA countries share the common feature that each is guided by central planning and decision making from a single center. In each of these three countries, all of industry can properly be regarded as a single organization subject to common direction. In each, the appointment, promotion, dismissal, and monetary rewards of managers of suborganizations (e.g., of enterprises) are determined by a common central authority. While the methods of direction by the center differ substantially among the three countries, all are directed to the same goals: efficient execution of the center's decisions.[1]

This characterization does not apply, however, to contemporary Yugoslav industry, which cannot properly be conceived as subject to the decisions of any single authority. Instead, Yugoslav enterprises should be regarded to a considerable degree as independent power centers, whose actions are coordinated primarily through the market place.

Thus, while the market serves as a major mechanism of coordination in both Hungary and Yugoslavia, its function is fundamentally different in the two economies. In Hungary, it is the chosen mechanism for carrying out central decision making; in this regard, market transactions among enterprises are comparable to interdivisional sales within a single large and decentralized capitalist firm. In Yugoslavia, on the other hand, the market is the mechanism for interrelating genuinely independent organizations.

This major discontinuity leads me to pose somewhat different questions concerning CMEA and Yugoslav industry. Since the managerial systems of the three CMEA countries are all designed to solve the same problem—the efficient coordination of the country's industry to carry out

---

[1] One justification given for the Hungarian move in 1968 to considerable decentralization is that it was intended to lead to the strengthening of central control, in the meaningful sense of more efficient and thus more effective implementation of central objectives (J. Zala, "Central Intention and Planning," *Acta Oeconomica*, 7, 3-4, 1971, pp. 289-301).

centrally determined objectives—they will be analyzed within a common framework; the same analytic factors in managerial control are relevant to all three. But the Yugoslav economy is organized to reach rather different objectives, and thus it is convenient to examine it within a different analytic framework.

The purpose of this chapter is to discuss in general terms the main factors which are examined in each country study, and to present a rationale for selecting these particular factors for emphasis. The particular analytic frameworks are chosen precisely because they are built around those factors which will serve as the heart of the empirical analysis of the remainder of this book.

National Managerial Systems: the Three cmea Countries

If it is accepted that Romania, the G.D.R., and Hungary are all centrally guided and controlled, then the state-owned industry of each country can be treated as though it were all part of a single, national corporation. National Communist Party and government decision makers, together with the planning committee and functional ministries as their staff support, and branch ministries as their line organs of command, can be compared to a corporate headquarters. Intermediate organizations —the *centrale* in Romania, the vvbs and *Kombinate* in East Germany, and the giant enterprises in Hungary—can be compared with divisional headquarters of a corporation; individual enterprises in Romania and the G.D.R., and factories in Hungary, can be compared with the field units of a capitalist firm. The relevant approach to coordination of cmea industry is in terms of managerial theory.

The orthodox model. In the recent past, western analysis of the operation of enterprises in centrally planned socialist economies has rested primarily upon an implicit form of a model which is closely related to microeconomic theory of the operation of capitalist firms.[2] Enterprise managers are conceived as maximizing a clearly defined objective function subject to constraints; this objective function is the managers' own personal incomes both in the current year and in the time-discounted future. Managerial bonuses are assumed to be a useful proxy for such income. These bonuses, in turn, are a nonlinear but well-specified function of quantified measures of the enterprise's performance compared to planned performance. Managers are thus motivated to concentrate their efforts upon the achievement of those measures of success which are most important in the bonus function (these are called "success in-

[2] The first section of Chapter 4 spells out the features of this model.

dicators" in the literature), but to avoid major overachievement relative to plan because this will lead to the raising of plan targets in the future and thus to the reduction in the sum of all discounted bonus receipts.[3]

This analysis treats the managers as independent and maximizing decision makers. Planners influence managerial decisions through their choice of the parameters which affect managerial bonuses: (1) the selection of the particular success indicators which are to influence bonuses, and the weighting of these indicators in the bonus function; (2) the level at which the planned indicators are set for a given enterprise in the current year, and (3) the degree to which the increase in this planned level in future years is influenced by the enterprise's current performance; (4) the shape of the nonlinear bonus function relating achieved performance to the planned indicators.

This model has the attraction that it can be used to explain where and why decisions of enterprise managers will lead to results which are dysfunctional from the viewpoint of the central authorities. The model is based upon an assumption that is clearly comparable to the profit-maximizing assumption for firms which is the basis of microeconomics of capitalist economies. It permits the construction of a microeconomics of socialist economies which is the counterpart to the microeconomics of capitalist economies.

There is, however, a fundamental difference in the justification which can be offered for the assumption of managerial-income maximization in socialist enterprises and for profit maximization in capitalist enterprises. The latter assumption is justified on the basis that enterprises which do not act in this fashion are unlikely to survive in the long run. In a planned socialist economy, however, the survival characteristics needed for enterprise managers to retain their functions are not determined through the working of a market economy, but rather by the administrative decisions of higher authorities. What is required for socialist economies is a managerial analysis, and the "orthodox model" described above is only one possible subset of relevant managerial models. Although this specific model may have considerable value as applied to the Soviet Union, the country for which it was most particularly developed, it may be a poor tool in analyzing other Soviet-type economies.[4]

I shall argue in the country studies that, in fact, the elaborated ortho-

---

[3] Critical here is the concept that bonuses in any given year are a highly kinked function of plan fulfillment, with bonuses being high for 100 percent plan fulfillment but thereafter increasing relatively slowly as performance improves.

[4] No generally accepted model exists to explain the behavior of managers at divisional and field-unit level in capitalist firms. The problem of explaining their behavior is quite parallel to that of explaining the decisions of enterprise managers in CMEA economies.

dox model is a poor tool for analyzing the behavior of production units in either Romania or the G.D.R. Furthermore, it is clearly not relevant to Hungary, since central plans are not developed in that country below the level of the ministry. Thus a broader—and therefore, unfortunately, less specific—framework is required which can encompass both this and other models.

Like the orthodox model, the framework to be presented rests upon a distinction between the enterprise and the center. It also conceives of enterprise managers as economic men, and ignores considerations of ideology and the public weal in analyzing their behavior. Where it differs is in the breadth of factors going into economic reward for managers and, more significantly, in the choice of instruments of influence which are available to the center.

Key factors of the managerial analysis.[5] The following two equations summarize the postulated relationships, the independent variables being those which will be given particular attention in this book.

(1) MANAGERIAL EFFECTIVENESS = f (SIGNALS RATIONALITY, SPECIFIC INDICATORS, PLAN AMBITION, MEASURED-SUCCESS REWARD)

(2) MEASURED-SUCCESS REWARD = f (BONUSES, CAREERS, INCOME INEQUALITY)

The terms are defined as follows:

MANAGERIAL EFFECTIVENESS. Managerial effectiveness of the industrial system at the level of individual branch ministries. Effectiveness is indicated by the ability to achieve objectives desired by the center.

SIGNALS RATIONALITY. Degree of rationality of cost, pricing, and other signals (such as weighting of different products in an output index) that serve as methods of aggregation and are provided to enterprise managers. The criterion used for rationality is that of guidance to actions desired by the center.

SPECIFIC INDICATORS. Degree of central use (backed by penalties and rewards) of *specific* quantified performance indicators and detailed resource allocations for enterprises.

PLAN AMBITION. Degree of ambition incorporated in planned targets given to enterprises, whether these planned targets be expressed through the medium of many specific indicators or in one or a few

[5] For an articulated model dealing with these factors, see Granick, "A Management Model of East European, Centrally-Planned Economies," *European Economic Review*, 4 (1973), 135-61.

generalized indicators, and with this level of ambition of plans being enforced by penalties or rewards.

MEASURED-SUCCESS REWARD. Degree of differential reward of managers dependent upon overall *measured* success. Such success may be measured by a weighted average of a large number of specific indicators, or by a single aggregative indicator such as profits. The relevant feature is only that it be quantified in some fashion.

BONUSES. Nature of bonus system used for enterprise managerial personnel.

CAREERS. Nature of career lines of enterprise managerial personnel.

INCOME INEQUALITY. Degree of income inequality between ordinary workers, rank-and-file engineers, and the various levels of management within enterprises and in managerial organs above them. Particular stress is placed upon the degree of income inequality between rank-and-file engineers and the various managerial groups.

The literature dealing with socialist planned economies has given considerable attention to SIGNALS RATIONALITY and PLAN AMBITION. It is the treatment of the remaining variables, as well as one aspect of PLAN AMBITION, which is somewhat original here.

The fewer the specific performance indicators both incorporated in the indices of plan fulfillment of enterprises and taken seriously by the enterprises, the more important is the effect of SIGNALS RATIONALITY (defined as the degree of rationality of aggregate measures of inputs and outputs which are provided to enterprises) on the decisions made within enterprises. However, no planning system—no matter how centralized— eliminates the problem of choice for the enterprise managements; even if all indicators were expressed in physical terms, many would still be aggregates reflecting a weighting of the components. (Output indicators almost inevitably combine different products within a single indicator with different weighting, enterprises would be motivated to fulfill a specific output indicator with a different mix of products.) Increase of the amount of SIGNALS RATIONALITY has an unambiguously positive effect on MANAGERIAL EFFECTIVENESS, and thus we might expect to see efforts to achieve such an increase made in both centralized and decentralized planning systems.

The greater the number of specific performance indicators, and the greater the detail of resource allocation provided to enterprises (i.e., the higher the value of SPECIFIC INDICATORS), the greater is the degree of potential central control[6] over the economy, and the larger the poten-

---

[6] Throughout this section, except where otherwise stated, all administrative and planning organs above the level of the enterprise are subsumed under the common rubric of "central" organs. However, such bodies as Romanian *centrale* and East German *Kombinate* are defined as enterprises.

tial for detailed coordination of the operations of different enterprises. The counterpart is that less decision making is left to the individual enterprise; i.e., the management function of industry is concentrated above the level of the enterprise. Enterprise management becomes simply an intermediary between true management and the labor force, much as has historically happened to foremen in large private companies in the West.

One problem involved in such an attempt at detailed coordination is that it may result in the realization—as opposed to the potential— of considerably less achievement of central goals for the development of industry than might otherwise be attained.[7] Central managers find that their time is fully taken up with efforts to achieve consistency among the various performance indicators and resource allocations provided to enterprises, and that little opportunity is left for consideration of efficiency and direction. At the extreme, such a managerial system would be governed by consistent directives, but would be essentially out of control in that it would be unresponsive to changes in welfare functions, technological knowledge, or input availabilities.

As a compromise, detailed coordination may be pursued through a three-tier system. At the top are decision makers concerned with the direction of the economy and with setting only broadly defined goals for groupings of enterprises. In the middle, but still within the central apparatus, are located those managers responsible for integrating the operation of the industrial system and for helping individual enterprises meet the broad goals set for their sector by the top decision makers; the integrating solutions found by these middle-level managers are expressed through specific performance indicators and resource allocations. At the bottom are enterprise managers who fulfill the functions of junior executants, not too dissimilar from foremen.

Such a three-tier system would imply the concentration of managerial resources at the middle level rather than in the enterprises. Responsibility for working out measures by which to fulfill top decisions would be focalized here. The managerial effectiveness of the system would depend primarily upon the relationships between the top and middle tier, and the enterprises would represent a relatively uninteresting area for managerial investigations. The relevant degree of use of SPECIFIC INDICATORS would not depend upon the degree of specificity of goals and resources provided to the enterprises, but rather of those provided to this middle tier.

[7] The Hungarian economist Julia Zala has made such a case in application to Hungary, arguing that the "central will" was better realized during the years of decentralized control (1968 and afterwards) than earlier. However, her inability to define convincingly the desires of central authorities makes it difficult to evaluate her position (Zala, pp. 289-301).

A three-tier system of this type has in fact been developed through the creation of *centrale* in Romania and of *Kombinate* in the G.D.R., and through the merging of what were earlier independent enterprises in Hungary. In all three countries, the creation of this system has implied the sharp reduction of the management role in individual factories. However, the *centrala* and *Kombinat* simply replaced the enterprise as the basic managerial unit, and in fact the former enterprises have tended to lose many of their earlier legal rights. This can be interpreted, as has legally been the case completely in Hungary and partially in Romania and in the G.D.R., as meaning that it is these new units which are in fact the "enterprises." Central control and coordination are unaffected.

Putting aside the three-tier case, there is the question of the degree to which a large number of specific performance indicators and resource allocations can be enforced upon the enterprises. The less consistent such indicators are with one another, the greater the extent to which the enterprises must choose which indicators they are to heed and which to ignore. The greater the degree to which central authorities are concerned with directing change in the economy, the less time they have available to give attention to insuring consistency among the indicators. Furthermore, consistency is easiest to attain when the level of performance required by each indicator is low; in this case, there is considerable slack at the enterprise level which can be used to meet the various indicators even when they are inconsistent at that performance level which had originally been projected for the enterprise. (I.e., performance can be sufficiently improved beyond the planned level so that all indicators are met or surpassed.) But if the central authorities set ambitious enterprise objectives, then the existence of indicators which are inconsistent at the level of performance originally projected by central authorities compels the enterprise managers to engage in trade-offs among the various measures of performance as shown by the different indicators. It is at this point that the enterprise managers inevitably become true decision makers.

Normally, therefore, central authorities must choose between, on the one hand, actually enforcing a large number of performance indicators established ex ante, and on the other hand both exercising genuine control and incorporating at least a reasonable degree of annual improvement factor into the performance indicators chosen. In the above sentence, the operational word is "enforcing." There is no reason to believe that the number of enforced indicators is necessarily a function of the number which are promulgated in plans or directives going to the enterprises; a reduction of the number of indicators promulgated might actually be accompanied by an increase in the number of indicators which are enforced. To take a historical case, there seems little reason to believe that the sharp reduction in the number of indicators promulgated in the Soviet Union after 1965 was accompanied by a reduction in the number actually enforced. Not only may the existence of a large number of unenforced performance indicators be a product of self-deception within the central apparatus, but it may perform the functional role of at least reminding enterprise managers that these indicators should not be totally ignored. To the extent that the enforced indicators do not measure the total activities of the enterprise—e.g., if, under conditions of a sellers' market, they are limited to sales and/or profit indicators and do not include quality of product—one can make a good case for the existence of at least some unenforced indicators.[8]

While we may rule out the existence of any really large number of enforced performance indicators at the level of the individual enterprise, this in no way implies that there cannot be significant differences in their number as between various socialist economies. The more such enforced indicators, the greater the number of constraints within which enterprise managements make decisions. It is in this sense that we can consider the degree of decentralization to the enterprise level to be inversely correlated with the number of enforced indicators and resource allocations. On the other hand, there seems no reason to expect any necessary relationship between the number of enforced indicators and resource allocations and the level of difficulty of the tasks set for the enterprise managers.[9]

So much for the factors described by SPECIFIC INDICATORS. Turning now to the variable of PLAN AMBITION, let us briefly examine the effects of the degree of ambition incorporated in the enforced indicators.

An ambitious level of planning by central authorities has the advantage of mustering a high level of effort on the part of enterprise management, since only thus can management avoid the penalties for failure to realize the enforced plan indicators. The disadvantages, however, are threefold.

First, a high value of PLAN AMBITION reduces the ability of central authorities to coordinate the activities of the various enterprises; a sub-

---

[8] Clearly, the level of enforcement of promulgated indicators need not be considered as being either 0 or 1. A more realistic treatment is to consider them as either 1 or as some small fraction which always remains positive. A third alternative is to posit a group of "enforced" indicators with differing high-fraction weights, and a group of "unenforced" indicators with weights not too far above zero.

[9] The above treatment ignores the specific content of the indicators. It seems preferable to consider the issue of such content under the heading of SIGNALS RATIONALITY rather than under SPECIFIC INDICATORS.

For a fuller treatment of much of the above discussion as it applies to the Soviet Union in its "classic" period, see Granick, *Management of the Industrial Firm in the USSR* (Columbia University Press, New York: 1954), chapters 5 and 9, and Granick, *Metal-Fabricating and Soviet Economic Development* (University of Wisconsin Press, Madison and London: 1967), chapter 7.

stantial rate of enterprise failure to fulfill plans must be expected. In addition, the less slack left to enterprises, the more are they forced into trade-offs in heeding inconsistent performance indicators.

Second, a high value of PLAN AMBITION reduces the reliability of information received from enterprises by higher authorities,[10] and it makes suspect the planning proposals put forth by the enterprises. This is because the enterprise managements are forced into attempts to mislead their superiors in order to restrain the level of ambition of the plans approved for them.

Third, a high value of PLAN AMBITION may lead to lower performance by many enterprises than would otherwise occur. No matter how ambitious plans may be, there must be many enterprises which have the potential for surpassing them in individual years; this is because, if the stated plans were so ambitious as to make this impossible, they would be unenforceable. But enterprise managers are well aware of the fact that overfulfillment of the performance indicators will lead to higher plans in the succeeding period. Thus they are motivated to avoid substantial overfulfillment even when this could be readily achieved.[11]

As was the case for the variable of SPECIFIC INDICATORS, PLAN AMBITION relate to the ambitiousness of only those plans which are in fact enforced. Formal performance indicators for enterprises may be ambitious, while less than 100 percent fulfillment is accepted as satisfactory by superior organs. It is, of course, the level of performance which is accepted as satisfactory—whatever this may be as a proportion of plan—which is relevant for the determination of the value of PLAN AMBITION.

MEASURED-SUCCESS REWARD, the degree of differential reward dependent upon overall *measured* success, is a variable unrelated to the method of measurement: whether this be through a large number of specific indicators or through a single aggregative indicator such as profits. The degree to which reward of managers within an organization is linked to their measured success has apparently no readily observable relationship to the socioeconomic system of the country concerned. In the industry of the G.D.R., for example, this degree seems much closer to what we find within large American corporations than to what is the case either in the Soviet Union or in British companies.[12]

[10] See G. Grossman, *Soviet Statistics of Physical Output of Industrial Commodities* (Princeton University Press, Princeton: 1960), chapter 5.

[11] H. Hunter, "Optimal Tautness in Developmental Planning," *Economic Development and Cultural Change*, IX, 4, Part I (1961), 561-72, and S. Gindin, "A Theory of the Soviet Firm," *Economics of Planning*, 10, 3 (1970), 145-57.

[12] The discussion of MEASURED-SUCCESS REWARD represents a brief summary of the relevant portions of Granick, *Managerial Comparisons of Four Developed Countries: France, Britain, United States, and Russia* (The M.I.T. Press, Cam-

MEASURED-SUCCESS REWARD has a very high value in Soviet industry. Soviet enterprise managers, as well as their white-collar staff, receive substantial bonuses which are linked to their monthly and quarterly fulfillment and overfulfillment of specified plan indices. The amount of the bonus rewards depends upon the extent of overfulfillment of these quantified measures of success.

This type of managerial system offers a high degree of stimulus toward the maximum achievement of the plan indices, which presumably are chosen precisely because they represent those aspects of performance which senior executives consider to be of greatest priority. There is, however, a major disadvantage: namely, that enterprise managers give relatively little attention to aspects of enterprise performance which are not fully and positively reflected in the emphasized plan indicators. Since it is quite impossible for higher executives to express in periodic (e.g., monthly to annual) quantitative plan goals all of their desiderata, many of these are shortchanged in such a system. Soviet experience demonstrates that the neglected goals tend both to be those which are future-oriented (e.g., development of new products, and honest participation by enterprise managers in the formulation by higher authorities of future plan objectives for the enterprise) and those which are difficult to quantify (e.g., many aspects of product quality). Furthermore, enterprise managers are driven to suboptimize with regard to the ramifications of their decisions upon other enterprises, despite the fact that central authorities are really concerned with the effect of decisions upon the economy as a whole rather than upon individual subunits (enterprises).

A system with a high value of MEASURED-SUCCESS REWARD can be characterized by a conventional model of maximization under constraints. The individual subunits (the enterprises in the Soviet case) are rewarded for maximizing one or another specified objective (or a specified combination of a very few such objectives), subject to the constraint of meeting both a few other individual quantified objectives and a combination of other central objectives of which only some are quantified. In practice, most of the specified constraints—particularly those which are nonquantified—tend to have little force in Soviet industry and thus are nonbinding.

American corporate planning for the divisions and lower units within the organization is a system which seems to be characterized by a very low value of MEASURED-SUCCESS REWARD. As in the case of Soviet in-

---

bridge, Mass. and London: 1972), chapter 2. The elaboration there is both theoretic and in specific relation to planning in Soviet industry and in large American industrial corporations.

dustry, plans for the subunits single out a small number of critical plan objectives. In sharp contrast to the Soviet system, however, there is no substantial incentive for overfulfillment of these objectives. Rather, the plan targets serve as constraints which are to be met 100 percent but no more, and it is trusted that the residual efforts of the managers of divisions, factories, sales units, etc. will be directed to meeting the residual and only informally specified goals of the company central planners. Managers of subunits "satisfice" with regard to meeting their stated plan objectives; i.e., they make no efforts to exceed them.

For such a system to be successful, PLAN AMBITION—as expressed in the targets encompassed in MEASURED SUCCESS—must be restrained; otherwise there will be little residual managerial effort left to pursue performance objectives which are not fully and immediately reflected in these planning targets. In fact, high PLAN AMBITION in the measured targets for a given year may lead both to the reduction of performance by subunits in future years as measured by these same targets, and to reduction in performance by the same measures in the given year when performance is aggregated for the organization as a whole.[13]

A managerial system which has a low value of MEASURED-SUCCESS REWARD, and in which PLAN AMBITION in setting the measured targets is restrained, can be regarded as a very curious form of maximizing model. The managers of the subunits are rewarded for their success in maximizing some unstated combination of the less important, and often unspecified, goals of the organization's central planners, subject to the constraint of meeting the planned targets for the critical short-run goals (e.g., annual profit and share of the market in the American context). Assuming, as seems reasonable, that it is the goals set forth in the organization's plan which are regarded by its top executives as the most critical, this is a system which is likely frequently to lead to lower performance along these dimensions than the top executives might wish. (For the top executives cannot know, at the time that they formulate the subunit's plan for the year, either the precise capacity of the subunit under unchanging conditions or the ways in which conditions will change during the course of the year.) On the other hand, such a system renders feasible high attention by subunit managers to future-oriented and difficult-to-quantify objectives. It also substantially weakens the force of suboptimization in determining the behavior of subunit managers. This type of system would seem most appropriate in cases where the top

[13] In an American company-planning context, one American comptroller took the position in an interview that overly ambitious annual profit targets for individual divisions reduce the multiyear profitability of the division. Overly ambitious financial targets for managers of individual functions within a division may reduce even the short-run profitability of the division (Granick, *Managerial Comparisons*, chapter 2).

executives of the central organization have considerable confidence in their own ability to shape short-run plans which are both feasible and demanding, and thus where they are content when their subordinates meet but do not surpass the planned objectives.

In order to operationalize the variable of MEASURED-SUCCESS RE-WARD, we must link it to specific kinds of rewards made to managers of subunits of an organization. The two relevant rewards, whether we are thinking of a socialist or of a capitalist organization, are BONUSES and career advancement (CAREERS). The more they are linked to measured achievements within the planning period, the greater is the value of MEASURED-SUCCESS REWARD. Furthermore, the incentive of promotion is greater the larger is the degree of income advancement involved in such promotion (INCOME INEQUALITY).[14] This is the basis for equation (2) above, where MEASURED-SUCCESS REWARD = f (BONUSES, CAREERS, INCOME INEQUALITY).

Both in Soviet industry and in large American corporations, bonuses typically represent quite substantial portions of the income of managers of subunits. But there the resemblance ends. In the Soviet case, the amount of bonus depends upon the subunit's degree of success in meeting or surpassing one or more quantified plan indicators. In American corporations, bonuses are not linked to any objective measure of the subunit's success. Typically, they are a function of the profits earned by the corporation as a whole (not by the specific subunit for which the manager is responsible), of the career level of the manager concerned, and of a subjective evaluation of the manager's performance. The critical distinction is that the manager's performance is evaluated objectively in the Soviet Union, and thus is linked to one or a few quantified plan objectives, while in the United States it is evaluated subjectively. Thus the degree of fulfillment of the maze of central objectives which are not specified in the plan is of critical importance in determining bonus levels in the United States, while it plays almost no role in the Soviet Union.[15]

Career advancement of a manager in large American corporations is dependent primarily upon features other than his performance relative to planned indicators. Of course, American managers must meet their planned targets in order to be viewed as suitable candidates for promotion; but this is only a minimum and not very discriminating criterion. Overfulfillment of explicit planned targets is largely irrelevant.

---

[14] Since it is the income accompaniment of promotion or demotion which is important, the relevant comparison is between the various managerial and professional ranks. Both in Russia and in eastern Europe, the lowest income level to which managerial personnel can normally be reduced is that of a rank-and-file engineer rather than of an ordinary manual worker.

[15] See Granick, *Managerial Comparisons*, chapter 9.

Instead, American managers are promoted primarily on the basis of a subjective evaluation of their "potential." Here, the degree of imagination shown in their contributions to corporate planning plays a substantial role. Since successful careers typically cut across a number of functions and subunits within the company, concentration on meeting measurable success indicators would be a form of career-suicide for a manager. Thus a factory manager who attained superplan cost reductions by resisting too strenuously the marketing department's efforts to expand sales through widening the range of products produced in his factory, which would incidentally reduce the length of his production runs and so raise his costs of production, would find his career opportunities in the company sharply curtailed. The American subunit manager achieves his career rewards primarily through activities geared to goals other than the narrow ones specified in the plan objectives laid down for him.

It would appear that the degree of success shown in meeting and over-fulfilling planned targets has greater importance in determining the promotion of Soviet than of American managers. More significant, however, is the fact that promotional progress of managers in the Soviet Union since the Second World War has been extremely slow.[16] The discounted income of a Soviet manager, unlike that of an American, is much more likely to be determined by his bonus rate than by the evaluation made of him for promotion purposes. Thus the key reward for the Soviet manager is that of bonus, while the more important reward for the American is career advancement.

When we look at the east European countries, it is these aspects of BONUSES and CAREERS which we must examine in order to evaluate the relative value to be assigned to the variable MEASURED-SUCCESS REWARD in the different countries. However, while bonuses will be treated in the country studies, career patterns and the degree of income inequality will be postponed until Chapter 14.

Since in Romania, the G.D.R., and Hungary, all of industry is regarded as a single national managerial system, the analysis of each country's industry will be carried out in terms of the seven factors discussed above.

THE ANALYSIS OF YUGOSLAV INDUSTRY

Particularly since 1965, the Yugoslav economy has been organized on the "self-management" principle. The first critical feature of this fundamental Yugoslav dogma as it applies to the economy is that all individual enterprises should be genuinely autonomous in their decision making. Their tasks are viewed as not including that of applying central

---

16 Ibid., chapter 8.

policy; rather, enterprises are expected to develop independent policies. The second critical feature is that control should be kept in the hands of representatives elected by the employees of the individual enterprise, and that full-time managers should be held strictly subordinate to these representatives; moreover, the elected representatives should be replaced frequently, with consecutive reelection being limited.

In the light of this self-management principle, our analysis of the organization of industry will focus on two problems: the nature of the objective function of the individual enterprise, and the coordination of the enterprises through the market place. Specifically, we will concentrate upon three issues:

(1) The degree to which the individual enterprise is genuinely self-managed rather than directed by local government and regional-republic authorities. As we shall see, a major question in treating this issue is the degree to which the enterprise's policies are in fact shaped by its full-time general director as opposed to the elected workers' representatives; the question arises because governmental units are in a much stronger position to exercise influence upon the general director of an enterprise than upon its workers' council.

(2) The relative strength of different forces within the enterprise itself in determining enterprise policy as articulated by the workers' representatives, and the degree to which the different groups have conflicting interests. This analysis is critical for an evaluation of the claims that Yugoslav self-managed enterprises pursue significantly different goals, and thus respond to identical stimuli in significantly different ways, than do capitalist firms.

(3) The resultant interactions of Yugoslav enterprises in the market place. The issue here is that of how the market mechanism, together with whatever nonmarket mechanisms are present, functions in coordinating the actions of enterprises which are pursuing somewhat different objectives than those of firms in any other economy.

CONSTRAINTS

Common to the analysis of all four countries is the treatment of political constraints. None of the governments is free to pursue in an untrammeled fashion its immediate economic objectives of rapid growth, structural change, income distribution, and the like. All are constrained to pursue such objectives within fairly rigid bounds imposed by doctrinal views, which strongly favor the interests of important groups within the society, and which can be bent only slightly in the short run.

For the three CMEA countries, the principal constraint with which we shall be concerned is that of full employment, defined in a particularly rigid fashion. The existence of this constraint does not radically affect the nature of the economic system in Romania or the G.D.R. But in Hungary, the bounds which it has established on policy have seriously deformed the course which the economic reform would otherwise have taken.

What is significant about the full-employment constraint is not so much that the rate of aggregate unemployment which can be tolerated is considerably lower than that accepted as a government policy objective in any capitalist country. Rather, it is the fact that it is considered impermissible, except in very rare circumstances, to dismiss workers on grounds other than those of gross incompetence or continued violation of factory discipline. It is considered morally wrong to force workers to change either their trade or their place of work because of the abolition of their existing post.

This job-maintenance policy stems from the fact that socialists' greatest reproach against capitalism has been the fact that workers are constantly threatened with the loss of their posts. The abolition of such a threat has become one of the key ingredients of socialism as it has been interpreted de facto in eastern Europe, and any relaxation of a rigid job-maintenance policy would doubtless be perceived by many workers as an abandonment of socialism.

As we shall see later in our treatment of the Hungarian economy, the job-maintenance policy is consistent with reliance on a market mechanism only if conditions of a sellers' market exist throughout the economy. Despite the fact that a market mechanism operates very inefficiently under conditions of a sellers' market, and that this fact has been fully recognized, Hungarian authorities have had little choice but to retain the conditions for such a market. Up to the present, the effectiveness of the Hungarian reform methods has been unable to transcend the limits set by this constraint. So long as this constraint remains binding, there is in my opinion very little likelihood that the reform can produce the efficiency results which might otherwise be possible.

In the case of Yugoslavia, the binding constraints have been the related ones of containment of the country's nationalities' conflict, and of rigid interpretation of the self-management principle.

The conflict among major nationalities has historically been far more virulent in Yugoslavia than in any other of the east European countries. Almost any significant action by the national government is interpreted as favoring one or another nationality group at the expense of others. The method for containing this conflict which has been used since the 1960's has been that of increasingly withdrawing matters of domestic policy from the purview of the national government.

The self-management principle has served as the justification for this withdrawal, and this principle has become one of the great "myths" of Yugoslav society which is virtually immune from attack from within the system. Individual work organizations are to be fully autonomous; where this is impossible, their autonomy should be interfered with by the local communities or, at most, by the regional republics. National decision making is interpreted as bureaucratic interference and as a flagrant violation of the rights of self-management.

This principle has played an exceedingly useful role in the development of the economy. Perhaps nothing but the raising of this principle to the level of an unchallengeable dogma could have restrained the forces pushing for a reintroduction of central planning as a response to the problems of the market economy of the 1960's and early 1970's. But precisely because it has become such a forceful dogma, self-management has prevented not only detailed central planning but even the effective use of central monetary and fiscal policy. The result is that, in many important respects, present-day Yugoslavia bears more of a resemblance to the type of liberal market economy envisioned by Adam Smith than is the case in any country of western Europe. The most elementary lessons of Keynesianism have proved inconsistent with the dogma of self-management, and the Yugoslav economy has suffered accordingly.

My analysis of the working of the post-1965 Yugoslav economy and of the post-1967 Hungarian economy must, of course, accept their political constraints as given. Pessimism as to the effectiveness of the economic reforms undertaken in these two countries is heavily conditioned by the existence of these constraints. If these constraints should be lifted in the future, as may of course occur, then both economies would presumably function in markedly different ways than those observed in this book. But the breaking of these constraints would involve change even more radical than the reforms of the 1960's.

PART I

Romania

Romania is a country at an early stage of development, and her rapid growth in national income has been due in considerable part to change in the structure of the economy. The industrial labor force has increased rapidly, primarily by movement out of agriculture. The capital stock of industry has also shown very high percentage increases. The expansion of industrial output has been fueled more by extensive (increase of inputs) than intensive (improvement of overall productivity) means, and this is neither surprising nor unfitting for her level of general economic development.

Highly centralized methods of planning and plan enforcement have been frequently described as more appropriate for countries at an early stage of development, where the prime problems are those of mustering manpower and investment resources and directing them to structural change, than to more mature and complex economies. Thus it should not astonish us that the industry of Romania is administered in a more centralized fashion than that of the other two CMEA countries which we shall examine, let alone (although for different reasons) than that of Yugoslavia.

True, as in other countries, there has been talk for some years of what amounts to economic reform. The first experimental measures were introduced into industry in 1967, and were generalized in 1969. Primarily, the Romanian reform took the form of the creation of *centrale*[1] as large production units which were to be given certain powers formerly kept in the hands of the industrial ministries. Just as in the purely domestic economy, there has also been some decentralization of decision making in foreign trade matters.

But such decentralization has not amounted to much. Part I of this book is based primarily upon a study of the economy in the fall of 1970 when the decentralization had progressed about as far as it was to go through the end of 1973 (the time of writing these lines); it describes a pattern of administering industry which seems quite centralized even by the high standards set in the USSR during the 1930's. The restructuring of the *centrale* in early 1973 suggests that the aims of the 1969 reorganization were being abandoned; at least, the *centrale* were being consolidated along precisely those lines which Ceauşescu had long warned would amount to the recreation in substance of the branch directorates within ministries, directorates which had been abolished in

---

[1] *Centrala* is the singular form, and *centrale* the plural. These Romanian terms will be used throughout.

1969. Thus an analysis of Romanian industrial administration need pay little attention to the forces of decentralization and reform.

Yet curiously, when we turn to the microeconomic level of the *centrala* and enterprise, behavior appears to be rather different from what analyses of the Soviet Union have led us to expect in centralized socialist economies. The standard model for explaining enterprise management's behavior in the Soviet Union does not appear to have much explanatory value for the Romanian production unit. Thus my analysis of Romanian administration suggests that industry in centralized CMEA countries can be directed through devices which, while outwardly similar, encourage rather different attitudes on the part of managers of microeconomic units in the various countries. It is this which is by far the most interesting conclusion of Part I.

Chapter 2 is a background chapter, intended to provide an orientation to the specifically Romanian scene before the reader plunges into an examination of the mechanisms by which industry is coordinated and directed. Here I begin with a survey of the economy, proceed to a description of the organizational pattern of industry, estimate the proportion of professional manpower in industry which is employed in coordinating units above the level of the *centrala*, discuss the limited development of a rational system of producer prices and the implications of this for decision making, and end with an examination of the educational level of industrial management.

Chapter 3 offers an analysis of decision making at the level of the industrial ministry and the State Committee for Planning. It is at this level that the important economic decisions which affect both the development and the day-to-day operations of industry are made, or at a minimum where the main staffwork for them is done. While this chapter pays some attention to decisions which represent an arbitrage between the interests of different major branches of the economy (as these branches are represented by the ministries which administer them), prime attention will be given to decision making within major branches. The high degree of centralization above the level of the *centrala* makes this chapter of particular importance for understanding the decisions generated by the Romanian administrative system.

Chapter 4 turns to the microeconomic level: that of the *centrala* and, to a lesser degree, of the enterprise. Here, an orthodox model of the socialist production unit is presented, and data are mustered from a substantial sample of *centrale* and enterprises to show that this model does not fit Romania. The chapter concludes with a treatment of decision making at the microeconomic level, and with an attempt to demonstrate that such decision making is essentially technical rather than economic. In key respects, the *centrala*'s general director is more comparable to a foreman than to a member of even middle management in an American enterprise.

These three chapters on Romania rest upon a richer data base of interviews, but a considerably poorer base of published materials, than do any of the following country studies. The published economic literature of Romania is peculiarly unrewarding. Furthermore, the literature that exists was to a considerable degree inaccessible to me because less has been translated or summarized in languages I know than is the case for the other countries.

On the other hand, Romanian managers and administrators proved peculiarly accessible. Lengthy interviews were conducted in nine production units distributed among seven branch ministries, in the headquarters of seven of Romania's thirteen industrial ministries (primarily with officials at the level of department chief),[2] and in the State Committee for Planning. An integral part of the interview strategy was to discuss identical or similar problems both in the production units and in the ministries which supervised them, so as to obtain the perspective both of the operating unit and of its control body; discussions in the Committee for Planning provided the perspective of still a higher control level. This strategy was pursued with considerable success in Romania, although it was not possible to implement it in either the G.D.R. or Hungary.

Romania was the only country in which I had considerable control over the choice of the production units in which I interviewed. Guided by a set of criteria which I had elaborated, my host agency provided me with a list of about forty *centrale* and enterprises from which I was permitted to make my own selection. On the basis of advice from both foreigners and Romanian colleagues (none of whom were associated with my host organization, and all of whom had had considerable experience with the top managements of many of these production units), I selected eight units and also requested to see a ninth which was not on the original list. Interviews were arranged in all nine without exception, and I was permitted to decide unilaterally as to my distribution of time among the units. Thus the time constraint on interviewing within each unit was imposed by me rather than by the Romanians.

Furthermore, I received the impression that the managers of units in which I interviewed had been requested to be quite frank with me. In the first unit, I interviewed one functional director who ducked my questions completely. Alerted to this fact by my interpreter, my host organization immediately intervened. A few days later, the general di-

---

[2] These seven ministries administer sectors of the economy which range from the highest to the lowest national priority, and considerably more than half of the industrial labor force of the country work within their confines.

rector of this unit apologized in my interview with him for the "misunderstanding," and was himself prepared to go over the relevant ground. Since I did not encounter similar avoidance of questions in any other Romanian production unit, it is my surmise that interviewees were told that such avoidance was frowned upon by the Romanian authorities.[3]

[3] Of course, such Romanian cooperation was only possible because I was careful to avoid questions which could be construed as relating to state secrets. For example, I never asked for absolute production or investment figures.

CHAPTER 2

The Romanian Industrial
Setting

This chapter is intended to set the stage for discussion of Romanian managerial behavior at the ministry, *centrala*, and enterprise level in 1970. It does not enter into substantive matters of managerial decision making.

SURVEY OF THE ROMANIAN ECONOMY

Romania, with a population of twenty million, is one of the two larger of our four countries. It has two national minority groups of some size: Hungarian (8 percent of the population) and German (2 percent); 6 percent of all students through secondary education attend schools taught in a national-minority language. Unlike Hungary and the G.D.R., Romania has a nationalities problem and there are claims—which are vigorously denied—that nationality discrimination exists in the choice of top managers.[1] But clearly this nationalities problem is much less virulent than that of Yugoslavia.

Like Yugoslavia, Romania is still a heavily agricultural country: 49 percent of the labor force is engaged in agriculture. The absolute number of those working in agriculture has been declining since the middle 1950's, and this decline has made possible a very high and continuous growth in industrial employment: from 12 percent of the country's labor force in 1950 to 23 percent in 1970. The Directives for the 1971-75 Plan (adopted in August 1969) appear to have called for a halving of the rate of growth of the industrial labor force, but the later Draft Plan for 1971-75 (adopted in May 1971) seems instead to have required a continuation of the 1966-70 tempo. This latter decision implies roughly a 10 percent decline in the agricultural labor force over these five years.[2]

The shift of manpower from agriculture to industry has led to the latter sector being constantly fed with a large flow of relatively untrained

[1] N. Ceaușescu, the head of the Party and the state, said in March 1971 that there are some sectors with too few leading personnel of Hungarian and German nationality (*Romania: Documents-Events*, 1971, 18, p. 22).

[2] Nicolae Ceaușescu, *Speech at the Festive Meeting Dedicated to the Semicentenary Anniversary of the Romanian Communist Party, May 7, 1971* (Meridiane Publishing House, Bucharest: 1971), pp. 27 and 32.

TABLE 2.1: Change in Absolute Number of the Labor Force over Five-Year Intervals (percentage)

Years	Industry	Agriculture
1951-55	+ 22	+ 5
1956-60	+ 18	− 5
1961-65	+ 29	− 12
1966-70	+ 23	− 11

SOURCES: Computed from Direcţia Centrală de Statistică, *Anuarul Statistic al Republicii Socialiste România 1971*, table 48, p. 124.

manpower, inevitably creating serious problems of on-the-job training. Nevertheless, the dimensions of the problem have been contained by the quite moderate rate of growth of the country's total labor force: 1.3 percent annually during 1951-60 and 0.4 percent during 1961-70. In 1965, only 21 percent of the industrial labor force was less than twenty-six years old, and only 30 percent had less than five years of service in paid employment of any type (i.e., excluding work on agricultural collective farms).[3]

No general figures exist as to labor turnover. While one would expect it to be high because of the influx of young and untrained workers, data from four *centrale* suggest that both turnover and unjustified absenteeism are moderate to surprisingly low.[4] In any case, the Romanian govern-

[3] Data are for April 25, 1965 (Direcţia Centrală de Statistica, *Forţa de Muncă in Republica Socialistă România*, Bucureşti: 1966, pp. 222-23 and 258-59).

[4] The annual percentage of those leaving for any reason, including retirement, death, and being called into the armed forces, are as follows:
In a large mine with one thousand employees, the average for 1968 and 1969 was 47 percent. In a construction *centrala*, the annual average for skilled workers was 15 percent. In an iron and steel *centrala*, the annual average was 5 to 6 percent; somewhat earlier, prior to the introduction of seniority bonuses, the average here was 8 to 9 percent. A textile *centrala* reported that its turnover was almost nil.
Since mining and construction are relatively high-turnover occupations in all countries, these figures appear quite low by international standards.
Published data seem somewhat higher than in the above *centrale*, but are still on the low side. Data for five and one-half years for three enterprises of Braşov show an annual average of 27 percent; but this figure must be interpreted in terms of the fact that the data for one similar large city suggest that perhaps one-fifth of the labor force of the city consists of people with only temporary residence. A small sample studied in Slatina yielded a 24 percent annual figure for manual workers during three and one-half years; one Bucharest plant had an annual rate varying between 17 and 20 percent over seven years. It is also stated that the 1969 turnover rate was only 25 percent in that industrial branch (construction materials) which had the second largest rate of all of the approximately twelve industrial ministries; but this figure should not be relied on too greatly since the newspaper article from which it stems is internally contradictory in the statistics presented. (See T. Bogdan and others, *Procesul de Urbanizare în România - Zona Braşov*, Editura Politică, Bucureştì: 1970, p. 112; M. Constantinescu and others, *Procesul de Urbanizare în R.S. România - Zona Slatina*, Editura Academiei R.S.R.,

ment does not appear to consider labor turnover as a serious problem. Since the end of 1967, the only penalties for changing jobs without enterprise permission have been reduction in sick pay and the elimination of seniority bonuses;[5] pension and vacation rights have remained untouched.

The rapid rate of labor movement out of agriculture would, of course, have been incompatible with full employment without an elevated rate of urban investment. Romania appears to have been investing a very high proportion of its national income in comparison with the other two centrally planned economies of our study.[6] Although the 1969 Plan Directives for 1971-75 called for a reduction in the ratio of net investment to income, the revision in early 1971 called for an increase over the ratio realized during the previous quinquennium.[7] This revision is particularly striking evidence of a desire to maintain the high rate of investment, since it was announced at a time when the impact of the Polish events of December 1970 might have been expected to lead to reverse behavior. As a Romanian bitterly commented to me when explaining the exceptionally sharp jump in housing rents which occurred in 1968 and 1969, "Romania has a very bold government."

With the heavy movement of both labor and capital into industry, it is not surprising that the rate of increase of industrial output has also been exceptional. The officially calculated rate of growth of industrial output has held up remarkably well since 1958 (although it was lower in the second half of the 1960's than in the first half), and this record is more

---

Bucureşti: 1970, p. 331; Honorina Cazacu and others in *Lupta de Clasă*, June 1970, p. 87; M. Chiţu and S. Fomino in *Muncă*, March 27, 1970, pp. 1 and 7. I am indebted to Professor Kenneth Jowitt for pointing out to me all but the last of these sources.)

Unmotivated absenteeism ran only 2.5 days annually per worker in the mine in which I interviewed, and 1.5 days in the iron and steel *centrala*. It appears to have been even smaller in the published study concerning Slatina.

[5] These latter peak at 10 percent of salary.

[6] The Romanian ratio of net investment (net fixed investment plus increase of inventories as a ratio of the socialist-countries' normal definition of national income) was 30.3 percent during 1966-70. This compares with the Hungarian ratio of about 22 percent in 1968-69, and the G.D.R.'s ratio of some 21 percent. The Yugoslav ratio during 1968-69 was some 29 percent, roughly the same as the Romanian. All of these figures are official, and no effort has been made to standardize among the various countries for the effects of national differences such as price structure. Despite incomparabilities in the statistics, it seems reasonable to say that the difference between Romania on the one hand, and Hungary and the German Democratic Republic on the other, is marked.

[7] The ratio of net investment achieved in 1966-70 was 30.3 percent. That planned in August 1969 for 1971-75 was 28 to 30 percent, and the revised range announced in May 1971 was 31 to 32 percent. (Communiqué on fulfillment of the plan for 1966-70, *Romania*, 1st year, 9, p. 1; Ion G. Maurer, *Report on the Directives of the Tenth Congress of the Romanian Communist Party*, Agerpress, Bucharest: 1969, p. 24; Ceauşescu, p. 34.)

or less supported by an American estimate. The 1971-75 Draft Plan predicted an additional 2 or 3 percent decline in the annual rate of growth of industrial production, but the final plan adopted in late 1971 called for a similar rate of growth to that achieved in 1966-70 (Table 2.2). Rates of growth of factor productivity (net industrial production divided by capital and labor inputs) have also been quite high.[8]

TABLE 2.2: Annual Rate of Growth of Industrial Output (percentage)

Years	Official Index	Lee-Montias Index	Alton Index[a]
1951-55	15.1	10.6	7.7
1956-60	10.9		9.2
1961-65	13.8		10.8
1966-70	11.8		
1956-58	9.7	9.5	
1959-60	13.1	15.4	
1961-63	14.0	12.2	
1964-65	13.6		
1966-68	12.1		
1969-70	11.4		
1971-75			
Directives	8.5 - 9.5		
Draft Plan	8.8 - 9.8		
Final Plan	11.0 - 12.2		

SOURCES: John M. Montias, *Economic Development in Romania* (The M.I.T. Press, Cambridge, Mass.: 1967), p. 56. T. P. Alton, "Economic Structure and Growth in Eastern Europe," in Joint Economic Committee, 91st Congress of the United States (2nd session), *Economic Developments in Countries of Eastern Europe* (U.S. Government Printing Office, Washington, D.C.: 1970), p. 50. *Anuarul 1971*, pp. 166-67. Communiqué on fulfillment of the plan for 1966-70, *Romania*, 1st year, 9, p. 4. N. Ceauşescu, *Speech at the Festive Meeting Dedicated to the Semicentenary Anniversary of the Romanian Communist Party, May 7, 1971* (Meridiane Publishing House, Bucharest: 1971), pp. 20 and 27. *Romania: Documents-Events*, 1971, 63, p. 4.

[a] Industry and handicraft.

The officially recorded rate of growth of real wages has also been substantial, though it must be remembered that Romania is still the poorest of the three centrally planned economies we are studying. Real wages are said to have increased by 20 percent during 1966-70 (against a planned 25 percent). The Draft Plan and Final Plan for 1971-75 call for another 20 percent increase, compared with an earlier planned figure of 16 to 20 percent in the Directives for the same period.[9] Since the

[8] John M. Montias, *Economic Development in Romania* (The M.I.T. Press, Cambridge: 1967), table 1.17, p. 56.
[9] Ceauşescu, p. 27; Ceauşescu, *Report Delivered at the National Conference of the Romanian Communist Party* (Meridiane Publishing House, Bucharest: 1967),

planned rate of net investment rose between the announcement of the Directives and that of the Draft Plan (a phenomenon which can be expected to have negative effects on the rise in consumption levels), and since the planned rise in real wages had not been achieved during 1966-70, it seems likely that the actual percentage rise in real wages will be lower during 1971-75 than it was during 1966-70. In any case, it is perfectly clear that there is to be no dramatic shift in policy toward a more rapid increase in consumption standards than has occurred in the past. The contrast with the situation prevailing in Hungary is striking.

In short, Romania is still quite an underdeveloped country, but one engaged in massive shifts out of agriculture. Its rate of growth of industrial output has been exceptionally high, although now perhaps tapering off somewhat. The same seems to be true of industrial productivity. The percentage growth in real wages has been substantial but not outstanding. No major change in these respects appears to be foreseen for the five years following the period of my visit.

THE ORGANIZATIONAL PATTERN OF ROMANIAN INDUSTRY: THE *Centrale*

In the fall of 1969, one year prior to my interviews in Romania, the organizational structure of industry was basically altered through the creation of *centrale*[10] to cover the vast majority of enterprises in manufacturing, mining, and construction. Formerly, enterprises had been placed in direct subordination to branch directorates located in the headquarters of their sectoral ministry; now the branch directorates were abolished, the number of personnel in the ministerial headquarters was reduced by about 35 percent, and virtually all enterprises were combined into *centrale* which are intermediary between the enterprises and the ministries.

Roughly two hundred *centrale* were formed to cover a workforce in industry and mining under republic-wide (as opposed to local) jurisdiction of 1.6 million people. This gives an average of 8,000 people per *centrala*. Two of the *centrale* (in mining and machine building) had about 100,000 employees each, but their creation seemed to represent a temporary de facto maintenance of the previous branch directorates of the ministries. Some sixty-eight others were regional organizations in

---

p. 98; *Communiqué on Fulfillment of the Plan for 1966-70*, p. 44. In late 1970, the Directives' range of 16 to 20 percent was apparently interpreted as 17 percent.

[10] These bear a variety of names: most commonly *centrala, kombinat*, or trust. (However, I did come across one case where a *kombinat* was simply a unit within a trust.) Differences in nomenclature to a considerable extent represent the varying customs of different industries rather than differences in organization. The term *centrala* will hereafter be used to refer to all indiscriminately.

the food and woodworking industries, and were generally relatively small. As a rough guess, the remainder averaged about 9,000 people each. If one also eliminates light industry, in which the *centrale* also tended to be somewhat small, the other *centrale* must have averaged about 11,000 (Table 2.3).

Judging by American and west European experience, organizations of this size are not so large that their leadership cannot provide concrete guidance in the solution of current problems. Unlike the previous branch directorates of the ministries, they are of a size small enough to be operational units. Certainly this was the intention of the reorganization.

TABLE 2.3: *Centrale* and Enterprises in Seven Ministries, late 1970 (number)

Ministry	Centrale	Enterprises within Centrale	Independent Production Enterprises	Number of Personnel within the Ministry (000)
Light industry	47	287	3	400
Machinebuilding	11-12	120	0	. . .
Mining	12	. . .	2	180
Industrial construction	22	. . .	5	170
Construction materials	5	56	0	65
Iron and steel	7	. . .	2	. . .
Chemicals	10	50a	. . .	110b

NOTE: The above data were given orally, although by informed sources, and must be taken as only approximate. This table accounts for seven of the thirteen production ministries. It seems clear from a comparison of the number of enterprises with those listed in the *Anuarul 1970*, table 70, p. 154, that the definition of enterprise used here is considerably looser than that of the Central Statistical Board. The above numbers represent the definition used operationally within the ministries. (It was stated without contradiction at a meeting which I attended of directors of various *centrale* that within the Ministry of Light Industry only *centrale*, and not the enterprises subordinate to them, are registered with the Ministry of Finance as independent bodies for purposes of tax payment. The stated implication of this was that each *centrala*, by its own uncontrolled decision, could change any or all of its enterprises into production "sectors." If this is so, it would not have been unreasonable for the Central Statistical Office to have treated the Ministry of Light Industry as though it had only fifty enterprises: i.e., to count only the organizations registered with the Ministry of Finance.)

a Total number of enterprises within the ministry.

b Total number of personnel within the branch under all ministries of republic-wide jurisdiction, irrespective of the particular ministry in which these people were working.

The *centrale* have been organized along varying principles, from that of including all enterprises of a subbranch which is scattered geographically to that of including all food enterprises of a given region so as most easily to centralize the process of collecting the branch's raw materials.

But the preferred type, comprising 88 percent of the total number as of late 1970, is one in which the *centrala* headquarters is located physically in its major enterprise, with the *centrala* managers acting simultaneously as managers of this enterprise. In this type of *centrala*, the other enterprises ideally become purely production units which are managed in a fashion little different from that used for the larger production shops of the major enterprise. The general directors of these smaller enterprises may even be subordinate to the production director—rather than to the general director—of the *centrala*.

An example of what was considered by the Romanians to be a markedly unsuccessful *centrala* was one which combined only three enterprises, one of which carried out two-thirds of the total activities of the *centrala*, but where the headquarters was separate from that of any of the three enterprises. A manager of the principal enterprise held that it was the branch ministry and not the *centrala* which in fact made all decisions exceeding the competence of the enterprise. The Ministry of Labor seemed at the time to agree with this characterization. The *centrala* headquarters consisted of a total of fifty-six people (perhaps two-thirds of whom were at the professional level), and this number was regarded as quite insufficient to provide operational leadership. As a result, the Ministry of Labor was then considering recommending the abolition of the *centrala* and the coordination of the three constituent enterprises directly from the sectoral ministry itself.

In early 1971, Ceaușescu, the head of the government and Communist Party, strongly criticized the structure of some *centrale*, arguing that it made them coordinating bodies rather than production units; he saw little difference between them and the former branch directorates of the ministries. However, such *centrale* then constituted only a fairly small minority of the total.

The period after 1971 saw some change in the position of the *centrale*, but its significance was unclear even in mid-1973. As of early 1972, the *centrale* were sometimes called supervisory rather than operating bodies,[11] and the enterprises which belonged to the *centrale* were being given additional independence.[12] During March and April 1973, there

[11] See C. Catuti in *Probleme Economice*, May 1972, pp. 37-42, translated in *JPS*.

[12] This increased independence was probably greatest in light industry and in the foodstuffs industry. (For light industry, see the interview with Ion Bazac in the article by V. Salagean, *Scînteia*, September 14, 1971, translated by *RFE*.) In both of these industries, *centrale* had been greatly consolidated along product lines and had been reduced in number by about two-thirds. In light industry, for example, the size of the average *centrala* was increased from 8,500 to 34,000 employees, and two-thirds of the consolidated *centrale* were headquartered in Bucharest. (See the list of all *centrale* as of January 1972 which was published in *Viața*

was massive concentration of the *centrale* throughout industry, and the average size of the *centrala* may well have tripled. It was claimed that this regrouping was accompanied by a substantial shift of engineering personnel from the staff of the *centrale* to that of their component enterprises. The 1973 development in particular might well be interpreted as the transformation of the *centrale* back into the ministerial branch directorates which they had replaced in late 1969.

On the other hand, Ceaușescu repeated in March 1973 his long-held position that the *centrala* headquarters should be grafted onto the main enterprise subordinate to it, and that the *centrala* should take over from its enterprises all of their functions except that of production.[13] Clearly this was inconsistent with the consolidation of the *centrale* which appears to have been decided at the same time or even earlier. How the matter will be resolved seems uncertain, and thus these developments will be ignored in the description and interpretation of the *centrale* to be given below; this description will deal with the *centrale* as they existed in late 1970 at the time of my interviews in Romania.

In my judgment, the creation of *centrale* represented a significant reorganization of industry, but one which cannot properly be designated as either centralization or decentralization. On the one hand, considerably less power was left to the enterprise (except for the large ones which now took over the management of their parent *centrale*). For, where previously the ministerial branch directorates had possessed sufficient professional manpower only to coordinate the enterprises rather than to manage them, the new *centrale* were given sufficient manpower to take on a true management function. On the other hand, the abolition of the ministerial branch directorates, combined with the 35 percent reduction in the number of personnel at ministerial headquarters, implied that the ministries could no longer exercise the degree of coordination which they had carried out previously.

The creation of *centrale* was also expected to strengthen the link between both development and design functions and that of production by placing all under the same *centrala*. One year after the creation of the *centrale*, about two-thirds of the institutes (and personnel) for applied research and design of new facilities were directly subordinate to the *centrale*. Previously they were all subordinate to the ministries, with the production units (then the enterprises) possessing no more than laboratories. Of course, it was far too early in 1970 to judge whether the placing of much research and design under the *centrale* would yield the

---

Economică, 1972, 3 and 4, translated in *JPS*.) On the other hand, the number of *centrale* in the machinebuilding industry had roughly doubled since 1970.

[13] Ceaușescu report to the March 1973 plenum of the Central Committee, as reported in *RFE*.

desired result; the improvement in the coordination of these activities with production is bound to be a lengthy process.

Tables 2.4 and 2.5 view the creation of the *centrale* from another standpoint. To the degree that the *centrale* headquarters are located at major enterprises, one would expect their regional distribution to bear a reasonable relationship to the regional location of such enterprises. On the other hand, to the degree that the *centrale* headquarters are heavily manned by personnel formerly in the branch directorates of the ministries, there would be a strong temptation to locate them in Bucharest.

Table 2.4 indicates that in 1970 there was indeed a disproportionate concentration of *centrale* headquarters, relative to industrial labor force, in Bucharest. But the degree of such concentration was limited at that time; even when one eliminates from consideration the food and woodworking *centrale* (which were then regional), only two-fifths of the remainder of the *centrale* were headquartered in Bucharest. By January

TABLE 2.4: Regional Location of Headquarters of All *Centrale* in Industry and Mining, Beginning 1970

	In Bucharest		Outside of Bucharest	
	(number)	(percentage)	(number)	(percentage)
Headquarters of all *centrale*	54	28	136	72
Headquarters of all *centrale*, excluding those of the food and woodworking ministries[a]	47	38	78	62
Total industrial labor force under republic jurisdiction (thousands)	289.2	18	1,339.7	82
Total number of industrial enterprises under republic jurisdiction with over 2,000 manual workers[b]	38	19	162	81

SOURCES: *Centrale: Viaţa Economică*, 1970, 2, p. 9. Data are for December 31, 1969.

Labor force and enterprises: *Anuarul 1970*, table 68, pp. 150-53, and table 71, pp. 162-63.

[a] Since the food and woodworking *centrale* were organized regionally, only a very small percentage of them could have been located in Bucharest.

[b] If one considered only enterprises with over 3,000 manual workers, the Bucharest figure would rise to 22 percent.

TABLE 2.5: Immediately Previous Posts of *Centrale* Directors of 1970

	Centrale Headquartered in Bucharest		Centrale Headquartered Outside of Bucharest		All *Centrale*[a]	
	General Directors	Other Directors	General Directors	Other Directors	General Directors	Other Directors
I. Ministries for which I have full coverage of all *centrale*[b]						
All directors (number)					47	
Directors whose previous post was in a ministerial headquarters (percentage)					21	
II. All other ministries[c]						
1. All directors of *centrale* in which interviews were conducted						
All directors (number)	0	5	3	24	3	29
Directors whose previous post was in a ministerial headquarters (percentage)		0	0	0	0	0
2. All *centrale* directors who studied at the national Management Development Center during 1970						
All directors (number)	2	24	17	37	21	73
Directors whose previous post was in a ministerial headquarters (percentage)[d]	50	12	6	3	5	7
III. Total of sample						
All directors (number)	2	29	20	61	71	102
Directors whose previous post was in a ministerial headquarters (percentage)[d]	50	10	5	2	18	5

[a] These include *centrale* whose location of headquarters is unknown.

[b] Source I provided data only as to general directors, and failed to indicate where their *centrale* were headquartered.

[c] All directors other than general directors are included, regardless of ministry.

[d] These percentages are underestimated to an unknown degree because it was not always possible to determine the location of the previous post for the sample taken from the Management Development Center. I do not think, however, that the bias introduced is very great.

1972, the degree of concentration of *centrale* headquarters in Bucharest had increased sharply; 42 percent of the total were now located there compared to 28 percent originally.[14]

The greater the degree to which the new *centrale* were headed by others than the 8,000 or so people who had been squeezed out of the ministries in late 1969, the higher is the presumption that the *centrale* in fact bore a different relationship to their enterprises than had the former branch directorates of the ministries. Table 2.5 shows, for a sample which is presumably fairly representative, that only 18 percent of all general directors, and 5 percent of all other directors, came from the ministry headquarters.[15]

The evidence of Tables 2.4 and 2.5 strengthens the presumption that the creation of the *centrale* represented something genuinely new. It was primarily top managers of the former large enterprises, rather than ministry executives, who were placed in charge of these new bodies, thus strengthening the relative power of managers whose experience had been essentially in production units. Of course, this tells us nothing as to whether the new effect was helpful or deleterious to the efficiency of the system. Moreover, the short-run direction of effect might be quite different from that which will occur over a number of years.

ORGANIZATIONS ABOVE THE LEVEL OF THE *Centrala*

Figure 2.1 shows the hierarchical structure of administration in Romania; this table of organization ends, for industry under republic-wide jurisdiction, at the level immediately above the *centrala*. There is nothing here which will strike the reader, if he is at all knowledgeable as to administration in CMEA countries, as unusual.

---

[14] *Viaţa Economică*, 1972, 3 and 4, translated in *JPS*.

[15] It should be noted that the nature of the data is such that these results do not indicate that any difference exists between these two groups. The difference in the percentages is entirely due to source I which did not provide figures for "other directors."

It is not clear what happened to the men forced out of ministerial headquarters when the *centrale* were created. Ceauşescu reported that less than 10 percent of them went to production units (clearly including *centrale*) located outside Bucharest. (*Scînteia*—written *Scanteia* in the citation—February 25, 1971, cited by *RFE*.) If one assumes that all the nonprofessionals found other jobs in Bucharest, then perhaps 15 percent of the professionals went to *centrale* and enterprises outside Bucharest. Many of the others must have gone to responsible positions in Bucharest *centrale* and enterprises within their own ministry. The ministerial reduction in staff was also taken as the occasion for a large-scale retirement of personnel. Still, it is difficult to see how all this could have totaled anything close to 100 percent. It seems possible that many took whatever job they could find simply in order to stay in Bucharest, and that the 1971 and 1973 concentration of *centrale* in Bucharest provided them once again with the possibility for responsible posts.

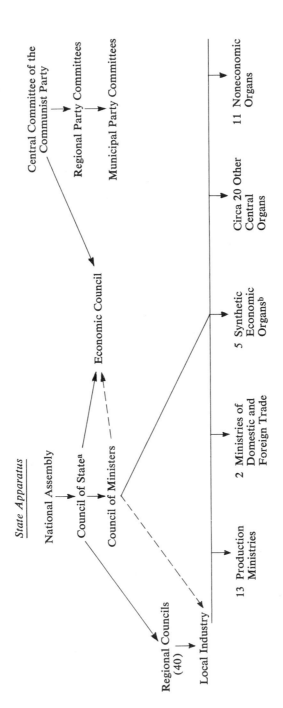

FIGURE 2.1: Organizational Structure above the Level of the *Centrala*, 1970

NOTE: Dotted lines indicate the absence of formal hierarchical authority.

[a] This is the executive organ of the government. It rules when the National Assembly is not in session, being empowered to decree laws subject to later ratification.

[b] The State Committee for Planning, the Ministry of Finance, the National Bank, the Central Statistical Office, and the Ministry of Labor.

More interesting than the details of organization is the question of the number of people engaged in the coordinating activities carried out by this suprastructure above the microeconomic units. This quantitative approach should offer some insight into the existing degree of central coordination of industry. Clearly, the fewer such people the less detailed the coordination which can be carried out. On the other hand, one might expect that, if the numbers were very large, some work would be found for them.

Data have been collected as to the number of full-time professionals in many of the organizations above the level of the *centrala*. (Professionals are defined as those who have either completed higher education or who have a rank normally held by such a person.)[16] The figures are not precise, but in each case they were given by Romanians in a position to know.[17] My confidence in the figures is strengthened by the fact that my informants were unwilling to make guesses as to the numbers in other organizations with which they were not personally familiar. In evaluating the significance of these figures, it is important to realize that manpower requirements were affected by the fact that the relevant organs had very little regular access to computers at the time of my study; the State Committee for Planning, for example, had no such access.

These figures are clearly of considerable importance for a study of the Romanian economy. But their import is broader. So far as I am aware, no similar data are available for any other centrally planned socialist economy. Thus their rough magnitudes have a greater significance than they would otherwise deserve for an understanding of the functioning of such economies in general.

Industrial branch ministries. The bulk of all professionals above the *centrala* level who are engaged in coordinating industrial activities is located in the headquarters of the branch ministries. The estimate of Table 2.7 suggests that the proportion is some 55 to 75 percent, and the true figure is probably toward the upper end of this range.

Good data are available for six ministries which coordinate about half of the total manpower in all republic-wide jurisdiction industrial min-

[16] The number of people in professional rank who have not completed higher education appears to be very small. According to a law which seems to have been enforced, only those who had filled such a position prior to 1961 were allowed to occupy professional posts; moreover, such people could not be promoted after 1960.

[17] Generally, my informants could make a close estimate of the total number of personnel in these organizations. But since the guards, cleaning women, chauffeurs, and secretaries do not play a coordinating role, I preferred a less reliable estimate of a more significant figure. This they were willing to provide. My impression is that there were not very many medium-level technicians in these organizations.

istries (Table 2.6). Although no comparable figure can be developed as to their share of total industrial capital stock or of recent industrial investment, the nature of the industries which they govern suggest that these figures would be of the same order of magnitude. Given the size and nature of our sample, it would appear quite representative of the total population of industrial branch ministries.

Total professionals employed in organizations above the level of the centrala. Interview data are presented in the Appendix to this chapter which permit an estimate of this total number. The estimate is restricted to those essentially engaged in coordinating the activities of that part of industry (82 percent in 1970) which was administered by central

TABLE 2.6: Total Personnel in the Headquarters of Six Branch Ministries, late 1970

Personnel in Headquarters[a]		Total Personnel under the Ministries		Personnel in Headquarters as Proportion of All Those under the Ministries	
Professionals[b] (number)	Others	Professionals[b, c] (number)	Total[d]	Professionals[b] (percentage)	Total
1,645	830	46,000[e]	975,000	5.3[e]	0.25

a These numbers do not include personnel in organizations directly subordinate to the ministry such as research institutes and foreign trade enterprises. However, in the case of two ministries, separate organizations which were not a part of formal headquarters had been temporarily established in order to carry out, as a part of their functions, tasks normally performed by ministerial headquarters. In the case of these two ministries, the professionals executing these specific tasks are included as working at ministerial headquarters.

b Number of staff with higher education or with job classifications normally held by such people.

c Data are available for one large ministry as to the proportion of personnel working anywhere in the ministry who did not have the level of education required for their job classification; the figure was 2 to 3 percent. This proportion has been used to expand the number of personnel with higher education which was estimated as working under the relevant ministries.

d Ministerial data are available for four ministries with 815,000 personnel. Data for the remaining two ministries have been estimated from published information on the number working in the relevant branches under republic-wide ministerial jurisdiction.

e The total number of professionals in ministerially supervised industry is a rough estimate taken from the national stock of all employees in the country with higher education. The stock of those with higher education working in industry was assumed to consist of the stock of all those who had graduated from industrial technical faculties and half of those who had graduated from economic faculties. It was then further assumed that the proportion of this group which worked in the six ministries was the same as the proportion of the labor force of these ministries to the entire industrial labor force. Fortunately, the calculated percentage is quite robust with regard to reasonable modifications of these assumptions.

Anuarul 1971, table 98, p. 229 provides data for the total number of people filling higher-level and middle-level positions under most of these ministries. If one assumes that all of these posts but no others required higher education as normal qualification, then my figure of 46,000 is underestimated by about 15 percent. However, no indication is given in the source as to what is meant by either higher-level or middle-level positions; the latter particularly may well include some positions for which higher education is not a normal requirement.

TABLE 2.7: Estimate of Number of Full-time Professionals, above the Level of the *Centrala*, Engaged in Coordinating the Activities of Industry, late 1970

Organization	Number of Professionals[a]
Economic Council	25
Secretariat of Council of Ministers	30
State Committee for Planning (working on the entire economy)	535
Ministry of Finance (working on the entire economy)	600-800
Ministry of Foreign Trade (working on the entire economy)	100-200
Ministry of Labor, restricted to staff engaged in improving economic efficiency (working on the entire economy)	183
Communist Party Committees, staff working on all economic matters[b]	200-500
All industrial branch ministries	3,300
Total, all industry	4,500-6,000

[a] Number of staff with higher education or with job classifications normally held by such people.

[b] Staff working in regional and municipal committees are included here. Full-time Party secretaries of individual enterprises are not included.

ministries rather than by regional or local authorities. Table 2.7 summarizes the resulting estimates.

If we consider the degree to which these coordinating organs represent a major investment of the manpower of industry as a whole, the figure is of course derisory (less than half of 1 percent) as a proportion of total manpower. It is more significant as a proportion of the total number of industrial personnel with higher education: an estimated 6.4 to 8.5 percent. The investment becomes one of major dimensions, however, if taken as a proportion of the fully job-trained personnel with higher education who have moved a notch above the position of rank-and-file engineer. My estimate is that some 20 to 35 percent of such personnel (the correct figure is probably closer to the upper range) must be working in organs above the level of the *centrala*.[18]

From the absolute number of people employed there, it does not appear that the ministries and their counterparts should be considered over-

[18] In the one ministry headquarters for which such data are available, no professionals below the rank of senior engineer are employed. While senior engineer is a position below that of section chief, it represents a fairly high degree of recognized competence. In the State Committee for Planning, all professionals must have first worked elsewhere as engineers or economists for eight years.

staffed. Doubtless the need for concentrating such a high percentage of medium-level and senior industrial professionals at levels above that of the operating unit is severely aggravated by the apparent failure to utilize nonprofessionals or very junior professionals in ministerial head-quarters. But the essential Romanian problem is that the country, be-cause it is moderately small and relatively unindustrialized, has no choice but to place in coordinating bodies a large proportion of its skilled in-dustrial professionals if it is to operate a centrally directed economy.

The Formation of Enterprise Prices

The appropriateness of relative prices plays a significant role within any economy in affecting the degree to which managers either in a micro-economic unit or in a supervisory agency can correctly evaluate the likely effects of alternative decisions. Since aggregation in money terms is a peculiarly convenient device, and probably one which cannot be wholly avoided, the development of a proper system of weights (i.e., prices) for such aggregation would seem an important prerequisite for achieving high efficiency at the economy-wide level.

Nevertheless, Romanians have done little to develop a satisfactory system of relative producer prices. In this respect, the country lags con-siderably behind the G.D.R.; the word "lag" is used here advisedly be-cause of my impression that Romanian administrators do not regard this as a matter of principle, but rather as a result of their inability to work out as yet the necessary preconditions. At the same time, it must be admitted that there are no indications that relative pricing is viewed as a problem area to which significant manpower resources should be de-voted.

Prices paid to and by enterprises were last changed in 1963-65 (eight to nine years after the previous change), and as of 1970 the next price change was not expected before late 1972 or 1973 at the earliest. While the desirability of such long-term price stability had been under some attack, there was no indication in 1970 of any policy change in this regard. However, at the end of 1971 a new system was legislated which provided for planned changes in producer prices every year; it was be-lieved that the new system would result in the abolition of the need for general price changes once a decade.[19]

The determination of enterprise prices was still highly centralized in 1970, with the system laid down back in 1954 remaining in force. About three-quarters of the total value of production was covered by prices set by the Council of Ministers. Almost all remaining prices were estab-

[19] G. G. Maria, chairman of the State Price Committee, in *Lupta de Clasă*, January 1972, pp. 19-30, translated in *JPS*.

lished by those individual branch ministries which are the principal producers of the relevant products. As of late 1970, decentralization of price-setting authority was expected in the near future, with the *centrale* to be given increased authority.

Just as significant as the location of price-setting authority, however, is the placement of power to change individual prices between general price revisions. Only a ministry can change a price originally established by an enterprise or *centrala*, and only the Council of Ministers can alter prices set by the ministries. Extreme price rigidity has been the natural result.

The 1963-65 prices—as well as those set more recently for products not in production at that time—were established on the basis of cost plus an average planned profit margin (percentage of cost) of 4 to 10 percent depending on the branch of industry. The profit margins used for setting individual prices varied still more widely. The price change of the 1970's was not expected to introduce anything new into this system of price determination; in fact, however, a law passed at the end of 1971 followed the example of the other CMEA countries by shifting the profit margin incorporated in prices from a percentage of cost to a percentage of capital employed.[20]

While it would have been possible to use the variation in profit margins to make prices reflect demand and supply conditions, such a concept of price formation seems in fact to have played very little if any role. To the extent that any general principle governed the variation in profit margins among branches, it seems to have been expected future reductions in costs per product unit over the lifetime of the new prices. Variations in profit margin among individual intermediate products within a branch are said to reflect mainly the desire to have similar prices for goods which can be readily substituted for one another. In reality, the prime determinant in the differentiation of profit margins was doubtless no single principle, but rather that amalgam of miscellaneous reasons grouped under the term "social considerations."

At best, therefore, prices paid to and by enterprises[21] are based on average costs. Conceivably, this could mean that prices reflect an anticipated long-run equilibrium of supply and demand,[22] but there is no

---

[20] Ibid.

[21] Highly differentiated sales taxes are levied on goods sold to consumers, but they are almost nonexistent for goods sold to enterprises.

[22] Two conditions would be necessary for this to be true. The first is the varying of planned profit margins between products and branches in such a fashion as to offset expected future shifts in costs for any reason, including changes in the scale of production; this condition was partially realized. The second condition is that planned production expansion both of branches and individual products is such as to equate the amount of a product supplied with the quantity demanded at the established price; no great effort has been made to fulfill this condition.

indication that they are even intended to be set at such a level. Certainly they could not reflect short-run equilibrium.

In fact, monetary cost under Romanian conditions is a very poor reflection of the resources required to produce a product. At the most basic level, the allocation of costs between different products produced within a single enterprise is extremely primitive. In general, all overhead costs—from maintenance and amortization to the salaries of foremen, designers, and managers—are distributed between products in proportion to the direct labor costs of the products.[23] Furthermore, the pricing of semifabricates for transfer within a *centrala* has additional weaknesses. Thus, one *centrala* I visited produced a highly differentiated set of semiprocessed goods from different elements of a common raw material, and then used some of the semiprocessed goods for further production while selling others outside the *centrala*. This *centrala* divided the cost of the common raw material among the various semiprocessed goods in strict proportion to the weight of the raw material used for each; this was done despite the fact that one would have expected the different elements of the raw material to be valued per ton in a highly differentiated fashion—as, indeed, they are in foreign markets.

A second defect of Romanian costing practice is that, until at least 1972 or 1973, there was essentially no charge made for capital, use of land, or the exhaustion of natural resources.[24] The profits planned to be earned on the sale of different products have not been related to the capital invested in their production. The only major concession to the

[23] In multiproduct enterprises (and these are the overwhelming majority) in the United States, a major attempt is usually made to allocate overhead costs to those products which are responsible—in terms of an average-cost concept—for their incurrence. Thus amortization expenses are allocated by product according both to the value of the equipment used and the proportion of the working time of this equipment which is employed in manufacturing the particular product. Design costs are allocated by attempting to determine how much time was spent on each product. These apportionment systems often, of course, yield results which vary widely from apportionment according to direct labor cost. Since overhead costs usually constitute a major proportion of total costs, the calculation of the average cost of a product is highly sensitive to the apportionment system used.

[24] Sales tax has been charged on both petroleum and resinous woods, and this can properly be interpreted as a charge for exhaustion of natural resources. Beginning with 1970, some of the centrally planned investments were financed by credit; in 1970, this share constituted about 19 percent of all industrial investment. But the annual interest rate is insignificant: some 0.1 percent for equipment and 2 to 4 percent for buildings. Another 2 percent of industrial investment was financed in 1970 by decentralized bank credit at an interest charge which was quoted to me by different sources as being between 1 and 8 percent provided that the credits are repaid on schedule. Increases of working capital since 1970 are also subject to a charge averaging 3 to 4 percent.

At the end of 1971, following the example of the other CMEA countries, a general charge on capital was legislated. No information is available as to its having had a significant effect on pricing.

desirability of reflecting in cost calculations the existing scarcities of nonlabor inputs has been that amortization rates, since their 1969 revision, are much more differentiated than earlier and are intended to take account of obsolescence.[25]

Improvement in the allocation of overhead costs would be a major undertaking which could only be done at the enterprise or *centrala* level, and which would require a considerable investment of skilled manpower. Yet without this, even significant charges for the use of capital and other nonlabor inputs would improve the character of pricing to only a limited degree. Moreover, such limited improvement would have considerable short-term disruptive effects. The absence of any input-output table for the economy implies, as was stressed to me by a Romanian economic expert, that planners would have no idea of the implication of major changes in input prices (based on revision of calculated costs) for the costs of production and therefore for the consistent pricing of other goods. Thus it is not surprising that the Romanians have been reluctant to involve themselves in major alterations of cost calculations which would be reflected in enterprise prices.

The result of the failure of enterprise prices to reflect actual scarcities in the Romanian economy is, of course, extremely damaging to decentralization. As we shall see in Chapter 3, branch ministries make investment decisions on the basis of attempting to minimize "social costs" rather than monetary costs. Decisions as to the best methods of production to employ are not based on least-cost solutions. The recognized inability to treat prices of different inputs as reflecting their relative scarcities is bound to lead to poor decisions, whichever organs make the necessary choices. But at least officials in the headquarters of branch ministries, if only because they act in constant consultation with the headquarters of other ministries, are in a better position to sense the underlying economic realities of the economy than are managers of the *centrale*. Thus decentralization of decision making could well lead to a deterioration in the quality of decisions.

Although the Romanian government opted in 1969 for giving some former ministerial powers to the operational units (*centrale*), it has made little effort to bring prices more into line with scarcity relations. No such efforts seem envisioned; even if they were to be pursued, and in a fashion unhampered by ideological constraints, it is unlikely that they could be successful in less than a decade. Decentralization of ministerial powers was being implemented in 1970 without creating the pre-

---

[25] Some fifteen hundred different linear amortization rates are in fairly frequent use. Passenger cars have a five-year amortization period and ordinary lathes are amortized over ten years. Both of these periods appear short enough to be taken as reflecting obsolescence.

condition for effective decentralized choice; furthermore, this was the only option if decentralization were to be attempted anytime in the reasonably near future. This fact may be expected to place sharp limits on the degree to which *centrale* actually exercise their new powers as well as on their effectiveness in using them.

While the problem of decision making by *centrale* under these conditions will not be treated until Chapter 4, the difficulty is also acute at the ministerial level. In evaluating ministerial planning, as it is described in Chapter 3, the reader should constantly keep in mind the constraint within which it must be carried out.

HIGHER EDUCATION

The efficiency of the management of any country's industry is bound to be affected by the level of education of the industrial labor force and particularly of its managers. Romania exhibits several surprising features in regard to education.

First, the percentage of the population with higher educational degrees—1.4 percent—appears to be almost midway among the CMEA countries of eastern Europe. This is higher than the proportion in the G.D.R. or Poland, and is not abysmally below the proportion in the country (Hungary) which has the largest percentage (1.9 percent).[26] When one considers the percentage of the Romanian labor force which is in agriculture, where relatively few people have higher education, the proportion with higher education in the rest of the labor force is surprisingly high. Furthermore, half of the engineers in 1970 had graduated before 1960, and thus had had time to accumulate substantial experience.

Basing itself on this educational accomplishment, the Romanian government in 1960 decreed a set of positions for which higher education was a requirement, and insisted that no one could be newly named or promoted to such a position unless he possessed a higher degree. As we saw exemplified in a note to Table 2.6, this law appears to have been enforced effectively. (One *centrala* director complained that, when two engineers went on leave because of pregnancy, and manual workers acted

[26] See *Statistisches Jahrbuch der Deutschen Demokratischen Republik 1970* (Staatsverlag, Berlin: 1970), appendix, p. 4. It seems quite possible, however, that the source exaggerates the Romanian figure in comparison with the East German since, while it separates East German graduates of higher educational institutions from those having finished only junior colleges (*Fachschule*), it apparently does not make such a separation (although claiming to do so) for Romania. But it should be noted that Romania had had no junior college graduates since 1958.

There is no indication as to how the East German statistical office calculated the percentages for the other CMEA countries, and thus this source can be accepted only with reserve. However, I know of no other sources except those based upon obviously improper comparisons of educational levels.

as their temporary replacements, it was not possible to pay them engineers' salaries.) Similar job requirements exist with regard to completion of secondary education, though these seem to be more laxly enforced. Although the rigidity of educational requirements leads to some complaints by managers, the government stands firm on the ground that it wishes to avoid foreman-type management. The government view that experience is no substitute for education is in sharp contrast to industrial practice in the other three countries we shall study.

All directors in enterprises (except for small ones in such branches as commerce and the food industry) are required to have completed higher education. So too are all heads of production departments in enterprises, and all heads of functional departments except for those of personnel and administration. Even at the level immediately below management, no one can be appointed as a foreman unless he has completed a two-year evening course in foremanship.

The most serious shortage in Romanian industry appears to be among people with pre-university technical training. Junior-college programs were abolished in 1958, and started up again only in 1968 or 1969. I have heard it claimed that many secondary school graduates who are not admitted to higher education prefer to work as skilled manual workers rather than as technicians, since they can earn more in the former posts. In any case, the result is that graduate engineers have to fill many positions which could readily be handled by technicians—if these existed in sufficient numbers.

Since 1967, a major effort has been made in management training. Economics training until about 1968 or 1969 consisted essentially of Marxist theory. Today, I am told, the bulk of economics students study in fields which are comparable to business school subjects.[27] Concomitantly the number of entering economics students seems roughly to have doubled in some four years, while it is said that there has been a small reduction in the number of engineering students.

All in all, for a less-developed country where major industrialization has been recent, industry appears to be remarkably well stocked with a cadre which has had relevant university training. Clearly, Romania has made a major effort in this direction to compensate for the lack of industrial experience and traditions among a large part of its industrial work force.

[27] Of the first-year class in economics in 1969-70 in all Romanian universities, 79 percent of those students who were divided by specialty were studying business subjects. (See M. R. Jackson, "Report on Economic Education and Research in Rumania," *ACES Bulletin*, xiv, 2, 1972, p. 4. This breakdown does not include the four universities outside of Bucharest which have only one economics faculty, but Jackson reports that the bulk of their students were also pursuing programs of business studies.)

THE MAJOR purpose of this Appendix is to present available data for late 1970 as to the numbers of full-time professionals employed outside of the industrial branch ministries, but who were engaged in coordinating industrial activities. The second purpose is to provide an indication of the functional tasks performed by those working within the branch ministry headquarters. All data were collected through interviews with the relevant organizations.

Working our way down the hierarchy shown in Figure 2.1 of Chapter 2, and presenting data wherever they are available, we have the following picture:

The Economic Council. This is the most senior staff body for industrial matters, and serves both the Council of State and the Central Committee of the Communist Party. It carries out long-run studies for both bodies (in this regard, serving essentially as a check on the State Committee for Planning), and also provides the entire staffing for the provision of daily key operating figures to the Party Central Committee which has no economic staff of its own. For its long-run studies, the Council relies heavily on study groups formed from specialists outside its own staff; thus two functional directors at the headquarters of one branch ministry reported that they were constantly members of one or another such group.

The Council has two or three full-time professionals to cover branches which account for 6 percent of the industrial labor force and 14 percent of the industrial capital stock, and which absorbed 15 percent of all industrial investment during 1966-69.

Secretariat of the Council of Ministers. This staff deals exclusively with operational matters. For example, it treats such questions as why a particular ministry did not provide the specific goods it was supposed to deliver to another ministry. This is the second most senior staff body dealing with industrial affairs.

Here, six professionals handle the problems for a group of industries accounting for 15 percent of the industrial labor force and 23 percent of the industrial capital stock, and which absorbed 48 percent of all industrial investment during 1966-69.

Below this level are about fifty organs (including noneconomic ones) of ministerial rank. Let us begin with three of the five organs which exist for synthesizing information.[28]

[28] I do not have information about the other two.

The State Committee for Planning. Including the bodies attached to it which can be considered as constituent parts, the committee has a total staff of about 535 professionals. This is divided roughly as follows:

Branch sections[a]	200	professionals
Functional sections[b]	160	
Of this, foreign trade		40
Coordinating section	40	
Department for Coordination of Supply[c]	60	
Research organizations[d]	75	

NOTES:

[a] Each such section corresponds in coverage to one or more production ministry.

[b] There are separate sections for at least the following functions: man-power and wages, investment, foreign trade, education, research, finance, territorial distribution, and economic cooperation with foreign countries.

[c] The professionals counted here work out materials balances and develop norms of consumption of materials and of final consumer products. Not in-cluded are operational personnel working in the regional enterprises (sub-ordinate to this department) which provide supplies in less-than-carload lots to the branch enterprises located in their respective regions.

[d] This was quite a new and developing part of the Planning Committee in late 1970, and has since probably expanded rapidly. It included an inter-ministerial group working on developing the first input-output table of the Romanian economy, a group of model builders and mathematicians for the Committee's computer center (although the computer itself had not yet been received), and a tiny research institute.

Of the 400 professionals working for the Committee itself, close to two-thirds had had an economic education; the rest were engineers who worked primarily in the branch sections.

Ministry of Finance. While this appears to be the largest of the min-istries, I would estimate that it has only 600 to 800 professionals (if one excludes the local inspectors who constitute a force of probably another 200 to 300). The bulk of the Ministry's personnel are em-ployed within sections, each of which is charged with financing a group of branches of the economy (all industry and construction is covered by one such section); each of these sections has some 100 to 150 pro-fessionals.

Ministry of Labor. The data provided here cover only one major segment of the Ministry: that concerned with improving the general efficiency of the economy. About 183 professionals are engaged in this activity. The work is carried on by three sections:

Section for Organizational Studies[a]	42
Section of Staffing Norms[b]	37
Section of the national Management Development Center[c]	104

NOTES:

[a] Half of the professionals in this section are occupied in working out recommendations to the Council of Ministers on how best to organize branch ministries, *centrale*, and enterprises, and on how to develop a proper national information system. The other half are engaged in more operational tasks: acting as consultants to *centrale* and enterprises, and providing professional guidance to the regional centers of management training.

[b] This section is involved primarily in developing the methodology for determining the appropriate number and composition of personnel in enterprises and *centrale*; its methodology is then passed on to the individual ministries with the instruction to apply it. The section has also worked out manpower ratios which can be applied directly to certain groups of administrative personnel. One-quarter of its staff consists of field inspectors charged with assuring that the section's methodological instructions are properly applied.

[c] These are operational personnel, directly involved in running management training courses for middle and senior managers, giving courses for computer programmers, and conducting management research whose main purpose is to improve the training programs.

If, however, we eliminate the staff concerned directly with management training and consulting for operational units (*centrale* and enterprises), only some 72 professionals are left.

Of the two ministries of trade, rough data are available only for the *Ministry of Foreign Trade*. My figures for this ministry are probably the least reliable of any I am presenting. I have been told that the Ministry has only 100 to 200 professionals when one excludes those in the Ministry's institute for studying foreign trade possibilities in foreign countries, and also those in the five export-import enterprises which remain under the Ministry's jurisdiction.

State Price Committee. This is an interministerial committee (apparently run basically by the Ministries of Finance and Domestic Trade and by the State Committee for Planning) whose tasks are to work out the methodology for determining new prices and to give its "opinion" as to price changes recommended by line bodies such as branch ministries. The number of professionals is not known; but it is said to be certainly fewer than 100, including a fair number of inspectors. Their tasks, however, do not include that of setting individual prices.

Party Committees. The full-time professionals who are both attached to the Central Committee and are engaged in economic work number virtually zero. However, the second Party level (consisting of the forty regional committees) and the third level (the municipal Party committees) do employ professionals.

Data are available for one region, which had four to five full-time professionals attached to the Party regional committee and working entirely on economic matters. Four professionals worked on economic matters (mainly industrial) in one of the country's nine municipalities with 150,000 to 200,000 population (excluding suburbs);[29] two worked in a medium-sized municipality of 40,000 population. As we shall see in Chapter 4, such regional and municipal Party committees play an important de facto role in administering enterprises and *centrale* in their areas. Thus it is important to take account of the size of their full-time staffs.

The industrial branch ministries. I have collected data of varying degrees of reliability as to the number of full-time professionals working in each of the functional sections of three of the six branch ministries in which I conducted interviews. As one might expect, both the precise tasks carried out by sections bearing the same name, and the proportion of professionals employed in each section, vary somewhat among ministries. Nevertheless, comparison with the data of the other two ministries allows me to conclude that the figures for the one large ministry which provided precise numbers can be taken as reasonably representative.

From Table 2.8 we can see that roughly one-third of the ministerial headquarters staff are concerned with problems of production and improvement in technology. Over one-quarter deal with the allocation of

TABLE 2.8: Number of Professionals by Section in One Ministry's Headquarters Staff, late 1970 (percentage)

Procurement, distribution, and sales	28
Planning	11
Finance, accounting, costing, and pricing	9
Personnel and education	3
Law and arbitration	1
Technology	18
Production[a]	14
Organization, control, and inspection	11
Administration	2
Advisers to the Minister	1

[a] In half of the six ministries, this function was performed by two to four sections which were distinguished by subbranch. In the other ministries, a single section was in charge of this function for all subbranches.

[29] Only Bucharest is larger than this size category.

materials to the units of the ministry and with the distribution of their products. Planning, finance, and pricing constitute the occupation of another fifth. Data from two ministries suggest that 55 to 60 percent of the ministerial staff have engineering degrees, with the rest having degrees in economics.

CHAPTER 3

Romania: Integration of the Economy Above the Level of the *Centrala*

This chapter is based primarily upon interviews conducted partly within the State Committee for Planning and the Ministry of Foreign Trade, but above all in the headquarters of seven of Romania's thirteen industrial ministries. It represents an interpretation, taken from the standpoint of the branch ministries, of how the economy is coordinated.

In Romania, much more than in any of the other three countries covered in this book, the economic decisions of the economy are concentrated above the level of the production unit. Thus my materials on the methods of economic decision making in Romania are concentrated in this chapter.

PLANNING IN GENERAL

Absence of economic research. It must be stressed at the outset that virtually all nonacademic economic work, whether done in the ministries or even in the State Committee for Planning, is operational. Research designed to provide a better understanding of the structure or functioning of the Romanian economy is almost nonexistent. Thus efforts at improvement of the economic working of the system are inevitably of an ad hoc nature.

Until 1970, the entire staff of the State Committee for Planning was involved in handling current problems. No one there had time for basic studies. The same was true in other ministerial-level organizations. One result was that Ph.D.'s—whether in economics, natural science, or engineering—were rarely found in any of these bodies. Of more than five hundred professionals working in the State Committee for Planning, only several tens of them had any higher education beyond the first degree.

Furthermore, it would appear that academic economists involved in research and teaching have made relatively little contribution to the improvement of planning. The principal relevant economic research body is the Institute of Economic Research of the Academy of Social and Political Science.[1] The researchers here who deal with the Romanian economy have been primarily involved in historical studies. They appear to have had little or no access to unpublished data, and no significant relations have been developed between them and such bodies as the State Committee for Planning. No system has yet developed in which they can take leaves of absence to work at a ministerial-level organization for a year or two. Thus they have not served as a significant complement to the work of the administrative organizations.

Only toward the middle of 1970 did the State Committee for Planning establish a small research institute of its own. Over the next few years, its contribution will probably be limited primarily to the development of an input-output table of the Romanian economy.

Of course, this does not in any way suggest that the personnel in ministerial-level organizations are incompetent. My impressions as to the analytic and managerial competence of directors and department heads at ministerial headquarters were quite favorable; those with whom I talked seemed on an average to be a notch above their counterparts in the enterprises and *centrale*. They were clearly, however, operational people. In this respect, executives working in ministerial headquarters and even in the State Committee for Planning are quite similar to those engaged in the company headquarters of very large American firms. Their misfortune is that they receive virtually no backup from research-oriented economists in the creation and organization of basic economic knowledge about Romania.

Five-year plans. The operational plans for the economy are drawn up annually. But "perspective" plans are also employed; the five-year plan is intended to coordinate the development of the various economic sectors, while plans for ten to fifteen years are established for a few individual sectors (e.g., energy and the development of the Danube) in which investment decisions require a longer perspective. Since the inauguration of the 1966-70 plan, the five-year plans have included branch production targets for each individual year. There is talk of moving to a system of "rolling" five-year plans beginning with 1972; under this system, a new five-year plan would be drawn up each year and extended one year beyond the last. It is unclear to me, however, whether this notion of shifting to a "rolling" plan is taken seriously by the planners concerned.

A fair amount of work goes into the formulation of the five-year plans. Work on the 1971-75 plan began in 1967-68 with the formation of commissions whose membership included representatives of individual min-

[1] There are also three other economic research institutes in Romania: for agricultural economics, for the analysis of consumer demand, and for foreign trade.

istries as well as experts appointed in their individual capacities. Following a year of meetings of these commissions, Directives for the plan were adopted by a Party congress in late 1969. In June 1970, the State Committee for Planning gave proposed tasks to the individual ministries, which then subdivided the tasks to the level of the *centrale* and enterprises. These production-unit tasks were further discussed at regional Party committee meetings, and the *centrale*'s reactions to them were expected to reach the State Committee for Planning by mid-October. The State Committee for Planning expected that revisions on the basis of these reactions would be very minor, and that a law for the five-year plan could be adopted in December 1970. In fact, it was only in May 1971 that the Party Central Committee adopted a "draft plan"—and this differed substantially from the 1969 Directives. Even at this point, the planning process was incomplete. The degree of change which was still to come is shown by the fact that the final plan, adopted in October 1971, called for a rate of growth of industrial production which was 25 percent higher than that of the draft plan.

The planning head of one rapidly growing and capital-intensive ministry gave the following description of the formulation of his ministry's five-year plan. The ministry begins by setting output targets for each of its major product groups. (For the 1971-75 plan, this of course occurred long before June 1970 when the ministries received their first product tasks from above.) Consultations with its major direct supplier ministries indicate whether these output targets are realistic from the viewpoint of probable receipts of the necessary materials. Having modified its targets on this basis, the ministry comes to the State Committee for Planning with a request for a specific monetary allocation for investment. The State Committee for Planning evaluates this request in the light of similar requests from other ministries and reduces it accordingly.

On the basis of the reduced investment quota, the ministry in turn reduces its proposed production program for the latter years of the plan period. Simultaneously, it informs its customer ministries as to the product groups for which it will have to reduce shipments below those originally estimated. Since its products serve as inputs for these ministries, they in turn reduce their proposed output and, correspondingly, their intended investments. A new set of ministerial investment requests is now made to the State Committee for Planning, and a second iterative process has begun.[2]

At least in this particular ministry, the sequence of iterations includes only output, material input requirements, and investment requests. Dur-

---

[2] Presumably, the State Committee for Planning does not in the first round(s?) of iteration reduce the sum of the requested investments to the total amount scheduled for the entire economy.

ing the iterative process, no account is taken either by the ministry or by the State Committee for Planning of the possibilities for labor/capital substitution.[3] Rather, only at the very end of the process (during the last two or three months of formulating the five-year plan) does the ministry calculate its "synthetic" indexes (primarily profit margins and labor productivity). No lengthy iterative process is used to adjust these. This fact does not mean that the resulting synthetic indexes are immune to review; in fact, this particular ministry has been subject to more pressure on labor productivity targets than on any others. But central effort to increase ministry-planned labor productivity occurs primarily through insistence, rather than through an iterative trade-off between investment and manpower needs.

The national five-year plan, as it is finally adopted by the National Assembly, is a very brief document. The detailed five-year instructions are not contained in appendixes, but rather are issued by the Council of Ministers in orders to the relevant bodies. These instructions are said to remain unmodified throughout the five-year period.

It is not surprising that the five-year plans are fulfilled in more widely varying proportions than are the annual plans; not only is it more difficult to make accurate predictions for a longer time span, but also there is a greater likelihood that central government decision makers will change their views as to relative priorities. What is more interesting is that the Romanian five-year plans do not represent the most accurate predictions available at the time that the plans are established.

It was explained to me at the State Committee for Planning that actual annual production plans are expected to be higher than the plan stipulated for that year in the five-year plan. The essential reason for this practice, it was claimed, is that the five-year plan is particularly concerned with establishing balance between the various sectors of the economy, and that underfulfillment is considered a more serious problem than overfulfillment since the latter can be readily restrained. Thus the five-year plan is deliberately biased downward.[4]

But this need not be true of all aspects of the five-year plan. An informant in late 1970 from the State Committee for Planning expected

[3] In successive iterations, the ministry does not respond to reductions in its investment allocation by reducing the level of mechanization which it had originally projected. Nor, on presenting an investment request to the State Committee for Planning, does it inform the Committee of the expected effect of mechanization on labor productivity.

[4] The logic of this viewpoint would appear much sounder as applied to sectors which are not heavily dependent upon scarce inputs produced by other sectors, than to those which can be considered as coming later in a vertically integrated process. (This assumes, as is probably reasonable in Romania, that the input-output matrix—if such a matrix had been worked out by Romanian planners—would be triangular.)

that the 1971-75 plan for aggregate cost reduction would end up unrealistically optimistic; the logic behind the Committee's setting unattainable cost targets, according to him, was that such targets would lead ministries and *centrale* to increase the priority given to cost reduction measures. Staff personnel at the Committee differed as to whether export plans also deliberately overstate the expected results. It should be noted that failure to fulfill aggregate cost reduction or export plans does not represent the threat to structural (input-output) physical balance of the economy which is involved in underfulfillment of the production targets for goods which are inputs into further production.

At one of the ministries, I was told that its allocation of investment in the five-year plan has always been less for the last year of the plan than for the preceding year; the quantity of investment realized in the last year has, on the contrary, been higher. The reason given for this state of affairs was that the Council of Ministers wishes to keep larger investment reserves for the later years than for the earlier ones, so that it may more easily add investment resources to those sectors where they are most needed. The result is that this ministry has always counted on receiving a larger investment allocation than provided in the five-year plan.

In a second ministry, the increase in the labor force provided in the 1966-70 plan was two to three times higher than the increase which actually occurred. The ministry, however, fulfilled its overall production target. Discussions at the ministry headquarters indicated that the staff there had never taken seriously the increase in the labor force which had originally been promised, and had operated from the start on the assumption that their sector would have to show much greater improvements in labor productivity than were called for in the plan.

The result of this approach toward five-year planning is that, even if the economy were to function throughout the five years exactly according to the best estimates made at the time that the plan was drawn up, the five-year plan instructions would not be precisely fulfilled. For the five-year plan is a combined result of prediction, the holding of hidden reserves, and the setting of targets based on their expected incentive effect. The same is also true of the annual plans, of course; but there the relative weight of prediction in determining the plan appears to be much more important.

In the future, however, the importance of accurate planning two years ahead is supposed to be considerably greater than was the case prior to 1971. This is because, as will be discussed below, it is hoped that annual production targets for *centrale* will be established on the basis of prior delivery contracts which they will have signed with their customers. This system was not implemented successfully during the first contract negotiations which took place during 1970 for 1971; however, the failure was traced in part to the lack of annual global output targets, because the 1971-75 plan had not yet been adopted, which the *centrale* could use as a guide in their negotiations. If this contract system is to work better in the future, it is important that the *centrale* receive such targets at least one year in advance and that these be viewed as good predictors of the tasks to be set later in the annual plans. Thus improved five-year planning takes on increased importance; here, probably, is the motivation for the "rolling" plans. But the experience of both the Soviet Union and of large American companies suggests that it is dubious whether such "rolling" plans can actually be developed without devoting to them an unacceptably large amount of planning resources.

In other socialist countries (e.g., the Soviet Union and Hungary), the notion has developed in recent years that production units such as enterprises should be guaranteed the immutability of certain aspects of their five-year plans.[5] While it is unclear whether such guarantees will actually be observed, it is interesting that as yet the very concept is foreign to Romanian planning. Here the view is held that five-year plan indicators for *centrale* should be taken only as predictive of the annual plan indicators, and that even the latter should be subject to change at the whim of the organ which originally approved the plan.

Annual plan indicators. The annual operating plans, both for the ministries and for the organizations below them, are composed of a wide variety of indicators. Only a few of those indicators, however, are considered of genuine importance. The important ones appear to be the following:

1. Total production, measured in value terms in constant prices.
2. Outputs of certain specific, major products.
3. Labor productivity, defined as total value of output divided by the number of employees.
4. Profit margin as a percentage of value of output.[6]
5. Export deliveries both to East and West. (For bodies below the ministry level, this is a new indicator provided only in mid-1970, and one which it was said might well prove only temporary.)

This list of major plan indicators does not cover five major aspects of economic performance which should clearly be of concern to government authorities: measurement of efficiency by return on capital; quality im-

[5] Such guarantees relate to financial norms governing the portions of profits which can be used for bonuses and for investments.

[6] Presumably this was changed for the planning-year 1973 to a percentage of capital.

provement; introduction of new products; mechanization and improvement of technological processes; and concentration on the product mix desired by consumers.[7] The question thus arises of how the planning system deals with these aspects of performance.

Judging from my interviews at ministries, the problem is approached in two ways. First, emphasis is placed on a very limited number of new products and process improvements which can be specifically spelled out in the annual plan given to the ministry. This approach is most appropriate for an economy whose structure is relatively simple: one in which final consumers have a low living standard and thus are comparatively satisfied with any goods meeting their basic needs; in which the central government authorities are primarily concerned with attaining structural shifts away from agriculture toward industry; and in which the sophisticated products that are required in relatively small quantities are heavily imported. All of the above features are peculiarly characteristic of Romania.[8] Under these conditions, the importance of advancing across-the-board efficiency is less than would be the case in a more advanced economy.

Second, the targets established for the ministries do not appear demanding. My impression from discussions at the ministries is that it is quite exceptional for them to fail to fulfill plan indicators of importance.[9] Longevity in ministerial headquarters staff posts is great, and

[7] Of these five areas, so far as I am aware only new products and quality are covered by even minor plan indicators. Beginning with 1971, the ministries were each to receive an annual target for the percentage of their total output which was to consist of items not produced in Romania in 1970. But since this target might be met by the proliferation of minor product changes of no benefit to anyone, the fulfillment of this indicator could not be treated as of prime importance. Aside from this, the areas of new products and technology are handled simply by specifying a few major products and projects which are to be introduced. Quality improvement is said to be covered by an indicator of the proportion of output which is to be of "superior" quality according to national quality standards; but I never heard this indicator referred to except at the State Committee for Planning.

[8] Sales of consumer goods at reduced prices, for example, constitute only a minor phenomenon in Romania, in sharp contrast to the situation in Hungary. Apparently the Romanians encounter no serious problem of consumer sales resistance.

[9] I also have the impression, although I was not given any systematic data on the subject, that it is also exceptional for a ministry to have its plan indicators changed during the course of the year. In one ministry, it was stated that the Council of Ministers is normally asked by this ministry to make one or two changes each year—but that these requests are generally refused, and were in fact so refused in the last full year. In a second ministry, there were also no changes made in the preceding year. In a third, it was expected that a revision of one indicator would have to be requested for the current year; but it was already late November when I was told this, and the request had not yet been made.

It is interesting that there is no uniform procedure for changing plans, whether they be for a ministry or for a *centrala* or enterprise. It is true that a cut in targets is expressed through a formal reduction in the official plan; but plans may be in-thus dismissal or transfer is not a serious fear. Furthermore, no substantial portion of the earnings of the professional staff working at headquarters is dependent upon the degree of fulfillment of plan indicators. Thus the ministerial headquarters personnel are under no great pressure to concentrate exclusively on those economic objectives whose attainment is reflected in the plan-fulfillment figures. Since ministries can afford to broaden their focus of interest beyond the indicators specified in their plans, government authorities are in a relatively good position to use ad hoc measures to direct the attention of individual ministries to other problems when and if the authorities find this advisable.

A good example of the treatment given even major plan indicators is the handling of product-mix assignments for a ministry with a wide product assortment. This ministry's outputs of about one hundred major products or product groups are specified by the Council of Ministers. In fact, however, there is no objection to the ministry's slighting these assignments so long as the pattern of "demand" by other ministries is not too seriously violated. Thus the ministry is never compelled to go to the Council with a request for revision of its product-mix plan. A responsible official in this ministry cited a particular major product group for which the Council of Ministers provides a four-way assignment breakdown according to the dimensions of the individual product produced. According to him, the ministry can in fact ignore this four-way breakdown so long as the purchasing ministries are not so grievously treated as to be moved to protest to the Council. At any one time, the Council follows and enforces the assignments for only some twenty of the hundred products which it officially plans.

This ministry follows a similar procedure in specifying the outputs of particular products for its *centrale*. In fact, the ministry does not bother to revise the annual product-mix plans of its *centrale* until December of the very year covered by the plan; the fulfillment of product-mix targets is regarded as too uncertain for it to be worthwhile making formal changes in the "plan" any earlier in the year. Both the Council of Ministers and the ministry itself show no interest in the quarterly differentiation of the output programs for individual product groups.

In another ministry, I was told that the ministry is expected to establish relative output levels of substitute products mainly according to the criterion of profit for the economy as a whole (taken as a percentage of value of output). Since prices do not reflect the utility (average or marginal) of the different products to the using ministries, there is no

---

creased either through a formal change or by an addition of extra tasks which do not formally enter into the plan. There does not appear to be any established set of conditions which causes one or the other approach to be used.

expectation that this criterion should lead to the same product-mix decisions as would the criterion of profit earned by the ministry. The headquarters of this ministry appears to consider the index it receives for its ministerial accounting-profit margin as having no binding force, and it disregards it in making its product-mix decisions.

In two ministries in which I interviewed, labor productivity was said to be a very important plan indicator. One of these ministries was extremely capital intensive and the other labor intensive. But in a third, highly labor-intensive ministry, the labor productivity index was considered of quite minor significance and its fulfillment was not taken seriously. (This seems to be because of its inappropriateness to the production of this third branch, since the ratio of value-added to the total value of production differs widely within the ministry from one period to another.) For this ministry, the Council of Ministers appears to be interested only in output figures. The ministry's approach toward its own *centrale* appears to be similar.

Thus it can be seen that the branch ministries are subject to systematic control only with regard to a very small number of plan indicators, and that there is variation among ministries with regard to the degree that the individual indicators within this group are taken seriously.

LABOR FORCE AND WAGES

Both the ministries and their subordinate bodies are obliged to fulfill their annual plan indicators within three constraints; the total size of the labor force allocated to them, the total amount of wages they are allowed to pay, and the materials allocations which they have received.

There are two formal constraints upon the size of the labor force in an organization: the total number of blue-collar employees and the total number of white-collar employees. My impression, however, is that neither of these is normally an operative constraint; the plan indicator for overall labor productivity appears to provide the effective control over the size of the labor force which the ministries and their *centrale* attempt to recruit.[10] No doubt the practical labor force limitation arises far more from labor market conditions than from any constraints imposed by planning quotas.

In theory, the ministry subdivides its manpower quota to its *centrale* and enterprises. They, in turn, can hire only within the limits of their

[10] The evidence for this impression is twofold. In my interviews in most ministries, no mention at all was made of the labor force constraints. In the one ministry where they were discussed, the ministry had more men than its allotted quota. Nevertheless, the planning director of this ministry showed no disturbance over this excess, and he was not trying to bring the above-quota *centrale* into line.

quotas; the mechanism to assure this is that when they hire at the gate —which is the normal procedure—they must first get clearance from the local labor office, which is expected to give permission only within the quota assigned to the enterprise. In practice, however, such permission was regarded as a mere formality in the one ministry where I discussed this matter, even though the ministry was then above its planned manpower quota.

I would conjecture that the main means currently employed to direct labor into the desired industries stems from the existence of the phenomenon known as "closed cities." In late 1970, all or virtually all of Romania's cities with more than 100,000 population were "closed," meaning that it was exceedingly rare for a nonresident of the city to receive permission to become a permanent resident.[11] However, the number of temporary residents is large: in the one city for which I have such information, 15 percent of the total population—and perhaps 21 percent of the labor force—was composed of temporary residents.

It is the municipality itself which grants the privilege to an individual to reside in a closed city as a temporary resident, and such permission seems to be given for less than a year although it can be renewed. Clearly this device can be a potent means for directing labor to those enterprises within the city which would otherwise suffer most from labor shortage. While this device is applicable only to activities located in closed cities, approximately half of the country's urban labor force seems to be employed in these localities. Thus it seems reasonable to estimate that something over 10 percent of Romania's total labor force in industry, mining, and construction is subject to the de facto job direction which is imposed upon temporary residents of closed cities.

The wage fund quotas which the ministries receive appear to be taken more seriously than do the manpower quotas. Each ministry receives a wage fund for white-collar workers which is invariant with the degree of plan fulfillment; the wage fund for manual workers, on the other hand, is changed roughly in proportion to the degree that the planned target for value of output is fulfilled.

People at the Ministry of Labor claim that national wage outlays normally are slightly less than the wage funds allotted, and that it is rare for assigned wage funds aggregated to the ministerial level to be overexpended. The aggregate underexpenditure is explained on the basis that each organization must be sure not to overexpend its fund, and that it cannot plan exactly both because of its lack of control over labor force quits and because sick pay is not paid from the wage fund.

[11] An estimated hundred to one hundred fifty people receive such permission annually in the single city for which I have data.

On the face of it, this claim is puzzling. Some 47 percent of all manual workers are paid by piece rates, and piece norms are readily "adjustable" by enterprise management in order to provide higher earnings. Similarly, managers can easily classify workers into higher skill (and thus pay) categories than their actual abilities warrant. If managements are primarily motivated to fulfill physical output targets, one would expect them to compete with one another for labor by using such mechanisms to raise the earnings of their employees; this would cause them to exceed their allotted wage funds. In the Soviet Union, for example, strong pressure has to be placed on enterprise managements not to exceed wage funds. (Any such overexpenditures are deducted from the fund for white-collar bonuses.) Why is it that Romanian industry seems to live within its wage fund without the use of such pressure methods?

Part of the answer seems to be that only mining and construction suffer from serious shortages of manpower, presumably because of the rapid inflow of labor from agriculture. A second reason is the existence of wage fund reserves within ministries which seem to be sufficient to allow for a 2 to 3 percent annual slippage.[12] But the principal reason is that there is little incentive for overfulfillment of planned output targets at the *centrala* and enterprise level, and that the established targets are not overly ambitious. Thus there is no strong motivation for wage fund violation.

Wage fund allocations are made on the basis of what is required to assure designated average earnings. Norms of piece rates appear to be set within this constraint. In construction, for example, the head of one trust said that he cannot pay higher than planned average earnings to his workers even if he could thereby get along with fewer workers and a smaller total wage fund. Nor are actual piece-work wage payments in this trust allowed to fall below the planned weekly wage level. Since the trust would lose its workers if they earned less than what they expected, the foremen when necessary make adjustments in individual output norms so as to bring earnings up to the necessary level. In another ministry, no additional wage payments at all are made to piece workers producing more than a specified amount.

In theory, earnings are determined according to a national wage and salary system differentiated both by skill and by the branch of the economy. In practice, however, they are more determined by the planned wage fund for the unit: a fund which is determined statistically rather

[12] In one ministry, the planning director believed that the wage fund reserves were 1 percent at the level of the ministry and an average of 0.2 percent at the level of the *centrale*; but he stated that a total of 3 percent reserves were permitted. In a second ministry, it was believed that reserves at all levels of the ministry totaled about 2 percent of the ministerial wage fund.

than by a detailed analysis of the labor force composition. Thus within one ministry, wage funds are allocated on the basis of the average earnings in the unit during the previous year, plus an expected 1-1/2 to 2 percent increase in fulfillment of work norms and thus of earnings.

The Romanian concept of wage increases is that for any branch they should be concentrated within a single year of the five-year period. In practice, however, work norms are only raised at the same time that basic wages are augmented; thus the actual annual increases in average earnings during 1966-70 were evened out through steady expansion in above-norm piece-rate wage payments during all years when there was no increase in nominal wages, and by sharp reductions in such payments in the year (primarily 1970) of nominal wage increases.

Materials Allocations and Product-Mix Decisions

Materials allocation must be judged as quite centralized when one considers together the allocations made by both the Council of Ministers and the individual branch ministries. Through 1970, the Council of Ministers determined allocations to user branch ministries of some 180 different groupings of materials and equipment.[13] The Council's allocations are made on the basis of materials balances developed by a staff of some sixty professionals in the State Committee for Planning. Further allocations—both of the same product groupings in greater detail and of other products—are carried out by the branch ministries producing the materials and equipment. An estimate by a very well informed Romanian source is that only some 10 to 12 percent of the economy's value of materials and equipment escape both of these allocation systems.[14] For all controlled materials and equipment, the allocations are made to the user ministries which in turn make the further allocations to their own *centrale*.

The process of drawing up materials balances within the State Committee for Planning appears to be primarily an internal matter, with negotiations taking place between the materials balances department and the various branch departments of the Committee. Discussions with Committee officials indicated no clear standards for determining substitution of materials, only a listing of relevant criteria. Clearly, relative monetary costs play some role; so far as I have been able to determine, this internal

[13] In addition, the Council of Ministers approved norms of materials consumption for specific products; six hundred such norms were approved for 1970. The number of groupings of materials and equipment allocated by the Council of Ministers was expected to be reduced by 45 percent in 1971.

[14] These unallocated products are, of course, those for which demand does not exceed supply. Apparently there is frequent change from one year to another with regard to the specific products which are left unallocated.

work of the Committee is the only place in the economy where shadow-rates of foreign exchange (differentiated by country source) are used.[15] The branch ministries themselves appear to play no role in this process; apparently, their interests are considered to be represented by the appropriate branch departments of the Committee for Planning.

Romanian authorities appear to have no illusions as to the accuracy of the materials balances. This is shown by the rather large reserves of planned production which remain unallocated to user ministries at the beginning of the planning year; such reserves are estimated as averaging 4 to 6 percent of planned output. In addition, of course, the user ministries maintain their own reserves, to be allocated to the individual *centrale* only during the course of the planning year.

For all materials and equipment, including those balanced at the level of the Council of Ministers, decisions as to the detailed product mix to be made available to a user ministry are determined by the producing ministry. Thus the producing, rather than the consuming, bodies have the whip hand in deciding which specific items are to be produced.[16] This applies even to imports, since in general foreign exchange allocations are provided to producing rather than to user ministries; it is the former which decide—within their foreign exchange constraint—which products they will produce and which they will import. Although user ministries have the right of appeal, they—and even more their *centrale* and enterprises—are in a weak position to get the precise product mix which is most beneficial to them.[17]

The above system represents an extreme concentration of procurement decisions at the levels of the ministries and the Council of Ministers combined. In my opinion, such concentration has significant advantages. Partly this is because the Romanian pricing system constitutes a totally inadequate guide for consuming *centrale* and enterprises as to the relative national shortage of the various materials which can be substituted for

[15] Here, for example, a different shadow-rate of exchange is used for each socialist trading partner, rather than a single percentage multiplier of the official rate for all of them lumped together. These shadow-rates are not determined ex cathedra for a given planning year, but are themselves derived by an iterative process.

[16] This bias may have been reduced slightly by the creation in late 1971 of the Ministry for Supply of Materials and for the Supervision of the Management of Fixed Assets. This new ministry had under it a commission charged with resolving precontractual disputes (*Buletinul Oficial*, I, 1971, 109, pp. 718-24, translated in *JPS*). Previously, the supply function had been fulfilled by an agency subordinate to the State Committee for Planning; the new ministry was at a higher hierarchical level than the agency it replaced.

[17] The Ministry of Domestic Trade, which is often dissatisfied with the product mix it receives, engages in a fair amount of exchange of such products for other consumer goods produced abroad. Hungary, the Soviet Union, and Yugoslavia are the main trading partners in such exchanges, but enterprises in capitalist countries also take part.

one another. Partly it is because producing enterprises and *centrale* are less to be trusted than are their ministries to soft pedal the product-mix effects on fulfillment of their own planned output, productivity, and profit-margin goals when deciding on the product mix to offer. Nevertheless, Romanian authorities have been more impressed by the disadvantages of this centralization, and they therefore attempted in 1970 to decentralize the procurement system.

Decentralization consisted of two elements. The more important was the legislation requiring that supply contracts between *centrale* precede rather than follow the setting of production plans. The second element was a reduction in the number of materials balances determined at the Council of Ministers level, and the transfer of many ministerial balances to coordinators operating at the *centrala* level. While this new system was supposed to go into effect in 1970 in preparing the 1971 plan, my impression is that relatively little was accomplished then. A description of the program (as of late 1970) for the 1972 plan is thus of more relevance. Unfortunately, no information is available to me as to the progress, if any, in decentralization after 1970.

It was expected that, in the fourth quarter of 1970, *centrale* would receive total profitability targets and also planned value of output targets for their main product groups. On the basis of these preliminary indicators, producing and user *centrale* would sign contracts during the first half of 1971 for the delivery of specific products. The balance-coordinators at the level of the producing *centrale* or ministries would guide the contract negotiators. Their task would be to transform what would otherwise be a sellers' market into an equilibrated one by specifying the purchasing units with which any given producing organization could negotiate; thus, since the producing *centrala* would have to sign with these few purchasers sufficient contracts to meet its own production targets, it would be forced into being responsive to detailed demands for product-mix and delivery terms. At the same time, the producing *centrala* would negotiate as to product mix within the constraint of the profitability target it had already received.[18]

On the basis of these contracts, the ministries and the State Committee for Planning would both revise the preliminary planning indicators and make them binding and more detailed. This could, of course, lead

[18] Perhaps partly with this in mind, profits which are greater than 10 to 12 percent of the value of production are to go directly into the state budget rather than be counted as *centrala* profits. This should reduce the degree to which the producing *centrale* gear their contracts to those products which have the most favorable prices. But not only does this regulation apply only to "selected products," but the extent to which it will be actually enforced is unclear. While it officially went into effect in mid-1970, units below the ministerial level seemed totally unaware of it in late 1970, and even the branch ministries offered widely diverging interpretations of the regulation.

to the revision of contracts signed earlier—and no compensation would be paid to user *centrale* when their contracts were so revised. The entire process was expected to be completed during the fourth quarter of 1971.

Obviously there are many problems and uncertainties involved in such a procedure. In view of the vested interests of the producing *centrale* in obtaining a detailed product mix which makes it easiest for them to meet the preliminary planning targets, it may prove quite impossible to allow the balance-coordinators to function at this level. Just as important, the contract making of the first half of the year is likely to be a fiasco unless the preliminary planning indicators of the different *centrale* are fairly consistent with one another; this will require the original materials balancing to be completed some half to three-quarters of a year earlier than has traditionally been the case. In a discussion of these problems at a meeting which I attended of *centrale* directors and a representative of the State Committee for Planning, heavy emphasis was placed upon establishing long-term relations between producing and user *centrales* (thus reducing flexibility)[19] and upon the need for producing *centrale* to base contract negotiations on their informal knowledge of their markets when planning indicators were insufficient. In view of these problems, it is hard to be optimistic as to the likely success of the attempt at decentralization.[20]

INVESTMENT PLANNING

According to a very responsible source, two things may be said about national investment strategy. First, the binding constraint on the rate of movement of the labor force out of agriculture is believed to be the amount of investment funds for industry (i.e., the absorptive capacity of industry) rather than the threat which a faster labor exodus would represent to agricultural production.[21] Consistent with this, it is asserted that investments in agriculture are directed exclusively to expanding agricultural output, and that increases in labor productivity in agriculture are simply a fortunate byproduct. This general strategic viewpoint would

[19] See the 1972 speech by Ilie Verdeţ, first vice-chairman of the Council of Ministers and member of the Presidium of the Central Committee of the Party, for a similar emphasis (*Romania: Documents-Events*, 1972, 4, pp. 39-40). In fact, however, hardly any use was being made of long-term contracts as of early 1972 (Ilie Verdeţ in *Lupta de Clasă*, May 1972, as reported by *RFE*).

[20] It was later reported that, in fact, there were a large number of cases in 1972 of enterprises and *centrale* beginning production without any contract, and of their waiting for their ministry to assign them a purchaser (C. Catuti, deputy director in the Ministry for Supply of Materials and for the Supervision of the Management of Fixed Assets, in *Probleme Economice*, May 1972, pp. 37-42, translated in *JPS*).

[21] Balance of payment considerations and the capacity to organize new urban projects were mentioned as secondary constraints.

lead us to expect that the central authorities would press for capital-saving rather than labor-saving types of investments throughout the economy, at least in choosing the technology to be used in realizing a predetermined product structure.

The second strategic principle which it is said has been generally followed, although accompanied by considerable criticism, is the concentration of industrial development on the production of items which can be produced in large volume, coupled with dependence on imports for low-volume products (mainly equipment). This implies an emphasis on producing products of relatively simple technology. Thus lathes are produced in large series, but numerically controlled machine tools are not produced. For a country at the Romanian level of development, this is probably a reasonable policy.[22]

Planning of total investment at the level of the State Committee for Planning includes not only all state and cooperative investment, but also an estimate for total individual investments in housing and barns. This is because all planned monetary investment can be realized only to the degree that materials and equipment are allocated for it.

The Council of Ministers allocates all planned investment to ministerial-level users. Of this, some 60 to 80 percent is assigned to specific projects after they have been worked out in detail. The specifications for each of these investment projects include capacity, production technology, and the proportion of production of major products which is intended for exports. One industrial ministry for which exact data are available was left to plan independently 25 percent of its investment allocation for 1970. Of this, three-fifths was used for projects planned in detail by the ministry, and only the remaining two-fifths (together with materials allocations needed to make the investments possible) was left to the semidiscretion of the *centrale*.

Even for the 10 percent of the investment fund which was placed at

[22] The major exception to this policy which was cited to me was the production of transistors; but, when pressed, the Romanian authority agreed that these no longer represent a complex or novel technology by international standards. Clearly, the decision to build a plant to produce computers under foreign license represents a more serious violation of this strategy; my informant seemed to be quite embarrassed to have to defend this decision.

Automobiles represent a second exception, at least as of 1973. Automobile assembly had begun in 1968, and parts production had developed progressively. However, full production of a complete car was to begin in 1973 in a factory with a capacity of only 50,000 annually (H. Hummel in *Die Wirtschaft*, 1972, 24, p. 22).

The policy of depending upon imports for low-volume products may, however, be in the process of change. In February 1971, Ceauşescu (the head of both the Party and the state) called for producing such items instead of importing them; he particularly singled out dyestuffs and control apparatus (*Romania: Documents-Events*, 1971, 6, p. 14).

the disposal of the *centrale*, the ministry gave a list of medium-sized and small projects (a maximum for each project of less than $4 million at the official rate of exchange) which were to be constructed. The *centrale*'s freedom was restricted to that of determining how much money and materials to spend on each of the projects on the list.[23]

For all of industry, only about 2 percent of investment is truly unplanned and is left at the complete discretion of the *centrale*.[24] Such investment is financed partly by bank credit, and partly from profits earned by the individual *centrala*. The distinction in financing between planned and unplanned (decentralized) investments is not particularly important.[25] What is vital is that no materials allocations are granted to support unplanned investment. Thus *centrale* can use unplanned-investment funds to purchase allocated materials and equipment only when surpluses of these are available somewhere in the economy; the ministry provides some informal help in searching out such surpluses, but essentially this search is the responsibility of the *centrala* itself. As one might expect, the funds seem to be used primarily to hire additional labor to carry out minor construction or to produce small pieces of equipment for the *centrala*'s own needs. The goal of such unplanned investments appears to be primarily to expand labor productivity rather than to increase output or profitability.

Even though it is the Council of Ministers which specifically approves the projects which comprise the bulk of investment in industry, the analysis of the projects and all but the final stamping of approval is normally done at the level of the individual ministry or through consultation between the headquarters staffs of the several ministries involved. Thus the ministries constitute by far the most important administrative level at which to observe the application of investment criteria and the methods of choosing between alternative investment possibilities. The remainder of this section focuses on these issues as they are treated in ministerial headquarters.

Choice of location of new investment projects is, of course, affected by

[23] Prior to the creation of the *centrale*, enterprises had such freedom only up to a limit of 5 percent of the maximum funds per project which were permitted in 1971 to the *centrale*.

[24] This rate has been increasing and is expected to increase further, but still to be well under 3 percent by 1975.

[25] Credits are used as the source of financing for part of planned as well as unplanned investment. In calculating the proportion of total profits to be paid into the state budget by each *centrala*, the ministries differentiate between *centrale* according to the financial demands placed upon them to repay credits which had been granted earlier both for planned and unplanned investments. If a *centrala* begins an unplanned project from its own funds or from bank credit in one year, the ministry may give it additional funds as a straight grant the following year if this is necessary to complete the project.

the local availability of labor. But once the location is determined, the decision as to the plant's technology is conditioned by the degree of national labor shortage in the industry, not by excess or deficit labor supply in the given region.[26] Thus investment location and investment technology are treated as two independent questions.

To the degree that cost and profitability considerations affect investment decisions, it is current prices which are used. No attempt is made to adjust current prices by a set of coefficients which would make such prices more reflective of present or future scarcities.[27] The result, of course, is that investment choice according to lowest-monetary-cost calculations is a poor proxy for choice which minimizes the "real inputs" involved in producing a given volume of product. This was all the more the case prior to 1972 or 1973 in that there was no charge other than depreciation (and interest on some planned and unplanned investments) on capital nor a rental fee for land.[28]

In at least one ministry, investments for purposes of replacing imports or for expanding exports are evaluated with the aid of foreign currency coefficients provided by the Ministry of Foreign Trade rather than by the use of official exchange rates. But even such shadow exchange rates are kept stable over a period of years, rather than varied with foreign trade conditions.

It is quite clear that the period of payback of an investment from expected profits on production is relevant to investment decisions. But the cut-off period chosen differs widely, not only among ministries but

[26] Officials in one ministry were quite adamant on this point. This ministerial attitude of refusing to differentiate according to location the technology built into new projects might be interpreted as part of a search for technological solutions which yield a minimum average monetary cost of production. (This is because wage rates are set on a national rather than on a regional basis, and thus local shortages or surpluses of labor have relatively little effect on the monetary labor costs of operating a new plant.) But such an interpretation would be overly strong; productivity improvement is an independent ministerial objective, quite apart from its effect on costs, and is given differing weight in the various ministries and subbranches. The ministerial approach promotes both least cost and highest productivity solutions, both interpreted narrowly from the ministerial rather than the national standpoint.

[27] The only temporary exception was for the years 1970-71. The rate of profit projected for an investment analyzed during these two years was to be figured on the basis of "calculated" rather than actual prices for a few major products which were either direct production inputs or outputs of the investment project. These "calculated prices" were said to be set according to the rule that the ratio of profit to the cost of the product was to be no more than 5 to 10 percent. This modification in investment calculations was introduced in anticipation of general price changes then expected to be introduced about 1973, and it was expected that the system of "calculated prices" would be abandoned at that time.

[28] Such charges, following the example of the other CMEA countries, were legislated at the end of 1971 (Maria in *Lupta de Clasă*, January 1972, pp. 19-30, translated in *JPS*).

even between different products within the same ministry. In one ministry, two to three years was regarded as a reasonable payback period for an investment to expand one group of products, while seven to eight years was used for a second group. The use of different norms within the same ministry was justified to me on the ground that product prices did not reflect relative scarcities. The planning director of a ministry which was applying widely varying payback periods for investments in the expansion of different products explained that the ministry was under no overall profit-margin constraint in its investment planning.

Different payback periods are also used to evaluate output-expansion investments and labor-substitution investments. Labor-substitution investments are heavily favored in industry and mining, in sharp contrast to what I was told concerning agriculture. In the industrial ministry where a seven to eight year payback is the upper limit used for output-expansion of a major product group, a ten to twelve year payback is regarded as acceptable for recouping the cost of introducing automated equipment. In other ministries, labor-productivity improvement is regarded as an independent goal which takes precedence over payback analysis.

However, while financial analysis in investment decisions is subject to many caveats, discussions with ministerial officials showed that it is still basic. "Social" considerations such as the providing of industrial employment in labor-surplus regions seem, for example, to play only a marginal role in the ministries where I interviewed. It is true that other desiderata are given consideration and that the standards of financial analysis are confused. (Both the maximization of profit as a percentage of cost and its maximization as a percentage of investment are used simultaneously.) Nevertheless, Romanian authorities have backed away from trying to treat individually all the multitude of input-substitution decisions, and have tended to handle them essentially through converting the alternative physical inputs into the common denominator of money costs.

Despite the reliance on financial criteria, major investment decisions and even analysis of major individual projects are to a considerable degree concentrated in ministerial-level bodies. There are two reasons for this. First, given the high proportion of nonagricultural investment to total capital stock in the Romanian economy, location decisions for new investment projects frequently involve several different ministries; this is because the appropriate location of a new plant is dependent upon the location of other investment projects by both its supplying and user ministries.

Second, rate-of-return calculations are not employed to determine in which industry an investment should be made in order to realize a given end result. For example, if higher-quality nonferrous metal ores are supplied by the mining ministry, with resultant higher investment costs per ton of metal content, this will cheapen production costs and reduce investment needs in the metal smelting industry. But the relative prices of lower-quality and higher-quality ore may well not reflect this difference in costs to the smelting industry. A similar problem arises in determining whether new production should be concentrated in plants with low-cost production which would be so situated geographically as to require supplementary investment in railroad track; railroad rates do not properly reflect the investment in tracks. Thus such decisions are made through interministerial consultations with the aim of minimizing the investment in the economy as a whole, and the necessary investment funds are then allocated to the appropriate ministry through the Council of Ministers.

The above paragraphs suggest that financial criteria do not play the all-decisive role in total investment decision making that they do in those decisions where the analysis is limited to the confines of a single ministry. Nevertheless, taking investment projects as a whole, their location and the technology built into them are heavily influenced by the deviation of current prices from relative scarcity values. The resultant distortion of Romanian investment decisions is modified—although in an unknown direction—by simultaneous consideration of such other independent goals as improving labor productivity and emulating the "best" international technologies. However, the relatively small size of the professional staff at ministerial headquarters prevents any serious analyses of the opportunity costs of alternative projects—as measured by a direct trade-off between physical quantities of different inputs—in terms of a ministerial "welfare function." The trade-offs can be examined only after the physical quantities have been transformed into monetary values through the use of current prices.

The misleading nature of the price system, coupled with the ministerial decision-making process described above, suggests that decentralization of at least smaller investment decisions to the level of the *centrala* would have lower decision-making costs than might at first be expected. For the existing price system seems to mislead the ministries almost as much as it would mislead the *centrale*.

FOREIGN TRADE PLANNING

This section rests on a much weaker data base than do any of the previous ones. The officials whom I queried on foreign trade matters struck me as both less competent and more secretive than my informants on other matters; whether the former or the latter or both are in fact the case, this section suffers as a result.

To begin with a rough picture of the significance and structure of Romanian foreign trade, total exports are estimated to constitute about 15 percent of the country's national material product.[29] In 1969, some 28 percent of exports went to the Soviet Union, 23 percent to the other CMEA members, and 20 percent to West Germany, Italy, France, and Britain.[30] The commodity composition of 1969 trade is shown in Table 3.1. Here we can see the following breakdown of net exports and imports by category: Foodstuffs constituted 49 percent of net exports (see the table for the definition), consumer industrial goods 27 percent, and petroleum products 19 percent. Machinery constituted 60 percent of net imports, and nonpetroleum fuels, minerals, and metals (mainly iron ore and coke) were the remaining 40 percent. Cotton is also a major import. A substantial trade in both directions exists for many products; for example, gross exports of rolled steel constituted about 20 percent of total tonnage produced, while gross imports constituted 31 percent. The net imports of machinery come primarily from western Europe.

The procurement situation for imports is even tighter than that for domestically produced products. Enterprises and *centrale* must normally state their precise import needs for materials one to two years ahead of time if they are to have a reasonable hope of receiving them. Equipment orders from CMEA countries must be placed two to three years before delivery, even for types of machinery whose design is rapidly changing on the international market.

There was until 1971 no place for direct foreign investments in the Romanian economy.[31] Joint companies did exist, but these were restricted to commercial organizations for selling Romanian products abroad. However, it is possible to consider sales of foreign equipment on credit, with repayment in the form of production from this equipment, as a form of indirect foreign investment in industry.[32]

The five-year plans for individual ministries divide their exports and imports into three categories: transactions with socialist countries, trans-

[29] See the estimates of 12.5 to 14 percent for 1960 and 1964 in John M. Montias, *Economic Development in Communist Rumania* (The M.I.T. Press, Cambridge, Mass.: 1967), p. 147.

[30] Direcția Centrală de Statistică, *Anuarul Statistic al Republicii Socialiste României 1970*, table 229, pp. 563-67. Twenty-six percent of Romania's imports came from the above four capitalist countries. These proportions are computed using the official foreign exchange rate of the lei with other currencies, and doubtless overstate the real share of total Romanian trade which is conducted with the CMEA countries. The commodity composition data of Table 3.1 suffer similarly from the failure to adjust for price differences in Romania's trade with its various partners.

[31] While joint companies were permitted as of early 1971, I was told by a Romanian official in early 1973 that none were yet in production.

[32] Such investments can be used by foreign companies as a substitute for investment in the expansion of their own capacity for producing the final products.

TABLE 3.1: Commodity Composition of Romanian Foreign Trade, 1969 (percentage)

Commodity Group	Gross Exports	Gross Imports	Net Exports[a]
Fuels, minerals, and metals (other than petroleum products)	13.3	28.4[b]	− 17.0
Petroleum products	7.3	... [b]	+ 7.3[b]
Foodstuffs, foodstuff raw materials, and live animals	21.9	3.8	+ 17.8
Vegetable and animal raw materials	10.3	9.1	+ 0.6
Consumer industrial goods	15.7	5.7	+ 9.7
Chemicals, fertilizers, rubber	7.1	6.7	− 0.1
Building materials and fittings	2.7	2.0	+ 0.6
Production machinery and equipment	21.7	44.3	− 25.5
Total	100	100	− 6.6

SOURCE: Direcţia Centrală de Statistică, *Anuarul Statistic al Republicii Socialiste România 1970*, tables 230-31, pp. 568-71.

[a] Each item in this column consists of the gross exports minus gross imports of the appropriate product group, all divided by the total of Romania's gross exports of all products. The figure in the last row represents the year's balance of trade.

[b] I have assumed for purposes of this table that no petroleum products were imported except from the Soviet Union; these latter were minuscule. However, this assumption may be substantially incorrect; in 1971, Romanian gross imports of oil (all from sources other than the Soviet Union) constituted 21 percent of domestic production (*Viaţa economică*, 1973, 8, pp. 19 and 23 as cited in *ABSEES*, July 1973).

actions in convertible currencies with nonsocialist countries, and transactions in nonconvertible currencies with nonsocialist countries. Each ministry receives an export plan for each of these categories.

In general, import quotas are allocated to that ministry which is the main producer of the relevant product grouping and which, therefore, is given the task of allocating supplies of these products among final consumers. The sole exception in principle is for plant and equipment intended for investment; these quotas are allocated to the ministerial-level final recipient. Thus, in the case of equipment, it is the final recipient ministry for the investment funds which can exercise whatever choice is delegated by the Council of Ministers in determining which units of equipment shall be imported and which shall be taken from domestic production. Presumably this system has been adopted for investment goods so that the recipient ministry, having the greatest stake in assuring that equipment of good quality and modern design is purchased, should be in a relatively strong position to assure that it is not saddled with Romanian domestic products where these are not up to international standards and where such a deficiency is of importance. For all other products, it is the producing ministry which is given the choice as to which items to produce and which to import. This distinction in procedure seems to reflect the Romanian authorities' priority on modernity and quality in the development of new production capacity.

Realization of foreign trade plans is easiest in the case of CMEA trade, where all transactions are either governed by five-year bilateral agreements or are negotiated as annual barter supplements between the respective national ministries responsible for a particular group of products. It is known that at least the Ministry of Domestic Trade, the Ministry of Construction Materials, and the Ministry of Iron and Steel engage extensively in such barter agreements. Half of total gross steel exports are of this barter type; these permit the iron and steel ministry to concentrate its production on a much more limited range of rolled steel profiles than would otherwise be possible. There seems no reason why such barter arrangements should be limited by organs above the ministry level, and I know of no such limits except for supervision by the Ministry of Foreign Trade over the terms of barter established.

Plans for the remaining half of Romanian trade, and particularly for exports to the nonsocialist world, are more difficult to fulfill since they depend upon the vagaries of foreign markets. Here the main emphasis of both the Ministry of Foreign Trade and the branch ministries appears to be on eliminating uncertainty as to the balance and terms of trade. Barter arrangements with private firms are strongly preferred to one-way sales and purchases;[33] sometimes these are through direct barter of goods within a given year, but at other times they consist of the purchase of equipment on credit which is to be repaid by products built with the purchased machinery. In addition to barter, long-term contracts are also used to reduce uncertainty. In the State Committee for Planning, it was agreed that such arrangements probably are not efficient in the sense of yielding optimal terms of trade; but the greater certainty is considered to be worth the cost. In the Ministry of Foreign Trade, a deputy minister welcomed my observation that Romanian ministries and *centrale* seem to prefer long-term contracts for exports to higher-priced

---

[33] An official of the Foreign Trade Ministry, in commenting on a draft of this manuscript, disagreed with this statement. He pointed out that, in any case, barter transactions are very few.

short-term contracts; he regarded the hunt for short-term profits as a temptation to be avoided.

Until the year 1970, production enterprises played no role in foreign trade. Import and export transactions were carried out directly by some thirty-odd foreign trade enterprises that were both administratively under the Foreign Trade Ministry and whose operations required licenses from this ministry. Production enterprises delivered planned quantities of goods for export to these trading enterprises, and were paid the same price as applied to domestic deliveries.

Some decentralization of foreign trade operation to the level of the *centrala* occurred in 1970.[34] Thirty-two of the thirty-seven foreign trade enterprises were subordinated either to the relevant branch ministries or to *centrale*, rather than to the Foreign Trade Ministry, and a number of *centrale* were authorized to engage in foreign trade directly. By 1973, there were seventy-six Romanian organizations authorized to engage in foreign trade operations; at least twenty-one of these were individual *centrale* and at least six were inter-*centrale* bodies.[35]

All *centrale*, whether or not they handled their foreign trade operations directly, were made responsible for selling their export quotas. The head of the export-import section of one *centrala*, who had previously worked for almost twenty years in similar operations under the Ministry of Foreign Trade, pointed out that there was considerable advantage with regard to customer contacts in consolidating sales, production, and technology within the same organization. Furthermore, he argued, the export-import house in which he had formerly worked was concerned only with its total exports rather than with those of any individual sub-branch; he thus thought that exports would sell better under the new system.[36]

Nevertheless, although the *centrale* were made responsible for negotiating their planned volume of exports, they seem to have been given very little authority or material interest with regard to the prices received for them. As of the end of 1970, there was dispute as to whether decentralization in this regard would proceed much further in the future; in fact, it does not appear to have done so through 1972. Although payment to *centrale* was in principle to be made by converting export earnings at the official rate of exchange or some multiple thereof,[37] generally

[34] This was codified by a law of March 1971.

[35] *Romania: Directory of Foreign Trade Companies 1973* (Romanian Embassy, New York: 1973).

[36] M. Radian in *România Liberă*, July 25, 1972, p. 2, translated in *JPS*.

[37] I was told that in one ministry the rate used was three times the official exchange rate, but that this same three-to-one exchange rate applied to all sales whether in hard or in soft currencies. In three *centrale* of three additional ministries, export earnings were counted in at least the index of "total value of pro-

95 percent of the gain or loss (aside from assigned foreign trade subsidies) relative to the domestic price was borne by the budget.[38] In the one ministry for which I have relevant information, *centrale* were not permitted to accept on their own authority any foreign purchase orders at less than the Romanian domestic price (converted at a standard exchange rate).[39] Thus the financial interest in exports given to the *centrale* was minuscule, as was the authority granted them. So long as all currencies earned are exchanged into lei for the *centrala* at either the official exchange rate or at rates proportional to the official rate, despite the fact that the balance of payments situation of the country is quite different as between different currencies, it is scarcely possible to make the *centrale* genuinely responsible for export sales.

The foreign trade enterprises not under the *centrale* are commission agents and seem to have no policy-making authority. They are said to negotiate only with respect to such matters as delivery times, precise product mix, quality, and packaging; even in regard to such questions, they require the approval of the *centrala* which is their principal. Their probable lack of authority is best indicated by the fact that they make their purchases and sales at the official exchange rate, and appear not to have received even informal shadow exchange rates. In view of the fact that the Romanian lei is inconvertible, and that thus the balance of payments problem is not aggregative but rather must be regulated separately for each trading partner, the foreign trade enterprises do not have the necessary relevant information to permit them to make sensible foreign trade decisions. Their actions in 1970 were directed partly by the branch ministries, which had to approve any pricing agreements, and partly by the Ministry of Foreign Trade which licensed all of their transactions. The five *centrale* within the Ministry of Light Industry which were given the right to export directly were similarly bound. The expected future transfer of many of the foreign trade enterprises to subordination to the *centrale* would not have changed this picture in any significant way.

---

duction" at some multiple of the official exchange rate. In one of these *centrale*, a multiple was used for sales to capitalist countries while none was used for sales to socialist countries; but even in this *centrala*, all exports within either the group of socialist or capitalist countries were treated identically.

[38] In early 1973, an official of the Romanian Foreign Trade Ministry told me that he thought, although he was not sure, that the 95 percent absorption rule was still in force. In any case, some degree of such budgetary absorption of gains and losses from foreign trade was still occurring at the end of 1972 (N. Ceaușescu, speech at the Central Committee plenum of November 21-22, 1972, as reported in *Romania: Documents-Events*, 1972, 44, p. 38).

[39] The branch ministry had the authority to grant permission to go 5 percent below this price on individual transactions. Any further reductions required a decision of the Ministry of Foreign Trade.

From the above it can be seen that, in the area of foreign trade, the significant issues of decentralization do not lie in the decisions permitted to enterprises and *centrale*. Rather, the decentralization question is restricted to the division of authority between the Ministry of Foreign Trade and the branch ministries in interpreting and carrying out the foreign trade plan.[40]

In principle, the branch ministries receive foreign trade plans—for imports as well as exports—which are broken down both according to product and according to the proportion of the transaction volume to be conducted in nonconvertible currencies with socialist countries, in nonconvertible currencies with capitalist countries, and in convertible currencies. In the Ministry of Machine Building, for example, the export plan is subdivided into one hundred eighty product groupings. The only link which is supposed to exist between a ministry's exports and imports is that a ministry is allowed to keep a percentage of its above-plan export receipts (regardless of the prices received for exports) in order to finance additional imports; moreover, a high official in the State Committee for Planning denied that this linkage has any practical significance in view of the ambitious levels at which the ministry export plans are set.

In order to fulfill their plans, the ministries must apply to the Ministry of Foreign Trade for both export and import licenses. It is through its power to grant or refuse such licenses that the Ministry of Foreign Trade directs transactions to one or another trading-partner country according to balance of payments considerations relating to each partner individually. This operational control could obviously be of great importance; however, it is difficult to see how the Ministry of Foreign Trade can exercise very detailed control with its relatively small staff. Doubtless the workload pressure upon the Ministry is a major reason why it presses for long-term contracts. The inability of the Ministry to evaluate carefully all license applications inevitably decentralizes considerable power over foreign trade to the level of the branch ministries.

For imports, the State Committee for Planning allocates much of the foreign exchange to the purchase of individual products.[41] But much is also left in a global allocation to the ministry responsible for distributing a whole category of products to final users.[42] In general, this ministry

---

[40] Both are subordinate in foreign trade matters to a vice-chairman of the Council of Ministers who is in charge of foreign trade (Ceauşescu speech at the Central Committee meeting of February 10-11, 1971, as reported in *Romania: Documents-Events*, 1972, 8, p. 38).

[41] It is said that this is done according to assumed average foreign prices. If actual prices turn out to be higher, the quantities which can be imported are reduced accordingly.

[42] At least formally, such global allocations to ministries were to be abolished for 1973; the resources were instead to be kept in a reserve of the Council of

allocates the imported goods among final-user ministries as it sees fit. But, of course, there are limits to its discretionary power, and inter-minis- terial consultation is frequent. Thus it is the Ministry of Light Industry which receives the annual allocation to import cloth; but the imported cloth is divided between the Ministry of Light Industry (for clothing pro- duction), the Ministry of Domestic Trade, and the cooperatives through bargaining among the three groups within the State Committee for Planning.

In determining imports of equipment for a new factory, planning begins with the percentage of the value of equipment which is to be im- ported—a percentage which normally reflects no more than a historical projection. Working from this percentage, a joint-team from the design institutes of both the Ministry of Machine Building and the recipient ministry specifies the items to be imported; during the process of draw- ing up the specifications, the team collaborates with the Ministry of Foreign Trade to be sure that the specific foreign currency needed will be made available. At the end of the exercise, the team brings its rec- ommendations to a technical council formed from the two ministries; the technical council may decide that more or fewer imports are needed than had been originally projected for the project, but this decision is made within the constraint that the recipient ministry cannot spend more than its total allocation of foreign currency for all investment projects together.

Some 80 to 85 percent of one ministry's value of exports is specified by the State Committee for Planning according to product groups. The product mix of the remainder is determined by the branch ministry, subject only to licensing by the Ministry of Foreign Trade. According to officials of this branch ministry, their principal criterion in deciding on these residual exports is the net[43] foreign exchange earned per lei of domestic costs. But since these earnings are computed at the official exchange rate, an active role by the Ministry of Foreign Trade is essen- tial if balance of payments considerations are to be properly reflected in export decisions. The branch ministry is permitted to expand its sales by entering new markets at a price which is abnormally low, but the approval of the Ministry of Foreign Trade is required for each such transaction.

In fact, although not in theory, there is a link (additional to the the-

Ministers (N. Ceauşescu, speech at the Central Committee meeting of November 20-21, 1972, as reported in *Romania: Documents-Events*, 1972, 44, p. 39).

[43] The foregone foreign exchange earnings from direct inputs of materials and fuels which could otherwise have been exported are deducted from gross foreign exchange receipts, regardless of whether these materials and fuels are produced within the same ministry.

oretic but apparently nonoperative one earlier mentioned) between the exports and imports of individual ministries. At a minimum, this occurs in the approval of investment projects by the Ministry of Foreign Trade, which may require future exports of the plant's products as a precondition for approval of equipment imports. Furthermore, a branch ministry is constrained by an informally expected net foreign exchange position. It can receive permission to import goods which it would otherwise have to produce itself for the Romanian economy only to the extent that its planned exports will leave it in the desired position of net balance; thus its bargaining with the State Committee for Planning over its import plan is closely tied to the size of the export plan it is willing to accept.

A complex example of the export-import link is one cited to me by an official of the Ministry of Machine Building. The problem is that of whether a specialty machine tool should be produced domestically or imported, under conditions where no import allocation has been made for it and where it is technically feasible to produce the item within Romania but only under disadvantageous conditions. If the Ministry of Machine Building agrees that the item is needed, but prefers that it be imported so that the Ministry will be freed from a burdensome production obligation, it can have its way provided that it agrees to supply for export several ordinary machine tools over and above its ministerial export plan. If, however, it is the recipient ministry which is pressing for the specialty item against the desire of the Ministry of Machine Building, the item may be accepted for domestic production provided that the recipient ministry takes over a compensating amount of the Ministry of Machine Building's export plan. Alternatively, the recipient ministry may import the item by agreeing with the Ministry of Foreign Trade to a compensating export above its own export plan. From this example, it is easy to see that considerable three-cornered bargaining between two branch ministries and the Ministry of Foreign Trade may be involved in import-export decisions.

An interesting example was cited in another ministry which had requested an export license to a country with which Romania then had an active trade balance. The Ministry of Foreign Trade was reluctant to grant the license, but did so when the recipient ministry arranged to import from that country in the same year equipment which was beyond its annual ministerial import and investment plans. This arrangement was only possible, however, because the purchase by the ministry of similar equipment had previously been scheduled for the following year.

A third branch ministry pointed to the free commingling of foreign exchange funds allocated for imports of equipment for its own use with funds allocated for the purchase of products to be supplied to other ministries. Economies from funds planned for imports of products similar to those produced by the ministry could be used for equipment imports; conversely, when the ministry was unable to meet its production targets for domestic deliveries, it had been forced to import these items and pay for them out of the allocation of foreign exchange for its own equipment needs.

From these examples we can see that foreign trade planning is in practice rather more flexible than it is in theory. The difficulty with such flexibility is that all decision-making bodies except the Ministry of Foreign Trade and the State Committee for Planning make their decisions on the basis of criteria which implicitly assume that the Romanian lei is convertible, and that the official exchange rate (or, as an improvement, a rate higher but proportional to this for all countries or, at a maximum, a single such rate for all socialist and a second for all capitalist countries) is properly applicable to all exports and imports regardless of the trading partner. Inevitably, this throws a tremendous burden upon the Ministry of Foreign Trade to effect rationality from the national standpoint through its licensing policies. Particularly since the Ministry of Foreign Trade's licensing staff is quite limited in size, this can only mean that foreign trade decisions suffer both from poor information and from casual empiricism.

CHAPTER 4

Romania: *Centrale* and Enterprises

THE TASK of this chapter is to investigate the scope, objectives, and process of decision making in the operating units of Romanian industry: the *centrale* and enterprises. Their activities are guided by annual plan indicators, detailed instructions, and allocations received from branch ministries. Other organs—particularly the powerful regional committees of the Communist Party—also exercise a direct influence. How much freedom, and in what areas of decision making, is left to the *centrale*? What goals do they pursue within the limits of freedom they possess? How effective do these operating units appear to be in exercising the powers which are left to them?

The first and major section of this chapter will consider the orthodox model of the behavior of socialist enterprises, and test its pertinence to Romanian industry. The second section will deal with the constraints on managerial decision making, and the third will deal with this decision making itself.

Over the course of many years, and owing particularly to the early work of Joseph Berliner, a widely accepted model has been developed to explain microeconomic behavior in Soviet-type economies. This model views managers of production units as maximizing subject to constraints, with their own bonuses constituting their objective function. It posits a system in which enterprise managers orient their behavior to achieving the "success indicators" to which bonuses are attached, and suboptimize with regard to society's goals as these are perceived by central authorities. This theory of the firm has been used as a principal intermediate analytic instrument to connect planners' decisions and the macroeconomic behavior of the economy. Specifically, it is critical (even if usually only by implication) in the explanation of types of suboptimizing behavior by individual enterprises which lead to macroeconomic malfunctioning.[1] The model has been developed particularly with regard

---

[1] Not only does such an orthodox treatment as that of Alec Nove rest upon this microeconomic model, but so too does the quite unorthodox treatment of Ames (see E. Ames, *Soviet Economic Processes*, Irwin, Homewood, Illinois: 1965, chapters 4 and 7).

It is true that the same results may be derived from a microeconomic model which rests upon rapid job mobility of enterprise managers, with such mobility being strongly linked to the performance of the enterprise as judged by success

to the Soviet economy, but has also been applied to Hungary of the 1950's and to Poland of the 1960's.

This orthodox model constitutes a subset of the model of the firm which has long been dominant in the microeconomics of capitalist economies; in lieu of capitalist enterprises acting so as to maximize the discounted stream of their present and future profits, Soviet enterprise managers are assumed to attempt to maximize the discounted stream of their present and future personal earnings. In order to do this, Soviet managers should consider the effect of their actions on their own expected future base salaries (which are a function of their likelihood of being promoted or demoted) as well as on the current and future bonuses which they may earn. The critical assumption of the model is that the discounted stream of current and future bonuses, subject to a relatively minor constraint with regard to avoiding dismissal, is an appropriate proxy for this maximand.

My Romanian interviews in *centrale* and in ministerial headquarters suggest that the accepted theory of the firm in Soviet-type economies has no explanatory power with regard to Romania. This is particularly curious since the Romanian system of formal central controls over production units, and the formal framework within which the latter make decisions, are closer to the traditional pattern of the Soviet Union than is the case for any other east European country.

The basic data used in my examination of the applicability of the orthodox model to Romania consist of materials covering 1969-70 for six of the country's thirteen industrial ministries. Statistics presented cover all of the production units within the ministries indicated. Because the statistics are available at the microunit level, it is safe to say that no materials of their comprehensiveness, and covering such a broad sample, have ever before been available to western scholars for any socialist country.

One reader of the draft manuscript has suggested that it is troubling that these basic data come entirely from interviews rather than from published sources. Quite aside from the fact that such comprehensive published data do not exist, I would suggest that such interview materials are more likely to be reliable than would published statements. This is because I was in a position not only to evaluate the likely access to the raw data of each individual informant, but also—and even more

indicators (see D. Granick, "An Organizational Model of Soviet Industrial Planning," *Journal of Political Economy*, LXVII, 2, 1959, 109-30). But such high mobility has not in fact characterized the Soviet economy since World War II (D. Granick, *Managerial Comparisons of Four Developed Countries: France, Britain, United States, and Russia*, The M.I.T. Press, Cambridge, Mass.: 1972, chapter 8).

important—to question him as to the meaning of the figures quoted. Comparable information is rarely available for published statistics of socialist countries.

PLAN INDICATORS AND BONUSES

The orthodox model. Both socialist and nonsocialist writings on the operation of enterprises in centrally planned socialist economies have leaned heavily on an implicit form of the following model:[2]

(1) Managers are assumed to attempt to maximize their expected personal incomes in both the current year and in the future.

(2) The proxy for such maximization of discounted future earnings is taken as the maximization of discounted future bonuses expected to be earned while managers hold their current positions, subject to the constraint of avoiding actions which are likely to lead to dismissal. The justification for the use of this proxy is twofold. First, bonuses are assumed normally to constitute a substantial proportion of total managerial income. Second, the evaluation of individual managers for possible future promotion is assumed to be made by the same criteria which determine their bonuses.

(3) Managerial bonuses constitute a well-defined function of the degree of fulfillment of specified plan indicators. This function is highly

---

[2] For varying pieces of this model, spelled out with differing degrees of explicitness, see the following: J. S. Berliner, *Factory and Manager in the USSR* (Harvard University Press, Cambridge, Mass.: 1957) and "Managerial Incentives and Decisionmaking: A Comparison of the United States and the Soviet Union," in Subcommittee on Economic Statistics, Joint Economic Committee, 86th Congress of the United States (1st session), *Comparisons of the United States and Soviet Economies* (Washington, D.C.: 1959), Part I, pp. 349-76; H. Hunter, "Optimum Tautness in Developmental Planning," *Economic Development and Cultural Change*, IX, 4, Part I (1961), 561-72; A. Nove, "The Problem of 'Success Indicators' in Soviet Industry," *Economica*, new series, XXV, 97 (1958), 1-13; D. Granick, *The Red Executive* (Doubleday, N.Y.: 1960); J. Kornai, *Overcentralization in Economic Administration* (Oxford University Press, London: 1959); J. G. Zielinski, *On The Theory of Socialist Planning* (Oxford University Press, Ibadan, Nigeria: 1968). The most explicit use of bonuses as the mainspring of a microeconomic model is in S. Gindin, "A Model of the Soviet Firm," *Economics of Planning*, 10, 3 (1970), 145-57 and M. Keren, "On the Tautness of Plans," *Review of Economic Studies*, XXXIX, 4 (1972), 469-86. The emphasis upon the importance and role of bonuses stems from Berliner. Kornai draws upon the experience of Hungary during the 1950's, Zielinski upon the experience of Poland, and all the others upon the Soviet experience.

With regard to the key role of bonuses, Zielinski goes even further than this model. He states that "observation of the behaviour of Polish enterprise managers reveals that their goal is to maximize the volume of bonuses for a given volume of effort exerted." He reports that when he presented this view in Poland in 1967, it met with hardly any serious opposition (J. G. Zielinski, *Economic Reforms in Polish Industry*, Oxford University Press, London: 1973, p. 198).

kinked, with very little or no bonuses being paid for anything less than 100 percent plan fulfillment.

(4) Annual plan indicators are set at levels which are quite ambitious in relation to the potentialities of a high proportion of enterprises. The managers of such enterprises are thus unable to fulfill these indicators 100 percent except by violating other plan instructions which are less important for the awarding of bonuses. The decision-making powers of the managers stem from the fact that they must choose which instructions to violate and in what degree; they are guided in their trade-offs by the effect on the bonuses which they are maximizing.

(5) The constraint on managers' behavior (which consists of avoiding actions likely to lead to dismissal) is not overly severe, and it leaves a great deal of room for such trade-offs. The justifications for this critical hypothesis are that the ministries are themselves primarily concerned with the fulfillment of those plan indicators to which enterprise bonuses are attached, and that the ministerial staff recognize that such fulfillment is impossible except through violation of other ministerial instructions.

(6) Overfulfillment of plan indicators in one year is followed in the next by the setting of a higher plan for the enterprise than it would otherwise have been given. The greater the overfulfillment, the higher the plan in the following year. Enterprise managers are well aware of this process.

(7) Because of the above effect of overfulfillment, combined with the fact that bonuses constitute a kinked function of the percentage of plan fulfillment, enterprise managers avoid excessive overfulfillment in any year. "Excessive" is defined as a percentage of plan overfulfillment which is believed to jeopardize 100 percent plan fulfillment in the following year. This is a further specification of (1).

In testing this model against the available data for Romanian industry, I shall begin by examining the percentage of annual plan fulfillment achieved by enterprises. From the first sentence of feature (4) of the model, we would expect a substantial percentage of enterprises to fail to fulfill their annual plans, and many by a substantial proportion. This follows from the hypothesis of ambitiousness of plans, linked with the assumption that ministerial planners would not wish or be able to take into account the differential competence of managers and labor force in different enterprises in setting their respective plans.[3] On the

---

[3] Since the degree of such competence might be expected to vary substantially among enterprises, a ministry which achieved an average of 100 percent plan fulfillment—or even one which attained a few percentage points of overfulfillment —might be expected to encompass many enterprises which did not individually fulfill their plans.

Underfulfillment of plan by a high proportion of enterprises could be avoided only if plans were modified during the course of the year as a function of observed

other hand, because of feature (7) of the model, we would not expect to find a symmetrical variance of plan fulfillment above and below the bonus function's kink point of 100 percent fulfillment.

The above model assumes that annual plan indicators are relatively immutable. To the degree that they are in fact frequently changed within the year, the effort by enterprise managers to achieve at least 100 percent fulfillment of the final targets would cease to be a predictor of their trade-off behavior as between different possible outcomes of the production process.[4] One would only be able to predict that, ceteris paribus, managers would give greatest attention to those indicators which are least liable to change during the final months of the planning year. Thus my second task will be to examine the degree of alteration of enterprise plans during the course of the year.

The third empirical task of this section is to examine the system of managerial bonuses used in Romania, and to see whether it is consistent with the nature of bonuses postulated in the model.

Plan fulfillment. My best source of information consists of data provided at six ministerial headquarters concerning the distribution of *all* of their operating units according to the degree of fulfillment of specified annual plan indicators. These data vary in reliability and detail. For some ministries, the units described are enterprises; where enterprise data were unavailable, it is the group of enterprises consolidated into a *centrala* which is taken as the unit of analysis. In total, three hundred operating units are covered by these statistics. Data relate to the units' plans as finally approved, rather than to the plans originally given to the units at the beginning of the year.

Exact data were provided in Ministry No. 1, and are presented in Table 4.1.

Ministry No. 2's information is precise only for those units which failed to fulfill their plans. All manufacturing units are included in Table

---

performance. Although it is true that there indeed are plan modifications for individual Soviet enterprises, there is no indication that they occur primarily as a function of performance of these enterprises themselves—rather than because of changes in plan goals or as a result of performance by supplier or customer enterprises. If plans for Soviet enterprises were indeed widely modified as a function of performance, they could not successfully fill the "target" role which both the Soviet and foreign literature posit for them.

[4] American corporate planning for internal divisions displays a great reluctance to change annual divisional plans during the course of the year. The reason for this is that, once the principle of plan changes is accepted, it becomes extremely difficult to evaluate managerial performance. Divisional management's efforts might be spent at least as profitably in lobbying for reductions in plan goals, and in supplying results which would seem to justify such changes, as in attempting to meet difficult plan targets. Presumably the same applies to socialist enterprises with regard to changes in the plans laid down for them by their ministries.

TABLE 4.1: Plan Fulfillment in 1969 by 49 Units in Ministry No. 1 (percentage of units)

Plan Indicator	Percentage of Plan Fulfillment			
	95 or less	96-99	100-103	More than 103
Total production[a]			49	51
Finished-goods production[b]			92	8
Labor productivity[c]			84	16
Total profits in lei	4	2	47	47
Profitability[d]	2		98	

[a] This is measured in constant prices of 1963-65. Unfinished production is excluded in at least some units, but certain products produced by a subunit which also serve as inputs to another subunit are double counted.

[b] Measurement is in current prices. All finished goods intended for sale by the unit are included, whether or not these goods have actually been shipped.

[c] Total production divided by the total labor force. Labor force appears to be defined differently in different units: sometimes as the average labor force on the books of the unit, and sometimes as the average number who were physically present at work.

[d] Total profits as a percentage of finished-goods production.

4.2's coverage, but five construction enterprises are excluded. The planning director of the ministry reported that only one or two of the manufacturing units had achieved less than 100 percent plan fulfillment for all of the three critical indicators listed in Table 4.2. For the indicator of total production, the planning director said that 5 to 6 percent overfulfillment was about the maximum achieved by any enterprise; in fact, he said, it is rare for large enterprises to surpass 1 percent overfulfillment. For the profitability indicator, on the other hand, individual enterprises get as high as 20 to 22 percent overfulfillment.

The planning director of Ministry No. 3 provided me with his estimate, as of the end of October, of the probable plan fulfillment in 1970 by fifty units. For all of the three principal plan indicators (total pro-

TABLE 4.2: Plan Fulfillment in 1969 by 51 Units in Ministry No. 2

Plan Indicator	Percentage of Plan Fulfillment					
	Percentage of units					
	85-91	92-95	96-99	100-103	More than 103	Ministry as a whole
Total production	4	6		80-82	8-10	100.5
Labor productivity		6	6	78-80	8-10	100.1
Profitability	2	2	4	82-84	8-10	100.2

duction, productivity, and profitability), he expected that two or three and possibly four (i.e., between 4 and 8 percent) would fail to meet their planned targets. He expected that even these units would fulfill 97 to 98 percent of their targets. He predicted that seven to eight enterprises (15 percent) would overfulfill their plans by more than 105 percent, and that the top enterprise would reach 107 to 108 percent of plan. He considered this performance to be reasonably representative of that of recent years in his ministry, and said that it has been typical for units to overfulfill their plans by between ½ and 1½ percent.

In Ministry No. 4, an official of the planning directorate limited his rather general remarks to fulfillment of the plan indicator of total production. Speaking of the one hundred twenty units in the ministry, he said that there were years when all fulfilled their plan, and other years when five to ten (i.e., 4 to 8 percent) failed to fulfill it. He believed that it was very rare for a unit to produce less than 95 percent of planned output or more than 102 percent; in fact, he seemed to regard as rather exceptional any enterprise which deviated by more than 1 percent in either direction from its planned target.

The planning director of Ministry No. 5 reported as to the performance of his six units in 1969. All units fulfilled or overfulfilled their plan targets for total production, labor productivity, total profits, and profitability, and all remained within their planned wage fund. Each of the units also met its quarterly plans for total production and for productivity; but each quarter saw two or three of the six failing to meet their profit and profitability plans. None of the six units surpassed its annual plan target for total production by more than 3 percent. The range of percentage of plan fulfillment during the last two or three years was very narrow for all the units. In evaluating the above information, the reader should be aware that the reporting units are much larger and more heterogeneous than in the other ministries; this naturally reduces their variance in plan fulfillment.

Ministry No. 6 has by far the worst record of all, but the data provided by its planning director refer only to the first three quarters of 1970 rather than to the entire year. The significance of this reporting period is that no possibility was available—in contrast to the situation in the other ministries—for improvement in plan performance through reduction of plan targets during the last quarter of the year.

Out of twenty-two units, 18 percent had failed to fulfill their targets for total production; 49 percent had failed to fulfill their productivity targets; 49 to 64 percent had failed to meet their profitability goals; and about 32 percent had more than their planned number of personnel, although all of these last units were said to be within their wage fund limit.

Table 4.3 sums up the degree of plan fulfillment of the six ministries. For those ministries for which we have fulfillment data related to the plan as it was finally revised (i.e., excluding Ministry No. 6), a maximum of 12 percent of the units of any ministry failed to fulfill their plans. Substantial overfulfillment (defined as more than 103 percent of plan) was reasonably symmetrical with total underfulfillment in four ministries, and greatly exceeded it in one. Comparing substantial underfulfillment with substantial overfulfillment (more than 3 percent deviation from 100 percent), we find many more units overfulfilling than underfulfilling in Ministry No. 1, and a pattern varying between this and equality (depending on the plan indicator) for Ministry No. 2.

TABLE 4.3: Summary of Annual Plan Fulfillment by 298 Units in Six Ministries, 1969-70

Plan Indicator	Ministry	Number of Units	Units not Fulfilling Plan	Units Overfulfilling Plan by more than 3 percent
			Percentage of units within each ministry	
Total Production				
	No. 1	49	0	51
	No. 2	51	10	8 to 10
	No. 3	50	6 (circa)	15[a]
	No. 4	120	0 to 8	near 0
	No. 5	6	0	0
	No. 6[b]	22	18	. . .
Labor Productivity				
	No. 1	49	0	16
	No. 2	51	12	8 to 10
	No. 3	50	6 (circa)	15[a]
	No. 5	6	0	. . .
	No. 6[b]	22	49	. . .
Profitability				
	No. 1	49	2	. . .
	No. 2	51	8	8 to 10
	No. 3	50	6 (circa)	15[a]
	No. 5	6	0	. . .
	No. 6[b]	22	49 to 64	. . .

NOTE: All production units in all six ministries are covered by these data. Precise data are available for Ministries Nos. 1, 2, and 5, and also for 6 except for profitability. Data for Ministry No. 5 are not comparable to those of the other ministries because the reporting units are much larger and thus average out under- and overfulfillment by their subunits. Data for Ministry No. 6 are noncomparable for the reasons indicated in note b.

[a] More than 5 percent.

[b] Data are for three quarters of a year, and thus do not take account of plan changes instituted during the fourth quarter.

These results are radically different from what would be predicted from the orthodox model; this prediction would have been that a high proportion of units would not fulfill their plans, and that a much larger percentage of units would underfulfill substantially than overfulfill substantially. This prediction from the orthodox model should apply even more strongly to the Romanian than to the Soviet economy, since our Romanian data relate to three principal plan indicators rather than to the single one which has been characteristically treated for the Soviet Union. The ability of almost all enterprises to fulfill their plans for all three principal indicators should be less than for a single indicator, since the potential for trade-offs is less.

The results also differ radically from the only aggregative figures which are available for the Soviet Union (these are consistent with the orthodox model); in the USSR during each year of the 1951-54 period, between 31 and 40 percent of all industrial firms failed to fulfill their most important annual plan indicator (value of total output).[5]

In searching for an explanation of the low proportion of Romanian operating units which fail to fulfill their annual plans, the data for Ministry No. 6 provide a suggestion. The explanation may lie in the revision of unit plans during the course of the operating year. In order to explore the likely significance of this explanation, let us now examine the number of plan changes which have occurred in the various ministries and *centrale*.

Plan changes. The data from ministry sources as to the amount of change in enterprise and *centrala* plans is much poorer than the information concerning fulfillment of the final plans. The planning directors of the ministries do not keep such careful track of the number and significance of changes.

The planning director of Ministry No. 2 took the position that deviation of units in either direction from 100 percent plan fulfillment was primarily due to errors in the plan assignments which he had given them, rather than to the operating performance of the units themselves. Thus he normally felt at ease with his conscience in reducing the levels of plan indicators for units which would otherwise fail to meet their targets. He was limited in his ability to do this, however, by the fact that the summation of all the unit plans could not fall below the ministry's own plan target; therefore, lowering one unit's plan targets usually required a compensating increase in the plans of other units, and such increases during the course of a year were resisted strongly by unit directors.[6]

---

[5] *Pravda*, August 10, 1955, p. 1.

[6] The explanation for such resistance is, presumably, that plan increases would

Furthermore, an individual unit might be the only one producing a particular product mix established by the Council of Ministers; in this case, no reduction in its planned output volume was possible. He recognized that, as a result, there were times when units were left with unchanged plans which they could not possibly fulfill—even though such underfulfillment might not at all be the fault of the unit managers. Nevertheless, he estimated that about 50 percent of the units in the ministry had their planning indicators changed during the course of each year.

Two conclusions as to the approach of this ministerial planning director emerge from the above remarks. The most important is that he regarded his planning task as including changing the plans of the units under him sufficiently throughout the year so that all units would come as close as possible to hitting their targets. While it is true that he was constrained in these efforts, he regarded the unit plans much more as predictions of performance than as targets. Second, he appeared not to regard the percentage of plan fulfillment as a good indicator of the unit's performance. This interpretation is reinforced by the fact that, in this ministry, it has not been the same units which failed to fulfill the plan indicators in successive years; for individual units, the percentage of plan fulfillment in successive years appears to have been generated by a stochastic process. Since, clearly, some units must be better managed than others and consistently perform better in relation to their objective possibilities, a reasonable ministry official faced with these statistical results could scarcely give much weight to the percentage of plan fulfillment in his evaluation of the unit managers.

Ministry No. 4 provided data as to the fulfillment of the plan indicators for those products or product groups whose output is planned by the ministry itself. As of the end of September 1970, output targets for 30 percent of these product groups had not been met; for one-tenth of the number of product groups, the degree of underfulfillment was greater than 10 percent. However, this ministry makes all its changes in product-mix assignments in December of the operating year; my informant expected, on the basis of the ministry's past record, that the changes would result in final plans according to which the output of only 5 percent of these product groups would fall below plan targets. This difference be-

---

augment the effort required from managers and the labor force, while at the same time adding to the possibility of plan failure.

While, certainly, plan targets for enterprises can be increased—the compensating benefit for the enterprise being reduction of plan targets in other years when they are difficult to meet—it seems reasonable that there should be a lack of symmetry in the ease with which a ministry can increase or decrease the planned targets for its constituent units.

tween 30 percent and 5 percent underfulfillment seems to be due primarily to plan changes.

The finance director of Ministry No. 4 reported that the planned profitability indicator of each of the one hundred twenty enterprises in the ministry had been revised twice during the first eleven months of 1970, and that the wage funds of twenty to twenty-five of the enterprises had also been altered.

Table 4.4 summarizes the available data as to plan changes in the units in which I conducted interviews. It should be noted that managers were reluctant to admit changes in their plans, and so additional changes may have occurred.

The above data seem to suggest that changes in important plan indicators for individual units during the course of the planning year are quite common. Enterprises No. 2 and No. 3 of Table 4.4—the units in which the least changes in plan were indicated—were in Ministries No. 2 and No. 4 where ministerial staff had provided figures showing very substantial plan changes. The other three units of Table 4.4 were from two different ministries. From Table 4.4 one might conclude that plan changes are more prevalent in consumer goods ministries; however, Ministry No. 2—where, as we saw earlier, half of the units receive changes in a normal year—is in charge of a producer goods industry. There is no evidence that such changes are more or less prevalent in higher priority sectors. Changes appear to be much more frequent for financial plan indicators and product mix than for targets measuring the volume of total output.

Ambitiousness of original plan indicators. The above material for two ministries and five production units suggests that the prevalence of plan changes during the course of the operating year goes a long way in explaining why only a small proportion of operating units fail to fulfill their most important plan indicators. It is my impression, however, that a second explanation is that the original plan targets are not set at a particularly demanding level.

The evidence for this impression is threefold. First, as was seen in Chapter 3, officials of the State Committee for Planning considered that the only five-year plan indicators for ministries which were set at demanding levels were those of profitability and, perhaps, of exports. But, of all the major annual plan indicators for operating units, it was the financial and export indicators which were taken least seriously, and it was probably the financial indicators which were most easily changed. Second, the officials of branch ministries reported that they and their units both had "reserves" built into their annual plan targets. Third, none of the managers in operating units complained that their major plan

TABLE 4.4: Plan Changes in Units

Unit	Industry	Years Covered	Plan Indicator and Type of Change
Centrala No. 1	Consumer goods	1970, first three quarters	Total production: reduced in one quarter Domestic sales: reduced for the year because exports were increased Profitability: reduced each quarter Total profits: reduced each quarter Wage fund: increased each quarter
Centrala No. 2[a]	Consumer goods	1970, first three quarters	Exports: reduced for period as a whole Profitability: reduced each quarter Total profits: reduced each quarter Marketed goods paid for: reduced for period as a whole
Enterprise No. 1[b] (very large)	Intermediate producer goods	1969, all four quarters	Total production: reduced in each of three quarters[c] Finished-goods production: reduced in each of three quarters Profitability: reduced in each of three quarters Total profits: reduced in each of three quarters Product Mix: annual change[d]
Enterprise No. 2 (very large)	Machinery	1970	Total production: increased by less than 1 percent
Enterprise No. 3	Producer goods	1966-70	Total production: increased in only one of the five years

[a] In the principal enterprise of the *centrala*, there had been little revision over five years in the plan indicators for total production or for finished-goods production, or in a very broad product-mix indicator.

[b] Over ten years, there had been no changes which increased the planned wage fund. In 1970, the only plan changes for the *centrala* in which this enterprise had been placed were for product mix.

[c] For 1969 as a whole, the reduction in plan totaled 1.5 percent. This reduced annual plan indicator was overfulfilled by 1.8 percent.

[d] Major changes in the product-mix plan were made during two of the last four years.

indicators were set at unreasonable levels; if many of them had regarded these indicators as terribly demanding, it seems likely that some of them would have said so.

This does not mean, of course, that there is complete honesty between the operating units and their ministries in the setting of the original plan indicators. The general director of one enterprise told me that he always proposed lower plan targets than those which were in fact established by his ministry. The planning chief of another enterprise said that he always requested higher materials allocations than he was granted. Neither seemed disheartened that their recommendations were not accepted.

But I was assured in both a *centrala* and in an enterprise that the unit had "reserves" which were not incorporated into its original plan indicators. The plan indicators were seen as being raised by the ministry over those of the previous year primarily on the basis of technical improvements already introduced into production in the unit, as well as of new investments in the unit which were planned to come into operation during the current year. The reserves consisted of most of the technical improvements which the unit was prepared to introduce but had not yet begun to utilize.

For example, an enterprise general director told me that, immediately after his annual plan indicators are given to him, he sets above-plan tasks for the subunits of the enterprise and indicates the specific means by which these can be accomplished. That these are realistic and not simply exhortatory is suggested by the fact that in 1969 the above-plan output tasks totaled no more than 1.5 percent of the planned production indicator for the enterprise.

All in all, I believe that Romanian industry is poorly described by the orthodox model of enterprise operation, which posits that managements' abilities are severely strained by the need to fulfill annual plan indicators.[7] As a corollary, we might expect that Romanian managements would not feel compelled to engage in the predicted amount of violation of the less important plan instructions. In these regards, Romanian operating units seem markedly different from Soviet enterprises.

Bonus funds of centrale *and managerial bonuses.* The orthodox model for the operation of enterprises which was presented at the beginning of this chapter is based upon certain critical assumptions as to man-

---

[7] In late 1972, the head of the Party and the state voiced the view that normally the enterprises' annual plans should be fulfilled by December 15th, but that the remaining half month should be devoted to preparations for production in the following year rather than to above-plan output (N. Ceauşescu, concluding speech at the Central Committee plenum of November 20-21, 1972, as reported in *Romania: Documents-Events*, 1972, 44, p. 62).

agerial bonuses. Specifically, bonuses are assumed both to be substantial as a proportion of total managerial income and to constitute a well-defined function of the degree of fulfillment of specified plan indicators. However, these assumptions—which appear to hold in the case of the Soviet Union[8]—are invalid for Romanian industry.

For all except a few experimental enterprises, the current bonus system for production units was introduced only in January 1970. However, by far the most important source of variations in income for top management personnel has been, both before and after January 1970, payments received from the ministerial bonus fund. The amount and method of distribution of this ministerial bonus fund were unaltered by the change in the system of enterprise and *centrala* bonus funds. Since our concern is centered on bonuses paid to upper managerial personnel, and since the critical features of these remained unaffected, we need not be troubled by the January 1970 change. I shall concentrate in my treatment of the enterprise bonus fund on the system in force after 1969, but the bonus statistics of Tables 4.5 and 4.6 lump together both 1969 and 1970 data.

Let us begin with a brief description of the pre-1970 system. Through 1969, rather substantial bonuses were paid to all personnel. Aside from payments out of the ministerial bonus fund which will be described below, bonuses in 1969 averaged 17 percent of the total wage fund in one ministry and 18 percent in a *centrala* of a different ministry. A Ministry of Labor source estimated that senior managers of enterprises had received 19 to 23 percent of their income from bonuses: i.e., much the same percentage as rank-and-file workers.

These pre-1970 bonuses were paid out of the wage fund rather than from enterprise profits. The amount of bonuses available to the enterprise for distribution were in theory linked to the fulfillment of plan indicators, although it appears that no additional bonuses were paid for overfulfillment.[9] Thus bonuses were theoretically a function of fulfillment of well-defined plan indicators, with a kink to an absolutely horizontal line at the point of 100 percent plan fulfillment.

This system was abolished because of the belief that it was unworkable and that in practice it provided no incentive effect. Since the entire industrial labor force was involved in the system, and since bonuses represented such a substantial portion of income, it was regarded as politically and humanistically impossible to avoid paying bonuses regardless of the degree of plan underfulfillment. Presumably this was

---

[8] See Granick, *Managerial Comparisons*, chapter 9.

[9] This was specifically stated to have been the case in one large *centrala*. The method of funding bonuses makes it likely that this was general throughout industry.

particularly the case because it was difficult to defend eliminating bonuses for ordinary workers in months when plan fulfillment by their unit was reduced for reasons quite outside their control. Thus bonuses were in fact regarded as no more than delayed wage-and-salary payments. As of January 1970, previous bonus payments were incorporated into normal wages and salaries, and the earlier system was abandoned.[10]

Introduced in its stead was a four-part system:

1. An annual bonus fund was created for each *centrala* as a percentage of its total profits,[11] but it was to be fully paid only if other indices of plan fulfillment were met. The percentage of profit intended for bonuses differs between *centrale*, but it is computed so that the annual bonus fund will constitute about 2 percent of the *centrala*'s wage fund if the planned indicator of profits is exactly fulfilled. It seems highly unlikely that many—if any—*centrale* would earn sufficiently more or less than planned profits so that these bonuses would go outside the limits of 1 to 3 percent of the wage fund.[12]

Three-quarters of the annual bonus fund is to be distributed annually, and each worker or employee is to share in his unit's fund in direct proportion to his wages. The remaining one-quarter can be used during the year as an advance on the fund, and is paid out at the discretion of the *centrala*'s management as a reward for special services or accomplishments. This discretionary part of the fund is intended primarily for manual workers and lower-level employees; the top-management cadres of the *centrala* and, in some *centrale*, of its constituent enterprises are specifically banned from sharing in these awards.

Given both the small size of this annual bonus fund and its method of distribution, it would seem that it should be regarded primarily as a

[10] The previous three years had seen a sharp rise in the share of basic wages in the total earnings of manual workers in industry. This had been accomplished primarily through increasing basic wages sharply at the same time that norms of output for piece workers were increased, thus reducing extra earnings paid to workers exceeding their norms. By early 1970, it was claimed that base salaries of manual workers in industry constituted about 90 percent of their total earnings, in contrast to an average of 78 percent earlier (see the article by Petre Isac and Andrei Burlă in *Scînteia* of March 10, 1970, and the article by Teodora Sersun in *Muncă* of January 10, 1970, both summarized in *RFE*).

[11] The experimental enterprises placed on this system prior to 1970 had received a far greater percentage of above-plan profits than of planned profits for their annual bonus fund. When the system was made universal, these differing percentages were renounced on the ground that some enterprises were believed to have received unreasonably large funds. Only the few *centrale* which receive budgetary subsidies for operating expenses are given a high proportion of above-plan cost economies for their bonus fund.

[12] One indication that no great incentive effect is expected from this bonus fund is the fact that, in two *centrale* of different ministries in which I conducted interviews, the percentage of profit to be used for bonuses in 1970 had not yet been determined even in October 1970.

form of delayed wage payment. Clearly it is no more than this for top-management personnel. Its current function appears to be symbolic: both to interest all the employees in the success of their *centrala* and, specifically, to interest them in the attainment of profits. This last is particularly important since central authorities in Romania are concerned with upgrading the importance attached to cost reduction.

An additional possible effect is to create some minor rank-and-file pressure on the managers of individual *centrale* which do not earn the planned bonus fund. One may speculate that the insignificant size of the fund will make it politically possible for higher authorities to withhold it from individual laggard *centrale*, while they could not afford to do this earlier for the much larger bonus funds then being distributed. National propaganda concerning these funds may conceivably give them a role in the minds of ordinary workers which their economic importance does not deserve.

It is possible that this primarily symbolic significance will change in the future, since at least certain groups in the Ministry of Labor hope that the fund can reach one month's salary by 1975. If this in fact occurs, the discretionary one-quarter of the fund would begin to become quantitatively significant. In any case, however, this annual bonus fund can scarcely serve as any real direct incentive to top management personnel.

2. Two additional bonus funds have been created at the *centrala* level to reward specific accomplishments in reducing the required labor force and in economizing on materials. In late 1970 when I did my interviewing, there was still great uncertainty as to the criteria of eligibility for these new payments. Some *centrale* considered that these funds were only for people who made innovating suggestions, and that even lower-level managers were ineligible. Others considered that all the personnel involved in achieving the economies should share in them. In general, neither fund seems to have been very large; in one *centrala*, however, the fund for economies of materials did amount to 5 percent of the wage fund. Although in one enterprise it was a department head who received the largest single bonus for economizing materials, the funds in 1970 appear in general to have been used primarily to reward manual workers rather than managers.

3. In contrast to the first two items, the introduction of a system of salary reductions for nonfulfillment of plan was directed particularly at middle and upper management.[13] It is true that all personnel except

---

[13] The relevant indicators of plan fulfillment differ according to the *centrala* and are determined by its branch ministry. In one *centrala* in 1970, marketed production, profitability, and the degree of fulfillment of specified tasks were the three main indicators used; labor productivity and export sales were also used as minor

manual workers paid by piece rate are subject to the provisions. But rank-and-file workers and employees are to have their salaries cut by only 1 percent for every 1 percent failure to fulfill plan, constrained by a maximum reduction of 20 percent; on the other hand, top managers of enterprises and *centrale* are subject to a 4 percent reduction for every 1 percent failure to fulfill plan, and their constraint is a maximum reduction of 30 percent.

In defining plan fulfillment for this purpose, only those working in the *centrala*'s apparatus are judged according to the plan fulfillment of the *centrala* as a whole, and only those in the enterprise's apparatus by the overall results of the individual enterprise. Others are judged according to plan fulfillment by the lowest-level subunit in which they work. Financial indicators of plan fulfillment are relevant only to personnel who have at a minimum completed secondary education.

Salary reductions are applied in relation to actual versus planned results for each month. However, if a shortfall is made up in the succeeding month, 90 percent of the salary reduction is returned; if made up later in the same quarter, 80 percent; if made up at any other time during the year, 70 percent.

Data as to salary reductions are available for one ministry as a whole, for two *centrale*, and for one large enterprise. These data provide some coverage of four separate ministries.

In Ministry No. 6 of Table 4.3, where the percentage of units not fulfilling plan during the first three quarters of 1970 varied between 18 and at least 49 percent for major plan indicators, 10 to 15 percent of all the top managers of these units had suffered salary reductions in at least one of the nine months. The maximum salary reduction in any month was 10 percent. As of October, none of the salary reductions had been returned. An overlapping 9 percent of these top managers suffered an additional reduction during two months in the "personal indemnization" portion of their salary. (Personal indemnization is an addition to the base salary for the post, and its amount is a function of the qualifications of the individual officeholder. Normally, it comprises some 10 to 15 percent of the total salary of managers at this level.) It is clear that salary reductions for top management had some quantitative importance in this ministry, but the morale effect was probably much more significant. It is also clear that not all the units which failed to meet plan targets were punished by salary reductions.

---

indicators. In two other *centrale*, marketed production, profitability, and export sales were used, and ministry officials decided on an ad hoc basis whether overfulfillment of one indicator could be considered as compensating for underfulfillment of others. In a fourth and fifth *centrala*, marketed production and profitability were the only two indicators used.

In one *centrala*, none of the directors of the *centrala* was penalized at any time during the first ten months of 1970. The director of the largest enterprise of the *centrala* was penalized 30 percent in one month, but received back nine-tenths of this the following month; thus his total loss was 0.3 percent of his salary for the ten months as a whole. About twenty additional people were penalized in that enterprise for the one month's performance; they received 10 to 20 percent reductions, but also recouped nine-tenths of this in the following month. The director of a second enterprise (of the four in the *centrala*) was similarly penalized by a 30 percent reduction in one month, and similarly received nine-tenths of it back in the following month.

In a second *centrala*, there were no salary reductions at all during the first ten months of 1970. A very large enterprise of a third *centrala* had reduced salaries for about 1 percent of all its personnel in each month of the first three quarters of 1970, and for about 5 percent of its professional and managerial personnel. However, the same individual was rarely subject to such penalty in more than one month, and the vast bulk of the salary reductions were returned during the following months.

From these data it can be seen that salary reductions for even top managers had little monetary significance. It seems unlikely that any were penalized in nonreturned reductions by much more than 2 percent of their annual salary.

4. For top management, the most significant variations from base salary come from a source which has continued from the past. This is the ministerial fund, constituting 0.1 percent of the total wage fund of the ministry as a whole, which is used for bonuses paid at the discretion of the minister. Unlike the other three items discussed above, payments from this fund are not tied to any specific plan indicators.

It was claimed at several of the branch ministries that the ministerial fund is used primarily for rewarding entire units for special efforts; in one ministry, it was asserted that the principal uses are as rewards for bringing new investments into operation sooner than planned and for reducing downtime of equipment while it is under repair. In fact, as Table 4.5 shows, the bulk of the fund in three out of the four ministries for which such information is available was used to finance bonuses for top managers.[14]

Table 4.6 provides full coverage of all top managers at the designated ranks in six ministries. While there is a good deal of variation among ministries, the great majority of top managers appear to receive bonuses regularly from the ministerial fund. The average seems to be between 4

[14] This was the case at least in Ministries Nos. 1, 2, and 5 if "top management" is defined as the top 1 percent or so of all employees.

TABLE 4.5: Use of the Ministerial Bonus Fund

Ministry	Year	Use
Ministry No. 1	1969 and 1970	About 50 percent was paid to the general directors, chief engineers[a] and assistant chief engineers of the enterprises and *centrale*
Ministry No. 2	1969	52 percent was paid to the same group as indicated for Ministry No. 1[b] 10 percent was paid to manual workers
Ministry No. 5	1969	Less than 20 percent was paid to manual workers and first-line foremen
Ministry No. 7	1969	23 percent was paid to general directors and chief engineers 42 percent was paid to manual workers

[a] Chief engineer is a title given to some directors and also to some nondirectors.
[b] There were three hundred twenty such people in these posts within Ministry No. 2, about one-half of 1 percent of the ministry's personnel.

and 9 percent of annual salary. The difference between flat failure and major success in bonus performance for individuals seems to be about 12 percent of salary.

The bonuses described above, are, of course, reasonably substantial. But they scarcely appear to be of a magnitude to bear the weight placed upon them in the orthodox model of enterprise behavior.[15] Even if the reader should disagree with this analysis, however, what is more important than the relative size of managerial bonuses is the criteria by which they are rewarded.

Fundamental to the orthodox model is the attachment of managerial bonuses to measured performance. Romanian bonuses, on the other

[15] Comparisons may be drawn between these bonuses and those paid in Soviet and American industry in the middle 1960's. In the Soviet Union, the variable portion of income of unit managers was two to three times as large a percentage of income as in Romania (Granick, *Managerial Comparisons*, chapter 9).

For the United States, 1967-68 data are available for nine industrial companies; all of these are among the top one hundred fifty American firms ranked according to sales in 1966, and they include one-fifth of the top twenty-six companies. Considering bonuses as a proportion of base salary for the 2.5 to 9 percent of professional and managerial (i.e., "exempt") personnel whose positions made them eligible for managerial bonuses, six of the companies can be considered as having "high" bonus plans, with a seventh being similarly rated as regards the top six managers in each division. "High" bonus is defined as one which normally runs at least some 20 to 60 percent of base salary, depending upon the individual's position, with factory managers' normal bonus typically lying in the 60 percent range. For the counterparts of the Romanian top managers in *centrale*, stock options would have to be added to gain a full appreciation of the importance of variable earnings in the incomes of American managers (ibid., chapter 9).

It is against the background of these Soviet and American data that one may conclude that Romanian managerial bonuses are quite modest.

TABLE 4.6: Size and Regularity of Ministerial Bonus Fund Payments to Top Managers of *Centrale* and Enterprises

Ministry	Year	Group of Managers	Bonuses Paid
Ministry No. 1	1969 and 1970	Assistant chief engineers and above	Bonuses averaged about one month's salary
Ministry No. 2	1969	Assistant chief engineers and above[a]	81 percent of the group received bonuses during 1969[b] For those receiving bonuses, the average bonus was 46 percent of one month's salary
Ministry No. 3	1970 (nine months)	The general directors of *centrale*	All received bonuses, 90 percent during the second two quarters Bonuses averaged one month's salary. The range of bonuses was between 45 and 145 percent of one month's salary
Ministry No. 4	1969	Enterprise directors	Directors of all or virtually all enterprises received bonuses Bonuses averaged half of one month's salary, with very little variation
	1970 (nine months)	All	No bonuses had yet been paid
Ministry No. 5	1969	Assistant chief engineers and above in *centrale*	All received bonuses
		Same group in enterprises	Almost all received bonuses
		Same group in *centrale* and enterprises together	Bonuses averaged one month's salary
		General directors of *centrale*	Bonuses averaged one and one-half month's salary
Ministry No. 7	1969	All directors of enterprises and *centrale*	Directors in some *centrale* received no bonuses Bonuses averaged half of one month's salary

[a] There were three hundred twenty such posts in this ministry.

[b] In this ministry, 10 percent of the enterprises failed to fulfill their plan indicators for total production, 12 percent for labor productivity, and 8 percent for profitability.

hand, are not paid in relation to any of the individual indicators of plan fulfillment or to any combination of them. It is true that the figures of Table 4.6 for Ministry No. 2 are consistent with the hypothesis that top managers of units which fail to fulfill some major plan indicator do not receive bonuses. However, I was explicitly told in Ministry No. 6 that some of the top managers receiving bonuses were in units which fulfilled neither their productivity nor their profitability plans, despite the fact that these two indicators are considered as among the most important. All informants both at the ministerial headquarters and in the *centrale* were unanimous that bonuses were distributed according to the subjective evaluations of the minister and his vice-ministers, and that the top managers of units could not predict their bonuses from their success as measured by the various plan indicators.

Payment of managerial bonuses according to subjective evaluations by superiors creates the danger of arbitrariness and favoritism. I have no evidence as to this in Romania. It should be noted that, while such a system of awards is not used in the Soviet Union, it is the prevalent pattern employed in large American companies.[16]

In at least one ministry, individual *centrale* are provided with a fund similar to the ministerial fund: this is used to finance special bonuses for the top two or three managers in each enterprise, but not for the managers of the *centrala* administration itself. In 1970, the enterprise managers in two *centrale* received an average of about three-quarters of a month's salary from this fund. Here again, however, the size of the bonus awards is not linked to any indicators of plan fulfillment.

The unimportance of bonuses as a motivator of managerial behavior holds even more sharply for those in the ministry apparatuses than for those in the production units. Although the ministries do have a bonus fund designated explicitly for personnel at their headquarters, all of the ministries studied seem to use this fund almost entirely to finance social benefits for persons below middle-management level. The fund's main function appears to be to help individuals faced with personal financial crises. Bonuses as such are virtually nonexistent at the ministerial level, and earnings normally consist solely of salary as in most western civil services.

Romanian industry and the orthodox model. The above evidence strongly indicates that the orthodox model of operation of production units— which was developed particularly for application to Soviet industry, but which has also been applied to Hungarian industry of the 1950's and to Polish industry—is inappropriate for explaining the working of Romanian industry.

[16] Ibid., chapter 9.

The orthodox model is predicated on the assumption that managers attempt to maximize their bonuses, and that this effort causes them to respond in a well-defined fashion toward achieving major plan targets at the expense of lesser objectives.

However, the variable portion of income of Romanian managers of *centrale* and enterprises seems too small to act as this powerful motivating force. Executives within the apparatus of branch ministries have virtually no variable income at all. Much more important, the overwhelmingly dominant financial source of income variations in enterprises and *centrale* (i.e., bonuses from the ministerial fund) is distributed according to subjective rather than objective evaluations of managerial performance. Therefore, even to the degree that managers do indeed intend to maximize their bonus earnings, such an attempt provides no guide as to what their actual managerial behavior will be.

The orthodox model proceeds on the basis of the bonus-maximizing assumption, combined with others presented earlier, to predict that a large proportion of production units must fail to fulfill their plans, and that a much greater percentage of units underfulfill substantially than overfill substantially. But our analysis of Romanian industry led to a rejection of both of these predictions, as might have been expected from the radically different role of bonuses in Romanian industry from that in the orthodox model.

No satisfactory information is available for Romania as to the basis upon which managerial promotions and demotions are made. But it is quite clear that the criteria employed are subjective, and that the degree of fulfillment of key plan indicators is not given dominant weight. Thus the applicability to Romania of the orthodox model cannot be rescued by substituting career advancement for bonuses.

We are thus left with a theoretic tabula rasa in explaining the managerial process of deciding on trade-offs between objectives in Romanian *centrale* and enterprises. I shall approach the problem of explanation by first examining the constraints within which decisions are made, and by then analyzing some areas of trade-off and the criteria used there for decisions.

CONSTRAINTS ON MANAGERIAL DECISION MAKING

Constraints emanating from the branch ministries. These constraints, of course, are the principal ones affecting the *centrale* and enterprises. They consist in part of annual plan indicators established by the ministry, in part of direct instructions, materials allocations, and limits on labor inputs.

Let us begin with a relatively complete list of plan indicators which was given to me by the planning director of one *centrala*. For this director, the annual plan indicators of significance were the following:

(1) Total production, expressed in constant prices of 1963-65. Unfinished production is included here. Certain products, but not others, are double-counted when they are both produced within the *centrala* and are used within it in the production of a final product of the *centrala*.

(2) Finished-goods production, expressed in current prices. This includes all finished goods intended for sale by the *centrala*.

(3) Marketed production, expressed in current prices. This includes all goods for which payment has been received.

(4) Product mix, expressed in physical terms. Almost the entire product mix was specified for this *centrala*, although the aggregation was into a small number of very broad categories.

(5) Number of personnel, referring to all those listed as employed in the *centrala* rather than to the number physically present at work. This was subdivided between manual workers and all others.

(6) Wage fund, subdivided according to that paid to manual workers and to all other personnel.

(7) Productivity, defined as total production in constant prices divided by the average number of total personnel listed on the books of the *centrala*.

(8) Profitability or cost plan. This is defined as the total costs in current prices per thousand lei of finished-goods production, also measured in current prices.

(9) Total profits.

(10) Specific new products to be brought into production.

(11) Specified research and development studies which are to be carried out.

(12) Capital/output ratios for specified major types of equipment in use, with both capital and output being defined in physical terms.

(13) Materials usage per unit of product for specified inputs and outputs, both numerator and denominator being defined in physical terms.

(14) Exports, measured in foreign exchange and subdivided according to the three categories of destination described in Chapter 3.

Along with the above indicators of performance, some allocative indices were also established. These were:

(1) Investment coming from the State budget (90 percent of total investment for this *centrala*), and the component of this intended to finance construction and installation. The usage of these investment funds is specified in detail.

(2) Materials allocations, fully specified.

(3) Amount of working capital owned by the *centrala*.

A second *centrala*'s directors said that they were given approximately eighty plan indicators. In addition to indicators similar to those listed above, additional items were included which are exemplified by:

(1) Total sales tax to be generated from sale of products.

(2) The maximum number of railroad cars to be used.

(3) The amount of electricity to be used at different hours.

But even the sum total of the plan indicators given to a production unit does not constitute the entire list of objectives and constraints which management must heed. In at least five out of the nine *centrale* and enterprises in which I interviewed, the broad categories set forth in the annual product-mix plan indicators served as no more than a framework for further negotiations between their ministries and the client ministries. On the basis of interministerial agreements, the producing ministries gave the *centrale* far more detailed product-mix instructions than were incorporated in the *centrale*'s formal plans. Furthermore, significant changes in technological methods require ministerial approval.

The importance of the minor plan indicators and of detailed instructions is not completely clear. On the one hand, the planning director of the second *centrala* above stated that the need to consider eighty indicators left the *centrala* with little room for possible trade-offs. On the other hand, while he could cite exact figures as to the *centrala*'s plan fulfillment according to several major plan indicators, he did not know, or apparently care, whether all eighty indicators had been met. The financial director said that product-mix decisions by the *centrala* were completely unaffected by the differentiated rates of sales tax levied on the various products produced, and that there were never any difficulties if changes in product mix led to below-plan generation of sales tax revenue for the state budget.

In the first *centrala* above, the planning director had no difficulty in picking out the major indices used in evaluating the work of the *centrala*. These were only five (with one of these being almost a mathematical function of two of the others): total production, marketed production, number of total personnel, profitability, and profit. In other *centrale*, however, some of these indices were not considered important, and others were substituted for them in the list of truly significant indicators.

The creation of *centrale* in Romanian industry was viewed in these production units as an effort to provide the units with more de facto power to engage in trade-offs among the minor plan indicators, so long as they respected the most important indicators. However, one general director spoke of his unit as still "breathing with the lungs of others" (i.e., of his ministry). I have previously described the relative ease of meeting the final revised major plan indicators; the frequency of change in these indicators during the course of the planning year, and the difficulty of explaining under what conditions changes favorable to the *centrala* are made; and my inability to specify either a clear objective function for the *centrala* or binding constraints on its choices. Given the above, it is not possible to generalize as to the degree to which production units stand ready to sacrifice fulfillment of minor plan indicators and instructions in order better to fulfill the major plan indicators. It is only possible to say that, if and when managers become convinced that they cannot meet major plan indicators without violating the minor constraints established for them, and when they are also convinced that they cannot persuade their branch ministry to make the appropriate changes in the major indicators, then they may be expected to make trade-offs which violate the less important plan indicators. This set of conditions may well apply to only a very small minority of production units in any given year.

Committee direction. The current system of formal internal controls over management has existed since 1968. A council was established within each ministry to discuss top managerial decisions; this council meets at least monthly in the one ministry for which I have information. *Centrale* have both a board of directors (meeting monthly or quarterly) and an executive committee (meeting about weekly). Each enterprise has both its own board and a workers' council. In principle, the internal control bodies must approve certain major decisions of the general director of the *centrala* or enterprise before they can enter into force.

In practice, however, these collective organs do not exercise any serious restraint on the decision-making powers of the head of the unit concerned; if they should disagree with him, and if the disagreement cannot be ironed out between them, the dispute would go to the next highest hierarchical body for decision. It is the individual head of the unit who is still held individually responsible for the unit's performance.

Elected workers' councils exist only on the enterprise level, and not on that of the principal microeconomic unit (the *centrala*). Membership is quite large, and in the more substantial enterprises normally consists of fifty or so delegates. Their role appears to be essentially pro forma: approval of the annual and five-year production plan, analysis of plan fulfillment, and the adoption of measures to improve plan fulfillment. Occasionally, however, these tasks can be genuine if minor. The director of one enterprise told me that he had come to the workers' council the previous year with projects for surpassing the production plan by 1 percent. To his surprise, one of the delegates—anxious to use this forum to show his own competence—made additional proposals which would result in a 1.5 percent overfulfillment, and the council adopted these proposals. The general director then proceeded to try to implement them.

The ministerial council, and the board of directors and executive council of the *centrala* and enterprise, have a more substantive function than do the workers' council. Nevertheless, despite the fact that many decisions of the *centrala*'s general director require the formal approval of either his board of directors or executive committee, it is clear that these are essentially consultative committees. Furthermore, and equally important, they represent primarily the top management of the unit rather than a broader constituency.[17] Since in only one of the three *centrale* for which I have information do all the employees elect members to the board of directors, and in none are there elections for any of the posts on the more important executive committee, it cannot be said that these bodies exist so as to provide even an illusion of mass participation. One ministerial manager explained the existence of these committees on the ground that it was useful to force the general director of a *centrala* to defend his decisions before some informed group, if only to reduce the likelihood that he would make purely arbitrary deci-

---

[17] In the one ministry for which I have information, the members of the council consist of the six top men at ministerial headquarters, the general directors of all of the *centrale*, the secretary of the trade union of the industry, and three or four specialists (mainly university natural science and engineering professors) from outside the ministry.

The composition of the boards of directors is known for three *centrale*. Each of these boards has twenty-nine to thirty-five members. The directors of the *centrala* and of its constituent enterprises are all on the board, constituting about one-third of the membership. In each case, the trade union secretary of the main plant is a member. No Communist Party secretary is a member unless he is there in another role, but normally the Party secretary is present without a vote. Only one of the three boards has representatives from outside the *centrala*; in this case, there is one from the ministry to which a large part of the *centrala*'s products are sold, two from research institutes of the *centrala*'s own ministry, and one teacher from the engineering institute from which the bulk of the *centrala*'s engineers are recruited. In one *centrala*, the bulk of the remaining members are middle managers chosen by the *centrala*'s general director, and the rest are junior managers and professionals similarly chosen. The second *centrala* has, in addition, four elected manual workers from the main enterprise; but the workers in the other enterprises have no elected representatives. Only in the third *centrala* are some 40 percent of the board members elected by all the employees of the *centrala*.

The executive committees of the three *centrale* are made up exclusively of top management. In one case, it consists only of the seven directors of the *centrala*. In a second, the six *centrala* directors are supplemented by three other top managers from *centrala* headquarters. In a third, the *centrala* directors are supplemented instead by the three heads of constituent enterprises.

sions from which he himself would voluntarily withdraw if forced to examine their rationale.

Role of the Communist Party. The Party organizations within the *centrale* occupy a potentially important position in constraining the behavior of top management. Not only is political power in Romania completely concentrated in the hands of the Party, but some 15 percent of all adults —and a substantially higher percentage of urban adults—are members of the Party.

However, these Party organizations do not appear to exercise any significant control over the decisions of the general director. Rather, their task (aside from political functions which have nothing to do with the economic role of industry) appears to be essentially to improve morale and mobilize worker effort for plan fulfillment. This is exemplified by the fact that no Party organization exists at the level of the *centrala*; although Party committees and Party executive committees are elected by the Party members in each plant, and others are elected by members working in the apparatus of the *centrala* itself, none are elected to represent the entire Party membership of the *centrala*. Nor have I come across any instance of full-time paid Party functionaries for a *centrala* as a whole; such functionaries exist in large factories, but the first secretary elected by the Party members in the administrative apparatus of the *centrala* seems always to hold a regular job within the apparatus and to exercise his Party function in his spare time.

Moreover, to whatever limited degree the Party committees of industry do exercise genuine supervision over management, statistics on the one *centrala* for which I have data suggest that their supervision is under the heavy influence of the managerial personnel being supervised. In this *centrala*, in which 20 to 25 percent of the total workforce belonged to the Party, three out of seven of the members of the Party executive committee of the *centrala*'s central apparatus were department heads, although management at that and higher levels comprised only 6.9 percent of the total number of employees of the apparatus. In the principal plant, seven members of the Party plant committee (i.e., 26 percent) were department heads or higher, and two members of the Party's plant executive committee (i.e., 29 percent) were at the same level of management.

It is at the regional and municipal levels, rather than in the factory or *centrala*, that the Party committees and secretaries play a significant economic role. Their functions here appear to be three: providing the intraregional coordination of the economy which exists in no other organization, supplying the branch ministries with local and relatively impartial information about their *centrale* and plants, and offering managerial recruitment services.

Since 1969, the position of Party first secretary for a region or municipality has been linked to the post of the top government official for the same district.[18] Party regional committees receive regional economic plans of their own, coordinated through the State Committee for Planning. Prior to the approval of the plans for individual enterprises or *centrale*, the relevant Party regional committees check such plans as they come from the respective ministries: both with regard to how they fit into the regional plans, and also with regard to the demands they make upon local sources of labor supply, road building, and materials. Thus the Party municipal, and especially the regional, committees exercise an important administrative role which parallels that of government organs. After their plans have been approved, the ministries and *centrale* must keep in close touch with the regional Party committees for the same reason that they have regular contact with other suppliers of necessary inputs.

A second important function of the regional Party committees is to exercise broad supervision over all the production units in their territory. Regular meetings are devoted to examining the progress of such units. The committees can order specific technical measures to be introduced in enterprises, but more normally they will limit themselves to checking factory proposals before these are sent on to the factory's ministry.

The planning director of one ministry, describing to me the usual role of the Party in the visits which he would periodically make to inspect his *centrale*, said that he would begin his visit by first spending half a day at the regional Party committee, talking with two or three full-time Party secretaries about the *centrala*. He felt that this was the most objective source he could tap as to the *centrala*'s problems and prospects. After spending two or three days at the *centrala*, he would then return to the regional Party headquarters to discuss his provisionary decisions and to arrange for local help to the *centrala* where this was needed.

In this ministry, all of the ministerial department directors and assistant directors spent an average of twenty days each during 1970 in visiting *centrale*, enterprises, and Party headquarters in this fashion. A representative of this ministry, at the above level or higher, normally participates each year in two or three day-long sessions with each of some ten regional Party committees, over and above the meetings with

---

[18] This Party-state link was further extended at the end of 1972 (N. Ceauşescu, speech at the Central Committee plenum of November 21-22, 1972, reported in *Romania: Documents-Events*, 1972, 44, p. 45).

individual regional Party secretaries. In a second ministry, the ten top officials of the ministry each spent about eight days during 1970 attending regional Party committee meetings.

The first Party secretary of a large city told me of the role of his Party organization in choosing top managers (the top three to five men) for enterprises and *centrale* located in the city. An individual may be nominated either by the factory director, the factory Party organization, or the ministry; the nominee's qualifications—both professional and in terms of social relations—will then be discussed with the city's Party secretaries or in its Party committee. Since the nominee is usually a local man, and may well have been active in municipal or regional Party affairs, the local Party organization is generally in a position to voice an opinion as to his suitability. In these cases, however, the city Party organization is presented with only a single candidate whom it can veto or approve; but it is not given a slate from which to choose.

Nevertheless, there are instances in which the municipal Party committee plays a more active role in searching out managerial candidates. This is where a suitable candidate cannot readily be found within the ministry which must fill the slot. In such a case, the municipal Party committee asks the Party organizations of other plants in the area if they can provide a candidate. Two or three such candidates may then be invited to appear before both the municipal Party committee and the general director of the enterprise concerned, be orally tested as to their technical and economic knowledge, and one of their number be selected for further interviews in the appropriate ministry. While the ministry will still make the final decision, it will interview only the one candidate unless it rejects him. In this large city, there are perhaps two cases a year in which the municipal Party committee goes through this procedure.

A final interesting device of Party "control" is that each member of the national Central Committee is made personally responsible for one large unit. Of the organizations in which I interviewed, one very large enterprise had above it a Central Committee member who was not otherwise linked to industry at all; the general directors of two *centrale* were themselves members of the Central Committee.

This device is said to have been adopted for two reasons, neither of which is that of control. The first is as a means of educating the Central Committee members who are not personally connected with production units. The second, however, is to provide these large units with a form of normal access to a level of authority higher than that of its own ministry; through its Central Committee supervisor, the unit can appeal for aid which its own ministry may not be in a position to provide.

The role of the banks. The financial affairs of the *centrale* and enterprises are supervised by the National Bank and, since it was split off from the National Bank in mid-1970, by the Investment Bank as well. The National Bank concentrates on working-capital credits and expenditures of the wage fund; the Investment Bank supervises use of investment funds provided either through credits or state grants.

Centrale and enterprises finance most of their working-capital needs from state budget funds, which are granted to them as part of their capital. It would appear that 90 percent or more of the industrial credits from the National Bank are limited to loans on finished goods which have been shipped to customers; these loans are provided automatically, and are normally liquidated within ten to twelve days. Additional credits are granted to finance above-plan accumulation of stocks;[19] interest rates on these loans vary considerably depending on whether the bank considers that they have been necessitated by deficiencies of the production unit's management. The supervisory work of the local office of the bank is concentrated on these supplementary credits; even when the unit's bank account as a whole is positive, the bank can insist that individual operations be financed from loans made at 12 percent interest where these specific financial needs are judged to result from managerial failures.

The Investment Bank is primarily concerned with assuring that investment grants and credits are paid out only in proportion to the investment work actually done. In addition, it makes sure—through sample surveys—that equipment, and especially imported equipment, is fully utilized. When it finds improper usage, it can recommend that the underutilized equipment be transferred to another production unit; but it is the appropriate branch ministry which makes the decision. Finally, the Investment Bank checks as to the economic justification of investment projects before paying out any money for them from the state budget account; these checks, however, seem purely pro forma, in contrast to the situation in the German Democratic Republic. (In the one large enterprise for which there is information, neither the Bank nor its predecessor body has ever played an active role in this regard.)

Since neither of the two banks can refuse to provide credits or to pay out state investment grants, their supervision would seem to have potential significance to the production units' managements for only two reasons: first, because of the effects on profitability of high- versus

---

[19] From the information which I have received, it is unclear whether above-plan expenditures of wage funds are covered by bank loans or solely from additional allocations by the production unit's superior organization. I presume that it can be from either source.

low-interest loans, and, second, because of their reports on managerial performance, which get back to the unit's own branch ministry. In my judgment, the relatively low priority and frequent changes in plan of the profitability indicator of *centrale* render the interest-rate consideration of very minor importance. Thus only the second consideration requires analysis.

The National Bank has a full-time resident bank inspector, and the Investment Bank a half-time inspector, in one very large enterprise where I carried out interviews. Two National Bank inspectors worked full-time in a *centrala* of a different industry. Since these are the only people not working for the production unit who spend so much of their time concentrating on it, it is not surprising that the production units should regard them as peculiarly well informed about the unit's operations; two financial directors, in fact, asserted that these inspectors have a better overall perspective as to the unit's work than does any one person employed in the branch ministry headquarters.

Only in the large enterprise, however, was it asserted that the bank inspector acts as the eyes of the branch ministry and thus plays an important supervisory role. This was denied in a second enterprise and in a *centrala*. Discussions in the headquarters of a branch ministry (none of the above-mentioned production units were in this ministry) seem to corroborate the denials. During 1970, this particular ministry received only four or five reports from Bank inspectors warning of potential trouble in ministerial units; before the creation of the *centrale*, the ministry had received perhaps fifteen or twenty such reports annually. A somewhat larger number of such reports were channeled to the ministry through the central office of the National Bank, but I received the distinct impression that the ministry officials regarded such reports as quite exceptional; in any case, they explicitly denied that the bank inspectors acted as the watchdogs of the branch ministry.

My general conclusion is that the banks do not represent an important supervisory body over the *centrale* or enterprises, and that the managers of production units do not feel significantly constrained by the potential actions or reports of the bank representatives.

The role of the trade unions. Romanian trade unions appear to represent much less of a constraint upon managerial authority than is the case not only in the United States or western Europe, but even in the Soviet Union. Unfortunately, this statement rests primarily on the evidence of an interview with a single trade union plant president; in general, it proved extremely difficult to arrange interviews with trade union enterprise officials.

Trade union committees are organized similarly to Party committees in that it is the enterprise, rather than the *centrala*, which forms the significant unit. The data I have comes from the full-time trade union president of a factory with 6,000 employees; this president had held the post for five years, having earlier worked in the factory as a technician (with secondary education), and can be taken as knowledgeable about his own organization.

It is the trade union executive committee which is the principal union organ in the factory; its members are elected by the thirty-seven man plant committee, which in turn is elected biennially by the union members. In this factory, all nine of the executive committee members were Party members and had been on the executive committee for more than five years. Only three of the nine were manual workers; the remaining six came from the 2 percent of the plant employees who were supervisors or professionals. Of these six, one was an engineer and department head, three others were also engineers, and two were foremen. Thus the commanding positions in this factory trade union were all held by people who were politically reliable and who had long tenure in office, and two-thirds of the positions were filled by supervisory and professional personnel.

The president explicitly characterized the principal trade union roles as being the following two: mobilization of workforce effort behind fulfillment of the production plan, and the organization of cultural, artistic, sports, and vacation activities for the employees. Although I expressed considerable skepticism and pushed him hard on the subject, he was insistent that no worker complaints have ever been taken up by the trade union at the factory level. Specifically, he insisted that there had been no processing of complaints concerning favoritism by foremen, inappropriate piece-rate norms, workers being placed in a lower skill category than appropriate, or promotions. On the very rare occasions that individual workers complained about such matters, their complaints were handled at the level of trade union production shop meetings and never rose higher before settlement.

The above picture of union inactivity in the direct job-interest of workers is modified somewhat by an article written by a trade union official reporting on two large industrial branches.[20] During 1969, the year in which piece-rate norms were revised and sharply increased in light industry and in the food industry, there were 16,000 complaints by the 437,000 manual workers of these two branches as to the application of the new system. The figure of 16,000 complaints includes those which were settled on the spot and never reached joint union-

[20] Teodora Sersun in *Muncă* of January 10, 1970 as summarized in *RFE*.

management committees or the factory level of the trade union.[21] Although the resulting figure of 3.7 complaints per hundred manual workers is substantial, it seems rather low when one remembers that one would have expected it to peak sharply in that year. The figure should be compared with statistics for normal years of 2.3 in Yugoslavia and 0.9 to 2.9 in the USSR, with these latter statistics excluding the mass of complaints which were settled prior to reaching a worker-management committee.[22]

The situation of trade union inactivity in processing worker complaints which was described earlier for the Romanian factory contrasts sharply with that of the Soviet Union as depicted by Mary McAuley from the records of five Leningrad enterprises during the period 1957-65. Using a broader sample taken from several regions, Dr. McAuley estimates that some 3 to 10 percent of the Soviet industrial labor force are involved each year in disputes handled by either the shop or factory trade union bodies. In the five Leningrad enterprises which Dr. McAuley studied intensively, the factory trade union committees rejected about half of management's requests for dismissal of unsatisfactory workers (in the Soviet Union, the union committee has absolute power of rejection), primarily on humanitarian rather than legal grounds. They engaged in frequent disputes with management as to the proper length of annual holiday for individual classes of workers, since this is an area where the legislation, in many cases, is sufficiently confusing to lend support to both sides. Well over half of the many cases coming before the Leningrad plant labor-management committees or the trade union committees were finally decided in the workers' favor without going to the courts.[23]

Although in Romania annual trade union agreements are drawn up with each factory management, rank-and-file members have no easy access to the terms of the agreement. In the one enterprise for which I have this information, only two copies of the agreement exist: one is kept by the factory management and the other by the factory trade union secretary. Ordinary union members would have to make a very special effort even to learn whether the contractual terms were being observed—terms relating to such matters as the number of apprentices, safety, and social benefits.

It is perhaps not surprising that the trade union president denied that there had ever been a strike in his factory, even one which was limited

[21] Presumably, however, only those disputes were counted which reached the attention of some trade union representative.

[22] Table 12.2 of Chapter 12.

[23] Mary McAuley, *Labour Disputes in Soviet Russia 1957-1965* (Clarendon Press, Oxford: 1969).

to a single production department and lasted only a few minutes. In fact, he was quite amused at my questioning him about strikes; while he knew that they occurred in Yugoslavia, he seemed to view them as inconceivable in the Romanian context.

Since labor turnover and absenteeism do not appear to be particularly severe problems in Romanian industry (see Chapter 2), it would seem a fair conclusion that neither the trade unions nor informal worker pressure represent even as much of a constraint on managerial behavior as do the banks.

DECISION MAKING AT THE *Centrala* AND ENTERPRISE LEVEL

The preceding section has shown that the significant constraints on decision making by managements of production units come primarily from their branch ministries, but also to some degree from the regional and municipal Party committees. Constraints emanating from other organizations or groups within the unit need not be taken seriously.

This might suggest that managements of *centrale* and enterprises exercise very broad decision-making powers. In fact, however, this does not seem to be the case—at least if we define decision making as the trading-off of gains in one area against costs in another. One very important Romanian management figure explained this to me on the basis that department heads refuse to exercise responsibility, and instead buck decisions up to the directors of the enterprise or *centrala*. The result, in his opinion, is that top management is completely immersed in what should be middle-level management decisions, and that no one in the production units concerns himself with strategy or with trade-off problems. The real top management functions either are carried out by the ministries or remain totally neglected.

Of course, technical decisions are made continuously in the enterprises and *centrale*. The reorganization of production lines, the setting of maintenance schedules, temporary changes in design of product to take account of material shortages: such matters are the bread and butter of Romanian management. In one integrated textile *centrala*, the technical director had to determine the appropriate man-machine ratio in spinning, with the knowledge that a decrease in the ratio reduces the amount of cleaning work done by the operators and so reduces the quality of the yarn. This, in turn, requires more labor input in the weaving process in order to produce the planned quality of cloth. Here, indeed, is a trade-off; but it is one which can be expressed in terms of the single factor of labor productivity. On the other hand, where we find a woeful lack of decision making is in the areas where efficiency can be defined only in economic rather than in technical terms. I attempted to explore such decision-making areas in all of the *centrale* and enterprises in which I carried out interviews, and this section of the chapter will be devoted to presenting the results of these interviews.

"Economic" options will be defined much more broadly, and more relevantly for Romanian conditions, than simply as "financial" options. Economic options are defined as including all those requiring the comparison of costs and benefits expressed in terms of some common weighting system; unlike financial options (e.g., those differentially affecting money costs and profits), the weights used need not be current money prices. For example, a choice between two product-mix options which affect total value of output and labor productivity (both of which are measured in constant prices of 1963-65) will be defined as an economic option. Furthermore, the definition is extended to include choices involving improvement of the production unit's performance along one dimension of importance to the unit management's supervisors (e.g., value of output), at the expense of worsening it along another dimension (e.g., natural units of output). The textile example cited above is not economic in the sense used here, since the only vital dimension of performance affected by the decision is the overall productivity of the *centrala*,[24] and thus no weighting system of costs and benefits is necessary. It is true that the textile decision would have been converted into an economic one if the production director had also considered the effect on wage fund expenditures, since average wages are higher in weaving than in spinning; but because, in fact, the production director apparently ignored this ramification of the problem, his decision was narrowly technical.

In all of the *centrale* and enterprises in which I interviewed, there were managers who recognized that economic options exist at their level. Choice of product mix, decisions in the process of design, timing of decentralized-investment expenditures, and the lot-sizes to use in production runs were mentioned. But in all except one *centrala*, it was also pointed out that the choice among economic options has very little effect upon the degree of plan fulfillment. The effect is minor, it was claimed, because of the binding constraints of the detailed plan indicators under which the units function. Of course, this does not mean that the existence of such economic options is unimportant to the *centrala*; minor shifts in performance may lead to 100 percent fulfillment according to all major indicators. But it does suggest that the making of choices among such options is perceived as a poor area for a *centrala*'s management

[24] This is because the ministry is interested only in total labor productivity of manual workers, and not in the productivity of the group of spinners or weavers taken separately.

to pick as a focal point in which to invest managerial time. Such time is seen as better devoted to improving the technical decisions, since the quality of these decisions is believed to be much more important in determining the unit's success.

For example, the planning director of an equipment-producing enterprise which manufactures only in small batches and single units pointed out that his enterprise does have some power of choice as to its product mix. The enterprise's branch ministry sets for it the value of production or the tonnage (depending on the item) to be produced for each customer and for each major type of equipment, but within this constraint the enterprise can negotiate to manufacture to those specifications which it finds most advantageous. Nevertheless, he believed the constraints are such that the enterprise's degree of plan fulfillment cannot be greatly affected by the outcome of these negotiations.

Under these conditions, it is not surprising that the chief accountant asserted that his department plays no role whatsoever in such product-mix negotiations, and provides no information which might be used to guide them. From this we might conclude that, even where the commercial director of the enterprise does attempt to select a product mix which would be most advantageous to the enterprise, he has no sound basis for predicting the effect of alternative mixes on such important plan indicators and plan constraints as profitability, observance of the planned wage fund, and ability to finance work-in-process inventories without bank credits.

More opportunity for economic choice exists during the preplan period than after the annual plan indicators have been laid down. An example of this period differentiation is the choice of lot sizes in which to produce identical items. As the lot-size increases, unit manufacturing costs decline but inventories of work-in-process increase.

This choice problem was discussed in one *centrala* in terms of the constraint laid down by its branch ministry that the *centrala* cover all inventories from its own working capital rather than from borrowing; during at least the previous six years, the largest unit of the current *centrala* had never borrowed to finance inventories, and the *centrala*'s financial director saw no likelihood of this policy being changed. Given this constraint, and barring exceptional expansion of owned working capital, analysis of the most economic lot-size could scarcely have resulted either in much absolute cost reduction or in improvement of the *centrala*'s fulfillment of its cost-reduction plan.

A second *centrala*, however, was developing a computer program for the analysis of optimum lot-size. The criterion used in this program was the maximization of output during the planning year, without account being taken of the interest costs of holding larger inventories. The rationale for this flagrant departure from optimum-lot-size formulas used in capitalist firms was left unexpressed but, nevertheless, was clear; the *centrala* would request larger working capital from its ministry on the basis of its computer programs, and would be spared any interest charges on this additional capital. When and if the program is successfully developed, and if results are accepted by the ministry, the *centrala* will be able to show higher output, productivity, and profitability than is currently the case. But, of course, it may be expected that its annual plan targets will be raised accordingly, and thus there is no reason to expect that the *centrala*'s performance relative to plan will improve.

A second example of economic choice in the preplan period is that of a *centrala* in the industrial construction industry. The key planning indicator for this *centrala* is labor productivity, and its general director believes that each year it will continue to be given the task of increasing productivity by some 6 or 7 percent. In order to achieve this result, the *centrala* management is careful—to the degree that it has a choice—to reject jobs which would show low productivity: e.g., reconstruction of factories while they continue in operation, or projects whose geographic location would make it difficult to recruit and hold the necessary labor mix. The *centrala* insists on carrying out its projects with as much prefabrication as possible, even when this raises transport costs so much that the total costs of construction increase as a result of the prefabrication methods. The general director of this *centrala* was perfectly cognizant of the fact that his—and also his ministry's—interests could be in flat contradiction to that of the economy as a whole and of the state budget.

However, the possibilities of such managerial behavior were highly limited once the year's plan had been adopted. In 1970, this construction *centrala*'s projects and their technology were 100 percent predetermined by its branch ministry, and the same was expected for 1971. In the past,[25] the *centrala* had never been granted power of selection over more than 5 to 15 percent of its annual work program. Thus its "rejection" of undesirable projects primarily took the form of advice given to its own ministry before its annual plan was formulated, and presumably its productivity targets were set after this advice had been taken into account.

Economic choice in the preplan period may be quite important in improving a *centrala*'s record of improvement from year to year, but its effect on the percentage of annual plan fulfillment is much more dubious.

[25] This *centrala* had been in existence for a long time prior to 1969, although without the legal status of a *centrala*.

Hence, enlargement of such economic decision making by production units seems to have a rather low priority in the organizations I visited; indeed, given the major deviations of the criteria used in the examples cited above from those which would have been appropriate for the Romanian economy as a whole, such low priority is perhaps fortunate for the country.

Of all the nine organizations in which I interviewed, only one shoe *centrala* had elevated the problem of economic choice to a key consideration of top management. This was because of a unique marketing situation facing both the *centrala* and its industry: namely, a shortage over several years of demand relative to supply. This situation had forced the *centrala* into major efforts to procure export orders on short notice.

The *centrala*'s most important annual planning indicators—and also the most taut and the most difficult for it to have changed during the course of the year—are the following three: the number of shoes to produce and sell, the maximum number of employees, and the total allocation of leather. (The last is computed as a function of the product mix produced in the previous year.) Since 1969, the Ministry of Domestic Trade has been unwilling to purchase its normal proportion of the *centrala*'s production; as a result, the *centrala* has been forced to push exports much more heavily than previously. But the *centrala* management does not believe that it can continue to compensate with expanded exports for the shortage in domestic sales, and therefore it finds itself in a weak bargaining position relative to the wholesalers of the Ministry of Domestic Trade. In theory, both the *centrala* and its domestic customers (the wholesalers of the Ministry of Domestic Trade) are free to negotiate the product mix of shoes, except for a restriction on the proportion having leather uppers. In practice, and under the guise of such negotiations, the wholesalers have been able to reduce their purchases below the amount scheduled for domestic purchase in the plan set for the shoe *centrala*.

The *centrala* management believes that the only way to expand sales of shoes to Romanian consumers is to provide more fashionable styles. But it sees the wholesalers as a bottleneck to this solution: not only are they conservative in the styles they select, but they also give priority to selling their existing stocks, and thus new shoes are not placed before domestic consumers until they have lost their fashion novelty. Due to the excess supply in the shoe industry, the *centrala* is in no position to place pressure upon the wholesalers to accept those styles which the *centrala* would prefer to manufacture.

Faced with this market situation, the shoe *centrala* responded in mid-

1970—like the others of its industry, under a special dispensation from the Council of Ministers—by establishing its own retail stores in which it could promote its fashionable styles. This solution has the second hoped-for advantage of permitting the *centrala* to sell domestically the same styles which are demanded on the export market; in this way, the *centrala* can accept export orders for individual styles even when these orders by themselves would be too small to warrant production of the style. Thus the *centrala*'s entry into retailing is seen as the mechanism for the desired expansion of both domestic and foreign sales.

As of the fall of 1970, the future of this experiment in having producers sell directly at retail was wide open, and was heavily dependent on the efforts of the individual shoe *centrale*. The Ministry of Domestic Trade seemed skeptical as to the value of the experiment; the Ministry of Light Industry estimated that, by 1975, 10 percent of all shoe production might be sold through this channel; the general director of the *centrala* was aiming for an eventual 25 percent figure; and the commercial director of the *centrala* believed that, in one or two years, he would be able to sell 50 percent of his total production through his own retail stores. In short, this was a sphere in which the shoe-producing *centrale* were being given a very free hand.

Even in this sphere, however, the analysis engaged in by the *centrala* was minimal. Only two or three people in the entire *centrala* were involved in marketing analysis, and the rapid expansion of retail stores was being managed from the commercial director's hip pocket. More important, apparently little thought was being given to the implications for fashion production of the planning-indicator constraints of shoes-per-worker and leather-per-shoe.

The planning director of the *centrala* believed that fashion shoes for export require higher labor inputs per shoe than do standard domestic production. He also believed, although another director held the reverse view, that leather utilization per shoe is higher in these fashion shoes. If one assumes that the planning director was correct in his beliefs—though he had not assembled any quantitative data in support of them—one might speculate that labor and leather shortages would quickly force a halt to the *centrala*'s sale of fashion shoes in its own retail stores, and would compel the *centrala* to sell at retail the same styles of shoes which the Ministry of Domestic Trade was willing to purchase. If this should prove to be the case, the development of retail trade by the *centrala* would prove to have been totally misguided. It is difficult to conceive of a large capitalist firm going into a major retailing venture with so little prior analytic investigation. Of course, no capitalist firm would be faced with the type of uncertainty inherent in having to guess future years' planning constraints on shoes-per-worker and leather-per-shoe.

SUMMARY

This chapter has shown that the orthodox model of the operation of production units in centrally planned socialist economies is of no help in explaining managerial behavior in Romanian industrial *centrale* and enterprises. Managerial bonuses are too low as a proportion of managerial income, changes in plans during the course of the year are too frequent, and original planning targets for production units are apparently insufficiently taut to lead to the sort of suboptimizing behavior which the orthodox model would lead us to predict.

How, then, do Romanian managers of *centrale* and enterprises decide between alternative objectives: The constraints provided by planning indicators are at most no tighter in Romania than they have been in the Soviet Union—the country for which the orthodox model was originally designed. Nor are constraints other than those imposed by the unit's branch ministry particularly restricting. The possibility for choice should be present.

The answer would appear to be that enterprise and *centrala* managements have no clearly delineated objective function. Economic decisions at their level are kept to a minimum. Since, even where such choices are made, very little prior analysis is carried out,[26] the consequences must frequently be quite different from what the unit's management had expected. Instead, the attention of *centrala* and enterprise managers has been almost exclusively centered on improving technical efficiency—what Leibenstein has called "X-Efficiency."[27]

It is rather at the branch ministry level that economic decisions in Romanian industry are centralized. Despite the fact that *centrale* in 1970 were large units averaging some 8,000 employees, the functions of their top managers were much more comparable with those exercised by foremen and junior managers in western capitalist firms than with the functions exercised by top or even middle management in these western companies. As a result, Romanian *centrale* and enterprises suffer amazingly little from the evils of "success indicator" suboptimizing which have plagued Soviet industry.[28] Instead, they fall prey to the de-

---

[26] See the cases of the equipment-producing enterprise and the shoe *centrala* cited above.

[27] H. Leibenstein, "Allocation Efficiency vs. 'X-Efficiency,' " *American Economic Review*, LVI, 3 (1966), 392-415.

[28] This is not to deny that such suboptimizing does exist. I have come across a complaint that steel rolling mills attempt to maximize physical output at the expense of producing particular sizes in strong demand (*Viața Economică*, 1971, 11, pp. 3-4); that machinebuilding enterprises refuse to introduce innovations for fear of not meeting their plans (*Probleme Economică*, January 1971, pp. 29-36); and that the shipments of materials are uneven during the course of the month (*România Liberă*, November 16, 1971, pp. 1 and 3). (The first two sources are summarized in *ABSEES*, July 1971, and the third is translated in *JPS*.)

ficiencies of lack of initiative below the ministerial level. Either economic decisions are prepared and taken in the ministries or higher bodies, or they are not taken at all. Romanian national leaders clearly wish to remedy this state of affairs, and this is why the *centrale* were created in 1969. As of late 1970, they had a very long way to go.

To some degree, the difference between the management of Soviet and Romanian industry is simply a matter of the size of the two countries. But this case should not be overdrawn. For Romania is a land of 20 million people, with 1.6 million of them in the industrial labor force working under central ministries. Individual ministries reported on in this chapter have between 65,000 and 400,000 employees each. One could not say that Romania is a land of petty industry, and that this is the explanation as to why the orthodox model of enterprise behavior in Soviet-type economies does not apply.

PART II

The German Democratic Republic

THE German Democratic Republic is by far the most highly developed of the four countries we are studying, and is one of the two most industrialized nations within the CMEA bloc. There have been frequent statements, made both from inside and outside of the socialist camp, that highly centralized methods of planning and economic administration are more appropriate to economies at an early stage of development than to those that are relatively mature. In the light of this contention, it seems particularly important to have a study of the practice of economic administration in the G.D.R.

The older centralized system of planning began to be reformed in 1963, but the reforms were implemented most thoroughly during the 1967-70 period. The resulting "New Economic System" constitutes an interesting combination of centralized and decentralized planning and operational-decision-making procedures, quite different from the system in force in any of the other three countries we are studying. Part II is primarily concerned with describing the functioning of this system at its high point during 1970 when I conducted interviews in the G.D.R.

There have been claims[1] that this system was replaced de facto at the end of that year. It seems to me that, to some degree, such claims represent both a misunderstanding of the distinctive features of the New Economic System and an overhasty burial of a system because of what may be only temporary shifts in policy. Nevertheless, a reading of the East German press through the middle of 1974 has convinced me that the evidence supports the view that there have indeed been major shifts which far transcend in importance any changes which have occurred in the other three countries studied in this volume.

To a significant degree, therefore, Chapter 6—which describes the East German economy at the time of my interviews—represents a study of a historical period other than the present. Nevertheless, it seems to me to have contemporaneous importance for two reasons. First, it describes a socialist industrial system intermediate between that of the Soviet Union and Hungary:[2] one which both functioned with considerable success and is likely to be reinstated in some form either in the G.D.R. or in some other CMEA country. Second, it describes significant features of the contemporary East German industrial system which are

---

[1] These have been most strongly stated by Michael Keren in "The New Economic System in the GDR: An Obituary," *Soviet Studies*, XXIV, 4 (1973).

[2] The Romanian system is more centralized than either.

probably impossible to perceive except on the basis of such interviews as those which I was granted.

Chapter 5 begins with a survey of the East German economy, describes the organization of industry, and then proceeds to set forth the broad principles of the New Economic System as it existed in 1970. Finally, it treats the educational backgrounds of industrial managers and professionals and the role of the central trade unions. Of the materials in this chapter, only the description of the New Economic System seems partially obsolete as of late 1973.

Chapter 6, written primarily on the basis of my interviews with managers in six East German industrial organizations, discusses the planning system of 1970 as it affected individual enterprises, *Kombinate*, and vvbs. This is the most significant of the chapters, but also the one which is most dated.

Chapter 7 draws conclusions as to the New Economic System on the basis of the materials of the earlier chapters, and suggests the ways in which the system seems to have been modified during the 1971-73 period.

CHAPTER 5

The East German Industrial Setting

THE German Democratic Republic and Romania are at opposite ends of the macroeconomic spectrum covered by East European countries. The G.D.R. is highly industrialized, with little possibility for adding further to the labor force employed in industry. Its population enjoys a relatively high standard of living and has a plenitude of urban and industrial skills but, partly owing to substantial emigration, is little larger than that which existed in the same territory before the Second World War. Finally, the country is heavily dependent for its raw materials upon trade with other CMEA countries.

The G.D.R. shares with Romania a high degree of formal centralization of industrial administration which contrasts sharply with the systems in Hungary and Yugoslavia. But even in this regard the two countries differ somewhat, for the G.D.R. places much greater emphasis upon financial planning indicators at the expense of physical ones. Moreover, the managers of German production units exercise considerably greater de facto decision-making authority than do Romanian managers.

While our study of Romanian industrial management illustrated the operation of a centralized planning system in a rapidly developing but still primarily agricultural country, that of the G.D.R. shows its functioning in a mature, industrialized economy.

SURVEY OF THE G.D.R.'s ECONOMY

The East German population numbers seventeen million, 15 percent smaller than the Romanian. However, not only is this the same size as it was in 1939 but, despite the closing of the frontiers in 1961, there was even a small decline between 1962 and 1970. On the one hand, this is unfavorable from the point of view of economic growth because of its implication as to lack of expansion of the labor force. This is particularly the case because of the unfavorable age distribution: 19.5 percent of the population were past pension age in 1970 compared to 15.9 percent of the same age in West Germany. On the other hand, the requirements of funds both for new housing and for additional productive investment are substantially less than would have been the case if the population were growing.

In view of this labor-supply and capital-demand situation, although it is true that the labor force has grown somewhat because of an increasing rate of labor participation,[1] we might expect new investment to be biased more toward capital intensity than it is in Romania—with favorable effects on labor productivity.

Already in the prewar period, the territory of East Germany was highly industrialized; per capita industrial output was then slightly greater than in West Germany.[2] The industrial labor force was well trained and had traditionally acquired skills. Although this favorable pattern was disturbed by an estimated net emigration of two million people between 1949 and 1961,[3] and by a rise in the proportion of women in the industrial labor force from 36 percent in 1952 to 43 percent in 1970,[4] the industrial-skill situation was not thereby seriously altered. However, the result of the major emigration ending in 1961 was to strip the country of a major portion of its professionals and managers.

Thus, while the industrial labor force through the level of foreman has the high quality to be expected in a mature, industrialized society, the managerial part of the industrial labor force is of recent origin and has a youthful age structure. This last is partly a result of emigration, partly of the heavy death rate during the Second World War among the generations which would normally have been expected to fill the middle and top management posts, and partly of the political requirements for managerial positions which are set forth in all Communist countries and which are peculiarly difficult to meet for those who received a university or even gymnasium education in prewar Germany. The combination of these three factors is unique to the G.D.R.

Gross investment in the G.D.R. has been historically relatively low by the standards of CMEA countries. While it rose very rapidly as a proportion of gross national product between 1955 and 1960, and less rapidly thereafter until 1966, a western estimate suggests that in the middle

[1] Between 1952 and 1970, the labor force grew from 40 to 46 percent of the total population. While the population fell by 0.6 percent between 1963 and 1970, the labor force (excluding apprentices) rose by 1.6 percent. A 1964 comparison of East and West Germany indicated a substantially higher labor force participation rate in the G.D.R. for those between the ages of sixty and seventy. ("Materialien zum Bericht zur Lage der Nation 1971," Drucksache VI/1690 in *Verhandlungen des Deutschen Bundestages*, 6. Wahlperiode, Bonn: 1970/71, p. 237.)

[2] Edwin M. Snell and Marilyn Harper, "Postwar Economic Growth in East Germany," in Joint Economic Committee, 91st Congress of the United States (2nd session), *Economic Developments in Countries of Eastern Europe* (U.S. Government Printing Office, Washington, D.C.: 1970), p. 559.

[3] Ibid., p. 579.

[4] Staatliche Zentralverwaltung für Statistik, *Statistisches Jahrbuch der Deutschen Demokratischen Republik 1971* (Staatsverlag, East Berlin: 1971), pp. 57-58.

1960's it was still little higher than the West German ratio.[5] The investment ratio began to increase again in 1969 and 1970, continuing the trend of rising toward the general CMEA level, but it dropped off once more in 1971 and 1972. These relatively low levels of gross investment have helped to maintain high consumption levels; but the rising ratio of investment has nevertheless had its counterpart in a continuous decline in individual consumption as a percentage of net material product from 81 percent in 1955 to 74 percent in 1960, 72 percent in 1965, and 67-68 percent during 1970-72.[6]

Per capita personal consumption, according to official data, rose by 3 percent per annum during the first half of the 1960's and by 4 percent during the second half.[7] (However, a western estimate for the first half of the 1960's showed only a 1 percent per annum growth rate.)[8] The official 4 percent figure for 1966-70 is rather high for an industrialized country, being at the same level as the increase of real wages in Romania during the same period.

But the increase in income does not appear to have been distributed in equal measure among the various groupings of the population. The minimum wage was raised in two stages between 1967 and 1971 at an annual rate of 13 percent; moreover, in both years the lowest-income 13 to 18 percent of all wage and salary recipients had their incomes increased differentially toward a plateau of 57 to 60 percent of the average wage of state employees.[9] Large percentage increases were also received by groups (such as teachers and medical personnel) whose incomes were perceived as out of line.[10] Farm incomes and incomes of self-em-

[5] Snell and Harper, pp. 563-65. According to the estimates of "Materialien," p. 327, the East German ratio was lower in all years through 1969, except for the West German recession year of 1967.

[6] *Jahrbuch 1973*, p. 42.

[7] Calculated from *Jahrbuch 1971*, pp. 3, 40, and 42. Data from "Materialien," p. 328 give the same results; it would appear that this semiofficial West German source accepts the East German figures.

[8] Snell and Harper, p. 589. This western estimate is based upon 1955 weights; the intercategory weights for four groups of consumer goods are based on estimated expenditures of G.D.R. households, while the intracategory weights are based on West German retail prices.

[9] Walter Ulbricht, *Zum Ökonomischen System des Sozialismus*, Volume 2 (Dietz, East Berlin: 1968), p. 342, and Willi Stoph, *Zum Entwurf des Volkswirtschaftsplanes 1971* (Dietz, East Berlin: 1970), p. 31.

[10] Despite the increase in minimum wages in 1967, and the resulting higher-than-average wage increase for the very lowest income group, overall income distribution among worker and employee households remained quite stable over the years 1960-70, and probably also through 1972. The proportion of such households receiving a net income of less than 50 percent of the average remained between 9 and 10 percent of the total, while the proportion receiving more than 150 percent of the average stayed between 10 and 11 percent. (Calculated from *Jahrbuch 1971*, pp. 350-51. Data for 1972, as calculated from *Jahrbuch 1973*, pp. 340-42, provide the same result for the lower-income population but do not permit an

ployed people are said by a well-informed source to have risen considerably more rapidly than those of state employees. There has been a substantial upgrading of the educational level of the labor force, with a resultant rise in the proportion of the labor force which falls into higher-income categories. The result has been that large groups of industrial employees, who did not improve their skills but at the same time had incomes substantially above the legal minimum, seem not to have received any wage increases at all during the second half of the 1960's or in 1970-71.[11] These substantial groups failed to share in the increase of prosperity, and the effect on their morale may be readily imagined.

A unique feature of the East German economy—which was, however, abruptly abolished during the second quarter of 1972—has been the significant role played outside of agriculture by private and semiprivate enterprises.[12] In industry and nonconstruction handicrafts, over one-fifth of the entire labor force was employed in these enterprises in 1970, as shown in Table 5.1.

The principal reasons for preserving such private ownership of the means of production were doubtless political and social: a desire to appeal to those within the G.D.R. who value such private ownership, and to display to the West the moderation of the regime. But a secondary reason appears to have been the desire to maintain an already func-

---

estimate for the upper-income group.) This stability is presumably due to selected higher-income groups also having received larger-than-average salary increases. (Examination of the data for specific-size households, using the same source, shows only an erratic pattern with regard to greater or lesser income equality over the period. This is true with regard to compression both from the low-income and the high-income side.)

A West German estimate of net income by quintiles for worker and employee households for 1960, 1964, and 1967 shows a growth in income equality in both the 1960-64 and 1964-67 periods, but the changes indicated are quite slight. (Deutsches Institut für Wirtschaftsforschung Berlin, *DDR-Wirtschaft*, Fischer Bücherei, Frankfurt am Main and Hamburg: 1971, pp. 198-99.)

[11] The best statistical evidence for this concerns low-income workers and employees. In mid-1967, before that year's wage increase for low-income workers, 13 percent of all workers and employees earned less than 400 marks monthly. Almost four years later, the proportion earning less than 435 marks was 18 percent. These data suggest that during four years there were no increases at all for those posts earning between 400 and 435 marks. (See Stoph, p. 31, and Ulbricht, Volume 2, p. 342. The percentages are of all workers excluding apprentices; if apprentices are included, then the figures become 12 and 17 percent respectively.)

An individual worker told me in mid-1970 that he was working at the same job that he had been on four years earlier, and that his monthly earnings were unchanged.

[12] The latter are enterprises in which ownership is held jointly by private entrepreneurs and the state, with the entrepreneurs serving as the managers and sharing in the profits according to their proportionate ownership of the capital. Semiprivate companies are discussed at length in Chapter 6.

TABLE 5.1: Employment of the Labor Force in Private and Semiprivate Enterprises, September 1970 (percentage of total employment within the given production sector)

Sector	Semiprivate Enterprises		Private Enterprises	
	Total labor force	Labor force employed for wages	Total labor force	Labor force employed for wages
Industry	12.5	12.4	2.7	2.6
Handicrafts (other than construction)	0.0	0.0	65.7	94.4
Subtotal	11.0	10.6	11.8	7.2
Construction	8.4	10.3	9.1	7.4
Trade	8.2	4.8	8.8	6.1
All sectors	6.2	6.9	8.5	6.6

SOURCE: Staatliche Zentralverwaltung für Statistik, *Statistisches Jahrbuch der Deutschen Demokratischen Republik 1972* (Staatsverlag, East Berlin: 1972), p. 53. Apprentices are excluded from the labor force. See *Jahrbuch 1973*, p. 53 for comparable data two years later.

tioning small-parts and maintenance sector, since such work is small-scale in its very nature and private industry can very usefully fill the interstices of nationally planned production. In point of fact, I have the impression that these activities have functioned rather better in the G.D.R. than in other socialist countries where they have long been socialized.

While all of the CMEA countries have sharply reoriented their trade since prewar years, it is the G.D.R. which has been by far the most heavily affected. In 1936, the territory of present East Germany (without Berlin) received 45 percent of its total net consumption of agricultural and industrial goods from other parts of the German Reich; today, this share stands at little more than 2 percent.[13] As a result of the separation of the two parts of Germany, East Germany is much more self-contained economically than was the case prewar; one estimate is that, as of 1965, the G.D.R.'s imports stood at only 82 percent of their 1936 level while West Germany's were 413 percent as high as in 1936.[14]

[13] Werner Bröll, *Die Wirtschaft der DDR* (Günter Olzog, München-Wien: 1970), p. 118. Bröll's 2 percent estimate excludes imports of the G.D.R. from that part of Poland which formerly belonged to the German Reich.

[14] Snell and Harper, table 6, p. 569. This estimate for the G.D.R. is higher than that implied by the Bröll estimate given in footnote 13. Another American estimate for the G.D.R., after the 1964 figure given there is updated to 1965 by the official index of imports in comparable prices, is 67 instead of 82 percent (Maurice Ernst, "Postwar Economic Growth in Eastern Europe," in Joint Economic Committee, 89th Congress of the United States [2nd Session], *New Directions*

The need to develop far more self-sufficiency than existed prewar—due to the inadequacies of CMEA countries as sources of the supplies previously purchased from West Germany—has had two major implications for the G.D.R.'s economy. First, it has required highly capital-intensive investments in order to provide energy and semifabricate needs, thus leaving much less productive investments for labor-saving mechanization than would otherwise have been the case.[15] Second, it has tended to prevent the development of production in such a fashion as to gain the greatest economies of scale, and has instead compelled the production of an exceptionally wide product range—especially in the machine-building industry.

After Bulgaria, the G.D.R. is the CMEA country whose exports are most concentrated on sales to other members of the bloc (69 percent in 1970) and to the Soviet Union in particular (38 percent in 1970). This concentration of foreign trade has further contributed to the failure to attain desirable economies of scale, since it has necessitated a wide product mix of machinebuilding exports.

It is frequently stated that the G.D.R.'s access to the West German market without the payment of tariffs makes the G.D.R. an unofficial member of the Common Market insofar as its own export opportunities are concerned. This leads to the claim that this is an important ingredient in the G.D.R.'s economic success during recent years. In fact, however, the percentage of the G.D.R.'s exports which have gone to West Germany has been fairly stable throughout the 1960's and early 1970's; during the thirteen years 1960-72, the percentages of 1968 and 1969 were surpassed in six of the eight earlier years, and even the 1970-72 percentages were below that of 1960. There is no indication in these figures that the G.D.R. has been able to use its preferential entrance into the West German market to gain equal access to those of the other members of the Common Market.[16]

THE ORGANIZATIONAL PATTERN OF INDUSTRY

Figure 5.1 depicts the organizational structure of East German industry, including those state organs which most significantly influence its operations. The vast bulk of state-owned enterprise (except for the

---

in the Soviet Economy, U.S. Government Printing Office, Washington, D.C.: 1966, Part IV, p. 899).

[15] By 1968, East Germany had a substantially higher proportion of its industrial capital invested in mining and metallurgy than did West Germany: 22 versus 16 percent (DDR-Wirtschaft, p. 274).

[16] See Bröll, pp. 118-38 for an interesting treatment of G.D.R.-West German trade.

FIGURE 5.1: Organizational Structure of Industry, 1970

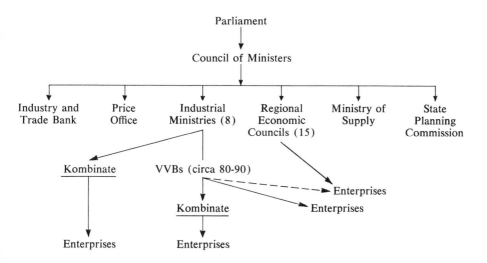

foodstuffs industry) has been placed under eight different industrial ministries. Private enterprises, almost all semiprivate enterprises, and various smaller state-owned enterprises operate under fifteen regional economic councils, whose industrial activities are in turn under the Ministry for Regionally Administered Industry and for Foodstuffs.

VVBs. The Unions of State Enterprises (*Vereinigung Volkseigener Betriebe*; hereafter, these will be referred to by their initials as VVBS) are the main intermediate organs between ministries and production units. There were about eighty to ninety of these in 1970,[17] and each covered

[17] Eighty is an estimate given me by a knowledgeable East German. A 1970 study refers to an analysis (presumably, from the context, recent) of eighty-eight VVBS, but without indicating whether that was the total number in the country (H. Mann, "Die planmässige Ausnutzung . . . ," in *Die ökonomische Stimulierung der sozialistischen Produktion*, Verlag Die Wirtschaft, East Berlin: 1970, p. 124). The only complete figure which I have seen in East German publications was for early 1964, when there were eighty (Ulbricht, Volume 1, p. 413). A West German source estimates that the number of VVBS was reduced by about 25 percent between mid-1967 and 1970 (*DDR-Wirtschaft*, p. 66). A Russian source reports that the number of VVBS declined from eighty during 1968-69 to fifty-five at the beginning of 1973 (A. Nagovintsin in *Planovoe Khoziaistvo*, 1974, 2, p. 89). A figure of about ninety for 1972 was claimed to have been quoted in an East German newspaper (*Neues Deutschland*, August 14, 1972, as cited by M. Gamarnikow, "Balance Sheet on Economic Reforms," in Joint Economic Committee, 93rd Congress of the United States [2nd Session], *Reorientation and Commercial Relations of the Economies of Eastern Europe*, U.S. Government Printing Office, Washington, D.C.: 1974, p. 175), but I cannot find this in the original source.

a given sector of industry. Probably a majority of the vvbs are located outside Berlin; the stated practice is to place the headquarters of each in the principal region of its sector.

The role of the vvbs is somewhat ambivalent. This is exemplified by the fact that they did not receive a clearly defined legal status as part of the New Economic System until 1973, although this System was introduced back in 1963.

The organizational distinction most commonly accepted by East German managers between the functions of the different hierarchical bodies of industry hinges on the issue of responsibility for current operations. Using this criterion, the vvbs are grouped with the ministries in contrast to the *Kombinate* and enterprises. Both vvbs and ministries are regarded as supervisory bodies.

An alternative view, however, is that a strong distinction should be made between the ministries and the vvbs. The well-known Hungarian economist Csikós-Nagy regards the East German system as similar to the Czechoslovak reform model of 1968, in that both emphasize the autonomy of industrial branches (as consolidated under the vvb in the G.D.R. and in the huge enterprise in Czechoslovakia) rather than the autonomy of individual enterprises within the same branch as is the case in Hungary.[18] For Csikós-Nagy, the significant locus of independence of decision making in the G.D.R. is the vvb rather than the *Kombinate* and enterprises which are subordinate to it.

Presumably, what Csikós-Nagy has in mind is that the vvb is expected to finance most of the investments of its branch out of that portion of its net profit which is not siphoned into the government budget, and thus that the rate of expansion of the branch is partially dependent upon its financial performance. The vvb also bears considerable responsibility for determining the product mix of the branch. VVB managerial personnel normally earn bonuses just as do *Kombinat* and enterprise managers, and are not civil servants on fixed incomes as are the executives of ministries.

In the above respects, however, the vvbs do not differ from their *Kombinate* and enterprises. All three types of organizations normally finance their investments from their own profits. For all three, between 40 and 70 percent of net profits are absorbed into the state budget, and the actual percentage is determined within these bounds by the next higher organization in the industrial hierarchy. In branches where more rapid investment is planned than can be financed either in this fashion or from credits granted against future profits, budgetary investment

---

[18] Béla Csikós-Nagy, seminar held on November 19, 1971 at the Institut d'Etudes Politiques of Paris, *Revue de l'Est*, III, 1 (1972), 25.

grants are available. *Kombinate* and enterprises, just as vvbs, play a role in determining their own product mix.

Usually, the vvb is described as the organization below the ministerial level which is most concerned with long-run development. However, the general director of one *Kombinat*, who had previously been general director of a vvb and thus had had experience at both levels, took the view that the vvb is primarily concerned with the short-run profits of the branch while it is the *Kombinate* which take the longer view. Thus, even in this regard there is no strict demarcation of functions or viewpoint; presumably, the various branches differ depending upon the personalities involved.

One can distinguish between the ministry and the vvb in that the ministry is not responsible for financing its own investments. But since all the component units under the ministry do have this responsibility, and since the ministry itself cannot meet its obligations unless these units are successful, this distinction is not particularly important.

On the other hand, one can distinguish the vvb from the *Kombinate* and enterprises by the fact that the former is not an operating body. The vvb, for example, does not have any significant resources of its own nor does it receive credits. The resources of the *Kombinate* and enterprises are increased, and because of this the constraints on their decision-making powers are widened somewhat, to the degree that their performance improves within a planning period covered by fixed financial norms; this is true for the vvbs only if they alter the *Kombinat* and enterprise norms of planned financial performance at the same time that their own norms remain unchanged, and such practice seems unusual. These distinctions appear more significant than that of financial responsibility. It is for this reason that I prefer the interpretation of the East German managers to that of Csikós-Nagy.

Kombinate. Traditionally, enterprises have functioned directly under the supervision of the vvbs. However, especially since 1968, an additional body has been created: the *Kombinat*. The *Kombinat* is quite similar to the prototype of the Romanian *centrala*, grouping a number of enterprises which are usually located within a small geographic area. In the *Kombinate* which I observed, the tendency is to absorb the non-production functions of the individual enterprises into the *Kombinat* headquarters (which may or may not be located in the principal enterprise), thus transforming the enterprises into purely production units. Since this process is being carried out only gradually, the enterprises within many *Kombinate* still retain at least some of their old functions of marketing, comptrollership, personnel, etc. Nevertheless, it is the

Kombinat rather than its constituent enterprises which should be considered as the basic operating unit.[19]

Although *Kombinate* exist primarily in sectors of heavy industry, I have also come across them in light industry. At least one hundred thirty existed in industry and construction in 1970.[20] Their prime function is described as that of coordinating within a single organization the various stages of product development and production leading to an end product. Not only is the creation of *Kombinate* intended to bring former subcontractors within the same organization as the final producer, but it is also believed to make feasible greater division of labor among the main enterprises than would otherwise be practicable because of the undependability of deliveries between independent enterprises. This prime function of coordination, it seems to me, should be seen as the counterpart to the increased development since 1967 of market relationships among operating units. On the one hand, highly detailed coordination by central authorities of the relationships among production units has been viewed as inefficient, and thus the market relations of the New Economic System have been introduced. On the other hand, wherever a comparatively small relevant sphere of control can be delineated, direct administrative controls are still regarded as the most effective; therefore, the creation of *Kombinate*.

A second function of the *Kombinate* appears to be that of improving the reconciliation between the goal of making operating units primarily self-financing and the paramount objective of promoting rapid technological change and product development. Since major technological advances require large investments in development expenditures and new equipment, they would be beyond the resources of an individual enterprise. A *Kombinat* can better finance such change for a limited range of products and production departments in any year out of the gross income of all the enterprises within the *Kombinat*.

A third function of the *Kombinate* is that of linking into one unit both efficient and inefficient enterprises. This may improve efficiency in the weaker organizations, because they can be provided with better managerial services from the *Kombinat* headquarters. It seems also to be sometimes regarded as a useful prelude to concentrating production in the more efficient plants—along with increased investment there—while phasing out production in the less efficient units.

Although a number of the *Kombinate* have been subordinated directly to the industrial ministries (the number had increased to thirty-seven by

---

[19] Sometimes a *Kombinat* is even described in the literature as an enterprise (*Cf. Lexicon der Wirtschaft: Industrie*, Verlag Die Wirtschaft, East Berlin: 1970, p. 484).

[20] *DDR-Wirtschaft*, p. 86. New *Kombinate* were still being formed in 1970.

the middle of 1971, and to forty-three at the beginning of 1973),[21] most have been placed under the vvb of their industrial sector. This has meant the creation of two organizations between the ministry and the enterprise, rather than one as previously. Some knowledgeable East Germans have suggested that this may well be only a transitional stage, and that the vvbs will in time be liquidated. To my knowledge, however, there are no official indications as to this.

Enterprises. Enterprises themselves appear to be largely single-plant organizations (i.e., establishments), although on occasion small neighboring plants are included in the rubric of a single enterprise. Statistics for the average of 1970 indicate that 29 percent of the labor force in socialist industry is employed in enterprises with more than five thousand employees, and that an additional 45 percent are in enterprises with between one and five thousand employees. However, *Kombinate* are included as enterprises in these statistics, and enterprises which are within *Kombinate* are excluded. The statistics as to enterprise size are thus no more meaningful in the case of the G.D.R. than in the case of Romania, and for the same reason.[22]

While a great many state enterprises remain outside of the *Kombinate* and are supervised directly by the vvbs, no information is available as to their share of industrial capacity. What was certain in 1970, however, was that such capacity was still diminishing in favor of that organized through *Kombinate*.

The "New Economic System"[23]

Beginning in 1963, but particularly since 1967, reforms were introduced into the East German planning and integrative system for industry. The new pattern was entitled the New Economic System. It followed upon a marked slowdown of economic growth during 1961-64 when the G.D.R.'s rate of expansion was the slowest of all the CMEA countries except Czechoslovakia.[24]

The purpose of this section is to describe the system as it functioned

[21] Nagovintsin, p. 89.

[22] See *Jahrbuch 1973*, p. 110 for the treatment of enterprises and *Kombinate* in the statistics. With the creation of the *Kombinate*, the proportion of the labor force of socialist industry which is located in enterprises with more than five thousand employees rose from 21 to 30 percent between 1967 and 1969 (*Jahrbuch 1969*, p. 110 and *Jahrbuch 1971*, p. 110).

[23] The two best general sources here are: *Planung der Volkswirtschaft in der DDR* (Verlag die Wirtschaft, East Berlin: 1970) and *Eigenerwirtschaftung der Mittel im ökonomischen System des Sozialismus* (Dietz, East Berlin: 1970).

[24] *Jahrbuch 1970*, p. 100 and appendix, p. 34; Snell and Harper, p. 589; Ernst, pp. 880 and 883.

in 1970. Since I was unable to arrange any interviews in the headquarters of branch ministries, it is impossible to provide a detailed description of the actual working of the system above the level of the vvb. This section is based primarily upon the East German literature and upon interviews with experts holding nonoperational positions.

East German industrial coordination constitutes a mix of the detailed physical planning which was traditional in all of the CMEA countries through the middle 1960's (and which we have seen to be still dominant in Romania), with looser parametric planning through financial instruments. While this section is devoted to a description of the mix, the key question—i.e., the relative weights given to the two sharply distinct components of physical and parametric planning—will be postponed to Chapter 6. There I shall rely on data from enterprises, *Kombinate*, and vvbs in which I conducted interviews.

Industrial coordination under the New Economic System has not been geared primarily to the achievement of rapid increases in measured output. For example, Ulbricht (the Party general secretary) proudly told a Party congress in 1967 that recent accomplishments of the G.D.R. were exemplified by the fact that the growth rate of national income had been stabilized at the *average* rate of advanced industrial countries.[25]

Instead, four objectives are said to have been given prime emphasis. (1) There is the development of new industrial products and new technology. This is intended both to promote efficiency within the G.D.R. to the extent that these new products are consumed within the country, and also to improve the terms of trade by allowing the G.D.R. to capture short-run semimonopolistic profits to the degree that these products are exported to other members of the CMEA bloc.[26] (2) Heavy emphasis has been placed upon the production of quality products in a product mix which corresponds to the desires of both industrial users and consumers. (3) Efficiency in the use of resources within individual branches has been stressed; this has been interpreted to mean economic rather than simply

[25] Ulbricht, Volume 2, p. 244. It is true that the Party Congress of 1965 took as its planning criterion the attainment of the highest possible rate of increase of national income. But experience through the late 1960's is said to have shown that profitability and labor productivity—which can be taken as measures of efficiency in promoting national income growth—have been lower in the "structure-determining" sectors, precisely those whose expansion is stressed most heavily, than in the rest of industry. Presumably, the highest rate of growth of national income is interpreted very broadly; not only is this goal pursued solely in a long-run perspective, but also it takes account of such aspects of growth as the development of new products and the improvement of quality, whether or not these are directly and fully reflected in the prices paid for these products. (Cf. *Planung der Volkswirtschaft*, pp. 26, 48, and 233-35.)

[26] The freezing of the prices of goods traded among the CMEA countries for the duration of each five-year trade agreement has limited relevance to new or genuinely improved products.

engineering efficiency. This last objective is to be promoted particularly through increased specialization of individual factories and by an expansion of subcontracting; but, unlike the situation frequently encountered in the traditional centrally planned economy, such specialization is to be guided by economic considerations—and financial results are taken as the appropriate proxy for economic results.[27] (4) Stress is placed upon the regularity more than the speed of economic development.

The first objective (technical progress) seems to be viewed as best promoted by extreme centralization. Partly this is because specific subobjectives can thus be given high priority in the command of resources. But it is also because a coordinated approach—from research and development to the manufacture of improved materials and components to the output of the final product—is believed to be more fruitful than isolated attempts. Not only is this true for the development of new products, but also for the development and utilization of new technology: e.g., automation and the use of computer systems.

To some degree, such centralization can be promoted by the creation of *Kombinate* which serve as larger operating units than their constituent enterprises. This appears to be why *Kombinate* are said to be particularly prevalent in the high-technology sectors. *Kombinate* are also viewed as an organizational form of promoting increased specialization among enterprises by bringing them within the same operating unit.

But since it is not feasible to carry out such coordination of all projects within the scope of a single *Kombinat*, central authorities are also heavily involved. This seems the main explanation why (as we shall see below) a high proportion of industrial professional manpower is concentrated in administrative work in the branch ministries, the vvbs, and the product groups.

The second and third objectives (high quality, desired product mix, and economically efficient choice of inputs) are considered to be best attainable with the help of market relationships and through the linking of operating units' success to financial profits. For this reason, decentralization through the market place has been made an intrinsic part of the New Economic System.

In the pursuit of these diverse goals, industry (and the economy as a whole) has been divided into two sectors. One consists of products and tasks which are said to determine the economic structure of the econ-

[27] On the one hand, it has been intended that operating units should increase their usage of individual inputs where this permits sufficient reduction in the use of other inputs to yield a net economic advantage; on the other hand, individual units should concentrate on that product mix which yields them the greatest financial returns per aggregate unit of input—within the constraint that the national desideratum of product mix be produced in the economy as a whole.

omy (hereafter, these will be called "structure-determining" items);[28] the second sector consists of the large residual. The structure-determining products and tasks are planned in great physical detail from the center; if anything, traditional centralized planning appears to have been reinforced in this sector. In contrast, market relationships and financial criteria are given a major role in the development and co-ordination of the nonstructure-determining sector.

Strictly speaking, "structure determining" is defined broadly enough so that it means nothing more than priority. In general, however, the term seems to be applied primarily to the introduction of new products and new technology.[29] Thus the separation of industry into two sectors should be interpreted as an embodiment of the viewpoint that extreme centralization is appropriate to the goal of introducing advanced technology.[30]

"Structure determining" is sometimes used to refer to entire enterprises and even *Kombinate*, but more normally it refers to individual products and tasks. It is held that the number of such products should be kept relatively small; one writer declared in 1968 that the number of such products in the 1971-75 plan would be about eighty. However, individual vvBs treat additional products as structure-determining from the viewpoint of their own organization; this means that they give to their *Kombinate* and factories more detailed programs concerning these items than concerning the main mass of products.[31]

Most significantly, while many and probably most enterprises have no structure-determining products or tasks, few if any produce only structure-determining products. Thus all or virtually all enterprises in the G.D.R. are directly affected in important aspects of their work by decentralized financial methods of planning.

Physical planning. Operating units of East German industry normally (although not invariably) receive annual production plans as to the value of goods they are expected to deliver to customers. The degree to

[28] *Strukturbestimmenden.*

[29] See R. Scheibler, K.-H. Reuss, B. Gierke, and D. Casper, *Die Planung nach strukturbestimmenden Erzeugnissen und Erzeugnisgruppen* (Series of Planung und Leitung der Volkswirtschaft, 40, Verlag die Wirtschaft, East Berlin: 1968), especially pp. 8, 26, and 32, and Ulbricht, Volume 2, pp. 233-34. Unfortunately, the full list of structure-determining products is treated as a state secret and is therefore not available. As a result, my interview discussions on the content of the structure-determining principle were rather unsatisfactory.

[30] It is true that one can find East German statements that it would be preferable if parametric methods provided sufficient incentives to *Kombinate* and enterprises so that central orders for structure-determining products and tasks would be unnecessary. But this is regarded as a currently unrealizable goal. (See *Planung der Volkswirtschaft*, pp. 48-49.)

[31] *Planung nach strukturbestimmenden Erzeugnissen*, pp. 62-63.

which these are broken down according to detailed product mix differs, but is greatest for the structure-determining products.

Physical allocation of materials, semifabricates, and investment goods is also widely used. The importance of the Ministry of Supply is indicated by the fact that, when the industrial ministries were created at the end of 1965 in a splintering of the previous Economic Council, it was the former chairman of the Council who was named as Minister of Supply.[32]

While some material inputs are allocated centrally, most are "balanced" by producer bodies, normally the principal national suppliers, which are responsible for equilibrating the supply (including imports) and demand of individual subgroups of products. These balancing bodies include not only branch ministries but also, and more normally, vvbs, *Kombinate*, and even individual enterprises. Although they have sometimes concerned themselves only with meeting the needs of those consumers who are using the materials in order to produce structure-determining items, this practice is considered an aberration.

This "balancing" system[33] is not a direct allocation system, but does bear a close relationship to it. The balancing organ is not responsible for deciding how much of each product will be supplied by specific producers to individual consuming organizations; this is determined by the contracts signed by these bodies themselves. But the individual purchase contracts must, in sum, be consistent with the national balance drawn up for the relevant product by the balancing organ—and it is the balancing organ's task to assure that contracts which violate this constraint are not carried out. In the signing of contracts, both balancing organs and the producing firms which sign contracts are instructed to give top priority to consuming bodies which need the item in order to maintain the routine functioning of the economy. (E.g., enterprises engaged in maintenance of electrical equipment and wiring will get top priority for the purchase of copper.) Second priority goes to the producers of structure-determining products. No special priorities are set as between other purchasers.

Clearly this system, in which the balances for substitute products are developed by a number of different organizations not in close contact with one another, can work effectively only if the shift for efficiency

---

[32] Gert Leptin, "Das 'Neue ökonomische System' Mitteldeutschlands," in K. C. Thalheim and H.-H. Höhmann, *Wirtschaftsreformen in Osteuropa* (Wissenschaft und Politik, Köln: 1968), p. 129.

[33] See especially "Rechtsvorschriften zur Durchführung der in der Grundsatzregelung für die Gestaltung des ökonomischen Systems des Sozialismus in der Deutschen Demokratischen Republik im Zeitraum 1971 bis 1975 enthaltenen Aufgaben," approved by the Council of Ministers on April 29, 1970, *Die Wirtschaft*, 1970, 19/20, Supplement 15, pp. 42-48.

reasons of net effective demand from one type of input to a substitute item is limited. In all likelihood, such shifts are heavily concentrated among the structure-determining producers, since it is these which represent the sector of changing technology. For the other enterprises and *Kombinate*, the possibilities of substitution are restricted by the constraints on contracts which are imposed by the balancing organs. An organ finding itself faced with excess demand would doubtless, as its first step, void those increases in contracted supply which are due to substitution by nonstructure-determining users. Nevertheless, even such users have considerably greater possibilities of input substitution under this system of "balancing" than would be the case if all balanced items were directly allocated.

Special "product groups" are formed within the producer bodies in order to carry out the balancing functions. (When these are formed in the enterprises and *Kombinate*, they serve only as the legal agents of their vvb.) Their location in the producing bodies, as opposed to within a "neutral" body such as the Ministry of Supply or even solely in the producing branch ministry headquarters, should lead us to expect their behavior to be biased toward favoring the product-mix interests of producing rather than of consuming organizations. At the very least, it places the vvb in the awkward position of being, on the one hand, responsible for the production and financial success of its own branch, and on the other hand of being expected to act as the judge between the interests of its own branch and those of consuming branches. Why, then, are the product groups located here?

The logic of this location appears to be that the product groups spend much more of their time dividing up the supply tasks of the balance among producing enterprises than in determining the distribution of the products between consumers. If this task were carried out within a neutral body such as the Ministry of Supply, it would be difficult to muster the professional competence needed to determine which enterprises have a comparative advantage in which products. If it were carried out in the branch ministry, it would require roughly a tripling in the number of professional personnel located there.[34]

In its determination of enterprise supply tasks, the product group fulfills four functions. First, such determination serves as the basis for the formulation of product-mix plans for the enterprises and *Kombinate* within the particular vvb which is the principal producer of the group of products concerned.

Second, a very significant function up to 1972 was to link these enterprises to the private and semiprivate enterprises which subcontract for

[34] See my estimate below as to the number of personnel currently working in product groups within *Kombinate* and enterprises.

them. The product group determines the nature of the subcontracting relations, assures materials for the subcontractors, and provides technical aid to these smaller plants. This function was in 1970 probably the most time-consuming one for the product groups, and it was then expected that in the future they would be given increased professional staff so as to be able to perform it more effectively. The product groups' role here is a striking counterpart to the work done by large American and Japanese companies in supervising their host of small subcontractors and improving their efficiency. It has been peculiarly important in the G.D.R., in contrast to all other socialist countries, because of the large number of such small private and semiprivate manufacturing concerns and the considerable amount of subcontracting done by them.[35] With the elimination of private and semiprivate concerns in mid-1972, it is possible that their plants will be consolidated into larger enterprises and that the importance of subcontracting, and therefore of this function of the product groups, will be much reduced.

Third, the product group also makes recommendations of tasks for the private and semiprivate enterprises, where these tasks are for the production of complete products rather than components. Here the product groups have only advisory powers; it is the regional economic councils, to which these enterprises are subordinate, which are empowered to make the final decisions. In a nationally integrated physical-planning system, however, some group must provide coordination on a branch rather than a regional basis.[36] In the G.D.R., this task is performed by the product groups. As in the case of the second function, the importance of this third task may be reduced sharply after the abolition of the private firms in 1972.

The fourth function is that of advising as to the product tasks of enterprises and *Kombinate* in other VVBS, to the degree that they produce items included within the group of products of the product group. My impression is that this function is quite unimportant; I have never heard it mentioned in the product groups where I conducted interviews.

In summary, even for nonstructure-determining products, enterprises and *Kombinate* are not free to shift their product mix at will. Their prime product-mix task is to "meet economic needs," whether or not these

---

[35] The future development of such small firms was seen in 1970 as lying in the expansion of output of components at the expense of final products (*Planung der Volkswirtschaft*, p. 64). In contrast, Romanian regional authorities in the same year seem to have done very little subcontracting, and to have been very anxious to surrender such tasks as soon as possible even when the work was being done for the Romanian counterpart of structure-determining products and enterprises.

[36] This branch-coordinating role for regionally administered enterprises is not important in Romania. This is because the regionally administered industry in that country primarily produces for the local needs of final consumers in the specific region rather than for the national market.

are incorporated in their plan indicators. They are required to obtain the agreement of balancing organs (which are often the product groups) as to their product-mix decisions and as to the contracts which they sign with consuming bodies.[37] If they wish to cease the production of an item, they or their product group must find some other enterprise in the country which will produce either it or a substitute product.[38] Here is a major restriction on the degree to which enterprises and *Kombinate* can respond to economic incentives.

Enterprises and *Kombinate* are also set a fixed maximum number of workers and employees which they may hire, although it is the responsibility of the enterprise itself to recruit the permitted numbers. For production of structure-determining products, the decision as to the maximum number of employees is made by national organs and, finally, by the enterprise's own vvb. But the regional economic council in whose territory the enterprise lies has the last word in determining the maximum labor force for all other products, although it operates within guidelines set by the State Planning Commission. This power is granted to the councils because the labor-force balance of supply and demand is drawn up regionally, and it is the regional economic council which is entrusted with the task of assuring that its labor-force balance is roughly in balance: i.e., that enterprises will in fact be able to come close to recruiting the maximum number of employees which they are allowed.

Financial indicators. The parametric elements of the "New Economic System" function only within the constraints of the physical planning system. They represent an attempt to provide the *Kombinate* and the independent enterprises (i.e., those directly subordinate to the vvbs) with both a strong motivation to pursue economic efficiency and with the authority to make economic choices. This authority is much greater for the nonstructure-determining producers, for whom physical planning of output is relatively aggregative, than for the producers of what are considered to be critical items. Similarly, authority to engage in input substitution is greater for those enterprises that use material inputs which are only loosely balanced than for those whose balances are regulated in considerable detail.

[37] See "Grundsatzregelung für die Gestaltung des ökonomischen Systems des Sozialismus in der Deutschen Demokratischen Republik im Zeitraum 1971 bis 1975," approved by the Council of Ministers on April 15, 1970, *Die Wirtschaft*, 1970, 18, Supplement 14, p. 12.

[38] See ibid., p. 12. Restrictions on the transfer of products between enterprises were strengthened in November 1970; since then, an enterprise or *Kombinat* cannot cease production of an item until another enterprise has mastered the technology of manufacturing this product and is already producing it under stable conditions. (Paul Verner, *Bericht des Politbüros an die 14. Tagung des ZK der SED*, Dietz, East Berlin: 1970, p. 26.)

Within the bounds of the planning system, *Kombinate* and enterprises are instructed to maximize their net profits. Bonuses and social expenditures for all the employees of the *Kombinat* or enterprise depend upon the amount of these profits, and such profits also serve as a constraint upon the expansion of the operating unit. This latter is because increases in both fixed capital and working capital of existing units are financed almost entirely from retained profits and from bank loans which must be repaid from a combination of amortization and future profits, rather than by grants from the state budget.

Independently of the effect on profits, *Kombinate* and enterprises are also motivated to increase their labor productivity. This is because increases in wages depend upon increases in labor productivity. Although wages for different skills are in theory determined centrally, in practice they are decided at the individual enterprise level. The constraint placed upon them is the planned determination of a fixed average wage fund per employee (within a maximum total wage fund) for the enterprise or *Kombinat*; this does not increase during the planning year if output alone exceeds plan. But within a given year, and for some selected *Kombinate* and enterprises between years, the wage fund is increased by a percentage which is some ratio of the degree to which labor productivity has increased more than was planned.[39] The ratio of the above-plan percentage increase of the wage fund to the above-plan percentage increase in labor productivity differs among industries and enterprises; it averaged one-fifth in the two VVBs for which I have information.

The funds left to enterprises for bonuses, social expenditures, and investments are determined by a set of financial norms. After deduction of a capital-value tax (which is normally 6 percent, but can vary between branches) from the difference between gross revenue and materials, labor costs, development charges, interest, and amortization, there remains net profit. Some ratio between 40 and 70 percent of this net profit is siphoned into the state budget;[40] the specific ratio used varies sharply between VVBs, as well as between *Kombinate* and enter-

[39] This basis for increasing the wage fund during the planning year was modified in early 1972, when its application was limited to cases of above-plan production which are of "special social interest" (*Gesetzblatt der Deutschen Demokratischen Republik*, II, 1972, 10, p. 127).

[40] One source suggested that 70 percent would be usual, and that most enterprises or *Kombinate* for which heavy investment was planned would normally still be subject to a 50 percent rate. On the other hand, an author publishing in early 1970 considered 50 to 60 percent to be the usual range (Mann in *Die ökonomische Stimulierung*, p. 132).

A minimum payment to the budget out of net profits is established for each enterprise or *Kombinat*. This is the multiple of planned net profits and the percentage applicable to the unit. Thus, if net profits are less than planned, the actual percentage of retention by the enterprise is less than that called for by its norm.

prises within the same vvb. The remaining profits are left to the enterprise or *Kombinat*.

The enterprise thus has at its disposal a portion of net profits which is determined by a financial ratio specific to it; all or a portion of the amortization charges on its fixed capital, this again being determined specifically for each enterprise; and, in some cases, a portion of the normal capital-value tax. From this sum, other financial norms—again specific to the enterprise—set the percentage of net profits which can be used for bonuses and for social expenditures. (However, the bonus norms apply fully only if key aspects of the enterprise's annual plan have been fulfilled.) The remaining net profits plus amortization are available to the enterprise to finance new gross investment and to repay outstanding bank loans.

This system may appear at first sight to be one in which posttax profits are left to each enterprise; but this interpretation would hold only if we incorporate the notion that tax rates are specific to each unit. The reason for the differential tax rates stems from the logic of the enterprise expenditures from its net profits. In determining the ratio of net profits to be retained by the enterprise for its social expenditures and bonuses, the enterprise's superior organ begins from the premise that all enterprises which are equally successful in plan fulfillment should receive roughly the same ratio of funds for social expenditures and bonuses to total wage fund. Thus the retention ratios are primarily a function of wage fund and planned net profits. It is only to the degree that actual net profits earned differ from planned profits that the enterprises are expected to gain or lose in social expenditure funds and in bonuses. From this reasonable proposition, it follows that the norms should be individualized by *Kombinat* or enterprise—although there are efforts being made to combine enterprises into groups with common norms—so as not to favor or disfavor employees in enterprises with high or low planned profits per employee.

The case for individualizing norms is even stronger when it comes to the residual of the net profits left to the enterprises. In essence, fixed investments and increases in working capital are planned for each enterprise. This implies that the retention norm of net profit plus the retention norm of amortization must be planned together so as to yield the funds needed for such investment, minus what can be borrowed that year from the bank. The effect of deviations of net profits from their planned amount is intended to affect investment funds available both because of the absolute difference in each year, and because of the effect of this on the bank's appreciation of the enterprise's credit worthiness. To the degree that the enterprise's retained net profits are greater or less than planned, the enterprise may invest more or less than called for in its plan. But aside from this, the total profit realized is not intended to have any effect on the amount of investments which the individual enterprise or *Kombinat* can finance.

The East German government recognizes that, if the financial norms for enterprises and *Kombinate* were to be changed every year, the motivation for the enterprise management to strive for higher earnings would be weak. Thus it has accepted the notion of fixing financial norms for a longer period than one year—although the longer this period, the weaker will be the correspondence between the planned retained net earnings and the financing needs as indicated above. Two-year norms were established for 1969-70 (unfortunately, I have no information as to the extent to which the enterprise norms in fact remained unchanged throughout the two years), and five-year norms (with only minor changes being permissible) were set for 1971-75. However, the five-year norms were predicated on the assumption that the 1971-75 plan would be fulfilled with much greater precision than has ever yet been the case for a five-year plan. In fact, fundamental changes in the financial norms were introduced in January 1972; among other changes, bonus fund receipts were linked to the degree of fulfillment of the annual plans rather than to improvement compared to previous years.[41]

The East German government has been anxious to avoid giving enterprise and *Kombinat* managers an incentive to strive for minimum annual plans for net profits. This is why they have linked norms of retained profits to total net profits, not differentiating in this regard between planned and above-plan profits. In fact, planned retained profits are more advantageous to operating units than are above-plan retained profits, since it may well be impossible to procure investment goods which the above-plan profits could finance. Of course, operating units still have an incentive to scheme for a low net profit in their five-year plans, since the norms for the five years are based on this. However, provided that they have confidence that these norms will not be changed, they have no such incentive during the course of the five years.

Just as profit maximization is intended to motivate enterprises and *Kombinate* to attain the greatest economic efficiency in the production process, so too a financial device exists for motivating the development of improved products for further use in production. The producers and users of such products are encouraged to sign agreements for sharing the cost-reducing advantages to the user of receiving these improved items. Beyond the normal price, the user pays an additional sum computed as a share of its financial savings; this amount is usually highest in the first year or two of the output of the improved product, and then quickly declines to zero. During the period of such payments, they

[41] *Gesetzblatt*, ii, 1972, 5, pp. 49-53. These changes were still in force in 1974.

are retained completely by the producing firm and may be used for bonus payments; no portion of the extra profits thus created are taken as taxes into the state budget.[42] Here we have the counterpart to Schumpeter's notion of temporary monopoly profits being earned by innovating capitalist firms.

Excluding such sharing of cost-reducing advantages, profits are likely to be considerably higher on products which have been in production for some time. This is because prices are based upon average costs of the product at the time that the price was originally set, whereas actual costs for specific products generally decline over time. But even if total profits are no higher for these new products than for preexisting items, the enterprise gains substantially because none of its cost-reducing share is taken by the budget.

This section has sketched out the formal structure of the profit-maximizing schema which affects *Kombinate* and enterprises. How much liberty this in fact leaves to these bodies remains, however, an open question, and one which must be left to Chapter 6.

Pricing and costing. A profit-maximizing nexus in a centrally planned system is reasonable as a guide to economic decisions (i.e., to those which substitute alternative inputs and alternative outputs) only to the degree that the prices of materials and products express their opportunity costs in the eyes of the central planners. For sales by industrial enterprises and *Kombinate*, the G.D.R. today uses fixed prices based upon average cost plus a profit mark-up as a percentage of value-added costs; the intention is to shift by 1975 primarily to cost plus a profit rate computed as a percentage of capital employed.[43] An allowance for research

[42] One source told me that only structure-determining products are eligible for this system of additional compensation to the producing firm. However, this source was not overly reliable.

In the metalworking industry, the producing enterprise is allowed to share up to 30 percent of the financial savings during the first year of production. This share normally goes down to zero in about four years. One constraint, however, exists: the shared portion of financial savings cannot exceed the gross profit used in the calculation of the basic price. (Mann, in *Die ökonomische Stimulierung*, p. 137, states that these figures applied throughout industry.) In one machinebuilding VVB where I conducted interviews, it was estimated that approximately 80 percent of the new products developed during the previous two years were being sold on the basis of shared financial savings.

It has been claimed, however, that the scope of this sharing of advantage between producer and customer was considerably narrowed after passage of the pricing law of November 17, 1971 (*Die Wirtschaft*, 1973, 30, Supplement 20, p. 12). This 1971 law also appears to treat the producer's share of the net advantage as subject to the normal treatment of profits (see *Gesetzblatt*, II, 1971, 77, p. 673).

[43] See Mann in *Die ökonomische Stimulierung* for a good treatment of this subject. The changeover began for new products in 1969 (*Die Wirtschaft*, 1968, 36, Supplement).

and development expenditures is incorporated into the calculation of costs.

The price reforms of the mid-1960's, which were completed in 1967, eliminated most state subsidies to entire branches and went a considerable distance toward equalizing profit rates (although as a percentage of value-added costs) on different products. Thus, in 1970, the machine-building industry generally employed a 22 percent profit mark-up except for spare parts, where a 44 percent mark-up was used. While these prices are not intended to equilibrate supply and demand, and instead the "balancing" system is relied upon for this task,[44] enterprises which attempt to arrange their purchases of different material inputs so as to minimize their own average financial costs will, under these conditions, most probably be reducing opportunity-cost expenditures for the economy as a whole.[45]

The East Germans regard prices which are properly linked to full costs as important for the effectiveness of decentralized decisions guided by profit maximizing. But they are also needed for central decision making. Since it is recognized that central authorities are able to use physical-unit planning to regulate only a very limited range of producers and users, meaningful prices constitute a critical input into central planning decisions. While shadow-prices would be preferable to cost-based prices, the latter are considerably superior to prices which are unrelated either to real costs or to shadow values.

Although prices in the G.D.R. are in principle fixed,[46] efforts have been made since 1969 to maintain a fairly stable cost-price relationship for individual products even when technology changes. The problem is that, since the relative average costs of different products are bound to change

[44] As in the case of all of the CMEA countries, differential sales taxes levied on consumer goods act roughly to equalize supply and demand on consumer markets. This is why rationing of consumer goods is not necessary. The system appears to break down completely in the G.D.R. for only a few goods like automobiles; the government is said to be unwilling to raise such consumer prices to equilibrium levels because it rejects the notion of prices which would be so high as clearly to limit certain goods to purchase by a small income segment of the population. Only for nondurable luxuries like French perfume and fur coats is the principle of very high, equilibrium prices accepted.

[45] Financial costs and national opportunity costs for specific material inputs may, of course, differ widely. But inputs for which these differences are very great are allocated to user enterprises through the "balancing" system, and there is presumably little impact from the effort of purchasing firms to minimize average costs. This is why efforts at cost minimization are unlikely to have a substantial negative effect when judged from the national standpoint. Consequently, the positive effects from some such efforts are not fully counterbalanced by negative effects from others.

[46] In theory, they have been set as "maximum" rather than fixed prices since near the end of the 1960's. But this change is said to have had no practical significance, except for some seasonal variations in the prices of consumer goods.

over time, prices should also change if they are to reflect costs. The method introduced for achieving this is to set limits—which vary somewhat between industrial sectors[47]—for the profit rate earned on any product group, defining profit rate as a percentage of gross fixed plus variable capital. When the profit rate reaches the upper bound of this limit, the average price of the product group is supposed to drop sufficiently so that the profit rate falls to the lower bound. Thus prices of products produced under conditions of declining costs should drop every few years, thereby maintaining a more stable price-cost relationship among products than would be the case with stationary prices.[48]

Of the organizations in which I conducted interviews, this system of declining prices had been implemented in only one machinebuilding VVB. Here, as of the middle of 1970, products comprising 4 to 5 percent of the value of production of the units in the VVB had had their prices reduced during two years by an average of 10 percent. Future price reductions in this VVB were expected to run at the rate of 1 percent per annum. According to a West German study—which, however, cites no sources—price reductions in all of industry must have averaged well over 1.5 percent in 1969.[49]

The above system of declining prices operates, of course, to reduce the motivation of *Kombinat* and enterprise managements to lower costs by improving efficiency. Such reduction of motivation appears to be accepted with regard to the incentives linked to financing of fixed investments, expansion of working capital, and social expenditures. But it is eliminated so far as bonuses are concerned; the bonus norm is applied not only to net profits but also (and here, in fact, it is raised by 20 percent) to what would have been earned as additional profits if the

---

[47] The limits are said to be normally set between 12 and 16 percent. But in one branch where I interviewed, they were established between 18 and 24 percent.

[48] However, the intention is that no prices should rise. Flexibility of prices refers only to prices paid by organizations rather than by individual consumers. Long-run stability of consumer prices appears to be a preferred policy, so as to enhance the possibilities for increasing the real income of preferred groups.

In the VVBs, *Kombinate*, and enterprises in which I discussed this system, the rationale was always described in terms of the objective of price-cost stability. On the other hand, Hahn (a university professor) treats the system as the means chosen for shifting from profit as a percentage of cost to profit as a percentage of capital (*Die ökonomische Stimulierung*, p. 125). Clearly it could perform both functions simultaneously.

[49] The study reports that there was a 10 percent average price reduction during 1969 in a group of products which included the total output of iron and steel, foundry products, and electricity, and what appears to be about one-third of the output of industrial consumer goods. Price reductions during 1969 just for this 15 percent of gross industrial production totaled 1.5 percent of the gross value of all G.D.R. industrial products produced in that year. (*DDR-Wirtschaft*, p. 73, and *Jahrbuch 1970*, p. 104.)

enterprise's product prices had not been reduced during the period of stability of the financial norms.

The linkage of price to cost makes sense only to the degree that costs are computed accurately in enterprises producing a variety of products. As of the mid-1960's, cost calculation still seems to have been very similar to the Romanian system, although the East Germans recognized that this was a mistake. In other words, overhead costs were allocated between products in relation to the direct-labor wage bill for each product.[50] But since about 1967, there appears to have been a major effort to update cost accounting methods and to improve the procedures for allocating overhead costs. Of course, the East Germans have had a major advantage over the Romanians in this regard, since they inherited a prewar tradition of relatively sophisticated accounting methods.

Exports. Although foreign trade is still one of the most centralized sectors of the economy,[51] exports (although not imports) have been made the responsibility of the relevant industrial *Kombinate* and enterprises. Contracts are drawn up by foreign trade enterprises—most of which work directly under the Ministry of Foreign Trade, although some are under the industrial vvbs—but they operate on a commission basis. It is the responsibility of the industrial enterprises and vvbs themselves to realize and fulfill sufficient foreign trade contracts to meet their export plans.

The price received on the foreign market rather than the domestic price has been used since 1970 in calculating both the sales and the profits of industrial enterprises. Export prices in foreign currency are converted into East German marks by a series of conversion coefficients, which are differentiated according to both the destination of exports and the broad product groups involved. The difference between the calculated export price and the domestic price is called, when positive, an "export profit." Norms (differentiated by enterprise) are established for the share of the "export profit" which can be counted as part of the net profit of the enterprise.[52] Subsidies may be paid to the enterprise for products sold at an "export loss," provided that the enterprise or *Kombinat* as a whole does not earn net "export profits."

[50] *Planung nach strukturbestimmenden Erzeugnissen*, pp. 145 and 148, and *Eigenerwirtschaftung der Mittel*, pp. 82-83.

[51] See Karl-Heinz Nattland, "Organisatorische und Finanzpolitische Massnahmen zur Exportförderung in der DDR," *Berichte des Bundesinstituts für Ostwissenschaftliche und Internationale Studien*, 1970, 70, p. 26. This is the best source I have seen dealing with the current East German export organization.

[52] For the year 1971, however, this system was restricted to selected exporting enterprises and *Kombinate* ("Beschluss über die Durchführung des ökonomischen Systems des Sozialismus im Jahre 1971," *Gesetzblatt*, II, 1970, 100, p. 733).

Sharing in the "export profit" is intended to motivate enterprises and *Kombinate* to give special attention to foreign customers. A second, but apparently much less significant, incentive has been that of being permitted to use 70 percent of above-plan gross export proceeds to finance above-plan imports from the same currency area.[53] Foreign currency may also be borrowed from the bank in anticipation of such earnings.

The banks. Direct relations with ministries, vvbs, and lower units are carried out by sectoral banks. It is these banks which make all loans. Their notes are discounted by the State Bank, which stands at the apex of the East German banking system. Although different interest rates are charged to the enterprises for varying kinds of loans, the rate of rediscount charged by the State Bank is adjusted accordingly; thus the sectoral banks have no financial incentive to demand high interest rates from their customers.

The State Bank plays two roles. The first is that of developing each year a credit balance for the national economy, with a planned volume of rediscounting for each of the sectoral banks. This is particularly important for controlling the amount of above-plan loans granted by these banks. The second is assuring that the sectoral banks raise their interest rates on loans granted for investments which have been yielding below-normal rates of profit to the enterprises (except for loans to expand structure-determining production). The State Bank does this by raising the rediscount rates charged to the sectoral banks when the average profit rate earned by the borrowing enterprises on the loan-projects falls.

From discussions with high officials of the State Bank, it appears that the banking system makes no attempt—either by rationing of credits or through changes in interest rates—to adjust credits within a given planning year as a reaction to unexpected inflationary or deflationary pressures. Instead, the main mechanism for consciously adjusting aggregate demand in the economy appears to be the alteration of government decisions as to the amount of wage increases to be given to particular groups during the year. Also (although this was not told to me), unplanned investment credits must have served until at least 1971 as an additional, if minor, form of adjustment. Since the government keeps no reserves of materials or capacity to supply these unplanned investments, enterprises and *Kombinate* apply for such credits only when they find supplies available on an ad hoc basis. Thus annual changes in the volume of requests for unplanned investment credits reflect unexpected changes in spare capacity, and—in view of the method by which wage

[53] This was abolished for 1971 (ibid., p. 742).

funds for enterprises are planned—they have relatively little impact on the demand for consumer goods.

The sectoral bank of concern to us is the Industry and Trade Bank, which deals with the entire large sector designated in its title. Since about 1968, this bank appears to have played a significant role in determining the amounts and types of planned investments to be carried out by the *Kombinate* and enterprises.[54] It also has granted above-plan loans for research and development and for minor investment funds which can be spent without having to draw upon centrally allocated materials.[55] Finally, as part of its task of granting working-capital credits, it exercises independent supervision over the general efficiency level of the enterprises.

Two officials of the Industry and Trade Bank illustrated its influence on planned investment with rough statistics for a recent year. Of all industrial and commercial investments which required planned credits and which were proposed by enterprises, VVBs, or ministries, the Industry and Trade Bank refused credits in about 25 percent (by number) of the cases. The rejected projects were then reexamined; two-thirds were either modified to the satisfaction of the Bank or were pushed through over the Bank's original disapproval, but one-third were abandoned as not being credit worthy. Thus 8 percent of all original investment proposals were abandoned, and another substantial percentage were revised, because of the Bank's opposition. It is true that many of these proposals might have been abandoned or revised in later stages of investment decision making even without the opposition of the Bank; nevertheless, these figures indicate that the Industry and Trade Bank does play a role of some significance in investment decisions.

The Industry and Trade Bank has two independent powers, in addition to serving in state decision-making bodies dealing with planned investments, and here being the only organization whose concern is almost solely with the rate of profit on the investments and with the likelihood of the credits being repaid on schedule. The first of these independent powers is that it can alter the rate of interest charged to enterprises depending upon their financial performance, thus multiplying the effects of performance on the enterprises' net profits. The second is that it can successfully demand review of any project by

---

[54] See especially Gertraud Seidenstecher, "Reformmassnahmen im Bereich der Planung und Finanzierung von Investitionen in Osteuropa," *Berichte des Bundesinstituts für Ostwissenschaftliche und Internationale Studien*, 1971, 29.

[55] In 1971, however, loans for above-plan investments appear to have been abolished (ibid., p. 36).

experts outside the normal industrial channels of project review. While a third alternative of simply refusing credits is also cited, this does not in fact seem to be a decision which the Industry and Trade Bank can make on its own authority.

The Industry and Trade Bank is organized into both industrial branch offices and regional offices. A given branch office normally handles credits for four or five industrial subsectors, and works primarily with the VVBS in charge of these subsectors. The office itself is given three targets: the rate of profit to be earned on capital by each VVB; the percentage of fixed investments and expansion of working capital which are to be financed by the VVB and its enterprises rather than through credits; and the maximum period for which individual investment credits may be granted. These are the terms of reference within which the branch office makes both its recommendations and its interest-rate decisions, and which it uses as guidelines in its supervision of the current work of the VVBS.

The regional offices of the Industry and Trade Bank have lower-quality staffs than do the branch offices, and seem to operate under their guidance. Regional offices work directly with the enterprises; their principal function appears to be to review operations when enterprise-profitability or the terms of credit agreements are threatened. They also review investment projects of individual enterprises within the general credit agreement of the VVB and the branch office.

In one such credit agreement (for 1969), an industrial enterprise was pledged to achieve its planned rate of profit on capital, its planned output/capital ratio, its planned ratio of sales to average working capital, and its planned net profit for internal financing purposes. If these were not achieved, the Industry and Trade Bank could charge a penalty rate of interest 10 percent above the normal rate.[56] The local office of the bank would investigate threatened violation of these terms, and would be empowered to decide as to the imposition of the above penalty.

My impression is that the banking system in the G.D.R. plays a much more significant role in planning industrial investments and supervising the operations of production units than is the case in any other CMEA country except Hungary. This, however, is not because of its formal powers, which do not differ radically from those available in Romania or in other socialist lands. Rather, the East German banks gain their strength from the emphasis placed by the entire economic system upon financial results. In countries where net profit has much less significance for enterprises than it does in the G.D.R., one could hardly expect a financial institution's advice and decisions to have great weight. For

[56] *Eigenerwirtschaftung der Mittel*, pp. 181-82.

the same reason, it is reasonable to assume that the East German banks' influence is at a minimum in the case of structure-determining products and enterprises. It seems likely that, since the end of 1970, the importance of the banking system has declined along with the emphasis placed upon profitability.[57]

It is also possible that the East German banks exercise a strong position in the economy partly because of the historically well developed role of the Banks as supervisors of enterprises in prewar Germany. But if this cultural factor is relevant at all, it is probably not important in view of the long hiatus of influence which existed until about 1968.

Summary. The New Economic System should be viewed as one in which physical criteria of decision making and evaluation of enterprise performance predominate in the structure-determining sectors, but in which profit criteria play an important role elsewhere. This dual system stems from the East German viewpoint that, if central authorities are to plan effectively in physical terms, they must restrict the scope of such efforts to a relatively small portion of the economy. For the remaining bulk of industry, it is held that efficiency will be best promoted if decisions at all levels—from the Council of Ministers down to the individual enterprise—are strongly guided by the criterion of maximum return on capital.

The logic behind the emphasis upon financial criteria is not particularly that they aid in providing incentives to the operating units; rather, it is that central authorities must choose between careful analysis of the physical parameters of a limited number of decisions and a cavalier treatment of the physical parameters of a much wider range of issues. Having opted for detailed, centralized attention to a limited number of products and enterprises, central authorities are forced to restrict themselves to aggregative planning for the rest.

Thus the reliance on profit criteria appears to be essentially a policy of faute de mieux.

NUMBER OF PERSONNEL COORDINATING INDUSTRIAL ACTIVITIES

Western treatments of the New Economic System have customarily regarded it as a system of decentralization of decision-making power, and have given the impression that it represented a deconcentration of authority.[58] The view presented in the preceding section shifts the em-

---

[57] See Chapter 7 for a treatment of developments in the economy as a whole during 1971-72.

[58] See, for example, Michael Keren, "The New Economic System in the GDR: An Obituary," *Soviet Studies*, xxiv, 4 (1973).

phasis: that it was intended to permit central authorities to conserve their own scarce manpower resources for what they considered to be the most important tasks.

An estimate of the number of professional people involved in coordinating functions in industry would seem highly relevant to this question of emphasis. As we shall see, it would appear that the G.D.R. in 1970 employed a substantially higher proportion of its industrial labor force than did Romania in coordinating the activities of enterprises and *Kombinate* (*centrale*). This is not what we would expect in a system devoted to decentralizing authority to the *Kombinat* and enterprise level.

The number of coordinating personnel is not available from any reliable source. But an extremely crude estimate can be made on the basis of data from individual organizations, as provided in interviews. All figures refer to full-time professionals.

Ministries: There were eight industrial branch ministries, with an estimated average of 80 professionals in each. This gives a total of 640 professionals.

VVBS: There were a minimum of 80 VVBS with an average of 120 professionals in each. This gives a total of 9,600 professionals.[59]

Product Groups: These are formed in enterprises and *Kombinate* as well as in the VVBS. Their task is to determine the total volume and distribution of output and usage of each of the products, wherever they may be produced or consumed. It is estimated that some 1,600 professionals work in these product groups inside organizations other than the VVBS and ministries.

The above numbers total to 11,840 professionals. The Romanian counterpart subtotal (there the professionals counted are those working only within the industrial branch ministries) was shown as 3,300 in Table 2.7. If we consider that the East German professionals are supervising at least the labor force employed in their own ministries, and if we make allowance for the number of the above East German professionals who are engaged in coordinating the work of additional firms outside their own ministry, we find that 0.51 percent of all the workers and employees of industry are occupied with the coordination of the activities of operating units. This is exactly twice the proportion which we found in Romania (see Table 2.6).

Unfortunately, I have no basis for estimating the number of professionals working in the functional ministries and in the Communist Party. It is difficult, however, to see how these could constitute a smaller percentage of the industrial labor force than they do in Romania. In view of the much greater importance of financial matters in the G.D.R. than in

[59] Following the same procedure as was used for Romania, professionals working in research and development institutes attached to the VVBS are not included.

Romania, of the existence of a Ministry of Supply in the G.D.R. which in 1970 had only a far feebler counterpart in Romania, and of the greater East German tendency to use full-time Party functionaries, it is conservative to assume (as I do) that the national ratios estimated for the industrial sectoral ministries are proportional to the overall national ratios of coordinating professionals to the industrial labor force.

In the case of Romania, I estimated that 6.4 to 8.5 percent of all industrial personnel with higher education worked in organs above the levels of the *centrala*. Although the proportion of university graduates to the total population in the G.D.R. is much the same as in Romania, it would be unwarranted to conclude that the proportion of East German university graduates in industry who work above the level of the *Kombinat* is far more than the Romanian 6 to 9 percent. This is because Romanian professionals in such organizations are virtually all university graduates, while a large proportion of the East Germans have only a junior college education.[60] I would guess that both countries have in their coordinating organs rather similar proportions of all industrial personnel with complete higher education at the university level.

In theory, the best professionals in the East German industrial branches below the ministry level are concentrated in the VVB headquarters, and all those working there should be capable of running an enterprise. A director of one VVB in light industry estimated, however, that only about one-fifth of the professionals in his headquarters would in fact be able to handle such a task without further training. This does not seem very different from the situation in Romania, and thus we might conclude that—as in Romania—one-fifth to one-third of all those in industry who are doing work a notch above that of a rank-and-file engineer are engaged in coordinating the activities of operating units.

The above estimates are very crude, and I place no great confidence in them. However, their orders of magnitude are sufficiently correct to support the following three implications.

The first is that the East Germans, like the Romanians, utilize a very high proportion of their skilled professionals in coordinating activities. The second is that, both because the East German industrial labor force is larger than the Romanian and because the East German government does not insist that all its coordinators have university degrees, the G.D.R. is able to allocate many more people (the estimate is three to four times as many) to coordinating functions than do the Romanians. Partly, it is true, this is necessitated by the more complex problems involved in organizing a more advanced economy with a wider range of products. To some degree, however, so long as there is any relationship between

---

[60] In the one machinebuilding VVB for which I have information, only half of the professionals at headquarters had university degrees.

the inputs of manpower and the output of performance, we might expect the G.D.R. to be able to do a better administrative-coordination job than the Romanians.

It is the third implication, however, which is the most interesting. This is that, despite the effort under the New Economic Policy to rely upon the market system to provide much of the coordination of the activities of industrial *Kombinate* and enterprises, it is clear that East Germany still leaned heavily—in 1970, at the height of the New Economic System—upon direct coordinating orders from higher bodies to operating units. This should warn us that we must beware of exaggerating the significance of the shift toward market coordination in East Germany under the New Economic System.

HIGHER EDUCATION

An appreciation of the size and quality of professional manpower resources available within the East German economy is important for understanding the significance of the decision to continue the concentration of much of it at levels above that of the *Kombinat*.

A substantial proportion of East Germany's university graduates emigrated during the period through 1961. The result is that the country's stock of university graduates in 1970 was only 1.4 percent of the population: lower than in Hungary, Bulgaria, Czechoslovakia, or Yugoslavia, and the same as in Romania.[61] On the other hand, 1970 admissions into universities constituted some 16 percent of the relevant population, and admissions into junior colleges were another 21 percent.[62] Higher educational degrees awarded each year are substantially higher on a per capita basis in the G.D.R. than in West Germany: the ratio of the two countries in 1968 was 143 percent for university degrees and 124 percent for junior college degrees, and these ratios are rising.[63]

[61] *Jahrbuch 1971*, appendix, p. 4.

[62] *Jahrbuch 1971*, pp. 374-75 and 382. *Universitäten* and *Hochschulen* are considered as universities, and *Fachschulen* (with three-year education) are treated as junior colleges. These figures were derived by first comparing the number of admissions to full-time study with the population aged nineteen; this comparison yielded figures of 11.9 and 8.9 percent respectively for universities and junior colleges. These percentages were then multiplied by the ratio between all admissions and the admissions to full-time study alone. The justification for this expansion is the assumption that evening and correspondence school admissions of the students above the age of nineteen will be compensated in the future by later admissions of the present nineteen-year-olds.

The same methodology shows that 36 percent of the relevant population were attending universities or junior colleges in 1970.

[63] In 1969, the ratio for junior college degrees was 156 percent. Official data are used for both countries. Degrees awarded to foreigners are excluded. For purposes of comparability, West German graduates of teaching colleges are in-

The East German attitude toward the importance of higher education has been intermediate between that of the rest of the CMEA bloc and that of West Germany. On the one hand, the East Germans are very proud of the social investment they have made in higher education, and of the greater opportunities which exist for such studies in East than in West Germany. For example, when members of one quite ordinary household group expressed to me their bitterness over the fact that many West Germans boast to East German friends of their higher living standards and minimize the accomplishments of the G.D.R., it was the East German improvements in education which they stressed the most heavily as counterarguments. On the other hand, the G.D.R. in 1969-70 still had the smallest proportion of university students to total population of any CMEA country except Mongolia.[64] The number of university admissions was allowed to run down in the 1960's, and did not again reach the 1960 level until 1969. The same pattern occurred in the junior colleges, where even 1970 admissions did not reach the 1960 level. It has been only since 1967, and then only for three to four years, that the G.D.R. has engaged in a major reexpansion in its admissions: in three years, 74 percent in the universities and 36 percent in the junior colleges.[65]

In Romania, as was described in Chapter 2, virtually all middle and upper managers in enterprises have long been required to have completed university education as a condition of appointment. This is still not the case in the G.D.R., especially in light industry. In one light industry enterprise with 1,200 employees, none of the five top managers in

cluded among the university graduates, and West German graduates of *Fachschulen, Ingenieurschulen*, and *Technikerschulen* are all treated as junior college graduates. An adjustment has also been made (following "Materialien," pp. 161-62 and 370-73) for the fact that teachers of the lower grades receive a junior college education in East Germany and a university education in West Germany; this adjustment increased the number of university graduates in the G.D.R. by 6 percent. Even with adjustment, the data for junior college graduates are not really comparable because the average length of junior college studies is somewhat longer in East than in West Germany.

Further useful comparison of East and West German higher education is available in "Materialien," pp. 147-64.

[64] *Jahrbuch 1971*, appendix, p. 18. This statement cannot be credited with too much significance without a prior evaluation of the level of university education in the different countries. It is quite possible, for example, that engineers graduating from the three-year G.D.R. junior colleges are at least the equal of university engineers in some other countries. But I am in no position to evaluate the different nations' respective university systems.

[65] *Jahrbuch 1971*, pp. 375 and 382. Admissions in 1970 were 33 percent higher than those of 1960 in the universities, but were still 5 percent lower than in 1960 in the junior colleges. On the other hand, admissions to the universities fell by 12 percent between 1970 and 1972, while they rose by 7 percent in the junior colleges (*Jahrbuch 1973*, pp. 362-63).

1970 had a university degree and only three of the five had even a junior college degree. In a vvb headquarters of a different branch of light industry, until 1967—three years after the vvb was formed—none of the six directors had a university degree. Even in 1970, less than 10 percent of that portion of the hundred professionals in this same vvb's headquarters who were more than forty years old had received a university education.

This is not to suggest that East German authorities have been indifferent to higher education as a criterion for choosing and promoting managers. Such is decidedly not the case. Particularly in the sectors of modern industry, East German leaders have been concerned with assuring technical progress—and they have considered higher education as a prerequisite for this.[66] At least since the middle 1960's, a veritable revolution has occurred in the composition of management; younger, more educated men have replaced the older executives. (This revolution was made possible by a tripling between 1961 and 1970 of the stock of university graduates working in industry, and an increase of 135 percent in the number of junior college graduates.)[67] In the vvb mentioned earlier, where as of early 1967 none of the six headquarters directors had had a university education, all six directors in 1970 had degrees. Five of the original six of 1967 had been demoted; their replacements were all between thirty-two and thirty-nine years old in 1970. But the East Germans have not felt it necessary to move so rapidly in insisting upon higher education for their managers as to oust experienced men before competent as well as educated replacements are available.

Those sent to universities have primarily been younger men rather than experienced professionals whose qualifications are being upgraded. Between 1960 and 1972, full-time students rose from 60 to 77 percent of all new entrants into the universities, with the proportion of evening and correspondence students declining proportionately; full-time admissions constitute a fair proxy for those beginning university education within a few years of finishing secondary school.[68] The East Germans

[66] In 1963, Ulbricht complained bitterly of the low percentage of factory employees with higher education in enterprises of such industries as chemicals and electronics compared to their West German counterparts (Ulbricht, Volume 1, pp. 222-23). Ulbricht repeated the same complaint in 1967; this time his comparison was with the Soviet Union in the engineering industries (Ulbricht, Volume 2, pp. 481-84).

By 1970, 1.7 percent of all employees in East German industry were university graduates, and 6.0 percent were graduates of junior colleges (*Jahrbuch 1971*, p. 66). For most sectors, the combined percentage is believed to be higher than is the case in West Germany (*DDR-Wirtschaft*, p. 40).

[67] *Jahrbuch 1973*, p. 66.

[68] On the other hand, judging by the same proxy, the majority of entrants into junior colleges remained older people. Because of growing efficiency in graduating evening and correspondence students, the proportion of graduates who had en-

have insured that the vast bulk of university students receive the best quality education which—despite protests to the contrary—simply cannot be provided except in full-time study.

TRADE UNIONS

Although not strictly relevant to the purposes of this chapter, a word about the role of the central trade unions seems appropriate to a description of the East German industrial setting. I shall concentrate here on the trade union functions at the national level, relying entirely on a lengthy interview with the chairman of one of the largest unions.

In order to fit the unions' national functions into their proper setting, however, it is important to note that full-time trade union officials appear to be considerably more numerous in the G.D.R. than in Romania. In the G.D.R., all of the enterprises I visited—even one with only seven hundred employees—had a full-time trade union secretary. In Romania, by contrast, small enterprises have no full-time trade union representatives. This difference parallels that for full-time Party representatives, who are also commonly found in East German enterprises; even each of the VVBS (unlike the Romanian *centrale* and ministries) has a full-time Party secretary.

In one of the very largest trade unions in the country, there is at least one full-time representative in each enterprise, and roughly one additional for every extra five hundred employees.[69] Supplementing these are thirty-five officials and employees in the national union headquarters and about two hundred ninety officials in the various regional headquarters. Thus the investment of manpower is substantial.

Prior to 1963, the trade unions played no substantial part in the formulation of the plans of state organs at either the national or enterprise level. Their functions were limited to aid in the execution of plans and to criticisms of "errors" in execution which prejudiced workers' interests. Since 1963, however, it is claimed that they have been active in the preparation of decisions prior to their formulation in state plans.

The chairman of the trade union explained the union's role in planning as consisting of representation of a special interest. He argued that, although officials of all organizations share the same common goal of advancing socialism, the attention that they give to different aspects of this broad objective differs depending upon their organizational affiliation. It is for this reason, he said, that the trade unions—in contrast to ministerial and enterprise executives—pay more attention to the social

---

gaged in full-time studies actually fell in both the universities and junior colleges during the decade of the 1960's (*Jahrbuch 1971*, pp. 374 and 382).

[69] The trade unions are organized on industrial rather than craft lines.

aspects of decisions than to their production-efficiency aspects. As might be expected, he offered this representation hypothesis not as an indication of conflict between interest groups, but rather as an explanation as to how balanced consideration of all aspects of a problem can be assured through special pleading by the different organizations concerned. Where the trade union cannot come to agreement with the relevant state body, he said, it would appeal its case to the next higher body; the line of appeal would normally be restricted to the state rather than the Party hierarchy.

In this trade union—and the chairman considered it to be quite typical in this regard—officials have generally spent their careers within the trade union hierarchy. Very few have come from either managerial or Communist Party posts. Thus they have had long work experience in representing the point of view demanded by their current position. Furthermore, tenure in post tends to be quite lengthy. Most officials in the national headquarters of the trade union have worked there for the last ten to fifteen years.

On the national level, this trade union participates in planning through presenting official comments to the Council of Ministers concerning the draft of the plan prepared by the ministry in which its members work. Attention is particularly concentrated upon issues of wages, social expenditures by industry, safety, and interenterprise production competitions. After the meeting of the Council of Ministers, the normal procedure is for the ministry to be instructed to rework its plan in the light of the comments made at the meeting—including those by the trade union. While I was talking to the trade union chairman, he had on his desk a letter of about six pages from the ministry indicating how it was responding to the union's recommendations.

Four examples were cited of conflict between the trade union and its ministry. The first transcended the level of any single union, relating to changes in the level of earnings in different branches of the economy. The trade unions accept that there should be larger wage increases in high-priority than in low-priority industries, but they object to stagnation of earnings for any group and insist on the principle that no group should ever suffer a reduction in earnings. At the time that I was interviewing, the draft plan of the ministry called for a stagnation of earnings for some worker groups and an actual reduction for a few. The trade union was currently engaged in a struggle to have these tentative decisions reversed.

A second issue which the union had taken (successfully) to the Council of Ministers was the question of the norms of social expenditures by enterprises. Social expenditures on nurseries and kindergartens, vacation homes for children and adults, dining room subsidies, factory shops, and a host of smaller items are financed out of a predetermined percentage of the enterprise's net profits. The ministry (through its individual VVBS) had in its draft plan established the percentage for each enterprise on the basis of realizing a more or less constant ratio of social expenditures to total wage expenditures in all enterprises of the ministry. But the trade union objected to this procedure on the ground that enterprises with a higher proportion of women workers should have higher social expenditures per worker, whereas the adopted procedure would have yielded lower social expenditures in such plants since, on average, women hold lower-paid jobs than do men. At the time of my interview, the ministry had altered its norms to the satisfaction of the union.

A third issue raised some years earlier had been the methods of implementation of the national changeover to the five-day week. The trade union had had to appeal several times to the President of the Council of Ministers, or to the Council itself, in disputes with its ministry over this matter.

A fourth issue was that the trade union wished the ministry to establish a center for research on labor matters: safety, analysis of the work process, norms of social objectives, etc. The trade union had formulated this suggestion two years earlier; the ministry had formed several working groups to consider the matter, but had still not arrived at a decision which was satisfactory to the trade union. At the time of my interview, the union had decided to take the matter higher in order to speed a resolution. It had just written a letter of complaint to the ministry, sending a copy to the vice-president of the Council of Ministers who was in charge of overseeing that particular ministry. The union chairman thought that this action would be sufficient; but he had determined that, if the matter were not satisfactorily resolved within two months, he would write requesting an opportunity to present his case before the executive committee of the Council or before the Council itself.

These four illustrations of dispute between the trade union and the ministry for which its members work seem to bear out the trade union chairman's analysis of the union's role. They are the kinds of issues which the personnel director of a large capitalist firm might well take for decision to the executive officer of the company. The dispute between the trade union and the ministry on these matters does not necessarily indicate any disagreement over final objectives; it probably represents only varied degrees of sensitivity to the different effects of any decision. Nevertheless, not only is it very important for the smooth running of industrial operations that such an advocacy system should exist—within a centrally planned system just as much as within a large, capitalist company—but it is also of considerable advantage to rank-and-file workers that they have some organization as their recognized advocate. That the central trade union does no more than act as personnel department for the Council of Ministers does not denigrate its role. It should be remembered that strong personnel departments have developed within large capitalist firms in the United States only after the challenge of independent trade unions had become serious. It is to the credit of the G.D.R. that, at least in this industry, it has developed the same sort of managerial function without the pressure of independent unions of the western variety.

CHAPTER 6

East German VVBs, *Kombinate,*
and Enterprises

I SHALL discuss in this chapter the nature of the planned tasks given to VVBs, *Kombinate,* and enterprises, and the behavior of these organizations within the constraints established by these tasks. Managerial bonuses will be discussed inter alia. There will also be a limited discussion of the role of the Party, the trade unions, and the Industry and Trade Bank in influencing the above units.

NATURE OF THE INTERVIEW SAMPLE

The source of information consists of interviews conducted during the summer of 1970. The interviews ran an average of twenty-five hours per organization in each of the following: one machinebuilding VVB, one of the *Kombinate* subordinate to it, one state garment enterprise, and one of the larger semiprivate enterprises of a different branch of light industry. In addition to my reasonably intensive studies of these four bodies, I also conducted interviews of several hours' duration with the head of the *Kombinat* to which the garment enterprise was subordinate, and with one of the directors of the VVB which supervised the semiprivate enterprise.

While this sample of six organizations is small, I believe that it is reasonably representative of large-scale East German industry. Both structure-determining industry and sectors of very low priority are covered in the sample. Only three of the six organizations are located in Berlin. The machinebuilding *Kombinat,* although described to me by an outside source as ranking among the better production units in the G.D.R., was as of the middle of 1970 in no better than a three-way tie for third place in a competition among the six *Kombinate* of its industrial branch.[1] Thus, by the criterion of plan fulfillment rather than absolute standards—and it is the former which is a better indicator of the kinds of pressure placed upon management—this was an average *Kombinat.* The garment enterprise had done sufficiently poorly in 1969 so that none of its upper managerial personnel received customary end-

---

[1] The competitive standing of the different *Kombinate* was based on a weighed average of percentage fulfillment of four different plan indicators during the previous half year.

of-year bonuses for that year. The semiprivate enterprise seems to have been picked for my visit both because of its large size for this form of enterprise and because of the political position of its principal director; it did not appear to be a showcase enterprise with regard to efficiency.

Although, in contrast to the situation in Romania, I was given no choice as to the units to visit, my main host insisted that I had not seen any of the very best enterprises or *Kombinate* in East German industry. While he did think that my sample units were somewhat more efficient than average, he also believed that they were quite typical with regard to the characteristics most important for this study: namely, the relationship between the different levels of organization, and between the unit management and the Industry Bank, the Party, and the trade unions.

Pursuant to my request, I studied only units which produced a variety of products and were in a technological position to alter their product mix markedly and rapidly. All units had a substantial proportion of their output directed both to the internal and to the export markets. The marketing issues they faced covered the gamut of those normally encountered by East German industry.

In the light of this description of the six organizations studied, I believe—despite the small size of the sample—that it is not unreasonable to lean heavily on my interviews as a means of inserting content into the primarily formal description of the New Economic System which was presented in Chapter 5.

PLAN INDICATORS

In order to evaluate the degree of flexibility left to bodies below the level of the industrial ministries, it is useful to describe the annual plan indicators received by these bodies and to distinguish between those considered obligatory and the rest.[2] Let us begin with the plan indicators given to the machinebuilding vvb. A complete list of its *obligatory indicators* for 1971 as they had been established as of the summer of 1970 (i.e., prior to increased centralization) is as follows:

1. Specific assignments in the field of research and development, both for products and processes.
2. Specific assignments for automation and mechanization of production.
3. Labor productivity (value-added per employee).
4. Minimum number of marks to be paid from net profits into the

[2] A full list of the obligatory plan indicators and of calculating-indicators for the year 1971 for the entire economy are given in "Beschluss über die Durchführung des ökonomischen Systems des Sozialismus im Jahre 1971," *Gesetzblatt der Deutschen Demokratischen Republik*, ii, 1970, 100, pp. 732-33.

state budget. This is calculated as planned net profits multiplied by the ratio given in (5).

5. Percentage of net profits which are to be paid into the state budget.

6. Minimum number of marks to be paid from amortization into the state budget.[3]

7. Percentage of amortization costs which are to be paid into the state budget.

8. Wage fund for workers and employees. (This is a single, maximum figure, which is reduced in proportion to the degree that the average number of workers and employees in the year is less than had been planned. It is, however, increased in some stated proportion to the degree that labor productivity is higher than was planned.)

9. Gross profits as a percentage of the year's average of fixed capital and working capital.

10. Sales of finished consumer goods. (For this vvb, such sales constitute an insignificant proportion of the vvb's total production.)[4]

11. Exports to socialist countries (in marks).
    a. As part of this, exports specifically to the Soviet Union.

12. Exports to nonsocialist countries (in marks).
    As part of this:
    a. Exports to developed capitalist countries.
    b. Exports to less developed countries.

The calculating-indicators–targets given to the units, and for which reports as to plan fulfillment are collected, but which are not considered as plans which the units are obliged to meet—for the vvb for 1971 were:

1. The number employed in research and development activities.
2. Total sales (in marks).
3. Total investment (in marks).
   Of this:
   a. In buildings.
   b. In equipment.
4. Ratio of total output to fixed capital.

[3] This plan indicator is used, in addition to (7), in order to avoid a situation in which the vvb retires more of its equipment than was planned, and so reduces its amortization payments below the expected amount. However, if the percentage-deduction from amortization costs is greater than this minimum, the larger amount is paid into the state budget.

[4] The existence of this indicator was described as a leftover from the situation of the mid-1950's, when all plants were expected to produce such goods in order to compensate for the fact that new investment was not going into factories specifically designated for the manufacture of industrial consumer goods.

5. Number of youngsters just leaving school who are to be employed.
6. Average number of workers and employees for the year. (This is a maximum figure.)
7. Percentage reduction in the value of materials used as a proportion of total production.

A third category of information-figures is also set forth for the year. These have the least significance, and for 1971 were as follows:

1. Total value-added (in marks).
2. Gross profits plus those additional contractual payments by consuming organizations which are paid as a means of sharing the projected cost reductions to be realized from new products produced by the vvb.
3. The projected average rate of price reductions for the vvb's products.

There are a number of notable omissions from the obligatory plan indicators for this vvb. The most glaring is the value of production—either in terms of total value or value-added—for the internal East German market. Although the absence of this indicator was far from universal throughout East German industry, it is striking that it should have been missing in this important branch. The reader should remember that in Romania this is the single most important plan indicator, and such was also the case up to a few years ago in this vvb.

A second noteworthy absent category is that of investment during the year. The absence of such a planned figure gives meaning to the formal right of the Industry and Trade Bank to refuse credits for investment purposes. A third category missing is the total number of workers and employees; but this is probably only because, as was seen in Chapter 5, it is the regional economic councils which set these limits, while the vvbs transcend any single economic region. A fourth category which one might have expected to be obligatory is the rate of price reduction; perhaps its absence is due to the recency of the policy of reducing prices paid by industrial users. Yet a fifth missing category is any indication as to the vvb's product mix, although it is true that in fact the minimum outputs of certain specific structure-determining products are determined at a level above the vvb and are treated as obligatory tasks.

However, by December 1970 all these categories except the fourth were listed as items to be included as obligatory plan indicators for all vvbs, *Kombinate*, and enterprises in the G.D.R.[5] To some degree this represents an expansion of the planning constraints placed upon the

[5] "Beschluss über das ökonomische System 1971," p. 732.

initiative of all organizations below the ministerial level; but the change can also be interpreted as little more than an explicit formulation of what had previously been implicit.

The most significant feature of the set of obligatory indicators is the emphasis placed upon financial tasks and limits, as opposed to physical ones, even in a high-priority sector of industry.

In the garment *Kombinat* which I visited, the general director singled out the five most important criteria of the *Kombinat*'s work—the only ones for which he personally followed the results closely. These five were:

1. Gross profits as a percentage of total output.
2. Gross profits as a percentage of fixed capital.
3. Working capital as a percentage of sales.
4. The development of new products.
5. The reorganization and expansion of the *Kombinat* as a whole.

For one state enterprise within this garment *Kombinat*, total production and the average number of workers and employees were added to the obligatory targets we have seen earlier for the vvb. In this enterprise, the total number of units of product to be produced during the year were also determined by plan, and these were divided into the two broad categories of winter and summer garments. Here is the first obligatory task for product mix which we have encountered; but it was not very restrictive, as a finer breakdown of assortment would have been into at least thirty to forty categories.

The semiprivate firm—because of its ownership status—was not given any obligatory financial plan indicators except for the constraint on the wage fund. Its second constraint was the average number of workers and employees. In addition to these constraints, it was given the following obligatory plan indicators:

1. Production (in marks). This was divided into only two product groups: one consisted of the total mix sold by the enterprise, and the second of jigs and fixtures produced by the enterprise for its own use.

2. Production for sale was determined (in marks) for six different markets. The internal East German market was one; exports to socialist countries comprised a second, with exports to the Soviet Union being specifically singled out within this with a special plan indicator; the last three consisted of three different markets (convertible currency areas, West Germany and West Berlin, and nonconvertible currency markets) within the nonsocialist group of countries.

From this survey of obligatory plan indicators in four industrial organizations, it would seem that managements are left considerable leeway. This is so in determining both the mix of output and the particular combination of inputs (e.g., types of labor) to employ. The only obligatory restrictions other than the plan indicators listed were the minimum output levels to be achieved for all structure-determining products, and the amount of specific centrally allocated materials which can be used.

In reality, however, these plan indicators do not constitute the total restrictions within which the industrial organizations operate. Each is obliged to work out many additional aspects of its annual plan such as the amount of working capital to be borrowed, the precise products to be delivered to purchasers and the scheduling of these deliveries, and the utilization of noncentrally allocated materials. What is important concerning these aspects of the plan—which are not centrally determined—is that they require agreement not only with the partner organizations (the Industry and Trade Bank, purchasers, and suppliers) but also, and more significantly, with the industrial body immediately superior to the one for which the plan is made. In this fashion, the enterprise is controlled by the *Kombinat*, the *Kombinat* by the vvb, and the vvb by the ministry, in many aspects of their work which are not originally set forth as obligatory plan indicators.

But there is a great difference between this kind of planning and that which I observed in Romanian industry. In East Germany, the unit itself bears primary responsibility for determining its annual plan, and for then winning the consent of the necessary agencies, rather than having this plan imposed upon it with only minor opportunity for negotiation. The most significant area of semi-independence of the unit is in the formulation of its own plan; here it operates only within the two constraints of meeting its obligatory plan indicators and of gaining the agreement of its partners and of its immediate hierarchical superior.

SALES AND THE DETERMINATION OF PRODUCT MIX

Sales procedures. The actual degree of independence of the unit is best judged in the formation of its sales plan.

In the machinebuilding vvb, some 50 percent of the value of sales consists of structure-determining products. For these products, the vvb receives central orders as to the minimum amount which is to be supplied, and these orders are distributed to the *Kombinate*. The amount of flexibility left to the vvb and *Kombinate* is slight; the machinebuilding *Kombinat* which I studied estimated that, for its most important structure-determining product, it had an additional 5 percent capacity which it could use to fulfill supplemental orders.

For the remaining 50 percent of its capacity, the vvb begins with a statement of annual requirements received from the Foreign Trade

Ministry and from the single ministry which is its customer for sales within East Germany. In its attempt to meet these requests, the vvb is constrained by the need to assure the planned net profit for the vvb as a whole;[6] the vvb coordinates the work of the various product groups, both within vvb headquarters and in the *Kombinate*, so as to balance the target of meeting customer demands within each specific product group with the constraint of meeting the vvb's own overall objectives. Since different products provide widely varying rates of profit (as a percentage of cost, these ranged within this vvb from negative to at least 30 percent), the profit plan constitutes a fundamental constraint in determining the quantities of different products which can be supplied. Once the vvb has a rough notion as to the product mix which will be produced, it is in a position to distribute its own net profit tasks among the subordinate *Kombinate*.

The machinebuilding *Kombinat* takes on the sales task at this point. For shipments within the G.D.R., the *Kombinat* begins by coming to an agreement with the purchasing ministry on the total value of sales to be negotiated that year.[7] Afterwards, it negotiates contracts with the purchasing enterprises; it is only in this process that the *Kombinat*'s detailed product mix—except for structure-determining products—is decided. The coverage of these contracts must, however, meet with the approval of the vvb.[8] The contracts then become part of the annual plan of the *Kombinat*.

As to exports, it is the machinebuilding *Kombinat* which is responsible for realizing the planned value of sales. For socialist countries, export contracts are signed within the scope of government agreements. But since in most cases these do not specify individual products, it is up to the *Kombinat* to undertake its own sales efforts. It is partly for this reason that the *Kombinat* participates in international fairs as far east as Volgograd in the Soviet Union, shipping at its own expense the heavy equipment it produces.

Aside from the four-way regional constraints on exports set forth in the compulsory plan indicators for the vvb and for the *Kombinat*, the *Kombinat* is not formally restricted by any further division of sales among individual countries. In reality, however, the *Kombinat* "consults" with the vvb as to the proportion of its output which is to go to

[6] Literally, there was in 1970 no planned obligatory task for net profit. But the term was used in all East German organizations, and was taken as the minimum amount to be paid from net profits into the state budget, divided by the percentage of net profits which were to be so transferred.

[7] Prior to this, the vvb has itself negotiated with the purchasing ministry as to the minimum value of sales to be provided by the vvb as a whole.

[8] Normally, this approval is given through the medium of the product groups described in Chapter 5.

individual countries. Furthermore, the *Kombinat* general director would inevitably talk both with his minister and with Party functionaries about such a matter as substantial sales to India, since political as well as economic considerations would be involved.

In the garment industry, there are no structure-determining centrally planned products. Nevertheless, the VVB balances demand and supply, and the *Kombinat* balances it further in more detail. The individual enterprise works out its own product-mix plan, but this must be approved by the *Kombinat*'s product group or be returned by it to the enterprise for reworking. Balancing is done both for basic types of clothing and for the materials from which the clothing is made; but it does not relate to style. For the enterprise I studied, fifteen to twenty different categories of clothing were singled out in the balance.

The product group of the garment *Kombinat* is itself guided by a set of product-mix priorities which have been laid down by its branch ministry. These priorities would be established at a level of aggregation which takes all exports as a single item, confirmation dresses as a second, children's clothing as a third, and all other production within the product group as the fourth. In the light of these priorities, the product group would examine the demand—expressed in number of units rather than in marks—by the foreign trade export monopoly group for textiles and by the relevant domestic trade body, and would approve or reject the garment enterprises's product-mix plan. But the product group works only in physical units of clothing (e.g., number of women's coats), while what matters to the enterprise is the value of its production.

Within the scope of its annual plan, the garment enterprise negotiates contracts twice a year for its deliveries within the G.D.R. These contracts are signed some two months before the beginning of deliveries for the summer season, and four months before that of the winter season. Ten to twenty percent of the enterprise's capacity is not covered by contracts at all, and is available for additional deliveries of new products throughout the season.

The semi-annual contract negotiation begins with the weaving enterprises displaying to the garment enterprise the patterns of cloth which they have available for the season. (Prior to this, the enterprises will have signed contracts for the total amount of cloth to be delivered during the year, but not for the patterns, colors, and yarn-counts.) The garment enterprise need not commit itself as to the precise cloth to be ordered from the weavers until eight to twelve weeks before delivery is wanted.

On the basis of its knowledge of the available kinds of cloth, the garment enterprise makes up samples which it shows to the single internal trade organization, indicating the number of units of each type it is prepared to sell. Since the trade organization is in a monopsonist position, the garment enterprise is prevented from taking full advantage of the conditions of a sellers' market. In fact, the garment enterprise seems typically to have had to prepare a second set of samples for the trade organization before it could contract its entire capacity for the season.

Export contracts for all socialist countries except the Soviet Union are handled on the same basis of seasonal contracts as is used for domestic sales. Exports to the Soviet Union (the principal foreign customer) have a much longer leadtime; as of June 1970, the garment enterprise knew the entire Soviet order in full detail for all 1971.

In preparation for its export contract with the Soviet Union, the garment enterprise submits samples and indicates the number of units of each type of garment which it wishes to sell. The Soviet trade organization responds by eliminating some items which had been offered and increasing the volumes for others. If the enterprise does not wish to supply the additional volumes of the selected items, it then offers additional samples to the Soviet buyer and the process is repeated.

If the volume requested by the Soviet Union is greater than the exports to that country incorporated in the garment enterprise's plan, the enterprise cannot sign contracts for the excess unless it believes these can be met from above-plan output. What is done, instead, is to transfer one or more of the items ordered by the Soviet Union to another East German factory; the only restriction is that the two factories must have as their supplier the same weaver. The garment enterprise has the right to choose the factory to which the order is to be transferred, and it does so on the expectation of reciprocity in another year when its own orders will be insufficient to meet its export plan.

Since the garment enterprise exports solely through a foreign trade enterprise to all its socialist customers, as well as to its customers in the one capitalist country which represents its principal nonsocialist market, it is interesting to note the tasks performed by this monopoly trader. First, it carries out all price negotiations not conducted at a higher government level: long term in the case of socialist markets, and spot prices for sales in capitalist countries. Second, it sometimes holds stocks abroad, although only in capitalist countries. Third, it handles all negotiations as to the precise quality characteristics of the sample items ordered, and thus on the appropriate price for them within the terms of long-term price agreements. Finally, it plays an important role in restricting the number of East German enterprises which are to export to a given socialist market; its function here is to assure that the orders each exporter receives for individual items are large enough to make possible proper economies of scale in production. But the remaining terms of the export agreements—such as delivery dates, packaging, and quality control procedures—are negotiated by the garment enterprise itself.

The semiprivate consumer goods firm handled its sales in a fashion rather similar to that of the garment enterprise, since neither of them produced structure-determining products. All of its output for the domestic market was covered through a single long-term contract with a monopsonist wholesale trade organization, although a portion of these sales were distributed through two private wholesalers. In 1969, a contract was signed for 1971-75 (the previous contract had been for two years). However, if the enterprise's approved annual plan of deliveries to the domestic market were to be reduced below the level called for by this contract (e.g., because export obligations were raised), the long-term contract would be automatically modified without penalty. Thus this multiyear contract does not seem to have been very significant. The really critical contracts—the ones detailing product mix—were signed semiannually with the same monopsonist.

Exports to socialist countries were made under annual contracts, with full details spelled out by September for the coming year. In contrast, exports to western Europe were all on a spot basis and without annual contracts. Considerable flexibility in the scheduling of such spot export deliveries was obtained by the enterprise through leniency in contract interpretation by the domestic wholesale monopsonist; although the domestic sales contract called for specified monthly deliveries, there was no difficulty in altering the schedule without penalty when the supplier firm requested this so that it could meet export orders coming from western Europe.[9]

Sales objectives. We have so far restricted our attention to sales procedures in the enterprises and *Kombinate* I have studied. What are the objectives of these organizations in negotiating with their purchasers as to product mix?

Examining sales objectives from the point of view of the producing VVB and of its product groups, it is my impression that the VVB tends to treat the realization of planned net profits as a constraint rather than as its objective function. Within both this constraint and that of value-added labor productivity, it attempts to satisfy the product-mix requests of the domestic purchasing ministry and of the Ministry of Foreign Trade as fully as possible.[10] However, even after the decisions of the product

---

[9] It must be added, however, that these variations of delivery dates could not have been very major, since only some 7 percent of the enterprise's sales went to western Europe.

[10] This was explicitly stated by the deputy economic director of the machine-building VVB.

groups have been made, considerable room is still left to the *Kombinate* and enterprises within which to negotiate the detailed mix with their customers.

Here the criteria are less clear. It is my impression that the *Kombinate* and enterprises analyze customers' product-mix requests from the viewpoint of profit maximization until they feel assured of realizing their planned gross profit for the year. Beyond that point, however, other considerations are of at least equal importance.

In the machinebuilding *Kombinat*, for example, the general director was enthusiastic about the price-reduction policy recently introduced in East German industry. About 40 percent of the *Kombinat's* total production is exported to socialist countries, and he regarded this market as the one with the greatest growth potential. Since he believed that, at least in a multiyear perspective, his volume of exports depended upon the export prices charged, he welcomed export price reductions (which he apparently thought would follow from reductions in the domestic prices charged for the equipment); he wished only to be assured of sufficient retained profits to finance his fixed investments and growing working capital needs.[11]

In the garment *Kombinat*, the general director believed that a *Kombinat* should never show high overfulfillment of plan. He thought that if a *Kombinat* could exceed its profit plan by as much as 5 percent, it was the general director's duty to have requested a higher plan.

In view of this attitude, it was only to be expected that this general director would not regard profit maximizing as the obvious criterion to use for determining the mix of above-plan output.[12] (Providing that the

[11] See Chapter 5 for a discussion of pricing and profit distribution. Price reductions within East Germany are not automatically reflected in the contractual prices of exports to socialist countries, but they may be taken into account in contractual negotiations. (Cf. S. Ausch, *Theory and Practice of CMEA Cooperation*, Akadémiai Kiadó, Budapest: 1972, pp. 92-93, and P. Marer, "Postwar Pricing and Price Patterns in Socialist Foreign Trade, 1946-1971," International Development Research Center of Indiana University, Report 1, Part II-A.)

In the case of this *Kombinat*, investment was viewed primarily as a function of the degree of expansion of foreign demand. Consequently, higher export profits would not lead to any increase in the planned amount of expansion, and higher expected profits for the *Kombinat* could only cause the VVB to increase the proportion of net profits to be taken into the state budget. Given this situation, both short-run profit maximizing and long-run output maximizing might be rational objectives for the *Kombinat* top management, but long-run profit maximizing was not in the *Kombinat's* interest. The situation would be quite different for a *Kombinat* whose rate of planned investment depended upon the evaluation by higher authorities of its profit perspectives, rather than upon the absolute rate of expansion of its market.

[12] Once a *Kombinat* has achieved the planned output targets for the year, it is no longer restrained by its VVB's balancing procedure. It can produce what it wishes, subject only to its ability to sell the goods and to procure the necessary materials.

profit plan's achievement was assured, he considered it as quite reasonable to produce low-profit utility clothing.) Clearly, this *Kombinat* general director took the same approach to profit earning as did the machinebuilding vvB.

According to the sales director of the garment enterprise, the task of his sales organization is threefold. The most important mission is to insure, insofar as possible, a product mix which will balance the demands made on the capacity of the different production processes within the enterprise.[13] Winter clothing, on average, requires less finishing capacity, and more preparatory and sewing capacity, than does summer clothing; furthermore, the two types of clothing are produced at different times of the year. The sales staff can legitimately negotiate with the product group for an aggregative product mix which is most conducive to an even, and therefore full, use of the capacity of the different processes. But the main effort must be put forth in the negotiation of contracts for appropriate amounts of specific items in order to maximize the use of finishing capacity in producing the winter clothing mix, and to minimize its use for summer clothing. Success in this is important for the achievement of both profit and labor productivity objectives.[14]

The second assignment, which he regarded as much less important than the first, is to maximize the relative weight of those operations for which the enterprise's productivity and profitability are substantially higher than the national norms. Factory sales prices within East Germany are set in terms of "normed" values for each operation, with the norms determined on the basis of national standards in the year that the prices were originally established. Some 40 percent of the total profits of this enterprise came from keeping average cost below the normed level. As might be expected, however, actual enterprise costs vary from these norms in a highly differentiated fashion. For example, since this enterprise was more mechanized than many smaller ones, it found its West German sales to be highly disadvantageous because they required more elaborate cutting and more button sewing than was the case for the enterprise's principal sales to the domestic and Soviet markets.

The third duty is to increase the domestic sales of fashion products, since these are defined as high-quality products and sell for 3 to 5 percent more than would similar items which are not fashionable.[15] Although

[13] Subcontracting of work is an additional means for attaining such balance.

[14] It is only in the above sense of insuring a balanced utilization that full loading of capacity was considered by the sales organization to be a problem. The threat of insufficient demand to provide full use of the bottleneck capacity was regarded as unreal.

[15] The judgment as to whether or not an item is "fashionable" is made by the German Fashion Institute. The procedure of official determination of fashion has the disadvantage of insulating designers somewhat from the actual tastes of con-

another director of the same enterprise had said that there was excess demand on the domestic market for fashion articles, the sales director insisted that currently the enterprise was having considerable difficulty in getting the volume of fashion orders which it wished. In any event, it is obvious that increasing fashion output as a proportion of total production may well be a difficult sales task, and that different enterprises may have varying success in meeting it.

Even the semiprivate consumer goods enterprise showed less concern with short-run profit than might have been accepted. A suggestion had been recently made within the enterprise that a specific new product be added which would be more profitable than the existing line.[16] The main private owner and principal director rejected this suggestion on the basis of long-run considerations, claiming that he was here taking the same position as would a well-managed capitalist firm. He admitted that he was currently facing excess demand for his products, that he expected this to continue for the foreseeable future, and that he was unable to expand further because of national policy with regard to investment in the semiprivate sector. But he felt that, since his current customers would fail to "understand" his initiating a new line while unable to meet their demand for his current products, such a policy would invite reprisals in the long run.

Given the conditions of the market, the possibility for such purchaser reprisals seemed to be distant indeed. Furthermore, in light of the uncertainty which surrounded the future status of the semiprivate sector as a whole, one might have expected a heavy emphasis on short-run returns. In fact—perhaps because of the high marginal tax rate on profits earned by semiprivate firms—the enterprise's management seemed, if anything, to give rather less weight to profit considerations than did the state garment enterprise.

PURCHASING AND THE CHOICE OF MATERIALS[17]

Centrally rationed goods constitute a rather small proportion of the materials used by the enterprises studied. In the machinebuilding *Kombinat*, the figure was some 5 percent of all materials; but this percentage was so low only because foundry products, which would otherwise have

---

sumers, but it provides the counterpart advantage of reducing the possibility for manufacturers to use sellers' market conditions to place pressure upon the sales organization to pay a higher price.

[16] There was disagreement among the enterprise's top managers as to whether it would, in fact, prove to be more profitable. But what is relevant for our purposes is that the main owner and principal director believed that it would be.

[17] See Chapter 5 for a general discussion of rationing and balancing of materials.

been centrally allocated, were produced by the *Kombinat* itself and thus escaped the system. In the garment enterprise, 10 to 20 percent of the cloth used was centrally allocated. Only in the semiprivate firm did rationed materials constitute a "large part" of the total received.[18]

A director of a vvb producing consumer goods insisted that, within the Ministry of Light Industry which controls his vvb, the central allocation of materials between branches depends heavily on both the branches' respective profitability and their relative export intensity.[19] Thus, within such a broad sector as total industrial consumer goods, financial considerations seem to play a major role in determining allocations. To the degree that this vvb director is correct, here is a mechanism for introducing a degree of consumer sovereignty within the sector of nonfood consumer goods.[20]

In the machinebuilding *Kombinat*, it was pointed out that all purchase requests for the year—whether for centrally allocated items or for those which are only balanced by product groups—must be made at the latest by November 1st of the previous year. (This does not mean that full specifications have to be given at that time. Rather, the request must be stated in terms of the quantities needed at whatever level of aggregation is used by the relevant product groups in their balancing work.) After that date, additional supplies can be purchased only from production which is above-plan or otherwise outside the balancing system. But even some steel can be picked up by the *Kombinat* in this unplanned fashion.

The garment factory—which, as we shall see below, appears to have been in a particularly favored position within its branch—has been able to purchase outside the balancing system some 20 percent of its needs

[18] Centrally rationed materials in 1970 included all imports, alloy metals, wood, paper, some plastics, and some types of cloth.

[19] Profitability is measured both as a percentage of the value of output and as a percentage of fixed plus working capital. I am uncertain whether state receipts through the sales tax on goods sold to final consumers are included in "profit" as used for this purpose; one might expect that they would be.

[20] This process of allocation appears to be geared toward equalizing the profit rate earned on different consumer goods in sales within the domestic market, thus maximizing consumer welfare from the consumption of a fixed total of industrial consumer goods, although within the constraints imposed by current income distribution and relative consumer prices. This constrained consumer-welfare maximization can be attained by altering the supply coming from the various subbranches in accord with the rate of profit earned. (If, in fact, "profit" is not defined so as to include sales tax, this consumer welfare argument breaks down.) There are however, two limitations on this policy. First, since the government wishes to set relatively high or low consumer prices for particular goods which it disfavors or favors, the tendency toward equalization of profit rate cannot be allowed to affect all consumer items. Second, no such tendency toward equating profitability between consumer goods' and producer goods' sectors has been indicated to me by anyone in the g.d.r.

for cloth, thereby gaining a good deal of flexibility. Within the balancing system, its purchases of cloth are aggregated into six or seven different categories. Normally, requests must be made a year ahead of time, but sometimes a half-year period has been permitted. Detailed specifications are given to the supplying mills only eight to twelve weeks before delivery.

Thus enterprises have some flexibility in adjusting purchase orders throughout the planning year: primarily by further product-refinement of orders falling within a single category in the balancing system, but also through purchases made legally but outside both the balancing and the contract systems. Nevertheless, their most significant economic decisions as to substitution of materials are with regard to what they should request from balancing authorities. While such requests do reflect VVB instructions as to the preferred direction of substitution (e.g., plastics for metal), cost minimization appears to be an important criterion as well.

The managers of the units in which I conducted interviews did not particularly complain of difficulties in obtaining supplies, provided that they could place their orders early enough. Data for all East German industry under the jurisdiction of central ministries show that, as of the end of October 1970, arrears on the year's contracted deliveries constituted approximately one-fifth of one month's production.[21] Although contracts normally permit shipments to be made at the discretion of the seller at any time within a given month or quarter, this volume of arrears seems to corroborate that the macroeconomic problem is not overly severe.[22]

In the garment enterprise, an interesting example of the use of market power was observed. Under East German pricing regulations, no quantity discounts are given. Thus even though this enterprise's relatively large orders of specified patterns of cloth result in volume economies for the weaving firms, the garment enterprise cannot share in this advantage through lower prices.

However, since the garment enterprise is not limited to purchasing from specific weavers, it is in a strong position in dealing with its suppliers. For this reason, it is usually able to insist that the weaving mills produce some patterns for its exclusive use. Similarly, it is in a much more favorable position than a small enterprise in obtaining cloth without having signed a prior annual contract. In these respects, the

[21] Paul Verner, *Bericht des Politbüros an die 14. Tagung des ZK der SED* (Dietz, East Berlin: 1970), p. 8, and Staatliche Zentralverwaltung für Statistik, *Statistisches Jahrbuch der Deutschen Demokratischen Republik 1971* (Staatsverlag, East Berlin: 1971), p. 108.

[22] It should be noted that 1970 was a particularly poor year in the G.D.R.

purchaser and supplier enterprises function much as capitalist firms might do if they operated under equivalent pricing regulations.

WAGES AND LABOR USAGE

In examining the degree of freedom of East German *Kombinate* and enterprises in organizing production, we have already analyzed their control over the composition of both their output and their material inputs. This section will deal with the second major category of inputs: labor.

Three formal restrictions are placed on the hiring powers of the production units. The first is quantitative: the maximum average number of full-time workers and employees permitted during the year. The other two restrictions place limits on the ability of the unit to attract labor; these consist of the wage and salary rates determined nationally for all jobs, and the total wage fund available to the unit. Labor regulations leave the production unit completely free to substitute one type of labor for another. It is not free, however, to increase total labor expenditures in order to economize on materials expenditures, or in the degree to which it can increase total earnings within the enterprise as compensation for productivity improvements.

The maximum number of employees permitted for the year appears generally to be set at an unattainable height. In 1970, the machinebuilding VVB was unable to bring its employment over 98 percent of the indicator established for it; its structure-determining *Kombinat*, despite being the highest paying employer in the various towns where it has plants, ran 3 to 5 percent below its planned maximum figure. The managers of the enterprises of light industry seemed to regard recruiting and holding the number of employees allotted to them as their most difficult and important problem. I was told in the semiprivate firm that, although the enterprise gives monthly notification of its labor needs to the local labor office, it receives no help in its recruitment efforts and must depend exclusively on its own resources.

Of course, this is not to suggest that the limit set on a production unit's employment is totally meaningless, even as a short-run constraint. Perhaps its greatest practical importance, however, is with regard to housing, and here solely for structure-determining enterprises. Although enterprises do not own housing of their own, towns are frequently allocated housing-construction funds in order to satisfy the needs for expansion of their structure-determining enterprises; the resulting community housing will then be allocated by the town to personnel selected by the enterprise. In the case of the machinebuilding *Kombinat*, such access to housing—linked to the *Kombinat*'s limit on employment—

was very important in preventing its employment from running even further below the allotted limit than it actually did.

Wage and salary rates, established on a national basis, are generally so obsolete as to be without practical significance. This is because most wage rates were set long ago and have not been updated.[23] In the machinebuilding VVB, actual earnings in 1970 of the lowest grade of skilled worker were two to two and one-half times the official hourly rate.[24] Nor were actual earnings for different jobs kept in strict proportion to the official wage rates. In one enterprise, the ratio of hourly earnings to official wage rates was as follows for differing skill categories:

semiskilled workers[a]	177 percent
tool and die workers[b]	
lowest category	225 percent
highest category	197 percent

[a] Most workers in the enterprise were in this category.
[b] These are all within the top three skill categories in a seven-category system.

As for salaried white-collar workers, the machinebuilding VVB reported that all its managers in the enterprises and *Kombinate* were paid above the official salary range for their jobs. Presumably the same was also true for nonmanagerial salaried white-collar workers.

While an enterprise's actual earnings structure is subject to approval by the VVB, such approval appears to be purely formal. The machinebuilding VVB, for example, did not even bother to give approval to wages and salaries above the standard rate except in the case of upper managerial personnel.[25]

In reality, therefore, enterprises and *Kombinate* are bound only by changes in the minimum wage rate[26] and by the total wage fund established for the year; the latter implies, in practice, an average annual earning rate per full-time employee. The unit is free to respond to labor market pressures for different labor skills by varying as it sees fit both

[23] In one industry, they were last established in 1958, with minor revisions being introduced in 1965.

[24] This was further increased for workers on piece-rate pay who exceeded the norms set for the job; but such additional earnings were very minor in this VVB.

[25] This VVB does, however, set maximum salaries for new graduates from universities or junior colleges.

[26] Changes in the minimum wage rate for the entire East German economy, combined with legally binding increases for those up to a specified monthly wage, represent a constraint of some considerable importance in low-wage industries. Minimum monthly earnings were raised by 36 percent in 1967 and by a further 16 percent in 1971. In 1967, the proportion of all wage and salary earners in the economy who were covered by legislated wage increases was 13 percent; in 1971, 18 percent were covered.

the composition of its labor force and the earnings for different grades. The institutional pressures restraining management in this freedom seem to come more from the individual enterprise's trade union than from any other source.

Of course, noninstitutional pressures against raising earnings for selected groups can be quite severe. In the garment enterprise, for example, only one-third of the labor force worked on shifts. Because of quits by such workers, the percentage of shiftworkers was declining both in this enterprise and in its industry—rather than increasing as the government and enterprise management desired.

The enterprise's general director and personnel head both recognized that the monetary incentives for working shifts was so small as to have no effect. Both would have liked to increase sharply shift bonuses in order to use the enterprise's capital more intensively; however, although the enterprise was quite free to do so if it wished, such a policy was regarded as out of the question because of the necessary side effect of reducing the earnings of day workers.[27] These managers said that they could introduce higher shift bonuses only if this were to be made government policy, with compensating increases in the enterprise's total wage fund. They saw no prospects for this, and were thus resigned to a continued deleterious effect on the ratio of profit to capital investment.

An important implication of the previous materials is that the management and trade union of the individual enterprise and *Kombinat* must have a great deal of liberty in determining the relative earnings of different skill groups inside the production unit. Although it is true that their decisions are obliged to fall within the bounds imposed by the relative rigidity of the unit's total wage fund, one might expect that different enterprises would make different decisions as to relative earnings.

Unfortunately, no aggregative data have been published on the variation in earnings of the same skill group between different enterprises or *Kombinate*. My sample of enterprises and *Kombinate* is too small for me even to attempt to develop such data. But if considerable variation between enterprises does exist, then we would expect to see a high quit rate of the labor force. This is particularly so because of the extreme labor shortage in industry, the absence of freezing people in their jobs, and the lack of significant penalties attached to changing jobs.[28]

---

[27] As was pointed out in Chapter 5, large portions of the industrial labor force of the G.D.R. appear to have received no wage increases at all since the middle 1960's.

[28] So far as I am aware, the only rewards for remaining in the same enterprise are relatively minor additions to annual bonus and some possible effects on one's place in the housing queue. Those who already have as satisfactory housing as they are likely to get are unaffected by the housing queue. Since public housing in the G.D.R. is owned by the municipality rather than by the employing enterprise, a

While there are no national figures as to job turnover, the meager data which I have for two enterprises and one *Kombinat* do not suggest the high labor turnover rate which we would expect. In the two enterprises of light industry, both of which employed a heavy proportion of women, it ran 20 percent and some 8 to 12 percent annually. In the high-wage machinebuilding *Kombinat*, while no general figures were provided, there was a much lower labor turnover; total quits and retirements of white-collar employees were estimated at only 2 percent. As a standard of comparison, in Hungary—where individual enterprises are also free to vary relative earnings—the proportion of the total industrial labor force leaving their jobs annually varied between 29 and 35 percent during 1968-71.[29]

This leaves me with a conundrum. On the one hand, my labor turnover data may be quite unrepresentative of the general situation in East Germany. However, if we do accept these data as even crudely representative, then we must conclude that the individual enterprises have much less control over the relative earnings of different components of their labor force than my reasoning has implied. Reduced control might occur through informal pressure from the vvb; more likely, it is carried out through the medium of national wage policies implemented by the national trade unions. Unfortunately, I can say no more about this important matter.

Turning now to the procedure by which the wage fund per employee in an enterprise or *Kombinat* is determined, in principle the vvb increases the fund from year to year in relation to the planned increase in labor productivity.[30] In reality, of course, the vvb does not follow this principle strictly. Thus, while in 1969 the wage fund of the machinebuilding vvb was increased on the basis of 1 percent for every 5 percent increase in its labor productivity, the vvb used a ratio of 1 to 8.45 for one of its

---

worker who changes his job within the same community does not find his housing threatened. Similarly, a young worker who has only recently gotten onto the queue (e.g., because of marriage) normally faces such a long waiting period that a change of job is probably irrelevant. Workers who would be restrained from changing jobs are those who expect their turn to come soon to receive a new apartment allocated to their existing enterprise.

[29] These figures are calculated from Központi Statisztikai Hivatal, *Statisztikai Évkönyv 1969* (Budapest: 1970), p. 90; Központi Statisztikai Hivatal, *Statisztikai Havi Közlemények*, 1972, 5, p. 121; and Központi Statisztikai Hivatal, *Foglalkoztatottság és munkaviszonyból származó jövedelem 1968* (Budapest: 1970), p. 30.

[30] Although the vvb sets a total annual wage fund for each subordinate unit, this is calculated as the multiple of the wage fund per employee times the number of employees. If the average number of employees during the year is less than the maximum number allowed the *Kombinat* or enterprise (and if labor productivity is as planned), then the total wage fund is reduced correspondingly. Thus what really matters is the wage fund per employee, not the total wage fund.

enterprises which had particularly good opportunities for improving productivity. But the vvb's deputy economic director admitted that there was a socially imposed limit on the degree to which differentiation between *Kombinate* and enterprises could be implemented, and that in practice this constrained the vvb's possibilities of concentrating its productivity-investments in individual *Kombinate* or enterprises.

During the course of the year, a production unit's per capita wage fund for the current period is increased by some predetermined percentage of the above-plan increase in labor productivity. However, since the average proportion is on the order of 20 percent, significant overfulfillment of piece-rate norms would inevitably lead to overexpenditures of the wage fund.[31] Since changes in piece-rate norms are legally permitted only when technical conditions of work are altered, this would seem to leave the enterprise in an untenable position if productivity of piece workers should improve either because of greater labor intensity or because of movement upward on the learning curve in the production of a given line of products.

One might speculate that the result of this system of linking wage fund increases to productivity is to cause management to prefer not to have unplanned increases in labor productivity, at least for piece workers, except to the degree that they arise from changes which are clearly technical and require no additional worker effort. Piece workers, understanding the restriction on their earnings which is established by the enterprise's total wage fund, might be expected to hold back on overfulfilling their work norms. Some evidence that this latter does indeed occur is provided by the fact that there is very little overfulfillment of piece norms in the machinebuilding vvb. Thus the level of work effort might be expected to suffer in comparison with countries with a different incentive system for manual workers.

It is, of course, extremely difficult to test this last hypothesis by casual observation of a few factories. Not only is it difficult to evaluate work effort in individual workplaces by walking through a shop, but the intensity of effort is a function of the time of day, and thus random factors can have a major effect on one's observations. For what it is worth, however, my impression of three different factories in three different industries was that workpace was steady but rather slow. Work tended not to be machine paced, as by a conveyor, even when this could have been readily accomplished. No managers seemed concerned about the level of worker effort. When I suggested to the general director

[31] In a number of my interviews, it was denied that this was a problem. It was pointed out that productivity of overhead personnel would also rise in such a case, while their earnings would not change. This can be true, however, only in enterprises where the ratio of piece-rate workers is quite small: i.e., a maximum of approximately 20 percent in the vvb discussed earlier.

of one enterprise that the pace seemed slow, he brushed my comment aside with the statement that this was not so, since workers were fulfilling their "scientifically determined norms"; but he was clearly reluctant to pursue the matter.

In an assembly shop in which sixty people were working in a single shift, piece workers were each taught two or three quite specialized jobs and were compulsorily shifted between them every three to four weeks. While one advantage of this frequent job change was said to be a versatility which is useful in replacing workers who quit or who are absent on a given day, the main reason for the system was quite clearly to reduce the job alienation believed inherent in a combination of extreme and permanent division of labor. Here, management was presumably sacrificing productivity (achieved through continued specialization) for social goals.

Even more striking was the sacrifice by piece workers of productivity, and thus of potential earnings, for greater safety. In sharp contrast to the pattern which is so frequently observable in American factories, I saw no machines in East Germany from which workers had removed safety devices which slow down the rate of production.[32]

Of course, the disincentive to rapidly paced work has less economic significance in the G.D.R. than it would have in a country which was not as highly developed and had not inherited the work traditions found in Germany. By and large, the plants I observed were efficient manufacturing operations. Furthermore, despite the lack of any close supervision by foremen, I did not see workers absenting themselves excessively from their work places or remaining idle while there. Nevertheless, the prevalence of a slow workpace—particularly in the many activities I observed where productivity depended heavily upon individual effort —is bound to have its effect upon productivity.

PLAN FULFILLMENT AND PLAN CHANGES

The nature of East German planning for production units, as we have seen in Chapter 5 and in the material presented so far in this chapter, is substantially different from Romanian planning. East German managers of *Kombinate* and enterprises are judged much more according to financial criteria than are their counterparts in Romania, and they are given substantially more freedom to exercise economic choice.

---

[32] Perhaps related to this is the fact that the official statistics as to reported accidents on the job show only half as high an accident rate in the G.D.R. as in West Germany. I am indebted to Professor Lynn Turgeon for pointing this out. I suspect, however, that the standards of reporting are dissimilar. (*Jahrbuch 1971*, p. 74 and Statistisches Bundesamt, *Statistisches Jahrbuch für die Bundesrepublik Deutschland, 1971*, W. Kohlhammer, Stuttgart and Mainz: 1971, p. 380.)

Yet the orthodox model of microeconomic behavior in centrally planned socialist economies,[33] a model which was developed with the Soviet economy particularly in mind, does not seem to fit the G.D.R. any better than it fits Romania. Some of the deviations from the model, however, are radically different in the two east European countries.

In comparing East German behavior at the *Kombinat* and enterprise level with that implied by the orthodox model, I shall follow the same outline as that used for Romania in Chapter 4. But I should point out that an important modification of, and addition to, the conclusions drawn in this section are contained in the following section on bonuses. Here I deal exclusively with obligatory plan targets, while the following section deals with all targets which affect either bonus funds paid to the enterprise or *Kombinat* for general distribution, or bonuses which are specifically designated for its top managers.

With regard to both sections, it should be noted that my sample is much smaller in the East German than in the Romanian case, and the reliability of the results must be evaluated with that in mind.

Official figures for 1972 and 1973 show that 95 to 98 percent of all the enterprises operating under central ministries fulfilled their sales plan for the year in each of the two years; these, however, were declared to be the highest percentages ever achieved.[34] In the summer of 1970, a high official in the research institute of the State Planning Commission believed it was safe to estimate that at least 90 percent of all industrial enterprises fulfill at least 100 percent of *all* their obligatory planned tasks for the year. However, he also felt that, in general, they are reluctant to overfulfill their plans by any substantial precentage because of the probable effects of this on their following year's plan.[35]

During 1968 and 1969, the twenty or so enterprises of one VVB ranged in fulfillment of their annual plans for total production between 100 and 102 percent, and for net profits between 100 and 103 percent. For both these major plan indicators, median fulfillment was about 101 percent. For the first six months of 1970, the six *Kombinate* of the enlarged VVB ranged between 99.2 and 104.9 percent fulfillment of their labor productivity improvement plans, and they averaged 101.8 percent. These are the only production-unit data available which cover an entire subbranch of industry within the G.D.R.

[33] See Chapter 4.

[34] Plan fulfillment reports, *Die Wirtschaft*, 1973, 4, p. 15, and 1974, 5, p. 14.

[35] As was seen in Chapter 5, five-year financial norms were to be introduced in 1971 precisely so as to minimize this problem. But none of the managers I interviewed, who seemed reluctant to attempt substantially to exceed plan, volunteered to me that their attitudes would be changed in the future by the new regulations.

For the machinebuilding *Kombinat*, fulfillment of the net profit plan during the previous three years ran between 100 and 102 percent. For the eleven enterprises within the *Kombinat*, the range of profit fulfillment was between 97 and 105 percent.

In the garment *Kombinat* in 1969, each of the five enterprises was said to have fulfilled all of its major obligatory plan indicators by between 99.5 and 102 percent. In the same year, the garment enterprise in which I conducted interviews failed to fulfill its profit plan, but did fulfill its plan for total production.

The semiprivate firm fulfilled its output plan in four of the years 1965-69, but never exceeded it by more than 1.5 percent. In the one year during which it failed to meet the planned target by 4 percent, the failure was said to be due to nonreceipt of deliveries from a supplier enterprise.[36]

These data as to plan fulfillment appear to present a pattern for East German industry which is similar to that of Romania. It is true that the original aggregate annual plans for East German industry as a whole, both for total output and for labor productivity, were rather substantially underfulfilled during 1969 and 1970.[37] But there is no information as to whether this was due to underfulfillment in existing plants or to failure to bring planned capacity onto line at the expected speed. It is also the case that enterprise wage funds were widely overspent during 1970—and the usual penalty of deducting the overexpenditures from the enterprise bonus funds was not levied—but this is described as a very exceptional year.[38]

However, while the degree of plan fulfillment seems rather similar between the two countries, the situation is radically different with regard to plan changes during the course of the year. In the G.D.R., in sharp contrast to Romania, such plan changes seem to be of negligible significance.

All of the executives with whom I talked discussed plan changes during the course of the year as though they arose exclusively from alterations in the product-mix demands made upon production units by their superior organization, with compensating changes in the plan for net profits sometimes being made. Even such changes seem to be rare. I heard of no reports of changes in total planned production for the year.

---

[36] Evidence that this was indeed the reason is the fact the enterprise was exempted from fines for nonfulfillment of its sales contracts; such fines would normally be waived only if the enterprise were judged not to have been responsible for the failure.

[37] Deutsches Institut für Wirtschaftsforschung, *DDR-Wirtschaft* (Fischer Bücherei, Frankfurt am Main and Hamburg: 1971), p. 249.

[38] Paul Verner, *Bericht des Politbüros*, pp. 13-14.

Plans do not seem to be changed because of failures on the part of enterprises or *Kombinate* to meet the original plan targets, as is clearly the case in Romania.

A director of a light industry VVB insisted that there are never changes in the plan indicators for his plants. He pointed out that, even during 1970 when there was pressure for a national increase in exports to compensate for increased imports, domestic demand conditions in his industry prohibited any reduction in sales to the domestic market; as a result, export tasks were not expanded during the year, since there was no intention of increasing the target of total production.

In the machinebuilding VVB, the deputy economic director stated that, during the last two or three years, the VVB has received instructions during the course of the year which changed the product mix of 0.4 to 1 percent of annual production. The ministry has a reserve of 4 percent of the ministry's total planned net profit which can theoretically be used to compensate for the effect of such plan changes. In fact, said the deputy economic director, it is very rare for the VVB to receive during the year any reduction in its planned net profit task; the financial head of the VVB claimed that this VVB had never received any such compensation for changes in physical indicators.

In the garment enterprise, in contrast, there were apparently significant changes in product-mix plans during the course of both 1969 and 1970. In the latter year, exports were ordered increased at the expense of production for the domestic market; presumably in compensation for an unfavorable effect upon product mix, this change was accompanied by a reduction in the amount of the enterprise's net profits which were to be paid to the state budget. During the first quarter of 1969, an additional type of product—one produced from a synthetic cloth which the enterprise had not used previously—was substituted for part of its originally planned output. The enterprise ran into production difficulties as a result of this shift, and was only partially compensated by a change in its profit plan.[39]

The semiprivate firm had had its product-mix plan changed during the course of the year in only one year out of the last five. The change arose from a subcontractor having been ordered to produce a different product, which in turn forced the semiprivate firm to produce the previously subcontracted items.

These interview comments as to changes in plans during the course of the year can be summed up with the statement that such alterations appear to provide no significant explanation for the success of East

[39] Another director in the same enterprise insisted that the enterprise's troubles resulted, not from this shift in product mix, but from a different cause. The *Kombinat* general director took the same view. It is thus not clear whether the enterprise was indeed undercompensated for the shift in planned product mix.

German enterprises and *Kombinate* in meeting their targets for at least the major planning indicators. Targets were not reduced, as they often are in Romania, to match achievements. Instead, the explanation for the East German enterprise success would seem to lie in the fact that the original plans are not set at particularly strenuous levels.

The general directors of both *Kombinate* spoke of their having "reserves" built into their plans. One of them said that an advantage of the New Economic System, in contrast with the past, is that one can speak openly of the existence of such reserves. The second man laughingly stated that he was not afraid to speak to me about them, even though an official of the State Planning Commission was present at this interview.

Given the existence of such "reserves," the question naturally arises as to why one does not see greater overfulfillment of enterprise plans. Probably the issue is sharpest with regard to the profit plan. For, as we shall see in our discussion of bonuses, the only plan overfulfillment which was rewarded until 1972 was that of net profits (and of labor productivity, as we saw earlier, through an increased wage fund). Even more significant, slight improvements in efficiency or output are likely to have much larger relative effects on profits.

The answer is obvious enough: avoidance of substantial plan overfulfillment is a matter of conscious managerial policy. The general director of one *Kombinat* spoke specifically of increasing research and development expenditures in years when net profits would otherwise be "excessive." An enterprise director mentioned quality improvement as a means of avoiding excess profits. A vvb director said that enterprises used their freedom to choose the appropriate year to write off obsolete stocks of spare-parts production and of equipment in order to "manage" their profits. The general director of the second *Kombinat* spoke of choosing to produce low-profit items when he exceeded planned output. In the context of a discussion of the "management" of reserves, he said that his planning aid was the colleague whom he had to trust the most, even more than his first deputy.

Such avoidance of substantial overfulfillment, however, should not be regarded as a peculiar feature of a nationally planned socialist economy. Similar attitudes and results are found in large, decentralized American corporations; here, divisions seem to show the same reluctance to exceed their annual budgets of profit or profit percentages. The notion of divisional "reserves" against unexpected misadventures are accepted just as much by large American corporations as they are by East German ministries and vvbs.[40]

[40] For example, one division of a large American industrial company had, at the time of my interviews there, achieved its profit plan in five of the previous six

Directors of East German *Kombinate* and enterprises can use unneeded reserves existing in their annual plans so as to push further their efforts for future improvements in the products and technology of the unit. Second, they can use them to produce a higher proportion of low-profit goods. If this is indeed what occurs, as has been suggested in some of my interviews, then they are responding in a fashion rather similar to what has been observed in divisions of American companies: attempting simply to meet the critical quantitative parameters of their annual plans (i.e., to satisfice with regard to the formal plan indicators), and to use any additional resources in order to meet goals espoused— but not planned in detail—by executives in the organizational level above theirs.[41]

BONUSES

Bonuses may be treated under two headings: those paid from the enterprise's own fund and those paid as special grants by higher organs.

The enterprise's own bonus fund[42] is formed from net profits. The total maximum bonus money available for the enterprise's labor force is planned as a fixed percentage of the bonus fund of the previous year, plus a predetermined proportion of the increase in net profits of the enterprise during the current year. The percentage of the increase in net profits which is designated for the bonus fund is differentiated by individual enterprise, but it is normally to remain the same for five years.

While the maximum size of the enterprise's bonus fund is thus linked to the net profits earned, deductions from this maximum are made on three grounds. The organ above the enterprise is instructed to determine each year, at its own discretion, two plan indicators for the enterprise; nonfulfillment of these tasks reduces the bonus fund by 15 to 30 percent. Nonfulfillment of other plan indicators cannot lead to a reduction of the bonus fund, nor can overfulfillment of the two chosen indicators lead

---

years, and in the sixth year had missed it by only 10 percent. This was possible because of a hedge against uncertainty which existed in the profit plans. Yet, despite the existence of this demonstrated hedge, the division never turned in a single year's profits that were better than planned. (See David Granick, *Managerial Comparisons of Four Developed Countries*, The M.I.T. Press, Cambridge, Mass.: 1972, p. 36.)

[41] Ibid., chapter 2.

[42] This system which was intended to govern the years 1971-75 but was in fact changed in early 1972, is described in "Rechtsvorschriften zur Durchführung der in der Grundsatzregelung für die Gestaltung des ökonomischen Systems des Sozialismus in der Deutschen Demokratischen Republik im Zeitraum 1971 bis 1975 enthaltenen Aufgaben," approved by the Council of Ministers on April 29, 1970, *Die Wirtschaft*, 1970, 19/20, Supplement 15, pp. 85-87. The system was much the same during 1969 and 1970.

to an increase. Finally, if the annual wage fund is exceeded, or if improvement in labor productivity is less than was planned, the bonus fund is reduced accordingly.

The minimum enterprise bonus fund is virtually guaranteed at a sum equaling one-quarter of one month's earnings of an average employee in the economy; the maximum is established at one and one-third to one and two-third months, depending on the kind of enterprise.[43] It is my impression that the average bonus is about one month's wage. Individual worker and employee variations from the average seem normally to be kept within the range of one-third of one month's to one and one-half months' wage, and this range appears to apply to all levels of the hierarchy. The same pattern prevails in *Kombinat* and VVB headquarters. It is only in the ministries that no normal bonus is paid.

Most of the bonus fund (two-thirds to 85 percent in the enterprises for which I have information) is distributed in end-of-year bonuses.[44] All skill grades and managerial levels within a given enterprise must share in the end-of-year bonus in proportion to their monthly earnings, but individual variations are permitted within the range of one-third of a month and two months' salary. In practice, however, all upper-management personnel may be totally deprived of end-of-year bonuses.

The principles of distribution to individuals of these end-of-year bonus funds are decided independently for each enterprise by its management and its trade union organization. In one *Kombinat*, each department of each enterprise was graded monthly on the quality of its production; depending on the results, its workers were credited with between 80 and 120 percent of their "normal" end-of-year bonus earnings for that month. In another enterprise, the quality standards met by each individual worker affected his end-of-year bonus. There were also payments for seniority and for shiftwork.

The relatively small proportion of the enterprise bonus fund which is paid out during the year seems to be handled at the discretion of management. Most of this appears to be paid for results of competitions between sections of the enterprise, but this is sometimes interpreted as a standard additional payment to all workers of every section which meets its monthly production quota. There are also special bonuses which are awarded for a variety of activities such as a new production idea or attendance in a special Sunday shift.

---

[43] The maximum was established in marks by the legislation, but it is not absolutely certain whether this was for one year or for five (ibid., p. 86). Although one East German professor interpreted it as applying to the bonus fund for each year, I am here using the opposite interpretation provided by a VVB deputy economic director. (Certainly this interpretation was correct by 1971.)

[44] This has been the case since 1966 (*Die Wirtschaft*, 1967, 7, p. 2).

As was said earlier, the maximum bonus fund can be reduced sharply for nonfulfillment of two plan indicators chosen by the organ above the enterprise. Within the machinebuilding vvb, one of these two is always the export plan, at least for enterprises which have a substantial percentage of exports. The export plan in this vvb is stated in term of both the total amount of exports and the amount of exports to convertible currency areas in particular; moreover, it is divided into quarters, and failure to meet the plan in one quarter cannot be compensated in the next. This prerequisite for maximum bonus payment is stringent, particularly the portion dealing with sales to convertible currency areas where conditions of international competition may be the determining influence on fulfillment.

As for the second plan indicator chosen, this vvb makes varying choices for different enterprises, depending on what it considers to be the problems of the particular enterprise. A frequent plan indicator used is the ratio of annual production to fixed capital. For one enterprise, the second indicator was the supply of two specific structure-determining products in specified amounts by the end of March and the end of April; this indicator was used in order to control the speed with which new products were brought up to normal production volume.

For the garment enterprise, the two plan indicators for 1969 both concerned fulfillment of all sales contracts; one was for exports and the other for domestic production. The enterprise ran into difficulties in this year; although its annual production reached the planned level, it was unable to respect delivery dates and was penalized for violation of contracts. Following this, one new plan indicator was chosen for 1970. While the indicator of fulfillment of export contracts remained, the second indicator selected was fulfillment on schedule of the year's list of all rationalization measures planned. To cite an example, for the purchase of a new machine, this indicator included the date of installation and the date at which production on the machine should reach the level considered standard for that piece of equipment.

The example of the garment enterprise suggests that the choice of the two plan indicators whose fulfillment is to serve as a constraint on bonus fund earnings depends on the status of the enterprise. For 1969, the tasks chosen were those of achieving production and sales goals, but the means were not specified. However, after the enterprise's failure in 1969, one physical indicator for 1970 was of a highly specific and detailed nature; supervision over the schedule of fulfillment of this indicator gave the *Kombinat* much more detailed authority over the enterprise's management than it had had previously. The shift presumably reflected the degree of confidence placed in the enterprise's management by its supervisory body.

Deductions from the maximum bonus fund are in fact made for failure to achieve the two plan indicators used as constraints on bonus payments. This is seen from the experience of the machinebuilding vvb in 1969. In this year, all enterprises achieved at least 100 percent fulfillment of their planned net profit. However, deductions from the maximum bonus fund were imposed upon all but a few of the smallest of the twenty or so enterprises. For one large enterprise for which exact data were given me, these deductions constituted 14.3 percent of the maximum bonus fund earned.

Such determinants of the enterprise's bonus fund suggest that we must be careful in defining "plan fulfillment" for the enterprise or *Kombinat*. Earlier, I have defined plan fulfillment as the meeting of the obligatory plan tasks. But if we say that the type of plan fulfillment which really matters is that determining the size of the enterprise's wage and bonus funds, then we should define the truly relevant objectives as the following four: (1) Keeping within the allotted wage fund. (2) Achieving complete fulfillment of whichever two plan indicators are set as constraints on the payment of earned bonuses. (3) Earning of net profits, with overfulfillment of this plan increasing bonuses. (4) Achieving increases in labor productivity, with overfulfillment of this plan permitting increases in wage payments. The other plan indicators—whether obligatory or not—do not affect either the size of the wage fund or the size of the bonus fund.

This suggests that identical obligatory plan indicators are of differing importance to different enterprises, even those within the same vvb. Still more interesting, results which are not covered by "obligatory" plan indicators may be included among the two constraints on bonus payments, while "obligatory" plan indicators can be excluded. For example, the ratio of annual production to fixed capital was one of the most frequently used constraints on bonus payments within the machinebuilding vvb; yet this was only a calculating-indicator rather than an obligatory plan indicator for this vvb. Similarly, meeting of the precise terms of sales contracts constituted in 1969 both of the constraints for the garment enterprise; yet neither of the two was an obligatory plan indicator.

In addition to the bonus fund of the enterprise, the vvb and *Kombinat* have funds of their own for special bonus payments. These are used not only for awarding nonmanagerial personnel for special successes, but also to pay what appears to be the major portion of the total bonuses of the top-managerial personnel of the enterprises.

Data are available for the total bonuses paid during 1969 to the general directors of three of the major enterprises of the machinebuilding vvb, and these are presented in Table 6.1. It should be noted that all three of these enterprises fulfilled their plans for net profit, but all

TABLE 6.1: Bonuses of Enterprise General Directors from All Sources, for all 1969 (percentage of one month's salary)

	1st Enterprise	2nd Enterprise	3rd Enterprise
1. From enterprise bonus fund: end-of-year bonus	67	54 ⎫	
2. From vvb bonus fund:		⎬ 91	91
a. End-of-year bonus	83	91 ⎭	
b. Sum of small bonuses paid throughout the year	67	91	0
c. Special bonus for developing and placing into production a new product line	333[a]	0	0
3. Total bonus	550	236	91

[a] This was quite exceptional, and could be earned at most once every few years.

three also suffered deductions from the maximum enterprise bonus fund earned.

These enterprise general directors within a single vvb received in bonuses during the year between nine-tenths of one month's salary and five and one-half months' salary. (But the five and one-half months' bonus was paid largely for results which could not be achieved more than once every few years.) The range is widened if we include the garment making enterprise, where none of the seven top managers earned bonuses from any source in 1969. This is a fairly broad spread, and clearly much wider than that applying to employees other than top managers. Managerial bonuses are determined subjectively by the *Kombinat* or vvb general director, with approval required by the comparable level of the national trade union organization. However, I have seen one case of a management-by-objectives agreement being drawn up between the vvb and an enterprise general director; here, seven broad categories of objectives were listed which had to be met if the general director was to receive maximum bonus from the vvb's own fund.

Fines and salary reductions for managers do not seem to play any significant role in the East German system. I have heard of only one top manager who was fined, and the next year he received an especially high bonus as compensation.

If we consider plan fulfillment as constituting the meeting of all objectives which enter either into the payment of the enterprise bonus fund or into managerial bonuses, then the record of fulfillment by East German industry is much poorer than if one uses only the principal obligatory plan indicators. Yet it would not be unreasonable to consider the criteria used for bonus payment as the operational plan indicators. Using this standard of evaluation, it is not at all clear that the "plans" drawn up for East German enterprises are easy to fulfill.[45] The desire to meet all these bonus criteria as fully as possible helps further to explain why enterprises do not overfulfill their principal obligatory plan indicators, including that of net profit, by appreciable margins.

Enterprise Stocks and Bank Loans

It is my impression that the Industry and Trade Bank exercises a principal control over the level of stocks held in enterprises. The ratio of working capital to sales was not listed as even a calculating-indicator for enterprises, *Kombinate*, or vvbs in 1971, and only one of the units in which I interviewed regarded it as a critical indicator in its own right. It was not even listed as an available option for the vvbs to use as one of the two constraints on bonus payments by their enterprises.[46]

[45] Some key indices of plan fulfillment during the first half of 1970 for the six *Kombinate* of the machinebuilding vvb are worth noting here. It should be remembered that all the enterprises of this vvb had a record of fulfilling 100 percent of their annual plans for both net profit and total production. The three indices listed below (Table 6.2) were the only ones used in the inter-*Kombinat* competition within the vvb. (A fourth index—payments to the budget from net profit—was also listed. However, since such payments constitute a primary obligation of the *Kombinate* which must be met even if net profits fall below plan, a vvb director agreed that this index was meaningless.)

TABLE 6.2: Plan Fulfillment of Indices Used in the Inter-*Kombinat* Competition in the Machinebuilding vvb (first half 1970)

Plan Index	*Kombinate*						
	1st	2nd	3rd	4th	5th	6th	Unweighted Average for the vvb
				(percentage)			
Total sales shipments undelivered at the contracted date (percent of total sales)	0.1	2.1	0.0	1.2	1.5	2.8	1.3
Stocks held above plan (percent of planned stocks)	5.3	2.7	19.5	6.1	0.0	7.6	6.9
Increase in labor productivity[a] above that planned (percent of planned increase)	3.8	4.9	0.0	2.7	0.0	−0.8	1.8

[a] Measured in value-added.

[46] "Beschluss über das ökonomische System 1971," pp. 732-33, and "Rechtsvorschriften," p. 86.

Rather, the impact of deviations of the ratio from that planned seems to be felt primarily through the effect of increases in holdings of stocks upon the net profit of the enterprise. This effect, in turn, depends upon whether such accumulations are greater than planned and, if so, how the local office of the Industry Bank evaluates both the reasons for the above-plan growth and the efforts of the enterprise to get back to normal. When stocks increased in accord with plan in 1970, the marginal cost to the enterprise was usually 9.6 percent of that portion financed by credit,[47] and it could be as low as 7.8 percent. However, if stocks were larger than planned, the marginal cost could rise to 18 percent.[48] These rates must be interpreted in the light of the absence of inflation; i.e., they are real and not simply monetary interest rates.

The cost of even sharply excessive stocks is not prohibitive for those enterprises which are able to cover their planned net profit in spite of the capital charges; this is because 50 to 70 percent of the resultant reduction in net profits would have gone to the state budget in any case.[49] But all other enterprises must make the complete profit payments to the budget which had been planned for them, even though their net profits fall below the planned level; for them, the full marginal cost of the stock is a deduction from the net profits left to the enterprise.[50] Thus excess stock holdings cost these enterprises between 7.8 and 18 percent depending upon the evaluation of blame made by the local branch of the Bank. The difference between these two percentages can have a significant effect both upon the enterprise bonus fund and upon the availability of funds for expansion in the following year.

Not only is the local office of the Industry and Trade Bank expected to evaluate the reasons for above-plan accumulation of stocks, and to levy interest charges accordingly, but it also participates in the decision as to what the level of planned stock accumulation should be. In the

---

[47] Six percent tax on capital plus 3.6 percent annual interest charge. While I was told in one vvb that the 3.6 percent rate was "normal," a 1970 source declared that 5 percent was the "basic" rate. Both sources described 1.8 percent as the minimum interest rate. (W. Luchterhand, "Grundlegende Erforderniss . . . ," in *Die ökonomische Stimulierung der socialistischen Produktion*, Verlag Die Wirtschaft: East Berlin, 1970, pp. 240 and 247.)

[48] This is the rate which I was told that some enterprises in the machinebuilding vvb have actually paid.

[49] For the six *Kombinate* in the same vvb which were analyzed in footnote 45, only one was far above its planned stock level: namely, 19.5 percent in excess. It is perhaps no accident that this was also the only one of the *Kombinate* which, at that point in the year, had earned more than the planned net profit. This profit picture may explain why the *Kombinat* management felt it could take such liberties with stocks. Since it had in any case earned 2.4 percent above planned net profits, it probably had no concern for earning more.

[50] This situation was modified at the end of 1971 (see Chapter 7, footnote 27).

case of the machinebuilding *Kombinat* studied, the local office kept three university graduates (one of whom had worked in the headquarters of the *Kombinat*'s own ministry before transferring to bank employment) engaged half-time on the affairs of this one *Kombinat*. In view of the educational level of these inspectors and the career history of one of the three, it may be presumed that they were intended to exercise independent judgment rather than simply to rubber-stamp the views of the *Kombinat*'s VVB.

THE COMMUNIST PARTY, TRADE UNIONS, AND MASS PARTICIPATION

Managements of enterprises and *Kombinate* are supervised and controlled primarily by the official state bodies which we have discussed up to this point. In addition, of course, employee-participation organizations also play a role. From the fact that the Communist Party and the trade union each normally employ a full-time official in even the smaller enterprises and in the VVBs—and that this official's expected competence is suggested by a salary which ranges from that of a department head to that of a director—we might expect that these organizations play a larger role in the East German enterprise than they do in the Romanian. Unfortunately, I have not been able to form a serious impression as to their activity.

With regard to many issues, enterprise managers see no clear demarcation between government and Party channels. For example, directors of the machinebuilding *Kombinat* insisted that they discuss major matters with both lines of authority. The questions so treated are said usually to transcend economic issues and to affect social relationships. Examples cited were the direction and speed of growth of the *Kombinat*, new enterprises to be joined to it, and measures to be taken to prevent individual alienation as the larger *Kombinat* takes over the functions of the enterprises. But directors also treat through Party channels such issues as the choice of product lines to be developed over the period of the five-year plan,[51] and the individual countries to which sales priority should be given within the compass of the export tasks set for the *Kombinat*. These matters are discussed both with the regional Party committee and inside the *Kombinat* Party committee; the rationale given is that the Party has officials who are just as expert on these matters as the professionals of the state organizations.

[51] For a single year, these lines are fairly well determined for this *Kombinat* by the state's decisions as to structure-determining products. But the demarcation between structure-determining and other products is regarded as fuzzy when one goes beyond the bounds of one year.

The absence of clearly separated lines of authority also applies to problems of emergency aid. Thus, in the severe winter of 1970, one enterprise which rented factory space from the municipality found itself without heat because of a boiler breakdown. Complaints to the city did no good, but the problem was solved following an inspection visit by a regional Party official.

The regional Party committee must approve the appointment of the general director of an enterprise or *Kombinat*, and the Party committee of the enterprise or *Kombinat* must approve the appointment of other directors. The significance of this right, as one might expect, varies; one enterprise reported that pro forma approval was normally given, while in another enterprise it was claimed that the Party bodies play an active role in the appointment process. In any case, their authority to block appointments and to force removal of directors make it obvious that managers should not bypass them with regard to important issues.

The general pattern seems to be typified by the situation in one enterprise, where the personnel head insisted that he—rather than the Party secretary—was responsible for developing a promotion plan for the professionals and managers of the enterprise. Yet the Party organization had its own such plan for its own members, and this had to be synchronized with that of the personnel head. The possible conflict was considerably eased by the fact that the Party secretary had worked as an engineer on the plant's staff until his election five years earlier, and that the personnel head was also the deputy Party secretary who, when I interviewed him during the secretary's vacation, was so occupied with his Party role that it was more convenient for him to see me at his Party office than at his personnel desk. Nothing much would have been altered if the two men had exchanged jobs.

Much ado is made in the East German literature over the importance of mass participation in the running of industrial units. The trade unions of the individual enterprises are represented on a *Kombinat* committee, and those of the *Kombinate* on a vvb committee. Both the *Kombinate* and vvbs have advisory economic councils; these have as members not only outside experts, but also trade union and Party representatives as well as individual manual workers and employees who were chosen to participate. The enterprise plan and progress in fulfilling it are discussed both at mass meetings and at meetings of union shop stewards.

Nevertheless, emphasis upon secrecy sharply limits the possibilities for such participation. The full list of obligatory plan targets for the enterprise and for all higher units is secret, and available only to members of top management, the members of the Party committee, and the trade union secretary. In one enterprise, a director said that only he and the other directors—but no one else in the enterprise—knew the obligatory plan targets for his *Kombinat*, and that no one in the enterprise knew the list of targets for the vvb. Given this situation, the formal requirement of "acceptance" of the enterprise plan by the total workforce, or at least by a meeting of the shop stewards, can be only a formality. The general director of one enterprise regarded the function of mass participation as consisting primarily of mustering support for specific measures undertaken by the management in individual shops. The notion of "workers management" does not seem to play any significant role in the G.D.R.

The trade union in the enterprise is not regarded as an organization devoted to promoting workers' benefits which go beyond the net improvement called for in the plan; rather, it is intended to assure that these benefits are distributed equitably and that the division of the package is consistent with member wishes. The bonus system for the enterprise is determined and implemented by a joint union-management committee. Shop stewards are on hand for worker complaints as to work norms. An annual collective agreement between the enterprise union and the management spells out details of improvements in working conditions, amenities, and safety, and it specifies educational programs to be carried out at the enterprise's expense—sometimes even naming individuals who are to be sent to universities or junior colleges. Camps, nurseries, the distribution of cheap tickets to vacation spots, and the like are administered by the trade union from the enterprise's social funds.

In sum, the role of these organizations and of mass participation in East German industry seems to be quite the traditional one for CMEA countries. In contrast with Romania, there appears to be a higher proportion of paid union and Party officials; perhaps this indicates a greater level of activity by these organizations.

Semiprivate Companies

We saw in Table 5.1 that 12.5 percent of all East German industrial employment in 1970 was in semiprivate companies. Although these firms were nationalized during 1972, their importance at the time of my interviews warrants some comments on their operation. My analysis rests entirely upon interviews in a single such firm which was then one of the largest of its type in the G.D.R., and which was the principal national producer of a minor line of consumer products.

The enterprise had been founded in 1945 as a private firm with one employee. The owner had been a skilled worker before the war; thereafter he was a soldier and, after being captured, had worked at his trade in the Soviet Union. By 1956 he had taken a partner who handled the commercial side of the business, and the company had reached an employment of one hundred workers in a number of small shops located in rented buildings.

When in 1956 the East German government began purchasing participations in private firms, the two owners promptly offered to turn their company into such a semiprivate firm. The offer was accepted; the owners' share was evaluated at the book value of the business (with no credit for good will), and the government made up its share by contributing money for expansion.

The original owner, in analyzing his reasons for converting the business, listed three. First, he "felt safer" (presumably from the danger of expropriation) by contributing to socialism. Second, it represented a political awakening on his part. Third, it was the only feasible means of financing further growth. The high tax rate on profits effectively prevented any self-financing of expansion, and there was no private money available for investment. While it was true that the firm could borrow from the state bank, such credits never were granted in amounts above the owner's own equity. Thus sale of a participating share to the state was the only recourse for owners who viewed themselves as entrepreneurs. A fourth reason, which he did not list but which was major for many owners, was that an owner's net income after taxes might be raised substantially by converting part of what had been treated as profits into salary.[52]

The legal form that all the semiprivate firms were given was one in which directors could be discharged only for cause by the annual stockholders' meeting. The former owners were confirmed as the sole directors. If they were dismissed, they would continue to receive their share of profits as silent partners. But in fact, so the original owner told me, he personally knew of no owners in the G.D.R. who had been removed as directors. The state, he said, would not have purchased a participation if it had not had confidence in the business acumen of the men involved.

As the semiprivate firm expanded, the relevant ministry set for it medium-term output targets which would not be met in the existing rented space. Consideration was given to building a new consolidated factory, but raising the funds for this would have meant increasing the state share of ownership to some 99 percent. The private owners regarded this share as too high, and were fortunately able to resolve the problem by renting a new consolidated factory built by the municipality.

Clearly, there was some limit below which these private owners did

---

[52] The marginal tax on salary was 20 percent as compared with 90 percent on profits (Gert Leptin, *Die deutsche Wirtschaft nach 1945*, Leske Verlag, Opladen: 1970, p. 22).

not wish to see their share fall. However, the original owner made a strong case for the view that such an attitude was irrational. For the owner-directors had the same managerial powers whether they owned 2 or 80 percent of the business (this is the range which he thought actually existed in 1970 in semiprivate firms); if the expansion was commercially warranted, a reduction in their share would not reduce the absolute profits they received; and salaries earned as directors could only rise as the size of the business increased.

At the time of my interviews, the two owner-directors each earned as salary about four times the wage of the average worker in the plant,[53] or perhaps 10 percent more than they would have received (including bonuses) if they had been general directors of comparable state-owned enterprises. In addition, their share of posttax profits constituted a similar monthly sum. But since the posttax profits seem to have been devoted essentially or entirely to reinvestment, the net cost to the state— measured as the increase in resources devoted to consumption expenditures—of running the enterprise as a semiprivate firm rather than through complete government ownership was almost nil.

It was said in 1970 that it was often difficult to persuade the son of an owner-director to take over his father's position when he retired. The ambivalent social position was an uncomfortable one for younger men, and when they were professionally qualified for managerial positions they preferred simply to take their share of the profits and to work in the state sector.

The plans and regulations under which the company operated were much the same as those applying to state-owned enterprises. True, there were minor variations. For example, the bonus fund was partially constituted from the wage fund rather than entirely out of profits. Additional bonuses were paid as a sharply degressive percentage of total export sales, with no calculation being made of "export profits." No portion of the amortization allowances were channeled into the state budget, and the procedure for absorbing profits into the budget differed from that used for state-owned enterprises. But these were matters of detail which did not seem to cause significant differences in the actual operations of this enterprise from its state-owned counterparts.

A major distinction in form was that state organs such as the vvB had no authority to order a semiprivate firm to change its product mix in a designated fashion when this would be expensive for the firm. However, since the vvB could advise such a shift, the only substantive distinction seems to have been that the vvB might be forced to bear most of the costs. Moreover, if the firm had been a state enterprise, the vvB in such

---

[53] The firm was in a low-wage industry. Their salaries were somewhat less than three times the earnings of the average East German worker.

a case would have reduced both the enterprise's planned net profits and the percentage of these net profits taken by the budget; thus this limitation on the power of the state organ did little more than create symmetry between the position of the semiprivate and state-owned enterprise.

Of greater significance was the fact that the rate of expansion of the company might be restrained by the nature of its ownership. Two factors were at work in the semiprivate firm studied. The first was that net investments could be made only at a fixed multiple of the investments which the owner-directors could afford out of posttax profits, since the private owners held veto power over the diminution of their share of the business. Perhaps even more important was that government policy dictated that expansion of semiprivate enterprises should be slower than that of their state-owned counterparts in the same branch. It is possible that these restraints caused investments in the branch to be divided somewhat differently among enterprises than would have been the case if all had been state owned.

One would like to know whether owner-directors gave greater emphasis to earning profits than was the case in the state-owned enterprises. On the very slim basis of this single semiprivate company, my feeling is that no substantial difference existed.[54] A major reason is that the tax rate on profits received by owner-directors was so high as to provide little financial incentive for actions to increase these profits. While the owner-directors paid only the standard income tax rate of 20 percent on their salaries, they were taxed an average of 80 percent on profits. Of even more significance, the marginal tax rate on profits was said to mount to approximately 95 percent.

A leading manager of the enterprise thought that the two principal differences in practice between state-owned and semiprivate enterprises were the following: (1) The regulation of the semiprivate firms was less detailed. As an example, he pointed out that his firm did not employ the system of forms laid down for all state-owned enterprises of the branch for scheduling production and for the issuance of materials. (2) The owner-directors of semiprivate enterprises were usually older than the directors of state enterprises and were more cautious in their investment policies. It is noteworthy that this manager did not place great emphasis upon these differences.

One might expect that political control would have been particularly strict over semiprivate firms, and that the state would have had a

[54] In this company, for example, export demand in socialist countries was substantially more than the company could meet. Yet the firm had engaged in three voluntary price reductions since 1963, and had also improved quality at the expense of foregone profits. The principal owner-director explained this policy by saying that he was more concerned with market stability in export markets for the next ten to twenty years than in higher current profits.

"representative" in the company's management. Such did not, however, appear to be the case in the semiprivate company studied. Not only was I told this directly, but the statement seems to be borne out by the fact that the Communist Party organizaion of the company numbered only 2 percent of the total labor force, and that these members were all manual workers with the exception of one foreman. The Party secretary (who carried out this function in addition to his full-time job) struck me as rather incompetent; a management representative said that neither the Party nor the trade union secretary played much of a role in company decisions, even on such matters as allocation of the bonus fund or the setting of piece norms. I was told that there was also considerably less political activity in this semiprivate firm than was typically seen in state enterprises.

CHAPTER 7

Conclusions as to the New Economic System, and Modifications since 1970

CONCLUSIONS AS OF 1970

IN Chapter 4, we saw that the operation of Romanian enterprises and *centrale* departs sharply from that depicted in the orthodox microeconomic model of Soviet-type economies. There, however, it was because of extreme centralization of all economic decisions within the ministerial headquarters. While "success indicator" suboptimizing by individual production units was absent, so too was local initiative.

East German reality seems to be depicted no more effectively than the Romanian by the orthodox model. True, top managerial bonuses are more important than in Romania: the difference between major success and failure may well be rewarded by an annual increment on top of salary of some 20 percent or higher. But the bonuses are more a function of prompt and detailed fulfillment of all sales contracts than of such an aggregative index as that of value of sales or that of net profits under conditions of fixed prices. Thus the danger that suboptimizing decisions will be made in order to achieve designated success indicators is not overly great. Moreover, the critical constraints on payment of enterprise bonus funds—for whose nonattainment enterprises are penalized 15 to 30 percent of the funds earned—change from year to year for the same enterprise, and they cover in total a wide gamut of activity. By far the most substantial bonus recorded in Table 6.1 was paid to a general director for successful product development carried out over a number of years; thus the major bonus incentive observed in my records was for precisely the efforts which the orthodox microeconomic model describes as most sharply neglected because it is the least rewarded.

The Romanian and East German enterprises both deviate sharply from the orthodox model, and they seem similar in the degree to which they meet obligatory plan indicators and at the same time avoid "success indicator" suboptimization. Here, however, the similarity ends. Unlike the Romanian pattern, plan changes for East German units seem to be quite unusual. Financial indicators are given primary rather than secondary emphasis. Most important by far was the sharp difference in

1970 in the degree of authority given to and accepted by management at the enterprise and *Kombinat* level.

The most significant area of enterprise initiative and authority was in the planning process itself. For certain structure-determining products and tasks, the East German enterprise, *Kombinat*, and even the vvb were under strict central control. Aside from these, however, the production unit was given considerable liberty in a wide range of activities. The most important of these was the selection of its product mix and customers and, to an apparently lesser degree, of its material inputs. The second most important was the choice of methods of rationalization and of development of new products, upon which great emphasis is placed. The first set of decisions is incorporated into contracts, the fulfillment of which becomes probably the single most important criterion of an enterprise's success. The second is incorporated in the enterprise's plan, for which it is then held responsible. The degree of such freedom is considerably greater in light industry than in the production of producer goods, but a substantial amount was also seen in the machinebuilding *Kombinat* studied.

Even product "balancing," quite centralized in Romania and generally in the other CMEA countries where it exists (i.e., excluding Hungary), was a rather decentralized process in the G.D.R. The vvb had considerable control here, and individual *Kombinate* and enterprises were also important in the process. Thus, even before contracts are negotiated within the lines laid down by balancing decisions as to the distribution of each enterprise's product mix, the production unit has already exerted a surprising degree of influence.

The third area of liberty for the enterprise is in control over the composition of its labor force. Here it has operational freedom unrestricted by annual plans. The same is true with regard to changing the relative earnings of different skill-categories of employees, a freedom which is vital for its ability to recruit and hold the type of labor it needs. However, apparently-low labor turnover rates suggest the hypothesis that a good deal of uniformity in pay scales is imposed on the enterprises, most likely by the relevant trade unions.

Fulfillment of the major obligatory plan indicators does not appear to be an overtaxing task for enterprise and *Kombinat* managers. But, if we define "plan" as embodying all the conditions for full receipt of the enterprise bonus fund which is earned out of net profits, then the plan is a good deal stricter. This is shown by the fact that none of the important enterprises of the machinebuilding vvb which I studied had succeeded in meeting such conditions fully during 1969. "Reserves" are available to insure the meeting of total output targets and profit plans; but they are needed for the host of detailed problems whose solution is so important to the overall evaluation of the unit's management. This is particularly true because of the great emphasis placed throughout the East German economy upon product and process development; such investments in the enterprise's future can absorb an almost limitless amount of resources.

The emphasis upon financial criteria—least, to be sure, for the structure-determining sectors—deserves to be singled out. Not only was this true during the course of the year in the sense that operations were directed to achieving the critical profits plan but, far more important, financial considerations were vital in the planning process itself. Even in product balancing—let alone in the negotiation of detailed purchase and sales contracts—the balancing organ appeared to attempt to satisfy demand at existing prices only to the degree that such a product mix was consistent with the attainment of the profit plan. It is true that neither vvbs, *Kombinate*, nor enterprises attempt to maximize profits; rather, they "satisfice" at or close to the planned level. But in this regard they do not seem to differ appreciably from divisions in large, decentralized American corporations—and for fundamentally the same reasons.

A major restructuring both of costs and of prices of finished goods had been completed before my interviews in 1970, and a further restructuring was then in process. Prices, both of inputs and outputs, were based upon costs of production as of roughly 1966 or as of the time the product was introduced, whichever was later. Within individual branches, there was some degree of homogeneity of profit mark-up on value-added. A tax (generally, at a single national percentage rate) was levied on all fixed and working capital of the enterprise, so as to eliminate the earlier situation in which capital was treated as a free good. An allowance for development costs was included in price formation. A fair amount seems to have been done (although here the evidence is weak) to improve the distribution of overhead costs among products produced in multi-product operating units.

As of 1970, things were moving further. Depreciation regulations were being loosened to allow for rapid depreciation of types of equipment for which obsolescence was considered an important factor. Profit mark-ups were being shifted from a percentage of value-added to a percentage of capital employed. A system of continuous reductions of factory prices was being introduced, so that relative prices might change along with relative costs without the previous long lag. Most interesting of all, a link was being established between supply and demand for the various industrial consumer products by relating central allocation of materials and new investments within the sector of light industry to the profits earned by the individual subbranches. In this fashion, although factory prices of consumer goods were still formed without attention to current demand conditions, a tendency was developing for them to reflect long-run supply and demand equilibrium through the effect of profit rate on supply.

All this had created before 1970 the preconditions for partial reliance on financial criteria which simply did not exist in Romania. Furthermore, improvement of the basis for financial analysis was advancing relatively rapidly.

A problem which would appear to be important—but to which no apparent attention was being given—was that of improving labor productivity through greater labor intensity. Of course, particularly in the light of the demography of the country, great attention was being given to raising labor productivity through improvements in fixed capital resources and through rationalization. But the linkage between the increase in an enterprise's wage fund and that of its labor productivity was such as to discourage any rise in worker effort; in fact, this latter would be a positive embarrassment to management since it could be rewarded to only a slight degree. Thus it is not surprising that there seems to be little overfulfillment of individual piece norms by workers paid according to piece rates, and that workpace seemed rather slow in the factories I visited.

The implementation of the "New Economic System" has leaned particularly heavily on four factors:

(1) The traditional discipline of the Germans. Not only has this been important in preventing worker effort from decreasing below its current level, but it has also been critical in permitting the existing mixture of centralization-decentralization to function. Some executives in other socialist countries commented to me on the decentralized system of product balancing to the effect that, in their view, such a system could function in no other country than Germany. Here, the critical ingredient is discipline on the part of enterprise, *Kombinat*, and vvb management: i.e., restraint in using their powers to insure overeasy plan fulfillment by appropriate juggling of the sector's product mix.

(2) The heavy emphasis of national leadership upon development of new products and technology, both for the home and for the export market. No other socialist country appears to have given this degree of emphasis to the technological revolution of our times as expressed in nonmilitary goods.

(3) The considerable reliance upon private and semiprivate enterprises for maintenance work and small-parts production.

(4) Management development. This last factor requires some elaboration, since it has not been treated in Chapter 6.

First, the g.d.r. is the only one of the east European countries in which politically acceptable managers who were technically inefficient have been demoted on a fairly large scale. As mentioned in Chapter 5, five of the six directors of 1964 in the one VVB for which I have such information had been demoted by 1970. Generally, the places of such executives were taken by younger men with higher technical and economic education. East Germany—like the other east European countries—has of course also sent managers to junior colleges and universities, both on full-time study programs and on correspondence courses, and was in this way able to retain them in their posts. But only East Germany seems to have used demotions as a major device for improving managerial quality.

In view of the rapid industrialization which has occurred in Romania, it would have been difficult to follow such a policy there; competent professionals were needed in the new factories, and could not be spared to replace experienced managers. In Czechoslovakia, the one east European country at much the same level of industrialization as the G.D.R., the very prewar political strength of the Communist Party within the working class of the country made it difficult to replace the managers who had been promoted from the workbench at the end of the 1940's. Longstanding political debts were owed to these prewar Communists, and presumably their lengthy Party backgrounds provided them with political strength—at least as a group, if not as individuals—which their managerial counterparts in the G.D.R. did not possess.[1] In Hungary, where managers have backgrounds rather similar to those in Czechoslovakia, the political turmoil of the 1950's and the major reform movement of the 1960's would have made it politically dangerous to engage in mass dismissals of upper managers who had come from the workbench.

None of these conditions has existed in the G.D.R., and thus a policy of demotions for incompetence was much easier to implement there than elsewhere. Nevertheless, the regime deserves high credit for having carried out a program which is at best difficult and distasteful.

Second, judging from the sample of managers I have met in the various countries, East German upper managers, especially in the enterprises and *Kombinate*, are unusually young; they are seasoned in each organization with only the barest sprinkling of older and experienced top managers. This situation permits direction by men who combine the ambitiousness of youth with the up-to-date technical knowledge ac-

[1] One might also argue that the Czech regime until 1968 depended upon the Party to keep order and could not afford to endanger its stability. The East German regime, to the contrary, enjoyed the presence of the Soviet army. I would not, however, put much weight on the effect of this particular national distinction.

quired in higher educational institutions in the very recent past. Partly this is a result of the wartime deaths and of the emigration of managers from East Germany until 1961; doubtless it is also partially because the bulk of older managers and potential managers were viewed with political suspicion precisely because they had been adults under the National Socialist regime. The combination of all three of these conditions, of course, is peculiar to Germany.

Third, a point which will be developed in Chapter 14, the G.D.R. has not only engaged in managerial training of top managers but has also engaged in careful career planning for managers. Selected professionals are moved from one position to another so as to provide them with on-the-job training for higher posts. Here is a very fruitful accompaniment to a policy of rapid promotion of young managers. With the exception of the United States, East Germany is the only country with which I am familiar where a policy of career planning is widely employed.

Fourth, there is some indication that the top leadership of *Kombinate* includes a high proportion of men with previous experience at levels above that of the enterprise. Unfortunately, I have data as to the careers of only two *Kombinat* general directors. One of them had had two years of managerial experience in a VVB and three years in an industrial ministry. The second had been general director of his own VVB for seven years. This kind of background helps provide a level of broad experience and personal authority in the top management of the *Kombinate* which permits the exercise of considerable independence.

My impression of East German industrial top management was, on the whole, quite favorable. Most striking within the tiny sample I interviewed was the apparent willingness both to assert and to delegate authority. Thus the general director who had formerly worked in a ministry said that he had been unhappy there because it was necessary to consult constantly about all matters. In the *Kombinat*, he said, he took decisions. In talking of issues faced by the *Kombinat*, his conversation was studded with the phrase "That is my beer." Yet, in speaking of the authority left to his own technical director, he insisted that he himself was interested only in the number of workhours which the technical director's staff economized every quarter, and in the resultant addition to net profits. How the technical director achieved results "was his beer." Of course he had a plan for the technical measures to be taken, but the general director assumed that some measures would show better and others worse results than had been planned.

The slight opportunity I had for watching the relationship between enterprise directors and their subordinates suggests informality and easy relations. People entered directors' offices without knocking. Directors were not addressed as "Herr Direktor" or even as "comrade"; instead, the first name was used. In talking to me, directors referred even to manual workers as "the colleagues." A plant would usually have a single dining room shared both by workers and top managers. There was no indication of manual workers paying any special attention or speeding up their work when supervisors walked past.

The development of self-reliant and effective enterprise and *Kombinat* managers would seem to be an important precondition for the successful operation of the mix of centralization and decentralization which characterizes East German industry. An official of the research institute of the State Planning Commission took the view that the granting of the present degree of independence to enterprises had had to wait for the development of managers who were qualified to exercise such responsibility in operating large units.

CHANGES INTRODUCED DURING 1971-72[2]

1. The terminology of "structure-determining" products and tasks had disappeared from both the legal and economic literature by 1972. It was replaced by "important" products and tasks.

This terminological change was symbolic of a major shift in national economic strategy. The emphasis changed from the introduction of new products and new technology, and the alteration of the structure of industry in the direction of rapidly increasing the relative weight of the most modern branches, to instead assuring availability of energy and materials supply. It was recognized that the policy of changing industrial structure had been overstressed at the expense of guaranteeing supplies. As two economists of the research institute of the State Planning Commission wrote, "The experience of the last few years has taught us that a highly efficient economic structure cannot be achieved without a simultaneous maintenance of proportionality via the plan."[3]

The shift beginning with 1971 was dramatic. Energy production had grown less rapidly in the G.D.R. during 1966-70 than did total production in the economy, and fixed investment in the fuel and energy sector had actually declined by 8 percent over the period in contrast to an in-

[2] For a more detailed analysis, see M. Keren, "The New Economic System in the GDR: An Obituary," *Soviet Studies*, XXIV, 4 (1973); Kurt Erdmann, "Abkehr vom bisherigen Modell des Ökonomischen Systems des Sozialismus," *Deutschland Archiv*, 4, 8 (1971); J. Naor, "How Dead is the GDR New Economic System?" *Soviet Studies*, XXV, 2 (1973).

[3] G. Schilling and H. Steeger in *Einheit*, 1971, 5, pp. 542-43.

crease of 51 percent in industry as a whole. But during 1971 and 1972, fixed investment in fuel and energy grew by 17 and 32 percent in comparison with an increase of only 3 and 4 percent for all of industry.[4]

Similarly, the level of inventories in state-owned industry grew by at least 12 percent[5] during 1971, compared to an increase in total industrial sales of 5.5 percent. Furthermore, sales during 1971 of intermediate industrial goods by ministerially directed industry increased by 6.8 percent, compared to an increase of 5.6 percent in the sale of final goods. Comparing the first half of 1972 with the first half of 1971, the respective rates of growth were 6.5 and 4.5 percent. The 1972 plan for the Ministry of Processing and Transportation Equipment called for an increase of 14.8 percent in spare parts production[6] compared to a total ministerial increase of sales of only 5.6 percent. Clearly the emphasis had shifted away from improvement in the structure of industry, through emphasis upon high-value products, to the assurance of the materials inputs needed for the economy's smooth operation.

2. The number of obligatory plan indicators increased substantially during 1971-72, although they were once again reduced in the plan for 1973. The degree to which these changes added and subtracted constraints which were binding on the efforts of *Kombinate* and enterprises to fulfill their major tasks is unclear; to some degree, the changes probably reflected only formal recognition of the status quo. Nevertheless, it would appear reasonable to regard the increase and later decrease as reflecting direction of change in the number of genuine constraints.

3. The number of product groups for which "balances" are drawn up by central authorities at ministerial level or higher increased sharply during 1971 (from approximately five hundred to eight hundred) in preparation for the 1972 plan. The increase was due entirely to product groups balanced at the highest level; the State Planning Commission had formerly stayed relatively aloof from the balancing task, but was now directly responsible for three hundred balances.[7] On the other

[4] Staatliche Zentralverwaltung für Statistik, *Statistisches Jahrbuch der Deutschen Demokratischen Republik 1973* (Staatsverlag, East Berlin: 1973), pp. 43 and 47.

[5] A. Binz in *Die Wirtschaft*, 1972, 15, p. 11. Through November 30th, inventory levels rose by 18 percent; the December decline is estimated by me at the maximum level Binz suggests.

[6] H. Scholz in *Die Wirtschaft*, 1972, 17, p. 13.

[7] Naor suggests that the 1973 plan showed a major decrease in the number of central product balances used. The source he quotes is, however, ambiguous and seems to me to be more properly interpreted as referring to a special subset of balances. This impression is reinforced by the fact that an official of the State Planning Commission some five months later discussed the number of central balances, but made no reference to a decline for 1973 (H. Niderberger and K. Blessing in *Die Wirtschaft*, 1972, 26, Supplement 7, pp. 9-10).

hand, the total number of product balances in the economy as a whole appears to have declined somewhat from the earlier level.[8]

As an accompaniment of the reintroduction of the State Planning Commission directly into the balancing process, apparently for the first time since 1963, a major effort seems to have been made to sharpen the procedure used for determining materials inputs needed for individual products. For the first time, norms specific to individual products were developed above the ministerial level in preparation for the 1973 plan: norms for the inputs of 87 materials into the production of 145 products (making, however, a total of only 450 materials-specific product norms) were constructed. Coverage for the 1974 plan was to be further expanded to about 800 products.[9] This new task was undertaken as a reaction to the impression within the State Planning Commission that its own 1972 balancing experience had shown that requests for input requirements could not be effectively evaluated, and thus that its 1972 central balances were often unrealistic.[10]

4. For selected consumer goods, balances were drawn up for 1972 and 1973 showing the volumes to be sold within lower- and medium-price ranges. Clearly this innovation reduced the ability of the enterprises and *Kombinate* to select their product mix in such a way as to maximize profit, output, and labor productivity. But the quantitative significance of these new constraints for consumer goods industry is difficult to judge, since no indication is given as to the breadth of coverage of the goods treated in this fashion. Furthermore, while production in the lower- and medium-price range constituted an obligatory plan indicator for 1972, it was removed from this listing in the instructions for 1973.

5. The regulations governing the enterprise bonus fund were changed drastically in four respects in January 1972.[11] Most important of all, the guaranteed annual bonus fund per employee was changed from 200 marks to 80 percent of the planned bonus fund. If one assumes that 80 percent of the bonus fund was distributed in the form of year-end bonuses, and also that the planned bonus fund was equal to at least 90 percent of the actual bonuses paid out, then the guaranteed bonus fund in each enterprise per employee was increased from 200 marks in 1970

[8] Keren, p. 560, refers to 6,000 total balances for 1967, the last year for which he gives data. Two East German sources state that there were 4,500 or 5,000 balances worked out for 1972 (I. Grüning in *Die Wirtschaft*, 1972, 4, p. 7, and H. Milke and A. Mühlefeldt in *Wirtschaftswissenschaft*, 1972, 8, p. 1129).

[9] *Die Wirtschaft*, 1972, 7, p. 8; 1973, 21, Supplement 12, p. 2; 1973, 14, Supplement 7, p. 12.

[10] Interview with officials of the State Planning Commission, *Die Wirtschaft*, 1972, 4, p. 8.

[11] See *Gesetzblatt der Deutschen Demokratischen Republik*, II, 1972, 5, pp. 49-53.

and 1971 in ministerially directed industry to 585 marks.[12] Since the maximum annual bonus fund (in most firms) had formerly been 850 marks per employee, and for 1972 was raised only to 900 marks, the proportion of the enterprise's bonus fund which depended upon enterprise success was drastically reduced.

Similarly, wage overexpenditures compared to the planned wage fund had, through 1971, been deducted (at least in theory) from the earned bonus fund. Such deduction was abolished in early 1972.

The second aspect of change was to eliminate the previous pattern under which the amount of the enterprise bonus fund was linked solely to the amount of net profit earned, and instead to link it to both net profit and sales achievements relative to plan. This presumably reduced the effect of profit on the size of the bonus fund.

The third aspect of change was to eliminate the two side conditions for full payment of earned bonus fund to the enterprise up to the amount of the planned bonus fund, although they were retained with regard to above-plan payments into the fund. (Through 1971, the earned bonus fund was reduced by 15 percent if one of these conditions were not met, and by 30 percent if neither were fulfilled.) Beginning with 1972, the size of the bonus fund up to but not beyond the planned amount depended solely on profit and sales results, and the meeting of other obligatory plan indicators had no effect on it. On the other hand, the meeting of obligatory plan indicators—as well as others—remained important for the payment of bonuses to managerial personnel in the enterprises and *Kombinate*.

The fourth change was the renunciation of the attempt to set multi-year normatives relating the growth in the bonus fund to the growth in production and profits. Instead, firms were to have planned bonus funds for each year individually, and additional payments into the fund were related to performance above the plan for that year. This represented at least a theoretic return to the pre-1969 situation.

6. A reading of the East German economic press suggests reduced attention to the effort at making producer pricing more rational. Although both a 1971 and a 1972 law repeated the notion of developing profit mark-ups as a percentage of capital employed rather than of value-added, pricing discussion after 1970 has not revolved either around the issue of carrying out this reform in the pricing system, or around the closely linked question of bringing down wholesale prices as costs fall. Instead, concentration in the field of producer pricing has been on tightening central controls so as to minimize hidden inflation in the pricing of new products and tailor-made items. There is no re-

---

[12] For average payments of year-end bonuses, see *Die Wirtschaft*, 1972, 7, p. 10, and 1973, 15, p. 7.

jection of the pricing reform which earlier was expected to be instituted gradually during 1971-75, but one forms the impression that central authorities do not consider it of sufficiently high priority to warrant giving it the administrative attention which would be necessary for it to progress vigorously.

Similarly, the tone of writing about the role of financial considerations in the determination of product mix and input mix has shifted from that found in the economic press in 1970. First priority is given to producing that mix which satisfies "need" as determined by balancing organs and by requests of consuming bodies; improvement of an enterprise's profit position is no longer cited as even one among several bases for determining its product mix. The same is true with regard to input mix; minimizing costs are no longer cited as a major basis for such determination. Rather, financial criteria for judging the work of enterprises and *Kombinate* seem now to be viewed as ideally being no more than a measure of the production unit's aggregate success in producing a fixed mix of output with a fixed mix of inputs.[13]

7. The first half of 1973 saw the virtual elimination of all semiprivate firms in the economy, of private firms operating in industry and construction, and of cooperative enterprises of industrial handicrafts. It would appear that something in the order of 92 percent of these enterprises had been converted to full state ownership by the end of July 1972.[14] The social significance of this conversion is clear enough, but it is also suggestive of economic significance.

INTERPRETATION OF THE POST-1970 CHANGES

Any interpretation of the post-1970 changes must rest on one's understanding of the objectives of the New Economic System. In my view, this system was intended simply to rationalize and make more efficient a highly managed economy; decentralization of decision making was a tool of such rationalization rather than an end in itself. Moreover, in 1970—prior to the changes—the G.D.R. had approximately twice as high a proportion of the industrial labor force engaged in central coordinating functions as did highly centralized Romania.[15] There was never any

[13] As examples of this new spirit, see the article by H. Taut, president of the Industry and Trade Bank, in *Die Wirtschaft*, 1972, 12, pp. 4-5; B. Meissner in *Die Wirtschaft*, 1972, 11, p. 8; O. Sturm in *Die Wirtschaft*, 1972, 14, p. 6.

[14] As of the end of 1971, 11,865 such private, semiprivate, and cooperative enterprises existed (*Jahrbuch 1972*, pp. 118, 152-53, 192, and 196). By the end of July 1972, some 10,900 such firms had been converted to state ownership (*Die Wirtschaft*, 1972, 31, p. 9, and 1972, 36, p. 2).

[15] See Chapter 5. Personnel in East German *Kombinate* and Romanian *centrale* are not included as engaged in these coordinating functions, but those working in the East German product groups are included.

intention of implementing truly radical new mechanisms as has been done in Hungary after 1967. Industry as a whole continued to be organized in a fashion which allowed it to be compared with the organization of a large, conglomerate capitalist firm; the New Economic System was simply an effort to run this organization in a more decentralized fashion than earlier.

If this interpretation is correct, then the G.D.R. was in a position to move backward temporarily in the direction of greater centralization without jeopardizing its ability later to continue the decentralization trend. In this regard, it was in a fundamentally different position than that of Hungary since 1968. Important modifications of the Hungarian reforms could readily be viewed as a confession of basic error, and the earlier direction of the reform might not easily be taken up once more. This is because ideological issues were at stake. In the case of the G.D.R., backing-and-filling between differing degrees of decentralization was likely to be no more difficult than it is in an American corporation.

The real crux of the New Economic System may be summed up in three features:

(1) Emphasis on high technology items and modernization of the structure of industry. Clearly this feature was drastically modified in 1971, but one might well expect that this modification will be only temporary.

(2) Decentralization, and heavy use of financial criteria, for decision making with regard to nonstructure-determining products. This feature was also seriously modified after 1970, and the temporary nature of this modification is much more debatable.

(3) Slack planning, so that enterprise and *Kombinat* managements would be left with sufficient resources to pursue other goals in addition to fulfillment of their major plan indicators. This is perhaps the most fundamental feature of the New Economic System, and it has also been modified (at least with regard to the profit target).

All commentators are agreed that the root cause of the 1971 changes was a problem of disproportions as the East Germans call it, or taut planning in Keren's terminology. Weather conditions had led to bad harvests in 1969, 1970, and 1971. Electric power was a bottleneck at least during 1970-71. Delays in deliveries appear to have been more serious in 1970 than either earlier or later. Investment expenditures grew at a peculiarly sharp pace in 1970. For industrial output as a whole, 1970 was the only year since 1963 when the plan was taut in the sense that the plan of industrial sales both called for a higher growth rate than had been achieved in the previous year and was itself not fulfilled.

In the light of the disproportions problem, the switch of national priorities epitomized by the abandonment of the terminology of "structure-determining" products and tasks could be regarded as an eminently reasonable medium-term solution. Quite clearly, the East German leadership felt that it had been pushing the pace too hard. But there is no evidence that this switch was ever intended to mark the end of the modernization of industrial structure. By May 1973, Honecker—the East German Party leader—was again insisting on the need to increase more rapidly the share of high-technology items in total production.[16] This change could be readily interpreted as temporary and as representing no fundamental alteration of policy.

The same might be said[17] for the increase in the number of obligatory plan targets and for the creation of some three hundred balances drawn up by the State Planning Commission. Just as a large decentralized capitalist company tends to centralize in a period of economic strain, without necessarily compromising its basic decentralization philosophy, the same interpretation might be given for the tightening up which occurred in the G.D.R. during 1971. The fairly quick reversal with regard to the number of obligatory plan indicators, a reversal which took effect in 1973, could be taken as corroboration of this interpretation. But one would feel happier about it if there had also been a reduction in the number of centrally approved balances.

What is the difference between a balance which is established at the level of the State Planning Commission or a ministry in contrast to one determined by a product group in a lower organization? Partly, of course, it lies in the participation in the balancing process of officials of the central body; but it is clear that even enterprises and *Kombinate* may in fact be doing most of the balancing work for at least individual central balances.[18] Partly it is the problem that product groups have often been unable to enforce their production decisions on enterprises outside of their own VVB.[19] But probably the most important difference lies elsewhere.

Although accurate information is lacking, it appears that central balances are drawn up prior to issuing obligatory plan indicators to VVBs, *Kombinate*, and enterprises, while the reverse is the case for the balances drawn up by the product groups acting under the authority of

[16] Report of the Politbureau to the ninth session of the Party Central Committee, *Die Wirtschaft*, 1973, 22, pp. 4-5.

[17] As Naor does in the article cited above.

[18] H. Niderberger and K. Blessing of the State Planning Commission in *Die Wirtschaft*, 1972, 26, Supplement 7, pp. 9-10.

[19] See, for example, L. Kiehle in *Die Wirtschaft*, 1972, 8, pp. 8-9, and M. Kummer and D. Kowalewsky in *Die Wirtschaft*, 1972, 13, p. 9.

individual vvbs. If this is indeed the case, it means that the central balancing organs operate under quite different constraints than do the product groups. The product groups must draw up production assignments for the multiproduct *Kombinate* and enterprises which are reconciliable with the obligatory plan indicators which these bodies have already received, and in particular with their tasks for profit, output, and labor productivity. Thus the product groups cannot assign to a production unit a product mix which is too heavily weighted in the direction of low profit, low labor productivity, or a high capital/output ratio. They must pay strict attention to economic considerations, as expressed in these common denominators. Central balancing organs, on the other hand, are free of these restrictions. Similarly, during the course of the planning year, the central balancing organs have much greater freedom to change the product-mix requirements for producers, and the input allocations for users, than is the case for the product groups.

In a period dominated by the existence of national bottlenecks, it may seem reasonable to place part of the balancing task in the hands of central bodies which are in a position to give full weight to short-run problems.[20] But one cost to the economy is that aggregative plan indicators of efficiency must inevitably lose much of their importance. A second cost is that the State Planning Commission has been burdened with a major operating task from which it had been previously kept free; presumably, its ability to focus both on longer-run problems and on problems of short-run economic efficiency was reduced correspondingly.[21]

The expansion of balancing to include specific price categories for selected consumer goods is a development which is much more difficult to interpret as a response to an emergency situation. The purpose of this expansion of balancing was clear enough: to prevent hidden inflation through the shifting of consumer production to higher-priced lines. As such, it was part of the December 1971 pledge that no consumer prices would be raised during the period through 1975.[22]

Although there are no indications that the rate of such hidden inflation had increased during the previous year or two, one might explain the move as a consequence of the apparent failure of money wages of

[20] Ideally, this would mean balancing according to the shadow-prices generated by a national programming model, rather than according to prices which at best reflect long-run scarcity relations.

[21] It is possible, however, that the Planning Commission was relieved of its earlier task of detailed planning for the former structure-determining products. If so, this reduction of workload may well have offset the increase due to its new balancing task.

[22] *Gesetzblatt*, ii, 1971, 82, p. 725.

large groups of employees to have risen at all since the middle 1960's.[23] One might argue that by late 1971 it had become politically unacceptable to allow any further reduction of the real income of these groups.

But such an argument does not appear to me to be tenable. Real individual consumption in the G.D.R. as a whole had been rising regularly, and neither 1970 nor 1971 had been years of peculiar difficulty in this regard. Although the 1970-71 rate of increase was down slightly from 1969, both years showed somewhat better performance than had the period of 1963-69.[24] Money wages of many workers and employees had remained stable only because of the national distribution of wage increases; 1971, for example, had seen a major expansion of the wages of the very lowest wage categories. Total wage increases in the economy were sufficient so that, if central authorities had wished to distribute them in such a fashion, all groups could have had regular increases. Political authorities were free to have handled the problem of hidden inflation by concentrating wage increases during 1971 on those groups which had not had any for a number of years; they did not choose to make use of this possibility. Moreover, if hidden inflation were really a serious problem, one would have expected to see some spillover into the official consumer price index; in fact, no such spillover occurred.

Thus I cannot accept the thesis that the introduction of planning by price categories for selected consumer goods can be interpreted simply as a response to the problems of hidden inflation. Rather, it seems to have represented a deliberate decision to reduce the degree to which product mix was to be decided according to profit considerations, and to increase the role of "objective need" in its determination. It represented a distrust—not unwarranted under conditions of fixed prices— of the virtue of allowing individual enterprises to determine their own mixes.

This decision with regard to selected consumer goods thus suggests that the increased number of central balances for other products may have been more than simply a response to difficult bottleneck problems. It may well have represented a view that the role of profitability should be sharply reduced in determining enterprises' mixes of both outputs and inputs.

One might regard this view of the product-mix decision as resting upon the notion that the East German pricing system had not yet reached the maturity required to allow profitability decisions to be socially useful.

[23] See Chapter 5.

[24] Performance was better still in comparison with the entire decade of the 1960's. Data are both for personal consumption in real terms as measured in the national income accounts, and for real income per capita of worker and employee households (*Jahrbuch 1973*, pp. 42 and 334).

But if this were the case, one might have expected a resolute speeding up of the process of price reform. Instead, price reform appears to have languished—suggesting that it was given a low priority rather than the very high priority which this interpretation would have indicated.

The elimination of the semiprivate firms, of private firms in the sectors of industry and construction, and of cooperative enterprises of industrial handicrafts also suggests that the change in attitude toward the role of profitability was intended to outlast the temporary emergency. The very raison d'être of these forms of enterprise is to employ profitability as the principal criterion of decision making, however bounded the decisions might be by constraints imposed through the use of other criteria. If profitability were soon to be restored to its pre-1971 role, there would seem to have been little reason to nationalize these enterprises. Of course, one might argue that the nationalization occurred for ideological reasons and that its timing was coincidental. But if this is the true explanation, then it is a curious coincidence.

The bonus changes of early 1972 are the most difficult to interpret. One is tempted to say that they represent a reduction in the importance of all aggregate indices of *Kombinat* and enterprise success, whether these be profit, output, or labor productivity. At the same time that the implementation of socially desirable product-mix goals of outputs and inputs has been described in the economic press as the most important objective of all, it has been recognized that changes in planned product mix may lead to enterprise and *Kombinat* failure to achieve planned profitability, labor productivity, and even output.[25] The changes in the bonus fund regulations have gone very far in shielding nonmanagerial staff from enterprise failure to reach the planned goals of profitability and output, and have completely shielded them from failures with regard to labor productivity.

A further change one and one-third years later reinforced this downgrading of the importance of success indicators. In the computation of the annual planned bonus fund of an enterprise or *Kombinat*, the previous year's efforts to overfulfill that year's plan were eliminated as a relevant positive element. While it is not clear that actual overfulfillment would be ignored in the computation, this appears to be the implication. The result is that the longer-run positive effect on the unit's bonus fund of above-plan performance was further reduced.[26]

The special downplaying of the profitability indicator in determining bonus, in comparison with the pre-1972 situation, seems particularly appropriate in terms of the increased emphasis upon balances and the

[25] For examples of such recognition, see *Die Wirtschaft*, 1972, 11, p. 8; 1972, 10, p. 14; and 1972, 14, p. 6.

[26] *Gesetzblatt*, I, 1973, 30, p. 293.

meeting of "needs." Changes in the mix of inputs or outputs are likely to have a greater percentage effect upon profitability than upon output or labor productivity, while endless dispute is possible between the enterprise and higher bodies as to what was the precise effect on profitability in any given case. Thus the reduction of profitability in favor of output, as a factor affecting the enterprise's bonus fund, is a useful device for partially defusing this issue.[27]

It is the third change in the formation of the bonus fund which alone runs sharply counter to the interpretations offered above. The elimination of side conditions as a requirement for the full payment of earned planned bonuses appears to increase the importance of output, and even of profitability, in contrast to all other obligatory plan tasks. This change seems particularly relevant in terms of the actual bonus situation of individual units which was described in Chapter 6, where failure to fulfill completely the side conditions appeared to be the normal state of affairs. In fact, if we were to assume that managers attempt to maximize the enterprise bonus fund, and that obligatory plan indicators which do not affect the bonus fund are in reality not considered as obligatory, the economic situation in 1972-73 would appear to be much less centrally controlled than it was in 1970.

The last assumption would be a gross exaggeration, if only because managerial bonuses are said to be dependent on the fulfillment of obligatory plan indicators. Nevertheless, this removal of side conditions in the determination of the unit's total bonus fund (up to the planned amount, but not above) is a development which cries for explanation. Unfortunately, it is the sort of development which is peculiarly difficult to evaluate when one is dependent exclusively upon the published East German literature.

To sum up, the East German economic system has been modified since 1970 in ways which appear significant. In particular, financial criteria play a smaller role in decision making than was the case earlier. While this change was triggered by the structural disproportions in the economy which were revealed in 1970, it is unclear to what degree the extent of centralization should be regarded as a function of the gravity of these structural disproportions. Naor argues that it should be viewed as such a function, while Keren takes a reverse line and considers that the observed changes are likely to be at least semipermanent. My own view is intermediate.

---

[27] At much the same time as the bonus change, enterprises, *Kombinate* and VVBS were freed from their earlier obligation to pay into the state budget at least the planned number of marks, these being calculated as planned profits multiplied by a planned percentage deduction for the budget. Instead, when a unit fails to earn planned profits, payments due to the state budget are now to be reduced by 30 percent of the shortfall in profits (*Gesetzblatt*, II, 1971, 78, p. 686).

PARTIAL STABILITY OF THE 1970 MANAGERIAL MODEL

Keren has written that "by the end of 1970 there was little to distinguish the economic system of the GDR from the pre-1964 system and from that of countries farther east."[28] While this view appears exaggerated in general, it is particularly so with regard to the apparent maintenance of "satisficing" behavior by East German enterprises.

Critical here is the fact that the aggregate sales plans have continued to be set at levels which are not hard to meet. In 1972, in fact, 95 percent of the industrial enterprises which were under ministerial rather than regional jurisdiction fulfilled their annual sales plans—a higher proportion than had ever been reached in earlier years.[29] The proportion remained at the high level of 90 percent for the first half of 1973, and rose to 98 percent for the year as a whole.[30] Yet aggregate overfulfillment of industry's sales plan was only 1.7, 2.1, and 1.6 percent respectively; for the enterprises under ministerial jurisdiction, overfulfillment in 1973 averaged only about 0.8 percent.[31] These facts seem to show that, just as before 1971, this key plan indicator was set at a level which left "reserves" for the enterprises, and that the enterprises continued to exert their efforts in directions other than that of gross overfulfillment of plan.

It is true that the profit plans may be set more harshly. During the first half of 1973, one-third of the industrial enterprises under ministerial jurisdiction failed to fulfill their plans for cost reduction[32] and, presumably, most of them did not reach their profit plans. But these plan targets were probably considered less important than the sales targets, and the plan underfulfillment presumably reflects heavily the emphasis upon determining product mix according to "need" rather than profitability.

The very high figures for fulfillment of sales plan targets suggest that East German enterprise and *Kombinat* managers have continued to be able to exert their marginal efforts, after the fulfillment of the key targets, to meeting those goals which they themselves consider important for their units. In this important regard, they continue to look more like American divisional managers of decentralized firms than like Russian enterprise managers.

What does appear to have changed, however, is the degree to which the unit is itself primarily responsible for determining its annual plan,

[28] Keren, p. 554.

[29] Plan fulfillment report for 1972, *Die Wirtschaft,* 1973, 4, p. 15.

[30] Plan fulfillment reports in *Die Wirtschaft,* 1973, 29, p. 13, and 1974, 5, p. 14.

[31] This percentage is calculated on the assumption that enterprises under ministerial jurisdiction produced three-quarters of total industrial production in that year.

[32] *Die Wirtschaft,* 1973, 29, p. 13.

and then for winning the consent of the necessary agencies, rather than having this plan imposed upon it with only minor opportunity for negotiation. To the degree that the balances of inputs and the product mix of output are determined for the enterprises and *Kombinate* before they ever receive their obligatory plan targets, they are stripped of much of their earlier obligation of attempting to assure maximum attention to a desirable product mix within the constraints of profitability, output, and labor productivity targets. At the same time, they are also deprived of the possibilities of successfully struggling to assure that the various assigned tasks are all reconciliable. But it is not possible from the published literature alone to form a firm opinion as to the degree to which the production units have in fact lost their earlier influence on the shaping of their own plans.

Hungary

THE Hungarian economic reform, introduced at the beginning of 1968, represents the most radical change which has been maintained over a period of years in the economic system of any CMEA country. Individual state enterprises receive no plan assignments whatsoever, and they act much more autonomously with respect to their branch ministries than is the case in any other CMEA country. With minor exceptions, there is neither output planning to the level of the enterprise nor materials allocation. Although planning at the level of major branches does exist, these plans are carried out not so much through instructions as by the creation of financial incentives for the enterprises. Planning is primarily "indicative" in the sense that enterprises are motivated to act in accord with the plan because their own self-interest is best served in this fashion.

Part III will describe the situation at the time of my visit in early 1971—i.e., three years after the new system had been put into operation. My conclusions are different from those which have appeared in the informed western literature concerning the effect of the reform,[1] and my approach emphasizes the policy constraints within which the reform has functioned.

Chapter 8 begins with a survey of the Hungarian economy, proceeds to a brief statement of the conception of the post-1967 reforms, and ends with the further development of Hungarian attitudes toward the reforms during the early 1970's. The original part of the chapter, and the one most significant for understanding the materials of the following two chapters, is a treatment of three basic policy constraints which bound the reformed system.

Chapter 9 analyzes the functioning of the main economic mechanisms of the reformed system. Pricing, the creation of enterprise incentives and the influencing of managerial goals, the treatment of investments both in fixed and working capital, the use of subsidies and tax exemptions to direct the economy, and the sphere and mechanisms of control over foreign trade are the subjects examined. All of the economic mechanisms were partly shaped by the conception of the reforms, but were also heavily influenced by the requirements stemming from the fundamental

---

[1] Richard Portes and Béla Balassa are the two westerners who have written most authoritatively about the Hungarian reform. Both seem to regard the results to date as more positive and more radical than I do. (See R. D. Portes, "The Tactics and Strategy of Economic Decentralization," *Soviet Studies*, XIII, 4, 1972, pp. 629-58, and B. Balassa in M. Bornstein, ed., *Plan and Market*, Yale University Press, New Haven and London: 1973, pp. 347-72.)

policy objectives. It is the nature of the resulting compromises which is of prime interest.

Chapter 10 evaluates the economic significance of the reform. The evaluation rests primarily upon data provided by interviews in Hungarian enterprises, but it also makes use of macroeconomic statistics covering the first three to five years of the new system.

Although the Hungarian economic literature is vastly richer and more sophisticated than is the Romanian or East German, language problems have prevented me from exploiting more than a small share of it.[2] However, far more than in any other country, I consulted at length with a considerable number of well-informed academics and officials of the planning and financial organs. These consultations represent a principal data strength of this chapter, since these individuals were extraordinarily helpful and frank.

On the other hand, my interviews in Hungarian operating units were somewhat less successful than those in any other country. Since the greater independence of enterprises in Hungary than in either Romania or the G.D.R. would lead one to expect there to be larger variation in their behavior, I would have liked to have visited more enterprises in Hungary than in the other countries. Unfortunately, this was impossible; I was able to arrange visits to only five enterprises, and these visits were restricted to fifteen to twenty hours in each firm. Moreover, four of the five enterprises were located in Budapest, and there may well be regional differences in behavior of which I remain unaware.

However, the enterprises visited were in four distinct branches: light industry, machine building, heavy industry (manufacture of basic semifabricates), and heavy processing industry. Four of the five enterprises produced extensively for export as well as for the home market. All five manufactured a wide variety of products and enjoyed considerable technical opportunity for shifting the relative weight of their output between different items. All five were described by a well-informed Hungarian source as among the better managed enterprises of their branches; on the other hand, none of them was a showplace. Thus, with the exception of the criterion of regional location, they seem reasonably representative of the better—but not the best—managed industrial enterprises of the country.

The three major lacunae in my sources of information are with regard to the branch ministries, the Party, and the trade unions. Only one interview with a single high official could be arranged in a branch

---

[2] It should be pointed out, however, that the Hungarian journal *Acta Oeconomica* summarizes much of this literature in English, Russian, or German; the bulk of the articles are in English. *Abstracts of Hungarian Economic Literature*, published since 1971, has also been very helpful in easing access to the literature.

ministry; thus I am forced to portray the issue of branch ministry in-fluence on enterprises primarily through the eyes of Hungarians who were not working in ministerial headquarters. This limited perspective is in sharp contrast to what I could accomplish in Romania and, to a lesser degree, in the G.D.R.

Equally as serious, I was unable to establish contact with Party or trade union officials at the national, regional, or enterprise levels. Since both Party and trade union roles may have increased in importance as an accompaniment of the dismemberment of the former system of giving direct state instructions to enterprise managers, my inability to exploit these sources is particularly unfortunate.

A final word is necessary as to the confidence which can be placed in my sources. Both in their writings and in private discussions, Hun-garian economists and administrative theorists have been remarkably frank and self-critical with regard to their country's system. I judge their comments to be more reliable than those of their counterparts in Ro-mania and the G.D.R. On the other hand, there was a wider dispersion in the frankness and reliability of enterprise officials than was the case in the other countries; this has placed a greater burden upon me in Hungary than elsewhere in evaluating the trustworthiness of different people within the same enterprise. It is my impression, however, that I did meet frank and competent people in each enterprise whose remarks could be used as a yardstick against which to evaluate the comments of their colleagues.

CHAPTER 8

Hungary: Objectives of Decentralized
Planning and the
Constraints on the System

THE purpose of this chapter is to provide a background for the following two. However, even the reader who is informed as to the Hungarian economy is advised to read the section dealing with policy constraints.

SURVEY OF THE HUNGARIAN ECONOMY

Hungary has the smallest population (10.3 million) of the four countries studied. But within this small population, substantial changes have been occurring. First, population aging has been substantial; those over sixty years of age comprised 17 percent of the population in 1970 compared to 12 percent in 1949. Second, there has been a heavy shift of the labor force from agriculture to industry; the agricultural labor force fell to 28 percent of the national labor force in 1970 as a result of an absolute decline of one-third during the previous decade. The decade's decline in agriculture went almost entirely to expand industrial employment, which rose from 27 percent of the labor force in 1960 to 37 percent in 1970.

While national product has grown rapidly in Hungary since the Second World War, this growth has been almost entirely in nonagricultural production. Gross agricultural output rose at the rate of 1 percent per annum between the late 1930's and the late 1960's, but even this was primarily owing to the increase in industrial inputs; national income by origin in agriculture rose by no more than a total of 9 percent between the two high years of 1938 and 1969.[1]

Clearly a major reason for the absence of agricultural development has been the lack of incentives in this sector. In the collective farms, where the vast bulk of agricultural labor is employed, 34 percent of farm members are over retirement age and only 25 percent receive credit for more than two hundred working days per year.[2] In order to improve

[1] Hungarian Central Statistical Office, *Statistical Pocket Book of Hungary 1945-1970* (Budapest: 1970), pp. 19 and 161.
[2] F. Erdei, "The Changing Hungarian Village," *New Hungarian Quarterly,*

the agricultural situation, peasant incomes have been raised disproportionately to others since the end of the 1950's until, by 1969, peasant
personal income per capita was 88 percent of that of manual workers
in Budapest, 108 percent of that of manual workers in other towns, and
112 percent of that of village manual workers.[3] Only in late 1972 was
there any reversal. Within the state sector as well, interbranch earnings
differentials are quite small.

Partly because of the rise in agricultural incomes during the 1960's,
Hungarian income distribution is now highly egalitarian. This egalitarianism is essentially a reflection of the distribution of earned income, as
social benefits in cash (essentially pensions, sick pay, and family allowances) constitute only 10 percent of total income. There are complaints as to the lack of incentives inherent in the egalitarianism of
earned income, and it is recommended that incentives be reconciled
with egalitarianism of total per capita income by raising the amount of
social benefits in cash (particularly family allowances).[4] In fact, this
policy was pursued during the 1960's, when social cash benefits per
capita rose by 114 percent compared to 39 percent for per capita earnings, and when wage differentials were slightly widened.[5] But the combined effect of raising peasant incomes, enlarging social cash benefits
sharply, and continuing to provide rising real incomes for all major
social groups[6] leaves few resources available for the objective of increasing wage differentiation. Thus it can be expected that the monetary
incentive problem will continue to be serious in the Hungarian economy
for many years to come. (See Table 8.)

1970, 38, pp. 11-12. (I have corrected one of the figures for a misprint.) Data are
as of late 1967.

[3] Ö. Életö and Gy. Láng, "Income Level—Income Stratification in Hungary,"
Acta Oeconomica, 7, 3-4 (1971), 307-308 and 312. Households are classified according to the occupation of the head of household. The ratio of earners to de-
pendents is the same among peasant and manual worker households generally,
although it is higher in Budapest. By 1969, total per capita income of peasants was
equal to that of manual workers in the country as a whole, despite the fact that
their indirect social benefits (included in the total figure) were only three-quarters
as high (*Statisztikai Időszaki Közlemények*, 182, chapter 3, as translated in *RFE*).

[4] Ibid., pp. 321-22. Nyers, a member of the Hungarian Party's Politbureau, also
writes of the need for greater wage incentives while still pursuing the unequivocal
objective of equalization of income by classes and families (R. Nyers, "Hungarian Economic Policy in Practice," *Acta Oeconomica*, 7, 3-4, 1971, p. 268).

[5] Életö and Láng, pp. 321-22.

[6] The fundamental principle with regard to living standards has been declared
to be that of assuring that no major social group in Hungary should suffer a declining or even stagnant standard of living over a number of years. A study in
1965 showed that the threshold of perception of income increases for families is
a 2 to 3 percent rise per annum (I. Huszár, "On Living Standard Policy in Hungary," *Acta Oeconomica*, 4, 1, 1969, pp. 47-48).

TABLE 8.1: Distribution of Pretax Personal Income by Household[a] in Hungary and in the More Egalitarian of the West European Countries (percentage of personal income)

Quintile Groups of Households	Hungary (1962)	Norway (1963)	United Kingdom (1964)
Lowest	9	5	5
Second	14	12	10
Third	19	18	17
Fourth	23	24	24
Fifth	35	41	44

SOURCES: Hungary: "Social Stratification in Hungary" study carried out in 1963 by the Hungarian Central Statistical Office (English version, undated), p. 39. Norway and United Kingdom: United Nations, Economic Commission for Europe, *Incomes in Postwar Europe: A Study of Policies, Growth and Distribution* (*Survey of Europe in 1968*, II, Geneva: 1967), chapter 6, p. 15.

NOTE: No data are available for posttax income distribution. Income tax in Hungary is levied only on nonwage-and-salary income; employees, however, are subject to a progressive supplementary charge for pensions. Even including this latter as income tax, the posttax income distribution cannot differ radically from the pretax figures. Income taxes are much more progressive in the west European countries than in Hungary, while indirect taxes (sales taxes) are much more progressive in Hungary. The net effect of taxes on the relative equality of the different countries' posttax income distribution is uncertain. A comparison of the income distribution of wage- and salary-earners in the United Kingdom (1963/64) and West Germany (1964) with that of all Hungarian households displays a virtually identical quintile income distribution among all three countries. Such a comparison offers the advantage of eliminating the effect of most property income, in this respect better approximating a comparison of earned-income distribution in the western countries with that of Hungary. However, since pension incomes are not included for the west European countries, and since households headed by pensioners and other nonearners constituted 17 percent of the total number of households covered in the Hungarian survey, the Hungarian income distribution shown must be much less equal than would be a distribution limited to Hungarian wage- and salary-earners. (*Incomes in Postwar Europe*, chapter 6, p. 21, and "Social Stratification in Hungary," p. 21.)

[a] Hungarian data are by household. Norwegian and United Kingdom data are grouped by taxpayer; but, since the incomes of husband and wife are considered as one income, this distribution is presumably close to the distribution of household income.

Foreign trade is fairly evenly divided between socialist and nonsocialist countries; in 1970, only 53 percent was directed to socialist countries.[7]

[7] This calculation is based upon revaluing trade—which is published in "foreign exchange forints"—into domestic forints, so that it may be comparable between socialist and nonsocialist countries. Rather than using the arbitrary official exchange rate, which is the means used for converting receipts and expenditures in foreign currency into "foreign exchange forints," I have employed the rates currently employed in Hungary for converting export earnings and import expenditures of enterprises into domestic forints. These rates are differentiated between the ruble-bloc countries and the rest of the world; they were determined in 1968 as the minimum rates which would yield the same average profitability to

As one might expect in a small country, total foreign trade constitutes a high percentage of national income. But even given the size of the country, the magnitude of this percentage in Hungary is extraordinary. In 1970, exports constituted some 34 percent of Hungary's net domestic product.[8] It should be no surprise that much of the discussion by Hungarian economists concerning the objectives of reform has been concerned with finding improved mechanisms for carrying out this foreign trade.

Table 8.2 presents the commodity composition of Hungarian foreign trade. Raw materials and semifinished goods constitute by far the major item of net imports from both socialist and nonsocialist trading partners; equipment is a balancing net export to socialist countries and net import from capitalist countries; fuels are a substantial net import from socialist countries. Although agriculture is an important source of gross exports, the bulk of gross exports both to capitalist and socialist markets is provided by industry. Industrial consumer goods and foodstuffs rank equally as net exports in financing the net imports which go primarily to industry.

Particularly striking—and this applies to trade with both socialist and nonsocialist countries—is the large percentage of exports which are balanced by imports within the same broad product group. Using the five-way product grouping given in Table 8.2, such intrasectoral exports constitute 79 percent of Hungary's total gross exports.[9] This, of course, is precisely what we would expect in a country where gross exports are such a high proportion of national product.[10] Its significance

---

enterprises on sales in each of these foreign markets as on sales of similar products in the domestic market, given the constraint that the volume of exports to each of the two foreign markets must be sufficient to provide a balance of trade.

If one uses the official exchange rates for the ruble and dollar, then 65 percent of Hungary's trade in 1970 was directed to socialist countries.

[8] The same method as that described above is used to value exports. However, in terms of the criterion which the Hungarians employed in 1968 to establish the domestic conversion rates of foreign exchange, it appears that these rates overvalued the domestic forint in 1970. One prominent Hungarian economist, while asserting that no calculations had been made as to the degree of the overvaluation, provided his own guess in early 1971 that the number of forints paid per ruble was 10 percent too low, and that the rate applying to capitalist countries was 17 percent below the equilibrium value. If one recalculates the proportion of exports to net domestic product on the basis of these guesses, then it rises to 38 percent.

Net domestic product is valued in current domestic prices, and is defined so as to be comparable with the usual western definition rather than with the concept of net material product used in socialist countries generally (Központi Statisztikai Hivatal, *Statisztikai Évkönyv 1970*, Budapest: 1971, pp. 72-73).

[9] If we consider socialist and capitalist markets separately, the proportions are still 71 and 80 percent respectively.

[10] An earlier study by the Institute of Economic Planning of the Hungarian National Planning Office showed that the Hungarian proportion of intrasectoral to

TABLE 8.2: Commodity Composition of Hungarian Foreign Trade, 1970 (percentage)

	Gross Exports			Net Exports[a]		
Commodity Group	To socialist countries	To nonsocialist countries	Total	To socialist countries	To nonsocialist countries	Total
Foodstuffs, foodstuff raw materials, and live animals	17	33	25	+12	+10	+11
Raw materials, semifinished goods, and spare parts	23	42	32	−24	−25	−25
Machinery, vehicles, and investment goods	35	7	22	+ 7	− 6	+ 1
Industrial consumer goods	23	16	20	+11	+ 9	+10
Fuels and electricity	1	2	1	−11	+ 1	− 5
Total	100	100	100	− 6	−11	− 9

SOURCE AND METHODOLOGY: Központi Statisztikai Hivatal, *Statisztikai Havi Közlemények*, 1972, 2-3, pp. 53-54. In order to combine trade with socialist and with nonsocialist countries, I followed the procedure outlined in footnote 7; i.e., I used the foreign exchange rates currently employed in Hungary for converting the export earnings and import charges of enterprises.

[a] Each item in these columns consists of the gross exports minus gross imports of the appropriate product group, all divided by Hungary's total gross exports of all types to the relevant market destinations. The figures in the last row show the year's balance of trade with the relevant markets.

for our purposes is to suggest that a very substantial number of Hungarian industrial enterprises must supply some of their production to the export market.

Hungarian industrial enterprises are highly concentrated; the grouping of what had been formerly independent production units preceded in time the comparable movement in the G.D.R. and Romania. The Hungarian concentration occurred during the first half of the 1960's, prior to the planning of the reforms. The former enterprises completely lost their identity in the process, and the new amalgamations were given the old name of "enterprises." When the economic reforms were introduced in 1968, these new amalgamations were left untouched; it is these

total gross exports was even higher than that existing in Belgium and the Netherlands—two of the very few countries whose proportions of exports to national income are even higher than the Hungarian (M. Augustinovics, "A Comparative Analysis of Foreign Trade Impacts on the Hungarian Economy," *Acta Oeconomica*, 3, 2, 1968, pp. 147-48).

large units, rather than individual factories, whose activities were to be coordinated through the market place.

At the end of 1970, there were only 812 industrial state enterprises in the country, with an average of 7.0 plants per enterprise. Including industrial cooperatives, 291 enterprises employed 74 percent of Hungary's industrial labor force.[11] Furthermore, since enterprises seem to have been formed mainly according to the principle of horizontal combination, and since each normally carries on the bulk of its activities within a narrow industry grouping, the individual enterprises tend to possess great market power over their particular spheres of industrial production. Although there are Hungarian advocates of the policy of breaking up these enterprises in order to promote competition, no significant steps had been taken in this direction as of early 1971, nor were there indications of it through 1973.

While this structural component of industrial organization acts to restrict competition on the product market, the high geographic concentration within the urban population makes for competition in a large segment of the industrial labor market. Budapest alone in 1970 had 42 percent of the country's urban population; in addition, 26 percent of the city's labor force commuted to work from outside. This geographic concentration has made it feasible for Budapest workers to change enterprises freely, since other jobs are available to them without their having to find new housing. Partly as a result, and despite the enterprise-concentration of most sectors of industry, Hungary—both before and since the reforms—has been characterized by an exceptionally high rate of labor mobility between enterprises. The annual rate of departures from the labor force employed by individual industrial enterprises fluctuated between 32 and 36 percent during 1968-71, and at least the lower annual figures exclude students employed during vacation periods.[12]

[11] *Statisztikai Évkönyv 1970*, p. 171 and 174. Those working in industrial handicrafts are included in the industrial labor force.

[12] Different official series are not fully reconciliable, the problem being particularly severe for 1969. While no annual figure is available for 1967, comparison of third-quarter data with that of 1968 suggests that the 1967 annual figure should have been approximately 32 percent. (Központi Statisztikai Hivatal, *Foglalkoztatottság és munkaviszonyból származó jövedelem 1968*, Budapest: 1970, p. 58; *Statisztikai Évkönyv 1969*, p. 90; *Statisztikai Havi Közlemények*, 1970, 11, p. 110; 1971, 2-3, p. 116; 1972, 5, p. 121; and 1972, 11, p. 113.)

No serious penalties were levied until 1971 against workers who changed jobs, nor are there "closed cities" (as in Romania) to which a person can move only with special permission. However, the shortage of urban housing makes geographic movement quite difficult. In 1971, but only in Budapest and a few other cities, rent subsidies were ended for workers who quit their jobs. Since such rent subsidies in 1971 totaled no more than about 2 percent of household income (calculated from *Magyar Hirlap*, December 12, 1971, summarized in *RFE*), this penalty cannot have operated as an overwhelming deterrent to labor turnover.

The reformed system of the Hungarian economy was introduced in January 1968. Its immediate origins lay in the work of a large secretariat which met during 1965-66 and whose efforts were approved by the Party's Central Committee. Thereafter, government ministries and offices took over for another year and a half the task of preparing the detailed reform measures. This lengthy and detailed preparation of the reform is in sharp contrast to what occurred in Czechoslovakia during the middle 1960's, or in Yugoslavia prior to its major systemic changes.

Although 1965 was a bad year economically in Hungary, one cannot explain the fact that a market-oriented reform was introduced in Hungary and nowhere else in the CMEA bloc (except for a short period in Czechoslovakia) by particularly poor Hungarian performance. During the seven years preceding the introduction of the reform, net domestic product per capita grew by 4.8 percent per annum, personal consumption per capita by 3.6 percent, and industrial output by 7.4 percent.[13] Hungarian economic performance then, as well as earlier in the postwar era, may have been slightly on the low side in comparison with the total east European CMEA bloc; but on the whole, it was fairly representative of that achieved by this group of countries.[14]

Nor was the reform introduced because Hungary was at either a particularly high or low stage of development compared to the other CMEA members. Hungarian per capita production and consumption was clearly intermediate between that of the G.D.R. and Czechoslovakia on the one hand, and that of Romania and Bulgaria on the other.

Rather, the Hungarian objections to their traditional system of planning which went down to the enterprise level, and was expressed in physical as well as in financial terms, were identical to those voiced in other CMEA countries which have not followed the same path of reform. The fact that the Hungarian economy has evolved differently from that of its allies must be explained on political rather than on economic grounds.[15]

CONCEPTION OF THE REFORMED SYSTEM

While the reformed system had important preludes, dating back at least to an important document published in late 1957 by a large com-

[13] *Statisztikai Évkönyv 1970*, pp. 72-75.

[14] For a western comparison among these countries, see the papers by T. P. Alton and E. M. Snell in Joint Economic Committee, 91st Congress of the United States (2nd session), *Economic Developments in Countries of Eastern Europe* (U.S. Government Printing Office, Washington, D.C.: 1970).

[15] One might, however, legitimately argue that Hungary was peculiarly liable to those economic pressures for reform which stemmed from the unsatisfactory situation in all CMEA countries with regard to foreign trade. This is because foreign trade constitutes an especially large proportion of national income in Hungary.

mittee established by the Hungarian Party, one of its most remarkable features is its comprehensive nature and the fact that it was introduced as a whole at a single moment of time.[16] Earlier measures such as price reform and the introduction of capital charges, while significant in their own right, did no more than has been done in the other CMEA countries. The Hungarian approach was to reject gradual and piecemeal reforms as futile, and to move boldly to simultaneous major revision of most of the traditional mechanisms for directing the economy.

The fundamental objective of the reform was to improve economic efficiency by renouncing operational planning to the level of the enterprise, and to restrict the role of central authorities mainly to the setting of global goals and the adoption of measures which would stimulate enterprises to pursue these goals in their own interests. The integration of the economy was to be achieved primarily through the market place. This broad goal has been accepted without challenge.

An economy such as that of Hungary, which is peculiarly dependent upon foreign trade, might be expected to show considerable concern with improving its export performance. In the German Democratic Republic, the key to such improvement has been sought through development of goods incorporating a high level of technology. Hungary has shown no similar emphasis, but has instead concentrated upon developing flexibility of response to foreign market conditions. Emphasis upon market-oriented direction of the economy is an obvious means of pursuing such flexibility.

Of course, "temporary" measures have been employed which run counter to the reform objectives; but generally speaking, these former have been viewed as transitional devices. More significantly, important variations of viewpoint exist as to the degree to which direct central determination of such major features of the economy as investment and prices should be substituted for enterprise decisions. I shall here attempt to present my understanding of what has been the core of consensus as to the pattern at which the reform is aimed.[17]

The reformed system does not relax in any way the belief in central

---

[16] In December 1964, the Party Central Committee adopted a resolution ordering investigation into the possibility of comprehensive economic change. Various committees, under the leadership of a major Party figure, worked for a year on the problem. In November 1965, the Central Committee decided to go ahead, and it ordered these committees to elaborate the main directives for the reform. The directives were adopted in May 1966 by the Central Committee, and it was then determined to introduce the reform as a unit. The date of implementation (January 1968) was determined at still another Central Committee meeting of November 1967. (See W. F. Robinson, *The Pattern of Reform in Hungary*, Praeger, New York, Washington, and London: 1973, chapters 1-4.)

[17] The best single source in English is I. Friss (ed.), *Reform of the Economic Mechanism in Hungary* (Akadémiai Kiadó, Budapest: 1969).

governmental planning. In fact, one justification offered for the reform is that central objectives are better realized under the decentralized system than under the pre-1968 pattern; i.e., that central control, in the meaningful sense of implementation of central objectives, has been strengthened rather than weakened.[18] But clearly the meaning given to central planning has been drastically altered both from that which existed earlier in Hungary and from that prevalent in the other CMEA countries.

Central targets are now perceived as much more global than they are elsewhere in the CMEA group. Determination of the distribution of national income between investment and consumption is still a central target; so too are the total amounts of investment to be realized in a few key sectors, with the objective being that of promoting structural change in the economy; a desired distribution of disposable income among major occupational and income groups remains a policy target; both total export and balance of payment targets have been retained, as has also the goal of containment of inflation.[19]

The globality of these targets is almost universal; there is no concept of structure-determining products whose output should be tightly controlled, as there is in the G.D.R. Furthermore, it is intended that the internal consistency of these targets should be achieved by means other than direct instructions to operating units. Financial instruments are the most important measures used for establishing such internal consistency.

The integration of the economy through financial incentives to production units, rather than through direct orders passed down a hierarchical authority structure, is viewed in part as simply a choice of the more efficient mechanism. But it is also a planned objective per se. Thus the principal economic authority of the Hungarian Party's Politbureau wrote, in rejecting the relaxation of the use of financial incentives, that the "plan targets and the means of regulation are combined expressions of the national economic plan, that is, of social interest."[20] He justified this view on the basis of the importance of attaching workers' interests to

[18] J. Zala, "Central Intention and Planning," *Acta Oeconomica*, 7, 3-4 (1971), 289-301. (However, partly because of inherent difficulties in defining the "central will," her case does not seem to me very convincing.) The report of the Central Committee at the Party Congress of November 1970 stated that "as regards the majority of the indices of the national economic plan, fulfillment was significantly closer to plan targets during the past three years than in earlier periods." (Egon Kemenes in *New Hungarian Quarterly*, XII, 42, 1971, p. 205.)

[19] Only the five-year plans have obligatory, statutory force, and only central organs are bound by them. Annual plans are also drawn up, but these are not legally binding on any organization. According to a deputy president of the National Planning Office, even the five-year plan is not broken down to the level of individual ministries (O. Gadó, in O. Gadó, ed., *Reform of the Economic Mechanism in Hungary: Development 1968-71*, Akadémiai Kiadó, Budapest: 1972, p. 19).

[20] Nyers, p. 267. The sentence is underscored in the original.

that of their enterprises, declaring that worker adherence to such group interests is the only real way to achieve adherence to social (i.e., national) interests and "that the approximation and implementation of social interest is the most essential substance of socialism."[21]

The emphasis upon financial incentives as the principal motivating force for enterprise decisions is expressed in two ways: through linking the increase in disposable income paid to employees to increased posttax profits earned by their individual enterprises, and by attaching the expansion possibilities of the enterprises to their past and prospective profitability. The financing of industrial investment through budgetary grants and loans given on preferred terms is viewed as a policy to be restricted to a few sectors, although the proper dimensions of this part of the economy is a matter of disagreement; the bulk of industrial investment is to be financed either from enterprises' profits or through bank loans granted on the basis of anticipated future profits.

Given a socialist system in which there is almost no physical planning at the enterprise level, and in which the earning of posttax profits is the major indicator of an enterprise management's success, the issue of how prices are to be determined is critical. Although there is still disagreement on this matter, the objective appears to be a system in which most prices are allowed to fluctuate according to market conditions. It is the market mechanism, rather than the central planners, which should primarily determine the prices to which producing enterprises respond. The intervention of planners should take the form mainly of macro-influence on supply and demand through measures affecting income distribution, through change in the effective foreign exchange rates so as to vary the total supply of goods on the domestic market, and through promotion or restraint of aggregate investment by the rate of taxation levied on profits and by credit policy. The main microlevel state influences which appear to be envisioned as desiderata are those of expansion, through state-financed investment, of a few chosen sectors, and the protection of low- and medium-income consumers from being disadvantaged by major changes in relative prices.

Although, as we shall see, subsidies are rampant throughout the Hungarian economy, they are regarded as an evil rather than as a desirable part of the system. To the extent that they are needed, it is intended that at least the export subsidies be granted on an equal basis to all producers of specified goods, and that individual enterprises should not be singled out for preferential treatment. It is hoped that enterprises can be made to face financial conditions which hold for all competitors, rather than ones tailored by central planners to their individual needs.

[21] Ibid., pp. 272-73.

Finally, exports and imports are intended to be treated symmetrically with sales and purchases on the home market. Effective exchange rates, which are the same for all products although they may (and do) differ substantially from the official ones, are to determine which products are to be exported and imported and in what quantities. Central planners should implement balance of payments policies by changing these effective exchange rates and by differentiating them as between groups of countries. To the degree that planners have a foreign trade policy at all with regard to individual products, it should be implemented only through central budgetary investments intended to expand the domestic production of selected items.

The image of the objectives of the reformed economic system which has been portrayed to this point is one of great laissez-faire at the microeconomic level. Of course, the mechanisms described here differ substantially from those which have actually operated in Hungary during the period since the reform was introduced, the differences often being explained by the need for temporary and transitional measures. More relevant, however, is the question of the degree to which this ideal model reflects the consensus view of Hungarian leaders. There is some reason to believe that I have painted too sharp a picture.

For example, a 1971 Hungarian article insists that the central plan for individual sectors means more than a prognosis to which the individual enterprises can choose to be indifferent. The author writes that it is difficult to conceive that an enterprise would act contrary to the plan targets for its sector without being condemned and having sanctions applied to it.[22] While certainly this was a true picture of the actual situation in early 1971, it is difficult to determine the degree to which it was considered desirable. There may well have been important Hungarian figures who believed that this was a desideratum and not just a cruel necessity. Since this is a hypothetical question, it is not one concerning which we would expect to have seen a free and sharp public conflict if differing views were indeed held.

Thus it may well be that I have overdrawn the degree to which Hungarian leaders espouse the doctrine of renouncing central intervention at the microeconomic level. But even if this should be so, it would not matter greatly for our purposes. For it is clear that they are agreed on desiring much greater use of the free market mechanism than is currently practicable in the determination of microeconomic decisions.

[22] A. Harmathy, "A gazdasági szabályozók és a szerződések rendszere," *Gazdaság- és Jogtudomány*, 1971, 4, pp. 372-85, as summarized in Hungarian Scientific Council for World Economy, Scientific Information Service, *Abstracts of Hungarian Economic Literature*, 1971, 6, pp. 55-56.

POLICY CONSTRAINTS ON THE IMPLEMENTATION OF THE REFORM

It is obvious that, as is the case in all countries, the Hungarian government faces many practical constraints on the speed with which it can implement its objectives. But a more interesting set of constraints are those which arise from what I would hypothesize are fundamental policy objectives which take precedence over the objectives of the reform itself. These policy objectives will be elaborated in order to attempt to establish the bounds within which reform objectives can be pursued. Although I would not suggest that all or any of these restricting objectives are necessarily permanent, I believe that they are all binding for the medium term. One should add to the three constraints which I shall consider that of maintaining the overwhelming predominance of socialist rather than private ownership of the means of production, and that of carrying on some half of foreign trade within the CMEA system of an agreed-upon degree of balance of exports and imports within each major category of products and with each individual trading partner.

The employment constraint. The most basic of the policy constraints to be considered is that of full employment. On an aggregate level, the rate of open (including frictional) unemployment which can be tolerated is considerably lower than that accepted as a government policy objective in capitalist countries. But at least equally important is the fact that it is considered impermissible, except in very rare circumstances, to dismiss workers on any grounds other than those of gross incompetence or continued violation of factory discipline.[23] Thus, even when other jobs are readily available, workers cannot be forced to change either their trade or their place of work because of the abolition of their existing post.[24] Not a single industrial enterprise was closed during the first year of the reform,[25] and this situation has remained very similar thereafter.[26]

[23] For a rather similar view of the facts as to worker dismissals, see A. Bernard, H. Guillaume, B. Ullmo, et al., "Organisation et méthodes de la planification hongroise," *Economies et Sociétés* (Cahiers de l'I.S.E.A., Série G, 31), VII, 2-3 (1973), 335. This is a revised form of a report of a French Planning Commissariat mission to Hungary during October 1971.

[24] I am familiar with only two significant exceptions in Hungary. The first is in the coal mining industry, where a number of inefficient pits were closed. However, new industry was brought into these regions so that little geographic movement was required of the former miners. The second is a policy of moving some forty to forty-five plants, with a total employment of ten thousand, out of Budapest during the period of roughly 1971-75.

[25] Z. Komonyi, "Some Aspects of Enterprise Behavior," in Z. Román (ed.), *Progress and Planning in Industry* (International Conference on Industrial Economics of April 1970, Akadémiai Kiadó, Budapest: 1972), p. 339.

[26] On reading an earlier draft of this manuscript, Dr. Egon Kemenes of the

This job-maintenance policy seems to stem from what is considered to be a fundamental advantage of socialism over capitalism. Perhaps the greatest reproach which socialists have historically made against capitalism is that it functions with a reserve army of unemployed, and that workers are constantly threatened with the loss of their posts. During the quarter of a century that the Communist Party regime has been in power in Hungary, workers have had virtually complete job security. More than anything else, it is this feature which has given content in the mind of the ordinary worker to the slogan of a workers' state.

While the basic mechanisms of governmental control over the Hungarian economy have changed drastically under the reform, this strict interpretation of the "right to work" has gone untouched. Meddling with this fundamental right of Hungarian workers would raise in the sharpest form the issue of the abandonment of socialism: in the minds both of the population of Hungary and of leaders in the other CMEA countries.[27] Precisely because of the drastic reform measures undertaken, I would speculate that Hungarian leaders—whatever their own desires might be—would find any tampering with the current job-maintenance policy to be more politically dangerous than is the case in any other CMEA country.

But if workers are to be fully protected, at least so far as their jobs are concerned, both from the consequences of enterprise inefficiency and from the forced adjustments to changing product demands and technology which are their fate in capitalist economies, then two critical consequences follow.

The first consequence is that all high-cost enterprises must be shielded from the repercussions of their own inefficiency upon their output volume and thus upon their employment.[28] Since enterprises must sell their

---

Hungarian Scientific Council for World Economy commented that, while there have been no closings, there have been approximately twelve mergers of enterprises (as of early 1973) which have resulted from unacceptable financial losses. In these cases, there has been dismissal of managers and retraining of workers.

The most important such instance was that of the Vörös Csillag enterprise in Budapest which was the largest tractor enterprise in the country, and which at the end of 1972 was merged with an enterprise in another city. On merger, the Budapest factory shifted to the production of components of buses and trucks, these being the principal products of the parent enterprise. Thus the merger involved a complete change in product line, a replacement of about 70 percent of the plant's equipment, and retraining of its 2,500 man labor force.

[27] The Hungarian academician J. Bognár implies that abandonment of the socialist value system ("e.g., equality, *right to work*, free education and health service, inexpensive cultural facilities and services") would mean falling headlong into state capitalism. ("Economic Reform, Development and Stability in Hungary," *Acta Oeconomica*, 8, 1, 1972, p. 29. The emphasis is mine.)

[28] The most authoritative Hungarian with regard to economic policy writes that

products on the market place, this implies that at least one of the following three conditions must prevail. (1) A subsidy system must be used which is differentiated to the needs of individual enterprises. (2) Enterprises must be protected from competition by giving them monopoly rights over both their own products and those which are close substitutes. (3) Prices must be maintained at levels high enough to cover the costs of the most inefficient producers, and these must be assured of the possibility of selling their products at these prices.

All three of these conditions existed to some degree in Hungary in 1971. But all three have consequences which are repugnant to Hungarian reformers. The first implies that central authorities must closely supervise the subsidized enterprises and instruct them on how to improve their effectiveness; otherwise, the subsidies would be completely open-ended.[29] The second implies that the state must either determine prices, qualities, and product mix so as to prevent the monopolists from exploiting their positions, or that it must absorb monopoly profits into the state budget and—in order to do this—regulate the individual enterprises sufficiently closely so as to be able to determine what portion of their profits is due to their monopoly position. The third condition implies that central authorities must restrict the investment opportunities of the more efficient enterprises so that these enterprises do not expand sufficiently to threaten the market position of the less efficient. But it also implies either that the more efficient enterprises must be given maximum output quotas in the short run (i.e., return in fact to the system of physical planning of output), or that markets be maintained in permanent disequilibrum. Only by the maintenance of market disequilibrium can increases in output by the more efficient enterprises be prevented from either forcing the less efficient to lower production volumes than they require on employment grounds, or to sales at prices which would bring them financial losses.

Protection of jobs from changing product demands, and from alterations in technology which affect the skill composition required for the enterprise labor force, is much more difficult to provide by the first and second conditions than by the third one of price maintenance.[30] But

---

"competition cannot become a competition among capital; competition in Hungary does not endanger the existence of enterprises." (Nyers, p. 270.)

[29] It is perfectly true that enterprises may be warned—as has in fact been done—that their differential subsidies will be reduced over time; such warnings may motivate high-cost enterprises toward improved efficiency. But if the enterprises are not successful in reducing costs or improving their product mix, central authorities cannot withdraw the subsidies without jeopardizing the job protection of the enterprises' workers.

[30] The first alternative of differentiated subsidies might seem to some readers to

price maintenance implemented through short-run physical planning would represent a return to prereform conditions. The continued operation of a sellers' market would thus appear to be the preferred mechanism, even if it is used in combination with the others.

For these reasons, the second consequence of a national job-maintenance policy is that prices will generally be set below their equilibrium levels, while still being high enough to assure profits to the least efficient enterprises. This implies that the employment constraint which I have hypothesized as binding upon the Hungarian economy must prevent the government from leaving pricing decisions to the market place. Restraint over such price setting seems to be a necessary condition for satisfying the job-maintenance policy constraint on the system.

The disequilibrium pricing system which is characterized as a sellers' market is generally recognized to exist in Hungary as in the other CMEA countries.[31] The principal explanation for its existence which is usually

---

be less deleterious than the permanent maintenance of sellers' market conditions. There are, however, reasons for rejecting sole reliance upon it other than the necessarily ex post and open-ended character which such subsidies would have to take.

(1) Under Hungarian conditions, market-equilibrium prices in many spheres could only be those dictated by monopolies. It is true that monopoly profits could be taxed away through differentiating the sales tax even more sharply than it is today, but supply would still be determined through monopoly pricing. Furthermore, there would be strong ideological objections to having relative prices (particularly of consumer goods) heavily influenced by the degree of monopoly existing in the branch.

(2) The Ministry of Finance would doubtless exercise its parochial interest in combating the novel concept of open-ended subsidies which increase uncontrollably during the fiscal year with the decline in demand for the products of individual enterprises. Annual budgeting would be made much more difficult.

(3) There would be a fear that demand for certain products is extremely inelastic in the short run, and thus that the producing enterprises cannot—however much they may reduce prices—sell their existing product mix without reducing production and employment. Probably more important, even if demand is not so inelastic, enterprises may not (mistakenly) reduce prices rapidly enough.

[31] See, for example, János Kornai in *Közgazdasági Szemle*, XVIII, 1 (1971), translated as Working Paper 7 of the International Development Research Center of Indiana University. Kornai makes the same point in *Anti-Equilibrium* (North-Holland, Amsterdam and London: 1971), p. 327.

A survey (said to cover 80 to 85 percent of the large firms in industry and construction, and 20 percent of those in agriculture) as to the 1971-75 plans of individual enterprises showed that these enterprises were collectively planning on a rate of production increase which was 50 percent higher than had been attained during 1966-70 or was planned nationally for 1971-75; yet only 10 percent of these enterprises mentioned marketing factors as threatening their fulfillment of their own high goals (M. Siman in *Figyelő*, October 20, 1971, pp. 1 and 4, translated in *JPS*).

A questionnaire addressed in late 1968 to the three top directors of some sixty to seventy large enterprises, the results of which were believed by the group presenting the report to be typical of manufacturing, showed that only 12 percent of the

presented is that central planners consistently make greater demands upon the available economic resources than can be met.[32] Institutional reasons can be given for such excess demand. Pressure upon central planners from enterprises and from individual sectoral ministries for additional investments which sum to more than can be realized is one such reason.[33] Both political and incentive pressure for increases in the monetary disposable income of the population, which are greater than the resources which central planners are willing to allocate to the production of consumer goods, coupled with an unwillingness on the part of central planners to allow a compensating rate of inflation in the prices of consumer goods, comprise a second reason. These, however, constitute a rather ad hoc set of explanations which leave unexplained why central planners should consistently give in to these pressures. The alternative explanation that the job-maintenance constraint is the funda-

---

respondents believed that their own enterprise faced strong competition from domestic producers, and that 17 percent believed that it faced strong competition from imports (*Bulletin* of the Institute for Industrial Economics of the Hungarian Academy of Sciences, 6, 1969, and the tables in the Hungarian brochure to which the *Bulletin* refers). A ministerial conference in 1971 was said to have established that true competition exists only in the laundry detergent field (I. Friss in *Közgazdasági Szemle*, XVIII, 12, 1971, 1397-1411, translated in *JPS*); another source adds certain telecommunication items to the sphere of competition (J. Wilcsek in *Figyelő*, January 26, 1971, p. 3, translated in *JPS*).

A study of the reasons for consumer dissatisfaction with durable consumer goods in 1969 showed that 64 percent listed total lack of availability—in contrast with the remaining one-third listings of poor quality, lack of choice with respect to price, size, or fashion, lack of spare parts, and absence of proper sales timing. ("Kereskedelem-Politikai Közvéleménykutatás," *Marketing Piackutatás*, 1, 1970. p. 8, as referred to in G. P. Lauter, *The Manager and Economic Reform in Hungary*, Praeger, New York, Washington, and London: 1972, p. 75.)

Finally, the marginal rate of monetary saving (increase in savings deposits divided by the increase in monetary income) has been very high during 1968-71, and has indeed actually increased somewhat in comparison with the previous four years: from 41 to 46 percent (Hungarian Central Statistical Office, *Statistical Yearbook 1971*, pp. 332-33). If sellers' market conditions had been radically reduced during the reform years, we might have expected the marginal rate of saving to have become low or negative.

[32] See Kornai in *Közgazdasági Szemle*; his explanation leans most heavily upon the excess of investment plans. In *Anti-Equilibrium*, he goes further. There he presents as a working hypothesis the main factors which he views as immediately responsible for the disequilibrium that he calls "suction," and summarizes these factors as follows: "The reproduction of suction is ultimately related to the impatient chasing of economic growth, the forcing of the acceleration of the growth rate." Such suction, in his opinion, must either prevent or, at best, dilute the favorable results expected from the Hungarian reform (*Anti-Equilibrium*, pp. 313-21 and 327-29). There is nothing in his treatment either of the history or of the logic of suction to suggest any role at all for the job-maintenance constraint which I consider fundamental.

[33] See J. Drecin, "Investment Equilibrium: Mechanisms of Control and Decision," *Acta Oeconomica*, 7, 3-4 (1971), 275-87.

mental cause offers the attraction inherent in the principle of Occam's Razor.

I would argue, therefore, that the sellers' market in Hungary is not merely a flaw in planning, but rather a necessary condition for meeting a policy constraint which takes precedence over the objectives of the reform.[34] An analysis of the potential effectiveness of the reform measures in improving the working of the Hungarian economy must take this into account.

However, the force of the job-maintenance constraint is substantially lessened by a very high voluntary labor turnover in Hungary. As of September 1969, 24 percent of industrial blue-collar workers had worked in at least one other enterprise during the previous twenty-one months, and 41 percent had changed enterprises during the previous four and three-quarter years.[35] This high turnover makes it much easier for enterprises to contract their labor force or to change its skill composition over the period of a few years than would be the case if workers were more stationary. Since workers have been quitting their jobs at a much more rapid pace during the reform period than earlier,[36] the job-maintenance constraints can be met with somewhat less of a sellers' market than might have been predicted.

The price-stability inflation constraint. Rapid increases in the consumer price level are considered politically unacceptable. Memories of the hyperinflations in Hungary after both world wars, and of the steep price increases during 1950-52 which were accompanied by a major reduction in real wages, still seem to be sharp; the prospect of a rate of inflation comparable to American, let alone to west European rates, would be regarded as political dynamite. One Hungarian leader, while doubtless exaggerating somewhat, suggested to me that the entire reform might

[34] Nyers, p. 270, assures us that it is absolutely clear that early abolition of the sellers' market would be an unrealistic objective. He does not, however, present the reasons for his viewpoint.

[35] Központi Statisztikai Hivatal, *Az Állami Iparban Foglalkoztatott Munkások Létszámösszetétele, Munkakörülményei és Bérarányai* (Budapest: 1971), p. 36. The figures for such change during the previous twenty-one months ranged from 16 percent for skilled workers to 38 percent for unskilled. These figures are somewhat of an understatement, since official transfers between enterprises—as opposed to changes due to quitting or being dismissed—are not included.

[36] The proportion of the industrial labor force which quit its jobs (as opposed to leaving because of retirement, death, end of a short-term labor contract, reorganization, or dismissal) increased by 40 percent between the third quarter of 1967 and that of the first year of the reform period (*Foglalkoztatottság és munkaviszonyból származó jövedelem 1968*, pp. 30 and 58). For the economy as a whole, the number of quits more than doubled between the calendar years 1967 and 1969 ("Foglalkoztatottság és kereseti arányok, 1969," *Statisztikai Időszaki Közlemények*, 206, 1971, as referred to in *Abstracts*, 1971, 3-4, p. 118).

be abolished if the cost of living were to rise at even 3 percent per annum.[37]

The combination of this price-stability constraint and the employment constraint places narrow bounds on the set of feasible institutional solutions. Central planners must develop an economic system which combines virtually no unemployment with a very low rate of inflation, and must do this under conditions where all enterprises are assured by the state of sufficient financial means so that they need not dismiss workers. These constraints can be met only if the state exercises very tight controls over earnings since, in view of the tight labor market and the high rate of labor turnover, there exists considerable market pressure for wage inflation.

Furthermore, a policy of permitting wage increases only to the degree that they can be financed out of profits without raising prices would be insufficient. Such a policy would permit those enterprises which are most efficient, or which are in the best market position, to attract labor with the scarcest skills from the other enterprises, leaving these with a skill-mix which would be untenable for continued operations. The government could then maintain its job-maintenance policy only by providing the labor-losing enterprises with sufficient subsidies to permit them to raise wages in turn.

Reluctantly, but inevitably, the Hungarian government has placed tight limits on the percentage increases in average total compensation which may be provided by individual enterprises to their employees. It has recognized the deleterious effect on efficiency of such restrictions on worker incentives; worker interest in enterprise profitability is sharply reduced from what had been assumed when the reform was introduced. But even a limited relationship between profitability and earnings may be more than the economic system can handle within its constraints. The director of the Economic Institute of the Academy of Sciences has suggested that it may be wise to eliminate completely the link between wages paid and the enterprise's profitability.[38]

This state of affairs seriously jeopardizes the objective of attaching

[37] It is claimed that public opinion always perceives the loss through inflation as being larger than is in fact the case (B. Csikós-Nagy, "A magyar gazdasági reform eredményei és perspektívái," *Közgazdasági Szemle*, xix, 9, 1972). I am indebted to Paul Marer for pointing out that this is the reverse of J. M. Keynes' money-illusion argument: the greater the increase in nominal wages relative to real wages, the less is the perceived increase in real wages.

[38] I. Friss, "Gazdasági reformunk gyakorlati tapasztalatai," in *Közgazdasági Szemle*, xviii, 12 (1971), 1397-1411, as summarized in *Abstracts*, 1971, 6, p. 51. In late 1972, the problem was seen as one still defying solution. There was agreement only as to the limits within which measures could be devised: that workers should participate in enterprise profits, and that the financial instruments of wage control available to central authorities should be enlarged (Csikós-Nagy, p. 1016).

workers' interests to that of their enterprises, which Nyers has linked closely to "the most essential substance of socialism."[39] Under the circumstances, workers' self-management might be counted on to select the most conservative and inefficient choices available to the individual enterprises. One can only praise the wisdom of central authorities in having made no moves to enlarge the role of worker participation in the management of enterprises.

If enterprises are indeed to decide production issues according to their effects on enterprise profits, as is assumed by the reform system, it is top management alone which can be motivated to do this. But the psychological cost-benefit matrix facing top managers is very unfavorable for this. For one thing, they face a recalcitrant labor force which can be offered very little increase in earnings to compensate for the extra effort involved in accepting changes in technology, or even in the alterations of work patterns necessary for the adaptation of the enterprise's product mix to changing market demand. Pressure on the labor force in any individual enterprise may be expected to lead to a sharp rise in the quit rate. Thus profits may easily fall as a result of managerial efforts for greater efficiency. Second, pursuit of profit objectives would seem to pit managers against the workers of their own enterprises; this is a particularly awkward situation for managers in a society where the ideology is that of a workers' state. Third, benefits to managers from profit-increasing decisions can only be either personal financial rewards, or psychological rewards through acting in what they believe to be the interests of society as a whole.

Personal financial rewards to management from profit-increasing decisions are limited both by the absence of equity ownership rights in the enterprise, and by the national social pressures against compensating top managers too substantially for higher profits at a time when the vast bulk of the labor force cannot be rewarded for such successes. The strength of the social ethic in affecting managerial behavior is severely limited by a third policy constraint.

The constraint on rapid change of management. In 1967, immediately before the reform system was introduced, there were apparently extensive discussions as to whether enterprise directors who were regarded in the ministries as unqualified for work under the new conditions should be removed. The decision was against it.

Reasons cited ran the gamut from the need to follow a humane personnel policy, and the difficulty of finding replacements, to the politically harmful effects of such a policy. Doubtless all of these played their part;

---

[39] See the passage referred to in footnote 21.

one should not, for example, underemphasize the degree to which Hungary is still influenced by the *gemütliche* traditions of the former Austro-Hungarian empire rather than by efficiency considerations. But it seems reasonable to assume that political considerations were the most important. It was only sensible to avoid the creation of any powerful political group which would have had a strong interest in reversing the reform system, thus making it controversial internally in Hungary as it already was externally within the CMEA bloc. If large numbers of directors, after many years of job security, had been suddenly demoted or prematurely retired, the political ramifications might have been serious.[40]

The result is that enterprise directors, and especially the general directors, remained unchanged during at least the first three years of the reform. I was told in one of the major industrial ministries that a maximum of five or six of the ministry's general directors of enterprises, out of its total of one hundred fifty, are changed annually,[41] and that this pattern had not been affected by the reform; the ministerial official thought that the percentage is probably not surpassed in other ministries. The one removal of which I was told in another industry was a result of serious production failure: i.e., the same reason which would have been relevant prior to the reform. Generally, expert Hungarian observers spoke of the total lack of fear by enterprise directors that they might be demoted. Only one person claimed that at the end of 1970 there was a definite policy of increasing job mobility in general directors' posts; even he insisted that this was intended as a policy of gradualism, geared to avoiding the creation of fears among directors, and that it was a policy which shunned newspaper publicity.

Although there has been some talk of hoping to improve the managerial competence of enterprise management by bringing in new blood as "assistants"—younger men who have not spent their career under the system of physical planning which no longer prevails—their influence is much more likely to be on managerial efficiency than on managerial values. This is because enterprises appear to be run very much by their general directors, without even the formality of establishing collegial executive committees.

[40] However, see Table 14.8 of Chapter 14 for some evidence that enterprise directors were not a politically powerful group.

A Hungarian scholar who read a draft of this manuscript denied that political considerations played an important role in the decision. He also said that, in his opinion, the quality of top management in enterprises has been shown to be good during the postreform years. While he admitted that there both were and are opposing views as to this latter point, he believed that his view was the one generally held.

[41] Presumably these changes do not include retirements. I was told by a different source that a major study of the same industry indicated that the top three directors in each enterprise had an average tenure in post of ten to twelve years.

Thus, while the Hungarian reformed system can operate according to the goals set for it only to the degree that the top managers of enterprises internalize the profit motive, and resist the social pressures within the enterprise which counter change in products and in production methods, such strong espousal requires a revolution in the value system of men who are middle-aged or older. Moreover, these are men who were originally chosen partially for their political qualifications: i.e., for their acceptance of the previous values of the regime. It should be no surprise, for example, that a survey of the 1971-75 plans of individual enterprises showed a strong bias toward expansion of production: not only was the summation of their plans 50 percent higher than the production increase called for in the national plan, but their gross investment plans concentrated primarily on expansion of capacity, and provided for only a 2 percent annual rate of replacement of machinery.[42] A sample of general directors in late 1968 gave a weight of 25 percent to "satisfying demands" as a factor in their decisions as to product-mix programs.[43] Apparently, their product-mix decisions were heavily influenced by their subjective views as to the products which were most needed by society, rather than being determined by the market place through differential profits for different products. At least for consumer goods, the Minister of Light Industry has come out strongly in favor of these nonprice methods of determining product mix.[44]

In view of the characteristics of the general directors, it would be surprising if they would commonly pit themselves against the interests of the workers of their enterprises. One would not expect them to fight strongly for a high-profit ethic at the expense of other values to which they had been attuned over a long period.

Developing Hungarian Attitudes Toward the Reform

The first couple of years of the reform were marked by an apparent confidence that the "transitional" restraints on the blossoming of reform

[42] Siman, pp. 1 and 4.

[43] *Bulletin*, 6 (1969) and the tables in the Hungarian brochure to which the *Bulletin* refers. The study covered sixty to seventy large enterprises, and the results are described as characteristic of manufacturing as a whole. Differences between branches are generally quite minor.

Production motives as such (increasing production volume, utilizing capacities, and maintaining the employment level) were given an additional 34 percent weight. Thus "satisfying demands" does not appear to be a proxy for "realizing sales." Given the propaganda of the period for profit making, and the fact that the study was carried out under the auspices of the Academy of Sciences, it seems likely that the residual weights—essentially profit-earning—represent an overstatement.

Very similar results were obtained in a smaller study one year later by the same organization, this time based upon personal interviews (Komonyi, p. 345).

[44] Mrs. János Keserü, minister of Light Industry, in Gadó (ed.), *Reform*, p. 153.

could to a large degree be phased out in the fairly near future, combined with some surprise that employment and inflation constraints could be so fully observed during this transition period without markedly slowing down the rate of growth of the economy. Transitional measures which were particularly marked for elimination were central price controls, the remnants of materials allocation, subsidies for enterprises, controls over increases in worker incomes in individual enterprises, and foreign trade quotas and sharply differentiated export subsidies.

The early 1970's saw an increased realism of expectations as to the economic effectiveness of market mechanisms within the existing sociopolitical constraints. Only materials allocations had been substantially phased out, all other transitional measures remaining (although they were reshaped and somewhat eased in the area of wage restrictions). One Hungarian who commented in early 1973 on a draft of this manuscript pointed to increased recognition of the need for central controls. The director of the Office of Prices and Allocations noted the abandonment of the belief that the proportion of products governed by price controls or materials allocations should be reduced from year to year, and the substitution of the notion that their expansion or contraction should depend upon the projected tautness of materials supplies and of the balance of payments for the year; he insisted that no fixed policy with regard to their reduction should be followed even as far off as in the 1976-80 plan period.[45] It was authoritatively proposed that the number of sales tax categories should be increased.[46] The number of import quotas for 1972 rose rather than fell.[47] The prime minister said that there would be a temporary slowdown over the next few years in the pace at which reform measures were promoted.[48]

At the same time that this greater realism developed, there was also increased concern over the pressure of the constraints within which the reform mechanism functioned.[49] The director of the Economic Institute of the Academy of Sciences wrote that the country cannot forever accept the extraordinary disproportions which arise from consumer price supports, and that long-term plans must be developed for their elimination.[50] The prime minister—only a few months before he had said that there would be a slowdown for several years in the pace of reform— had urged that the macroeconomic employment and price-stability constraints could be met with less central interference on the market place,

---

[45] B. Csikós-Nagy in *Közgazdasági Szemle*, XIX, 9 (1972), 1016-1017.
[46] Ibid.
[47] I. Pardi in *Társadalmi Szemle*, 1972, 1, pp. 3-14, translated in *JPS*.
[48] October 1971 talk as reported in Robinson, p. 363.
[49] See Robinson, p. 355, for an account of this change of attitude.
[50] I. Friss in *Közgazdasági Szemle*, XVIII, 12 (1971), 1397-1411, translated in *JPS*.

and he had urged some withholding of subsidies for enterprises producing goods for which there was no satisfactory market.[51]

These reactions appear to be the mark of a system which, having become well established, is evaluated with increasing realism—including some cynicism—by those who function within its bounds.

[51] J. Fock, radio broadcast and *Népszava*, May 8, 1971, as reported in Robinson, pp. 334 and 354.

CHAPTER 9

Hungary: The Reform Mechanisms
in Practice

Tʜɪs chapter will deal with the main economic mechanisms of the reform, principally as they existed in early 1971. Their institutional development, as well as the ways in which they are used, are an adaptation of the conception of the reform to the various constraints which both grew out of the historical situation and resulted from higher-priority government objectives. While no Hungarian would assert that such adaptation was desirable per se, it is the result of this adaptation which represents the reform as it has actually functioned.

Pricing Policy

A basic change in the pricing system was considered a necessary prelude to the installation of the reform mechanisms, since these lean heavily on the free response of enterprises to market conditions; the new pricing system and the reform mechanisms were introduced simultaneously in January 1968, and both have remained essentially unmodified during at least the following five years.

The fundamental objective of the new price system was to make both producer and consumer prices reflective of current supply and demand conditions, as well as to transform prices into socially appropriate signals to enterprises as to what their total output, investment, product-mix, and input-mix decisions should be. A second goal, which still awaits implementation, was to bring the domestic price structure more into line with that prevailing in foreign markets, so that Hungary might become better integrated into the international economy through the medium of the price mechanism.

The fundamental pricing objective might have been implemented by removing the government entirely from the process of price setting and allowing prices to move freely at the dictates of the market, and by simultaneously stimulating investment finance to concentrate on those products and enterprises yielding the highest return to capital. Both of these policies have been followed to some degree, although always more in theory than in practice. But the objections to pushing them too far have up to now been persuasive: fear of inflation, the existence of monopoly and oligopoly conditions, the wish to keep certain goods low priced as a form of income-support policy for low-income families, and the desire of central planners to maintain considerable control over the intersectoral composition of industrial investment.[1]

The practice actually adopted was to introduce a new set of prices paid to producers which were to cover costs and were also to provide a more equal return on capital invested than had previously been the case. The number of differential sales tax rates on consumer products was reduced by two-thirds—still leaving, however, about one thousand different rates in 1968 and six hundred in 1970—so as to increase the impact on enterprise production decisions of consumer preferences for one type of product relative to another. A substantial portion of the new prices was set free, with producers being permitted in theory to vary them from the "reform price" as they saw fit.[2] Finally (as we shall see in a later section of this chapter), industrial investment in individual enterprises was to be partially financed from the enterprise's past profits and from credit sources weakly related to the enterprise's future expected profits, and partly from state sources whose volume was dictated by quite distinct considerations.

The producer prices which were introduced in January 1968 were expected to cover costs[3] and provide rates of return on capital which

[1] One might also list, as most fundamental, the need to maintain a disequilibrium sellers' market as an instrument for carrying out the national job-maintenance policy. However—in contrast to the reasons mentioned in the text—there is no evidence that Hungarian policy makers have explicitly recognized this as a justification for government price control.

[2] For a description of the pricing system introduced in 1968, see B. Csikós-Nagy (director of the Office of Prices and Allocations), "The New Hungarian Price System," in I. Friss (ed.), Reform of the Economic Mechanism in Hungary (Akadémiai Kiadó, Budapest: 1969), pp. 133-62.

[3] These costs included a 5 percent tax on capital, but also a 25 percent tax on wages: rates which had been imposed prior to the reform. The two taxes are counterbalancing in their effects on labor-substituting investment, and the imposition of both together seems to be a compromise between recognition that capital should be regarded as a scarce resource, and the notion that surplus value is earned through the use of living labor and that the budget should absorb this surplus value directly from the enterprises. The East Germans have been more single-purposed in restricting their factor tax to one on capital.

It is true that there is a potential advantage in having a two-channel tax (on both capital and labor) in that the combination of two instruments may be used to achieve both the desired amount of total investment and the desired degree of capital-labor substitution. However, I have never seen the two-channel tax defended on this basis. Committees created to analyze the reform experience of 1968-71 were, in 1972, considering recommending the maintenance of the existing rate of tax on wages while reducing the tax on capital; since everyone recognized that investment was much/too high, use of the two-instrument approach would have involved raising both taxes but—in order to promote capital-labor substitution as was wished—particularly raising that on wages. Probably it was the constraint against raising prices, and the lack of substantial sales tax revenues which might be reduced so as to absorb cost increases, which prevented this ap-

would vary from 1.6 percent in mining to 9.5 percent in the chemical industry. Partly, the sharp differentiation of rates reflected exceptionally high profits which could be earned on exports to the CMEA countries by individual sectors.[4] Low profit rates in mining, electricity, and steel reflected the belief that investments in these sectors must be so large that they could be financed only by the state, and thus that enterprises here need no substantial profits for investment purposes. The low profit rate for the food processing industry was partially a response to the desire to hold down consumer food prices. The result was an amalgam which departed seriously both from the notion that the profit rate on capital should be at the same average level in all sectors, with higher realized enterprise profits thus indicating greater enterprise efficiency, and from the alternative concept that higher profit rates should be reserved for those sectors which must expand particularly rapidly in order to equilibrate or keep up with demand.

While this new pricing system improved the degree to which Hungarian prices reflected costs plus a single, economy-wide rate of return on factors utilized,[5] the variance from this standard remained very great.[6] It would be difficult to argue that, given this price system, it would be reasonable either to reward differentially labor and management of the more-profitable compared to the less-profitable enterprises, or that investments should be channeled into those enterprises which provide the highest expected return on additional capital. The pricing system may have been an advance over the earlier one, but it was far from what would be desirable as the basis for a market-determined economy.

This might not have been too important if the new 1968 prices had been only the starting point from which enterprises could move freely in pricing policy. But, of course, the freeing of all prices would have raised major inflationary dangers, quite apart from other ill effects.

Although the Hungarians created four different kinds of prices, these can really be treated as two without much loss of accuracy: fixed (aside

---

proach from being followed. But the implication of this constraint is that the two-channel tax cannot be used as two instruments to achieve two separate goals. (For the 1972 state of Hungarian thought, see Csikós-Nagy, *Közgazdasági Szemle*, XIX, 9, 1972, translated in *RFE*.)

[4] E.g., by pharmaceuticals within the chemical branch, and by engineering products in general.

[5] For one measure of this improvement, see Csikós-Nagy in Friss, *Reform*, pp. 136-37.

[6] In 1970, observed rates of return on capital varied among forty-seven branches between 2 and 43 percent (J. Bokor and G. Ambrózy, "As ipar érdekeltségi és jövedelmezőségi viszonyai," *Gazdaság*, 1971, 4, pp. 49-59, as cited in Hungarian Scientific Council for World Economy, Scientific Information Service, *Abstracts of Hungarian Economic Literature*, 1972, 1, p. 90).

from seasonal variations) and free. The substantial bulk of finished producer and consumer goods has been sold by industry at free prices. Furthermore, free prices are also important for raw materials and intermediate products and for retail trade.[7] But this high proportion of free prices is quite deceptive.

According to a source in the Hungarian Office of Prices, the basic principle used in determining whether a particular price should be fixed or free was that the prices of a given product family need be controlled at only one state of the process leading from raw material to sale to the final user. Given such a fixed point for each product family, variations of the average free price for each product family could be restrained, while still gaining the advantage of fluctuating free prices at some stages of the process for individual products within each family. (Where it is the raw material or intermediate-product price which is frozen, the restraint on prices at successive stages rests upon the enforcement of "just" profit mark-ups.) If we think of the integrative process for individual products as consisting of three stages in cases where the products are sold to final consumers, and of two stages otherwise, it would appear from the figures of footnote 7 that this principle has been realized. This is all the more true when one remembers the important share of raw materials and intermediate products which are imported from other CMEA countries under five-year price agreements; for these items, no specifically-Hungarian price controls are needed in order to freeze the domestic prices of these materials and intermediate products.

But there is also a good deal of control over even the so-called free prices. Negotiations take place between the Hungarian Office of Prices and price-leader enterprises concerning not only fixed prices but also free prices; in this regard, no distinction is made between the two types. True, there are no legal restrictions of note over the free prices. But enterprises, as we shall see below, are engaged in constant negotiations with various interministerial committees over subsidies, tax rates, loans, imports duties, and rates of sales tax on consumer products; their managers would have to be extremely shortsighted to take a stiff-necked attitude in negotiations concerning their free prices. Moreover, there is social pressure against "profiteering" (i.e., raising prices where this is not compelled by increasing costs) from the local organs of the Communist Party and the trade union, as well as "advice" from the industrial branch ministry which is the administrative superior of the enterprise

[7] See Csikós-Nagy in Friss, *Reform*, pp. 148-51. In early 1968, 78 percent of the total sales of a broad group of processing sectors, 28 percent of a selection of raw materials and intermediate products, and 23 percent of all retail sales were made at free prices. In 1969, 25 percent of all retail trade was conducted at free prices, and the free-price proportion was 50 percent for the large sector of clothing and footwear.

general director; enterprise managers would have to be much more heavily motivated toward profit maximizing than is in fact the case for them to resist such pressure.

It is the combination of legal price control over most product groups at some point in their passage from raw material to sale to the final user, plus the bargaining power of interministerial committees and the administrative demands of branch ministries, plus the social pressure of organizations within the enterprise itself—all acting on enterprise managers who are themselves only weakly motivated to increase profits by actions considered socially irresponsible—which has succeeded in keeping the average cost-of-living increase to only 1 to 2 percent per year (3 percent only in 1972) in spite of general sellers' market conditions. Similarly, the January 1968 price reform led to only a 5 percent increase in the prices received by industrial enterprises, and thereafter the price increases were kept to 1 to 2 percent annually. Without the existence of general managerial acceptance of informal restrictions on their right to raise "free" prices, it is difficult to see how anti-inflationary jawboning by the Office of Prices could have worked so effectively.

In short, my impression is that enterprise managements feel reasonably at liberty to raise the "free" prices of individual products only so long as the average price of the products they sell does not rise by more than an agreed percentage. Clearly, enterprises have greater bargaining power over the amount of the average increase for free than for fixed prices. The liberty to change prices differentially is of value to the economy in adjusting the supply and demand for individual products within a given product family. But the distinction between "free" and "fixed" prices seems more marginal than one might think from the literature. At the end of 1970, two officials of the National Office of Prices and Allocations could still write that "the 1968 reform has hardly affected consumer prices."[8] Although there remains a real distinction between the mechanisms and effectiveness of price adjustment in Hungary and in the other CMEA countries, it is a thinner one in practice than is often supposed.[9]

[8] P. Vallus and L. Rásc in O. Gadó (ed.), *Reform of the Economic Mechanism in Hungary: Development 1968-71* (Akadémiai Kiadó, Budapest: 1972), p. 40.

[9] In early 1972, one Hungarian writer wrote that, since the first years of the reform, "the signaling function of prices has weakened to some extent, and the requirement of maintaining price stability has shifted increasingly to the forefront" (P. Vallus in *Figyelő*, January 19, 1972, pp. 1 and 3, translated in *JPS*). In late 1972, the director of the Hungarian Office of Prices and Allocations went so far as to declare that the extent of the deviation between prices and values of individual commodities is perhaps greater in Hungary than in any other CMEA country. Although value refers only to labor value rather than to total average costs, the passage treats the first as a reasonable proxy for the second; thus Hun-

MATERIAL INCENTIVES FOR ENTERPRISES

Since, under the reform system, individual enterprises ceased to receive plans from higher authorities which spelled out their expected production, product mix, or input mix, it became particularly important to motivate enterprise personnel both to make socially appropriate decisions and to work efficiently in terms of the pricing and market-demand parameters which faced them. Two methods have been used for such motivation: the first consists of awards directed to the enterprise's personnel as a whole, and the second of awards directed specifically to top management. Both methods attempt to link the material interests of the personnel involved to the increase in the profits of their particular enterprise, with profits being calculated on the assumption that average wages per employee in the enterprise will be the same as those paid in the previous year.

It would have been possible, of course, to leave each individual enterprise to decide how to spend these calculated profits: whether on wage increases, bonuses, social expenditures, or investments.[10] The problem with such a procedure, however, is primarily that it could have led to sharp wage inflation for the reasons discussed in Chapter 8; in addition, because prices of different products yield widely differing amounts of profit per employee, and because the government does have a policy as to the total volume of industrial investment, some restrictions had to be placed on the enterprises' rights to distribute profits between additional earnings for the workforce and investment.

Furthermore, increases in earnings determined at the level of the individual enterprise are also constrained by the fact that some increases are given to personnel in all enterprises as a result of national incomes policy. The most important example of this was in 1973, when manual workers in industry were to receive a special wage increase averaging at least 8 percent;[11] this was partly to be financed out of the state budget, and partly out of enterprise profits without the increase being subject

---

garian prices are viewed as deviating peculiarly strongly from long-run equilibrium. (B. Csikós-Nagy, "A magyar gazdasági reform eredményei és perspektivái," *Közgazdasági Szemle*, XIX, 9, 1972, p. 1016.) Even if this latter position should be somewhat exaggerated, it is reflective of the degree of meaningfulness of "free" prices.

In 1973, the second author declared that only about 10 percent of the value of consumer goods is sold at appropriate prices, and he forecast a transition period of change extending over ten to fifteen years (Csikós-Nagy in *Valóság*, 1973, 3, pp. 21-26, as summarized in *Abstracts*, 1973, 2, p. 43).

[10] Such a system would have been fully compatible either with a fixed percentage tax on computed profits, or with a tax rate differentiated by enterprise.

[11] This special wage increase was higher than the total percentage increase received by industrial manual workers in any previous year since the reform (*Statisztikai Havi Közlemények*, 1973, 1, p. 14).

to tax, and it was to be in addition to the normal wage increase. The purpose of this special wage increase was to permit industrial manual workers to regain the relative income position which they had been losing in recent years; but one effect, of course, was to exert considerable inflationary pressure on the economy even without the existence of decentralized wage increases.

The Hungarian government began in 1968 with a national percentage limitation on increases of average earnings in each enterprise taken as a unit. One result was a strong competition among enterprises to increase their employment of low-paid (i.e., low-skilled) personnel in order to provide more scope for raising the income of each individual employee without exceeding the permissible increase in average earnings. Enterprise managers told me that even in 1970, when this system had already been modified, they hired as many secondary school students as possible during the summer without any regard to their expected productivity;[12] the contribution of these short-term recruits was measured in terms of their effect on the enterprise's average wage rather than in pretax profit or output.

In 1971, when the regulations were more flexible than they had been in any earlier year of the reform, only a small percentage of the year's pretax profits could be used for increases in the earnings of the labor force. Let us take as an example an enterprise which increased its employees' average earnings by 4 percent (the average nominal increase in all socialist industry in 1971) and which also increased its profits per employee by 4 percent.[13] Table 9.1 shows both the average and marginal use of these profits which was possible under the governing regulations.[14]

[12] This practice appears to have stopped only after the summer of 1971. (See L. Horváth and J. Réti in *Munkaügyi Szemle*, 1973, 3, pp. 36-38, referred to in *Abstracts*, 1973, 2, p. 50.)

[13] The term "profits" is used here and in Table 9.1 in a sense different from the accounting meaning given to it in Hungary. It is used to include the additional earnings of the enterprise—including all taxes levied on the basis of such earnings, but excluding other taxes—which would have been received if nominal average earnings per employee had remained at the same level as in the previous year.

[14] The regulations first prescribe a local tax of 6 percent on all profits; 12.5 percent of the rest must then be placed into the enterprise reserve fund. The remainder is divided between the pretax sharing fund and the pretax investment fund, this division depending upon the ratio of total wage payments during the year to total capital employed. (The notion is that the higher the ratio of wage payments to capital, the higher the proportion of profits which can be used for the sharing fund. There is some differentiation between industries in the formula used.) The sharing fund is taxed at a rate varying between 40 and 70 percent, depending upon its magnitude as a percentage of all wage payments. The investment fund is taxed at a flat 60 percent.

The enterprise is free to increase wages for its employees as it sees fit. However, all increases in average wage payments are subject to a tax varying between 50 and 400 percent (in addition to the normal 25 percent tax on all wage payments); the rate depends both upon the average percentage increase in wages during the year,

Table 9.1 displays the high rate of profit tax, varying from 69 to 82 percent in our example. Even more important, funds available for increases in average nominal wages, for bonuses, and for social expenditures constitute only 5 to 14 percent of total pretax profits for the average industrial enterprise. The marginal share of pretax profits available for such purposes is 1.4 percent if used for wage increases, and is 6 to 12 percent if used for bonuses and social expenditures.

This tax structure provides enterprises with an incentive to use their available funds for bonuses and social expenditures rather than for wage increases.[15] This applies particularly to wage increases which are higher than the average for industry as a whole. Presumably, the logic of this policy is that increases in wages are more likely to spread to other enterprises than are increases in bonuses; the government is under greater pressure to provide the money needed for equalizing across enterprises the wages paid for similar work than it is to equalize bonus

---

and upon whether this percentage is higher or lower than the summation of profits plus the year's increase in wages-per-employee multiplied by the average number of employees, both divided by the average number of employees. Wage increases count as costs, and so are not paid out of the sharing fund or defined as part of profits.

All taxes on additional wage payments, however, must be paid out of the sharing fund. So, too, must all taxes levied on the pretax sharing fund. Similarly, taxes levied on the pretax investment fund are paid out of the investment fund.

The residual left in the sharing fund can be used to pay bonuses to employees and to make social expenditures for their benefit. Money in both the posttax sharing fund and in the posttax investment fund can be carried over to another year. In principle, repayments of bank loans are made from the posttax investment fund.

The addition to the enterprise reserve fund is best viewed as a tax, since the fund can be employed only under special circumstances, and the moneys used must then be quickly repaid into the reserve fund. The requirement as to the percentage of enterprise profits to be paid into the reserve fund has varied from year to year in accord with national fiscal policy rather than with the actual reserve needs of the enterprises.

It is important to note that subsidies from the government are included in the gross revenues of the enterprise; thus they help raise the enterprise's profits, and are taxed in the same fashion as any other source of profits. Some enterprises are liable to special "product taxes" on sales; these taxes are treated as a cost prior to calculation of profits for tax purposes.

[15] However, wage increases paid in 1971 are incorporated into normal costs for the following year and thereafter; in these successive years there is no special tax on them which must be paid from the sharing fund. The result is that, if the enterprise adopted a policy of increasing wages instead of paying bonuses in 1971, its net payout to employees (not discounted for time) would be the same after three years if one calculates at the "average proportion" rates of Table 9.1, and after nine years if one calculates at the "marginal proportion at 4 percent increase in earnings." When one adds a time-discount factor, which must be particularly high because of the uncertainty imparted by the earlier history of changes in the profit-tax system, one can only conclude that the tax structure is biased in favor of the payment of bonuses rather than wage increases.

TABLE 9.1: Use of Pretax Profits by an Average Industrial Enterprise, 1971 (percentage)

Distribution of Pretax Profits	Average Proportion		Marginal Proportion at 4 Percent Increase in Earnings		Marginal Proportion at Peak Tax Rate	
	If increase in average earnings over those of 1970 were all paid as:					
	Wages	Bonuses	Wages	Bonuses	Wages	Bonuses
Funds for increases in earnings of employees	5.3	13.9	1.4	11.7	1.4	5.5
Funds available for investment	17.0	17.2	17.0	17.2	17.0	17.2
Taxes on profits	77.7	68.9	81.7	71.0	81.7	77.3
Total	100.0	100.0	100.0	100.0	100.0	100.0

NOTES:
1. It is assumed that pretax profits per employee increased in 1971 by the same percentage as did average employee earnings, and that average earnings increased in 1971 by the average percentage for all socialist industry. If pretax profits increased by a higher percentage than average earnings, then taxes would take a slightly lower proportion of total pretax profits.
2. It is realistically assumed that the enterprise did not take advantage of the opportunity given it by law to divert funds from increases in employee earnings to investment purposes.
3. It is assumed that the enterprise is obliged to place two-thirds of its pretax profits in its investment fund. This has been described to me as the average situation in industry.
4. Money compulsorily placed in the enterprise reserve fund is treated here as a tax.
5. The percentages given for "taxes on profits" under the wages columns represent an overstatement, since they assume a 100 percent discount of wage advantages in future years which result from the increase in wages during the current year. As is explained in footnote 15, wage increases paid during 1971 are incorporated in the costs of future years.

payments. However, despite the tax advantage in paying bonuses, the effect of the high labor mobility in Hungarian industry, and the fact that employees are believed to change jobs more in response to wage differences than to wage-plus-bonus differences, is to place considerable labor market pressure upon the enterprises to use their available funds for wage increases.[16]

[16] One Hungarian author claimed in early 1972 that the overwhelming majority of blue-collar workers prefer wage increases to bonuses. He also stated that only a small proportion of blue-collar workers receive special bonuses during the course of the year; most receive their complete annual bonus only at the end of the year (J. Wilcsek in *Közgazdasági Szemle*, XIX, 1, 1972, pp. 12-22, translated in *JPS*).

During 1969 through 1971, a maximum of 5 to 10 percent of total wages paid in all state industrial enterprises was added on annually as end-of-year bonuses to all personnel in the enterprises, and this was distributed primarily in proportion to base salary.[17] (In four enterprises for which I have data, such year-end bonuses ranged from eight to twenty-seven working-days' earnings.) This can be compared with payments made in 1968, when year-end bonuses earned in the pre-reform year of 1967 were 7 percent of basic salaries.[18] From these and pre-1968 figures,[19] we may conclude that the bonus situation since the reform cannot be substantially different from that existing earlier.

Hungarian authorities hoped that the tax system whose effect was described in Table 9.1 would at the same time prevent wage inflation. As we shall see in Chapter 10, they appear to have been much more successful in accomplishing this objective than in providing profit incentive to the labor force. Since only 1 to 12 percent of an increase in profits can be used for the benefit of the employees, it is difficult to create high profit motivation on the factory floor. The lack of resolution of this dilemma has been fully recognized by the Hungarians themselves.[20]

When the reform was introduced in 1968, it was believed to be particularly important to provide material incentives to members of top management. Primarily because of this, but also because of a desire to increase the differentiation of income between people at different levels within the enterprise, the end-of-year bonus financed from the sharing fund was to be distributed quite disproportionately among the personnel. For close to 90 percent of the personnel of the enterprise, this could not

[17] Hungarian Central Statistical Office, *Statistical Yearbook 1970*, pp. 158-59, and *Statistical Yearbook 1971*, pp. 154-55. It is unclear, however, whether these figures include such other uses of the sharing fund as the payment of special bonuses during the course of the year, the payment of managerial bonuses, and the financing of social expenditures above the level spent in 1967. It is said that during 1970 the total sharing fund—which included all of these expenditures plus all wage increases above the 1967 level—was 14.4 percent of total wages paid during the year in industrial enterprises (Bokor and Ambrózy).

[18] Központi Statisztikai Hivatal, *Foglalkoztatottság és Munkaviszonyból Származó Jövedelem 1968* (Budapest: 1970), p. 164.

[19] In 1967, the year prior to the beginning of the reform, such end-of-year payments constituted 5 percent of basic wages in state industry (ibid.). In the same year, the total fund both for end-of-year payments and for certain bonuses was 6.5 percent of industrial wages. (Florian Antoniewicz, *Nyereségrészesedés és a vállalati ügyvitel*, Budapest: 1968. See also Laslo Ozhval'd, "O sisteme materi-al'nogo stimulirovania inzhenerno-tekhnicheskogo personala," in Institut Ekono-miki Vengerskoi Akademii Nauk, *Material'noe Stimulirovanie v Narodnom Khozi-aistve Vengrii*, Akadémiai Kiadó, Budapest: 1962, pp. 43-65.) This fund, like that created under the reform, was based upon the profits earned by the individual enterprise.

[20] See Csikós-Nagy in *Közgazdasági Szemle*, p. 1016.

exceed 15 percent of their annual wages (this limit was placed on the average for the group in the enterprise, not on individuals); for junior and middle management, the limit was placed at 50 percent; top management of the enterprise (1 percent of the labor force in state industry as a whole) was subject to a limit of 85 percent.

The significance of this differentiation was not that these limits were often reached,[21] but rather that end-of-year bonuses for 1968 were distributed (in 1969) among different categories of personnel in rough proportion to these limits.[22] Although the size of top management bonuses was indeed sufficient to provide these executives with a major stake in increasing profits, the side-effect was an explosion of protest on the factory floor when the amounts of the bonuses became known. The government responded by abandoning its three-way classification of enterprise personnel, and instead proclaimed that end-of-year bonuses should be proportional to annual wages for all groups within any given enterprise.

This public retreat did not, however, lead to any reduction in the new differentiation of total earnings.[23] Top managers were recompensed partially by an increase in their base salaries, partially by the creation of a new fund (financed out of the enterprise's sharing fund) for the award of special quarterly bonuses to management, and partially by the reinstatement of a fund at the disposal of each industrial ministry for the reward of its enterprise top managers. The result was that top management's total income was untouched, and that its bonuses related to profitability were reduced but still remained substantial.[24]

[21] The average end-of-year bonuses paid out in state industry on the basis of the 1968 results constituted less than half of the permitted maximum (*Foglalkoztatottság és Munkaviszonyból*, p. 164).

[22] The 0.9 percent of the labor force of all industry which was categorized in 1968 as top management received an average of ten times as much end-of-year bonus as did the 93 percent of the labor force categorized as rank-and-file (*Foglalkoztatottság és Munkaviszonyból*, p. 181). Although no data are available as to their relative basic earnings, one might guess that top management's was some two and one-half to three times as high. (This ratio is cited for an "average" enterprise by W. F. Robinson, *The Pattern of Reform*, Praeger, New York, Washington, and London: 1973, p. 322, quoting a 1970 Hungarian source.) Comparison of the two ratios suggests that top management's end-of-year bonuses were restrained somewhat (perhaps by one-third) compared to the rank-and-file's, in comparison to the maximum permitted to each group.

[23] A very authoritative spokesman for the regime wrote in 1971 that the current income differentials between different levels of the hierarchy were appropriate and should be preserved (R. Nyers, "Hungarian Economic Policy in Practice," *Acta Oeconomica*, 7, 3-4, 1971, p. 268).

[24] A case study of one construction enterprise, which was described as probably the poorest organization in its industry, showed that total bonuses paid to a sample of all categories of professionals and managers (excluding the general director) constituted 43 percent of their base salaries in 1970. Apparently, bonuses were genuinely differentiated according to the evaluation made of individuals; this is

I have data as to bonuses of top management for only two enterprises. In one of these, the total bonuses for the year of 1970 of the three top managers were approximately 35 to 50 percent of their annual base salary, and roughly one-third of these bonuses came from the branch ministry's fund rather than from the enterprise's sharing fund. The employees of this enterprise averaged, in contrast, some 5 to 6 percent total bonus as a percentage of base salary.[25]

In the second enterprise, top management received a salary increase of 30 percent starting with January 1970 in order to compensate for the reduction in its bonuses. Nevertheless, the top four managers averaged some 50 to 60 percent bonus in 1970, of which well over one-third came from the ministry's fund.[26] This second enterprise, however, paid much higher average bonuses to all its employees than did any of the other enterprises for which I have data: some 11 percent of base salary.

While these top management bonuses are very substantial as a proportion of base salary, it is unclear how closely they are in fact linked to the profitability of the enterprise. Only the portion of the bonus which comes out of the enterprise's sharing fund has any direct link, and even this is tenuous. When the profits of the first firm fell by 10 percent in one year, top management bonuses financed from the sharing fund alone fell at most from 30 to 25 percent of base salary. Bonuses financed from the ministry fund have no direct connection at all to the enterprise's profits.

In fact, the bonus of the general director—both the part financed from the enterprise's sharing fund and the portion from the ministry fund— is determined completely by the ministry. While the general director has a strong voice in determining the bonuses to be received by the other two or three members of top management, these will bear a close relation to his own bonus. Given the atmosphere of the reform, the ministries doubtless are heavily affected in their bonus decisions by the profit performance of the enterprise. But there is no reason to believe that they are indifferent to other criteria: "justice" (particularly in view of the belief that prices are not rationally determined), sale of desired exports,

---

shown by the fact that the variance of bonuses divided by the average bonus was three times as great as was the variance of base salary divided by average salary, and that a similar relationship existed for subcategories of professionals and managers. (Lajos Héthy and Csaba Makó, *A vállalati kontroll mechanizmus és a szervezetlenség*, Magyar Tudományos Akadémia, Szociólogiai Intézetének Kiadványai, Budapest: 1972, pp. 172-73.)

[25] Ordinary workers receive additional bonuses for superior quality of product, etc. But these are paid from the ordinary wage fund, and thus are not included here.

[26] A well-informed Hungarian source estimated in early 1971 that, in industry as a whole, top managers receive only about 10 percent of their bonuses from the ministry fund.

development of new products, production of an appropriate product mix, etc. Thus high top management bonuses, although they unquestionably provide a motivation for the search for profits, are not necessarily as strong a force as one might at first expect.

An important consideration for managers in many economic systems is the effects of their actions on the progress of their future careers. As was noted in Chapter 8, however, general directors of Hungarian enterprises seem to be fairly thoroughly shielded against the danger of demotion. Nor is promotion a serious possibility. Ministries have been reducing the number of their personnel and, in any case, movement to a ministry would probably involve a reduction in total money income. It is said that promotion from a medium-size to a large enterprise in the same industry would not provide much additional income or status. Thus top Hungarian managers can almost dismiss the issue of future personal career when determining the vigor with which to pursue profits.

Finally, as we shall see below, it is not at all clear that a general director who is concerned with improving the well-being of his enterprise is well advised to devote his energies to such activities as marketing, improving production efficiency, developing new products, and the like. Whether or not he is interested in expanding the enterprise's sharing fund or in enlarging its capital resources, political manipulations for greater subsidies, tax advantages, low-cost loans, and export privileges often offer a much larger pay-off than the search for higher profits through better operations.[27]

SUBSIDIES, TAX EXEMPTIONS, AND FOREIGN TRADE CONTROLS

The virtue of coordinating a socialist economy through financial mechanisms rather than by direct physical plans lies in the freeing of central authorities from the need for making decisions concerning each production unit. The resulting potential gain lies both in information processing and in improved motivation throughout the economy. But the requirements imposed by the constraints of Hungarian society seem to have largely frustrated the desired depersonalization of central controls. If before 1968 Hungary's economy was operated primarily by physical planning down to the level of the individual enterprise, Hungarian industry under the reform mechanisms has been governed by financial regulators whose provisions also are often specific to the individual enterprise.

[27] See the statement by a vice president of the National Planning Office as to the large role played by special grants and privileges (J. Drecin, "Investment Equilibrium: Mechanisms of Control and Decision," *Acta Oeconomica*, 7, 3-4, 1971, pp. 282-83).

One major reason for this lies in the exigencies of the pricing system. Particularly during the second half of the 1950's, enterprise costs (including taxes on capital and wages) rose sharply. But consumer prices were kept relatively stable,[28] the difference being compensated partly by reductions in sales tax, but also through extensive subsidies paid to enterprises producing particular consumer goods. Since the government wished to keep the pattern of consumer prices relatively constant, and since the rate of sales tax had always been highly differentiated among products, the use of subsidies was unavoidable.

Thus the reform period began with substantial payments being paid by the government to industrial enterprises according to the specific products which they produced. During the following years, enterprise requests for increases in fixed retail prices—as well as negotiations over increases in free prices—were sometimes resolved by leaving the retail prices as they were but reducing the sales tax. These actions, as well as reductions in import duties on specific materials, had the same effect both on the government budget and on the enterprises concerned as the granting of additional subsidies for specific products.

In addition to subsidies, some sectors (e.g., metal mining and various branches of food processing) were given partial or complete exemption from the 5 percent tax on capital, some were exempted from one-third of the payroll tax, and various of these sectors as well as others were partially or fully exempted from the profits tax levied on the investment and sharing funds. There are sectors which have been permitted to pay wage increases without any charge to the sharing fund. Additional sectors are allowed to allocate a much higher proportion of their pretax profits to the sharing fund (as opposed to the investment fund) than is the general rule for all enterprises in the economy, and their necessary investments are financed by other means. Thus branch subsidies, tax advantages, and special rights to increase wages and bonuses constitute a very complex counterpart to the low prices imposed on specific products.

The important group of subsidies and tax reductions described above is specific to products rather than to enterprises. However, the difference between the product and enterprise approaches is not as great as might at first be thought. As we saw in Chapter 8, a mere 291 enterprises employ three-quarters of Hungary's industrial labor force; these enterprises represent primarily horizontal rather than vertical combinations, and each carries on most of its activities within a rather narrow industrial category. As a result, subsidies or tax reductions for a specific product normally have their main effect on one or two enterprises. Decisions as

[28] Between 1956 and 1968, producer prices rose by 54 percent while consumer prices rose by only 4 percent (Csikós-Nagy in Friss, *Reform*, p. 135).

to the need for product-specific financial advantages seem to be made primarily on the basis of covering the cost and "reasonable profit" requirements of the leading enterprise producing each product.[29]

A second major reason for subsidies and tax advantages is the system utilized for converting foreign currency export earnings by enterprises into domestic Hungarian money (forints). One rate (40 forints = 1 ruble) is used for exports to socialist countries, and a second (60 forints = 1 dollar) for exports to capitalist countries. These rates were established in 1968 on the basis of equalizing the average return from sale of goods on each of these export markets with the return from domestic sales. However, since the price structure in each of these three markets differed substantially, both export subsidies and special taxes linked to high export profits were also required. In 1968, approximately two-thirds of all exporting enterprises received subsidies; these subsidies averaged 29 percent on trade conducted in rubles and 33 percent on trade with capitalist countries.[30]

Export subsidies—generally in the form of a given number of forints per ruble or dollar earned—were differentiated by individual enterprise during 1968-70. It was hoped that a single subsidy rate for all products exported by the enterprise would encourage it to choose its product mix for exports on the basis of relative prices in the domestic and foreign markets. As of 1971, roughly three-quarters of exporting enterprises were converted to an export-subsidy system based on about sixty sub-branch groupings; but the remaining quarter of the enterprises continued to receive subsidies whose rates were specific to themselves.[31]

The reverse side of export subsidies consists of special product taxes, levied on sectors which would otherwise show an exorbitant profit. Although such taxes may be levied on domestic sales as well as on exports,

[29] Negotiations as to price changes are conducted between interministerial committees, under the leadership of the Office of Prices, on the one side, and only one or two leading enterprises in a given branch on the other. Such negotiations cover price increases, subsidies, and tax reductions for the relevant products.

[30] I. Vincze in *Pénzügyi Szemle*, 1969, 11, pp. 881-93, as referred to by B. Balassa in "The Firm in the New Economic Mechanism in Hungary," in M. Bornstein (ed.), *Plan and Market* (Yale University Press, New Haven and London: 1973), p. 368. See also S. Czeitler, *Az új gazdasági mechanizmus bevezetésének tapasztalatai a külkereskedelemben* (Kossuth Könyvkiadó, Budapest: 1969), p. 35, as referred to in A. A. Brown and P. Marer, "Foreign Trade in the East European Reforms" (Working Paper 9 of the International Development Research Center of Indiana University), p. 35.

[31] Zs. Esze, "The Modified System of Export Incentives for 1971-1975," *Acta Oeconomica*, 8, 1 (1972), 63-64, and S. Czeitler, in Gadó, *Reform*, p. 118. Instead of subsidies, some enterprises received tax exemptions to compensate them for exports (Esze, p. 73). By 1972, reductions of profit taxes were also being used in one hundred fifty eight enterprises as a means of further encouraging exports specifically to convertible currency countries (I. Országh, in *Külgazdaság*, 1973, 11, pp. 813-24, as referred to in *Abstracts*, 1973, 6, pp. 26-28).

the vast bulk of them are on exports to socialist countries of products where the 40 forints to 1 ruble exchange rate would otherwise be unduly favorable.[32]

If subsidies and tax advantages were intended only to compensate for peculiarities of the pricing system, then there would be no need for them to be differentiated to the level of the individual enterprise to a greater degree than that compelled by the oligopoly nature of the Hungarian economy. But, as was seen in Chapter 8, the government is concerned with preventing bankruptcies, dismissals of workers, and even forced changes of occupations within the same enterprise. This has required the granting of subsidies to individual enterprises in addition to the subsidies by product and for exports which have been discussed above.

No data are published on the total of subsidies and tax advantages. But some notion of their importance is indicated by the fact that, during 1968-71, what appears to be an incomplete figure for subsidies paid to state-owned industrial enterprises constituted 54 percent of their pretax profits (including subsidies).[33] According to the plan for the 1971 budget, 38 percent of subsidies throughout the economy were to be given to provide compensation for low prices of consumer goods, 4 percent were to subsidize imports, 29 percent were intended to subsidize exports, and 29 percent were to be differentiated to the individual enterprise level for other than export subsidies.[34] It is primarily the latter two categories which are of interest for our purpose.

In view of the importance of subsidies and tax advantages in determining the financial results of most industrial enterprises, it should not be surprising that informed Hungarians do not appear to consider the profitability of individual enterprises—even those within the same broad branch—as reflecting their relative efficiency.[35] Nor is it surprising that enterprises which are so much at the mercy of financial decisions by interministerial committees should take great pains to avoid actions

[32] The main exception is with regard to taxes on domestic gasoline sales. This tax must be regarded as simply a substitute for a sales tax.

[33] *Statistical Yearbook 1971*, pp. 152-53. This percentage does not include product subsidies paid indirectly to industry through the internal trade network. I was told in Hungary that published subsidy statistics are a combination of gross subsidies for some enterprises and of subsidies net of certain taxes for other enterprises.

[34] One can roughly calculate from *Statistical Yearbook 1970*, pp. 77-81, and from *Statistical Yearbook 1971*, pp. 74-75 and 152-53, that subsidies paid directly to state-owned industrial enterprises during 1968-70 were divided as follows: 29 percent for compensation for low prices of specific products, 60 percent for export subsidies, and 11 percent for other subsidies allocated directly to individual enterprises. For 1970, the respective figures are estimated as 27, 60, and 13 percent.

[35] For example, see E. Huszti, "Az 1970-71. évi pénz- és hitelpolitika gyakorlati érvényesüléséről," *Közgazdasági Szemle*, XIX, 1 (1972), 23-40, cited in *Abstracts*, 1972, 1, p. 134.

which they are legally entitled to carry out but which would be likely to lead to financial reprisals. A Hungarian study undertaken during 1969 indicated that enterprises do not attempt to achieve profits which are so high as to jeopardize future subsidies or threaten repercussions on the permitted prices of their products.[36] Only very small enterprises —such as producer cooperatives and small state construction firms— seem to be relatively free from such financial pressure, since the subsidy-tax-pricing system cannot normally take account of the peculiarities of their individual positions. It is not surprising that it is these tiny enterprises which have created the most difficulties for the central authorities.

In addition to these financial influences which central authorities can exert on industrial enterprises, one direct means is predominant among those available to authorities other than the branch ministry directly superior to the enterprise. This direct influence lies in the field of foreign trade.

In principle, enterprises are free to export and import as they see fit and are guided only by financial considerations. By 1970, national import quotas were retained primarily only for consumer goods, and even in this sphere they constituted a genuine constraint on only a limited number of products. It is true that the great bulk of foreign trade is conducted through the medium of export-import enterprises,[37] each of which has a monopoly over trade in specified products and is subordinate to the Ministry of Foreign Trade; however, these enterprises are usually described as no more than commission agents for the principals (producing or trading enterprises) whom they serve. Export and import licenses are required, but these are said to be given quite freely.

Interviews, however, indicate a more complex pattern. Both exports and imports require licenses from the Ministry of Foreign Trade, and the power to refuse licenses apparently is not only used on occasion but always stands in the background in discussions between the industrial enterprises and the Ministry. Second, while many export-import enterprises regard their role simply as that of an agent for the enterprises they serve, others consider themselves to be primarily organs of the Ministry of Foreign Trade—and view their principal task as that of using balance-of-payments considerations in shifting exports and imports between trading partners.

During the second half of 1969, when there was a shortage of textiles

[36] This conclusion, however, was based on a study of only ten enterprises (M. Tardos, "An Econometric Study of Enterprise Behaviour," in Z. Román, ed., *Progress and Planning in Industry*, Akadémiai Kiadó, Budapest: 1972, p. 380).

[37] However, the total number of enterprises directly engaged in foreign trade increased from forty-two before the reform to one hundred nine in 1972; in the latter year, the majority of these firms were producing firms rather than purely commercial houses (J. Follinus in *The Hungarian Economy*, I, 1, 1972, p. 19).

on the internal Hungarian market, export licenses for textiles were widely refused. Export rights to socialist markets for particularly profitable goods have been allocated to individual enterprises according to their willingness to give up subsidies on exports to capitalist markets, while maintaining or even increasing the volume of such exports.[38] Other socialist exports have been allocated to those enterprises receiving the lowest subsidies on these exports. Requests for export licenses to socialist countries which are above the quotas determined by annual trade agreements have been judged individually, and competitive bidding has been used. In the granting of export licenses to nonsocialist countries, consideration is given to directing exports to those countries where the balance of payments is most in need of support.[39]

Import licensing is much stricter than export licensing, especially for equipment. Interviews with enterprise managers (including the heads of purchasing in two enterprises) indicated that goods, particularly those coming from capitalist countries, could not be imported simply on the basis of a comparison of the price in forints of imported and domestically produced items; one purchasing manager stated that he would not even attempt to divert purchases from domestic sources on these grounds, since he could be certain that an import license would be refused. Furthermore, one purchasing head insisted that he had been able to purchase equipment from capitalist countries only because this purchase was needed in order to expand exports to convertible currency markets. The maintenance head of the same enterprise stated that he could expand his imports of spare parts from capitalist countries above a stated amount only in proportion to the enterprise's convertible currency exports; this procedure was not enforced through import licenses, but rather directly through the willingness of the relevant export-import enterprise to execute orders for imports. In at least two enterprises, permission was received to import equipment from capitalist countries, when paying with the enterprises' own money, only after the enterprise agreed to increase its exports to convertible currency areas sufficiently to earn

[38] Esde, p. 71.

[39] This is particularly significant with regard to nonsocialist countries whose imports from Hungary are bought with inconvertible currency. But even when payment is made in convertible currency, bilateral trade considerations are relevant since excess exports may lead to future trade restrictions. The need for utilizing export licenses to nonsocialist countries arises because all such currencies are converted to nominal dollar values (presumably at par), and then into forint earnings for the exporting enterprise, at the common rate of sixty forints to a dollar. (It is true that I have come across one case in which the Ministry of Foreign Trade encouraged enterprise exports to a particular capitalist country by exchanging into forints the foreign currency earned at a rate 3 to 4 percent better than the customary one. Paul Marer in a letter has informed me that the Ministry of Foreign Trade has official funds set aside for such purposes. But the utilization of this technique seems to be rare.)

within a few years the foreign currency paid out. (In imports financed from loans, the same condition has generally been imposed.)

Especially with regard to imports, the extent of the impact on industrial enterprises of the new mechanism introduced in 1968 is doubtful. Responsible executives in two enterprises stated to me their belief that, in reality, they had no greater freedom to import under the new than under the old system. In a third enterprise, however, a trustworthy commercial head asserted that he had much greater freedom. Doubtless the reality differs considerably among enterprises, and is partially dependent upon the attitude taken by the particular export-import enterprise with which the producing enterprise is obliged to deal.

INVESTMENT AND BANK LOANS

One of the stated objectives of the Hungarian reform was to grant to the individual enterprises considerable authority in determining the level and nature of their investments. While it was always held that central authorities should determine the most important expansions in industry, the rest was to be left to the enterprises themselves. One reason for this was to assure that investments would be concentrated in the more profitable enterprises, since it would be these which would have the funds for expansion. A second reason was to provide enterprise managements with the incentive of expansion as a motivation for attempting to earn high profits.

About half of all gross fixed investments in the Hungarian economy in 1970 was financed centrally through the budget or through centrally determined loans. Roughly 10 percent was financed by ordinary bank loans, and over one-third of the money came from the enterprises' own amortization funds and posttax profits. However, the situation was radically different in manufacturing (industry other than mining and electricity); here, it is said, only about 16 percent of gross fixed investment was centrally financed, one-fifth came from bank loans, and two-thirds came from the enterprises' own funds.[40] If we assume that all replace-

[40] A Hungarian informant is the source for these figures. Although other Hungarians placed the figure for self-financing by manufacturing concerns a good deal lower, I do not believe that they were as well informed on this matter.

Independent confirmation is provided by data from the *Statistical Yearbook 1970*. Self-financing funds (amortization kept by the enterprises plus the accruals out of posttax profits to the investment fund) earned by state-owned manufacturing enterprises in 1970 constituted 67 percent of all fixed investments made in the total socialist sector of manufacturing in the same year. This percentage figure, however, is not comparable to the similar figure given in the text. On the one hand, an unknown amount of these self-financing funds had to be used to increase the enterprises' working capital expansion and to repay loans; in addition, they were available to finance 1971 rather than 1970 investments. On the other hand, our

ment investment was financed from the enterprises' own funds, then some 38 percent of net fixed investment in manufacturing was self-financed by the enterprises concerned.

On the face of it, these figures suggest that—at least in manufacturing —the investment decentralization objectives have indeed been realized. The explanation for the central authorities' sticking to this objective presumably lies in the sorry record of the earlier central control over investment. An analysis of a sample of six hundred investment projects in which production operations began during 1961-65 showed that only 34 percent began operations within the year scheduled, while 27 percent were between two and five years late.[41] It was strongly believed that decentralization of investment decisions to the level of those responsible for executing the investment projects would sharply speed up the process of completing investment projects. It was also believed that this desirable result would be promoted by increasing the volume of small investments in existing enterprises (financed out of profits) as a proportion of total investment.

In fact, however, the hoped-for improvement in investment performance has been one of the great disappointments of the reform. For the national economy as a whole, the annual increase in the value of incomplete investment projects averaged 2.8 percent of total national income during the first three years of reform—a percentage more than twice as high as that of the previous three years, and still worse in comparison with the earlier years of the 1960's.[42] A major reason for this was that total net investment in fixed capital moved even more out of control than it had been earlier, thus placing still more strain on the limited resources of the construction industry.[43]

investment figure includes manufacturing enterprises operated as cooperatives; these, at the end of 1970, owned 2 percent of the net fixed assets of manufacturing. I would conclude that the figure given for self-financing in the text is somewhat, but probably not grossly, overstated.

For detailed information concerning the sources of investment in the state sector as a whole during 1968, and those planned for 1969, see P. Marer and G. Pall, "Recent Developments in the Hungarian Financial System" (Contract U.S. Arms Control and Disarmament Agency/E-134, II, New York: May 1971), pp. 32-34.

[41] I. Neményi, "Investment Policy in Hungary in the New System of Economic Management" (Budapest: 1969, mimeographed), pp. 23-24. This sample covered the entire economy, rather than manufacturing alone.

[42] Központi Statisztikai Hivatal, *Statisztikai Évkönyv 1970* (Budapest: 1971), pp. 74-75. No similar data are available for manufacturing alone. Calculations made in 1970 showed that there had been no shortening of construction periods; state investments took an average of 6.3 years to complete, virtually double the time warranted according to the best foreign examples (Csikós-Nagy in *Közgazdasági Szemle*, XIX, 9, 1972, translated in *RFE*).

[43] Net investment in fixed capital constituted 17.5 percent of national income in 1968-70, in contrast to 14.9 percent during the previous three years and still

Part of the reason for the overinvestment relative to capacity was that the amount of money available for decentralized investment by enterprises was greater than had been expected.[44] Judging by the reaction of Hungarian authorities, however, this was not the principal cause. The Hungarian Politbureau member with prime responsibility for economic policy took the position in 1971 that the solution to the nation's investment problems lay in improved and better coordinated decisions within the realm left to central government, and he explicitly ruled out greater central control over the investment decisions made by the enterprises themselves.[45]

Why was the solution to investment problems not sought in 1971 through tightening central control over the enterprises' use of their own investment funds? The answer, I would suggest, is that a good deal of such control always existed; decentralization of investment was never so great as it would appear from our figures. Due to the rigidities and distortions of the pricing system, the extensive subsidies and tax exemptions which were intended to increase posttax profits of enterprises have had their counterpart throughout the reform years in special investment advantages given to many enterprises. Without this counterpart, general subsidies for enterprises would have had to be substantially increased, and this would have created an uncomfortably large expansion in the sharing funds of those enterprises whose investments central authorities wished to encourage.

To begin with, 60 percent of amortization allowances are normally left to the enterprises to reinvest as they see fit, while the remaining 40 percent is taken by the state budget.[46] But individual enterprises are allowed to keep a higher proportion of their amortization, one justification being that their equipment is relatively old and thus that their replace-

---

lower percentages during the earlier years of the 1960's (*Statisztikai Évkönyv 1970*, pp. 74-75). The year 1971 saw a very sharp further upward movement. In every postreform year through 1971, actual investments exceeded those planned (Csikós-Nagy in *Közgazdasági Szemle*, pp. 1013-14).

[44] In the first year of the reform, enterprise profits as a whole were 28 percent more than had been anticipated (R. Nyers, *25 kérdés és válasz a gazdaságpolitikai kérdésekről*, quoted by Z. Komonyi, "Some Aspects of Enterprise Behavior," in Z. Román, *Progress and Planning in Industry*, p. 339). In 1970, the deviation between actual and expected enterprise investment funds was five times greater than the margin which was considered tolerable (Drecin, pp. 280-81).

[45] Nyers in *Acta Oeconomica*, 7, 3-4, p. 260.

[46] Total amortization is calculated on the basis of being just sufficient for replacement needs. The reason for part of this being removed from the enterprises is to prevent those whose equipment is relatively new, or whose plant and equipment is planned to be reduced over time, from being left with excessive investment funds. In the absence of any significant capital market, this budgetary deduction is a device for making possible capital movement between enterprises and sectors by centralizing a portion of replacement funds through the budget.

ment needs are greater than the average for industry. Other enterprises may be compelled to place in blocked accounts part of the amortization funds left to them. The power of central authorities to determine the proportion of amortization allowances which is to remain at the discretion of individual enterprises gives these authorities considerable influence over the gross funds available for self-financed investment.

Second, much of the enterprises' investment funds have been committed to completing projects started in earlier years. Since many of these projects were begun before 1968, and thus were determined by central authorities rather than by the enterprises, much of the self-financing must go for projects over which the enterprises had no choice.[47]

Third, manufacturing enterprises have been dependent for major expansion upon external financing. Partly this has come from budgetary grants, partly from state loans, and partly from bank loans. Normally, however, money is not made available from any of these sources unless it is supplemented by the enterprise from its own funds. Thus, to the degree that the enterprise makes use of external funds for investment purposes, it loses control over the use of its own moneys.

Fourth, and probably most important, are the demands made upon the enterprises' investment funds for purposes of financing working capital needs.

At the beginning of the reform period in 1968, enterprises depended upon credits from the National Bank to finance an average of 25 percent of their working-capital requirements during the season of their minimum activity.[48] But individual enterprises were in very different positions, some receiving sufficient budgetary grants at that time so that they required no such credits. These credits, dating from January 1968, are in the form of loans with no date set for repayment. Probably most enterprises had not paid off any of these credits by the end of 1970, but one enterprise in which I conducted interviews had been obliged to repay a substantial portion. The ability of the National Bank to adjust its demands for repayment to the financial possibilities of the individual enterprise has given it considerable microeconomic control over the amount of resources left for gross fixed investment.

Just as important is the division of supplementary working capital needs into two categories. In theory, annual increases in working capital during the season of minimum activity are to be financed by the enterprise itself or, at a minimum, from loans repayable out of enterprise profits after they have been subjected to a 60 percent tax.[49] On the other

---

[47] While the enterprises are empowered to abandon these projects, one may presume that this has rarely been done.

[48] Huszti in *Abstracts*, p. 133.

[49] This has been the situation since 1970. During the two previous years, such

hand, all seasonal needs for working capital are financed from credits repayable from earnings on which no profit tax is charged. To the extent that the National Bank has permitted enterprises to opt for the second type of expansion of working capital, these enterprises were left with more funds for fixed investment.[50]

The significance of the differential policies followed by the National Bank with regard to individual industrial enterprises is illustrated by data from the five enterprises in which I conducted interviews. During the first three years of the reform, one enterprise used none of its own gross investment funds to finance additional working capital needs or repayment of working capital credits; at the other extreme, another enterprise was forced to devote 50 percent of its gross investment funds accumulated during 1968-70 to these purposes. Such differences were totally uncorrelated with the increase in working capital requirements of the various enterprises; they can only be interpreted as being a result of central control over the supposedly "free funds" generated from post-tax profits and from the amortization allowances left to the enterprises.

As the reform system was originally conceived, self-financing of capital investment by enterprises was to be supplemented significantly by a second source of capital investment which was also to be outside central control. This second source was loans to be made by the State Investment Bank, and to be repaid from posttax profits, for purposes of fixed capital expansion. While it is true that only a single bank (merged at the end of 1971 with the National Bank) was empowered to make such loans, this bank was expected to be guided in its loan policy by the expected rate of profit[51] to be earned by the enterprises on the new investments, and by the speed with which the loans could be repaid. Thus the distribution of loans was not viewed as an instrument of central policy, but rather as an advance against future posttax profits to those enterprises which could best use the funds.

In fact, these Investment Bank credits were rather smaller than had been intended because of the government's belief that funds for invest-

---

financing was intended to take care of increases in the average working capital used during the year over the previous year's average. (G. Csigaházi and K. Okruszky, "A vállalati alapok képzésének és egyöntetü kezelésének néhány idő-szerü kérdése," *Közgazdasági Szemle*, xix, 4, 1972, pp. 439-53, cited in *Abstracts*, 1972, 2, pp. 170-71.)

[50] A 1972 Hungarian article reports that enterprises have covered only 30 percent of their needs for additional working capital from their own resources (ibid., p. 134).

An additional major source of variation in treatment of different enterprises was introduced during 1970 and the first half of 1971, but on a one-time basis (M. Pulai in Gadó, *Reform*, p. 199).

[51] Profits have been calculated on a pretax basis and after deducting state subsidies.

ment were already too large. Moreover, about two-thirds of the money available for industrial loans in 1970 were allocated between different sectors of manufacturing by an interministerial committee, although the Bank could still choose the individual enterprises within each sector which were to receive loans. Some one-fifth of the credits were allocated on the basis of totally nonfinancial criteria.

Despite these restrictions, Investment Bank loans were granted to a large extent on the basis of at least formal financial criteria. In 1968, 31 percent of the total money loaned was expected to earn a pretax profit to the borrowing enterprises of over 30 percent;[52] in 1969 and 1970, the average profit was expected to be 20 to 30 percent. To the extent that these profitability estimates were taken seriously, I conclude that credits must have gone to a very major degree to those enterprises which were expected to earn the largest financial return on them.

However, there have been strong complaints that profitability has been grossly overestimated by enterprises, and that they have proved eager to acquire investment loans regardless of their realistically-estimated financial possibilities for repayment.[53] One Hungarian economist insisted to me that Investment Bank credits have often later been converted to state credits, thus allowing them to be repaid from pretax rather than from posttax profits. Since state credits are supposed to be granted by central authorities according to nonfinancial criteria, this suggests that such criteria may have been even more important than they first appear in the granting of Investment Bank credits. In one branch ministry, I was told that this ministry exerts great influence on the Investment Bank in determining which enterprises should receive credits, and that it even has the right to appeal to the Minister of Finance any decision of the Investment Bank on the allocation of credits among the branch ministry's enterprises.

In short, just as subsidies and tax advantages, differentiated to the level of the individual enterprise, imply that central authorities continued their prereform policy of attempting to determine the behavior of individual enterprises, the same holds to a considerable degree in the management of "decentralized investment." The fundamental principle of the reform was to move toward freeing enterprises from the control of central authorities, and to allow the enterprises to be guided by their managements within the constraints of the market place and of financial regulations which applied equally to all state-owned enterprises. The counterpart of this greater enterprise freedom was that central authorities should be able to concentrate upon macroeconomic policy. However, at

[52] Neményi, "Investment Policy," p. 65.

[53] Cf. B. Csikós-Nagy, "La politique économique de la Hongrie," Revue de l'Est, III, 1 (1972), 20-21, and the articles by Drecin and Nyers in Acta Oeconomica.

least through 1970, these objectives were accomplished to only a very limited degree. Rather, financial tutelage was substituted for the earlier physical planning. Supervision over the actions of the individual enterprise was retained in practice. It is the form of the supervision which changed.

CHAPTER 10

Hungary: Enterprises and the Success of the Reform

THIS chapter concentrates primarily upon the microunits of industry, analyzing their responses to the various reform measures. It then examines several types of organizations which exercise some degree of direct control over the enterprises, and also treats the relationship between the enterprise directors and the managers of the constituent individual establishments. Finally, it draws upon macroeconomic data to supplement microeconomic sources in providing an analysis of the progress of the Hungarian economy under the reform mechanisms.

MATERIALS ALLOCATION AND SUBCONTRACTING

One of the most prominent features of the prereform system in Hungary, as in all of the other CMEA countries, was the dominant role of materials allocation in supplying materials, semifabricates, and components to industrial enterprises, and in determining the subcontracting relationships among these enterprises. Although in all of the CMEA countries, including Hungary, the final users of consumer goods have been free to buy what they wished within the constraints of the money available to them and of their ability to find the desired items in the market place, physical rationing was the dominant means of distributing both intermediate producer goods and items needed for capital investment.

As of January 1968, the system of materials allocation in Hungary was reduced to very modest proportions, and by 1971 it had been almost abolished.[1] It would have seemed reasonable to predict major repercus-

---

[1] For the situation in January 1968, see O. Gadó, "The New System of Trade in Production Goods," in I. Friss (ed.), *Reform of the Economic Mechanism in Hungary* (Akadémiai Kiadó, Budapest: 1969), especially pp. 127 and 131-32. The elements which remained were progressively reduced thereafter; the difference between the remnants of the system of allocations to industry which still existed in 1968, compared to what remained in 1971, lay primarily in the freeing of the supply of nonferrous metals and of synthetics. A source in the Planning Office estimated that, by 1971, only 3 to 4 percent of the intermediate goods consumed by industry were subject to any form of central materials allocation.

In 1971, only meat still remained subject to classical quotas, which were given to specific regions within the trade network. As of 1968, both bread grain and fodder grain had also been included in the quota system, but these products were

sions from this changeover. In the short run, one might well have presumed that the former supply system would be only partially replaced by the new market mechanism, and that significant shortfalls in procurement would be suffered by many enterprises. One might also have expected considerable changes in the prices of intermediate products, resulting from the joint elimination of rationing measures and the decontrol of prices for the overwhelming majority of these items.

In the somewhat longer run, one would have expected positive features to emerge. While previously industrial enterprises had tried to hold substantial raw material and semifabricate reserves because of the dan-

---

removed in 1970. It is significant that none of these products is consumed by industry.

A second form of materials allocation is one in which several specific enterprises (a maximum of three in 1971 for any group of products) are allocated a minimum and/or a maximum amount of a given product for the year. The purpose of this regulation is either to assure supplies to a particular principal user or to restrict the consumption of the principal users so as to leave a sufficient supply for others. In 1971, seven groups of products were included under these regulations (gas and heating oil, domestically produced iron ore, buses, special trucks, pulverized coke, bitumen, and two types of paper). In 1968, some twenty-five to thirty groups of items had been handled in this fashion; copper and synthetic textile materials were particularly important among them.

A third form of allocation sets minimum or maximum (primarily minimum) quotas of certain goods which must be sold to the internal trade network rather than to industry. Fifteen articles—primarily construction materials—were included in 1971; some articles had been removed and others added since 1968.

A fourth form is that of naming one or a few specified enterprises as the exclusive purchaser of certain raw materials or semifabricates. Since these enterprises then serve as the sole channel through which the rest of the economy can purchase these goods, they are in a position to ration them if they see fit. In 1971, there were still about eight such groups of products (compared to some fifty in 1968); the only one really important for industry in 1971 consisted of all pine timber and sawn lumber imported from socialist countries. (These countries supplied the vast bulk of timber used in Hungary.)

The fifth form consists of the obligation placed upon the producers of certain products to sign contracts for deliveries for specified purposes. These obligations in 1971 appear to have related primarily to building materials and machinery required for major investment projects financed from the state budget; but they also included pharmaceuticals and medical instruments purchased by the national health service, gasoline and automotive tires, and some children's clothing which were unprofitable to the producing enterprises. For investment goods, this system provides state-financed projects with first call on the capacity of producers. For the other goods, it assures that major consuming bodies (e.g., the health service) or the trade network, rather than the producing enterprises, will determine the output of these products for domestic purposes.

For a summary of the number of product groups treated under each of the different forms of materials allocation during each of the years 1968-70, see O. Gadó (ed.), *Közgazdasági Szabályozó Rendszerünk Továbbfejlesztése* (Közgazdasági és Jogi Könyvkiadó, Budapest: 1970), p. 233, as referred to in G. P. Lauter, *The Manager and Economic Reform in Hungary* (Praeger, New York, Washington, London: 1972), p. 102.

ger of nonreceipt of the necessary allocations, a market system of supply would appear to eliminate this reason for stockpiling. In addition, the new emphasis upon profitability should have made enterprises much less eager than before to bear the monetary charges which fall on working capital. (These consist of capital charges paid to the budget and interest charges paid to the National Bank.)[2] Thus the excess stocks held by industry, for which Hungarians had strongly reproached the old system, might have been expected to be reduced fairly rapidly.[3] Second, it might have been predicted that enterprises would subcontract out to others much of the repair work and production of semifabricates which they had carried on themselves only because they could not trust the dependability of supply from external sources.[4]

In fact, not one of these predictions was realized. No special problems arose in 1968 or later as a result of the virtual abolition of materials allocations; all informants with whom I spoke in Hungary were unanimous on this point. Furthermore, a source in the National Planning Office, while unable to explain this success, insisted categorically that it was not due to imports being increased wherever shortages of materials and semifabricates appeared. From all accounts, the new mechanism for distributing intermediate domestic production took over quite smoothly. Nor was this takeover accompanied by substantial price changes for many intermediate products.

The medium-term positive expectations also failed to appear, at least within the first three years. Stocks of raw materials and auxiliary materials held by all socialist enterprises of industry increased by 33 percent between January 1, 1968, and December 31, 1970, and stocks of unfinished production and semifabricates increased by 30 percent.[5] This stockpiling was substantially faster than the rate of increase of industrial

[2] Although working capital financed from bank borrowing was exempt from the 5 percent capital charge during 1968, this charge was levied against it beginning in 1969.

[3] See, for example, Gadó in Friss, *Reform*, pp. 106-07 for such an implied prediction.

Prior to the reform, stocks in Hungary were very high compared to those in capitalist countries. In 1964, for example, stocks as a proportion of sales in manufacturing were two and one-third times as high in Hungary as in the United States (E. J. Fogaras-Zala, "The Stock Problem in Hungary," *The Review of Income and Wealth*, 14, 4, 1968, pp. 403-09).

[4] See D. Granick, *Soviet Metal-Fabricating and Economic Development* (University of Wisconsin Press, Madison: 1967), chapter 5, for a treatment both of the extent of such vertical integration within enterprises of the Soviet Union's machinebuilding enterprises and of the costs of such a policy. There is every reason to believe that Hungarian industry exhibited the same behavior as did the Russian.

[5] See Hungarian Central Statistical Office, *Statistical Yearbook 1970* (Budapest: 1972), pp. 156-57, and *Statistical Yearbook 1968*, pp. 130-31. Although the stock data are expressed in current prices, it should be remembered that the rate of inflation was only 1 to 2 percent per annum.

output during the same period; moreover, the difference cannot be accounted for by any increase of the growth rate of industrial output over that of the earlier period, since the growth rate declined somewhat compared to the previous three years.[6] Nor, since 1967 was by all accounts a year in which enterprises stockpiled in preparation for the changeover, can one explain the relative growth rates of stocks and of output by a shortage of stocks as of January 1, 1968.

One might legitimately choose to exclude changes during 1968 from the analysis, arguing that the original year of the reform was one of considerable uncertainty. If one considers only the growth of stocks during 1969-71, the picture is much better; but even then, industrial stocks of materials and unfinished production in real terms grew about as rapidly as did industrial output.

The evolution of these macroeconomic stock data is quite consistent with the information I received from interviews in enterprises.[7] In four of the five enterprises, I was told that the reforms had not brought any reduction in the long leadtime required between placing orders and receiving deliveries; the men in charge of purchasing saw no amelioration of the situation between 1967 and early 1971. The fifth enterprise did note an improvement, and this was offered as the explanation of why the enterprise's stocks had increased over a four-year period at only one-third the rate of increase in production. In this enterprise, however, two different managerial interviewees (including the purchasing manager) explained the improvement in procurement conditions for the enterprise by the more effective use of the enterprise's position as a major supplier of semifabricates to the vast bulk of its own suppliers; those partner enterprises which were accommodating in supplying the enterprise received in turn preferred treatment in rapid deliveries of semifabricates. This purchasing device of mutual aid was, of course, a nonmarket one and was probably almost equally feasible before the reform; in any case, it was not available to most enterprises. Thus, in

---

[6] Measuring the output of all socialist industry in constant prices, production during 1968-70 rose by 18 to 20 percent depending upon which definition one uses. With the same definitions, output had increased by 21 to 24 percent during 1965-67. (*Statistical Yearbook 1970*, pp. 64-65 and 68-69.)

If one extends the analysis by one year, stocks of raw materials and auxiliary materials during the first four years of the reform increased by 50 percent, and stocks of unfinished products and semifabricates by 26 percent, compared with an industrial growth rate of 25 to 26 percent (above sources and *Statistical Yearbook 1971*, pp. 60, 65, and 150-51).

[7] Survey data exist as to managers' views regarding changes during the first year of the reform. They indicate that much the same proportion of managers encountered worsening in supply conditions as those who encountered improvement (K. Szabó, ed., *A. Vállalati Belső Mechanizmus Helyzete és Fejlődésének Főbb Vonásai*, A magyar Szocialista Munkáspárt Központi Bizottságának Gazdaságpolitikai Osztálya, Budapest: 1969, p. 79, as referred to in Lauter, p. 103).

general, the need for stocks by enterprises does not seem to have been reduced by the reform.

In one enterprise supplying intermediate products to industry, a top production manager expressed the belief that his enterprise was able to maintain a more even production flow since the reform because it was less bound to delivery schedules, and thus could more readily readjust production schedules of individual products. He believed that the pre-reform state plan obligations, which specified deliveries to be made within a three-month period, had been more binding on the enterprise than were current contracts with purchasers; clearly this was because the penalty clauses of current contracts were both drawn up and interpreted under conditions of a seller's market.

No macroeconomic data exist as to changes in the degree of vertical integration in individual enterprises. However, I talked in four enterprises with managers who were knowledgeable about changes in the degree to which maintenance work and spare-parts production are done outside of their enterprise.

The chief engineer of one factory said that he had tried hard to expand the degree of such subcontracting, but had been quite unsuccessful. The period of waiting both for maintenance work and for those spare parts which had not been ordered a year or so in advance was simply too long for such orders to be practicable. Like the others with whom I spoke, he was fully conscious of the high financial costs to the enterprise of having to do this work itself rather than rely on specialists.

Managers in a second enterprise reported the same situation with regard to maintenance work, but felt that the spare-parts situation was much improved. The principal reason for the latter was that the enterprise was now allowed to import more spare parts from the western companies which had originally produced the relevant machinery than had been possible under the stricter foreign exchange control of the prereform period. (This same phenomenon was also reported in the fourth enterprise.) But a second reason was that purchases could now be made from a Hungarian enterprise whose prereform production for export of these same parts had been stopped when its export subsidy rate was set too low for such sales to be practicable. The latter reason, however, was peculiar to this enterprise's branch; the fourth enterprise reported precisely the reverse.

A plant director in a third enterprise said that the percentage of maintenance expenses which consisted of outside purchases was now just the same as it had been before 1968. He never attempted to expand such purchases simply in order to reduce costs; outsiders were used only where the enterprise did not have the technical capability of doing the work or when it suffered from shortages of capacity. On the other hand, both he and a manager in a fourth enterprise insisted that they now purchased new equipment in cases where before the reform they would have continued to maintain the old at greater expense. This was because they no longer required ministerial approval for all investments. (The saving from new investment rather than continued maintenance had to be substantial, however, for it to be worthwhile for the enterprise. This is because maintenance is financed as a cost, while the alternative new investment must be financed from the investment fund after payment of a 60 percent tax.)

The head of maintenance in the fourth enterprise, the only one located in a medium-sized town surrounded by a large rural area, reported success in expanding the proportion of its maintenance which is subcontracted out. This expansion went to local cooperatives, rather than to state-owned enterprises. The reason for this success appears to be that cooperatives are much more profit-oriented than state-owned enterprises and, since tax laws in force through 1970 permitted them to pay more to their workers, they could expand their labor force at the expense of state-owned enterprises. But such cooperatives were generally able to operate only in rural areas, and the other enterprises in which I interviewed did not make much use of them.[8]

This fourth enterprise also reported that maintenance conditions were easier since the reform because its branch ministry had earlier laid down the same schedule of preventive maintenance for all enterprises. Although this enterprise possessed newer equipment than the others and thus required less frequent maintenance, it had not been worthwhile for its management to raise the issue in the ministry; the enterprise would not have gained particularly from the resulting saving.

To sum up, it is true that three of the four enterprises reported an improved situation in maintenance compared to the prereform years. But the two principal reasons cited were the easing of foreign-exchange restrictions on imports of spare parts from capitalist countries, and the freedom from detailed controls by the branch ministries. In only one case did changes in domestic supply conditions improve the possibilities for subcontracting; moreover, this subcontracting was to cooperatives, whose services were used by the enterprise primarily because they

---

[8] See L. Rév, "Az ipari szövetkezetek gazdasági tevékenységének néhány sajátosságáról," *Közgazdasági Szemle*, xix, 3 (1972), 257-72, as referred to in Hungarian Scientific Council for World Economy, Scientific Information Service, *Abstracts of Hungarian Economic Literature*, 1972, 2, pp. 65-66.

During 1966-70, the rate of growth of industrial output was somewhat more than twice as high in cooperatives as in state-owned enterprises. In 1971, however, the rate of growth of such output in cooperatives fell by more than half, although it was still higher than that in state-owned firms (*Közgazdasági Szemle*, xix, 3, 1972, p. 260, summarized in *ABSEES*, July 1972).

could relieve labor bottlenecks rather than because they offered lower-cost services. Thus the improved maintenance situation reported in these enterprises must be considered as divorced from the abolition of materials allocation.

Our discussion as to the realization of the various expectations of what should have resulted from the abandonment of formal allocations leads to the conclusion—supported both by the macroeconomic data and by the limited sample of enterprises—that this major change in the economic system has been virtually barren of results. The only apparent effect was the very minor one of eliminating the extensive paperwork previously necessitated by the allocation system. The corollary of this conclusion is that the prereform materials allocation system had in fact been a purposeless excrescence on the economy, whose removal had no apparent significance.

In view of the omnipresence of formal materials allocation in the CMEA countries, except for the recent change in Hungary, this conclusion is nothing if not surprising. In order to test whether I was missing some obvious point, I suggested this conclusion at different times to a number of Hungarian economists. While they were all surprised at it, and no one expressed agreement with it, neither was any of them willing to assert that it was inconsistent with the facts.

How is the absence of significant effect from the abolition of the allocation system to be explained? Two minor factors lie in the prereform history of the Hungarian economy. One of these, which contributed to preventing chaos, was the introduction of price changes during the late 1950's which brought the supply and demand for intermediate products into better balance than had existed earlier.[9] Without this, the disequilibrium situation faced in 1968 would have been more severe than it was.

The second minor factor was the merger of enterprises in the early 1960's, so that an increased proportion of the provisioning of factories took place within the confines of a single enterprise; centralized materials allocation was irrelevant to such provisioning. However, since these mergers appear to have taken much more of a horizontal than a vertical form, it is unlikely that this factor was of great consequence.

If we put aside these two factors as unable to sustain much of the burden of explanation, we are forced to conclude that the formal system of allocations must have been replaced by an informal one. We know that traditional supply relations remained of great importance; one pur-

[9] Between 1957 and 1959, the price level of products of heavy industry—the main producer of intermediate products—had increased by two-thirds compared to the prices received by the producers of light industry products (B. Csikós-Nagy in Friss, *Reform*, p. 139).

chasing agent insisted that a supplying-enterprise's branch ministry would not permit it to cease delivering any product without having given the customer at least six months' notice. Managers in another enterprise said that they could not give up production of any item until they found some other enterprise which was willing to produce it, and that the search might take years.

The form taken by this informal rationing system is unclear. I have no information as to the relative importance of "advice" given by branch ministries; of pressure exercised by interministerial committees charged with granting price, credit, and tax privileges; of intervention by regional Party organizations; and of informal rationing conducted by the producing enterprises themselves to assure old customers of their traditional volumes of supply so long as they order long enough in advance. My guess is, however, that it is the last factor which is the most important. To the extent that this is indeed so, such informal rationing may be expected to work best so long as the structure of industry does not change radically from what it had been prior to the reform; it does not lend itself to great dynamism in adjustment of the product mix of final products to the demands of the internal and export markets.

It seems probable that the importance of foreign trade in Hungary's economy is of major consequence in making workable this system of informal allocations. The large role of gross exports, rather than of imports, is particularly critical here; gross exports of raw materials, semifinished goods, and spare parts constitute 11 percent of Hungary's total net domestic product.[10] To the extent that such exports—particularly those to the nonsocialist countries where long-term agreements do not govern the composition of trade—are treated as only residual claims on Hungary's capacity for producing individual intermediate products, it becomes easier to satisfy the primary claim of meeting the specific input needs of Hungary's own industry. Thus an informal materials allocation system should have greater flexibility, and be liable to less stress, than would be the case in a country whose gross exports of intermediate products are less substantial. As we shall see below, there is some evidence that a sizable proportion of Hungarian exports are residual in nature.

THE ENTERPRISE'S CHOICE OF PRODUCT MIX AND CUSTOMERS

Interviews in the five enterprises brought out clearly that production is oriented, ceteris paribus, to that choice of products and customers which is most profitable. It is, however, the content of the term "ceteris paribus" which is of importance here.

[10] 1970 data. See chapter 8.

An enterprise producing a wide product mix of semifabricates used throughout most of the Hungarian economy was said by its sales director to treat its key task as that of satisfying domestic demand. Although he acknowledged that different products produced for the home market provided varying degrees of profitability, he insisted that there was relatively little effort made to persuade domestic consumers to accept the more profitable items.

More significantly, this sales director claimed that he treated exports to nonsocialist countries simply as an outlet for surplus products. This was despite the fact that, during 1970, such exports had been two and one-half times as profitable as home sales. On further exploration of the subject, it appeared that all existing domestic customers were given priority for the quantities which they had ordered in earlier years, but that requests for increases in deliveries were not automatically honored by the producing enterprise. In 1971, with prices down substantially for the semifabricates sold in nonsocialist countries, the sales director expected to divert to the domestic market 20 percent of his previous year's sales to these foreign markets. His ability to do this would seem to indicate the degree of unsatisfied home demand for these intermediate products which had existed in 1970.

On the other hand, prices of a particular product group produced by the enterprise were up in 1971 in west European countries; the sales director expected to increase his sales of this product to these countries at the expense of his exports to socialist countries.[11]

In sum, the sales director's assertion that the enterprise gives absolute priority to fully satisfying domestic demand appears to have been an exaggeration.[12] Contrary to his assertion, profitability does act as a criterion in choosing between domestic and foreign customers, but apparently not to the degree of permitting either absolute reductions in shipments to any domestic customer or of permitting stagnation of total home deliveries. It is clear that the enterprise could take only limited advantage of the far greater profits to be earned from exports than from domestic sales.

[11] He explained that the trade agreements with socialist countries were sufficiently flexible for him to be able to substitute other products for part of his normal shipments of this group.

[12] But see the attitude expressed by the Party secretary of the May First Clothing Factory who insisted—contrary to the advice of a "high-ranking state official"—that her enterprise's priorities should be first that of meeting its domestic obligations, second of covering its orders from socialist countries, and only third to export to hard currency areas. This, she said, was regardless of the relative profitability of these different markets (Mrs. J. Hart in interview in *Társadalmi Szemle*, March 1972, as translated in *RFE*).

It should be noted, however, that this enterprise's current investment was concentrated in expanding the capacity of existing products rather than of an additional related item whose domestic demand was being met entirely from imports. The enterprise, with limited financial resources, chose to invest in the more profitable products; it had also prepared a supplemental project for investment in the import-substitution product, but it intended to move ahead with this project only in the very unlikely case that it could get special state financing.

In a second enterprise, the marketing head also regarded his enterprise's key task as that of meeting domestic demand. To him, profitability was of quite secondary significance in determining product mix, and exports to capitalist countries were treated simply as a means of utilizing specialized capacity which was temporarily in excess of domestic demand.

This enterprise enjoyed virtually a monopoly of both production and imports of a major product group used widely by other enterprises in Hungary. Imports from socialist countries comprised an important element in the total domestic usage of this product group; but import orders had to be placed in full detail one to one and one-half years before delivery, and even such contracts were usually not fulfilled in the precise product mix requested. The result was that the enterprise's production schedule had to be adjusted to meet the gaps for individual products which existed between domestic demand and imports. The enterprise was in no position to determine its product mix according to profitability considerations.

As a consequence, the marketing head believed in early 1971 that the enterprise's current sales on the domestic market were still quite uninfluenced by the reform. He viewed the reform as affecting only the choice among investments, and thus as having no short-run significance for the composition of production and sales.

A third enterprise, which produced semifabricates for a major consumer industry, was the only one which placed great stress on profitability as the key criterion in determining product mix. Even here, however, there were at least two serious constraints. The first was that there could be no reduction in the percentage of sales on the domestic market which consisted of cheaper (and less profitable) products. Even new products were put into production simply in order to keep up this ratio. The reason was that these cheaper semifabricates were needed by customers to produce less expensive consumer goods; a reduction in the supply of these latter would be interpreted by final consumers—and especially by the lower-income part of the population—as an increase in the consumer price level.

The medium of enforcement of this restriction is unclear. The department head who described the policy to me simply said that it was laid down by the enterprise's general director. Since the position of general director was also characterized as a political one, it is quite possible that he enunciated the policy because of his own conception of social responsibility. But it is more likely that he realized that there could be serious repercussions—from such diverse channels as his branch ministry, the regional Party organization, and the enterprise trade union—if he were to follow any other.

The second restriction was that exports could not be permitted to run down because of the failure to offer less-profitable items. The company was historically an important exporter, and a reduction in its earnings of foreign exchange for this reason would not be permitted by central authorities.[13] Since the enterprise was rapidly losing workers to higher-paying industries, and since it hoped to maintain production only through engaging in substantial labor-saving investments, net profits might well have been increased by allowing production to decline at the expense of such exports.

A fourth enterprise appears to have been in much the same position as the third in respect to production constraints. One of its products was continued in production purely for political reasons: consumer goods manufactured from it were viewed as important for the domestic market, even though there was an unwillingness to permit its price to rise. The enterprise's investment policy was geared entirely to replacing labor, which was leaving for higher-paying industries, and to increasing production; profitability considerations appeared to be negligible. While the enterprise was currently earning 18 percent pretax profit on its capital, it was hoped virtually to double the capital stock during the next five years at a prospective earning of the low figure of 8 percent pretax profit on the additional capital. The manager explaining investment policy to me insisted that profitability of investment was not a relevant consideration; what mattered was that it would be a scandal if production were to fall.

A second aspect of choice of product mix is that of quality. It had been hoped that the reform would motivate Hungarian industry to improve its product quality which, it was believed, suffered in comparison with that of western Europe owing to the same incentive reasons which apply to all of the socialist countries.

When I inquired of Hungarians engaged in planning, administration,

---

[13] The general director described the potential central pressure as the threat to stop export subsidies to the enterprise. But it seems likely that the issue was never in fact raised, and that the general director was only attempting to give me an explanation which was at least fairly consistent with the reform mechanisms.

and academic life as to whether these hopes had been realized, it was clear that no one had any data bearing on the question. Opinions on the subject varied sharply.[14]

In two of the five enterprises in which I conducted interviews, managers stated that the quality of their own enterprise's products had improved during the three years of the reform. But in both cases, these managers believed that quality had improved for reasons extraneous to the reform. A manager of a third enterprise, while expressing no opinion as to the change in quality of his enterprise's production, also asserted that the reform had had no effect on the dimension of product choice.[15]

The reasons for the apparent failure to improve quality are not clear. One obvious reason is the difficulty encountered in raising prices to compensate for improved quality.[16] But it may also be that enterprises

[14] This is quite a different question from whether the quality of goods available on the Hungarian market has improved. Particularly in the field of consumer goods, increased imports from western countries seem to have raised significantly the average quality of available goods.

Two Hungarian scholars who read this manuscript in draft form both felt strongly that there had been quality improvement in domestic production of consumer goods. Dr. Kemenes, in particular, held that the increase in imports of consumer goods from the west—from something in the order of 3 percent of total purchases by Hungarian wholesale enterprises of consumer goods from all sources in 1968 to 6.1 percent in 1971—is insufficient to explain the degree of improvement in quality which Hungarian consumers have perceived. (The percentages are calculated by me from the *Statistical Yearbook 1971*, pp. 266 and 306, the assumptions—which probably lead to understatement—being made for this purpose that the proportion of all consumer goods imports which came from the west was the same as that for industrial consumer goods alone, and that a foreign-exchange forint of trade with the west should be treated as worth 1.5 foreign-exchange forints of trade with socialist countries. A comparison with 1967 would probably show no greater change.)

On the other hand, a survey of managers about one year after the reform indicated no impression of improvement (Szabó, p. 80, as referred to in Lauter, p. 104). Commenting as to industry in general, the director of the Office of Prices and Allocations wrote in late 1972, "While one can observe an acceleration in the rate of modernization of products, . . . the elimination of unprofitable models and the introduction of competitive new models have either not proceeded at all or have done so only very slowly." (B. Csikós-Nagy, "A magyar gazdasági reform eredményei és perspektívái," *Közgazdasági Szemle*, XIX, 9, 1972, p. 1014.)

[15] No information on the subject was obtained from the other two enterprises.

[16] Greater differentiation of prices with regard to quality may, of course, lead to deterioration of quality because purchasers are unwilling to pay the higher prices. The firm producing semifabricates for producers' goods industries noted that it now had greater freedom to raise prices for off-standard items than was the case before the reform; since it in fact used this right, demand for these off-standard items had dropped sufficiently so that their production fell as a proportion of the enterprise's total output. I would expect, however, that higher prices for better quality or specialized items would, under Hungarian conditions, normally have a greater encouraging effect on the quantity supplied than a discouraging effect on demand (i.e., the principal effect would be to bring supply and demand for such products toward equilibrium along a price-elastic supply curve).

were responding to the same stimulus which was decisive prior to the reform: namely, the negative effect of the improvement of quality upon the volume of output.

A third aspect of choice is that of risk taking. One Hungarian economist indicated to me that he expected enterprises—particularly those in sectors where plants produced very small numbers of many different sorts of products—to adjust their mix to market demands much more rapidly than they had before the reform. He envisioned profit incentives as making these enterprises more sensitive to changing demand conditions, particularly to those in capitalist markets. He felt that this change was likely to be particularly important in improving Hungary's terms of trade with capitalist countries.

I have information from only two units which bears on the realization of this expectation; it is not encouraging. One enterprise's commercial manager told me that the enterprise's policy within capitalist markets was to continue to sell to the same customers in much the same proportions as earlier; this policy had been followed for the previous ten years, and was quite unaffected by the reform. He agreed that higher prices could have been gained for these exports if the enterprise had been willing to shift production to other customers, but he felt that there was little incentive to take the risks involved in this more active marketing policy.

A representative of a branch ministry strongly rejected the notion of producing items which are highly subject to the fads of fashion (hula hoops was our example). He felt that a risk which cannot be calculated should never be taken.

A study conducted in 1969 by the Hungarian Academy of Sciences showed that two-thirds of top managers in large industrial enterprises thought that Hungarian enterprises in general took too few risks, and none thought that they took exaggerated risks.[17]

Thus it would not appear that the reforms have led industrial enterprises to particularly adventuresome market-oriented policies. The reason would appear to lie, in part, in the weakness of incentives provided to managers for improving their enterprise's profitability.[18]

[17] Z. Komonyi, "Some Aspects of Enterprise Behavior," in Z. Román (ed.), *Progress and Planning in Industry* (International Conference on Industrial Economics of April 1970, Akadémiai Kiadó, Budapest: 1972), p. 340. The sample consisted of one hundred thirty seven enterprise managers; their enterprises employed 40 percent of the total labor force in state industry. Risk taking was defined in terms of choosing policies which promised a higher expected profit, but with greater uncertainty, than available alternatives.

[18] For one of many such statements, see G. Szenczi, "A nyereség és a jövedelem alakulása az iparban az új gazdaságirányitási rendszer első három évében," *Ipargazdaság*, 1971, 6, pp. 29-33, as referred to in *Abstracts*, 1971, 3-4, p. 259. The question of risk taking by enterprises will be discussed more fully below.

MISCELLANEOUS ENTERPRISE PHENOMENA

Control over the enterprise by state bodies. The principal single agency supervising the enterprises is still the branch ministry, of which there are five covering industry, agriculture, and construction. These branch ministries each appear to employ somewhere between one hundred fifty and four hundred professionals; these numbers were variously estimated in 1971 as still constituting 40 to 70 percent of those who had worked there several years prior to the introduction of the reform.

The power of these branch ministries is, of course, greatly diminished in comparison with the prereform days. Nevertheless, they continue to have hierarchical power over their enterprises. In early 1971, one ministry had the formal right of appointment and dismissal over the three principal directors of each enterprise subordinate to it, although its officials expected that this right would soon be restricted to power over the general director alone; presumably, much the same situation existed in the other ministries as well. The branch ministry also determined the bonuses to be paid to the principal directors of each enterprise. While the ministry has the power to give direct orders to enterprises where it feels this to be necessary, a high official of one branch ministry insisted to me that no such direct order had been given by his ministry during the three years since the reform had been introduced. On the other hand, this ministry does give "advice" to the enterprises, and doubtless it is often difficult to distinguish between such advice and orders. It would appear that operational "advice" by the branch ministries increased after the first few years of the reform.[19] Moreover, it is asserted that the branch ministries' prime interest is neither in short-run nor long-run profits, but rather in expansion of their respective branches' production and in improvement in the foreign trade balance.[20]

My impression is that the branch ministry exercises direct influence upon the enterprise primarily with regard to longer-run considerations: the extent and direction of new investments, research and development, relative expansion of different product lines, and the bringing into production of new products. Partly this is simply consultative: i.e., providing an expertise unavailable within the enterprises. Partly it is a fleshing-out

[19] See, for example, the statement by Árpád Pullai, a secretary of the Central Committee, that "operative action, if it serves the targets of the plan, is not an act of 'outside,' artificial intervention, but part and parcel of normal activity" (*Népszabadság*, December 13, 1972, as quoted in *RFE*). A Party resolution of November 1972 asserted that state authorities should closely follow the work of some forty to fifty of the largest industrial enterprises; these constitute about 20 percent of the total number of industrial firms, and produce 40 to 50 percent of total industrial production (T. Dániel and E. Horváth in *Pénzügyi Szemle*, 1973, 9, pp. 719-27, as referred to in *Abstracts*, 1973, 5, pp. 9-10).

[20] M. Tardos in *Közgazdasági Szemle*, XIX, 7-8 (1972), summarized in *RFE*.

of the decisions of interministerial committees in which the branch ministry is represented but not dominant; for example, if a particular industry were granted additional wage funds by government decision, it would be the relevant branch ministry which would distribute them to the individual enterprises.[21]

But it is perfectly clear that the enterprises cannot look for guidance solely to their branch ministries. The main decisions which affect them are made by interministerial committees: pricing, taxes, subsidies, grants, loans, exports, and the right of the enterprise to import equipment from specific sources. In all these matters, the branch ministry has a voice; but it does not appear to be the decisive influence. One well-informed Hungarian economist voiced to me the reasonable opinion that the fact that the branch ministries do not possess substantial sums of money which they can use as they see fit prevents them from exercising great power over the enterprises. It is the interministerial committees which dispose of the financial resources, and thus the key decisions are taken at their level. Therefore the many decisions which are made concerning the individual enterprises seem today often to be pushed up higher in the governmental hierarchy than was the case before the reform; matters which earlier a branch ministry could determine alone are now decided by committees representing a number of ministries.

From the enterprise's point of view, this situation has both its good and bad features. The negative side is that the enterprise can no longer, as before the reform, settle its affairs with ministry officials who are concerned with and responsible for all aspects of the enterprise's work and with whom the enterprise's managers are in permanent contact. The positive side is the greater independence given to the enterprise; for it is no longer dependent on decisions made by any single ministry.

An additional form of control was being experimented with in early 1971 in a number of enterprises: an enterprise board of directors consisting primarily or entirely of people from outside the enterprise.[22]

[21] A Hungarian scholar who read a draft of this manuscript felt that, while it is true that the functional central organs have come to the forefront of decision making since the reform, the branch ministries did not lose responsibility for the fulfillment of national plans by their branches. However, they have concentrated on the more important and long-run problems of their branch, despite the fact that the largest number of their decisions are in the realm of applying to the individual enterprises central decisions made at the level of an industry (e.g., the granting of additional wage funds).

[22] The most comparable body in western corporations is the German *Aufsichtsrat*. In one such Hungarian board for which I have information, seven members were appointed; six were officials of the branch ministry, and the seventh came from another enterprise of the same branch which was totally unconnected with the enterprise being controlled. A second enterprise had nine board members; two were officials of the branch ministry, one was from the enterprise's trade association, four were representatives of the enterprise's largest domestic customers, one

The board advised the branch minister on the appropriate bonuses for the top managers of the enterprise, and would recommend replacements for them if the issue arose. To some degree, the board acted as the representative of the branch ministry; but at least one of these boards also exercised financial supervision as the representative of the Ministry of Finance.

Intermediate between the branch ministry and the enterprise exist a number of associations. Most of these are, at least in form and probably to a large extent in reality, voluntary.[23] Some, however, have obligatory membership; for example, all metallurgical firms must belong for five years to that industry's association, and this association has been granted certain powers for scheduling purchase orders to the individual enterprises.[24] There exist also a very few trusts; these have varying powers over the constituent enterprises, and one informed Hungarian observer even expressed the view that at least one of these trusts has more power than do its enterprises. While the actual authority of these various intermediate organizations is unclear, it is certain that the existence of such organizations is exceptional. Normally, the formal line of authority leads directly from the enterprise to the branch ministry.

Communist Party and trade union control over the enterprise management. This is an important subject, but one on which I was not able to collect much significant information. Hungary is the only one of the four countries studied where it was impossible for me to arrange interviews with Party or trade union officials.

My impression is, however, that both the Party and trade union organizations in Hungary continue to play much the same role as they did prior to the reform, and as they do in other east European socialist countries.[25] A Hungarian study undertaken during 1969 observed that the enterprises examined were under the pressure of Party and "other"

---

was from an export-import enterprise (but not the one working with the enterprise), and one was from the enterprise itself. Clearly, most of the members of these two boards seemed to be present so as to represent their own parent organizations, but each board had one member whose own organization had no normal contact with the enterprise and who was chosen purely on the basis of his personal characteristics.

[23] I was told that, of two enterprises building television sets and equipment, one belonged to the telecommunications association and the other did not.

[24] While I do not know the extent of such powers actually exercised by the metallurgical association, it is clear that the enterprises retain considerable authority with regard to sales and to the scheduling of production.

[25] Robinson, however, makes a strong case for the view that the Hungarian trade unions, at least at the national level, stand out as a defender of worker interests in comparison with the unions of the other CMEA countries (W. F. Robinson, *The Pattern of Reform in Hungary*, Praeger, New York, Washington, and London: 1973, pp. 329-45).

organizations.[26] In one enterprise, I was told that all issues are coordinated by the enterprise's general director, the enterprise's Party secretary, and the enterprise's trade union chairman. The regional Party organization must approve the appointment of the enterprise's general director, and the enterprise Party organization must approve the appointment of the remaining directors of the enterprise.

Evidence is conflicting as to whether, since the reform, there has been expansion in the participation by the enterprise's Party secretary in the business affairs of the enterprise. Managers reported an increase in one enterprise and a decline in another; I would suspect that there is no clear overall tendency. While in Hungary, I heard only one comment (which came from an academic) as to the role of the regional Party secretaries; it suggested an enlargement of their role in the control of enterprises.[27] On the other hand, another Hungarian scholar who read the first draft of this manuscript held that there had been no general change in the responsibility and activities of the regional Party authorities. If there has been change here, it cannot be so marked as to be indisputable.

I have one instance of rejection of a managerial proposal by an enterprise's trade union. The management, faced with particular difficulties in retaining the workers in one major process of the enterprise, wished to increase their wages by 6 percent in the following year compared to 2 to 2½ percent for all other personnel. The enterprise's general director had won the agreement of the enterprise's trade union chairman, but could not gain the assent of the seventy-man trade union committee. As a result of this rejection, he dropped the proposal.

However, the power of the enterprise trade union to determine the enterprise's policy on relative wage increases for different groups of workers was less absolute than this example might suggest. The general director had not brought the proposal to the various plant Party organizations prior to bringing it to the trade union committee; if he had done this, and had won support there, presumably he could have carried the union vote. But he was anxious to avoid any widespread discussion of the proposal within the enterprise, for fear of arousing controversy and of giving time for an opposition to gather; thus he had wanted the matter settled at a single meeting. Even after the union committee had rejected the proposal, he could have brought it to his branch ministry and al-

---

[26] The observation, regarded by the author as an important one, was based on a study of ten enterprises (M. Tardos, "An Econometric Study of Enterprise Behaviour," in Z. Román, *Progress and Planning in Industry*, p. 380).

[27] An enlargement of their role is also suggested in *Népszabadság*, March 10, 1971, p. 3, summarized in *ABSEES*, July 1971, and perhaps also by a resolution of the tenth Party congress of late 1970 (*Stenographic Report of the 10th Party Congress*, Budapest: 1970, p. 196 as reported in *RFE*).

lowed the ministry and the national office of the trade union jointly to determine the matter. But this also he declined to do. Clearly he desired differential wage increases only if they could be adopted without a lengthy struggle.

The enterprise's internal organization. As was pointed out in Chapter 8, Hungarian enterprises were consolidated during the first half of the 1960's; this consolidation seems to have been primarily along horizontal rather than vertical lines. At the end of 1970, industrial state enterprises contained an average of seven establishments each, with 45 percent of the total labor force concentrated in large establishments employing over one thousand manual workers.[28]

While the reform has had a significant effect on the operation of enterprises, my interviews indicate that it has been almost irrelevant to the direction of the establishments. The individual factories continue to be operated within the bounds of production planning organized from the enterprise headquarters. Although two of the three enterprises for which I have data calculate profit at the factory as well as at the enterprise level, and although wages and average end-of-year bonuses can differ somewhat between factories within the same enterprise, the factories seem to have no more authority than they enjoyed prior to 1968.

Thus the longtime second-in-command of a large plant in one enterprise viewed his plant's operations as having been affected in only two respects by the reform. One of these was positive: Hungarian engineers could now travel to the west more easily than before, and thus international professional contacts had improved greatly. The other was negative: the quit rate of workers had risen drastically. Neither of these developments necessarily stems from the reform per se.

However, he did feel that the work of plant management had been revolutionized by the creation of the enterprise in the early 1960's. This was because plant autonomy had then been sharply reduced. While previously there had been only seventy people in the ministry to coordinate the activities of all plants in the entire industry, there were now four hundred people in the enterprise's headquarters who coordinated the plants of the enterprise and carried out some of their previous functions. As a result, the plant management now received much more detailed and operational instructions than had been the case around 1960.

One can conclude that, although the reform did promote decentraliza-

[28] *Statistical Yearbook 1971*, p. 165. According to the calculations of Wilcsek, the Hungarian industrial labor force is one of the most concentrated in the world at the establishment, as well as at the enterprise, level (J. Wilcsek, "Concentration and Specialization in the Hungarian Industry," in Z. Román, *Progress and Planning in Industry*, p. 304).

tion of authority down to the enterprise level, it has been largely irrelevant to the issue of decentralization to the establishment level. In fact, if one compares the situation in 1960 with that in 1970, there has been considerable centralization of authority in industry as viewed from the establishment's perspective.[29]

Both in academic and in central-planning circles, the views which I heard concerning the desirability of maintenance of large, semimonopolistic enterprises were almost uniformly negative. These views were based particularly upon the impossibility of organizing much competition within Hungary so long as these enterprises continued to exist. Perhaps this portends a future splitting apart of these enterprises into their constituent parts; as of early 1971, however, virtually nothing had been done in this regard.

Creation of a capital market. In a profit-oriented system of the type which the reform was intended to further, there is a clear danger that investment resources will be misallocated between sectors. This is so because enterprises are left with larger retained earnings than had been the case prior to 1968. To the extent that all enterprises reinvest these funds in their own expansion, there is the possibility of overinvestment in sectors which promise less profitability in the future than would alternative investments in other industries.

The section in Chapter 9 on investment financing in industry suggests that, in practice, this potential difficulty has been kept under control. State decisions as to central investment finance, as to allocation between subsectors of loans by the Investment Bank, and on the degree to which enterprises should be compelled to employ their retained earnings to finance their working capital needs have all had a strong impact; this impact has been sufficient so that enterprises in sectors which are considered to have a poor future have probably been able to do little more than finance their capital-replacement needs from their own resources. Nevertheless, there has been some mild concern in Hungary with this potential capital-misallocation problem.

One means of handling it has been to allow individual enterprises considerable room for diversification of production, although they are not allowed to move out of their own broad sector to become conglomerates. A second device is to pay interest to enterprises on their long-term deposits with the National Bank; but this has been totally ineffective.[30] A

---

[29] The Hungarian prime minister in 1971 deplored the fact that plant managements are "often" left with less freedom than they had prior to the mergers and reform (J. Fock as reported in *Népszabadság*, October 24, 1971, pp. 4-5, translated in *ABSEES*, January 1972).

[30] L. Tutzer, "A bankkamat szerepéről," *Közgazdasági Szemle*, XIX, 3 (1972), 288-96, as referred to in *Abstracts*, 1972, 2, p. 120.

third means is the right given them to invest—together with other existing Hungarian enterprises—in the creation of new enterprises. This last right is potentially important in permitting investments intended to take advantage of more profitable opportunities when these exist outside the product scope of their own enterprises.

As of early 1971, no joint investments by enterprises had yet been undertaken. But one enterprise in which I interviewed was considering making such an investment in the near future.

The project under consideration was a plant which would provide an early stage of processing of a basic raw material for the entire industry to which this enterprise belonged. The enterprise's interest in contributing to the necessary investment was not, however, based on any profitability calculations. Rather, it was grounded in the desire to assure itself —through partial ownership—a voice in determining the technology to be employed in the new plant, so that the plant's final product would be best adapted to the needs of the consuming enterprise.[31] The enterprise's management appeared to be considering the investment in the light of how much money it would have to put up in order to assure itself of this voice. Thus, in this case at least, the decision on the joint investment had nothing to do with extending the realm of placement of investment funds to more profitable sectors; rather, it was concerned with gaining, through partial ownership, some of the power over the quality of its material inputs which—in a more competitive market environment—it would automatically have derived from its ability to shift orders between suppliers.

STIMULATION OF WORKER AND MANAGERIAL EFFORT

One of the objectives of the reform has been to increase the concern of workers and managers with the fate of their individual enterprise, giving them a greater stake in its success than had been the case earlier. To the extent that this objective is achieved, one would expect to see increased inputs of effort and thought by industrial employees. Productivity should improve, other things equal, because of this greater labor intensity.

A national scale of base wages for workers and employees with different skills and in various industries has been maintained under the reform system, although the range of permissible wages for each skill category is said to have widened substantially in comparison with the pre-1968 situation. But what is significant is that this national scale has

---

[31] It seems likely that a second reason, although this was not expressed to me, was that refusal to invest would be regarded unfavorably (as a rejection of industry solidarity) by central authorities.

a sufficient spread for each category so that the existence of the scale does not appear to restrict managements from increasing wages wherever they have the funds and the will to do so. Since enterprises are also permitted to exceed even this generous scale for a portion of their workers, it would seem that payments for individual skills and to individual workers are determined almost entirely at the enterprise level; the national scale appears relevant only as a guide to both trade union and external pressures which may be placed on managers so as to counteract wage pushes emanating from the labor market.

As we have seen earlier, however, the constraints of the economic environment have largely frustrated the desire of Hungarian planners to reward workers for the profitability improvements in their individual enterprises. In 1971, the year when the tax regulations were most liberal in this regard, only approximately 1 to 12 percent of increases in enterprise profits—beyond that needed to finance the same percentage wage increase as the average paid out in industry as a whole during that year —could be used for further wage increases or for end-of-year bonuses. With such a high marginal "tax rate" on profits, the observer should not be surprised if workers failed to increase their work effort to any noticeable degree.

Although piece-rate systems of various sorts are widely used in Hungarian factories, enterprise management is in fact compelled to discourage major expansion of productivity through increases of worker effort. If worknorms are substantially exceeded because of greater intensity of labor, the tax system effectively prevents the management from increasing earnings proportionately. Thus management has no alternative but to reduce piece rates when they are exceeded, whether the reason for improved productivity is changed technology or expanded effort. Since regular reductions of piece rates as a reward for increased worker effort constitute a policy which managers must find untenable, it is not surprising that enterprise managers and workers normally are in accord in avoiding increases in job intensity.

A Hungarian sociological study was carried out during 1968-69 in three enterprises, these three being selected because their technological processes were particularly appropriate for the use of straight piece-rate pay. What is interesting about this study for our purposes is the method of payment actually employed in these enterprises. One of the three used an hourly-pay system; the second used piece rates, but with maximum total earnings placed at 100 to 110 percent of the standard rate; only one used unlimited piece rates, and these were reduced by 20 percent during a single year with resultant slowdowns by many manual workers. Moreover, the third enterprise—the only one in which a genuine piece-rate system was employed—suffered from a most unusual financial squeeze which forced management to attempt to cut costs; its workers were mostly from nearby villages and had less of the solidarity against "rate busters" than is commonly found among urban workers; and management seemed to have held a peculiarly powerful political position in the region.[32] It seems typical that only such an unusual enterprise was both forced to use piece rates, and was capable of using them, as a means of furthering labor productivity.

In the three enterprises for which I have comparable information from interviews, piece rates generally provided no incentives. In one enterprise, the average annual norm fulfillment had varied only within the limits of 101.2 and 102.4 percent during the previous eight years; the range of individual norm fulfillment was contained within 99 and 105 percent. The manager of one major plant confirmed that many of his workers were officially paid according to piece rates, but that this was not taken seriously; in fact, they earned an hourly wage. A second enterprise reported group bonuses for output; but the nature of production scheduling by management prevented these bonuses from having an incentive effect.

Only the third enterprise had effectively used incentive pay to increase work effort. Even here, the system was restricted to about 5 percent of the manual labor force: those operating bottleneck pieces of equipment. Prior to 1968, all of these operators had run two machines apiece. The management gave these workers the option of increasing their workload, and almost all had shifted to handling four machines. The management calculated that the work intensity of those handling the increased number of machines has been augmented by 40 to 50 percent (although their workload was still substantially less than that customary in Italy with the same equipment and raw materials), and they received 60 percent higher earnings than the few workers who continued with a two-machine load. This major increase in productivity and in earnings was possible because only a tiny percentage of the labor force was affected, and thus their higher earnings could be covered out of the posttax profit increase which the easing of the production bottleneck made possible.

I visited plants in three different enterprises, and in all three was struck by the poor workpace of manual workers. In one quite profitable enterprise, for example, one of the members of top management hazarded the guess that labor productivity could be increased by 60 to 70 percent without the purchase of any new equipment. Yet, because of the impossibility of providing significant incentives to workers, this plant was planning to realize a 35 percent expansion in its output over the

[32] L. Héthy and C. Makó, "Incentive Problems in the Centrally Planned Economy of Hungary" (Institute of Sociology, Hungarian Academy of Science, Budapest: 1972, mimeographed).

next five years purely through mechanization, which would entail an 87 percent increase in the value of its fixed capital. No improvement in the workpace of the individual worker was expected by management.

This lack of worker incentive cannot be regarded as due to the reform. The situation prior to 1968 seems to have been no better. Incentives in the German Democratic Republic are no higher, and that nation's apparently better labor productivity appears simply to be due to the differences in work traditions in the two countries. What can be said, however, is that the Hungarian reform does not appear to have provided any additional incentives toward greater work effort.[33]

The situation is somewhat better with regard to the stimulation of managers in enterprises. As was seen in Chapter 9, managerial bonuses constitute a substantial portion of base salary. Nevertheless, the data available suggest that these bonuses are not closely linked to the amount of profits earned by the enterprises. In one enterprise, the commercial director explicitly told me that he tries to avoid not only reductions in profit but also any sudden increases. As a result, managers—just like manual workers—seem reluctant to commit themselves to substantial increases in effort.

An example of this managerial reluctance can be seen in a second enterprise. This enterprise produces both directly and indirectly for the Hungarian consumer market; its broad product category is one in which retail stores are compelled by market pressures to dispose of approximately one-fifth of their annual turnover at mark-down prices of 20 to 30 percent. The reason for these mark-downs is that retail stores must on the one hand sell stylish products, and on the other must place their orders with manufacturers some six months in advance. The impossibility of predicting consumer demand for different styles this far ahead forces the retail trade network into an accumulation of stocks which it cannot sell at normal prices.

One would think that this situation would offer significant profit opportunities to manufacturing enterprises which are willing to supply goods on shorter notice but at higher prices. The opportunities for this would seem particularly good since manufacturers' prices in this field are mostly "free." The enterprise in which I interviewed has a three-

[33] At least through early 1971, Hungarian industrial workers did seem to respond to the greater incentives which cooperatives were able to offer under the tax regulations. State industrial enterprises suffered from the competition of these cooperatives for workers; in the cooperatives, it was possible both to work much longer hours and, apparently, to be rewarded for results. The cooperatives, however, employed only 13 percent of all industrial workers; this is why, without jeopardizing the national anti-inflation policy, they could be given considerably greater freedom in raising the earnings of their workers during 1968-70 than was deemed feasible in state-owned industry.

to four-month production cycle, but this could be cut in half if it were to stock semifinished products instead of waiting for detailed final orders before beginning production. Nevertheless, the enterprise insists that all orders for the fourth quarter of the year be placed on a firm and fully detailed basis in March.

In view of the obvious profit opportunities for the enterprise, as well as for the economy as a whole, which are implicit in changing the order-period demanded of customers, I asked the sales director why the enterprise did not change its policy. His answer was that such a change would doubtless be eventually forced upon the enterprise, but that there was no point in initiating it. The change would involve both more complex production scheduling, and a major effort to justify higher prices both to the national Office of Prices and to local popular organizations such as the trade union and Party organization. Given that the firm was already quite profitable, he did not see how the resulting addition to posttax profits and wages could possibly warrant the managerial effort involved.

OBSERVED MACROECONOMIC RESULTS OF THE REFORM

When one looks at the results achieved by the Hungarian reform during the first four years of its life, one must conclude that at best it has had little of either a positive or negative demonstrable effect. Indeed, this is not at all a bad record; for one might well have expected short-term deleterious results from a major change in the procedures by which economic decisions are made. But it does imply that a favorable evaluation of the reform must rest on expectations as to future effects rather than on demonstrated consequences.[34]

Ideally, one would wish to evaluate the macroeconomic effects of the reform through a regression model which includes all important independent variables affecting each year's results, and which treats the reform as a dummy variable. Since this is not possible, I shall simply compare results in the prereform and postreform years; changes in other variables will be indicated where these are known and important.

Labor productivity in industry showed no improvement at all during the first two years of the reform.[35] For the first four years (1968-71), it

[34] This, indeed, seems also to be the Hungarian view. A Hungarian scholar commented to me that Hungarian academics and officials are not at all sure that they have obtained an optimum combination of direct and indirect controls, and that the achieved record is an inappropriate yardstick to use in comparing the potential of the reformed system with that of the more orthodox socialist economic systems of the other CMEA nations.

[35] However, one of the Hungarian scholars who read the draft of this manuscript pointed out that there were methodological changes for these years in both

averaged slightly less than two-thirds of the rate of increase achieved during either the previous five or ten years.[36] It is true that there are offsetting factors to take into account: the reduction of the work week, and the absence of growth in the annual amount of net additions to the completed fixed capital stock during the first two reform years.[37] One might also argue that the productivity comparison contains some index-number bias, since enterprises prior to the reform were likely to select their changes of product mix in order to show increases in labor productivity, while after the reform they chose them so as to increase profits. Nevertheless, when one takes account of these factors, and also gives heavy emphasis to the record of 1970 and 1971 (on the basis that these represent the years of fullest adjustment of the economy to the reform), the best that one can say is that the reform per se did not reduce the growth of labor productivity below its normal rate.

Data are not available for comparing the rate of stockpiling in industry before and after the reform, although the material presented earlier in this chapter showed that industrial stocks of unfinished production and semifabricates continued after the reform to increase more rapidly than did industrial production. Table 10.1 does compare the rate of stockpiling in the economy as a whole prior to and after the reform. The rate of accumulation of inventories declined, but the rate of accumulation of the value of incomplete investment projects grew; the sum of the two expanded somewhat during the reform period. Since the reform was intended to reduce both rates, it cannot be judged a success in this regard either.

Although no data are presented in support of their statements, individual Hungarian authors assert that prereform expectations of improved regularity of production throughout the month, quarter and year

---

the calculation of industrial output and of the industrial labor force. These are not properly taken account of in the official statistics. According to experts using alternative adjustment methods, the total increase of industrial productivity over these years is understated by 1.5 to 2 percent as a result of the methodological changes.

[36] The unweighted annual average of growth of labor productivity in state-owned industry was 3.2 percent during 1968-71 compared to 5.1 percent during 1961-67. This is when production is measured by an index of physical output based on a sample of industrial products (*Statistical Yearbook 1971*, p. 110). The difference is diminished, but not by very much, when one measures production by industry's contribution to net national product (ibid., p. 65 and *Statistical Yearbook 1970*, pp. 68-69).

[37] *Statistical Yearbook 1970*, pp. 70-71. The second cannot be taken as much of an offset in view of the 34 percent increase in such net additions during the year before the reform. (Capital stock data are for the economy as a whole, rather than for industry alone.)

TABLE 10.1 Annual Increase of Inventories and Unfinished Capital Projects in the Hungarian Economy as a Whole
(Increases are taken as a percentage of each year's net national product)

Period	Increase in Inventories	Increase in Unfinished Capital Projects (percentage)	Increase in Total Net National Product
1961-67	5.9	1.1	5.1
1968-70	4.5	2.8	5.6

SOURCE: Hungarian Central Statistical Office, *Statistical Yearbook 1970* (Budapest: 1972), pp. 70-71.

NOTE: Data are in constant prices of 1968. Percentages are unweighted averages of the years included in each period. Data for 1971 from the same source (*Statistical Yearbook 1971*, p. 66) are clearly not comparable, but 1971 was a year of peculiarly high increases in each of the three categories.

have not been realized,[38] and that prereform anticipations of net movement of labor to the more efficient factories have also been disappointed.[39]

Some Hungarians claim that the reform was responsible for the 1968-70 national success in sharply increasing trade with nonsocialist countries. However, a comparison of 1972 with 1967 foreign trade (using official Hungarian price deflators) shows that Hungary achieved a faster rate of growth of trade in constant prices with socialist than with nonsocialist countries.[40] Moreover, prereform trade figures had shown a somewhat faster growth of exchange with nonsocialist than with socialist countries, and the 1968-70 reform years were ones in which business conditions in western Europe were good and thus its demand for Hungarian imports might have been expected to be unusually high. Therefore there is no reason to believe that, without the reforms, Hungarian imports would have expanded more rapidly during 1968-70 from socialist than from nonsocialist countries. Since the volume of trade with socialist countries is determined primarily by five-year and annual national agree-

[38] L. Tüü, "Az ipari termelés ütemessége 1968-1970," *Gazdaság*, 1971, 1, pp. 73-83, as referred to in *Abstracts*, 1971, 3-4, p. 154.

[39] A. Timár, "A magyar ipar termelékenységének vizsgálata," *Ipargazdaság*, 1971, 1, pp. 11-16, as referred to in *Abstracts*, 1971, 1-2, pp. 125-26.

[40] The increase to 1970 was 35 percent for imports from socialist and 40 percent from nonsocialist countries, and 28 and 31 percent for exports to the two groups respectively. However, the faster rate of expansion of imports from nonsocialist countries was reversed during the following two years; when 1972 is compared with 1967, the growth rates of imports are 56 and 44 percent respectively, and the growth rates of exports are 80 and 38 percent. (These figures have been calculated from *Statisztikai Havi Közlemények*, 1972, 2-3, pp. 51 and 105; 1973, 2-3, p. 107; and 1973, 4, p. 53.)

ments, it is difficult to maintain that decentralization of foreign trade decisions in Hungary could have had an appreciable effect on the volume of Hungary's trade with its socialist partners. Thus it does not seem appropriate to credit the reform with significant responsibility for Hungary's increase in trade with its western partners.[41]

It has also been claimed that the improvement in Hungary's overall terms of trade through 1970 was partly due to the reform's leading to an improved structure of trade and to better foreign trade operations.[42] The terms of trade with capitalist countries improved by 6.4 percent between 1967 and 1970, and those with socialist countries by 0.2 percent. But while the terms of trade with capitalist countries continued to improve over the following two years (by 1 percent) the terms of trade with socialist countries declined (by 3 percent) sufficiently to reduce by 2 percent the total terms of trade between 1970 and 1972.[43] It seems impossible to distinguish between the effect of the reform on the terms of trade and the effect of improved market conditions in western Europe.

The only clearly noticeable change during the first four years of the reform has been the sharp improvement in the position of consumers.[44] But it would not appear that this has had anything to do with the reform per se. Rather, it represents a political decision of the Hungarian government to lay more emphasis on meeting immediate consumer needs. Improvement in the quality and mix of consumer products made available seems to have been achieved, at least to a large extent, through imports from western countries.[45] The decision to raise sharply the priority given final consumers is one which was made more or less simultaneously with the decision to introduce the reform; the two grew out of the same political context, and the former took effect slightly earlier. Obviously,

[41] The whole issue might be considered a red herring, since considerations of international politics alone would have prevented Hungary from radically altering its distribution of trade between socialist and nonsocialist countries. Such considerations alone, however, would not have prevented Hungary from increasing its exports to nonsocialist countries sufficiently to balance its imports from them.

[42] I. Friss in *Közgazdasági Szemle*, xviii, 12 (1971), 1397-1411, translated in *JPS*. One of the Hungarian scholars who read the draft of this manuscript took the same position as Professor Friss.

[43] *Statisztikai Havi Közlemények*, 1972, 2-3, p. 105; 1973, 4, p. 53; and 1973, 2-3, p. 107.

[44] The quantity of goods and services consumed rose at an average annual rate of 5.7 percent during 1968-70, with the rate increasing each year to reach 6.9 percent in 1970. This compares very favorably with the rate of 3.9 percent during the seven years prior to the reform, although it is little better than the average for 1966-67 (*Statistical Yearbook 1970*, pp. 70-71). Data for 1971 are not comparable with earlier years, but the increase is shown as 5.8 percent, roughly the 1968-70 average (*Statistical Yearbook 1971*, p. 66). Only in 1972 did the increase fall below the prereform average.

[45] As noted in footnote 14, the degree of importance of such imports in quality improvement is disputable.

the decision to change the priority given to private consumption could have been made without the introduction of the reform, while similarly the reform could have been introduced without this accompanying policy decision.

To move beyond the range of purely economic results of the reform, it has sometimes been claimed that economc reform has been accompanied by major political reform.[46] While I have no view as to the justification of this claim, I would guess that, if it is correct, there exists no cause-and-effect relationship between the two phenomena. Rather, as in the case of the greater priority given to immediate consumer needs, both would be products of a joint cause: the political milieu.

In evaluating the contribution of the reform to improved economic efficiency in Hungary, there are no clear changes in the performance record which we can associate with the reform. From the very short record of four years, we cannot conclude that the major changes in the flow of information and in incentives have had a significant net effect in either a positive or negative direction. Therefore, an evaluation of the net efficiency of the present system, compared to the previous centralized planning, can rest only on the observer's view as to likely future results. The subjectivity imposed by having to rely on such a base is obvious.

CONCLUSION

At least through early 1971, the Hungarian reform of 1968 seems to be best categorized as consisting of a shift of central controls over enterprises from an individualized physical-planning base to an individualized financial-planning base. Central authorities continue to concern themselves with the short-term progress of individual enterprises, rather than limiting themselves to macroeconomic considerations as had been intended.

This is not to deny that the reform has encouraged somewhat more effective decision making by enterprise managements. Profit considerations do play a more important role in determining product-mix decisions. Two enterprises reported a substitution of replacement investments for the more expensive maintenance policy which they had earlier followed. One manager insisted that, in his enterprise, there was now substitution of alternative raw materials because of their relative costs. One enterprise increased its output of its principal group of final products by 20 percent during the first year of the reform, and increased it by a further 30 percent in the following year. This was accomplished without

[46] Robinson, p. 371.

appreciable investments, but rather by arranging for imports (mainly through barter arrangements) of an intermediate product for which the enterprise had formerly met all of its own needs through bottleneck capacity. A director of this enterprise insisted to me that such an expansion in final output would never have occurred prior to the reform; the ministry plan might have called for a 5 percent annual increase, and the plan might have been exceeded by 1 or 2 percent, but this would have been the limit of the output increases achieved.[47]

But such improvements of decision making due to the reform appear to me to have been fairly minor in the five enterprises in which I interviewed. (The one enterprise from whose experience the last example was cited is a possible exception.) Since the managements of these enterprises constituted a better-than-average sample of Hungarian industry, it seems unlikely that this conclusion would be reversed if my sample of enterprises had been larger and more representative.

The reform is to a considerable degree characterized by a shift in control over enterprises from the branch ministries to interministerial committees controlling price increases, subsidies, tax exemptions, loans, and foreign trade. This shift represents a considerable expansion in the relative power of functional ministries and national offices and banks at the expense of the branch ministries. It also grants more autonomy to the enterprises—if only because they are now less dependent upon a single chain of command, and thus are in a better position to play off one ministry against another.

But the net effect upon the economy's efficiency of the shift of the focus of decision making from the branch ministries to interministerial committees is unclear. Instead of a single hierarchical channel having responsibility for all decisions concerning a particular enterprise, there now exists a group of committees, each of which has jurisdiction over a specific source of financial privilege or extra financial burden. The likelihood of consistency between decisions affecting a single enterprise would seem to have been reduced. The need to bring the proper information about each enterprise before each separate committee would appear to represent a deterioration of the pre-1968 system of information processing.[48]

[47] Although I have reported this last example, I am exceedingly dubious of the claim that the enterprise's fuller utilization of capacity was a result of the reform. Since output increased because imports from socialist countries made it possible to use the enterprise's finishing capacity fully, the issue is that of why these barter arrangements were made in 1968 when they had not existed earlier. It seems to me likely that these arrangements were negotiated at a level higher than that of the individual enterprise, and that they could have been negotiated equally well under the previous system of ministerial plans.

[48] A Hungarian scholar who read a draft of this manuscript denied that there was any deterioration in this regard. He felt that the interministerial committees

Although no information is available on this score, I would speculate that the political aspects of the position of general director of an enterprise are even greater today than before the reform. As we have seen, the objectives of the Hungarian enterprise far transcend profit making, and they include many more "social" goals than is the case in capitalist firms in the west. Under the reform mechanism, no single ministry has authority to set the priorities as between these various objectives. The enterprise's general manager must do this himself—and on the basis of what presumably are much poorer sources of information than his branch ministry possessed prior to 1968.[49] In this regard, as in the case of the interministerial committees, it would seem to me that the availability of relevant information for decision making has probably deteriorated rather than improved under the reform.

If one considers the effect of the reform upon the quality of information available to decision makers, I regard the direction of change as an unsettled issue. On the one hand, to the degree that decisions other than those involving the weighing of different objectives are made at the enterprise level rather than higher, one would think that the quality of information available has improved because of the reduction in the necessary information flow. On the other hand, enterprise directors seem now to be forced into greater balancing of objectives than was the case earlier, and their knowledge of the relevant national social considerations must be inferior to that previously available in the branch ministries. Finally, decisions concerning individual enterprises which are made by interministerial committees would appear to be less informed than the central decisions earlier made in the branch ministries.

Comparing the situation in 1970 with that in 1960, rather than that immediately prior to the reform, the situation is even less favorable. This is because managers of individual establishments appear to have had greater decision-making powers prior to the merger of enterprises dur-

---

have a broader information base, and serve as a better forum for the clash of different interests, than did the branch ministries prior to the reform. Thus he believes that their decisions are more objective and better.

[49] In one enterprise, a member of top management told me that he viewed the position of general director as essentially that of representing the national Party viewpoint. In the light of this, he considered his enterprise's technical director as out of the running as a possible future successor to the general director, although he might possibly become a deputy minister since this was a less political post. It should be noted that the technical director had not only joined the Party by the time he was forty years of age, but was currently a member of the Party committee of the factory. Clearly this informant viewed the necessary political qualification of a general director as going considerably beyond Party membership and activity.

However, this informant gave no indication as to whether he viewed the political aspect of the general director's job as having increased or decreased in importance since the reform was introduced.

ing the first half of the 1960's than they had in 1970; some of their earlier decisions are now made at a higher (enterprise) management level, thus lengthening the flow of information coming to the decision maker.

With regard to the effect of the reform on the incentive pattern in industry, there are no particular indications that rank-and-file workers and employees are now provided with greater material incentives to concern themselves with the efficiency of their enterprise. Managers, on the other hand, have been given greater incentives; partly this is because of the increased differentiation of earnings as one moves up the managerial career ladder within the enterprise, and partly it is because of the larger role of bonuses in total managerial earnings. It is true that the slow rate of managerial mobility in Hungarian industry weakens the first managerial incentive, and the loose connection between enterprise profits and managerial bonuses weakens the second. But quite aside from monetary incentives, one would think that the very shifting of the locus of some decision making down to the enterprise level would encourage managers to greater activity since their ideas are more likely now than earlier to be put into effect.[50] I conclude that the incentive picture at the enterprise level has improved, but that the change is not very marked.

One of the hopes of the reformers had been that planning for longer periods than a single year would be promoted by the new mechanism. This hope rested primarily on the freeing of personnel in central bodies from the need for concern with the short-term activities of enterprises. A closely related objective was that of providing a much more stable environment of central regulations in which enterprises could make their own plans.

This effort to promote serious five-year planning and stability of central regulations affecting enterprises has, however, been no more successful in Hungary than it has been in the G.D.R. or in other socialist economies. While enterprises were expected for the first time to develop five-year plans (covering 1971-75), there is no reason to think that this exercise has been taken seriously. A decree of early 1971 permitted 25

---

[50] One of the officials in the National Planning Office explained on this basis the effort of enterprises to engage in heavy investments. He believed that top managers of Hungarian enterprises have a short-run approach to problems, and agreed that one would have expected this to have discouraged them from expanding investments, since these both increase their workload and involve some current costs without providing any current returns. He thought that the reason why top managers push investment is that they are under pressure from middle managers in their own enterprises; middle managers have taken the opportunity provided by greater enterprise authority to promote their pet projects, for which they could not earlier get a hearing at a level of decision making with which they were in personal contact.

percent of top-management bonuses to be withheld for a period of years (usually three to five) until evidence was available as to the successful attainment of long-run tasks; but 1971 saw no improvement in the realism with which enterprises prepared investment projects. A Hungarian author writing in 1972 stated that the time horizon of economic regulations has been, for all practical purposes, narrowed down from five to ten years to one year.[51] An interview study of one hundred thirty-seven managers of industrial enterprises during the summer of 1969 showed that they believed their greatest source of uncertainty in decision making stemmed from their lack of knowledge of what the national regulations would be in the future.[52] In view of the continued interventionism of Hungarian central authorities in the affairs of individual enterprises— although with different instruments than those used before 1968—it does not seem surprising that their success in providing a stable environment has been no greater than that of socialist countries which use physical-planning methods.

As was noted earlier in this chapter, risk taking by enterprise managements appears to be less than would be socially optimum. Hungarians correctly view this as a problem, and see it as caused by the incentive difficulties as well as by traditions inherited from the pre-1968 system. Sharp increases in enterprise profitability due to successful risk taking would tend to be negated by financial measures taken in response by one or another interministerial committee. Financial losses due to unsuccessful risk taking, while not extremely serious for either enterprises or their managers, have no significant counterpart in potential gain.

If, however, the incentive difficulties inhibiting risk-taking behavior were resolved, one might well wonder if the reverse problem of excessive risks would not become still more serious. So long as the present situation continues, where workers' wages normally cannot be effectively held down on the grounds of insufficient enterprise profitability, and where enterprise managers are safe from dismissal, the creation of significant rewards for successful enterprise risk taking could swing the balance of risk in the opposite direction from where it now rests. If unsuccessful risk taking continued to be liable to only the most minor penalties, it would be dangerous for the economy if successful enterprise risk taking were to be rewarded lavishly.

The problem is that of the organizational level at which major decisions embodying risk should be taken. Since the Hungarian managerial system is one of hierarchical appointment and dismissal, in which the

---

[51] E. Huszti, "Az 1970-71, évi pénz- és hitelpolitika gyakorlati érvényesüléséről," *Közgazdasági Szemle*, xix, 1 (1972), 23-40, as referred to in *Abstracts*, 1972, 1, pp. 133-34.

[52] Komonyi, p. 343.

enterprise general director is appointed by the minister and in which the remaining management team is effectively chosen by the general director, it would be difficult to penalize or reward in a major fashion either lower management or the rank-and-file of the enterprise for variations in the enterprise's success. Given the absence of any sort of workers' control over enterprise top management,[53] only top management of the enterprise can be held responsible for the decisions taken.

But what can be the practical implications, short of dismissal, of such managerial responsibility for insufficient profitability? Since such dismissal was rarely politically practicable during at least the first three years of the reform, no one in the enterprise could really be held responsible for failure in the sense that he would bear its costs. This meant that, to the degree that enterprises were given full decision-making authority, this could only be irresponsible authority. Small wonder that central organs have continued, just as before the reform although through different mechanisms, to exercise the ultimate control over enterprise decisions which were considered of major import.

If dismissal or transfer of unsuccessful managers had been freely engaged in by the branch ministries, then it would have been the high ministerial officials who would have had to be held responsible for the success of enterprises. This suggests that, even under such conditions, it would have been quite dangerous for them to have given enterprises more decision-making authority than is granted to individual product-divisions in decentralized private companies in the west. But although such western divisional managements are often granted considerable responsibility, subject to dismissal for failure, it is rare that their actions should be free of control by the company headquarters short of this ultimate penalty. Just as company headquarters in western companies have too much at stake to grant complete independence to divisions, so too the branch ministries and the interministerial committees could scarcely be expected to renounce interference in the really major issues facing the enterprises.

This analogy with large, decentralized capitalist companies suggests that Hungarian central authorities can never be expected to renounce completely an activist policy with regard to interference in the decisions of individual Hungarian enterprises, and that they would indeed be quite misguided if they were to do so.[54] Unless authority in Hungarian enter-

[53] Such workers' control exists only to the degree that the Party committees of the enterprise exercise control over the managers, that these Party committees in turn are responsible to the general Party membership, and that this membership is largely comprised of nonmanagerial personnel. Quite correctly, Hungarians consider this as so indirect a form of workers' control that they do not even refer to it in these terms.

[54] On reading an earlier draft of this manuscript, Dr. Kemenes of the Hungarian

prises were to become a syndicalist, worker-control type, and unless responsibility in the form of major reductions in earnings of all employees in an unsuccessful enterprise were accepted, it is difficult to see how central authorities could ever limit themselves to macroeconomic policy making. Barring such an evolution, it would appear that individual enterprise managements might either be as constrained in their authority as is the case for plant and divisional managements in centralized capitalist firms, or might alternatively be given as much authority as are divisional managements in the most decentralized of capitalist companies; but the bounds of authority which might be granted them can scarcely be far outside of these limits.

Beyond this issue, the performance and future prospects of Hungarian industry under the reform must be viewed in terms of the fundamental policy constraints which have restricted central decision making. In capitalist countries, avoidance of unemployment and inflation have served as the prime objectives of government policy to be traded off against one another. As we saw in Chapter 8, the Hungarian government has opted for extremely low unemployment—not only in the macroeconomic sense, but also in a degree of job protection which assures workers against being forced to change either skills or factories. Socialist ideology and traditions appear to have dictated this choice, leaving the government little freedom in this regard. But the government has also opted for restricting inflation to only 1 to 2 percent per annum. While the government has been highly successful in attaining both of these objectives, it has been so only at the price of creating a highly constrained environment within which the reform mechanisms could operate.

As was argued in Chapter 8, one element of the price paid was the continuation of a sellers' market for Hungarian industry, with its implications for the restricted possibilities of efficient central reliance upon the market mechanism as the means of determining enterprise decisions. The other element has been an incomes policy which has kept to a minimum the incentive offered either to workers or managers for improving enterprise performance.

This discussion, however, is not intended as an espousal of the conclusion which one auditor drew from a seminar I gave: that the Hungarian reform is a fraud. I would completely reject such an interpretation of my study. The shift from physical to financial planning has been a skillfully managed operation, surprisingly successful in that it had no serious negative short-run effects on the economy. In this sense, it is a

---

Scientific Council for World Economy agreed that such renunciation should never be expected; he seemed to find curious the very suggestion of such an eventuality.

remarkable accomplishment. It also offers the promise of significantly increasing efficiency in the future if the policy constraints which currently bound it should be lifted.

My own view is that the Hungarian reform cannot be expected to operate with markedly greater effectiveness so long as the system is constrained by policy decisions which impose a sellers' market and a fairly rigid incomes policy. I consider the employment constraint, and the resulting need for sellers' markets, as the fundamental one. Certainly the Hungarians have the right to make the choice of trading possible economic-efficiency gains for economic, social, and political stability; no one can fault them on the basis of purely economic analysis for this decision. Nevertheless, it seems to me important to recognize that the trade-off is a sharp one. Although it is certainly possible that the emphasis upon employment guarantees both at the micro- and macrolevels will be given up in time,[55] such a change would be much more fundamental than anything which has yet occurred in Hungary.

[55] One Hungarian scholar, commenting on a draft of this manuscript, suggested that increased manpower shortage may shift the employment constraint from the micro- to the macrolevel. I believe, however, that the constraint has ideological and political roots which are too strong to be uprooted for such a relatively minor reason.

PART IV

Yugoslavia (Slovenia)

Yugoslavia differs from the other three socialist countries examined in this book in that its economy is not centrally planned in the same sense as is that of the CMEA nations. The issue is not the absence of compulsory plans given to individual enterprises; in this regard, Yugoslavia is similar to Hungary. Nor is it even the more circumscribed and less detailed economic objectives of the Yugoslav central authorities as compared to those of the other nations. Rather, what is critical is that Yugoslav enterprises are independent of the central state apparatus, whereas industry in each of the other countries can be properly described as a single organizational network.

Romania, the German Democratic Republic, and Hungary share the common features that the top management of the enterprise (and of the *centrala* and *Kombinat*) is appointed and dismissed by a hierarchically superior state agency, and that both the salary and bonus awards of top management are similarly determined. In all three countries, it is the hierarchically superior state agency which is responsible for the activities and success of the enterprises under it. Such agencies exercise this responsibility partly by appointing and dismissing, rewarding and punishing enterprise management; but they also exercise it—as seems inevitable in such an organizational structure—by directly intervening in enterprise decisions when they believe this to be necessary.

Yugoslav industry is characterized by the absence of any chain-of-command linking the enterprise to central authorities. Enterprises are "self managed": i.e., enterprise management is responsible to no one outside the enterprise itself. While the legitimacy of the authority of enterprise management in all of the CMEA countries rests upon appointment by an agency superior to the enterprise, Yugoslav enterprise management legitimizes its decisions uniquely from sources internal to the individual enterprise itself.

The Yugoslav enterprise is in this regard similar to its capitalist rather than to its CMEA counterpart. The Yugoslav and capitalist enterprise differ both in the allocation of distributed profits (to the workforce in the former rather than to shareholders) and in the locus of final authority. The Yugoslav enterprise management gains its legitimacy from the unweighted votes of the enterprise's total labor force; the capitalist enterprise depends upon the votes of shareholders, weighted by their proportional ownership.

This peculiar position of the Yugoslav enterprise suggests the two questions which will concern us.

(1) The degree to which "workers' management" is a reality rather than a facade. Clearly, decisions which superficially are made by the workers' management of an enterprise may in fact be determined either by the upper full-time managerial personnel or by groups entirely outside the firm.

(2) The objectives which enterprises pursue, the behavior in which they engage, and the environment external to the enterprise which helps to shape this behavior.

The answers which I shall present to these questions pertain specifically to the period of my research: 1970. During 1972-73, the environment became somewhat more controlled. Most important, the Yugoslav Communist Party had become much more centralized on a national level, and a major potential source of national control was thus in the process of re-creation. Second, Party control over enterprise general directors was being implemented in a fashion which had not been seen for many years. Third, a temporary wage and price "freeze" restrained the self-management powers of the enterprises. As of late 1973, however, both the significance and the lasting nature of these changes was completely uncertain. In any case, none of these changes appeared to be of a nature and magnitude to affect fundamentally the answers which I shall give.

Chapter 11 presents the industrial setting existing in Yugoslavia in general and in Slovenia in particular. The meaning and significance of both self-management and workers' management are discussed in a general fashion, as are also the controls over the enterprise which have remained since the 1965 economic reform.

Chapter 12 concentrates on the question of the reality of workers' management. A major part of the discussion concerns the similarities and differences between control by full-time managers and control by workers' management bodies, when both are operating within the Yugoslav framework.

Chapter 13 treats the behavior of enterprises, concentrating upon finance and the various aspects of interenterprise competition.

Part IV, like the earlier parts of this book, is based upon both the national literature and my interviews. In contrast with the writings on the other three countries I have studied, and particularly on Romania and the G.D.R., the Yugoslav literature (both domestic and foreign) in languages that I know is relatively rich and useful. My generalizations from Slovenia (which was the core of the study) to the rest of Yugoslavia are based primarily upon this literature. However, it is important to note that even published writings deal primarily with the developed regions; not surprisingly, Yugoslav scholars are physically concentrated in these areas and so find it convenient to center their research projects there.

Interviews with academic sociologists and economists, as well as with government officials, were conducted in Slovenia, Croatia, and in the capital city of Belgrade. The underdeveloped southern portion of the country was completely unrepresented. Furthermore, my interviews in enterprises were almost entirely in those of Slovenia—the most economically advanced of Yugoslavia's eight regions. Thus my description and conclusions must be taken as applying more to the developed regions, and most specifically to Slovenia, than to Yugoslavia as a whole. In addition, they apply particularly to the population of firms with over one thousand employees; in 1970, this size category constituted 61 percent of the total Yugoslav industrial labor force.

Since Yugoslav enterprises are self-managed, there exist no branch ministries or counterparts from which interviews could elicit a view from "above." The nearest I came to drawing on this perspective was through an interview in the counterpart of the national planning committee, one in the national bank, and several from members of the central committee and politbureau of the Communist Party in Slovenia. In my interviewing, I concentrated on the production unit even more than I did in any of the CMEA countries. Within the Yugoslav enterprises, I was generally able to talk not only with management personnel, but also with leading elected representatives of the workers' management organs, of the Party, and of the trade union.

As will be seen below, my sample of large industrial Slovenian enterprises can be taken as representative of the relevant population of enterprises with much the same degree of confidence as is the case for my sample of production units in Romania, and with much greater confidence than in the G.D.R. or Hungary.

Eleven industrial enterprises and two business banks were studied through interviews; nine of the enterprises and one of the banks were in Slovenia. Of the seven enterprises with more than one thousand employees each, five produced primarily consumer goods and two concentrated on producer goods; the technology varied from the manufacture of large tailor-made product units to mass production. One of these seven larger enterprises was what is called a "political" factory: i.e., one which had depended on subsidies prior to the 1965 economic reform, and therefore was placed in jeopardy by this reform. Thus the mix of enterprises is sufficient to provide a broad picture of the larger enterprises of Slovenia.

The larger Slovenian enterprises studied were chosen by the Slovenian Chamber of Commerce, which was my host in this republic. My suggestion to two knowledgeable Slovenians that the sample of enterprises selected for me may have been biased toward efficiency was met with assurances that the firms included were not superior to the average of the larger industrial firms of the republic. I am inclined to accept this judgment.

Although eleven enterprises constitute a small sample in absolute terms, those in Slovenia represent a large proportion of the bigger Slovenian companies. One-fifth of all Slovenian industrial enterprises with over two thousand employees are included in my sample, as are 4 percent of the companies with between one and two thousand employees.[1] Of the eleven industrial companies included in Yugoslavia as a whole, two had more than ten thousand employees, three had three to four thousand, two had between one and two thousand, and four had fewer than five hundred. The four smaller enterprises were selected either because they were extraordinarily capital intensive or because they employed primarily highly educated personnel in coordinating work for other industrial enterprises. All of the smaller enterprises were chosen by me at the latter state of my interviewing, and were selected with the goal of widening the range of enterprise behavior studied.

[1] For the size distribution of Slovenian industrial enterprises, see Socialistična Republika Slovenija, Zavod SR Slovenije za Statistiko, *Statistični Letopis SR Slovenije 1972* (Ljubljana: 1972), p. 78.

CHAPTER 11

The Yugoslav Industrial
Setting

THIS chapter is intended only to introduce the two succeeding ones. It presents the industrial setting both of Yugoslavia as a whole and of Slovenia in particular, discusses the key concepts of self-management and workers' management, and treats those controls over the enterprise activities which remained after the 1965 economic reform. The reader who is well informed as to the Yugoslav economy will learn little here.

THE SLOVENIAN FOCUS OF THE STUDY

Yugoslavia stands out sharply among the four countries discussed in this book for its extreme regional diversity, both cultural and economic. Economic diversity is best shown by the degree of geographic variation in the level of gross material product per capita (see Table 11.1).[1]

Given this diversity, it seemed most fruitful to concentrate my interviews within the single small republic of Slovenia. This republic has almost double the national average gross national product per capita and is fairly close to the Austrian level. The study of self-management here permits us to see the working of this institution under conditions of considerable economic development and low unemployment. Furthermore, Slovenia's industrial traditions are older than those of the other republics and thus, in all probability, it offers the most favorable conditions for the exercise of self-management.[2]

[1] As one would expect, however, wage and salary differences are much less marked. In the same year in industry and mining, average net wages in Slovenia were only 15 percent higher than the Yugoslav average, while the poorest region (Kosovo) was 16 percent below the national average. (Socijalistička Federativna Republika Jugoslavija, Savezni Zavod za Statistiku, *Statistički Godišnjak Jugoslavije 1971*, Beograd: 1971, p. 477; hereafter, this source will be called *Statistički*.)

[2] A substantially larger proportion of the Slovenian than of the total Yugoslav population has completed both primary and secondary education. At the primary school level, only 53 percent of all Yugoslav children between the ages of eleven and fourteen attended school during 1952/53; the comparable figure in Slovenia was 82 percent. While the difference was sharply reduced thereafter, even in 1970/71 the figures were 82 percent versus 94 percent. As to secondary school education, 15 percent of the total Yugoslav population over the age of 10 in 1971 had received such training; in Slovenia, the figure was 23 percent (Z. Steinman, "Development of the Schooling System and Changes in the Educational Composition of the Population," *Yugoslav Survey*, XIII, 4, 1972, pp. 111 and 119).

In one important respect, however, Slovenia may not provide a healthy ground

TABLE 11.1: Gross Material Product per Capita of Republics and Autonomous Regions, 1970 (index: Yugoslavia = 100)

Republic or Autonomous Region	Population[a] (000)	Gross Material Product per Capita (index)
Kosovo	1,242.3	34
Bosnia-Herzegovina	3,716.8	64
Macedonia	1,611.1	70
Montenegro	531.2	73
Serbia proper[b]	5,254.7	99
Vojvodina	1,935.1	115
Croatia	4,346.4	124
Slovenia	1,697.5	188
All Yugoslavia	20,355.1	100

SOURCE: Socijalistička Federativna Republika Jugoslavija, Savezni Zavod za Statistiku, *Statistički Godišnjak Jugoslavije 1972* (Beograd: 1972), pp. 339 and 368.

[a] Data of March 31, 1971.
[b] The Republic of Serbia, excluding the two autonomous regions of Kosovo and Vojvodina.

There are several important respects in which we might expect that a study of Slovenian industrial enterprises may present a biased picture of self-management in Yugoslavia as a whole. These are the following:

(1) Slovenian workers and managers are more acquainted with work and life in an industrial setting. As such, they may be better able to make self-management function effectively.

(2) Unemployment is no problem in Slovenia, while it is a major concern in the other republics. One effect of this is that the labor force in Slovenian enterprises may be under much less social pressure to create additional jobs.[3] This could lead them to distribute more of their income in wages, rather than keeping it for investment, than is the case elsewhere. Similarly, it might lead them to more capital-intensive types of investments. A second effect which works in the same direction is that

---

for workers' management. In December 1970, 55 percent of its industrial labor force was classified as unskilled or semiskilled according to their level of training. In contrast, the proportion varied between 42 and 47 percent in six of the seven other regions of the country, and reached 49 percent only in Croatia (which was the second richest region) (*Statistički 1972*, p. 357). To the limited degree that these regional differences can be taken as more than statistical curiosities stemming from the use of varying definitions, and thus can be interpreted as representing the industrial sophistication of the labor force, Slovenia would appear to be peculiarly unqualified for genuine workers' management.

[3] Although theoretically possible, it is clear that the relatively low unemployment in Slovenia is not a result of greater social pressure for job creation in that republic than in the other parts of Yugoslavia.

the workforce of a Slovenian enterprise, having greater confidence in its ability to find jobs if necessary in other firms, may feel less pressure to keep a high proportion of its income for investment in order to maintain the competitive posture of the enterprise.[4]

(3) Operating in the opposite direction is the unusually high per capita income of the Slovenian labor force. Since, nationally, there is a positive relationship between the payment of high wages and the retention by the enterprise of a large share of income for internal financial use,[5] we might expect Slovenian firms to have exceptionally high investment ratios. This could be explained both by the fact that Slovenian workers, compared to workers of poorer republics, gain a lower marginal utility from additional funds distributed as wages, and by the fact that investments in Slovenian firms provide a higher return per worker employed.

(4) Particularly in the poorest regions of Kosovo, Bosnia-Herzegovina, Macedonia, and Montenegro, we might expect to see greater political pressure upon enterprise managers than is the case in Slovenia. This is because of the lack of industry in these regions, and the degree to which the local and republic authorities pin their hopes of economic progress on the success and expansion of a few large enterprises. As a result, such authorities are likely to be more activist with regard to enterprises' decisions than is the case in Slovenia.[6]

(5) Successful self-management may require a major learning effort on the part of the workers of the enterprise; this could be rather different for populations at varying stages of social development. It is possible that self-management compels a more rapid, yet easier, socializing process than does the usual capitalist or CMEA-socialist enterprise, and

[4] However, we would expect to see this reflected in a higher rate of labor turnover in the industrial enterprises of Slovenia than in those of the other republics. In fact, the Slovenian percentage has been quite close to the national average. It may be that the greater opportunities for employment in Slovenia are compensated in the other regions by the lesser willingness of recent entrants from agriculture to accept industrial discipline. But what is striking is that the total of labor quits and dismissals in all of the republics is quite low: in Slovenian industry in 1971, it constituted only 16 percent of the labor force (*Statistički* of various years, table 202-9).

[5] H. M. Wachtel, "Workers' Management and Interindustry Wage Differentials in Jugoslavia," *Journal of Political Economy*, 80, 3 (1972), Part I, 546-47. Data are for 1961-68, and compare SIC two-digit industries; I assume that the same relationship exists on an enterprise as on an industry level.

[6] In commenting on this paragraph in a letter of late 1973, J. Županov (professor of sociology at the University of Zagreb, and probably the most highly regarded of the Yugoslav students of management) expressed the view that my expectation was probably justified up to the end of 1971, but that since then the political pressure on enterprise managers had increased and was more uniform throughout Yugoslavia.

that this is most important for those populations which are just beginning to industrialize.[7]

SURVEY OF THE ECONOMY

Yugoslavia as a whole is more similar to Romania than to either of the two other CMEA countries we have analyzed. Its population, like Romania's, is twenty million. Its standard of living is similar. Its rate of growth has also been impressive: much the same as the Romanian in industrial production during the second half of the 1950's, although rather substantially less during the 1960's. In 1971, 37 percent of Yugoslavia's population was still agricultural; while this proportion is substantially less than that of Romania, it is still extremely high, and its decline over the last decade was much like its neighbor's.

A feature unique to Yugoslavia among socialist countries is the acceptance of large-scale emigration. Twenty percent of Yugoslavia's employed labor force worked abroad in western Europe in late 1971.[8] A second feature is the acceptance of open unemployment: the 1968 highpoint was 9.1 percent of the employed (not including the self-employed) population, and through 1972 the figure has never fallen below 7.2 percent (achieved in 1971) since the 1965 economic reform.[9] A third feature is the high rate of inflation; retail prices increased at an average annual rate of 7 percent during 1961-64, and 13 percent during 1965-70.

Slovenia has had a rate of growth very similar to that of Yugoslavia, and it has also been characterized by a high proportion of its labor force working abroad. But it is much less dependent upon agriculture than is the rest of the country, and this dependence has been reduced at a somewhat more rapid rate in Slovenia during the 1960's. Its rate of unemployment is about 40 percent of the national average, and its per capita gross material product is almost twice as high. As of 1970 and 1971, it was estimated that 21 percent of the republic's employed labor

[7] See I. Adizes, "The Role of Management in Democratic (communal) Organizational Structures," *Annals of Public and Cooperative Economy*, 42, 4 (1971), 399-420, for some interesting remarks about self-management at different stages extending to postindustrial societies.

[8] These are official figures collected by the host countries. Forty-four percent of these workers abroad had left during 1970-71 (*Borba*, December 4, 1971, p. 11, summarized in *ABSEES*, April 1972). The Yugoslav estimate for the end of 1972 was 24 percent (calculated from *Vjesnik u Srijedu* [*VUS*], April 25, 1973, p. 3, as cited in *ABSEES*, July 1973).

[9] For a treatment of the Yugoslav concept of unemployment, see C. Mesa-Lago, "Unemployment in a Socialist Economy: Yugoslavia," *Industrial Relations*, x, 1 (1971), 52-53. Unemployment is defined as all those registered with state employment offices; these registrants include some who are employed but, on the other hand, also exclude some unemployed.

force originated from lower-income republics; it would appear that those were overwhelmingly temporary workers.[10]

The proportion of the Yugoslav population with higher education degrees appears to be slightly greater than the Romanian proportion: 1.6 percent compared to 1.4 percent. This is midway among the socialist countries of eastern Europe. The Slovenian proportion is only three-quarters of the all-Yugoslav ratio, although this difference disappears if junior-college completions are lumped together with university degrees. Similarly, the Slovenian industrial labor force seems to have had somewhat less formal training than is the case for the Yugoslav labor force as a whole (see Table 11.2 on pp. 330-31).

SELF-MANAGEMENT

Self-management is one of the great "myths" (used in a nonpejorative sense) of Yugoslav society, and as such is immune to attack from within the system.[11] Probably even more than workers' management per se, it is regarded as the major Yugoslav contribution to democratizing the operation of socialist society. Yet it rests in uneasy balance with the need felt by all Yugoslav leaders for some degree of central planning and interventionism.[12] The self-management principle has had its greatest impact during the period since the economic reform of 1965. But

[10] *Borba*, September 1, 1970, p. 9 (cited in *ABSEES*, January 1971), and October 26, 1971, p. 4 (translated in *JTS*). Only 6 percent of the Slovenian population declared itself, in the 1971 census, to be non-Slovenian in origin; if non-Slovenian workers had all left their families in their native republics, but had declared their own permanent residence to be in Slovenia, they alone would have constituted 7 percent of Slovenia's population.

It is unclear whether the high proportion of Slovenia's labor force which comes from less-developed republics is due simply to the attraction of a relatively high-income and low-unemployment republic, or whether it reflects a pattern of migration in Yugoslavia toward nearby areas of higher income. In support of the latter explanation is the apparent fact that, in 1968, Slovenia's per capita share in labor force emigration to western Europe was 270 percent of that of the less-developed republics (i.e., excluding Croatia) of Yugoslavia. (See Z. Komarica, *Jugoslavija u suvremenim evropskim migracijama*, Ekonomski Institut, Zagreb: 1970, p. 8, as quoted in S. Djodan, "The Evolution of the Economic System of Yugoslavia and the Economic Position of Croatia," *Journal of Croatian Studies*, XIII, 1973, p. 81.)

[11] See the 1970 statement by D. Rihtman-Auguštin that it is "difficult to talk about any common values in this country, unless we affirm that it is self-management as an ideological project." (Fourth meeting of the Yugoslav Association for Sociology held in February 1970, as reported by B. Jakšić in *Praxis*, international edition, VIII, 3-4, 1971, p. 660.)

[12] See the 1971 statement in the Party press that, although any mention of the state sounds like heresy in Yugoslavia today, Communists in favor of self-management should not be against the state but only against an étatist state. The article's author finds it necessary to argue that the country indeed needs a plan, a long-term development concept, a taxation policy, and a policy of income distribution (*Borba*, August 1, 1971, p. 6, cited in *ABSEES*, October 1971).

many shudder at some of the economic features which have accompanied it: to name only two, almost a doubling of the rate of inflation, and a steady deterioration in the balance of payments from a favorable balance of 1.8 percent of gross trade imports in 1965 to a negative balance of 16.4 percent of gross trade imports in 1970.[13]

The distinction between self-management and workers' management is to some degree arbitrary, and is not normally made by the Yugoslavs. Workers' management can be considered an application of self-management to organizations other than political bodies. Nevertheless, the distinction is one which can be useful.

The concept of self-management embodies three different elements:

(1) Decisions of all types should be made at the lowest level at which an issue can be reasonably handled. The justification is the de-

[13] Although the balance of payments was less unfavorable during the second half of the 1960's than during the first half, the major improvement achieved during 1965 steadily deteriorated. Furthermore, as can be seen from the following table, the balance of payments during the second half of the 1960's was improved by a steadily increasing flow of net receipts from tourism and from remittances by Yugoslav workers abroad; the balance of trade deteriorated much more sharply than did the balance of payments.

	1960-64	1965-66	1967-71
	(Percentage: Average of Years)		
Deficit in balance of payments on current account as a proportion of gross trade imports[a]	−17.9	−1.3	−11.9
Deficit in balance of payments, minus net receipts from tourism and remittances, as a proportion of gross trade imports[a]	−23.3	−10.9	−32.5
Gross receipts from selected invisibles as a proportion of gross trade imports[a]			
emigrants' and workers' remittances	3.2	5.6	13.8
tourism	3.8	6.2	10.8

SOURCES: The first two rows are taken from *Statistički* of various years, tables 105-13, 105-14, and 105-16. What is called here the net receipts from tourism and remittances also includes, in fact, such other minor items as business travel, diplomatic representations, and social receipts.

The last two rows are taken from Služba Društvenog Knjigovodstava - glavna centrala, *Statistički Bilten*, February 1970 and February 1973, tables 46 and 48. All these figures differ somewhat in concept from those used in the first two rows, as they come from the balance of foreign exchange on current account rather than from the balance of payments account; but the differences do not appear to be quantitatively substantial.

Receipts from tourism do not include private transactions between foreign tourists and private Yugoslav citizens. A 1972 Yugoslav source estimates that this leads to a 25 percent understatement (*Vjesnik*, August 30, 1972, p. 7, cited in *ABSEES*, January 1973).

[a] Gross imports after 1960 exclude goods which are reexported, whether in a direct form or after further processing.

sirability of a pattern of direct democracy wherever this is feasible, and otherwise of a system in which decision-making bodies are in as direct contact as possible with the public which elected them. The political application of this principle is that as few decisions as possible should be elevated to the federal (all-Yugoslav) level, and as many as possible be relegated to the commune level; this is true both for government and for Communist Party (League of Communists) authority.[14] The economic application is that the individual enterprise should be given as much power as possible in relation to government authorities, and that within the enterprise there should be decentralization of authority to suborganizations called "economic units."

Traditional Leninist doctrine bears a superficial resemblance to this element of self-management, in that it also holds that decisions relating to particular applications of broad policies should be made at the lowest feasible level. But in Leninist doctrine, this amounts to no more than administrative decentralization—required so that central bodies should not be overburdened with petty issues, and so that the solutions of these issues be worked out at a level where the necessary detailed information is available. In contrast, the self-management concept provides for genuine autonomy of decision making at each level. Under self-management, lower organizational levels are not given the task of simply applying central policy; instead, they are intended to be relatively autonomous in developing their own policy.

This element of self-management is the direct antithesis of centralization, whether political or economic.

(2) Decisions at each level should be made, to the degree feasible, by elected representatives of the constituency or by meetings of all members of the constituency. Full-time bureaucrats (managers in economic organizations) should be kept under the control of elected representatives, where possible at their own hierarchical level within the organization.

(3) Elected representatives should be replaced frequently, with consecutive reelection being strictly limited. This rotation principle is designed to insure both that the elected representatives remain close in spirit to their constituency, and that the educational experience of serving on an elected body be shared over time by a high proportion of the total constituency.

The self-management principle acts as a counter both to centraliza-

---

[14] In reading a draft of this manuscript, Županov agreed that the application of "self-management" to the Party was to some extent observable through 1971. But he pointed out that the Yugoslav League of Communists had never renounced the principle of democratic centralism within the Party, and that this principle was strongly reaffirmed in 1972-73.

tion and to bureaucratic control, and applies to political as well as to economic decision making. In my treatment of self-management from this point on, I shall concentrate on the aspect of anticentralization; the other features will be treated as part of workers' management, since the two concepts overlap completely with regard to them.

TABLE 11.2: Selected Data on Yugoslavia and Slovenia (percentage)

Indicators	All Yugoslavia	Slovenia
Gross national material product per capita (1970; index: Yugoslavia = 100)	100	188
Annual rate (compounded) of economic growth[a]		
Material social product		
1956-60	8.0	8.3
1961-70	7.5	7.3
Industrial production		
1956-60	13.2	9.4
1961-70	8.4	8.8
Agricultural labor force as proportion of total[b]		
1961	57	37
1971	43	24
Annual rate (compounded) of increase in retail prices		
1960-64	7.0	. . .
1965-71	13.3	. . .
Unemployment as proportion of employed labor force (excluding self-employed)		
1965-70 annual range	7.3-9.1	1.8-3.7
Workers abroad as proportion of employment (excluding self-employed)		
September 1971	19.6	10
Industrial labor turnover, average annual rate		
1968-71[c]	15.5	15.1
Industrial labor force classified as unskilled or semiskilled by level of training (December 1970)	47	55
Proportion of population having completed higher education[d] (1971)	1.6	1.2
Graduates of higher educational institutions in 1971 per thousand population (index: Yugoslavia = 100)	100	95

SOURCES: *Statistički* and Socialistična Republika Slovenija, Zavod SR Slovenije za Statistiko, *Statistični Letopis SR Slovenije* (Ljubljana) of various years. *Borba*, December 4, 1971, p. 11 (cited in *ABSEES*, April 1972), for Yugoslav workers abroad. *Borba*, December 4, 1971, p. 11, and *Privredni Vjesnik*, July 12, 1971, p. 2 (cited in *ABSEES*, January and April 1972), serve as the basis for my own estimate of Slovenian workers abroad.

a The Slovenian data for 1956-60 are measured in 1960 prices, while all other data are expressed in 1966 prices. Thus these figures are not properly comparable. All figures are from official sources.

b The decline during the 1960's of the agricultural labor force relative to the total labor force is probably accounted for largely by Yugoslav employment abroad. Workers abroad are counted in the Yugoslav labor force (active population). If we assume that Yugoslav employment abroad is almost all nonagricultural, then the 1971 figure of all-Yugoslav agricultural labor force as a percentage of the total would have been 51 percent if there had been no net movement abroad between 1961 and 1971. On the same assumption, the 1971 ratio of agricultural to total domestic labor force was in fact 46 percent.

c This is calculated as twelve times the monthly percentage of those leaving enterprises, divided by the number there at the beginning of the month plus those who came during the month.

d Higher education is here defined as university level. The total number of living graduates in Yugoslavia was calculated as all those graduating from university faculties and arts academies between 1930 and 1971. The high death rate among the small number who graduated before 1945 is probably compensated by the number who received degrees abroad. The percentage calculated for Slovenia alone is slightly less reliable than that for all of Yugoslavia; the procedure followed was to find the number of Slovenian graduates as a proportion of the Yugoslav total for a comparable group, and then to apply this proportion to the Yugoslav percentage. The error introduced by this procedure cannot be great.

Census data are available for 1971 as to the proportion of the population which has completed either junior college or university education. The Yugoslav figure is 2.3 percent, and the Slovenian is 2.5 percent (*Statistički 1973*, pp. 351-52).

In the economy, the self-management principle has been taken to imply that the enterprise should be as unregulated as practicable, and that as little as possible of the country's gross material product should flow through the government (particularly the federal) budget.[15] During

[15] Thus the secretary of the commission for self-management of the council of the Confederation of Yugoslav Trade Unions wrote in 1972: "The process of the withering away of the state, and that of the realization of self-management, are in essence one and the same social process, designated by different terms." (N. Jovanov, "Définition théorique de la notion et de l'essence de l'autogestion en Yougoslavie," in *Participation and Self-Management*, papers presented at the December 1972 first international sociological conference on participation and self-management, Institute for Social Research, University of Zagreb, Zagreb: 1972 and 1973, I, 13.)

Unfortunately, the six-volume collection of papers of this conference, held in Dubrovnik, became available to me too late to be used in writing this book. Only

the last three years (1963-65) prior to the major economic reform, an average of 64 percent of the country's gross material product, and 68 percent of the gross material product produced in industry, was absorbed by the budgets of the federal, republic, or commune organs or by bank interest. In the five succeeding years (1966-70), these proportions were down to an average of 39 and 36 percent respectively.[16] Thus investment decisions were transformed essentially into self-management decisions. Subsidies diminished. The various enterprises were intended to be integrated primarily through the market place, rather than by government regulation or through central Party influence.

Where coordination of the various self-management units by devices other than the market is deemed desirable (e.g., in the case of wage restraint), the ideal form of coordination has been viewed as agreement among representatives of the various units rather than state or Party intervention. Thus the republic chambers of commerce are considered proper vehicles for such coordination. The syndicalist nature of this approach is apparent.[17]

---

the two papers given at the conference by Jovanov, and the paper by J. Obradović, were seen in mimeographed form and could be utilized.

[16] The only reason for lumping bank interest with government receipts is the aggregated nature of the data sources. Government receipts include not only all direct and indirect taxes, but also the commune reserve fund for enterprises and gross social security payments. (Calculations are made from *Statistički* of various years, tables 106-4 to 106-8.)

One Yugoslav calculation of the distribution of net material product of all enterprises in Yugoslavia shows a much smaller change since 1965 (D. Vojnich, *Aktualni Problemi Ekonomske Politike i Privrednog Sistema Jugoslavije*, Zagreb: 1970, p. 64, as quoted in E. G. Furobotn and S. Pejovich, "La structure institutionnelle et les stimulants économiques de la firme yougoslave," *Revue de l'Est*, III, 2, 1972, p. 185). A second, however, while agreeing with this one as to the dimensions of the change since 1964, shows the same change from pre-1963 to the late 1960's as the gross material product data show for the 1963-65 period compared to the latter 1960's (B. Šefer, "Income Distribution in Yugoslavia," *International Labour Review*, 97, 4, 1968, pp. 377 and 381). A western estimate, but one which cites only "unpublished sources," shows virtually no change between 1965 and 1969 in the proportion of enterprise net income (excluding interest) which was paid to government budgets (J. Dirlam and J. Plummer, *An Introduction to the Yugoslav Economy*, Merrill Publishing Company, Columbus, Ohio: 1973, p. 161).

[17] In commenting on this manuscript, Županov noted that such coordination has become much more important since the end of 1971. (So far as I am aware, however, this is primarily restricted to the important areas of pricing and of income distribution within the enterprise.) He said that the "market mystique" has been replaced by the self-management-agreement mystique.

However, Županov rejected my interpretation that this constitutes syndicalism. His rejection is based on the assertion that all such coordination is viewed as simply a part of the dictatorship of the proletariat, and that the Party plays a critical integrative role in the coordination. Županov holds that the Yugoslav pattern of the "dictatorship of the proletariat" is different from the Stalinist pattern, and that direct intervention in the decisions of trade unions and chambers of commerce

The ideology of self-management could be supported or attacked as a principle appropriate for universalistic adoption. It seems important to note, however, that it serves two political functions which are peculiar to Yugoslavia and to its political and cultural heritage.

The first function is historic. At the time of the break with the Soviet Union in the late 1940's, and for at least several years thereafter, there was a great need for mustering all possible sources of domestic support to counteract the dangers both of external intervention and of a domestic coup d'état. One might argue—as one Yugoslav academic did in private discussion with me—that it was important for this purpose to develop an official ideology for Yugoslavia which could be sold as a "differentiated product": differentiated both from the traditional doctrine of the world Communist movement and from the doctrines found in capitalist countries.[18] In this fashion, the notion could be combated that the struggle between Tito and Stalin was no more than a clash between strong personalities, while at the same time no ground was given to the charge that Yugoslavia was moving back to capitalism. Self-management, combined with workers' management, provided this differentiated variant of socialist ideology.

This myth of self-management also tied in well with the Second World War partisan background of all Yugoslav molders of public opinion. As late as 1970, a prominent former partisan defended self-management to me on the basis of its military virtues; in case of a Russian invasion, he argued, there would be no ready-made state apparatus available for the Russians to take over, and no bureaucracy at the local economic or political level which was accustomed to carrying out orders from the center. Partisan-type resistance could thus survive because of its local roots in a country where the national center exercised only very limited authority. Regardless of the realism of such a viewpoint, it would seem to be one which would appeal to those who had gone through the partisan movement, and who remained strongly linked to it emotionally. Self-management could thus take on some of the aura of the partisan movement itself, now enshrined in popular as well as official memories.

The second political function of self-management is to help keep within bounds the terrible nationalities problem of the country. Yugo-

---

is rare; he definitely does not consider such bodies as transmission belts of the Party. Nevertheless, he sees no room in Yugoslavia for centers of power autonomous of the Party. The issue of syndicalism would seem to me to lie in the degree of independence of the chambers of commerce with regard to the relevant issues.

[18] For a rather similar argument, see D. D. Milenkovitch, *Plan and Market in Yugoslav Economic Thought* (Yale University Press, New Haven and London: 1971), p. 294.

slavia as a national entity was a post-World War I creation. Its interwar history was one of struggle between the two major nationalities which together constitute two-thirds of the population. The Second World War was bloodied by mass killings along nationality lines: Serb vs. Croat, Serb vs. Moslem, and Serb vs. Hungarian. In Communist Yugoslavia, many of the Albanians have regarded themselves as a repressed minority within the republic of Serbia. Fears of disintegration of the country along nationality lines rose again in the early 1970's.

Complicating the nationalities issue is the north-south split of the country along economic lines. The northern republics of Slovenia and Croatia are relatively wealthy. The southern republics of Bosnia-Herzegovina, Macedonia, and Montenegro, and the autonomous region of Kosovo within Serbia, are desperately poor and number one-third of the nation's population. The second group favors a national investment policy which will channel expansion geographically so as to redistribute the nation's wealth among regions. The first group has urged that investments be regionally located primarily according to where they offer the greatest rate of return, a criterion which greatly favors the developed north.

Thus central economic policy immediately takes on overtones of the nationality conflict. Allocation of investment through the federal budget, subsidies to industry or agriculture, price controls (since these are differentially enforced for different products), foreign exchange allocations: all these are obvious focuses of such conflict. But so too, for example, is central bank monetary policy. Credit restraint is viewed as holding down the growth of the southern regions because of the limitations on bank financing of investment, and as promoting efficiency (and thus greater growth in the future) in the north because of the resulting reduction in the distorting influence of inflation. A strong and activist federal government must, regardless of its policies, inevitably create discord among the eight major nationalities.

The federal government has thus been faced with two choices: attempt to hold down the fires of nationality conflict by relegating most powers to a regional level where region and nationality are virtually homologous, or let the chips fall where they may and repress the conflict. Particularly during the second half of the 1960's and the very beginning of the 1970's, the government adopted the first position.

In Slovenia and in Serbia proper, regional boundaries and nationality bear a one-to-one relationship. But this is far from the case in the other regions (see Table 11.3). Thus, while relegating power to the level of the eight republics or autonomous regions would eliminate the strains of nationality conflict in Slovenia and in Serbia proper, it would go only part way toward solving the problem elsewhere in the country. It is only

TABLE 11.3: Proportion of the Population Which
Is Not of the Dominant Nationality of the Republic
or Autonomous Region, 1971[a] (percentage)

Republic or Autonomous Region	Percent Not of the Dominant Nationality	Other Major Nationalities	
Slovenia	6		
Serbia Proper[b]	10		
Croatia	21	Serb	14
Kosovo	26	Serb	18
Macedonia	31	Albanian	17
		Turk	7
		Serb	3
Montenegro	33	Muslim	13
		Serb	8
		Albanian	7
Vojvodina	44	Hungarian	22
		Croat	7
		Slovak, Romanian, and Ruthenian	8
Bosnia-Herzegovina	60	Serb	37
		Croat	21

SOURCE: *Statistički 1973*, p. 351.

[a] Presumably, the vast bulk of Yugoslavs who were temporarily working in other republics or regions than their place of origin are registered as domiciled in their republic (region) of origin. Thus this table understates the degree to which republics (regions) are heterogeneous in nationality composition.

[b] The Republic of Serbia, excluding the two autonomous regions of Kosovo and Vojvodina.

when power descends to the level of the commune (there were five hundred of these in 1970) that governing organ and nationality become as homologous as possible.

Political self-management means, in practice, the emasculation of the power of the federal government and the granting of power primarily to the commune, but also to the autonomous region or republic. Economic self-management implies leaving independent the individual enterprises and the economic units within them, and each of these is even more likely to be homogeneous with regard to nationality. Thus self-management can be properly viewed as a device of major importance in softening the conflicts between nationalities within the country.[19]

[19] In his comments on my manuscript, Županov felt that the granting of power primarily to the communes was a phenomenon of the early 1960's, but was being replaced with the grant of power to the republics at the end of the 1960's and

WORKERS' MANAGEMENT

Democratic decision making provides the basis for legitimacy of the autonomy element in self-government. Just as the legitimacy of political power in the communes rests on the selection of commune officials through popular vote, so legitimacy of economic power in the enterprises rests upon ultimate control of each enterprise by its own labor force. One aspect of workers' control is that the labor force plays the same role in Yugoslav enterprises as do stockholders in capitalist firms; the labor force, on a one-man–one-vote basis, is the ultimate repository of economic decision making. A critical difference, however, is that when a stockholder in a capitalist firm sells his stock and thus gives up his voice in the firm's activities, he receives a quid pro quo. When a Yugoslav worker leaves an enterprise (whether he quits, is dismissed, or retires), he gives up all his former rights without compensation.

Certain major powers are reserved for direct vote by the labor force: decisions on merger with another enterprise, for example.[20] But most powers are ultimately exercised by the workers' council of the enterprise, a group elected by the entire workforce—normally for a two-year term—which plays the role of a capitalist firm's board of directors. Operational decisions are made by the management board, which is elected by the workers' council, and under the board's supervision by the full-time management team headed by the general director. The workers' council has a complete veto and major voice in the choice of the general director, and can dismiss him at its pleasure.

Since all members of the workers' council and management board are full-time labor force participants in the enterprise, dependent for their livelihood primarily or entirely upon its economic success, they have a greater stake in exercising careful and genuine control over management than do the part-time members of boards of directors of capitalist firms. Similarly, the workers who elect them have a far larger interest in the affairs of the enterprise than do small capitalist stockholders. On the other hand, the slight acquaintance of most members of workers' councils with business matters pushes in the opposite direction toward de facto managerial control. Although it seems reasonable to expect somewhat less managerial control in the typical Yugoslav enterprise than in a capitalist firm which has no substantial stockholder grouping, this comparison cannot be taken as a particularly secure building block for

---

early 1970's. As of late 1973, he believed, both types of political decentralization had shown their incapacity to contain the nationalities problem.

[20] In 1967, two-thirds of the total of 203 referenda in Yugoslav enterprises concerned the splitting-up or merger of the enterprise (Drago Gorupić and Ivan Paj, *Workers' Self-Management in Yugoslav Undertakings*, Zagreb: 1970, p. 212).

the belief that workers' influence really matters. Just as small capitalist stockholders gain a significant power position only when there is a struggle for control between an existing management and a raiding group, so it seems likely that workers' control exercises its greatest influence when there is a policy split among senior managers within the enterprise.

Both self-management and its concomitant of workers' management have been taken, at least in the post-1965 period, as implying that the labor force of an enterprise is to enjoy the fruits of either its success or failure. Yugoslav enterprises are operated as individual cooperatives; net receipts, after deducting all expenses other than wages, are divided by decision of the workers' council between net investments and a wage fund distributed to the membership. Enterprises can choose to invest heavily at the expense of the current wage fund, speculating that they will increase future productivity—and thus per capita wage distributions —through current sacrifices by the membership. Alternatively, the workers' council is free to allocate nothing to net investment.[21] Quite apart from this decision as to the allocation of net revenues, the degree of business acumen of the enterprise management can make a substantial difference in the earnings provided to workers.

While no aggregative data are available as to the extent of differences between enterprises in the earnings of workers with similar skills, there is no question that the variation is considerable. Although a floor is placed by law under worker earnings, this minimum wage has no significance in a comparatively wealthy republic such as Slovenia. The only other restriction is that earnings paid out cannot be reduced to less than 80 percent of the previous year's wage. Relative pay for workers with different skills is decided by the individual enterprise's workers' council.

The labor force members thus have a very real stake in the decisions taken by the workers' council as to distribution of net income between investment and the wage fund, as well as on relative earnings of the different members of the labor force. They also have a vital interest in decisions concerning layoffs, working conditions, and the enforcement of working discipline. All this might be expected to cause the workers' council to play an active, decision-making role. At the same time, however, workers are also vitally concerned with the efficiency and financial success of the enterprise. It is this latter consideration which tempts them to permit managerial dominance of decisions, at least when the management's record is one of success. A workers' council which re-

[21] The freedom of the workers' council to determine the distribution of net earnings between the wage fund and net investments has been reduced somewhat during 1972-73 through the development of agreements among enterprises to restrict their wage payments. But this appears to be little more than a temporary incomes-policy device to fight inflation.

jects managerial advice on important matters would have to feel fairly sure of its ground, even more so than is the case for a board of directors of a capitalist firm since the workers' council has less business expertise available within its own ranks.

Until 1968, the enterprise management board—the operational organ of the workers' council—was required to have three-quarters of its members elected from among manual workers. But Amendment Fifteen of the Yugoslav Constitution, adopted in that year, gave each enterprise the authority to determine the membership of its own management board.[22] The result appears to have been that managerial personnel have come to dominate the membership of this key body. Although the national trade union organization struggled bitterly against the interpretation of Amendment Fifteen which made possible this expansion of managerial authority, workers' councils in 1970 seem to have given greater emphasis to improvements in efficiency than to preserving the aspect of workers' control which lies in the composition of membership of the boards. By late 1973, however, a workers' majority within the management board was once again legally obligatory.

If one interprets workers' control as meaning only that ultimate decision-making authority and responsibility reside in the hands of the entire labor force of the enterprise, then nothing has been lost by the post-1968 development. But workers' management has been interpreted much more broadly in Yugoslavia, and has been taken to mean that large numbers of ordinary workers should play a major role in the actual decision-making process.[23] This was the basis for the strong trade union objection to the 1969-70 interpretation of Amendment Fifteen.

One means by which substantial mass participation has been promoted has been the creation of "economic units" within the enterprise. These are lower organs of self-management, each of which either has its own elected body or is small enough to take decisions by vote of all those working in the unit. The creation of such units greatly expands the pro-

---

[22] In fact, the management board could be abolished. In some firms, it was replaced by a business committee consisting only of top executives; a number of such business committees were later renamed management boards (J. Županov, "Is Enterprise Management becoming Professionalized?" *International Studies of Management and Organization*, III, 3, 1973, p. 79). However, all of the enterprises in which I interviewed during 1970 had management boards and, by a 1973 court ruling, the business committees were no longer allowed to exercise any other role than that of an advisory committee to the general director.

[23] A 1968 survey covering enterprises with a total labor force of three-quarters of a million showed that 38 percent of the labor force took part, during the year, in one or another commission, board, or council. Double-counting of the same individual serving as a member of more than one commission or council was not, however, eliminated in the calculation of this percentage (Gorupić and Ivan Paj, p. 206).

portion of the labor force which can take an active part in the determination of policy; but, of course, the problem arises that such units may have no decisions to take which they consider significant or, on the other hand, that power within the enterprise becomes hopelessly decentralized. The latter danger is particularly serious in view of the effort to link the earnings of members of each unit to the business success of that unit itself, a policy which could lead to endless strife between units. Theoretically in some enterprises, it is the individual units which determine the proportion of their net revenue which is to be allocated to investment. My interviews suggest, however, that the first risk of powerlessness of economic units is usually the more real one. For, despite all ideology, Yugoslav workers as well as managers are deeply concerned with the efficiency of the enterprise as a whole.

A second mechanism of mass participation is provided by the general rule throughout Yugoslav society that the same person may serve only a limited number of years in any single elected public or political function. Thus membership in workers' councils, managing boards, executive committees of the Party organizations of the enterprises, etc. is rotating. In practice, however, some continuity is preserved by individuals being rotated from membership in one such organization to another within the same enterprise. For example, a member of the managing board may have previously been a member of the workers' council. Such "horizontal rotation" may be regarded as a travesty of the rotational system; but its elimination would probably have the de facto effect of further increasing the power of the professional managers in the enterprise.

Although the rotation principle has never been applied to professional managers in Yugoslav enterprises, periodic reelection of the general director by the workers' council after eight years was instituted in 1966, and was extended in 1968 to reelection after four years. In the three elections between 1966 and 1970, 81 to 85 percent of the positions voted on were filled by the incumbent director.[24] While this shows that reelection was the rule, nevertheless the average tenure of directors was not exceptionally long, either by CMEA or by American corporate standards. At the time of the 1968 elections, only 48 percent of the general directors had been in office for four years or more; in 1970, the percentage had fallen to 19 percent.[25]

[24] *Statistički* of 1969 and 1972, pp. 69 and 70, and Komisija za samoupravljanje pri RSS, "Reelekcija Direktorjev" (mimeographed, Ljubljana: 1968), p. 8.

[25] These percentages are calculated by comparing the number of elections in each year with the number of enterprises which elect workers' councils. This procedure may understate somewhat the true percentages.

The percentages do not appear to be substantially depressed by the creation of new enterprises. As will be seen in Chapter 13, comprehensive data for Yugoslav

The literature dealing with workers' management in Yugoslavia has concentrated primarily upon two features. First, there is the degree to which workers' councils actually dominate enterprise decision making and the degree to which there is effective mass participation in the organs of workers' management.[26] Second, there is the degree to which workers' management leads to decisions different from those which would be made by capitalist firms.[27] A third aspect however, which may be of even greater importance, is the link between workers' management and the autonomy aspect of self-management, neither of which feature exists in any other socialist country. Just as it would be difficult to imagine a general condition of autonomy of capitalist firms without stock ownership, so too the autonomy of the socialist firm provided in the doctrine of self-management requires workers' management to give it legitimacy. In both cases, whether reality is better described by managerial control or by stockholder (worker) control is much less important than whether a base of socially accepted legitimacy for enterprise autonomy has been found. Partly this is a matter of the myths upon which organizational reality rests; but even more important is the fact that both in capitalist and in Yugoslav society it is the supposed controlling groups of the individual enterprises (stockholders or total labor force as the case may be) which benefit or suffer to the degree that the enterprise wrestles successfully with its external environment.[28] In all other socialist countries, the main mass of the labor force has relatively little stake in the success of its individual enterprise; in short, there it is society rather than the

---

industry during 1961-62 show that such new entries were only 4.5 percent annually of the existing number of enterprises; these percentages probably did not change radically in the late 1960's.

Analysis of the position of president and chairman in six large American industrial corporations showed that 58 percent of the periods of tenure (sample size of twelve) were longer than three years. In view of the size of the American corporations compared to the Yugoslav enterprises, the position of divisional general manager may be more comparable with that of the Yugoslav general director; in the same companies, only 22 percent of the periods of tenure in this post (sample size of eighty) were for longer than three years (D. Granick, *Managerial Comparisons of Four Developed Countries: France, Britain, United States, and Russia*, The M.I.T. Press, Cambridge, Mass.: 1972, pp. 215-16).

Table 14.10 in Chapter 14 presents data as to the length of tenure of general directors in a sample of Slovenian, Romanian, Hungarian, and East German enterprises. The Slovenian average (5.8 years in a sample of eighteen) does not appear out of line with that of the other countries.

[26] See, for example, Ichak Adizes, *Industrial Democracy: Yugoslav Style* (The Free Press, New York: 1971).

[27] For example, H. M. Wachtel, *Workers' Management and Workers' Wages in Yugoslavia* (Cornell University Press, Ithaca and London: 1973).

[28] Of course, workers in CMEA socialist countries benefit somewhat from profit sharing, and workers in capitalist countries average higher wages when their industry (and even their individual firm) is particularly profitable. But these are only minor caveats.

members of the enterprise which is concerned with the enterprise's performance and with the success of its managerial risk taking. Only in Yugoslavia is society as a whole relatively shielded from the fate of the average individual socialist enterprise, in the same fashion that society as a whole in a capitalist country is relatively shielded from the fate of the average individual capitalist firm. This, in my opinion, is the most critical aspect of workers' management.

CONTROL FROM OUTSIDE THE ENTERPRISE

Control at the federal level. During the 1950's, the federal government exercised major influence over the individual enterprises, although its controls were of the present Hungarian financial type rather than being direct planning orders. Regardless of the technique used, however, investments, wage levels, foreign trade, and prices were all determined primarily at the federal level. Self-management was given little more than lip service, and the economic fate of the members of a given enterprise's labor force was determined primarily by national rather than enterprise policy. The organs of workers' management could play a major role in determining individual hirings and firings, work conditions, and the methods of exercising work discipline; but there was little room for these organs—anymore than for the enterprise director—to exercise critical influence on the economic decisions which are of greatest importance to the workforce: average levels of earnings in the enterprise, relative earnings of different categories of personnel, or the trade-off between current earnings and future earnings.

The economic reform of 1961, carried still further in 1965, drastically altered that pattern. In 1961, each individual enterprise became free to set the current earnings of its own labor force within its financial limits. After 1965, the federal government lost most of its control over investment; at least in principle, subsidies for current operations—other than exports—became of minor significance, and enterprises were left to survive as best they could in the open market place; in 1966, prices for one-third of industrial production had become totally free of control (de facto, and not simply de jure as in Hungary a few years later), and the relationship among different fixed prices was sharply altered by the federal government to the considerable disadvantage of various branches of heavy industry which had been previously favored. Although a substantial portion of imports remained subject to federal licensing, and enterprises could thus be compelled to export if they were to satisfy their individual import needs, the degree of control over imports was sharply diminished. By 1970, when I conducted my interviews, a semilegal—even if only a thin and loosely organized—market existed in

Yugoslavia for foreign currency purchases and sales by enterprises, and the value of the Yugoslav dinar in this market seems normally not to have exceeded the official rate by more than about 50 percent. Finally, the banking system was transformed into a collection of independent "business banks" which provided both short-term and long-term credit; federal control over this system was essentially limited to the reserve regulations and rediscounting procedure which are customary for central banks in capitalist countries.

In this new environment, central planning lost whatever significance it had previously had.[29] Five-year plans were expected to continue on an indicative rather than an obligatory basis. Annual plans were abandoned. In short, although interventionism (particularly with regard to import quotas and domestic prices) was maintained, central guidance of the economy became minimal.

The transformation of the Yugoslav economy to a genuine market basis is usually dated from 1965 in Yugoslav writings, and this is the date which I shall use throughout in statistical comparisons. Since workers' management is most meaningful under conditions where enterprises exercise genuine self-management, this is also the beginning date which will be used for analyzing the operation of workers' management. In fact, however, it is very difficult to pinpoint any particular starting year, and important changes occurred even in the 1970's.

The principal changes which occurred on or about 1965, and which justify this dating of the "reform," are the following:

(1) The establishment of a single rate of sales tax on retail sales only, rather than a multitude of rates.

(2) The abolition of subsidies to industrial enterprises for sales on the domestic market. The combination of these two changes implied a massive withdrawal on the part of the federal government from the determination both of prices and of the incomes of enterprises.

(3) The freeing of enterprise depreciation funds from partial blocking of expenditures by the federal government.

(4) The transformation of the banks from control by federal, republic, and commune authorities to primary control by those enterprises which both invested equity capital in the individual banks and which placed their bank deposits with them. This transformation appears to have had considerable effect upon the lending policies followed by the banks.

(5) The unification of foreign-exchange rates applicable to different sectors of the economy. (This had been attempted in 1961, but was not

---

[29] Aleksander Bajt, "Yugoslav Economic Reforms, Monetary and Production Mechanism," *Economics of Planning*, VII, 3 (1967), 203. Bajt is also quite skeptical about the coordinating power of national plans prior to 1965.

successful at that time.) Although differential export subsidies have made this last change less significant than it might at first appear, its importance has not been challenged.[30]

The early 1970's saw further reduction in federal economic influence, although now primarily to the advantage of the republics, autonomous regions, and communes. Funds which the federal government had earlier invested in enterprises were transferred to these lower government levels, and the interest payments and loan repayments by the enterprises were to be made to them. In some cases, these government units completely freed the enterprises from these debts; but, at least as of late 1972, this did not seem to be the rule.[31]

The 1965 shift to a genuine market economy was accompanied by placing the major emphasis upon microeconomic efficiency. Despite the national labor surpluses (which revealed themselves both in a high rate of unemployment and in considerable underemployment in privately owned family farms), enterprises were encouraged to expand output through higher labor productivity rather than through increases in the employed labor force. It was recognized that industrial enterprises were overstaffed, and the 1965 reform was intended to flush into the open the hidden underemployment existing in industry. In the face of an increase of the working-age population of Yugoslavia between 1964 and 1968 of about 3.9 percent, the absolute level of employment was allowed to fall by 0.6 percent.[32]

This shift of emphasis to microeconomic efficiency was accompanied by an innovation in the labor market which still remains unique among socialist countries. Since 1965-66, Yugoslavs have been permitted to take employment abroad for as long a period as they wish. The resultant large-scale exodus (primarily to West Germany and Austria) helped both to hold in check the rise in unemployment and to generate large amounts of convertible currency in remittances to families remaining in Yugoslavia. It involved a successful extension of the free-market principle to the foreign sector in the form of free international mobility of labor. Beginning in 1967, Yugoslavia also became the first of the socialist countries to encourage mobility of capital by permitting joint ventures inside the country with capitalist firms; however, this further opening of borders to factor mobility proved much less consequential.

By 1970, de facto federal control over the microeconomy seemed to be entirely consistent with the weak de jure position. Tax rates on en-

[30] See R. Bićanić, *Economic Policy in Socialist Yugoslavia* (Cambridge University Press, Cambridge, England: 1973), pp. 130 and 211-38.

[31] See the interview with Cemovic, the president of the interrepublic committee for monetary questions, *Borba*, August 8, 1972, p. 4, translated in *JPS*.

[32] *Statistički 1972*, pp. 78 and 89.

terprise income were uniform, differing neither by industry nor by enterprise. Federal controls were limited to foreign exchange and foreign trade, domestic prices, and investments.

Foreign exchange controls were the most significant in their effect both on enterprises and on the macroeconomy.[33] Enterprises could import some raw materials and consumer goods freely, for this purpose buying convertible currency from the state bank in unlimited amounts at the official exchange rate.[34] But other goods—and particularly capital equipment—could be imported at the official exchange rate only to the limit of each individual enterprise's exchange quota; beyond this, the necessary foreign exchange could be purchased solely at substantially higher rates, and with considerable uncertainty as to its availability at any price, through the very thin market for convertible currency. Import quotas (measured in the number of dinars which could be converted) were established for each enterprise according to ratios specific to the individual branch or, frequently, even to the large individual enterprise; these ratios linked the enterprise import quota either to its total exports or to its increase of them. In this fashion, federal authorities gained some degree of control over enterprise decisions on whether to buy and sell on the foreign market. But the substantial and growing deficit in the current balance-of-payments account showed the limited effectiveness of these controls.

[33] Both the exports and imports of Yugoslavia are heavily concentrated in industrial products. Their importance in 1970, relative to the country's gross material product, is shown in a somewhat distorted form in the table below. Unfortunately, both exports and imports have to be converted into dinars—for comparability with domestic production—at the official exchange rate; this understates the importance of exports, while tariffs lead to the overstating of imports.

Foreign Trade as a Proportion of Gross Domestic Material Product, 1970
(percentage)

	All Yugoslavia	Slovenia
Entire economy		
Exports	13	20
Imports	23	36
Industry and mining		
Exports	33	41
Imports	60	80

SOURCES: *Statistički 1971*, table 113-7 and *Statistički 1972*, table 105-5; *Statistični Letopis Slovenije 1972*, tables 5-3, 13-3, and 13-8.

NOTE: Reexports, whether in a direct form or after further processing, are excluded from both exports and imports.

[34] In 1970, 56 percent of industrial materials, 19 percent of industrial consumer goods, and 14 percent of capital goods were included under this free regime (S. Godevarica, "Price System and Policy," *Yugoslav Survey*, XIII, 3, 1972, p. 21).

The 1965 reform had unified the exchange rate for different commodities as between the dinar and foreign currencies. However, the system of multiple exchange rates was replaced (just as later in Hungary) by an extensive system of federal subsidies for different commodities. In 1970, such subsidies on exports totaled approximately 7 percent of the industrial gross material social product.[35]

In Hungary, export subsidies were individualized to the enterprise level and, in fact, seemed to remain largely individualized in this fashion even after the formal shift in 1971. Yugoslav subsidies, to the contrary, were by commodity group although, de facto, they must often have amounted to individual enterprise subsidies as in Hungary.[36]

Other than foreign exchange controls, direct state influence over the volume of imports of individual products primarily took the form of tariffs rather than quotas. In trade with other socialist countries, national trade agreements determined the total volume of imports of specific groups of commodities; but such agreements had more of an effect upon the national source of imports of these commodities than upon their total volume.

Federal price controls remained in force after the 1965 economic reform, continuing to affect something on the order of 50 percent of sales of manufactured goods.[37] These price controls, however, were much more similar to the French than to the Hungarian system. Unlike the Hungarian price-control system, the Yugoslav mechanism was not employed to restrain inflation throughout both the controlled and "free" sector; the 13 percent per annum rate of inflation between 1964 and 1971 illustrates this fact. The relatively free import and export of goods, as well as the very limited degree to which subsidies have been used to cushion the effect of wage inflation upon domestic prices, set sharp limits upon the extent to which prices could be restrained in the con-

[35] *Nedljne Informativne Novine* (*NIN*), April 12, 1970, pp. 10 and 12. These subsidies took the form of tax reductions, and thus were outside the budget.

[36] Although the industrial labor force is much the same size in Yugoslavia as in Hungary, Yugoslav industry is less concentrated. There were 45 percent more industrial firms in Yugoslavia than in Hungary in 1970; only 40 percent of Yugoslav industrial employment was in enterprises with more than two thousand employees, in contrast to 59 percent in Hungary. Nevertheless, almost two-thirds of the Yugoslav industrial labor force was employed in 363 enterprises; with this degree of concentration, subsidy by commodity must in many cases have virtually amounted to subsidy by enterprise.

[37] The proportion of industrial production covered by price controls fell from 65 percent in 1966 to 44 percent in 1968, and stabilized at that rate through October 1970. In that month, a freeze on further price increases of all manufactured goods was introduced; but this did not have even a temporary effect in slowing inflation. During the first half of 1972, over 90 percent of production was still subject to price control (*Privredni Vjesnik*, June 22, 1972, p. 3, cited in *ABSEES*, October 1972).

trolled sector relative to the free sector.[38] At best, price controls and the relative degree of freedom to import different products were used as a substitute for antitrust policy (preventing monopoly and oligopoly sectors from fully exercising their power over the prices of their products) and as a means of slightly delaying the effect of general inflation on the consumer price level.

Microeconomic investment control takes several forms. The most open is direct subsidization of new investments from the federal "central investment fund." But the total amount of this fund was sharply restricted after 1965,[39] and its use has been limited to the less-developed republics and autonomous regions and to infrastructure investments specified by law. Investment in industry in Slovenia, Croatia, and Serbia proper was out of bounds. The resources of the fund have been concentrated upon a few large projects primarily geared toward regional development.

The second more general instrument of investment control has been the allocation of foreign exchange quotas to individual enterprises. To the degree that investment by enterprises has involved purchase of imported equipment, such exchange control becomes an instrument of investment control.

The significance of this form of control is difficult to evaluate. Certainly, since both investment in domestically produced facilities and the use of the free market for foreign currency escape it completely, its power cannot be overwhelming. My interviews in enterprises led to no suggestions that investment control over the individual enterprise is indeed perceived by managements as a product of this quota system.

A third form of potential microeconomic investment control is federal influence over the individual short-term and long-term loans made by the business banks. My impression is that such influence can be virtually dismissed. In general, the strength of self-management ideology at the bank level is such that interference by federal authorities in the details of bank operations would be resented and would probably be self-defeating. Even the National Investment Bank, originally a creature of the

[38] Even when its industry is subject to price control, the individual enterprise is free to set the price of all new products. With the expansion of price controls, the number of "new products" registered with the Federal Price Bureau increased from about six thousand per year during 1967-68 to thirty thousand during the first quarter of 1971 (*Ekonomska Politika*, May 3, 1971, p. 4, cited in *ABSEES*, July 1971). This is an example of how price controls have been effectively avoided.

[39] As of the end of 1971, the assets of the federal investment loan funds constituted only 3.5 percent of the stock of total financial investment resources in the Yugoslav economy (National Bank of Yugoslavia, *Annual Report 1971*, p. 28). During 1966-71, however, such federal funds financed 12 percent of gross fixed capital investment in the sector of industry and mining (Služba društvenog knjigovodstva - glavna centrala, *Statistički Bilten*, February 1967-1972).

federal government, seemed by 1970 to be functioning as a normal Yugoslav business bank. Only in the field of agricultural and tourist loans have I seen any indication that the federal government may be exercising an influence on individual loans; even here, the evidence is at best only suggestive.

To sum up, it is my impression that microeconomic investment control by the federal government varies, in fact as well as in theory, from minimal to nil for controls other than the enterprise foreign exchange quotas. Certainly these other controls had no effect on any of the enterprises in which I conducted interviews.

Macroeconomic investment control by federal authorities is carried out through general regulations relating to reserves of business banks and to the rediscounting of their notes.[40] Here we have the normal operations of a central bank.

The relative failure of these macroeconomic controls is suggested by the high rate of national inflation and by the negative balance-of-payments on current account throughout the period since 1960 (except for a few years in the middle of the decade), as well as by the strong cyclical behavior of the Yugoslav economy.[41] Yet the Yugoslav economy has been most unusual in that inventory fluctuations have been generally countercyclical;[42] to the degree that this has been due to national credit policy, Yugoslav authorities should be credited with success in the use of this stabilization measure.

On average, the Yugoslav national bank appears to have been severely hampered since 1960 in its desire to restrain inflation and balance-of-payment deficits through monetary policy. The principal restraint has consisted of the nationality conflicts of interest in the issue of inflation versus growth. An anti-inflationary policy was carried out only during 1966-67 and parts of 1965 and 1968, and it had major negative effects on growth of output and on employment. The history of the period since 1960 shows federal authorities to have been peculiarly incapable, by standards both of socialist and capitalist countries, of exercising long-run monetary restraint;[43] nevertheless, the monetary restraint of the

[40] The Yugoslav economist Horvat writes that "Fiscal policy practically does not exist in the country." (B. Horvat, "Analysis of the Economic Situation and Proposal for a Program of Action," *Praxis*, international edition, VIII, 3-4, 1971, p. 550.)

[41] Branko Horvat, *Business Cycles in Yugoslavia* (*Eastern European Economics*, IX, 3-4, 1971), and Alexander Bajt, "Instability with Planning" (International Economic Association, Conference on Central Planning and Market Relations held May 4-8, 1970).

[42] Horvat, *Business Cycles*, chapter 9.

[43] The governor of the National Bank of Yugoslavia declared in 1970 that the increase of prices cannot be stopped by monetary methods (*Privredni Vjesnik*, July 23, 1970, p. 6, cited in *ABSEES*, October 1970).

mid-1960's, which ushered in the economic reform, demonstrated that the political constraints on effective policy are far from absolute.[44]

Thus far we have examined federal control only through government channels, and must conclude that it is quite weak. But since Yugoslavia is a socialist country with political rule by a single party, we should also inquire as to the significance of informal federal control through the League of Communists. The result of our inquiry appears to be much the same. Unlike the Communist Parties in other socialist countries, the Yugoslav League of Communists—at least throughout the second half of the 1960's and the beginning of the 1970's—has been more of a coalition of republic-level parties than a single unitary party with a unitary policy. On various key economic questions, the Slovenian and Croatian Party organizations have emphasized quite different things than have the southern Party bodies. But even on the republic level, the Party has been viewed as merely one of a number of power centers rather than as the only one.[45] The trade unions and chambers of commerce have been genuine sources of power rather than simply "transmission belts" as in other socialist lands. Thus control by the League of Communists, whether on a federal or republic level, cannot be viewed in the Yugoslavia of the 1960's or early 1970's as a genuine substitute for government control.[46]

[44] However, Horvat argued in 1971 that a "repetition of (the deflationary policy of) 1967 is no longer politically feasible" (Horvat, "Analysis," p. 547).

[45] This is doubtless one reason that 42 percent of the Party membership as of the end of 1960 left the Party during the following nine years, almost half of them without the Party's even having a record of their leaving. Nor was there heavy recruitment among the youth; the average age of Party members is forty-five, the second highest average in Europe (*Borba*, March 2, 1971, p. 4, and July 4, 1972, p. 5, cited in *ABSEES*, July 1971 and October 1972).

[46] It is possible that the situation changed somewhat in 1972 and 1973. Certainly after late 1971, there was an effort on the part of Tito to weld the different republic Party leaderships into a more unitary force and to strengthen Party discipline and control. This first took the form of removal of key people in the Party leadership of most or all of the republics; but it is too early to tell if this will have any significant effect upon the wielding of Party control over the economy in the interest of national, rather than republic, policy.

In commenting on a draft of this manuscript, Županov has argued that the pre-1972 situation is better described as one incorporating strong tendencies toward a coalition of republic-level parties, rather than as a reduction of the Yugoslav Party to a definite state of coalition. In his view, the hard core of a unitary Party was preserved throughout the period ending in 1971; if this had not been the case, he says, the sweeping change within the Party which occurred suddenly at the end of 1971 would be incomprehensible.

Furthermore, Županov argued that the trade unions and chambers of commerce were more apparent than real sources of power. In his view, it was the internal struggle among Party factions which gave the impression that these non-Party bodies constituted autonomous power centers. Another well-informed Yugoslav, who commented on the draft at the same time, claimed that recent trade union actions in defense of workers' rights and living standards show that the trade

Control at the republic and commune levels. The principal mechanisms of federal control—foreign exchange and foreign trade control, price control, and credit control—are all absent at the republic and commune levels. Nevertheless, the enterprises in Slovenia give the impression of being more under the influence of the government and social (Party, trade union, and chamber of commerce) organs at these lower levels than of those at the federal level.

Partly this is because both the republic and commune organs have some (if quite limited) funds for investing in and subsidizing their own enterprises,[47] while no such moneys are available from federal funds for enterprises of an advanced republic such as Slovenia. (Export subsidies, which are available for Slovenian enterprises from federal sources, are not normally allocated to individual enterprises.) Partly it is because the few business banks of each republic can be influenced by the republic and commune governments. Partly it is because the commune government plays an important role in nominating the general director of each enterprise.

But by far the most important reason for republic and commune influence on enterprise behavior is the informal pressure which both government and social organs at this level can place upon managers. Social pressure, including that of publicity, is important here; for example, this can be quite important in restraining the degree of disparity in the average income per head distributed by different enterprises of the same commune. Equally important, leading personnel of enterprises tend over time to move horizontally to similar-level posts in other organizations, and such moves are restricted to a considerable degree to the same commune, and almost certainly to the same republic.[48] To this

---

union movement has indeed become an independent and strong workers' organization; but he took no position as to its degree of autonomy from ultimate Party influence.

[47] In Yugoslavia as a whole, the assets of the investment loan funds of the republics and communes at the end of 1971 totaled 285 percent of the resources available in the federal investment loan funds. The former constituted 12.3 percent of the country's total financial investment funds. (National Bank of Yugoslavia, *Annual Report 1971*, p. 28.) During 1966-71, communes and republics directly financed 3 percent of gross investment in the sector of industry and mining (*Statistički Bilten*, February 1967-1972).

[48] I know the earlier careers of eight of the nine general directors of the Slovenian enterprises in which I interviewed. Two of the eight had held the post for eighteen years each, but none of the others had been general director in the same enterprise for more than seven years; three of the eight had been in office for one year or less.

Of these eight general directors, only one had long seniority in the enterprise before being elected as general director. Of the seven others, one came directly from a federal ministry, having earlier worked in the Slovenian republic administration; two came directly from municipal government posts; one came from a higher organization of the republic industry which had been dissolved; two had

degree, leading managers are dependent for their future career prospects upon powers outside of their own enterprise. Enterprises in their actions clearly do take into account the opinions of commune and republic leaders.

To an unknown degree, this implies that enterprise behavior is affected by nonmarket factors. It seems safe to say that such influence goes considerably beyond what is normal for private firms in most developed capitalist countries.

Nevertheless, it would be quite incorrect to view the typical Yugoslav enterprise as primarily guided by such external formal and informal controls. In essence, the Yugoslav enterprise is self-directed in the same fashion as is the capitalist firm. Both must pay attention to government and social pressures; individual enterprises in both types of economies —particularly those which look for government aid to help them out of a shaky financial situation, or which find their principal customer in government—can be strongly influenced by such pressures. But both are primarily creatures of the market place, and adapt to its requirements in a fashion qualitatively different from that of enterprises in other socialist countries including Hungary. In this regard, the Yugoslav enterprise, particularly since 1965, should be considered as more comparable to the capitalist enterprise than to the socialist enterprise of any other nation. Both the Yugoslav and capitalist enterprise share the common and crucial feature of being self-directed, which is a fundamental ingredient of self-management.

---

been general directors of other enterprises; and one had been a director of another enterprise. All of these latter seven either entered the enterprise directly as general director, or were elected to that post within one year of joining the enterprise.

CHAPTER 12

The Reality of Workers' Management
and Enterprise
Goals in Yugoslavia

THIS chapter is concerned with the significance of workers' management—other than as a legitimating device for the autonomy aspect of enterprise self-management—in the operation of Yugoslav enterprises. I shall approach this topic from three different perspectives.

The first is the Yugoslav counterpart of the familiar Berle and Means issue with regard to large American capitalist firms: managerial versus stockholder control. In self-managed socialist enterprises, this issue takes the form of managerial versus worker control. Much of the discussion of workers' management has been cast in this framework, with considerable evidence being presented that Yugoslav enterprises tend in fact to be management controlled.

To the degree that Yugoslav firms are indeed self-managed, higher full-time executives constitute the only alternative source of authority to that of the mass of employees as represented through the workers' council and other mass organizations within the enterprise. To the extent that social control by the government and Communist Party at commune, republic, and federal levels is important, such control can be exercised in only two ways. The first is by establishing conditions for the enterprise which cause firms to act in a particular fashion regardless of whether they are worker controlled or management controlled. This means will be ignored in this chapter on the ground that such socially determined conditions are simply part of the environment within which the enterprise must make its decisions.[1] The second means of control is through influence which can be exerted on full-time executives but not on the workers' organizations. This method will be treated here, but within the context of managerial versus worker control.

I shall not attempt in this first section of the chapter to specify the degree of managerial control, but rather shall explore the meaning of the issue. Specifically, I shall be concerned with the similarities and

---

[1] This is not to suggest that the degree of interference from outside the firm is irrelevant in determining the degree of mass participation in those decisions which are left to the enterprise. However, since I am examining only the recent period of Yugoslav history, I shall not consider changes in the degree of such interference. That is why this variable can be laid aside.

differences in interests and value systems between top management and the enterprise workforce as a whole, and thus with the effect on enterprise actions of the degree of managerial control which prevails.

The second section takes a different approach to the problem, dealing with the evidence as to the relative influence of full-time management in comparison with the workers' representatives in the various self-management bodies of the enterprise. Here we must beware of treating "management" as a homogeneous group, and must recognize the possibility that conflicts within the managerial group can take the form of struggle between the general director and the workers' management bodies.

This section also deals with the issue of self-management as an institutional device for providing a substantial proportion of the labor force with a sense of participation in the economic affairs of their unit, thus counteracting the sense of alienation said to be created by modern industry. This issue is related to the relative influence of workers compared to management, but it is not simply its "dual." For, while workers may be allowed to participate in decisions only within constraints which cause their decisions to be largely the same as those desired by the decisive power bloc of management, even this sort of participation may well counteract alienation.

The perspective of the third section is that of contrasting observed macroeconomic behavior in Yugoslav industry with that predicted on the basis of the twin assumptions that enterprises operate exclusively in the interests of the mass of their existing employees, and that such employees consider only their individual economic self-interest (the Ward-Domar model). The macroeconomic comparison of post-1965 reality with the model will shed some light on the question of the degree to which enterprise actions under the self-management system differ from the socially optimum, and correspond instead with those predicted for units genuinely controlled by workers' self-management. The results are consistent with the hypothesis that Yugoslav enterprises behave differently from enterprises in either a capitalist environment or a centrally regulated socialist system; however, these results are irrelevant to the issue of managerial versus worker control, since both groups may have identical perceived interests.

THE DISTINCTION BETWEEN TOP-MANAGEMENT AND WORKER CONTROL

The distinction between stockholder and management control has been investigated in American corporations in terms of whether the economic incentives provided to top management lead them to decisions contrary to the interest of shareholders in obtaining maximum return on capital. Although studies in this field have been inconclusive, it has been possible to frame the question empirically by comparing the performance of those large companies in which ownership control is quite concentrated with those in which there is no such concentration, and in which top management can thus normally exercise final authority.

No analogous empirical testing is possible for management-controlled versus worker-controlled enterprises in Yugoslavia. By definition, there can be no concentration of control of worker votes in the fashion feasible for stockholder votes. Control by any large group such as all the workers in an enterprise, or even the total elected body of the workers' council, is inevitably exercised through individual strong leaders or coalitions. If such a strong leader in one enterprise occupies the post of general director, while in another he is the chairman of the workers' council, there is no ipso facto reason for holding that the first enterprise is less worker controlled than the second.

There is, however, an important difference between the position of general director of an enterprise and that of a member or head of a workers' management organization, or of the Party or trade union executive committee in the enterprise. Only the managerial positions can be filled by the same person over an extended time period; the others are all subject to the rotation principle—with normally only one or two years in a post—which was described in Chapter 11. Thus it is much more difficult for an individual to dominate the enterprise's decision making from a position in workers' management, or in a social organization, than from the post of general director. Although in any case he must jockey for political power, only the general director has a permanent base from which to operate.[2] This justifies singling out the general director's post as the one to investigate in searching for a possible counter to workers' management.

What I shall do in this section is to look for the roots of possible conflict of interest between top management, as represented by the general director, and the mass of workers in the enterprise.

Excessive managerial income. One potential conflict is over the level of managerial income. This is because each enterprise is free to determine its own scale of relative wages, and to distribute as it sees fit its "profits" (defined as company income remaining after the payment

[2] The only apparent exception would be someone performing the role of a local American party "boss." But since such a person in a Yugoslav enterprise would have to work full time in an occupation other than that of "boss," and would almost always receive an income less than that of the general director, we might expect a person who has both this degree of influence and this interest in political maneuvering to take over the position of general director.

of all expenses, including the wages set by the firm itself at the beginning of each year).

If, however, we contrast the relative income distributions within the individual industrial firms which I have studied in Slovenia with those of Hungary, the German Democratic Republic, and Romania, two facts stand out sharply: (1) Slovenian earnings are high for rank-and-file engineers relative to semiskilled blue-collar workers. (2) Slovenian earnings are low for top management personnel relative to these engineers.[3] Since the general director in a large enterprise normally has an education similar to that of his engineers, the income comparison relevant for him is that of the rank-and-file engineers rather than of the semiskilled workers. It is thus clear that the monetary rewards attached to managerial posts are low, not only in comparison with capitalist countries but also in comparison with other east European socialist nations.

One might suspect that rank-and-file engineers in Slovenia enjoy high earnings relative to workers because the former are the best-informed nonmanagerial group, and thus constitute the stratum most strategically placed for giving leadership to workers' management organizations. But there is no evidence that this is the cause. Rather, their relative earning position seems to be fully explicable by their freedom to work abroad in higher-income countries (primarily West Germany). Engineers appear to form a disproportionately large share of the Slovenian workforce abroad; this is probably due to their better command of foreign languages and the greater geographic mobility of intelligentsia internationally. In mid-1970, experts from the Slovenian government organ most closely concerned with the matter estimated that at least one-fifth of all Slovenian university graduates currently go abroad upon graduation.[4] It is the competition of German industry which forces Slovenian enterprises to pay engineers relatively well.[5]

While the earnings of rank-and-file engineers are boosted relative to workers, those of general directors are not exceptionally high, by stan-

[3] See Table 14.17 in Chapter 14. In the Slovenian firms studied, the general director earned on average approximately 1.9 times as much as ordinary engineers in his firm who had three years of experience. The Romanian ratio was 2.9, the Hungarian was 4, and the East German was probably close to the Romanian.

[4] I estimate that in late 1971, Slovenian workers abroad constituted about 10 percent of the employed labor force in Slovenia (see *Borba*, December 4, 1971, p. 11, and *Privredni Vjesnik*, August 12, 1971, p. 2, cited *in ABSEES*, January and April 1972). It is conceivable that the proportion of young males working abroad reaches the 20 percent figure estimated for recent university graduates; but even if this should be the case, presumably still greater emigration of young Slovenian engineers is restrained only by the relatively high incomes which they can earn in Slovenia.

[5] Županov (probably the most highly regarded of the Yugoslav sociological students of management), in commenting on this manuscript in late 1973, completely rejected this explanation. But he was not able to offer an alternative one.

dards of socialist countries, in relation to those of ordinary workers. The result is that the income differential favoring top managers is small compared to what they could earn outside management ranks. When one considers that experts and technicians moonlight extensively,[6] and that top managers have no time to earn supplementary income, the differential becomes very small indeed.

Consistent with the observed small-sample differentials on which I have based the above discussion is the apparent difficulty in persuading capable engineers to accept top management posts. This is a complaint which I heard a number of times during 1970 in Slovenia. It appears to be supported by a survey of managers (from at least four of the six Yugoslav republics, but probably with a heavy Slovenian weighting) which was conducted in 1968; the overwhelming majority both of general directors and of other managerial personnel surveyed expressed the belief that directors' incomes were too low to serve as a stimulus to make professionals wish to compete for a general director's position.[7] The same survey showed that only a small proportion of general directors wished to retain such a post in either their own or in another organization.[8] Early 1972 saw the resignations of a number of managers from Slovenia's largest enterprises, as well as the threat of further resignations.[9]

Yugoslavia is the only country, socialist or nonsocialist, where I have heard complaints as to the difficulty of recruiting top managers from among the most competent personnel of industry. A reasonable hypothesis is that the meagerness of the income differential (such meagerness seems to be quite important in creating the observed state of affairs), is a direct result of workers' management. One might hypothesize that the very apparent self-interest of the general director in this question pre-

[6] Although there are no reliable estimates of the extent of moonlighting, one Yugoslav author describes total income earned outside of regular workhours as constituting more than 30 percent of the income of all employees (V. Svjetičanin, "Caractéristiques et dilemmes du socialisme autogestif yougoslave," *Praxis*, international edition, VIII, 3-4, 1971, p. 512). While this estimate would seem exaggerated, it does suggest that moonlighting is a widespread phenomenon.

[7] Josip Županov, "Is Enterprise Management Becoming Professionalized?" *International Studies of Management & Organization*, III, 3 (1973), table 19, p. 66. (This is a translation from *Moderna Organizacija*, 1968, 10.) A letter from the author indicates that the respondents were drawn heavily from large firms, and that there were probably few if any from enterprises with less than two hundred employees.

[8] Ibid., table 27, p. 76. No more than 15 percent of the sixty general directors surveyed said that they definitely wished to continue as general directors, but the author of the study thinks that the self-selection of the respondents (only those attending a symposium on management were questioned) probably makes them an unrepresentative sample in this regard.

[9] *Vjesnik u Srijeda (VUS)*, April 19, 1972, pp. 22-23, summarized in *ABSEES*, July 1972.

vents him from offering leadership to the workers' council in broadening the differential, even though such broadening would probably be to the longer-run advantage of all personnel in the enterprise. But an alternative hypothesis is that the mystique of egalitarianism, both within socialist countries generally and in Yugoslavia in particular, prevents the differential between the semiskilled worker and the general director from being enlarged,[10] and that rank-and-file engineering salaries must be linked to those offered abroad. In any case, I have heard of no clashes between top managers and the workers' councils of their enterprises over the issue of managerial salaries. Top managers express their dissatisfaction by looking for other jobs rather than by struggling within the firm.[11]

Attitude toward enterprise risk.[12] In comparison of managerial and stockholder control in capitalist firms, it has been suggested that top management is more motivated toward the avoidance of risk. We can express the objective function (goals) of both groups in the following equation:

$$O = f (P, {}^-R, {}^-V)$$

where

O $=$ objective function
P $=$ expected discounted value of future profits, beyond the opportunity cost of equity capital
R $=$ degree of risk with regard to earning the expected value of future discounted profits
V $=$ expected coefficient of variation between years in the realization of expected profits

[10] Županov argued at the 1970 meeting of the Yugoslav Association for Sociology that egalitarianism is one of the dominant values of Yugoslav society. He was, however, criticized for this view by V. Milić, J. Obradović, and B. Jakšić, who all viewed egalitarianism as a value which is accepted only by certain sectors of the society. (B. Jakšić in *Praxis*, international edition, VIII, 3-4, 1971, pp. 658 and 663-64.)

[11] Such search may be abroad, but more frequently it seems to be in other Slovenian economic sectors where pay for all categories of the labor force is higher. In either case, a Slovenian who accepts a post as general director can only rarely be viewed as making an investment in his own human capital on which he realizes through higher salary in his next position.

[12] The subject examined here is the degree to which different categories of employees are more or less receptive to the taking of risks by their own enterprise. This is a different question from that of the attitudes of the different groups as to which categories of employees will or should suffer the consequences of unsuccessful enterprise risk taking, or as to whether government should bail out unsuccessful enterprises. For a treatment of these latter two questions, shown in a mid-1966 survey of ten Croatian enterprises, see J. Županov, "The Producer and Risk," *Ekonomist*, 1967, 3, as translated in *Eastern European Economics*, VII, 3 (1969), 12-28.

Top management's objective function is viewed as giving higher weight to reducing R and V than is the case in the stockholders' objective function; this is because top management is subject to dismissal—and resultant major loss of income—if there are individual years in which the company has a particularly bad profit position.

Would we expect similar risk avoidance by top management, in comparison with workers' representatives, in the Yugoslav firm? The materials presented above on the low-income differentials for top managers, and on the difficulty of persuading competent experts to be candidates for such posts, suggest that the fear of dismissal after a year or two of bad enterprise performance would be much less of a deterrent to risk taking by Yugoslav than by capitalist managers.

Another aspect of this question, however, is the importance to managerial candidates of having good contacts within the organization for which they are to work.[13] The need for local contacts was suggested by many Yugoslavs with whom I spoke; proven competence is not sufficient in a society which still leans as heavily upon personal ties as upon proven competence.[14] Doubtless this is an important reason why, in the enterprises where I interviewed, two former general directors were working in lesser managerial posts. The difficulty of finding an acceptable position in another organization, and the psychological problems involved in working in a lower post in one's old enterprise, must serve as a deterrent to risk taking for many top managers.[15]

Going below the level of top management, we might expect that ordinary engineers and skilled workers in the enterprises of Slovenia would generally favor risk taking. This is because successful risks should lead to higher incomes for all members of the enterprise's workforce. The reduction in income resulting from unsuccessful risk can be countered by these personnel—in view of the full employment of the republic—by switching to another more successful enterprise. It is only groups which are peculiarly attached to the enterprise—foremen and older workers would probably constitute such categories—which are likely to be averse to risk.

Top managers might behave like one or the other of these two groups

[13] See Županov, "Is Enterprise Management Becoming Professionalized?" table 22, p. 70.

[14] See, for example, S. J. Rawin, "Social Values and the Managerial Structure," *Journal of Comparative Administration*, II, 2 (1970), 149-52.

[15] Out of a sample of general directors which was weighted toward Slovenians, and where the responses were given near the end of a recession period, half indicated that a general director who lost his post might easily remain jobless (Županov, "Is Enterprise Management Becoming Professionalized?" table 21, p. 68). From the context, however, it appears that those responding in this way may have meant only that they might not find a suitable position outside their own enterprise.

of nonmanagerial personnel, depending upon their self-perceived ability to find employment elsewhere. Those in Slovenia who are working in large urban centers and who have widespread personal contacts are most likely to react similarly to the first category; those in other republics, where the rate of unemployment is far higher, may well fall into the second. In any case, however, there is nothing peculiar in this regard about top management per se.[16]

Attitude toward growth and foreign operations. Growth of the enterprise is a sphere in which both upper and middle managers have a psychological stake which differentiates them from the remainder of the workforce. For, although growth as such does not seem peculiarly favorable either to an increase in the earnings per worker in the enterprise or to the greater security of such earnings, top managers who are concerned with the power and prestige of their posts find these increased by size itself. Middle managers in Yugoslav enterprises, just as in capitalist companies, are likely to find the opportunities for promotion augmented by the process of growth.[17] Thus, to the degree that power and prestige constitute managerial motivations, one would expect managers at all levels to be peculiarly favorable to growth.[18] In this regard, managerial interest is the same in both Yugoslav and capitalist enterprises.

An interest in foreign operations—particularly in western Europe—

[16] An additional reason for top managers to favor risk taking is that they may receive special individual bonuses linked to the increase in profits of the enterprise. Adizes describes this as existing in one of the two Serbian enterprises which he studied, and here even monthly variations in the income of top executives were very sharp (Ichak Adizes, *Industrial Democracy: Yugoslav Style*, The Free Press, New York: 1971, pp. 51-55). I myself have run across such top-management bonuses in only one enterprise, and this was in a firm which was in bad financial shape and with low earnings both for workers and for top managers.

Adizes, in commenting on a draft of this manuscript, offered an interesting explanation as to why Yugoslav managers may take less risks than do managers of capitalist firms. His argument is that risky enterprise plans are peculiarly liable to have to be altered, with resultant reductions of distributed income below that expected earlier. The need in Yugoslavia for directors to gain acceptance of changes by organs of workers' management causes plan modifications to be extremely difficult to push through, and causes them to be accompanied by interpersonal and intergroup conflicts. (See ibid., especially pp. 130-31, 159-64, and 230-31 for a treatment of these issues.)

[17] Even growth through merger is likely, in Yugoslav just as in capitalist firms, to provide such increased promotion opportunities for the middle managers of the "mother" firm. Although different Yugoslav enterprises in which I have interviewed have taken varied positions as to the retention of the bulk of top managers of the less-successful firms with which they have merged, in all cases there has been some increase of opportunities for middle managers from the original enterprise.

[18] A well-informed Yugoslav, commenting on a draft of this manuscript, rejected completely the view that managers and workers have different interests with regard to growth. He did not, however, attempt to justify his position.

seems to be another strong managerial motivation. Such operations provide opportunities for travel abroad in more developed parts of the world, for financial gains from travel expenses, and for the chance for some to live in western Europe for considerable periods while still retaining their ties in Yugoslavia. (Of course, I do not intend to suggest that these constitute the principal reasons why Yugoslav enterprises operate abroad; presumably, the enterprise itself generally gains from such operations.) The strength of such personal interest is indicated by an example in one enterprise in which I interviewed: the previous general director had resigned this position to take on the general directorship of a subsidiary company formed in western Europe. This managerial interest in foreign operations is one which is likely to be found particularly in enterprises—whether private or socialist—which are headquartered in less-developed countries.

Attitudes arising from differences in social values. A possible source of conflict between top managers and the mass of employees may be found in the different value systems of the two groups. Even where there is no conflict between their personal interests, one group may give more emphasis to certain desiderata relative to others because of systematic variations in their welfare functions.

For example, in a period of marketing difficulties for an enterprise, top managers might prefer to see dismissal of workers, while ordinary workers who themselves felt secure from dismissal might opt for a general reduction in wages within the enterprise.[19] Two possible explanations for such differences in attitude might be offered. The first is a difference in values, with top management emphasizing efficiency and seeing no need for the enterprise to act as a charitable organization for unneeded personnel.[20] The second is a different (better?) perception of consequences on the part of top managers; one general director who had pushed through dismissals within his own enterprise told me that an opposite policy would have led to reduced long-run viability of the firm because of resignations by the more efficient workers.

Attitudes toward profit maximizing might also be differentiated in this fashion. In terms of the purely economic interests of all existing em-

[19] Both enterprise reactions have been observed in practice in Yugoslav firms.

[20] This is suggested, although not shown, by the responses of political leadership and professional groups compared to workers and peasants in a national Yugoslav sample. Here, workers and peasants (unfortunately, a combined group in the study) gave substantially more emphasis to the importance of minimizing income differentials among all people and to the desirability of providing urban work opportunities for villagers. (M. G. Zaninovich, "Elites and Citizenry in Yugoslav Society: A Study of Value Differentiation," in *Comparative Communist Political Leadership*, David McKay Co., New York: 1973, pp. 231-32 and 248-50.)

ployees of a single enterprise, the enterprise goal of maximum earnings (in the form both of wages and net profits) per member of the labor force is the rational objective.[21] Yet managers seem often to be interested in the total amount of profits which can be earned with a given capital stock (such profits being computed on the basis of the existing wage scale set by the enterprise) rather than in profits per man. This managerial attitude might be explained in terms of the greater psychological stake of managers than of ordinary workers in enterprise growth. Alternatively, however, it could be explained by the fact that a maximum total profit goal is consistent with international managerial literature—whether coming from capitalist or from CMEA countries—and may thus be associated with "good management practice" in the minds of unsophisticated Yugoslav managers.

I know of no information as to whether such systematic differences in attitudes actually exist in Yugoslavia. But it is interesting to note that the single study of values in Yugoslavia of which I am aware points to a similarity of values among local political leaders (including enterprise general directors) and professional groups, in contrast to peasants and workers (including members of enterprise workers' councils).[22] If this should also hold for the values which are relevant to enterprise decisions, it suggests that top management's values are likely to be similar to those of ordinary engineers who, as previously noted, constitute the nonmanagerial groups most qualified to provide leadership to workers' management organizations. If such is the case, workers' management bodies are unlikely to develop positions which conflict sharply with top management values.

Attitudes toward participation in decision making by groups outside of top management. There would appear to be two distinct reasons why top management might hold a different attitude toward "worker management" than that held by the mass of employees.

The first reason is that top management may regard worker participation as a potential threat to its own decision-making power. So long as the workers' management bodies accept top-management recommendations, they are harmless. But the moment they adopt independent positions, they may be viewed as destructive of good management practices. Thus one study of managerial (heavily Slovenian) views showed that 82 percent of the general directors, and 67 percent of other higher and middle managers, felt that the general director has insufficient formal decision-making power. Items which were pointed to particularly were

[21] This is true, however, only when one takes as given the skill composition of the labor force.

[22] Zaninovich, pp. 229 and 249-50.

personnel questions (including discipline and rewards) and the choice of the other members of the director's "team."[23]

What, however, is the operational significance of such a top-management attitude? Unable to gain the desired formal power, one might expect top managers in enterprises to take actions designed to give them the actual powers which they consider desirable if they are properly to carry out their responsibilities. Presumably, the most effective way to achieve such a program is the attempt to structure the composition of the workers' management, Party, and trade union organs in such a way that they will support top-management recommendations. But this in no way differs from the approach of any other organized group in the enterprise, which can best advance its own ideas by pushing its own spokesmen for election or by forming coalitions with other groups in the workers' management bodies. Top management can here act only in the same fashion as other power groups within the enterprise, although admittedly it is in the best position to be effective.

The second reason is more interesting. Top management is unique among the various groups of the enterprise in that its members do not require any system of workers' management in order to get the pleasures of participation in decision making. As a consequence, in cases where efficiency of decision making is believed by all to be reduced by the lengthy processes of discussion which may be required in the workers' management organs, top managers may well have a different view of the resulting cost-benefit ratio.

To put the issue another way, top managers receive no personal benefit from reduction of "alienation" through the existence of workers' management organs, while the other members of the labor force do receive such benefits.[24] On the other hand, the time costs involved in the multitude of meetings of such bodies are born disproportionately by the members of top management. Even if the meetings can be depended upon to provide support for top-management views, it would not be surprising if top managers viewed such participatory democracy more negatively than does the rest of the labor force.

Various Yugoslav studies suggest that most workers view the benefit to them of workers' management as lying more in their having the op-

[23] Županov, "Is Enterprise Management Becoming Professionalized?" tables 9, 10, 11, and 12, pp. 57-59.

[24] It should, however, be noted that a survey among the workers in two Slovenian enterprises showed that the degree of participation in workers' management was uniformly placed at the bottom of the list of factors of employment having motivational importance (Arzenšek 1969 study as referred to in E. Neuberger and E. James, "The Yugoslav Self-Managed Enterprise: A Systemic Approach," in M. Bornstein (ed.), *Plan and Market*, Yale University Press, New Haven and London: 1973, p. 280).

portunity to present their views than in their power to make the actual decisions.[25] Thus "alienation" may well be countered even when top-management views always carry the day. Junior- and middle-management personnel, moreover, would seem to have a very special stake in workers' management; it is in these bodies that they can most readily bring themselves to top management's attention by well-argued proposals which cannot be dismissed out of hand, as well as being able to advance views which have been earlier rejected by their immediate superiors. For them particularly, workers' management would appear to be an attractive institution.

All this suggests that top management has a stake in reducing workers' management meetings to formalities which can be passed over quickly, while the other members of the labor force have a reverse interest. This is quite independent of the nature of the decisions which emanate from such meetings.

Social pressure upon top management from outside the enterprise. Perhaps the most significant element of top-management control is the fact that general directors appear to be subject to influence from the commune, republic, and federal levels (although particularly from that of the commune), while members of the workers' management bodies are relatively immune to such influence. Social pressure from both government and Party bodies at these levels can be placed on general directors to a degree which is quite impossible to exercise on the other members of the enterprise community. It is this which causes the general director's post to be viewed by many as highly political.[26]

Such social pressures provide a means additional both to the market place, and to such direct measures as price controls and foreign exchange allocations, for taking account of objectives external to the enterprise. Expansion of employment through the avoidance of capital-intensive investments is one possible example of such an objective.

[25] Ibid., p. 280.

[26] See Rawin, p. 142; B. Horvat, "Yugoslav Economic Policy in the Post-War Period," *American Economic Review*, LXI, 3, Part 2 (1971), 100. G. Lemân, "Ungelöste Fragen im jugoslawischen System der Arbeiterselbstverwaltung," *Berichte des Bundesinstituts für Ostwissenschaftliche und Internationale Studien*, 1969, 37, p. 28. The major study of value differentiation among different groups in Yugoslav society classifies general directors of enterprises as part of the political leadership, while members of workers' councils are classified simply as workers and peasants (Zaninovich, p. 229). In Županov's study of directors, over one-third of the general directors, and roughly half of the other upper- and middle-management personnel, considered that the population conceives the role of general director as being primarily a sociopolitical function (Županov, "Is Enterprise Management Becoming Professionalized?" table 1 and footnote 5, pp. 45 and 81).

Maintenance of a high ratio of internal savings by successful enterprises is a second example; this serves the twin objectives of expanding employment and of restraining inequality of employee income as between different enterprises of the same commune. Pressure to merge with unsuccessful enterprises and thus bail them out of their difficulties is a third example. Although such pressures constitute clear interference with the rights of self-management at the enterprise level, they provide a major method for taking account of externalities. They appear to be viewed as least objectionable, both politically and ideologically, when exerted by organizations at the level of the enterprise's own commune.

Commune and other extra-enterprise organizations can exert pressure in two ways. The first is to internalize into the self-managing enterprises the external economies: e.g., attempt to make otherwise-undesirable mergers a condition for bank loans and government aid. In reacting to this type of pressure, the enterprise general director has no special interest different from that of the workers' management bodies. In his fulfillment of the political role of negotiating with the extra-enterprise organizations, he is acting simply as the representative of workers' management—although, it is true, his awareness of the degree to which the externalities are internalized is likely to be far sharper than that of his colleagues, and he may thus be placed in the position of pushing unpopular decisions.

The second method of pressure by organizations outside the enterprise is quite different: it is to internalize with regard to the general director's own career, but not with regard to the welfare of the enterprise as a whole, the externalities described above. It is precisely because higher organizations do have such power over the general director, but not to any appreciable degree over other individuals involved in workers' management within the enterprise, that top-management control may be contrasted with that of workers' management. To the degree that such pressure is exercised effectively, a top-management-controlled enterprise will be one whose decisions are reflective of social (usually commune) considerations external to the enterprise itself. The behavior of such an enterprise might be expected to be rather different from that of a workers' controlled one.

General directors are fair game for commune political pressure partly because of the existence of a system of reelection every four years. At least until 1968 (and probably thereafter as well), a nominating committee, composed both of representatives of the commune and of the enterprise workers' council, has nominated a single candidate for general director. Although the workers' council can reject the nominee, it has been restricted in its choice of a candidate to one who has passed the nominating committee.[27] Yugoslav investigators take the view that political forces outside of the enterprise have a decisive impact on the reelection; the president of the local commune council and the head of the commune Party organization are said normally to have the last word.[28] Županov writes that the importance of political backing at the commune level became increasingly important for general directors in 1972 and 1973, and that without this they could be forced to resign.

The second reason that the general director is subject to outside political pressure is that, as previously noted, he is often concerned with finding a more attractive position in another organization. Only commune or republic political connections can serve him as a substitute for personal connections within that enterprise.

Finally, the general director is himself a part of the commune's political elite and, as such, is likely not only to have internalized at least some of the social considerations of this group but also to feel under a moral compulsion to accept its hierarchy of values.[29]

One might suspect that the same political pressures could be applied to the key people in the enterprise's workers' management organizations as to the general director. My impression, however, is that this is not the

[27] One foreign author (Albert Meister, *Où va l'autogestion yougoslave?*, éditions anthropos, Paris: 1970, p. 52) asserts that these nominating committees have been abolished; however, he cites no source, and insists that commune influence has nevertheless continued. A second foreign author (Stephen R. Sacks, *Entry of New Competitors in Yugoslav Market Socialism*, Institute of International Studies, University of California, Berkeley, Research Series, 19: 1973, p. 10) interprets the constitutional amendment xv of 1969 as abolishing all national requirements for commune representation on the nominating committee. Županov wrote me in late 1973 that, to his knowledge, the nominating committees had never been abolished; he agrees with Sacks' interpretation of Amendment xv. It appears, he wrote, that compulsory commune representation on these committees will once again be reintroduced by the new constitution. Although one of my sources in an enterprise said that these nominating committees were abolished in 1968, my other interviewees indicated that the committees continued. I would suspect that there is variation among individual enterprises.

In one interview, I was also told that there are a few enterprises where the republic government substitutes for the commune in having representation on the nominating committee. Roggeman writes of such representation as being additional (H. Roggeman, *Grundlagen des Jugoslawischen Betriebsverfassungs- und Unternehmensrechts*, Osteurope-Institut an der Freien Universität Berlin: 1968, p. 18, and Neuberger and James, p. 34).

In at least three of the firms in which I interviewed, the workers' council or managing board also elects the other members of top management. But there does not appear to have been any direct commune representation in the choice of these managers.

[28] This, for example, is the view of J. Županov.

[29] A well-informed Yugoslav who commented on my draft acknowledged the existence of these commune and other nonenterprise pressures upon general directors. Nevertheless, he felt that they are both weaker and less common than the reader would think from my writing. Županov, on the other hand, thought that I understate these pressures.

case except to the degree that they are themselves members of middle management, and as such subject to the influence of the general director himself.

From my interviews in enterprises, I have data concerning thirty-eight past and present key officers of workers' management bodies of eight enterprises. The positions chosen for such examination are: head of the workers' council, head of the managing board, head of the Party organization of the enterprise, and head of the trade union organization of the enterprise.[30] Although different enterprises have varying rules, generally none of the occupants of these posts can hold it for more than three years in succession, including reelections.[31]

Of the thirty-eight such officers for whom I have data, only three were reported as having held another post of similar importance in the same enterprise or in the commune,[32] and none were reelected to the same position after the passage of some years. While my data may be incomplete, it seems most unlikely that an accurate count would raise the figure to more than six. Generally speaking, these officers seem to have been members of the nonmanagerial power elite of the enterprise for only one or two years, and then to have dropped out of all prominence. While it is true that some of them doubtless continued to play an informal influential role in workers' organizations,[33] they were far from leading a continual and prominent political life in either the enterprise or the commune. They would seem to be in a very different position from that of the general director, and thus not susceptible to political pressure from outside.

The exposure of the general director to pressure from the commune is weakened to the degree that either of the following two conditions holds: (1) His enterprise is in fact free to reelect its own general director, being able to resist any commune pressures in this regard. (2) The

[30] While only the first two have formal powers in workers' management, it is clear that these are the four key nonmanagerial positions in any enterprise. In no enterprise was there any objection to my lumping these four posts together as the major nonmanagerial positions to study. For an analysis of the critical informal role of the "Political Active" in one enterprise, see Adizes.

[31] In only one enterprise was there a four-year term for the Party secretary.

[32] One head of a managing board with a one-year term had had, four years earlier, a similar one-year term as head of the Party organization of the enterprise. A second man had been head of a managing board for one year, and this term was followed consecutively by a two-year term as head of the workers' council; after this he was a member of the council of the city (which combined several communes). A third man had a term as head of a managing board followed by membership in the commune council.

[33] I received no information as to the degree that they served as ordinary members of the workers' council, managing board, Party committee of the enterprise, or union committee. To some degree, they doubtless rotated among these lesser posts, as well as among the host of others in the enterprise of still more minor importance.

general director has no strong interest in retaining this top management status, either at his own or at another enterprise.

I find it impossible to judge how effective commune pressure has been in shaping the decisions of general directors. It is true that one study shows that over one-third of a sample of general directors believed that the community conceives of their role as primarily sociopolitical, but on the other hand over 40 percent believed that this role should (normatively) be of little importance, and only 2 percent believed that it should be very important.[34] Unfortunately, no questions were asked as to the actual importance of this role.

To sum up, it is my impression that top management interests differ from that of the worker community of the enterprise in a variety of ways. While I have no means of evaluating the significance of these differences for decision-making behavior, my guess is that one should lay primary stress upon the differential interests in enterprise growth and on the peculiar exposure of the general director to social pressure from commune authorities.

THE WORKERS' REPRESENTATIVES

It is the workers' council which has the last word on decision making in the enterprise. Not surprisingly, the council normally approves recommendations made by the general director. Thus, in the two Serbian enterprises studied by Kolaja, 60 percent of all the suggestions accepted by the council of one enterprise, and 73 percent of those accepted by that of the other, were made by either the general director or by one of his close managerial aids. During the course of a whole year, only one recommendation by the general director in one enterprise, and two recommendations in the other, were rejected or modified.[35] Those directorial recommendations which were rejected or modified dealt with matters most closely linked to direct worker interests: housing allotments to individual workers, and the amount of the factory's contribution to the trade union fund.

A second study was carried out by a Yugoslav team through observation of all workers' council meetings in twenty companies, located in four different republics, over a three-year period ending in December 1969. A total number of 2,736 proposals were accepted by these workers' councils; the proposals were categorized by the research team according

[34] Županov, "Is Enterprise Management Becoming Professionalized?" tables 1 to 4, pp. 45-51. In the normative questions, a distinction was made between the sociopolitical role and that of leader of the collective.

[35] Jiri Kolaja, *Workers' Councils: The Yugoslav Experience* (Praeger, N.Y. and Washington: 1966), pp. 22-23 and 47. These data cover one year of records (1958/59) and thirty-nine council sessions which the investigator himself attended.

to subject, and data have been presented concerning the source of the proposals in the four categories covering economic problems in the most general sense (marketing, cooperation with other companies, internal economic activity, and distribution of wages and other personal income by groups of employees).

Of the total proposals accepted in these four categories, between 47 and 60 percent in each category were put forth at the meeting by a member of top management—although these managers constituted only 1.7 percent of the total number of workers and employees in the company. Only 16 to 32 percent of the accepted proposals came from nonmanagers, while this category constituted 92 percent of total employment.[36]

A foreign student reported on a workers' council meeting he attended in an enterprise of Bosnia-Herzegovina, where there was much discussion as to the recommended distribution of apartments and as to allocation of bonuses between departments of the factory. But on a much more critical issue for the enterprise—that of raising prices and of increasing nominal wages of different groups in the workforce in a regressive fashion —the general director's recommendation was adopted almost without discussion.[37]

These reports suggest that, on significant matters, managerial recommendations are normally accepted without ado. But it would be wrong to conclude that this implies that top management alone makes the decisions. Adizes reports on two other Serbian enterprises which he studied in some depth during 1967; one of these had a strong general director, but the other seemed in fact to have the basic decisions made by collective agreement. However, these collective decisions in the second enterprise were ironed out in meetings of top management, department heads, and the heads of the workers' council, Party, and trade union bodies. Once important questions reached the workers' council, they could be adopted without much discussion because all those who carried weight in the decision-making process were already in agreement.[38] Thus the evidence cited above from Kolaja, Obradović, and Riddell cannot be taken as proof that top management made the important decisions in the plants they studied.

Nevertheless, it seems certain that this is indeed the case in a large proportion of Yugoslav enterprises. It is true in one of the two enter-

[36] Josip Obradović, "Distribution of Participation in the Process of Decision Making on Problems related to the Economic Activity of the Company," in *Participation and Self-Management* (papers presented at the December 1972 first international sociological conference on participation and self-management, Institute for Social Research, University of Zagreb, Zagreb: 1972 and 1973, volume II).

[37] D. S. Riddell, "Social self-government: the background of theory and practice in Yugoslav socialism," *British Journal of Sociology*, XIX, 1 (1968), 66-67.

[38] Adizes, chapter 4, especially pp. 88 and 106.

prises studied by Adizes, and Kolaja suggests that he believes it was true in both the firms he studied. Of the Slovenian enterprises I studied, it was clearly the case in three, while it was not at all true in two of them. In one of these latter, in fact, the previous general director had been forced out of his position because his basic policy for the enterprise's development was unacceptable to the workers' council.

But who are the people constituting the workers' management bodies of the enterprise? If one considers the total membership of workers' councils of enterprises in 1970 in Yugoslavia as a whole, 68 percent were manual workers by education and only 10 percent had higher education (including junior colleges). In the managing boards in the same year, 44 percent were manual workers by education and 27 percent had higher education. Of all chairmen of workers' councils, the respective figures were 51 and 19 percent; of all heads of managing boards, they were 41 and 28 percent. These national figures indicate that approximately one-half of the workers' representatives had a manual worker's education, a proportion which appears to constitute a serious decline from the 1965 situation.[39]

The situation seems to be different, however, if we consider as a group the four most important positions in workers' management of the larger industrial enterprises in which I have interviewed.[40] Table 12.1 shows the work positions in the enterprise of twenty-seven current holders of these positions in eight enterprises; this is a complete tabulation of those for whom I have information from my interviews, and all but three were in the seven Slovenian enterprises of my sample. One-third of these major social positions were headed by members of middle management, and another quarter by junior managers; manual workers constituted only 7 percent of the sample. Very similar results are obtained if one also includes the former holders of these positions about whom I have data, and thus raise the sample size to thirty-eight.[41]

These sample results conflict sharply with the national data as to an educational proxy for the work positions of the chairmen of workers'

[39] *Statistički 1972*, p. 67, and N. Jovanov, "Odnos Štrajka kao Društvenog Sukoba i Samoupravljanja kao Društvenog Sistema," *Revija za Sociologiju*, 1973, 1-2 (translated into French in *Participation and Self-Management*, I, pp. 62-96). Jovanov treats the above figures as though they were good approximations for the proportions actually working as manual workers, but one would suspect that they might represent a serious overestimate of such proportions.

[40] Data here refer to the head of the workers' council, head of the managing board, head of the enterprise Party organization, and head of the trade union enterprise organization.

[41] For former leaders of workers' management, their work post is taken as of the date at which they held the social position. Sixty-one percent of the larger sample of thirty-eight were members of middle or junior management.

TABLE 12.1: Work Posts of Current Heads of Workers'
Management Organizations (sample size = 27)

Work Post	Number	Percentage of Sample
Member of top management[a]	0	0
Head of a major department[b]	9	33
Head of a small section[c]	7	26
Foreman	2	7
White-collar employee, nonmanagerial	7	26
Manual worker[d]	2	7

[a] These are the top four or five management executives of the enterprise.

[b] One example is the head of production for three factories. Another is the head of maintenance for the enterprise. A third is the head of the foundry shop in an enterprise where this was an important unit.

[c] One of these sections, for example, is composed of twenty to thirty assembly workers. A second is customer service for the enterprise. A third is design of new products.

[d] One of the two manual workers was a chargehand (sub-foreman).

councils and management boards.[42] I suspect that this difference is explained by the fact that I am dealing here only with larger enterprises (seven of the eight had over one thousand employees, and the eighth was extremely capital intensive); it was explained to me in several of these firms that manual workers did not have the necessary business experience to hold such posts. But it is also possible either that education is a poor proxy for job position, or that my sample reflects a peculiarity of the more-developed north of Yugoslavia.

If these key social positions are indeed to be of significance in the decision-making process of the enterprise, it is not surprising that some 60 percent of them should be held by managerial personnel. Partly this is a question of finding individuals who have the training needed to react with comprehension to the general director's recommendations.[43]

[42] Of my nine chairmen of workers' councils, four belonged to middle management (heads of major departments) and none were manual workers. Of the four heads of managing boards, two were members of middle management and none were manual workers.

[43] In no enterprise did I hear of the workers' council or managing board receiving independent outside technical advice, nor was this referred to in either Kolaja's or Adizes' accounts of the operations of workers' management organs. Even in one enterprise where the general director himself meets every month with an outside council of four university professors, the chairman of the workers' council told me that the council itself has no access to these or other outside opinions except in cases where the general director shows the council outside reports as confirmation of his own views.

A Yugoslav reader of my manuscript has pointed out that a new organ has been

Partly it is a question that, given the reality shown earlier in this chapter of the rotation principle, only managerial personnel have a degree of continuity of position which allows them to consolidate their experience and interest—and, perhaps, social power—in the general affairs of the enterprise. But it is also a question of the very limited free time during working hours which is allotted to these key social officers to carry out their obligations. In the two enterprises for which I have data, only one man spent more than twenty hours a month of paid worktime on his social duties.[44] None but managerial personnel, if even they, would have the opportunity to familiarize themselves in depth with the relevant issues except through the use of their own off-duty hours. This situation contrasts sharply with that of the CMEA countries, where enterprises of this size would have either one or two full-time—and long-term—officials of social organizations (the Party and trade union).

Where managerial personnel fill the key social positions, they may decide that it is preferable to withhold certain information from the workers' council on the ground that its members would not interpret it correctly. Thus in one enterprise where all four major social posts were held by members of management, the workers' council was regularly informed as to the total profits[45] of the firm—but was given no information as to the profits earned on individual articles. Because profits as a percentage of sales varied between 5 and 25 percent on major products, and their percentage of both capital investment and wages varied rather similarly, there was fear that the revelation of these differences would raise sharp questions as to the product mix of the enterprise and as to its investment program. Managers believed that the continued expansion of low-profit items was essential both for commercial reasons and in order to generate foreign exchange through exports;[46] but they did not wish to have to defend this position before the manual worker members of the workers' council. Since they were able to keep this critical information secret, it is not surprising that managerial programs for the allocation of investment funds were always adopted by the council; the members had absolutely no basis for evaluating these programs.[47]

---

created in enterprises, partly to deal with this problem. The "workers' control" organ is elected by all the employees in the enterprise, and at least three-quarters of its membership must consist of manual workers. It has the right to call on the advice of experts outside the enterprise.

[44] This exception was a salesman who headed the managing board of one of these enterprises, and who devoted about one-fourth of his worktime to this function.

[45] Profits in this company are defined as the net income of the enterprise after paying the wage rate determined at the beginning of the year.

[46] The earning of foreign exchange was needed in order to finance the firm's own imports.

[47] Another enterprise took out a loan in 1967 on the condition that it would

Yet there are no grounds for thinking that this dominance of the key social positions by middle and junior managers weakens the power of the workers' management bodies in relation to the general director. If anything, the reverse should be the case.

Sociological literature, particularly that dealing with small groups, points to the dominant role in participatory decision making of those having expert knowledge of the problems under consideration.[48] If this conclusion is correct, we might expect workers' management bodies to be most independent of top management when such bodies are guided by employees who themselves have expert knowledge. Such employees are most likely to be found in the ranks of middle and junior managers. This is not to deny, however, that it is precisely such managers who are likely to be offered the greatest temptations to participate opportunistically, because of the control by top managers over their personal promotional opportunities. The net effect of these counterbalancing factors is uncertain, but I would expect the first to predominate in Slovenia because of the limited incentive for rising in the managerial hierarchy.

The enterprise I visited which was most autocratically run as a one-man operation, by a general director with over ten years of tenure in post, was also the only one with no managerial personnel in any of the key social positions. Here, the general director told me that it is he who de facto chooses the head of the workers' council and that—despite the fact that his own long seniority implies that he himself has had the opportunity to select his managerial personnel—he generally chooses a foreman or chargehand. His preference was guided in part by the belief that such a person, while more knowledgeable than a manual worker, serves as a better source of information about worker morale and complaints than would an engineer. But also he felt that his own attitude of investing as much as possible of the enterprise's income would find greater support among these personnel than among either manual workers or engineers.

In a lengthy interview with the four key social figures of this enterprise, their views as to their own role were shown to be such as to please an autocratic general director. All considered that a key task of the workers' council was to provide the workers with a *feeling* of self-administration, but to make decisions only in the one area of determining which

---

be repaid in foreign currency. This critical condition was kept secret from the workers' council, presumably for a similar reason (*Vjesnik*, July 2, 1971, p. 5, summarized in *ABSEES*, October 1971).

[48] M. Mulder, "Power Equalization through Participation?" *Administrative Science Quarterly*, 16, 1 (1971), 31-38. See particularly the laboratory experiment reported on p. 34, and the reference to the work on Yugoslav participation by M. J. Broekmeyer, *De Arbeidsraad in Zuidslavië* (Meppel, Boom: 1968).

individuals should receive priority for housing credits. The trade union task was seen primarily as explaining the general director's viewpoint to the workers, rather than of representing the workers (this was said in the context of a recent strike in one shop of the enterprise).[49]

In contrast to this enterprise, it is interesting to look at another where the general director had recently failed of reelection and had been demoted to a lower post in the same firm. This second enterprise was not only peculiar among those in which I interviewed in that it had one of the highest proportions of managerial personnel filling the key social posts, but it was unique in the degree that current middle- and upper-management personnel had earlier held these social posts in the same enterprise. The general director's downfall was over a policy issue: that of pressing merger with other enterprises. This is precisely the kind of issue about which managerial personnel would be most likely to feel strongly, pro or con. It is thus not surprising that it is in a firm of this type, where middle and top managers with independent power positions dominated the workers' management organizations, that we find the only recent ouster of a general director.[50]

Economic units. As explained in Chapter 11, these are lower organs of self-management at roughly the shop level, and each has its own elected body or is small enough to take decisions by vote of all those working in the unit. Since their formation in 1959, their proponents have viewed them as a means of counteracting the tendency for the individual worker's voice to be lost within the self-management bodies of large enterprises. These economic units serve as the pattern for the "basic organizations of united work" which are prescribed in the new Yugoslav constitution.

Economic units are officially considered to have two functions. The first is to deal with the individual problems of its members: discipline problems, allocation of the unit's housing-credit funds, etc. The second function is much broader: to act as a semi-independent unit within the

[49] A well-informed reader of my manuscript expressed the view that, while this used to be (presumably during the 1940's and 1950's) a fair depiction of the trade union task, this is no longer so today. He held that the trade union viewpoint expressed above is an exceptional one. On the other hand, Županov generalizes that trade unions are unable either to organize or support strikes in enterprises (J. Županov, "Two Patterns of Conflict Management in Industry," *Industrial Relations*, 12, 2, 1973, p. 220).

[50] While one would normally expect workers' management to operate more effectively in small enterprises than in large ones, the consideration that small enterprises are likely to have no managerial personnel with training and experience to challenge that of the general director works in the opposite direction. I know of no studies which examine the degree of success of workers' management in small versus large firms.

As was noted earlier, the situation changed in 1972 and 1973 when general directors were also ousted for political reasons.

total enterprise. In fulfilling this second function, the economic unit may sell its products to other units within the enterprise—and sometimes even outside the enterprise—and derive an income which it has "earned" in the same sense that the enterprise earns its income on the wider national and international market. The economic unit, like the normal Yugoslav enterprise, is permitted to determine its distribution of income between payments to members and retained earnings. Retained earnings may be loaned—and an interest rate charged—by one unit to another within the same enterprise. At the extreme, the enterprise fades into relative oblivion and it is the economic unit which is all important. This is the theory of economic units, but practice deviates sharply from it.[51]

While all of the enterprises which I studied presumably have economic units, this second function was taken seriously in only two of eleven, and one of these had been chosen for study specifically because of its national reputation as an enterprise in which the institution of economic units was well developed. Thus the second function of semi-independence should not be viewed as having widespread application in present-day Yugoslav firms.

It is true that the wage system in use in a number of the other enterprises allows each economic unit to receive for income distribution whatever it "earns." In explaining this, it is necessary to begin with an exposition of the Yugoslav wage pattern. Normally, all personnel receive standard time wages (or piece rates) set for the enterprise as a whole. Added to this are "variable wages" distributed with the regular pay envelope; these sometimes depend upon the results (output or cost reduction) achieved by the enterprise as a whole, but more usually seem to be attached to the achievements of each individual economic unit. The sum of these two forms of wages are deducted from the income earned by the enterprise over the course of the year, and the residual of "profit" is allocated either to retained earnings or to further distribution to the workforce.

In six of the eight enterprises for which I have such information, the amount of "variable wages" depended on the results of each economic unit individually.[52] Conceptually, this not only gave each economic unit a direct incentive—and one relevant to all of its personnel—to improve the efficiency of the unit as a whole, but it also permitted the workers

---

[51] There are a very few Yugoslav enterprises, always or generally formed by merger, in which the enterprise is in fact essentially just a cartel and virtually all power is held by the constituent component bodies (see Sacks, pp. 12 and 62-63). These enterprises operate under a special charter. The term "economic units," as used in this section, does not refer to the constituent parts of these few enterprises.

[52] This system had also previously been used in a seventh enterprise, but the system had been renounced before the time of my visit there.

of each unit to determine for themselves the degree to which they wished to work more intensively for higher pay.

The "results" of each economic unit were measured against the plan for that unit as established by the enterprise management and approved by the enterprise's workers' council.[53] In order to reduce disputes between economic units, the annual plan seems often to have been based primarily upon the results of the previous year. In one enterprise where this procedure was followed most closely, the distribution of the enterprise's investment among the various economic units turned out to be the primary influence upon their relative percentages of variable wages during the following year or two. So as to avoid the quarrels among the economic units which result from this pattern of planning, another enterprise used the monthly plan (rather than the annual one) as the standard against which to evaluate "results," and the monthly plan was set so as to provide equal percentages of variable wages for all units; in an instance where even this procedure yielded different percentages between units, the plan was modified post hoc so as to solve the problem.

In two of the six enterprises which determined variable wages according to the results of the individual units, top management reported that in fact the percentages were always virtually identical between units.[54] In another enterprise which had abolished this system, the differences between units had been kept to between ½ and 1½ percent of the unit's wages. It was only in three enterprises that the variable wages differed significantly, and in one of these the differences depended primarily upon earlier investment over which the units had no control. The other two enterprises are A and B, which will be discussed below. These are the two in which the institution of economic units was taken seriously.

Although enterprise A is so organized that each of its six economic units has a very unusual degree of independence, nevertheless both the enterprise and each unit appear to be under unchallenged managerial rule. In the words of the head of the workers' council, it is felt that "one must trust the specialists." The decisive decision-making body of the enterprise is not the workers' council, but rather a collegium composed of the six management heads of the economic units plus the general director and his deputy.

[53] This was explicitly the case in five of the six enterprises; in enterprise B, to be described below, it was also the case de facto.

[54] No information was available for a third enterprise. For one where there were differences, no information is availabie as to the actual variation of percentages; but top management considered it significant. For a second such enterprise, the difference for 1969 as a whole between average earnings of a given skill grade of worker in the best and worst economic unit was about 10 percent of total earnings. For a third, the 1969 range was about 15 percent.

Each of the economic units handles its own sales, sets its own prices for sales outside of the enterprise, determines its own product mix, and decides on its own purchasing. Although it is the collegium of managers which determines the allocation to each of the departments of foreign exchange for imports, in fact this is fairly proportional to the earnings of each department through exports. However, it is the enterprise—rather than the economic units—which determines investments and sets wages. Thus, while most managerial decisions are decentralized to the level of the economic unit, those decisions of greatest interest to the workers are concentrated at the enterprise level.

Although the economic units are expected to develop their current plans in terms of profit-maximizing criteria, sales to other economic units within the factory are made at standard costs; since such standard costs remain unchanged for an entire year, despite the rapid inflation in the prices of purchased materials, this means that such intra-enterprise sales are made at prices below actual cost. These intra-enterprise sales are quantitatively quite important for some of the economic units; yet the manager of one unit, which sells 30 to 40 percent of its production within the enterprise, could see no harm in this pricing system. He insisted that economic units are neither reluctant to make such sales nor suffer from them, despite the sharply negative effects upon their profits.

This surprising outcome is made possible through the coordination exercised by the managerial collegium of the enterprise. This collegium gives each economic unit an annual plan (expressed only in money) for total sales and for total costs which include base wages. The members of each unit then receive monthly variable wages, or deductions from base wages, which depend upon the unit's actual profits relative to its planned profits. These monthly deviations can be between plus and minus 20 percent of base wage for personnel at the rank of foreman and higher, and half of that percentage for all other personnel. Presumably, an economic unit's profit plan is adjusted during the year to take account of changing conditions of intra-enterprise sales.

The variations by economic unit from base wages are, in fact, enforced. During the year before my visit to the enterprise, the difference between total annual earnings of people with the same base wage was approximately 10 percent between the most and least successful economic unit. During the month immediately prior to my visit, managers in one of the six economic units received only 80 percent of their base salary, and in a second they received only 90 percent; in the best department, they received 10 percent above base salary.

Clearly, this system must make for struggle between the economic units over their respective annual profit plans. The managerial head of one of these economic units believed that the enterprise suffered from the resulting difficulties of coordination of the six units and from what he considered to be excessive decentralization. However, as between years—although not as between individual months—the same economic units have remained in the top half of the total group as measured by plan fulfillment, and thus by variable wages.

But this enterprise's system is best described as one of extreme managerial decentralization, rather than as being geared to encourage greater worker participation than could be achieved through centralized management. Thus, while the system is espoused under the ideology of economic units and worker participation, its results do not seem particularly related to this goal.

Enterprise B was selected for interviewing precisely because of its national reputation as a leader in the development of economic units. The labor force of 14,500 is divided into sixty-three large economic units with an average labor force of 230 workers, and each of these in turn is divided into an average of five work units. All general meetings of the labor force occur at the level of the small work unit; but both the work unit and the economic unit have their own elected workers' councils.

Although many of the economic units carry on similar activities, and are divided into work units in identical fashion, the enterprise as a whole is sufficiently vertically integrated so that there are a great many transfers of semifinished goods between economic units. These transfers are carried out through intra-enterprise sales, and the price for a given semifinished item is the same regardless of which economic unit is the purchaser or seller. In fact, to the degree possible, these intra-enterprise sales are made at market prices. When one economic unit requires more investment funds than it has available from its own resources, its first source of finance will be the temporarily-surplus retained earnings of other economic units; the borrowing economic unit pays the lender an interest rate calculated as that which it would have had to pay for bank borrowing. Thus enterprise B not only has economic units which are about 2/7ths the size of those of enterprise A, but in theory enterprise B is still more decentralized with regard to the linkage between these units.

In fact, however, enterprise B was operated as a fairly centralized firm. Base wages are set by the workers' council of the enterprise. Although theoretically each individual work unit has the right to allocate its income after base wages between variable wages, investment, and reserves, in practice the economic unit makes recommendations which are unchallengeable.[55] The same applies to the recommendations coming

[55] The public relations spokesman of the enterprise, who was a strong ideologue for economic units, found inconceivable the notion that a work unit might reject these recommendations. He said that it was the task of the leader of the work

from the enterprise's workers' council to the economic unit itself.[56] While in theory each work unit determines its own production plan and product mix, in fact both the work units and economic units are completely guided in these respects by the enterprise's general management.

It is planned that individual economic units and work units will earn differing amounts of profit per employee, as one might expect from the system described earlier. What happens, however, is that the enterprise administration "recommends" to the different economic units that they allocate differing proportions of their profit for retained earnings, in this way leveling out the total per capita wage planned at the beginning of the year for distribution between the different economic units.[57] In fact, actual monthly earnings by members of different economic units who have similar base wages do differ substantially: the maximum range between the economic units in 1969 was approximately 15 percent. But this is due essentially to variations in the degree to which the different economic units earn their planned profit, rather than to differing percentage allocations for retained earnings. Within the individual economic units (or, at least, within the one in which I conducted interviews), a principle of "solidarity" is applied so that all work units normally receive the same percentage of variable to base wages.

Investment decisions are de facto decided completely at the level of the enterprise, with funds being taken from those economic units whose retained earnings are higher than their investment needs. Although accounts are kept as to loans made by one economic unit to another, and interest is calculated on these loans, this is purely a bookkeeping operation since the funds are used exclusively for investment.[58] Nor does an accumulation of credits on this account give any one economic unit a particularly strong claim for investment allocations in following years.

Thus we can see that the extensive use of the institution of economic units in enterprise B did not in any way lead to decentralization in matters of importance to the enterprise's well-being. The work units and

unit to persuade the membership to accept recommendations from its superior economic unit. On pressing, he finally said that the workers' council of the economic unit would keep sending back the same recommendations to the work unit until they were accepted.

[56] The only freedom in income distribution for the economic unit is between allocation to variable wages and to reserves; the latter are small, and are used solely to assure the economic unit's members against their earnings falling below 100 percent of fixed wages.

[57] While, on average for the enterprise as a whole, 80 percent of prewage income was spent on wages (both base and variable), the range between economic units varied from 67 to 97 percent.

[58] The enterprise director who told me the rate of interest charged on these internal loans thought that my questioning him as to this was quite amusing. Obviously, the interest rate used had no significance to anyone.

economic units have the right to make suggestions for their own production plans, and—a point which was heavily stressed—to ask for additional information concerning measures which are proposed to them. But their only real powers relate to the treatment of individual workers.

It is the work unit's council in enterprise B which determines the base wage of each worker within the unit, although this must be within the range set for the job by the workers' council of the enterprise. The council of the economic unit decides on disciplinary punishments (including dismissals) for the unit's members, and no appeal is permitted to the workers' council of the enterprise. Finally, new apartments are allocated to individuals by a commission of each economic unit's council. These were the only actual decisions which seem to be made by either unit.[59]

To sum up this section, unusually intensive development of economic units may—but need not—lead to managerial decentralization within the enterprise.[60] In no enterprise which I have studied has it led to significant worker participation at the level of the economic unit in determining questions of importance to the enterprise as a whole. Rather, economic units at their best perform three functions. (1) They serve as a means of providing group-incentive pay for all members of a given unit, with the amount of the incentive pay being linked to the degree of fulfillment of the enterprise's plan for the unit. (2) They decide matters affecting individuals within the unit. (3) They provide a mechanism through which members of the unit can insist upon additional information from the enterprise's central management. It is this last function which was most heavily stressed by the workers' management representatives in enterprise B.

Significance of worker participation. It is my impression that the significance of workers' management organs in Yugoslavia is not to be found in mass decision making on issues of major importance to the enterprise and to the collective as a whole. The nearest approach to this in any enterprise I have seen was the agreement by all four holders of the main social positions in one enterprise that workers' management leads to somewhat higher earnings, and thus to lower investments, than top management would wish if it had a free rein; but not only was this difference viewed as marginal, but these worker representatives all regarded it as an unfortunate concomitant of the objective of bringing the mass of workers into agreement with managerial decisions. My impres-

---

[59] At least, my hard questioning of the president of one economic unit's council, as well as of his full-time assistant, revealed no further areas of decisions.

[60] One Slovenian sociologist stated in private discussion that he considers such strengthening of middle management at the expense of the central administration as the main accomplishment of the institution of economic units.

sion as to this limitation of workers' management is fully in line with the conclusions of Yugoslav sociologists.[61]

In the enterprise in which I interviewed where the workers' management organs had recently shown their power by ousting the general director, a key decision had been taken shortly afterward which greatly broadened the enterprise's product mix, necessitated the hiring of a considerable number of new workers, and promised to commit a substantial portion of the enterprise's future investment funds. The managing board had discussed the issue for several consecutive days before approving the management's recommendation, but the workers' council limited itself to a single hour's discussion. The Party and trade union role was described as that of convincing the masses in the enterprise that the decision was a good one.

The heads of the workers' management bodies of the enterprise explained to me why their decision was so easy to make. The managing board was persuaded by two factors: first, that a business bank was willing to give an investment loan for the project, thus demonstrating that an independent body thought the project sound; second, that the Chamber of Commerce of the republic had given its approval for this expansion of product mix, indicating that it also thought that the marketing position was good. The workers' council granted its approval on the dual basis that the managing board had already investigated the proposal, and that other Yugoslav enterprises were currently carrying on profitable production in the new product range. No further investigation was considered necessary. Doubtless, however, all this followed agreement among the individuals in positions of social and managerial power within the enterprise.

A second enterprise provides an interesting example of another major issue: that of a strike in one department. Workers here were paid by piece rates, and a change in production methods had been followed by a change in output norms per worker. This resulted in a spontaneous strike.

The strike was handled solely by the head of the enterprise trade union; neither the workers' council, the managing board, nor the Party played any role. The trade union secretary explained to the workers the nature of norm setting, and convinced them to return to work by using the argument that they could gain nothing by striking. Following their return, there were two days of discussion with the workers; but again it was only the head of the trade union who was involved. The four heads of the workers' management bodies explained to me that it did not matter from which organization the spokesman came; what was im-

---

[61] See Neuberger and James, pp. 275-77, and their references to the work of Županov and Možina.

portant was that he be someone who was a convincing speaker and who was on hand at the time.[62] In an earlier situation where a strike had been threatened, the trade union, the Party, and the personnel section of management were all involved in "explaining" norm setting to the workers. In neither case did the workers' council or managing board play any role.

Two interesting features stand out in both of these instances of strikes. The first, of course, is the total absence from the scene of the workers' council or managing board.[63] The second is that there was no review afterwards of the new norms to see whether the workers' complaints were justified; it was simply assumed that they were not. The Party did indeed get into the matter after the strike was settled; but it was not to see whether the new norms were faulty, but rather to investigate why a better explanation of them had not been given by either the trade union, the Party, or the foremen, so that no strike would have been threatened.

The absence of true decision making by the workers' council on major questions fits in well with the results of a study linking reduction of alienation to membership on a workers' council.[64] As the alienation thesis would suggest, both general work satisfaction and specific job satisfaction are correlated with the individual's perception of the degree of his own participation in decision making.[65]

When, however, the authors turn to the effect of being a longtime workers' council member on degree of work satisfaction, they find quite different results depending upon the individual's stated desire to participate. For those with low desire to participate, membership in the workers' council does increase work satisfaction as the alienation thesis would suggest. But for those with high desire to participate, membership has no effect upon work satisfaction.

This suggests that workers with a positive but low desire to participate do have their alienation from work reduced by membership. Influence as

[62] The trade union head struck me as being, in fact, both quite intelligent and the dominant personality among the four heads.

[63] A possible explanation for their passivity is that of role conflict: both bodies are expected to be the supreme managerial bodies and, at the same time, to represent the workers. For such an explanation, see J. Županov, "Two Patterns," pp. 213-23.

[64] J. Obradović, J.R.P. French, Jr., and W. L. Rodgers, "Workers' Councils in Yugoslavia," *Human Relations*, 23, 5 (1970), 459-71. The sample consists of two hundred twenty longtime members of workers' councils and three hundred nonmembers, both groups drawn from factories at different locations and with varying levels of technology. Members are defined as those who have belonged to a workers' council for a minimum of two years (this need not have been consecutive service), while nonmembers are those who have never belonged to a council.

[65] The questionnaire described such participation in terms of degree of influence over decision making. Although the effect of perceived participation is in the hypothesized direction, it accounts for only 2 to 3 percent of the total difference in work satisfaction among individuals.

a member is sufficient to meet their needs. But those with high desire for participation find that such membership gives them nothing like the degree of influence over decision making which they desire.[66]

The principle function of workers' management which was emphasized in the enterprises where I interviewed was that of providing more information to members of these bodies, in this way increasing their feeling of taking part in the community of the enterprise. There was considerable emphasis upon the right to pose questions to management and to insist upon answers. Kolaja, from his study of two Serbian enterprises, stresses both this information function, and that of informing management as to worker attitudes, as being the principal roles of workers' councils.[67]

Indeed, the heads of workers' management bodies with whom I spoke were in general surprisingly well informed as to the situation in their own enterprises, although they usually seemed to accept unquestioningly top management's interpretation of events which had occurred or were occurring. If one assumes that the same was true, although obviously to a lesser degree, of a large proportion of the rank-and-file members of these bodies, then the educational role of passing on information would seem to be carried out effectively.[68]

When one considers the high degree of rotation of members of workers' management bodies, and thus the large proportion of the total workforce which is involved in the activities of one or another body during any five-year period, this information function can be of extreme importance in combating alienation among the workers—even when top management makes all decisions of importance to the enterprise. Workers are indeed involved in the community of the enterprise to a greater extent than that of simply selling their labor power. Furthermore, if one thinks of the future development of workers' management in Yugoslavia,

[66] The authors suggest this as only one interpretation of the data, although the one which they themselves choose. One would feel greater confidence in this interpretation if all managers had been excluded from the sample, and if "nonmembership" had been defined to include not only the workers' council but also both the management board and the executive committees of the Party and trade union organizations of the enterprise. One would also feel more comfortable if general work satisfaction were more strongly correlated with perceived participation.

[67] Kolaja, p. 77.

[68] It is true that in two of the seven enterprises about which I could form such an impression, some key information given to me was being withheld from the ordinary members of the workers' council. It is obviously quite possible that similar information was being withheld in the other enterprises as well. Nevertheless, both heads of workers' management bodies and lower-middle managers with whom I spoke had much more information as to broad policy issues facing the enterprise than was known to their counterparts either in the enterprises of the CMEA countries or in those of western Europe and North America where I have carried on similar interviews.

the labor force is receiving an education of great potential importance for such development.

A third possible function of workers' management is to permit people with a high desire for influence on decision making to play an active role in the formation of company decisions without having to take the path of rising through the managerial ranks.[69] This is perhaps of particular importance for those who do not have the education to allow them to move into management. But it also offers a second path of potential influence to junior and middle managers. Clearly this is not of relevance to any large numbers of workers, but it can be for those who become power figures (whether formal or informal) in the workers' management bodies.

This function, however, is also fulfilled in other societies: in capitalist countries, through the trade unions and shop steward bodies; in CMEA countries, through both the trade union and the Party. Thus Yugoslav workers' management should not be regarded as playing any peculiar role in this regard. In fact, the rotation principle in workers' management reduces the possibilities—compared to those in other countries —for such people to exercise a strong and long-run influence. More than in other CMEA countries, workers with such ambitions can satisfy them only by making their way into trade union, Party, or elected government positions at levels above that of the enterprise.

The fourth and most real decision-making function of workers' management is that of deciding issues affecting individuals rather than the entire enterprise or any sector of it. Disciplinary matters, choice of individuals for dismissal in case of the need to prune the size of the labor force, sometimes determining the precise fixed wage of individual workers within the range set for their job, determining allocation of enterprise housing or housing credits as between individuals: these matters are both the bread-and-butter of workers' management and the issues which excite real interest within the workers' councils and the councils of the economic units.[70]

It is not surprising that it is precisely in this general area of personnel that general directors complain most of lack of formal authority, as shown in the 1967 questionnaire of directors.[71] Yet even here, managers must have their own way frequently enough when it really matters. The only managerial complaint in this regard which I heard in my interviews

[69] In commenting on my manuscript in late 1973, Županov noted that this function was probably more important in Yugoslavia during the late 1950's and early 1960's than at the time of my interviews. He suggested that the importance of this function may grow in the near future.

[70] See Riddell, pp. 66-67, Adizes, chapter 6, and Neuberger and James, p. 280.

[71] Županov, "Is Enterprise Management Becoming Professionalized?" table 10, p. 58.

was as to the difficulty of dismissing workers who are inefficient or who flagrantly violate rules of labor discipline; this is the identical complaint which one hears in all the CMEA countries. Adizes, reporting on his study of two Serbian enterprises, states that in disciplinary cases there is no polarized worker-management confrontation within the disciplinary-review bodies; the worker members of such committees within economic units do not support workers per se, but rather attempt to be impartial.[72] In some cases, the worker members of these committees even take harsher positions in disciplining fellow workers than those recommended by management.

A comparison of a Yugoslav sample study for 1967[73] with various sample studies for the Soviet Union during 1958-63 casts an interesting light on the degree of protection offered to workers by the Yugoslav workers' management institutions in comparison with the Soviet system of worker appeals from management decisions. Table 12.2 indicates that a higher proportion of decisions are reversed within the enterprise in favor of the workers in the Soviet Union than in Yugoslavia. Moreover, where the final workers' council (or enterprise trade union committee in the Soviet Union) rules against the worker in dismissal cases,[74] the likelihood of reversal in the courts is vastly higher in Yugoslavia. The substantially greater degree of reversal by Yugoslav courts suggests that Yugoslav workers' councils feel far freer in sanctioning worker dismissals than do the Soviet trade union committees at the enterprise level.

There are three difficulties with the conclusion offered by Table 12.2 as to the degree of protection to the individual worker provided by the workers' management system. The first is that it is claimed by a reputable source that the Yugoslav statistics showing the high number of appeals are grossly at variance with the picture presented by trade union legal experts, who view workers as frequently helpless before arbitrary managerial authority. Partly this is because in Yugoslavia, unlike the situation in the USSR, there is no systematic grievance procedure. Partly it is because the workers' management organs tend to support management decisions. However, no means are available for reconciling the statistical picture with this impressionistic one, and there is no evidence that the

[72] Adizes, p. 169. Adizes draws his conclusion on the basis of a review of the written records of all disciplinary cases which took place over three years in the two enterprises, and of personal observation of two dozen cases. Adizes' writings on this point have been supplemented in a personal letter.

[73] This was a major recession period, and thus dismissals in this year were presumably particularly great.

[74] Dismissal cases numbered 53 percent of all appeals to the courts from workers' council decisions in Yugoslavia, and constitute the only significant category of such appeals for which a Yugoslav-Soviet Union comparison is feasible.

TABLE 12.2: Treatment of Worker Appeals from Managerial Decisions in Yugoslavia and in the Soviet Union (percentage)

	Yugoslavia	Soviet Union
Number of decisions appealed to worker-management groups within the enterprise in a single year, taken as a percentage of the labor force	2.3	0.9 to 2.9[a]
Appeals in which worker claims are upheld by the worker-management groups within the enterprise[b] Subject of appeal:		
1. Dismissal of worker	24	59
2. Remuneration	71	93
3. Holidays and vacation	41	91
4. Transfer to other work	32	78
Rejected worker appeals which are brought before the courts Dismissal cases	66[c]	Very few
Proportion of court rulings which are in favor of the worker Dismissal cases	32	33[d]
Appeals from original decisions in which the final ruling is in favor of the worker Dismissal cases	48	60 (Approximately)

SOURCES: Yugoslavia: D. Gorupić and I. Paj, *Workers' Self-Management in Yugoslav Undertakings* (Ekonomski institut Zagreb, Zagreb: 1970), pp. 217-23. The study was carried out in 1967 by the Federal Statistical Office, and covered 1,024 business enterprises and 740 noncommercial organizations employing a total labor force of 479,300 workers. Soviet Union: M. McAuley, *Labour Disputes in Soviet Russia 1957-1965* (Clarendon Press, Oxford: 1969), chapters 6 and 7. Samples vary in size from thirty to over one hundred enterprises, and probably cover several times that number of thousand workers.

NOTE: In the Soviet system of appeals, a management decision regarding either an individual or group may be appealed by the worker(s) to a joint union-management committee at the shop level. The worker (but not the management) may appeal the committee's decision to a joint union-management committee at the enterprise level. The worker (but again not the management) may appeal this decision to a committee composed solely of trade union representatives at the enterprise level. In the case of job-dismissal, the worker (but again not the management) may further appeal to the courts. In other cases, either the worker or management may appeal the trade union decision to the courts.

[a] McAuley estimates that, in a Leningrad sample of five enterprises with 21,000 employees, 3 to 10 percent of the labor force was involved annually in appeals. Since nearly one-quarter of the

appeals concerned more than five workers (usually five to twenty), I have assumed an average of 3.5 workers per appeal.

That the nature of the appeals brought before worker-management groups is not too different in the Soviet Union from that in Yugoslavia is shown by the following breakdown of appeals:

Subject of Appeal	Yugoslavia	Soviet Union	
		Union-management enterprise committee	Trade union committee
		(percentage)	
Dismissal of worker	14	11	27
Remuneration	41	32	50
Holidays and vacation	13	30	3
Transfer to other work	10	7	12
Subtotal	77	80	92

[b] Data are available (I have used weighted averages of McAuley's samples) for appeals in the Soviet Union both to the level of the union-management enterprise committee and of the trade union enterprise committee. McAuley states that data for four of her Leningrad enterprises suggest that a large proportion (well over half for the several hundred cases for which she has information) of all decisions by the shop union-management committees favored the workers. I have assumed that the shop committees' rulings on each type of appeal favored the workers in the same proportion as did the enterprise union-management committees.

[c] I have assumed that the court cases not yet decided during 1967 had the same proportion of dismissal-appeals as did the cases decided during that year.

[d] This is McAuley's estimate of court decisions for those dismissals which had previously been ratified by the enterprise trade union committee. Dismissals not so ratified were patently illegal, and this fact raised the national average of reversals of all dismissal cases brought before the courts to 53 percent in 1963.

statistics are unreliable.[75] Thus I would tend to lean more heavily on the statistics than on the reported impressions.

The second difficulty with Table 12.2 is that the Soviet data are weak concerning the number of appeals per hundred members of the labor force; it is possible that the Yugoslav worker is more prone to make appeals than is his Soviet counterpart (although both seem to partake in the practice to a considerable degree).[76] The third is that one might postulate that the Yugoslav managers are more cautious in making origi-

[75] The source for the above statements is Županov in comments on a draft of this chapter. See also, Županov, "Two Patterns," especially pp. 222-23.

[76] No comparable national data are available for the United States, but James Stern, a colleague in industrial relations at the University of Wisconsin, said that he thought these figures were in the range of the proportion of grievances which would be appealed to formal union-management negotiation in the United States.

nal decisions unfavorable to individual workers or work groups than are their Soviet counterparts. The first row of Table 12.2 suggests that, although either or both of these objections may be valid, we are not dealing with different orders of magnitude.

Of course, Yugoslav workers are upheld in a substantial proportion of their appeals to workers' management bodies: 44 percent in the case of all appeals, and 23 percent for appeals against job-dismissal after the end of a preliminary trial period as an employee and where the original dismissal was made solely at the enterprise's desire.[77] Workers' management bodies play a significant role in protecting workers against managerial arbitrariness or error. But the data for the Soviet Union suggest that there is nothing here which is unique to the Yugoslav situation compared to that of other socialist countries.

Summing up this section, the principal role performed by workers' management institutions in Yugoslavia in advancing general worker participation—if we take as our standard of comparison the situation in the CMEA countries—is in providing much greater access to information about the affairs of the enterprise and the alternatives facing it.[78] Not surprisingly, it is precisely this role which has been mainly emphasized in the enterprises in which I interviewed.[79] The second important role is to give the workers the accurate impression that they can overturn management policies and dismiss top directors if they believe that this has become essential for their own well-being.

Strikes and powerless groups of workers. Strikes are not legally prohibited in Yugoslav enterprises, and a minimum of 1,750 occurred between 1958 and 1969; in the latter years, an average of 17,000 workers were recorded as going on strike annually.[80] While this is an annual average of only one-half of 1 percent of the country's labor force, as a regular phenomenon it is enormous by the standards of other socialist countries where strikes are normally considered impermissible.

[77] If we consider the proportion of reversals of all decisions (whether or not appealed) in the categories for which appeals were made, the respective figures are 0.7 and 5.6 percent. As one would expect, the vast bulk of managerial decisions are not appealed (Gorupić and Paj, pp. 219-20).

[78] A well-informed Yugoslav, commenting in 1973 on a draft of this chapter, stated his belief that this conclusion is not correct for Yugoslavia as a whole. In fact, he was surprised at the answers I received in the enterprises where I interviewed.

It is, of course, possible that I have drawn an unrepresentative sample of enterprises with regard to the functioning of workers' management. But I see no reason to think so, and my results seem consistent with the views of Yugoslav sociologists who have studied the problem.

[79] At least this was the case after I had sharply queried some additional claims.

[80] However, only 31 percent of all strikers stayed out for more than one day (Jovanov, pp. 27 and 41). The recorded number of strikers is less than the actual number.

Three broad sets of reasons can be given for these strikes. The first is to call the attention of public authorities to market conditions which are beyond the control of the individual enterprise. While such strikes are generally for higher wages, it is recognized that only government aid to the enterprise or industry can permit these demands to be met.[81] This type of strike cannot be viewed as indicating a failure of worker self-management.

The second reason for strikes is a feeling by workers that they are powerless in the face of a managerially controlled set of workers' management bodies within the enterprise, who have different values from their own and against whom the strike is the only effective weapon.[82] This sentiment is exemplified in the situation described by the general director of one enterprise in which I interviewed, who said that when his workers are dissatisfied their first reaction is to quit and take work at another enterprise; their second reaction is to strike; only as a last resort would they seek redress through the workers' council.

The third reason is that an individual group of workers may feel that they have specific complaints—most frequently as to the relative level of their shop's variable wages or the piece rates set for their work. The two strikes about which I was told in enterprises where I interviewed were of this nature. In one of these enterprises, the strikes led to no reconsideration at all of relative wages. In the second, however, variable wages in the striking department were raised sharply compared to those paid in other departments.[83]

Strikes by individual departments within an enterprise are probably motivated primarily by this third reason.[84] Their relatively slight importance is shown by the proportion of the nation's strike-participants

[81] For an example of such strikes in mining and among dock workers, see *Le Monde*, June 24, 1970, p. 2, and Popov, "The Problem of Strikes in Yugoslavia," reprinted in *International*, 1, 7 (1972), 29-32. One Yugoslav author has argued that the majority of strikes are not against "bureaucratic management" but are rather of this type (R. Supek, "Some Contradictions and Insufficiencies of Yugoslav Self-Managing Socialism," *Praxis*, international edition, VIII, 3-4, 1971, p. 386). Jovanov (p. 39) points out that strikes have not occurred in the high-income sectors of the economy.

[82] See Popov (1972), p. 34, for a view that strikers are primarily workers who find that they have little influence on decision making. Jovanov views strikes as revealing class struggle.

[83] In this enterprise, variable wages for different departments depended upon performance relative to the department's plan. Members of the striking department then earned 30-35 percent lower variable wages than did workers with the same qualifications in other departments; two years after the strike, their variable wages were higher than those of any other department. When I suggested that this development showed that the strike had been successful, the heads of the enterprise's workers' organizations grinningly agreed.

[84] But Adizes (pp. 183-87) describes such a strike which is equally motivated by the second reason.

who have engaged in strikes which brought out only small numbers of workers: only 8 percent of all strikers were involved in strikes of fewer than fifty people, and only another 15 percent in disputes with fifty to one hundred strikers.[85] Strikes larger than this generally involve more than one work department.

It has been claimed that a growing number of strikes are broader than the bounds of a single enterprise;[86] clearly these must be motivated primarily by the first reason of placing pressure on public authorities. Each of such strikes must involve fairly large numbers of workers. However, only 8 percent of a large sample of strikers were involved in strikes with over two thousand participants, and only an additional 8 percent in strikes with between eight hundred and two thousand participants.[87] Strikes restricted to a single medium-sized enterprise seem unlikely to have much effect on the public authorities.

This is quite in line with data showing that, during the course of strikes, only 15 percent of a sample of strikers expressed grievances solely against groups or forces outside of their own enterprise, while 77 percent restricted their grievances to those against individuals or groups within the enterprise.[88]

The figures as to the proportion of strikers involved in strikes of different magnitudes suggest that something in the order of at least 61 percent of all strikers[89] have been reacting to a feeling of general powerlessness of workers within the enterprise's organs of workers' control. It is not surprising, therefore, that 74 percent of all strikers participated in strikes which were limited exclusively to manual workers.[90]

This does not mean, however, that manual workers active in self-management bodies stayed aloof from strikes. Eighty-five percent of all strikes, and those strikes which involved 93 percent of all strikers, included as participants one or more member of some workers' management body.[91] Membership in the Communist Party is said to be an irrelevant factor in affecting willingness to participate in a strike.[92] During the course of strikes, strikers have been mostly in direct conflict with

[85] Jovanov, p. 42. However, two-thirds of the number of strikes were of this category. These and other figures presented below from the Jovanov study are based on a questonnaire sent to all Yugoslav commune trade union councils and municipal assemblies at the end of 1969; they cover a total of five hundred twelve strikes throughout the country. Ninety percent of the strikes studied occurred during 1966-69.

[86] N. Popov, "Les formes et le caractère des conflicts sociaux," *Praxis*, international edition, VIII, 3-4 (1971), p. 359.

[87] Jovanov, p. 42. [88] Ibid., pp. 50-51.

[89] I.e., participants in labor disputes with one hundred to eight hundred strikers.

[90] Jovanov, p. 43. [91] Ibid., p. 45.

[92] Z. Mlinar (president of the Yugoslav Association of Sociologists), "Les conflits sociaux et le développement social en Yougoslavie," *Revue de l'Est*, III, 2 (1972), p. 38, and Jovanov, p. 55.

management and not with the workers' management organizations as such.[93] Apparently, activists may well feel just as powerless as other workers in the face of what they consider to be a set of managerially controlled workers' management organizations.

On the whole, strikes have been quite effective. Fifty-nine percent of the strikes (involving 55 percent of the strikers) were said to have gained their demands completely;[94] this, however, does not mean that the underlying problems were resolved, but rather only that the specific causes of the strikes were at least temporarily removed.

Yugoslav trade union leaders differ widely in their attitudes toward strikes, ranging from the view that—given a system of workers' management—they virtually border on sabotage, to the position that they are a normal occurrence in Yugoslav society and should be accepted as a component of the self-management rights of workers.[95] In practice, unions at the enterprise level opposed 66 percent of the strikes which occurred.[96] Nevertheless, despite the fact that the Yugoslav strike movement has had exclusively a wildcat nature, and that strikes have not been organized by any permanent institutions existing in society,[97] these work stoppages seem to represent a socially acceptable (although not a favored) alternative to attempting to muster electoral power within the workers' council.

ENTERPRISE BEHAVIOR AS EVIDENCE OF THE REALITY OF WORKERS' MANAGEMENT

The theoretic literature as to workers' management points to one clear conclusion and to one likely result. The clear conclusion is that a workers' management system should lead to greater capital intensity (through substitution of capital for labor) than would be appropriate either under capitalism or under a centrally regulated economic system; this is because the current workers of an enterprise serve their economic interests best by determining both the amount of new hirings and the types of

[93] This is said to be the case in 70 percent of the strikes, involving 68 percent of all strikers (Jovanov, p. 51).

[94] Ibid., p. 52. However, since 72 percent of the strikes broke out before the strikers had exhausted all the normal procedures for settling grievances (ibid., p. 50), doubtless many of the strike demands would have been fully met without a strike.

For an interesting set of interrelated hypotheses explaining this effectiveness, see Županov, "Two Patterns," pp. 219-20.

[95] Lemân, pp. 107-09.

[96] Moreover, the strikes which they opposed were particularly the larger ones; they involved 78 percent of all strikers. In two-thirds of the cases of trade union opposition to the strike, the trade union supported the strike demands (Jovanov, p. 53).

[97] Jovanov, p. 55.

investment undertaken in such a fashion as to maximize the flow of net income (including wages) per worker.[98] On the other hand, management under capitalism is concerned with the return on capital rather than on labor inputs, while under a centrally regulated socialist system, national concern is with raising the productivity of the labor force in the economy as a whole rather than in maximizing the return to labor within each enterprise individually.[99] Given the predicted tendency toward capital intensity in a workers' management system, we would expect this system to do particularly poorly in overcoming problems of the secular unemployment which has perenially plagued the Yugoslav economy.

The second likely result is that a workers' managed enterprise would be biased toward a high rate of pay-out of income to its workers rather than toward keeping up retained earnings for investment purposes. Partly this is because we might expect relatively low-income manual workers to have a high rate of time preference in comparison with either capitalists or a central state. Partly it is because workers lose all personal stake in the net income of the enterprise once they have left it through either labor turnover or retirement,[100] and thus have a much shorter time horizon for investment payoff than would either capitalist owners or the socialist state.[101]

The assuredness of this second result is weakened, however, by two factors influencing the Yugoslav enterprise. The first is that retaining enterprise income for investment purposes is usually a precondition for receiving bank loans,[102] and that such loans are made at what amount (given the rates of inflation of the economy) to at most 6 to 7 percent effective interest rates.[103] The linkage of self-investment to bank borrowing sharply raises the real rate of return earned on self-financed investments by the enterprise compared either to that earned by society as a whole, or to what enterprises might expect in a thoroughly capitalist society. The second factor is that a workers' management decision to reinvest income is influenced not only by the expected rate of return but also by the fear that failure to invest will make the enterprise non-

[98] Strictly speaking, this applies only when all labor has the same skill composition and so equal distributed income. This qualification is unimportant for purposes of analyzing capital intensity.

[99] See B. N. Ward, *The Socialist Economy* (Random House, New York: 1967), pp. 211-12, and Jaroslav Vanek, *The General Theory of Labor-Managed Market Economies* (Cornell University Press, Ithaca and London: 1970).

[100] Pensions in Yugoslavia are financed by the state rather than by the individual enterprises.

[101] See S. Pejovich, "The Banking System and the Investment Behavior of the Yugoslav Firm," in M. Bornstein, pp. 292-303.

[102] See Neuberger and James, p. 260. My interviews are corroborative of their conclusion that this linkage is the rule. However, Pejovich (pp. 305-07) assumes that there is no such connection.

[103] See Chapter 13.

competitive, and thus will lead to unemployment for the current workers; this concern is much stronger in a workers' management system, operating under Yugoslav conditions of substantial unemployment, than it would be in a capitalist enterprise.[104]

If we assume that workers of an enterprise would wish to determine both the amount and nature of investment and the volume of new hirings of workers in terms of their personal economic interests rather than in the light of their social conscience, we might hope to test the degree to which workers' management actually functions in Yugoslavia by the degree of realization of the theoretic predictions. Fortunately, we can do this through the use of historic data, as enterprises really became the masters of their own investment decisions only since the 1965 economic reforms.[105] A comparison of the pre- and post-1965 periods should thus be illuminating, and this is done in Tables 12.3 and 12.4.

Table 12.3 shows that the annual rate of growth of employment in the Yugoslav economy was reduced by two-thirds between 1960-65 and 1966-71; the same occurred in industry alone. This is despite the fact that the rate of unemployment was very high in both periods. Much the same occurred in the republic of Slovenia, where the unemployment rate was quite low. These data are completely consistent with the prediction that enterprises under workers' management will—once given the opportunity by the central government—restrict hirings and funnel investment in capital-intensive directions.[106]

[104] Other features of perverse reaction to increases in prices of inputs and outputs are stressed by Ward (chapter 8). But these follow from rather specific assumptions, particularly with regard to labor supply. (See the account in H. M. Wachtel, *Workers' Management and Workers' Wages in Yugoslavia*, Cornell University Press, Ithaca and London: 1973, chapter 3.)

Jaroslav Vanek emphasizes low price elasticities of supply compared to a capitalist economy (Vanek, *General Theory*); the countercyclical nature of inventory fluctuations in the Yugoslav economy is in line with this theoretic analysis. On the other hand, his view that "the labor-managed economy will be far less susceptible to long-range inflationary pressures," and that strong downward as well as upward price movement may be expected, finds no support in the admittedly brief post-1965 period. (See ibid., p. 391, and Vanek, *The Participatory Economy*, Cornell University Press, Ithaca and London: 1971, p. 29.)

[105] This view as to the historical facts is radically different from that of Jaroslav Vanek, who considers that Yugoslavia has been a labor-managed market economy since the early 1950's, and that changes during this period should, without exception, "be thought of as changes of policy instruments, rather than changes of the principles of participation" (Vanek, *The Participatory Economy*, pp. 39 and 41). Chapter 11 provided the justification for my using 1965 as the starting point of effective workers' management. Milenkovitch not only takes 1965 as the date at which investment planning was abandoned, but also considers that "the incentive for, and ability of, enterprises to maximize income per worker was severely limited" earlier (D. D. Milenkovitch, *Plan and Market in Yugoslav Economic Thought*, Yale University Press, New Haven and London: 1971, pp. 176 and 211).

[106] It is true that the case is much stronger for the years of monetary restraint (1966-68) than for the last three years. But even the last three years never reached

TABLE 12.3: Rate of Growth of Employment (percentage)

	1960-1965		1966-1971	
	Annual Average	Annual Range	Annual Average	Annual Range
All Yugoslavia				
Increase of employment	5.0	2 to 9	1.6	−2 to 5
Rate of unemployment	7.0	6.2 to 8.3	8.0	7.2 to 9.1
Slovenia				
Increase of employment	4.3	0 to 7	1.6	−3 to 5
Rate of unemployment	1.8	1.4 to 2.0	3.1	2.4 to 3.7

SOURCES: Socijalistička Federativna Republika Jugoslavija, Savezni Zavod za Statistiku, *Statistički Godišnjak Jugoslavije* (Beograd), and Socialistična Republika Slovenija, Zavod SR Slovenije za Statistiko, *Statistični Letopis SR Slovenije* (Ljubljana), annual volumes.

One might argue that the change in the rates of growth of employment was caused by another factor: namely, by the emphasis on the part of the national government, beginning in 1965, on improving efficiency in the enterprises rather than encouraging hidden unemployment there. But it seems difficult to believe that this factor alone could account for the fact that the 1964 level of Yugoslav employment was not reached again until 1969. Moreover, it played a relatively weak role during 1969-71. The employment data thus seem better explained by the workers' management hypothesis.

Table 12.4 suggests that Yugoslav enterprises took advantage of the opportunities given them by the 1965 reform to increase the proportion of their income distributed to members. The diminution of state investment sources allocated for enterprise investment was only very partially compensated by increased investment from enterprises' own funds, despite the sharp reduction in the share of enterprise income going to the state. As enterprise gained increased command over the distribution of their pretax income,[107] they shifted fairly sharply to increased payments to the labor force.[108] This shift from investment to increased consumption by workers is what we would have expected in workers' management enterprises.

---

the average rates of growth of employment of the earlier period, despite the fact that the earlier period included several years of monetary restraint.

[107] See R. Bićanić, *Economic Policy in Socialist Yugoslavia* (Cambridge University Press, Cambridge, England: 1973), pp. 112-13 and 211-12 for the limitations on enterprise freedom of distribution during the 1961-64 period.

[108] This argument is supported by the fact that, although enterprises immediately after the reform sharply increased their own share (from amortization and retained earnings) of their total gross investment in fixed assets, this share steadily declined thereafter. By 1971, the enterprises' share was barely more than it had been in 1964 before the reform (Pejovich, p. 302).

TABLE 12.4: Use of Enterprise Income for Payments to the Labor Force
in All Yugoslavia (percentage: unweighted average of annual figures)

Years	Payments to the Labor Force as a Proportion of Gross Product		Payments to the Labor Force as a Proportion of Gross Product, Excluding Sales Tax Receipts	
	Entire economy	Industry	Entire economy	Industry
1961-64	28.5	24.7	32.5	29.2
1965	32.1	29.8	35.2	32.4
1966-70	37.5	36.5	39.6	38.4
1966-70 average as percentage of 1961-64 average	132	148	122	132

SOURCE: *Statistički*, volumes of 1962-72, tables 106-4, 106-7, 106-8, and 204-12.

NOTES:

1. The remainder of the gross product of enterprises is used for enterprise gross investment, for repayment of bank loans, and for payments to government bodies including payments for social security purposes. It is not possible prior to 1967 to separate gross investments in the enterprises from general government payments. The exclusion of sales tax payments in the third and fourth columns of the table represents an attempt to do this to the limited degree practicable.

2. Gross rather than net product is used as the denominator in the ratios because amortization rates were not fixed by law during the second half of the period, and they include an unknown amount of rapid depreciation which individual enterprises could voluntarily choose to take.

However, it must be noted that this response to increased opportunities for shifting from investment to consumption did not occur under stable conditions. Despite this shift, real personal income per employed worker in the Yugoslav economy grew at a slightly slower pace during the postreform years (1966-70) than in the last three years before the reform, although somewhat more rapidly than in the last five years (1960-64) before the reform. One might well argue that Yugoslav workers have simply attempted to maintain their earlier growth in real earnings, and have treated enterprise investments as a residual category, rather than deliberately attempting to shift from investment to consumption.

The reality of workers' management during the post-1965 period is also suggested by the sharply declining rates of labor turnover in industry which have characterized both Yugoslavia as a whole and the low-unemployment republic of Slovenia (see Table 12.5). By 1971, the rate of industrial labor turnover in Yugoslavia was only 72 percent of that of 1965—a year with much the same rate of unemployment and a somewhat lower rate of growth in the industrial labor force. These sharply declining—and always quite low—rates of labor turnover suggest that

TABLE 12.5: Rate of Industrial Labor Turnover (percentage)

Year	Yugoslavia			Slovenia		
	Turnover in industrial employment (monthly average)	Growth in industrial employment (annual)	Unemployment rate in entire economy (annual average)	Turnover in industrial employment (monthly average)	Growth in industrial employment (annual)	Unemployment rate in entire economy (annual average)
1964	2.0	7.9	6.3	1.8	8.2	1.4
1965	1.8	4.4	7.3	1.5	1.8	1.8
1966	1.53	−1.4	7.4	1.33	−1.3	2.4
1967	1.37	−0.4	8.2	1.11	0.0	3.0
1968	1.22	−0.2	9.1	1.14	1.8	3.7
1969	1.28	3.7	8.5	1.28	3.9	3.5
1970	1.38	3.9	7.5	1.32	3.8	3.1
1971	1.29	5.3	7.2	1.31	4.4	2.6

SOURCES: *Statistički* and *Statistični Letopis*, annual volumes.

NOTE: Data for turnover in industrial employment do not appear to be available prior to 1964.

workers have indeed formed the long-term attachment to their individual enterprises which one would expect under a workers' management system.[109]

Despite the caveats that one may legitimately raise, it is interesting to find that the shifts in enterprise behavior were in the directions one would have expected as workers' management became much more free of state control since 1965. This suggests that workers' management is indeed a reality in Yugoslavia; even if enterprise general directors often govern de facto, they make the sorts of decisions we would expect workers to approve.

[109] A reader has suggested that an alternative explanation of the decline in labor turnover is increased fear of unemployment. However, the rise in national unemployment from 7.0 percent of the employed labor force during 1960-65 to 8.0 percent during 1966-71 has been far more than compensated by the opening of legal opportunities for employment abroad.

CHAPTER 13

Enterprise Behavior in Yugoslavia

CHAPTERS 11 and 12 have treated both the external environment within which the Yugoslav firm operates and the internal relationships of the workers' managed enterprise. In this chapter I shall consider the behavior of enterprises in relation with the external environment, basing myself heavily upon interviews.

Three areas of enterprise behavior will be given particular attention. The first is external sources of finance for industrial enterprises. The fifty-five business banks of the country play the primary role here; their operation as independent enterprises poses a particularly interesting problem for the efficient allocation of national capital resources. The functioning of these business banks is one major area in which the principle of self-management and the social interests of the larger community can be observed in the process of mutual adjustment.

The second area of behavior is that of mergers. Some mergers are a result of the motivations of those within the parent enterprises. Examples of such motives include managerial desire for growth for its own sake, and the search for higher profits through economies of scale, through consolidation of an oligopoly position, or through the more effective use of available capital by entering new markets. Other mergers take place in response to commune and republic pressure to bail out inefficient enterprises which would otherwise go to the wall. In both cases, mergers represent another area of potential clash between enterprise, community, and ideological concerns.

The third area of enterprise behavior to be examined is foreign trade. This is the principal field in which the free working of the market system for material inputs and products of industrial firms is distorted by state interference. For this reason, it is a particularly critical sphere in which to analyze the reality of market relationships.

All three of these behavioral areas involve market relationships. Banking deals with the market for financial capital; mergers deal with the markets for both capital and labor; foreign trade deals with the market for products. In all three, the principle of the self-managed enterprise is forced into compromise with the almost equally revered principle of social responsibility. The intertwining of the two ideals can be observed throughout.

EXTERNAL FINANCE AND THE BUSINESS BANKS

In industry, as in the economy as a whole, gross investment in fixed assets has been heavily financed by the business banks. Table 13.1 ex-

TABLE 13.1: Sources of Gross Investment in Fixed Assets in Industry and Mining, 1967-71[a]
(unweighted average of the years)

Sources	All Yugoslavia	Slovenia
	(percentage)	
Banks[b]	54	48
Internal finance by enterprises, including repayment of loans[c]	30	47
Government bodies	16	5
The Federation	13	...
Republics	1	...
Communes	2	...

SOURCES: For Yugoslavia: Služba društvenog knijigovodstva - glavna centrala, *Statistički Bilten*, February 1968-72, tables 38 to 45 in the respective issues. For Slovenia: Socijalistička Federativna Republika Jugoslavija, Savezni Zavod za Statistiku, *Statistički Godišnjak Jugoslavije* (Beograd), 1968 through 1972, tables 216-1 through 216-3.

[a] The total takes no account of foreign investment in joint ventures, which would appear to be on the order of 2 percent of the total. Nor does it include enterprise bonds purchased by individuals.

[b] This includes loans made by business banks from credits granted to them by communes and republics, although it excludes loans made by the banks from funds which they simply administer for government bodies. (My source is a letter from the research department of the National Bank of Yugoslavia.) Thus it includes loans from funds over whose use the banks have only partial control. In the case of the Slovenian Republic's investment fund, for example, the Slovenian government determines the total amount to be loaned from this fund to each sector of the economy, while the business bank (acting as the intermediary) determines which individual enterprises are to receive the loans and is itself responsible in case of default. In December 1969 and December 1970, 41 percent of the total (but not necessarily industrial) long-term credit resources of all business banks in Yugoslavia consisted of credits obtained primarily from governmental bodies.

[c] Includes an unspecified, but probably not very large, percentage of credits by Yugoslav suppliers of equipment, as well as an insignificant amount of inter-enterprise investments and loans.

amines such financing for the homogeneous period of 1967-71; somewhat over half of total financing in Yugoslavia was carried out by the banks. If one considers the financing of all gross investments (including inventories) of socialist enterprises, the share of the banks is not affected, but the expansion of the share of net trade credit granted by enterprises reduces the residual shares left to internal finance and to government bodies.[1] The share of the banks in net investment in fixed

[1] Bank loans financed 53 percent of all gross investments by socialist firms of

assets by industrial enterprises was still higher, since the proportion contributed by internal finance was only 14 percent.[2] Moreover, during the three years of 1967-69, 96 percent of the unweighted annual average of total net investments of all types by all enterprises in the economy were used for repayment of loans given by banks and government bodies.[3]

As of 1970, bank wages were determined by an interbank agreement which set the maximum proportion of net bank income which could be used for this purpose. Since virtually all banks distributed this maximum percentage, bank employees, just as employees of other Yugoslav enterprises, had a direct interest in maximizing their own enterprise's income per employee. Bank officials, like directors of industrial enterprises, are also motivated to expand profits in order to finance the growth of their own organization.[4]

This combined motivation on the part of loan officers suggests that bank loans would be made at the highest interest rates consistent with security and social mores. Various machinations are permitted and used to get around the legal maximum interest rate which may be charged; thus, at a time when 8 percent was the maximum legal rate, one Slovenian firm paid an average effective rate of 13.6 percent on all bank borrowings during 1969. In its case, the legal rate was exceeded because the enterprise was unable to borrow except on agreement to repay late —and thus be subject to a penalty rate of interest.[5] This is quite consistent with the national interest of assuring that bank loans are given to those enterprises which can use them most effectively.

---

all sectors during 1967-71 (unweighted average of the years), and expansions in net trade credit financed an additional 7 percent. Such data are not available for industry alone. (Organization for Economic Co-Operation and Development, *OECD Financial Statistics*, 1970-72.)

[2] Expenditures on replacement and maintenance of existing capacity levels in industry and mining are given in Socijalistička Federativna Republika Jugoslavija, Savezni Zavod za Statistiku, *Statistički Godišnjak Jugoslavije* (Beograd), 1969 through 1972 issues, tables 119-4 and 119-6. (Hereafter, this source is called *Statistički*.)

[3] D. Vojnic in *Vjesnik u Srijedu* (*VUS*), June 10, 1970, p. 22, translated in *JTS*. However, since net investments were presumably calculated after deducting amortization, and since enterprises were free to set their own amortization rates above a designated minimum, these figures can be taken only as crude and maximum approximations. The reader should note that, in contrast with the apparent definition of net investment used here, the definition of footnote 2 deducts actual replacement expenditures rather than amortization allowances from gross investment expenditures.

[4] This second motivation, rather than the first, was emphasized in an interview with a high bank official in one major business bank.

[5] An alternative device, said to be widely used in Yugoslavia, is the insistence that firms keep a substantial proportion of their long-term borrowings in the form of time deposits.

Social mores, of course, do limit the degree to which the banks' effective rate of interest can exceed the legal maximum. With the legal maximum only 60 percent of the rate of inflation during 1965-71,[6] the effective rate of bank interest in real terms must only rarely have reached 6 to 7 percent. It is not surprising that bank loans have had to be rationed.

Not only have social mores as to interest rate served as a constraint on income maximization by the banks, but the incentives to bank executives to strive for such maximization are less than in most other enterprises. Although bank wage increases are linked to expansion of income, a much smaller proportion of such expansion can be distributed to employees than is the case in industrial enterprises. Furthermore, while retained income can be used for bank expansion, increases in customer deposits constitute a more significant source of growth.

More important in restricting the search for bank income, however, is the fact that the basic loan policy of individual banks is not determined by their workers' councils, but instead by the assembly or executive board of each bank; the latter bodies represent founding shareholding organizations and major depositors rather than bank employees. The communes, and for some banks the republics, are given an important voice in these bodies because the major commune and republic investment funds were transferred to the banks during several years ending in 1965 and were incorporated as part of bank capital.[7] To the degree that the neighboring communes and the republic play a major role in determining any given bank's policy, one might expect that each bank would represent a small regional financial enclave and that the optimal national allocation of capital through the banks would thus be vitiated. If loans must in any case be rationed, then bank officials have little reason to combat the use of regionalism as the rationing principle.

With the exception of three former national banks (for investment, foreign trade, and agriculture), both founding organizations and major depositors tend to be local enterprises, although some large firms are

[6] The legal maximum was above the 1968 and 1969 rate of inflation, but below that of 1970 and 1971.

[7] This voice does not take the form of formal votes in the banks' shareholder groups, since no single government body can have more than 10 percent of the total votes in the shareholders' assembly. For all banks in Yugoslavia about 1970, government bodies had 19 percent of the votes in assemblies and only 9 percent of the votes in the executive boards. However, their informal influence has been very great (*Ekonomska Politika*, October 5, 1970, p. 15, translated in *JTS*). In addition, since 1969 the communes and republics have been empowered to withdraw their funds from the banks' capital; even earlier, they could withdraw both their deposits and the funds which they permitted the banks to manage for them on commission.

founders of several banks.[8] This localism is due to the business banks having been created only in 1965, when they were founded by enterprises and sociopolitical communities. The attraction for an enterprise of being a bank founder was that this—at the cost of putting up some capital—gave it a claim on the lending powers of the bank.[9] Such a claim however, was much more likely to be recognized if loans were also to the advantage of the communes in which the bank operated; for it was the commune governments themselves which originally invested much of the capital of the banks, have been able to withdraw it at will since 1969, and must have continually exercised considerable control over bank loan policy. Furthermore, since long-term loans are virtually restricted to enterprises making time deposits in the same bank, enterprises would be careful thereafter to reinforce their claims for loans by concentrating their time deposits in their local bank.

The degree of banking compartmentalization by region diminished sharply after 1965; bank mergers reduced the number of Yugoslav banks from two hundred twenty-five at the end of 1965 to fifty-five at the end of 1971.[10] But even at the end of this period, it was rare for a long-term loan to be granted to an enterprise outside the republic of the bank concerned.[11]

The allocation of bank loans is thus determined by a combination of the self-interest of the bank as a separate enterprise, the self-interest as potential borrowers of the enterprises which are shareholders and depositors, and the self-interest of the communes (and sometimes the republic) which were among the original founders and are still creditors and/or depositors. Since, given the high rate of inflation in Yugoslavia, it is socially impossible for the effective rate of interest to be brought up to the level needed to clear the loan market, it is not at all surprising

[8] One large bank reported that it had no large depositors who were not also founders. A large enterprise in which I interviewed was a founder of five different banks, although some of these were former specialized national banks.

[9] It is true that dividends on bank stock are sometimes paid, but such earnings were not a serious motive for purchasing bank stock. During 1968-69, dividends for all Yugoslav banks constituted only 1 percent of the capital which had been originally invested or later accumulated (*Ekonomska Politika*, October 5, 1970, p. 15, translated in *JTS*).

[10] National Bank of Yugoslavia, *Annual Report* of 1966, p. 59, and of 1971, p. 52. Moreover, by 1972 ten banks held 88 percent of all bank assets, and three banks held 45 percent (*Nedeljne Informativne Novine* [*NIN*], August 27, 1972, pp. 11-12, summarized in *ABSEES*, January 1973).

[11] The three former national banks, all located in the capital in Serbia, seem to be major exceptions to the rule of investing only in their own communes. Presumably as a result of this, and to a considerable but unknown degree because of bank loans made prior to 1965, about one-third of the assets of all Serbian banks as of 1972 had been placed outside this republic (ibid.).

that each bank should be heavily influenced by the desirability of restricting loans to its own shareholders and of financing expansion in its own geographic region.

Short-term credit is partially discountable with the National Bank,[12] but is primarily based upon demand deposits. Long-term loans are permitted only up to the sum of the amount of the bank's capital, time deposits of organizations, savings time deposits of individuals, foreign credits, and special funds usually emanating from one or another government source.[13] Reasonably enough, banks have been unwilling to lend to enterprises which do not normally hold time deposits with them; such time deposits are held by enterprises partially as a means of keeping available funds reserved for future investments, but primarily as a claim on current and future borrowings. Since in all business banks of Yugoslavia at the end of 1970, only about 26 percent of all long-term loan sources consisted of time deposits by organizations (and some of these were doubtless government bodies which did not borrow), time deposits have been eminently justified for the enterprises by the claim to borrowing which they bestow.[14] It matters little that the top interest rate paid to depositors by any Yugoslav bank has been little more than half the current rate of inflation.

Within the previously mentioned constraints as to potential borrow-

---

[12] During 1967-71, credits from the National Bank financed an annual average of 25 percent of the business banks' short-term lending operations (National Bank of Yugoslavia, *Quarterly Bulletin*, January 1973, p. 30).

[13] The system of permitting long-term loans to be granted only on the basis of long-term funds of business banks was formally abolished in 1972. It would not appear, however, that this formal change had a significant practical effect (ibid., pp. 39 and 44).

For business banks as a whole at the end of 1970, long-term credit resources for loans other than those made for housing and communal development were divided as follows: bank capital, 22 percent; time deposits, 30 percent; credit obtained primarily from government bodies, 41 percent; credit from the National Bank, 4 percent; credits from outside Yugoslavia, 3 percent (ibid., table 11a). The year 1970 (although it is quite similar to 1969 in the asset composition of banks) is particularly appropriate to analyze because it both partially postdates the withdrawal of federal funds from inclusion in the balance sheets of business banks although the banks had no real control over these funds, and predates substantial credits from the National Bank for funding the short-term debt of enterprises needed for permanent working capital.

Data for a single large bank in 1970 showed that 85 percent of all time deposits were held by organizations rather than by individuals.

[14] Nevertheless, not all enterprises have been granted long-terms loans, and some enterprises keep time deposits with their bank simply as a means of building cash savings to finance a future capital investment. Of the eleven enterprises in which I interviewed, four had done no long-term bank borrowing since 1965, two had borrowed, and no information was available about three others. (The remaining two enterprises were able to satisfy their capital needs from a special fund established by the republic government.) One of the nonborrowers was a founder of three banks.

ers, business banks would doubtless prefer to lend where the return is highest and security the greatest. For example, one industrial enterprise, although unable to expand its borrowings on the basis of its current product mix, was quite confident of its ability to borrow long-term if it entered a profitable new field. But other constraints have also bound the choices of the banks.

The most important of these has been the need to provide financial support for current customers. Short-term credit has apparently been normally renewed without much question, and additional short-term credits have been readily supplied to finance higher inventory requirements caused by inflation. Partly this has been a response to pressure from the communes, whose enterprises would otherwise have faced bankruptcy and closing; but it has equally been due to the need of the banks themselves to protect their outstanding credits from being swept away as bad debts. These dual pressures, most frequently working in the same direction, have greatly restricted the freedom of action of the banks by forcing them to act defensively.

A second constraint has been the interest of communes in promoting new enterprises and supporting existing ones in their own areas, both so as to increase employment and to expand the local tax base.[15] Communes have been frequently accused of adopting a nonchalant attitude toward the financial soundness of such enterprises, holding that some device could always be found for maintaining an enterprise once it was created.[16] While I have no notion of the degree of such commune pressure, or of the extent to which banks have felt forced to adapt themselves to it, doubtless such demands have represented some burden on bank resources.

An interesting example of this was the interest of one commune in financing the development of a new factory for one of its existing enterprises. The parent enterprise was primarily engaged in an industry suffering from overcapacity and thus from low prices, and its income position was poor. The new factory was to be engaged in a highly profitable line in which imports (despite tariff protection) were heavy.

As an aid to this enterprise, the commune loaned it some 30 percent of its total financial requirements at 5 percent interest; the enterprise itself put up 40 percent of the funds; and the business bank of the commune was persuaded to lend the remaining 30 percent (probably short-term) at 8 percent interest which, while it was the legal maximum, was

[15] See E. Neuberger and E. James, "The Yugoslav Self-Managed Enterprise: A Systemic Approach," in M. Borstein (ed.), *Plan and Market* (Yale University Press, New Haven and London: 1973), p. 270.

[16] One Yugoslav authority, while stating that such an attitude on the part of communes was now less common than it had been in the past, held that it was still a problem at the time of my interview with him in 1970.

substantially below the normal effective rate charged. During the following two years, the parent enterprise earned a return on its own capital of 100 percent annually; this profit constituted about 30 percent of the total profit (after the payment of wages) earned by the enterprise in these years. But clearly the bank suffered by the transaction.

It is probable that the action of the business banks in circumventing federal pressure, exercised in 1970 to reduce imports, represented a similar response to commune demands. The federal government introduced a requirement that a 50 percent deposit be paid to the federal government at the time of import orders, but the money deposited was much larger than had been thought possible. Shortly after these large deposits, the major business banks demanded additional credits in the amount of these deposits from the National Bank, stating that otherwise they would be illiquid and unable to meet their short-term obligations.[17] It seems unlikely that the banks would voluntarily have placed themselves in this difficult position.

A high official of one bank stated that his bank is unable even to insist that increases in short-term capital needed to finance expansion of physical inventories bear the market rate of effective interest charges. The banks, as he saw it, carry the legacy of having been government banks prior to 1965; they cannot suddenly renounce this heritage and operate on purely business principles, although they have moved a long way in this direction.

Normally, however, the interests of the bank and of its commune governments coincide for the reasons stated earlier. Still another example of this is the internal ruling by one large bank that it would give long-term loans only to enterprises which supply at least 70 percent of their investment needs from internal finance. Not only does this allow the region to get the greatest employment and tax leverage from its enterprises' use of internal funds, but it also provides desirable security for the bank.

Bank financing by loans represents virtually the sole source for enterprises of external finance other than government loans. While other sources exist, they were still quite unimportant in the early 1970's.

(1) One such source was equity investment in both old and new enterprises, which began in late 1969.[18] In my interviews, I came across two cases of new plants to be built by consortia of Yugoslav enterprises which would then share in the profits earned by the new enterprises. While both new enterprises were being financed partially by enterprises

[17] *Komunist*, November 26, 1970, p. 2, summarized in *ABSEES*, January 1971.
[18] See S. R. Sacks, *Entry of New Competitors in Yugoslav Market Socialism* (Institute of International Studies, University of California, Berkeley, Research Series, 19: 1973), pp. 15-17 and 56-58.

outside their industry, in neither case was this due to a search for a higher return on capital than could be earned elsewhere. In one case, the investment was being made by an enterprise facing marketing difficulties, which thus assured itself of being the principal raw material supplier of the new enterprise. In the second case, some of the investments came from contracting firms which were eager to gain an inside track on contracts to build and equip the new plant; other investments came from future purchasers of the new plant's product, who were guaranteed lower-than-market purchase prices. In both of these cases, the investors' motivation was commercial rather than financial.

Another of my interviews was in a business bank which was taking an equity position in an operating enterprise, thereby partially financing the enterprise's major expansion. Here it was unclear to me whether the bank's motivation was that of increasing its rate of return beyond what was feasible from a long-term loan, or whether it was that of providing a socially desirable investment without placing the expanding enterprise in the difficult financial position of having too high a debt ratio. My impression from a talk with a director of the bank was that both motives were present.

(2) A second additional source of finance is the issuance by enterprises of bonds which may be purchased either by enterprises or individuals. Such bonds were legalized only in 1970 and, once more, the attraction to the purchaser was other than financial. The principal automobile enterprise of the country, as well as a major tractor plant, have issued such bonds which carry with them the right to purchase the company's product at a low price or with quicker delivery time than is customary. In 1971, about 2 percent of the investment funds of the country were raised through the issuance of such bonds.

(3) A third source of external funds has been a system of compulsory loans by other enterprises. Investments in the electric power industry of Slovenia during 1965-70 were financed largely by a fifteen-year compulsory loan, paying only 5 percent interest, and levied on each nonelectricity enterprise of the republic as a proportion of its own gross fixed investments in each year. However, electric power is the only industry for which I have heard of this method of financing.

(4) The fourth source of external finance is foreign, and has taken the form of joint ventures with Yugoslav enterprises. Such foreign funds, however, have provided only a very minor amount of capital. Between mid-1967, when such joint ventures were legalized, and mid-1972, some fifty-two joint ventures were registered and about $93 million worth of capital (2 percent of the period's gross investment in fixed capital in all industry) was subscribed by foreign capital. Half of the total foreign capital subscriptions were in the automotive industry, and a minimum of

another fifth came from East German and Czech sources. The pace of subscriptions remained fairly constant from the beginning, showing no tendency to increase.[19]

The relative insignificance of these additional sources of external finance, added to the fact that industrial enterprises have provided only one-third of their own gross financial needs for fixed investment, has left the business banks as the main provider of investment funds. The regional character of these banks has had the negative effect on efficient use of capital resources which was noted earlier. But the economic importance of the banks has also placed them in a difficult political situation. On the one hand, it has led to claims that they undermine the self-management of industrial enterprises by dictating business policy, masterminding appointments of managerial staff, and draining away enterprise profits through interest and bank charges.[20] On the other hand, the very power of the banks has enticed commune and republic governments to attempt to influence their lending policies; not only does this weaken the independence of the bank directors, but it further exposes them to the charge that the intertwining of the banks and local governments is injurious to the self-management principle of the economy.[21]

MERGERS

The statistical picture. The merger movement among industrial enterprises received considerable attention in Yugoslavia toward the end of the 1960's, primarily in terms of the potential it offers for mobility of capital. Before discussing this movement, it is worth while to show its recency. Table 13.2 indicates the net change during different time periods in the number of industrial enterprises of different sizes.

During the five years immediately prior to the 1965 reform, there was only a 1 percent decline in the total number of industrial firms. Since the industrial labor force increased by 33 percent during this period, it is not at all surprising that the number of enterprises in the larger size categories increased sharply. There is nothing in these figures which suggests any major merger movement; if we base our estimate on the available figures for 1961 and 1962, it would appear that about

---

[19] *Privredni Pregled*, July 31 and August 1, 1972, p. 2, translated in *JPS*. Organization of European Co-Operation and Development, *Foreign Investment in Yugoslavia* (Paris: 1970), pp. 13-15.

[20] The fact that it is the federal government which is the principal supplementary source of investment funds for industry is far from a consolation to those Yugoslavs anxious to preserve the principle of self-management.

[21] See, for example, M. Tripalo (then a member of the executive bureau of the presidium of the League of Communists) in *VUS*, October 14, 1970, pp. 21-25, summarized in *ABSEES*, January 1971, and K. Gligorov (who held a similar position) in *Politika*, March 6, 1973.

TABLE 13.2: Number of Enterprises in Industry and Mining in All Yugoslavia (index for last year, with first year of each period = 100)

Size of Enterprise (number of employees)	1959-64	1965-68	1968-70
All enterprises	99	102	95
Enterprises with 126-250 employees	101	101	95
Enterprises with more than:			
250 employees	122	96	100
Of these:			
1,000-2,000 employees	139	96	107
More than 2,000 employees	143	107	108

SOURCE: *Statistički*, 1961 through 1972, tables 106-3, 106-5, 106-9, and 203-10 in the various issues. Employment data are average for the year, excluding apprentices. There is no good reason to doubt that these data are roughly comparable as between years. It is true that another source (M. Dautović, "Economic Integration," *Yugoslav Survey*, IX, 2, 1968, p. 77) gives much larger figures than those of *Statistički* for the number of enterprises in all sectors together during 1959-64, and roughly the same figures for 1965 and 1966. But the discrepancy does not appear to affect the earlier years' figures for industry and mining. (Compare Jan Vanek, *The Economics of Workers' Management*, George Allen and Unwin Ltd., London: 1972, p. 104. Vanek gives similar figures to those of Dautović for the total number of enterprises in 1961 and 1962; but his figures for the number of industrial and mining enterprises are comparable to those of *Statistički*.)

NOTE: Due to the rapid inflation, no categorization of enterprise size by sales or amount of capital would be warranted for an intertemporal comparison. Employment is the only valid aspect of size which is available.

3.3 percent of all industrial enterprises disappeared annually because of merger (see Table 13.3).

The three years following the reform constitute a period in which the industrial labor force was essentially stable (it registered a 2 percent decline), and in which the financial position of enterprises was particularly shaky. Yet the number of enterprises actually increased slightly, and this was especially true of the smaller ones.

It is only during the years 1969-70, when employment increased by 8 percent and for the first time surpassed the 1965 level, that mergers appear to have been vigorous.[22] They must have accounted for the bulk

[22] In industry, the number of mergers during 1970 were twice the average of 1965-66 (*Politika*, August 17, 1971, p. 8, translated in *JTS*, and M. Dautović, "Economic Integration," *Yugoslav Survey*, IX, 2, 1968, p. 78).

Using other data, Sacks concludes that the merger movement did not have a substantial effect on the measurable aspects of industrial structure at any time during the 1959-68 period (S. R. Sacks, "Changes in Industrial Structure in Yugoslavia, 1959-1968," *Journal of Political Economy*, 80, 3, 1972, Part I, pp. 573-74).

The merger movement developed at a much more rapid pace outside industry, with 24 percent of the total number of nonindustrial enterprises disappearing in these two years. Handicraft enterprises, agricultural and fishing units, restaurants and bars, and retail stores were the primary victims.

of the 5 percent per annum decline in the number of industrial enterprises with fewer than two hundred fifty employees, in addition to compensating for the additional small enterprises formed during these years.[23]

Unfortunately, the above materials deal only with the net change in the number of enterprises, whereas it is the gross change which should interest us. The only comprehensive data of which I am aware that treat the entry and exist of enterprises are rather old (see Table 13.3), but

TABLE 13.3: Entry and Exit of All Enterprises in Industry and Mining in All Yugoslavia, 1961 and 1962

	Enterprises	
Causes of Entry and Exit	Number	Proportion of total existing at beginning of 1962 (percent)
Total number of enterprises at beginning of 1962	2,781	100
Exits		
Total	258	9
Due to liquidation	75	3
Due to merger	183	7
Entries		
Total	248	9
Due to establishing new enterprises	215	8
Due to merger	20	1
Due to division of enterprises	13	—

SOURCE: Jan Vanek, *The Economics of Workers' Management* (George Allen and Unwin Ltd., London: 1972), p. 104. These data were assembled especially for the late Vanek by the Yugoslav Federal Office of Statistics.

NOTE: Changes in the number of enterprises due to their being transferred statistically in or out of the category of industry and mining are not included in the entries and exits.

[23] Liquidations cannot have been significant in this decline; they would have been more likely to have occurred earlier, and in any case appear to have been quite exceptional. (See, for example, B. Horvat, "Yugoslav Economic Policy in the Post-War Period," *American Economic Review*, LXI, 3, 1971, Part 2, p. 105.) Slovenian industry showed a pattern which was fairly similar to that of Yugoslavia as a whole, but mergers seem to have played less of a role in that republic. With an 8 percent increase in industrial employment between 1968 and 1970, the number of industrial enterprises with less than two hundred fifty employees registered a 4 percent per annum decline between December 1968 and December 1970. However, the total number of industrial enterprises declined by only 1 percent, and there was a substantially sharper increase than in Yugoslavia as a whole in the number of enterprises with more than one thousand employees. New hirings by existing enterprises, rather than mergers, probably played a larger role in Slovenia than in the rest of Yugoslavia (Socialistična Republika Slovenija, Zavod SR Slovenije za Statistiko, *Statistični Letopis SR Slovenije*, Ljubljana, 1970 and 1972 issues, tables 4-10 and 4-3 respectively).

there is no reason to think that the entry rate has substantially increased. Entry of enterprises due to the establishment of new units (rather than because of mergers or division of enterprises) accounted for an average of only 4 percent of all enterprises each year. Moreover, the data available are for two years (1960 and 1961) in which the rate of increase in industrial employment was higher than in any postreform year. Exits in industry and mining due to merger were 6 percent during the two years of 1965-66 compared to 7 percent during 1961-62; i.e., virtually the same.[24] Thus it seems unlikely that knowledge of the gross figures of entry and exit would radically alter the picture presented above.

The industrial merger movement of 1969 and 1970, primarily affecting enterprises with fewer than two hundred fifty employees, was an accompaniment of difficult financial times in the Yugoslav economy as a whole. Since mergers were a response to economic conditions, it seems appropriate to relate them to the economic situation of the previous year; unfortunately, the financial data available to me apply to all enterprises rather than to those of industry alone. During the first three quarters of 1968, 43 percent of all enterprises were unable to meet their financial obligations regularly; during the same period of 1969, this figure rose to 55 percent.[25] Fourteen percent of all Yugoslav enterprises suffered net losses for the year 1968, and 15 percent (employing 12 percent of the Yugoslav labor force) for 1969.[26]

Yet, despite the fact that enterprises were supposed to pay only 80 percent of the previous year's wages if they had suffered losses for the year as a whole, only 2 to 3 percent of all Yugoslav enterprises in 1969 in fact obeyed this legal restriction.[27] In Zagreb, for example, enterprises which together employed one hundred thousand workers were exempted

[24] Dautović, p. 78. In 1965, 92 percent of the participants in the mergers were enterprises with fewer than two hundred fifty employees.

[25] Calculated from *Ekonomska Politika* of December 8, 1969, as referred to in G. Lemân, "Die jugoslawische Unternehmung in der Wirtschaftsreform," in W. Förster and D. Lorenz (eds.), *Beiträge zur Theorie und Praxis von Wirtschaftssystemen* (Duncker & Humbolt, West Berlin: 1970), pp. 208-09.

[26] *Naše Teme*, 1970, 1, and *Komunist*, September 17, 1970, p. 2, summarized in *ABSEES*, July 1970 and January 1971. These figures exclude enterprises, such as one in which I interviewed, in which bookkeeping manipulations hid actual losses. This enterprise, having suffered heavy losses during the first half of 1969, produced substantially for inventory accumulation during the second half and came out for the year with a slight profit. This profit can only have reflected the price which it set on its inventories.

[27] See *VUS*, March 4, 1970, pp. 22-25, summarized in *ABSEES*, July 1970. Those enterprises paying the minimum wage are added in to form this percentage. The total percentage of Yugoslav employees covered was, however, somewhat higher than this.

According to Lemân, p. 209, the number of enterprises affected was considerably higher, but still vastly smaller than the number which should have been.

from the regulation by the municipal Party committee.[28] Bankruptcy proceedings were started against only 198 enterprises in 1969—1.4 percent of all those in Yugoslavia.[29] In my own interviews, I came across only one industrial firm which had been placed into formal bankruptcy; its plant, moreover, was taken over on the next day by another enterprise and continued to operate and provide employment for its labor force.

Clearly, such financial difficulties posed a serious problem for the communes and republics. Due to their own restricted resources, only limited aid could be given directly to enterprises by the government bodies themselves. But pressure could also be placed upon the business banks to come to the rescue. Within extremely broad limits, suppliers could be forced to take up some of the burden by extending trade credit.[30] Still another major form of aid available was to persuade the stronger enterprises to absorb the weaker; sometimes—but almost certainly not always—this was in the interest of both.

Mergers discussed in interviews. This section will treat all mergers and attempted mergers in which the industrial firms of my sample both took part and about which they told me.

I know relatively little about the first case, since my informants were involved only at the tail-end of the proceedings. Here a rather unsuccessful enterprise (A) of one commune was merged in 1967 with a second (B) of the same industry in the same commune. Later that year, on the basis that it was losing money, A was split off from B and joined to a third enterprise (C) in a nearby commune. A year later, two other portions of B—also losing money—were similarly split off and joined to a fourth enterprise (D) of its own commune. Another year and a half later, considerable pressure was being placed upon a fifth enterprise (E)—this time, at least, a highly successful one—to take over C, which was now in a bad liquidity position and suffering from an inability to sell its products (it had already had to stop production of the original product line of A).

From the information available, this series of mergers would appear

---

[28] *VUS*, March 4, 1970, pp. 22-25.   [29] *Naše Teme*, 1970, 1.

[30] During the five years of 1967-71, increases in trade credits to enterprises (in the whole economy, not just in industry) averaged four times the increase in short-term bank credit to the same enterprises (*OECD Financial Statistics*, 1970-72). The average number of days between the sale of goods and the receipt of payment increased from sixty-eight in 1968 to one hundred four in late 1971 (*Privredni Vjesnik*, October 14, 1971, p. 3, summarized in *ABSEES*, January 1972). The first stoppage of deliveries to business customers for nonpayment of debts did not occur until August 1971; similar earlier threats (for oil by-products, gasoline, and electricity) had not been carried out. Only as of January 1973 were illiquid firms obliged to reduce their workers' incomes by 10 percent compared to 1972 wage payments.

to have been forced upon unwilling partners in the same and in a neighboring commune: precisely what we might expect in the case of absorption of unprofitable enterprises. But perhaps, as the remaining cases would suggest, this appearance is a reflection only of my lack of detailed knowledge.

The second case is a merger which would also appear, on the face of it, to have been a shotgun marriage. A large enterprise merged in 1969 with two medium-sized and unsuccessful neighbors in the same industry, thus increasing its size by two-fifths. At the time of the merger, the general director of the parent enterprise had stated publicly that the result would probably be that wages of workers in the original enterprise would increase more slowly for the next three or four years than would otherwise have been the case; in fact, this prediction seems to have been born out during at least the first year of the merger when there was no increase at all in real wages, even though worker earnings in the absorbed enterprises had not been brought up to the level of those in the parent firm. Rather substantial bank debt by the absorbed firms was accepted as an obligation by the parent enterprise, although it is true that this was converted to twenty-year credit at 1 percent interest, and with a three- to five-year total moratorium on payments of principal and interest. The willingness of the banks to accept these bad terms is convincing evidence that the absorbed enterprises had been virtually bankrupt.

A sweetener for the merger consisted of loans which must have been conditional upon it. Three new plants were to be erected by the enterprise; internally generated funds would be needed for only one-fifth of this investment, with the rest coming from banks at 4½ and 6 percent interest—perhaps one-third to one-half of the customary effective market rate.

The prime reason for the merger, according to a number of executives of the parent firm, was the belief that it was necessary for marketing reasons. This belief was predicated on the hypothesis that only very large enterprises could market successfully, although no case which seemed reasonable to me could be made for this position as it applied to the particular industry. In fact, it was perfectly clear that the parent enterprise had faced no current marketing problems up till then and that it anticipated none in the forseeable future. The assistant general director put the marketing argument to me in terms of having to plan for the year 2000.

Why, then, the merger? Should it be explained solely on grounds of social pressure both on the parent enterprise and on the banks which sweetened the proposition? From my talks in the enterprise, I doubt it. Executives at all levels—as well as the heads of the workers' organizations—seemed to be obsessed with the necessity for growth, and with the fear that a rival some fifty kilometers off would have absorbed these enterprises if their own firm had not done so. In so far as I could judge, the obsession was totally unreasonable in terms of objectives either of short-run or long-run earnings per worker or of return on capital; the issue of reasonableness, however, is irrelevant to the question of whether desire for growth was indeed the major motivating factor.

The third case is a merger in 1970 with an obsolete factory which was to be immediately torn down and replaced by another facility built on a different site. Two justifications were given for this merger: the first was that the parent enterprise could not otherwise have received a loan for the new construction, since the banks would have rejected any proposal involving additional competition for a weak enterprise in the same commune. The second was social: the assistant general director in the parent enterprise told me that, in a socialist economy, one cannot work solely for the advantage of one's own enterprise.

A fourth case was that of the absorption in 1969 of an enterprise in the same commune which had actually gone bankrupt, and whose facilities were considered quite incapable of competing in the market for the plant's existing product line. The general director of the absorbing enterprise justified the take-over by stating that he needed the extra plant space and was getting the factory very cheaply.[31] Indeed, he did proceed promptly to transfer products to it from his parent plant.

This might seem to be a straightforward case of an enterprise taking advantage of a bargain in order to meet its needs for expansion. But, in fact, the parent enterprise was expanding rapidly into a variety of product lines which were considerably more profitable than its basic line. Would it not have been more profitable to have restricted itself to its old plant and labor force, and to have reduced its output of its principal product line as rapidly as possible, rather than expanding both? The general director denied that this was possible because of the issue of economies of scale within a given line, but his argument appeared to me somewhat doubtful.

This take-over was accompanied by a complete replacement of the management of the absorbed enterprise with junior and middle managers of the parent firm. This was the only complete managerial replacement after merger which I have encountered in Yugoslavia; in the other cases, only the top layer of management was forced to leave. Nor were the workers of the absorbed enterprise left unscathed; they were compelled to accept the higher intensity of work and lower piece rates which had long been traditional in the parent firm.

---

[31] The bank debts of the absorbed firm were converted to a twelve-year loan at 5 percent (one-third of the effective rate the absorbing enterprise was currently paying for bank credit), and with a moratorium for the first two years.

The fifth case is a 1969 merger across republic lines. Interestingly, this is the first one where the parent enterprise was acting purely in its own self-interest.

The absorbed enterprise had low labor productivity and was in a dangerous financial position. Half of its total production was purchased as subcomponents by the absorbing firm. It was clear that the enterprise would be absorbed by some company, and in fact it first negotiated with a competitor of the firm with which it finally merged. It was believed to have a good product line and modern facilities; the absorbing firm believed that its problems were really limited to poor top management.

Three reasons were given for the merger. The most important was competitive: the parent enterprise was unwilling to become dependent on a Yugoslav competitor for a major subcomponent, and it perceived the alternative to merger as being the construction of its own subcomponent plant. The second major consideration was commercial: top management believed that it would be easier for it to market its products in other republics if it proved that it was a real "Yugoslav firm" by having facilities outside its own republic. The third reason was that top management was convinced that the merger was a sound financial investment (presumably, the investment consisted of taking responsibility for the bank debt of the absorbed firm) and that it would prove profitable.

The first few months of the take-over saw the replacement of all the seventeen top managers in the absorbed firm, except for one man who was retained on a trial basis. The workforce was cut by 12 percent with no reduction in output, clearly showing that ready improvements in productivity were feasible. The merger promised to be a success.

This merger was accompanied by an interesting agreement with the workers' council of the absorbed enterprise. The parent firm provided a sharply increasing guaranteed output for each year between 1969 and 1975, and was planning on bringing wage levels in the absorbed plant up to those of the parent firm by 1974 or 1975. The latter program, however, was conditional on the factories all having attained equal labor productivity. This plan for attaining equality of wages within six years is particularly striking since the parent firm was a very high-wage enterprise even for Slovenia.

The sixth case involves the merger of three enterprises (one merger occurred prior to 1965 and the second in 1967) in two different republics. The three enterprises were all in the same industry, and all produced competing products. The merger achieved specialization by product among the different factories.

Two aspects are interesting about this case (unfortunately, I have only limited knowledge concerning it). First, it is another instance of interrepublic merger, although here the reasons for this are unknown. The second is that, although more than half the total employment of the merged enterprise was in one poorly developed and low-wage area, virtually all of the post-1965 investment of the merged firm has been in the different region of a second of the original three enterprises. Apparently, the location of investment within the merged firm was guided by profitability considerations, rather than by the desire to provide equal employment opportunities in all communes or to concentrate such opportunities within the commune where the majority of the enterprise's workers lived. This fact provides some justification for the position of a manager in another firm, which was then strongly resisting merger, who insisted that there is an advantage for a commune in having its own independent enterprises rather than in seeing them merged into larger concerns which are headquartered elsewhere.

The seventh and final case consists not of a merger, but rather of unsuccessful efforts to negotiate one. Here, an enterprise supplying about one-third of the total Yugoslav market for its types of product attempted in 1969 and early 1970 to merge with two other large enterprises (one of them being in a different republic) in order to achieve greater market power. Cartelization was the unabashed objective and, in line with this purpose, only a loose linkage of the original enterprises was desired.

Of these seven cases of merger or attempted merger, only two clearly had no element of rescue of an enterprise in trouble as the motive for the absorbing firm. Four cases obviously involved such considerations. Yet in only one case (the first) is there no evidence that the absorbing firms thought that the mergers were in their own self-interest; moreover, this is one of the two cases about which I have the least information. The use of bank credits to finance new investment is the most prominent method used for pushing mergers which would otherwise have been unacceptable.

Of the four merger cases which clearly included considerations of rescue, three were restricted to a single commune and the fourth affected a nearby commune. This is what we would have expected, given the localism of Yugoslav politics. But it would be a mistake to conclude from this that medium-sized and larger enterprises generally have their labor force entirely restricted to a single commune. In 1960 and 1961, prior to the merger movement, the number of enterprise divisions located in communes other than that of the headquarters of the enterprise constituted 90 percent of the total number of industrial enterprises with more than two hundred fifty employees.[32] By 1970, however, despite the

[32] See Vanek, *The Economics of Workers' Management*, p. 104, and *Statistički*, 1961-63. Of course, much fewer than 90 percent of these enterprises were involved, since many of these enterprises must have had more than one such division.

mergers and the starting up of new departments by existing firms, this proportion was undoubtedly much lower; for the number of communes had been reduced by 34 percent, from seven hundred fifty-nine at the end of 1961.

Among the six cases in which mergers were completed, two involved enterprises of different republics. Interrepublic mergers promised in 1969 and 1970 to become of increasing importance;[33] since such mergers are not motivated by hopes of rescuing unsuccessful enterprises, but rather by good investment prospects, they would serve as a means of helping to bring the regional allocation of capital in Yugoslavia more into line with the regional efficiency of capital. But the exacerbation of strife among the republics in the early 1970's appears to have stopped this movement. One well-informed Yugoslav told me in mid-1972 that, in fact, mergers going beyond the level of the individual commune had become relatively rare.[34]

COMPETITION AMONG ENTERPRISES

Yugoslav enterprises differ from the CMEA enterprises not only in the degree to which they are free of any unified government control, but also in that the competitive economic environment in which they operate is quite similar to that of western capitalist countries. True, we do see commune and republic governments intervening to prevent physical liquidations of enterprises and the mass dismissal of their labor force. But worker incomes vary substantially as between financially successful and unsuccessful enterprises, and at least the top layer of management appears normally to lose their positions when an unsuccessful enterprise is absorbed by another.

The sellers' market conditions which exist in Hungary are far from the rule in Yugoslavia. Purchasing agents insist that they receive different price quotations for the semifabricates and components they need. Sufficiently large discounts are received for quantity purchases so that one enterprise could claim that it has completely financed the amortization of new expansion by the additional rebates on purchases which such expansion made possible. Substantial excess capacity exists in some product lines, and there are enterprises which have been compelled to abandon completely the production of certain lines in which they had

[33] In 1970, 5 percent of all mergers in the country crossed republic lines (*Politika*, August 17, 1971, p. 8, translated in *JTS*).

[34] In the economy as a whole, even though only about 40 percent of mergers since 1965 have involved enterprises of different communes, the majority of merger-dissolutions have been of such enterprises (*Privredni Vjesnik*, April 6, 1972, p. 3, summarized in *ABSEES*, July 1972).

earlier had large sales. Price competition forces even successful enterprises to tear down obsolete facilities and build new ones. Quite unlike the situation in Hungary, a leading textile producing firm in which I interviewed was able to sell only 30 percent of its output on annual contracts, with the rest being sold on spot contracts; even the 30 percent contracted for annually might in reality be returned by the wholesalers, with the textile enterprise being unable to demand fulfillment of the contract because of the resulting loss of future markets.

To some degree, competition is fed by entry of new firms into the economy. But Table 13.3 showed that such entry was relatively slight in industry during 1960-61. Although no data are available to me for entries since the reform of 1965, there is no reason to think that the number has substantially increased.[35] Aside from enterprises created mainly by a grouping of firms already within the same industry, these would have to be financed primarily by communes or republics. The demands on the funds of government units for the support of existing enterprises appear to be so large, relative to the resources available, that little would be left for financing the creation of new enterprises.

Considerably more important, however, is the branching out of existing enterprises into new fields. One of the enterprises in which I interviewed was constantly entering new spheres; acting primarily as an assembly and marketing firm, it would import products until the national market developed sufficiently to warrant home production, and then would take over the manufacturing operation. It was engaged in a constant search for new product lines, and at the time of my interviews was even preparing to extend beyond its broad field of metal fabrication.

A second enterprise moved from the building of large tailor-made units of equipment into the assembly of automobiles. A third enterprise remained in the area of light metal fabrication; but during the past four years, it had entered the manufacture of a variety of products which had a similar technology of production but very different end uses; about one year before my interview, it had begun to produce a product which promised high profits and had previously had only one producer in all of Yugoslavia. A fourth enterprise was remaining entirely in textile production, but was attempting to shift from bulk production to high-price speciality items.

By the time of my interviews, three manufacturing enterprises in my sample of eleven had begun opening their own retail stores to sell their products. One firm was prepared to invest heavily in tourism over the

---

[35] Data on the net changes in the number of enterprises classified in each of one hundred three branches of industry (three-digit sic classification) suggest that net increases were fewer during 1963-68 than during 1959-63 (Sacks, "Changes in Industrial Structure," pp. 563-64).

next five years. Two were establishing export-import units to handle general commission business as well as their own foreign trade.

In short, the majority of the enterprises in which I interviewed were constantly on the alert for new products—and even completely different lines of activity—which promised to be more profitable than their old ones. In this regard, their orientation was heavily geared to marketing —quite the reverse of the situation prevailing in the enterprises of the CMEA countries.

Moreover, these new activities were only partially carried out in the current facilities of the enterprises. To a considerable degree they required new investments—and not always in their own communes. It is existing enterprises which are in the best financial position to attempt to enter activities promising high profits; thus it is not surprising that much of Yugoslavia's capital mobility, both between different products and even quite different sectors, should occur through the branching out of these firms. For it is existing enterprises which not only have the largest amounts of internal finance available, but are also in the best position to approach the business banks for loans.

The present workers of an enterprise which invests in new activities to be carried out elsewhere are able to make what amounts to an equity investment. To the degree that such activities are profitable, the income (calculated prior to wage payments) per member of the expanded labor force of the enterprise will be increased, and it is up to the workers' council of the enterprise as a whole to determine how the wage portion of this income will be distributed among the workers in the different activities. Workers in the older and less-profitable activities can be paid more than their production brings in to the firm. This is the type of Yugoslav direct equity investment which offers the greatest possibility both for profit and for continued control; it is not surprising that it should be particularly extensive.

Such investments do, however, carry a special element of risk. Under Yugoslav law, individual units within an enterprise can choose to become independent; obviously, this is tempting for units established to carry out particularly profitable activities.[36] While such decomposition of enterprises does occur, the managements of those firms in which I interviewed did not seem particularly worried about the possibility. Perhaps their greatest protection is that the business bank which had given the loan to finance the investment would have to approve the decomposition until the time the loan was paid off, and the bank would be most likely to side with the parent organization which was almost certainly a founder of the bank.

[36] See Sacks, *Entry of New Competitors*, pp. 11-12 for an account of the relevant legislation.

A variant on such investments by enterprises is to develop subcontracting relationships with smaller firms. One large enterprise in which I interviewed derived about 15 percent of its profits from purchasing and reselling goods within its own line of products from seven other firms, each with one hundred or fewer employees. The contracting enterprise provided marketing services—fitting the smaller firms' products into its own line—as well as supplying technical services, quality control, and product development. It viewed this arrangement partly as a means of directly boosting its earnings, but secondly as a means of controlling production which might otherwise have led to price competition.

A second enterprise was considering providing a similar service in an industry which was completely foreign to its own. It envisioned a potentially profitable market in plastics, and was interested in matching this market with the capacity of a number of leather-working factories in the neighborhood which were currently operating at a loss. The enterprise was thinking of organizing them through a subcontracting relationship; in this case, the contracting enterprise would itself have put up some of the necessary funds for production conversion, and bank loans would have been available only because of its participation in the venture.

The formation of voluntary associations of enterprises requires quite minor investments by the member enterprises, but can be significant in improving their competitive position. Such associations began in 1958, and by the beginning of 1967 there were two hundred ninety of them in the economy as a whole.[37] Their functions can be seen from the following four examples which turned up in my interviews.

The first association numbered about thirty enterprises from all but the single republic where the giant of their industry is located. This association fulfilled two primary roles. The first was selling—half through its own retail shops—about one-sixth of its members' total production of consumer durables; the second was providing maintenance service to consumers for all the products sold. By belonging to this association, the member firms were placed in a much stronger competitive position ɹlative to the industry leader.

This association was also intended to play the cartel role of reducing competition among its members. As part of its effort to eliminate product duplication, it has attempted to develop new products to offer to members as a substitute for existing items whose production they renounce. But my impression from interviews is that this aspect of the association's activities has not been particularly successful.

A second association in a different industry kept its membership open to all enterprises of the industry, but was in fact almost entirely re-

[37] Dautović, p. 80.

stricted to a single republic. Its activities were primarily in the lucrative field of exporting and importing for its members, none of whom could afford to maintain the necessary skilled staff for this purpose. Not only does the existence of the association permit the members to integrate vertically into an area of high profit, but it also provides a mechanism by which they can avoid price competition with one another on foreign markets.

A third association was formed by nineteen equipment and engineering companies, mainly within a single republic, to work as a general contractor in industrial construction. While the association operates as though it were an independent enterprise, and while it meets its engagements by buying equipment from all sources, its members would appear to be given preferential treatment as suppliers.

A fourth association, like the first, has been successful in two functions but not in a third. It has handled for its members all of their exports and approximately half of their domestic sales. It also has handled all of their larger purchases so as to receive quantity discounts. It has been unsuccessful, however, in persuading its members to specialize their production so that the group as a whole would gain the maximum economies of scale.

Generally, then, these associations appear to be aimed at improving the sales, and sometimes the purchasing, facilities of the members. Efforts at cartelization through the medium of the association have, however, been effective in only one association, and even there only for exports where it was unlikely that such cartelization would have much impact.

It is certainly true that Yugoslav enterprises have striven for restrictions on competition, and that the existence of a large number of product markets in which there are few firms[38]—a phenomenon virtually inevitable in a small country because of the economies of scale in large production—would seem to have encouraged such efforts. Governments have done virtually nothing to promote competition, perhaps because powers reside primarily in commune and republic governments and their interests are parochial.[39]

[38] See Sacks, "Changes in Industrial Structure," p. 272.

[39] Acts in restraint of trade, and particularly market sharing and price fixing, are prohibited under a federal law of 1960 (although retail trade price maintenance agreements are legal). But in fact such acts have been condoned and often encouraged by government. The absence of seriousness in enforcing antitrust legislation is exemplified by the situation in Croatia, where cases filed with the Croatian Supreme Economic Court under "unfair competition" relate almost exclusively to copyright infringement (ibid., p. 566).

Price controls and tariff rates are the only other federal weapons available against cartel abuses, and there is no indication that they have been utilized significantly.

Yet efforts at restricting competition within individual industrial branches have not been particularly successful. Such unsuccessful efforts were observed both within the associations and in the case of the unsuccessful merger cited earlier. Another example is a product line which has only three producers in Yugoslavia. A new product within this line was developed by the dominant firm of the industry in 1966 and proved quite profitable. After two years, the other two enterprises also began producing the same product—but they sold it at a 15 percent reduction from the original price, although their new price was immediately matched by the first firm. Still another case is that of a firm which failed to raise its prices when price restrictions were lifted from its products because of its fear of encouraging entry of new competitors. One association's efforts to carry out a market study for its industry were encountering great difficulties in 1970 because enterprises were unwilling to reveal their plans, and even their past and current sales, to the association.

The failure to exploit the potential advantages of oligopoly seems to be due primarily to the financial weakness of most industrial firms, which both forces them to concentrate upon short-run gains and prevents the larger ones from using financial power to police the market by threatening below-cost sales.[40] For these reasons, and not because of enterprise restraint on social grounds, oligopoly in the Yugoslav market has been much less of a problem than might have been expected.[41] In this regard, it should also be noted that four-firm concentration ratios in Yugoslav industry in 1963 were no higher than Canadian concentration ratios in 1948,[42] and that they do not seem to have changed appreciably between 1959 and 1968.[43]

Yugoslav complaints about monopoly abuse have not focused upon industry, but rather have concentrated upon the sectors of banking, export-import houses, and wholesaling. Some Yugoslav authorities have even insisted that capitalist exploitation within enterprises has been replaced by the exploitation of entire self-managed industrial enterprises

[40] One may ask why business banks do not jump into the breach. Presumably, it is because of the social restrictions on the effective rate of interest that they can charge.

[41] Imports also act as a competitive force. However, the high level of Yugoslav tariffs on competitive imports, which stems to a considerable degree from the balance of payments situation, makes the threat of expanded imports less of a restraint on oligopoly behavior in most sectors than might have been expected.

[42] T. A. Marschak, "Centralized versus Decentralized Resource Allocation: the Yugoslav 'Laboratory' " Quarterly Journal of Economics, LXXXII, 4 (1968), 583.

[43] This is true for all subperiods (excluding 1961-63 when there was a decline) both for three-digit and four-digit branch classifications. See Sacks, "Changes in Industrial Structure," pp. 563, 565, and 573.

by these service sectors, and they have called for a new "nationalization."[44]

Indeed, income differentials between different sectors sometimes reach surprising heights. In 1972 within the single commune of Split, average salaries in the bank, the Chamber of Commerce, and foreign trade enterprises were ten times as high as the average in the economy of the commune as a whole.[45]

Nevertheless, the exploitation complaints would appear to be grossly exaggerated. It is true that the geographic fractionalization of banking has made this into a monopoly industry, but I have shown above that the business banks have been in no position to exploit their position. Export-import firms have indeed seemed to be highly profitable, but this would appear to be because of the quasi-rents enjoyed by their labor force due to the lack of personnel experienced in foreign trade.[46] Moreover, in view of the profitability of these operations, industrial enterprises appear to have begun to engage in them on a substantial scale, both directly and through their industry associations.[47]

Wholesale trade has perhaps profited most from monopoly conditions; the main responsibility for this is borne by the republics and communes, which have placed obstacles in the path of "foreign" concerns from other republics. Wholesalers in a variety of fields began to expand into retailing in the late 1960's in order to strengthen their oligopolistic position. Nevertheless, while all the enterprises in which I interviewed were respectful of the power of wholesalers, three of them had entered the retail field themselves in the late 1960's in order to challenge the wholesalers' grip on local markets.

As one might expect, nationalism also plays a role in fostering local monopolies by manufacturers. Thus one major Slovenian enterprise

[44] See, for example, the interview with Miko Tripalo, then a member of the executive bureau of the presidium of the Yugoslav League of Communists, in *VUS*, October 14, 1970, pp. 21-25. See also the analogy drawn by Bakarić, at the Second Congress of Self-Managers, between the worker-capitalist relationship and that of the enterprises and banks in Yugoslavia. (*Vjesnik*, May 7, 1971, p. 2. Both sources are summarized in *ABSEES*, January and July 1971.)

[45] Research paper of B. Vuckovic reported on in *Borba*, February 8, 1973, and summarized in *ABSEES*, April 1973.

[46] Foreign trade operations were really freed only in 1965, and naturally there were few Yugoslavs at that time who were familiar with foreign markets. Although export-import houses require licenses to operate, these are granted to all organizations which have sufficient personnel with the appropriate training.

[47] In the four and one-half years ending in November 1970, the number of enterprises and associations engaged in foreign trade operations more than tripled. During 1970, foreign trade firms handled only 54 percent of the country's exports (Z. Pivarski-Stojićević, "Foreign Trade Enterprises," *Yugoslav Survey*, XIII, 1, 1972, pp. 74 and 80).

reported in interviews that it had great difficulties in selling in Croatia (the neighboring republic) because wholesalers would not carry its products. But the industrial enterprises are not without weapons in such a situation; this firm had broken into the markets of one major Croatian city in 1968 by establishing its own retail store there, and also by aiding a wholesaler who had never sold there before to enter this area. Encouraged by its success, it was in the process in 1970 of carrying out the same strategy in a second major Croatian city.

Another aspect of exploitation of production units about which Yugoslavs complain is the expansion of existing enterprises into new and more profitable activities by creating new subsidiary units. Such expansion into tourist facilities, for example, is a favorite field for complaint. When such enterprise equity investments are successful, this does indeed constitute exploitation—but only in a peculiar sense. Wages paid in the new unit could indeed be higher if the finance had instead been available from a business bank, and wages in the investing enterprise would have been lower without such investment. But clearly the complaint consists of a grievance that those actually working in a sector favored by market conditions cannot reap all the gains from this situation, but must instead share them with the workers of an enterprise which had had free capital available for investment. A minor variant on this theme of exploitation is the charging by trading companies of a high fixed rate of interest for medium-term loans; but since the highest rate of which I have heard is 20 percent on a one-year loan[48] (which, in view of the inflation of that year, amounted to only 7 percent real rate of interest), this complaint would appear to have little substance.

In short, it is my impression that the Yugoslav economy is quite competitive, that the many sectors of high concentration are relatively free from oligopolistic abuse because of the financial weakness of the oligopolists, and that sectors of high profits are subject to considerable invasion by enterprises seeking additional and more profitable activities. Monopoly exploitation, although much noted in the nonindustrial sectors, appears peculiarly vulnerable to the forces of competition from enterprises established in other sectors.

This competitiveness is not at all due to the socialist nature of the economy. It is not unreasonable to suspect that it is due in large part to the newness of genuine independence of enterprises at the time of my interviews, and that competition will be reduced in time as some enterprises become financially powerful, and many become sufficiently sound financially to be able to reject the short-run gains from price

---

[48] Twenty percent is also the figure quoted as the black market rate in early 1971 (*Privredni Vjestnik*, March 11, 1971, p. 2, summarized in *ABSEES*, July 1971).

cutting. In any case, the nature of the competition does not differ particularly from that found in capitalist countries.

In this competitive environment, there is very little centralized coordination of enterprise investment. Fears have been expressed about the development of capacity in certain sectors which will shortly become surplus, but no central regulatory controls exist. Even in the case of the highly capital-intensive electric power industry of Slovenia, where investment through 1970 was carried out from a loan fund centralized at the republic level, and where a republic-wide coordinating body was established, investment was coordinated to only a very limited degree. Not only did the republic coordinating body analyze investment projects solely from a republic rather than from an all-federation standpoint, but also the individual enterprises of the industry were free to ignore its recommendations. Both the advantages and the disadvantages of capitalist interfirm competition appear to be replicated in Yugoslavia.

FOREIGN TRADE ACTIVITIES BY INDUSTRIAL ENTERPRISES

With industrial exports constituting one-third of total Yugoslav industrial production,[49] and with substantial imports of materials and semifabricates being required by almost all enterprises, the treatment of foreign trade is of considerable significance for the financial health of the firm. Decisions as to both exports and imports are made by the industrial enterprises themselves, although federal approval of most of their imports is required.

The enterprise is expected to convert its foreign exchange earnings into dinars at the official exchange rate, which is a unified one for all sectors of the economy. In addition, export subsidies in the form of tax-remissions are paid to industrial enterprises; in 1970, these subsidies totaled approximately 22 percent of the total value of industrial and mining exports.[50] But in spite of such subsidies, five of the enterprises in which I interviewed indicated that they either suffered losses on exports to convertible currency countries, or at best earned less on such sales than on those in the home market; the same may well also have been true for other enterprises in which I interviewed. One firm exported in 1969 at a price (including subsidy) which was only 75 to 80 percent of the price received on domestic sales; yet despite this, 40 percent of its total production for the year was exported.

[49] See Chapter 11, footnote 33.
[50] For the total amount of such subsidies, see *NIN*, April 12, 1970, pp. 10 and 12, summarized in *ABSEES*, July 1970. As no such subsidies seem to be paid for agricultural products, they must virtually all be concentrated upon industrial and mining products. Subsidies in the three firms which gave me such information varied between 12 and 17 percent.

Given these disadvantageous financial conditions, what is the motivation for the enterprise to export? Very clearly from my interviews, the dominant reason is the need to finance imports. Enterprises are allowed to retain the foreign currency value of a portion of their exports, and this serves as the prime source for their financing import needs.[51] Although some raw materials can be purchased without such earnings, many—as well as capital equipment purchases—are dependent upon these exports.

Export-retention quotas vary substantially among enterprises; firms in which I have interviewed have had quotas varying between 7 percent and 80 percent.[52] According to an informant in one enterprise, the percentage for any given enterprise differs from one year to another. The Ministry of Foreign Trade, the Ministry of Finance, and the Chamber of Commerce together decide on quotas for different industries, and then varying quotas are set for individual firms (at least for the larger ones) within each industry. In two enterprises, experience has shown that the export-retention quota percentage increases with the proportion of the enterprise's total output which is exported; the experience of a third enterprise was the opposite. Clearly, export-retention quotas are set having in mind not only the incentive effect, but also the need of the individual firm for imports which must be financed in this fashion.

Since licenses for imports seem to be freely given—their existence has been explained to me as aimed at protection of Yugoslav industry, and thus as complementary to tariffs—an enterprise is quite free in determining how to utilize its available foreign exchange. For example, goods may be imported which are available within Yugoslavia but are cheaper abroad; however, in determining to use foreign exchange quotas in this fashion, an enterprise must take account of the fact that it must usually sacrifice income by exporting rather than selling at home.

In one enterprise in which I interviewed, the entire marketing strategy of the firm was based upon having a substantial foreign exchange quota. The firm was attempting to enter one field of consumer durables' manufacturing after another as the Yugoslav market developed, since it was able to profit from a quasi-monopoly position only so long as the individual product lines were relatively new to the market. Because production was uneconomic until volume sales were achieved, it normally entered a new field by first importing the items from western Europe. As of early 1970, it had developed the manufacture of two major prod-

[51] In addition, they are allowed to import capital equipment up to a standard percentage of the minimum legal amortization rate of their equipment.

[52] The export-retention quota was, in principle, set at a common flat rate as of January 1972. But exceptions still continued (*Ekonomska Politika*, February 28, 1972, pp. 17-23, translated in *JTS*).

uct lines in this fashion, and was currently preparing to use the same device for establishing itself in a third.

We have seen earlier that firms with free financial resources can and do expand into new activities, often rather distinct from their earlier ones, which they think will be more profitable. But not only financial resources in dinars are necessary for this purpose; so, too, are unutilized foreign exchange reserves. An enterprise heavily engaged in exports is thus, other things equal, in a better position to expand profitably than is a firm producing essentially for the home market. This is an additional incentive for exports.

One trade-off between direct use of foreign currency for an enterprise's own needs, versus concentration on those types of investment which require only domestic dinars, is for an enterprise to sell foreign currency to its own business bank or even to keep it on deposit with its bank. Since such foreign currency is particularly useful to a bank in providing a legal base against which it can borrow abroad, such sales and deposits appear to play a significant role in banks' credit-rationing decisions as to which enterprises should be granted long-term loans.

Still another trade-off approach, this one semi-illegal, is for an enterprise to purchase foreign goods needed by a second firm which does not itself possess sufficient foreign currency, and to sell these goods for dinars to that firm. This, of course, amounts to the sale of foreign currency at a black-market rate.[53]

A final trade-off approach has been to sell foreign currency directly to other enterprises, a procedure which in 1970 was also semi-illegal but was generally accepted (at least in Slovenia). This market for convertible currency has been a very thin one,[54] and my enterprise sources insisted that they could not depend upon it as a provider of foreign exchange; in fact, they said, it would be regarded as quite unethical to purchase foreign exchange for any except unusual requirements.[55] Executives familiar with this market in Slovenia told me that the rate charged

[53] Not all such transactions are motivated by the expectation of a profit on foreign exchange. One enterprise in which I interviewed was purchasing semifabricates from a foreign concern, and these were paid for by exports to the same foreign concern of different semifabricates by a second Yugoslav enterprise. The second Yugoslav firm was attracted to the deal because in this way it was able to expand its production of these semifabricates by one-third, thereby reaching economically attractive production runs.

[54] According to an estimate made in July 1970 by the head of the directorate for foreign exchange transactions of the national bank, about $20 million of foreign exchange were purchased annually in this market—a bit less than 1 percent of total 1970 imports from nonsocialist countries (*Ekonomska Politika*, July 20, 1970, p. 4, translated in *JTS*).

[55] However, one enterprise in which I interviewed was making such purchases to finance imports of equipment and the payment of foreign consultants.

for foreign currency varied widely, and reached 160 to 200 percent of the official rate; but one firm in 1970 was currently making purchases at a remarkably low mark-up, paying only 125 percent of the official exchange rate.[56]

Given the comparatively unattractive prices (even allowing for export subsidies) which seem generally to be received for exports to convertible currency markets, it is not surprising that many enterprises determine their volume of exports according to their own foreign currency requirements for imports. The absence of a fully recognized open market for foreign currency has doubtless led to foreign trade inefficiencies when judged from the national viewpoint, with the national product mix of exports being somewhat different from what would exist if the dinar were fully convertible. Nevertheless, the situation must be vastly better in this regard than is the case in Hungary; the relatively low rates charged in 1970 for foreign currency on the Yugoslav semi-illegal market are evidence of this.

This suggests that, although foreign currency is a major area of federal interference in the market place—both through subsidies and through the determination of export-retention quotas—such interference has in practice been relatively restrained.

ENTERPRISE INCOME AND INCENTIVES

Western models of worker-managed enterprises suggest that the Yugoslav system should lead to ever-increasing differentials between the per capita incomes of different enterprises. Using the assumption that enterprises attempt to maximize their income per employee, there is no incentive for a firm to hire additional workers simply because their marginal product is greater than what they can earn in other enterprises; this eliminates the tendency toward equalization of worker earnings which exists in capitalist societies. Moreover, the richer enterprise has a stronger incentive to acquire labor-saving machines than has the poorer one (because the cost of labor is greater for the richer firm), and it also

---

[56] These rates contrast sharply with those of 1953, when such rates reached 680 percent of the official exchange rate, and of 1960 when they reached 1,230 percent (Horvat, p. 125).

As of January 1973, an official foreign-exchange market was to be established in Yugoslavia, with banks being eligible to deal on this market both on their own account and on that of their customers. The law establishing this market even allowed dealing in futures. However, it was expected to become effective only gradually, and the federal Secretary for Finance regarded it as illusory unless inflation was first brought under control. (See *Službeni List SFRJ*, 1972, 36, pp. 741-55, and *Borba*, July 1, 1972, p. 4, translated in *JTS*.)

has greater possibilities of investment (both because it need not distribute to labor as high a proportion of its discretionary funds as must the poorer enterprise in order to compete successfully for labor or to pacify its workers, and because it is a better credit risk for bank loans). Thus inequality should increase overtime.[57] Wachtel, treating the enterprise as though it invested only within its own industry, concludes that a trend toward increasing interindustry inequality of per capita income emerges from the worker-management system of decision making.[58]

Short-run institutional restrictions exist on interenterprise and interindustry differentials in income paid out to workers. Probably the most important of these restrictions is the fear of violating the individual community's mores as to appropriate earnings; here, comparisons extending beyond the limits of the commune seem to be irrelevant. A second restriction exists in a few industries (in 1970, apparently only banking and electric power generation) by interenterprise agreements sponsored by the federal government. A third restriction on increased wages in high-income enterprises was imposed by federal and republic laws during 1971-72; but this incomes policy, intended to control inflation, did not appear to be particularly strict. To the degree that such restrictions have any effect, they lead to an increase in the self-financing of investment by the richer enterprises, and should thus further increase the long-run dispersion of income levels between firms.

There are however, offsetting factors which arise partly out of the nature of competition among worker-managed enterprises, and partly out of commune and republic pressures and aid. Enterprises with free capital funds or with access to bank loans expand into the high-profit sectors, and this tendency must have the effect of reducing interindustry (and, perhaps, interenterprise) income differentials. Mergers have been important in 1969 and 1970 (and, perhaps, thereafter); many of these —intended as rescue operations for poorer enterprises—have undoubtedly reduced interenterprise differentials. Another offsetting factor is that wealthier enterprises are expected to make "free gifts" and loans to their communes;[59] one enterprise in which I interviewed contributed annually 1.5 percent of its total income payments to members as a gift to its commune; a second enterprise had contributed 3 to 4 percent until two years earlier, and was currently contributing 8 to 10 percent. Finally, communes and republics provide aid to weaker enterprises; sometimes this is in the form of direct loans, sometimes in the form of

[57] See Marschak, p. 580, who is here expanding on the Ward-Domar model.
[58] H. M. Wachtel, "Workers' Management and Interindustry Wage Differentials in Yugoslavia," *Journal of Political Economy*, 80, 3 (1972), Part I, 548 and 558.
[59] *VUS*, October 27, 1971, pp. 8-9, summarized in *ABSEES*, January 1972.

pressure upon both local business banks and other enterprises to offer assistance, and sometimes in the form of political influence to gain new and profitable activities for these enterprises.

No conclusive data are available as to the relative force of these conflicting tendencies. If we use interindustry wage differentials as a proxy for interenterprise ones, these differentials increased between 1956 and 1966 but stabilized after the reforms (between 1966 and 1969).[60]

Absolute wage differentials for workers with similar skills between enterprises of the same region are substantial, but by no means astonishingly high. A comparison of two Slovenian enterprises with roughly the same skill composition showed that the highly profitable one paid 35 percent higher average wages than did its marginally profitable colleague. If one assumes that wages normally increase with the degree of urbanization, then this percentage represents an understatement of the differential; for the high-wage enterprise was located in a small town, while the low-wage firm was in a large city. A second Slovenian comparison within a single city showed a similar difference between workers of identical skills employed in different enterprises. A third Slovenian comparison of identical work skills in an electric generating enterprise (one of the highest-income industries), contrasted with the average for the city in which the enterprise was located, showed a 21 percent difference.[61] A fourth comparison is a statistical sample drawn from all enterprises of the relevant industries in Belgrade and Zagreb during 1963 and 1964; of seven occupational specialties studied in each of these two cities, four showed a greater difference in wages between enterprises of the same city than within enterprises—a difference which must be rather large, since skills and piece-rate performance vary considerably within any given enterprise.[62] A fifth comparison does not deal with workers of similar skills, but shows (for all Serbia, about 1966-67) that the best-paying enterprises, which employed 1 percent of the labor forces of all enterprises in this republic, paid three times the republic's average per capita wage.[63]

These differences in wages, paid by more and less successful enterprises in the same region, seem sufficient to provide greater incentives for the rank-and-file workforce than exist in the CMEA countries. In Yugoslavia, higher productivity can be rewarded. My impression from factory

[60] Wachtel, "Workers' Management," pp. 548-49.

[61] These three sets of comparisons are for 1970 and are drawn from interview materials.

[62] Marschak, p. 582. The interenterprise differences in wages (compared to the intra-enterprise differences) are significant at the 5 percent level.

[63] Popov, "The Problem of Strikes in Yugoslavia," reprinted in *International*, I, 7 (1972), 50-51.

visits in Slovenia is that the amount of worker effort there was rather greater than that which I saw in Hungary, the German Democratic Republic, or Romania. Yugoslavia would appear to be doing relatively well in resolving the problem of providing work incentives in socialist enterprises.

SUMMARY

Our examination of the behavior of Yugoslav enterprises has proceeded from the hypothesis that the enterprise attempts to pursue its own self-management goals, meaning by these the interests of the members of the enterprise collective rather than those of society in general. The role of the different groups within the enterprise in the setting of these objectives was treated in the previous chapter, and has not been further considered here. The objectives themselves, whatever they may be, are taken to be revealed through market behavior. Market behavior, however, is also affected by social control from nonenterprise sources (these consisting particularly of groups at the commune and republic, rather than federal, level at least until 1972 and probably thereafter) as well as by a sense of social responsibility on the part of those directing the enterprises. It is the amalgam of these influences with self-management interests which has been this chapter's subject.

Let us begin with the fact that the distinctive self-management interests of the enterprise are solidly based in Yugoslav institutional reality. Not only do top managers have a stake in successful enterprise growth because it implies for them increased personal power, responsibility, and influence; not only do middle managers have a similar stake because of the opportunities created for managerial advancement; but, most important of all, the entire labor force of a given enterprise shares a common interest in the enterprise's prosperity because the latter implies relative individual prosperity for themselves. The evidence is not available to allow us to determine whether earning differentials among workers of similar skills in different enterprises within the same region are greater in Yugoslavia than in capitalist countries. But there can be no question that such differentials are sharp by CMEA standards, particularly if we consider only those differentials which are due to relative enterprise success rather than to government policy regarding priorities among sectors. Thus a solid foundation of self-interest of individuals supports the efforts of enterprises to achieve self-management goals in the market place.

What is the market place milieu within which these enterprise interests find expression? Despite the efforts of existing firms to create cartel conditions, the apparent paucity of new firms, and the absence of any serious government actions to promote competition, the economy appears quite competitive. This competitive environment cannot be attributed to the socialist nature of the economy, but is rather a result of two other factors. First, it is caused by the willingness and ability of Yugoslav enterprises to broaden their activities both into new sectors and, through vertical integration, into new functions such as retail sales; this is a product of the search both for growth and for increased per capita earnings. Thus sectors showing above-normal profits appear to attract new entrants; these new entrants, however, are not newly created enterprises, but instead are existing ones from other sectors. Second, existing firms in all markets suffer from financial weakness due both to their lack of cash reserves and to their limited ability to obtain funds on the capital market. As a result, they are incapable of exploiting fully the potential advantages of oligopoly because of their need to concentrate upon short-run gains; furthermore, they are unable to ward off invading firms by the threat of engaging in substantial below-cost sales as a means of maintaining market power.

It is the merger movement which has been the main mechanism for the apparent breakdown of what would be otherwise oligopolistic power, and this movement has increased in strength after 1968. Mergers appear to be the principal form of transferring capital from one sector to another, and they seem to be strongly motivated by the fact that the workers of one enterprise can make what amounts to an equity investment through taking over the operations and employees of a second firm. However, since reaping the fruits of such equity investment may be regarded as a form of exploitation of the workers in the absorbed firm, mergers across republic (and thus nationality) lines are risky endeavors. It should not be surprising that the interrepublic merger movement is still in its infancy.

The second important mechanism for capital movement is through loans by the business banks. Despite the fact that these banks are themselves enterprises and exercise a fair degree of self-management independence in their lending policy, their loans tend to be limited to customers in their own communes and, certainly, to customers within their own republic. This is due both to the method by which the banks were originally founded and to their current sources of funds. Furthermore, compared with the loan-granting capabilities of the banks, there exists a substantial excess of demand for credit at any rates of interest which are socially acceptable. Thus the banks have little motivation to attempt to break out of their existing regional circle of customers and to create a national capital market.

It is true that the Yugoslav press has long been filled with bitter complaints as to the abuse of monopoly power, but what they point to is exploitation of the industrial sector by banks, export-import houses, and wholesale establishments. They also complain of exploitation, both through merger and through the creation of subsidiary units, of workers in sectors such as tourism by enterprises originally outside it. But all this seems to amount to no more than objections to quasi-rents in a profitable sector being shared with the workers of those units which provide the capital necessary for successful operation and expansion, rather than being gained solely by those actually working in the sector (tourism is the prime activity involved), and to the fact that enterprises supplying capital through merger receive a return which is often considerably above the very low socially accepted real bank rates.

I have argued that mergers and enterprise investment in new facilities perform the two socially useful functions of strengthening competition within individual sectors and of transmitting capital between sectors. A third function is that of strengthening the managerial capabilities of production units which are poorly directed. A fourth, similar to the movement of capital, is transfer of the scarce resource of foreign exchange from surplus sectors to deficit ones. Given the institutional constraints of the Yugoslav environment, it is enterprise expansion in the form of conglomerates which seems to be the driving force behind both the mobility of nonlabor factors of production, and the advance of whatever tendency exists for the equalization across sectors of marginal returns to all factors.

Up to this point, the summary has concentrated exclusively upon the expression of self-management interests. As was said at the beginning, this is only a portion of the story.

Although mergers often occur simply because of the perceived interests of the two parties, they also occur because of a combination of both local government and Party pressure upon the stronger enterprise, and of social responsibility on the part of those guiding that enterprise's decisions. In four of the six cases for which I have sufficient information to judge, considerations of rescuing an enterprise in trouble played a part in the merger motives. However, the absorbing firm in all but one of these cases also thought, whether correctly or not, that the merger was to its own advantage. Thus perceived self-interest of the absorbing enterprise coincided with perceived social interests in most of my small sample of those mergers which actually occurred.

The allocation of bank loans is also partly determined by commune and republic pressure, rather than solely by the self-interest of the banks. I would guess that social considerations and pressures, as contrasted with self-management interests, play a larger role in the distribution of bank loans than they do in the merger process.

I conclude that, at least as of 1970, perceived self-interest played a considerably greater role in determining the behavior of Slovenian industrial enterprises and banks than did either government and Party pressure or attention to social considerations by those guiding the enterprise decisions.

PART V

Managerial Careers and Earnings
and Conclusion

CHAPTER 14

The Managers: Backgrounds, Careers, and Earnings

THE FOUR country parts of this book have dealt with the behavior of enterprises, and with the methods and degree of their coordination. But they have been concerned only casually with the decision makers themselves. Yet it is obvious that managerial decisions will be influenced both by the characteristics of the decision makers and by the systems of rewards and punishments which they face.

The first section of this chapter deals with certain characteristics of managers: their sociopolitical background, age, and education.

The second section treats their careers, which can be viewed from two different perspectives. The first is that of on-the-job training for current posts; different career paths not only provide varying qualities of preparation, but prejudice managers in favor of alternate kinds of actions. The second perspective is the reward system facing managers, and the strength of those rewards which are embodied in career advancement. The more rapid the flow in the promotion channels, and the wider the demotion channels, the more likely it is that managers will act in a fashion to reap the monetary and career rewards of the system; in this sense, career advancement plays a role comparable to that of bonuses which we have already examined in earlier chapters. To the degree that career opportunites are relatively slight, and that bonus differentiation is minor, managers' actions are less likely to respond quickly and faithfully to the changing priorities of superiors.

The third section is concerned with educational programs for existing top managers and with career planning for managers.

The fourth section attempts to measure the strength of material incentives for career advancement, a feature which may also be significant in affecting the responses of managers to signals which they receive from superiors.

Unfortunately, the nature of our data often precludes serious intercountry comparison among the east European managers. Backgrounds and careers will be examined by means of a sample of 533 managers; but for many questions, sample size is satisfactory only for Romania and Slovenia. In these cases, we shall have to be content with a general evaluation of managers in the four countries taken together.

The sample. Table 14.1 describes the sample which is the data base of the first two sections. All managers studied are well within the upper 1 percent of the labor force hierarchy of their industrial branch. For most of our purposes, however, further differentiation is needed. Those working within Romania's ministries or the G.D.R.'s VVBS are separated from those employed in the *centrale, Kombinate,* or enterprises. Since Hungarian enterprises are comparable in size to Romanian *centrale* and to East German *Kombinate,* Hungarian factory managers are also included in the sample; they are comparable to enterprise managers in the other countries.

TABLE 14.1: The Sample of Managers (number)

Category	Hungary	Slovenia	Romania	German Democratic Republic
Organizations above the level of production units[a]				
Top-level managers[b]	0	0	45	17
Second-level managers[c]	0	0	9	0
Centrale or *Kombinate*[d]				
Top-level managers[e]	4	0	37	2
Second-level managers[f]	20	0	103	10
Third-level managers[g]	21	0	0	0
Enterprises[d, h]				
Top-level managers[e]	31	18	35	6
Second-level managers[f]	18	60	29	10
Third-level managers[g]	6	52	0	0
Total	100	130	258	45

NOTE: The lowest-level manager included is the head of a major production department or functional section in an enterprise.

[a] In Romania, these consist of branch ministries and of the State Committee for Planning. In the G.D.R., they consist of VVBS—the organizations immediately below the branch ministries.

[b] In Romania, these are ministers, vice-ministers, and heads of major directorates within a ministry. In the G.D.R., they are general directors and functional directors of the VVBS.

[c] Heads of sections.

[d] In Hungary, enterprises which are comparable in size to *centrale* and *Kombinate* are included in that category.

[e] General directors.

[f] Functional directors (normally, the top four to eight managers directly below the general director). On occasion, managers without the title of director are listed here because the personnel director of the organization said that in fact they held a comparable position. Similarly, some managers with the title of director are placed in the third category instead of this one.

[g] Heads of major production departments or major staff functions.

[h] In Hungary, factories within large enterprises are included in this category.

These upper managers are also subdivided by level. Top-level managers are general directors; second-level managers are the four to eight functional directors (production, engineering, sales, etc.) directly below them; third-level managers are the heads of major production departments or major staff functions.

The main source of the sample is information provided by the personnel managers[1] of the production units in which I interviewed; this information covered *all* the current managers at these levels in the organization, as well as their recent predecessors in the positions about which I asked in some of the units. Not infrequently, the personnel manager consulted a colleague on points as to which he was uncertain. In some cases, information was supplemented directly by the manager concerned. Information as to individuals was refused in only one enterprise (Slovenian), where I was told that the enterprise regulations forbade it to be given. The fact that the information was given orally has the advantage that I could query my informants as to internal consistency.

The virtue of this method of collecting the sample is that bias in selection of individuals (but, unfortunately, not as to the completeness of information regarding the individuals selected) could come only from bias in the selection of the organizations themselves. In earlier chapters, I discussed my reasons for believing that the units in which I interviewed were reasonably representative with regard to level of priority and performance; I have no knowledge as to whether this is also the case with regard to the backgrounds of managers.

While the reliability, and particularly the completeness, of the information collected from personnel directors is substantially lower than that which might be obtained from personnel records, the personnel directors who served as informants all had sufficient personal contact with the high-level executives included in the sample so that the information may be considered of acceptable quality.

In Hungary and Slovenia, information was collected as to all executives in an organization at any of the three managerial levels. This was not practicable for third-level managers in Romania or the G.D.R., and thus third-level managers in these two countries have been excluded from the sample.

In Romania, a second source of information was also used. This consists of autobiographical forms which had been filled out by *all* students who had attended any of the top-level courses (intended particularly for *centrale* directors) offered during 1970 by the Romanian Management Development Center. These materials were kindly placed at my dis-

---

[1] In the case of organizations above the level of *centrale* and *Kombinate*, the source of information was a head of a section or of a directorate in the organization.

posal by the Center. They are the source for biographical data as to 51 percent of my Romanian sample of top-level managers, and 71 percent of the sample of second-level managers. Since the students at these courses were essentially selected by their superiors rather than being self-selected, and since it was expected that all managers of their level in all *centrale* would in any case eventually attend, I doubt that major sample bias is introduced here.

Sample size is rather unsatisfactory for Hungary and East Germany; the Hungarian subsamples seem larger than they in fact are, since much of the data supplied as to individuals is incomplete. Information as to Romania and Slovenia is much better.

MANAGERIAL CHARACTERISTICS

Age. Table 14.2 shows the ages of managers in the four countries. Those in Romania and, especially, East Germany are considerably younger than their Hungarian and Slovenian colleagues. This, indeed, is what we would expect. Romanian industry has had a particularly rapid post-war expansion, and East Germany has had a combination of high war-time deaths and, in particular, a need to replace managers who emigrated prior to 1962.

Education. Table 14.3 shows the level of education. In all four coun-tries, completion of higher education (at least at the three-year junior college level) is the rule for general directors. Only in Hungary and Slovenia are there any appreciable number of managers at any level who have not reached this educational level; these latter are also the two countries in which managers are somewhat older.

The most striking feature of the table is that, in all four countries, occupants of the most politicized post (that of general director) have at least as high a level of education as do their subordinates whose tasks are more narrowly technical. If we consider education as a proxy for technical ability, there is no indication that promotion policy has been constrained to exercise a trade-off between political and technical char-acteristics.

It is true that East Germany is notable for the high proportion of man-agers who are graduates of junior colleges rather than universities. The point is not that East German managers have a lower level of education than do their colleagues (I am unable to compare the three-year East German higher education with the four- or five-year university degree in the other countries), but rather that the East German regime was in 1970 still forced to employ upper managers who had not received what

TABLE 14.2: Age Distribution of Managers Whose Ages Are Known

Organization and Age	Hungary		Slovenia		Romania	G.D.R.
	Top- and second-level managers	Third-level managers	Top- and second-level managers	Third-level managers	Top- and second-level managers	Top- and second-level managers
Ministries and vvbs						
Under 40 years (percentage)					4	23
Over 49 years (percentage)					19	8
Managers whose ages are unknown (percentage of total sample)					2	24
Managers of known age (number)					53	13
Centrale, Kombinate, and enterprises						
Under 40 years (percentage)	12	5	18	33	26	68
Over 49 years (percentage)	37	58	26	29	7	9
Managers whose ages are unknown (percentage of total sample)	33	30	25	13	3	21
Managers of known age (number)	49	19	61	45	197	22

NOTE: Similar results are obtained when top-level managers are separated from second-level managers. The only exception is for a small subsample of seven top-level managers in the G.D.R.'s *Kombinate* and enterprises; here, the number in each age group is equal (29 percent).

the regime considered to be a top quality education. It is my impression, however, that this was not due to a political versus education trade-off, but rather because of a shortage of university graduates of the proper age groups who were working in industry outside of design.

Comparison of the first and second columns of Table 14.3 suggests that intragenerational mobility by means of delayed higher education has been common in all four countries. The proportion of university-graduate managers whose higher education had been either delayed or received only through evening studies is about 50 percent in Romania, Hungary, and Slovenia, and is substantially higher in East Germany.

TABLE 14.3: Educational Level of Managers Whose Education Is Known

	Early University Graduates[a]	Total University Graduates	Lesser Education than Complete Junior College[b]	Sample Size of Those with Known Education
	(percentage)			(number)
Hungary				
Enterprises and factories				
Top-level managers	30	74	4	23
Second-level managers	58	81	6	31
Third-level managers	39	67	17	18
Slovenia				
Enterprises				
Top-level managers	45	82	18	11
Second-level managers	32	38	43	47
Third-level managers	21	51	26	39
Romania				
Ministries				
Top-level managers	60	100	0	30
Second-level managers[c]	50	88	0	8
Centrale and enterprises				
Top-level managers	52	100	0	61
Second-level managers	53	94	2	124
G.D.R.				
VVBS				
Top-level managers	36	86	0	14
Kombinate and enterprises				
Top-level managers[c]	0	33	0	6
Second-level managers[d]	12	38	0	16

NOTE: The proportion of all subsamples for which education is known is quite high, ranging between 61 and 94 percent. Thus lack of information about members of the original complete sample gives little ground for fear as to lack of representativeness.

[a] Entered university within two years of the normal age of graduating secondary school.

[b] Junior college is used as a translation of the German term *Fachschule*. It normally refers to a three-year higher educational institution.

[c] The size of the subsample whose education is known is very small.

[d] Data are also available for what appear to be the functional directors of eight VVBS of the Ministry of Heavy Machinery. Of a sample of 174 directors, 41 percent were university graduates, and 7 percent had less than a complete junior college education. The period covered is not stated, but is presumably during the 1960's. (Frank Grätz, "Wirtschaftsführer in Ost und West. Versuch eines Vergleichs," *Deutschland Archiv*, 1971, 10, p. 1029.)

This might be taken to suggest that ordinary workers who show potential on the job have a reasonable possibility of mounting the managerial ladder by being singled out for further education. The problem with this conclusion, however, is that the data of Table 14.3 may reflect essentially the situation facing the older generations, whose members could not have been chosen by the current regime for immediate higher education after secondary school.

The apparent solution to the problem is to examine only younger managerial cohorts: those born in 1930 or later. This solution has two problems of its own: small subsample size, of course, but equally serious is the fact that accession to higher management levels at an unusually low age will always, in any country, tend to be reserved for those who have taken all the preliminary steps (i.e., those steps which are well regarded in that society) as early in life as possible. Thus the proportion of early graduates among managers under forty must be taken as a maximum estimate of the situation which will characterize all eventual managers from that age cohort.

Table 14.4 shows the results for what they are worth. Sample size is enlarged somewhat by considering graduates from both universities and

TABLE 14.4: Likelihood of Early Graduation from University or Junior College: Effect of Date of Birth of Managers

Top-level and second-level managers of *centrale, Kombinate,* and enterprises	Proportion of Early Graduates[a] to All Graduates of Universities or Junior Colleges[b]		Sample Size of All Graduates of Universities or Junior Colleges[b]		Of all Managers Born after 1929	
Country	Managers born after 1929	All managers	Managers born after 1929	All managers	Less education than junior college[b] degree	Unknown level of education
	(percentage)		(number)		(percentage)	
Hungary	67	51	6	51	0	0
Slovenia	80	58	5	36	36	9
Romania	87	55	47	182	0	4
G.D.R.	67	27	6	22	0	7

[a] Entered higher education within two years of the normal age of graduating secondary school.
[b] Junior college is used as a translation of the German term *Fachschule*. It normally refers to a three-year higher educational institution.

junior colleges. In Hungary and the G.D.R., one-third of this youthful cohort of educated fast-risers in management ranks had had their higher educational studies interrupted. The comparable proportion in Slovenia and Romania was 15 to 20 percent. Since these figures must be taken as minimum estimates of the lifetime chances in management for that part of this age-education cohort whose education was interrupted, it may be expected that a very substantial share of all the members of this age cohort who eventually reach upper-management ranks will have started as rank-and-file workers or employees, whose accession to higher education should be considered as part of their career advancement rather than as a prelude to it.[2]

Table 14.5 displays a major difference from the Soviet Union's pattern as to the nature of higher education. Although, as in the Soviet

TABLE 14.5: Field of Higher Education of Managers

Level of Manager	Economics or Business				Economics or Business Combined with Engineering				Other Non-engineering Education				Sample Size			
	H	S	R	G	H	S	R	G	H	S	R	G	H	S	R	G
						(percentage)								(number)		
Total sample of managers with known field of education	28	35	19	33	6	0	4	17	2	12	1	0	64	80	219	30
Of this, top-level managers	14	50	4	44	5	0	7	19	0	0	0	0	21	10	91	16

NOTES:

1. H is Hungary; S is Slovenia; R is Romania; G is G.D.R.

2. Higher education is defined to include both universities and junior colleges; managers with incomplete higher education are included in this table. Information is available as to field of education for almost all managers known to have had higher education.

3. Data are available for a sample of one hundred sixty-two second-level managers in *Kombinate* of the G.D.R. The corresponding percentages are 40, 0, and 1; it appears that the author has no category corresponding to our second column, and some of those whom I would have placed there may here be placed in the first column. (For the source and description of the data, see Table 14.3, footnote d.)

Union, engineering education predominates, one-quarter to one-half of these upper managers have had an economics or a mixed economics-engineering education. While the proportion of general directors with this type of education is only 11 to 19 percent in Romania and Hungary, it is over 50 percent in the G.D.R. and in Slovenia. It would appear that, with the exception of law, traditional patterns of higher education have continued. Conceivably, this mixed pattern of educational fields among

[2] It should be noted that this small sample suggests that advancement to upper management without at least graduating from junior college is virtually impossible in any of the three CMEA countries. While such advancement is common in Slovenia, the four Slovenian managers without a degree all had incomplete higher education at the time of my interviews, and none were general directors. To the limited degree that one can generalize from such small samples, higher education appears to be a virtual requirement for younger men if they wish to attain to upper-management posts.

the upper-managerial cadre may promote improved adaptation to the possibilities of decentralized management. If such should indeed be the case, here is a source of weakness for Hungarian decentralization compared to either East German or Slovenian.

Socio-political background. Membership in the Communist Party is a rudimentary test of political activity in socialist countries. Table 14.6 presents the available data for those countries and categories for which the data are sufficiently complete.

TABLE 14.6: Proportion of Managers Who Are Members of the Communist Party (percentage)

	Slovenia		Romania			
	Enterprises		*Centrale*		Enterprises	
	Top-level managers	Second-level managers	Top-level managers	Second-level managers	Top-level managers	Second-level managers
Party members as proportion of all whose membership status is known	100	60	100	97	100	100
Known Party members as proportion of the entire subsample of managers[a]	61	45	100	94	83	72

[a] This row is included because, when an informant is ignorant of the Party status of some of the managers on whom he is reporting, the representativeness of the sample for which Party status is known may well be destroyed. This row gives a minimum estimate for a more representative sample than that treated in the top row.

Both in Romania and Slovenia, Party membership appears fairly universal among the general directors who constitute the top level of management. This is not surprising, since their posts are regarded as being at least as political as technical. More interesting is the contrast between the two countries at the second managerial level (of functional directors, immediately under the general director). In Slovenia, unlike Romania, this level of management appears to be viewed as technical and without political prerequisites. Since workers' representatives have a voice in choosing these directors in Slovenia in contrast to Romania, one might have anticipated the opposite result on the basis that local organs tend generally to be most orthodox in their interpretations of central doctrine. This suggests some confirmation of the interview statements made in 1970 which downgraded the importance at the local level of the Party organizations in Yugoslavia.

In Yugoslavia, a more significant test of political reliability than Party membership is considered to be previous membership in the partisan movement of the second world war. Since this was an extremely youthful movement, it seems appropriate to treat the relevant age group as consisting of those who were nineteen years of age or older at the end of the war. Table 14.7 shows the proportion of this age group of managers who had been partisans. Comparison of the data for second-level and third-level managers confirms the previous Party-membership results, suggesting no great emphasis upon political activity at the second level.

TABLE 14.7: Managers in Slovenia Who Are Former Partisans, as Proportion of the Age Group 45 Years and Older

	Enterprises		
	Top-level managers	Second-level managers	Third-level managers
Former partisans as proportion of all whose status is known (percentage)	75	11	24
Known former partisans as proportion of the entire subsample of the appropriate age group (percentage)	25	8	13
Managers of the appropriate age group (number)	18	60	52

A third measure of sociopolitical background is the proportion of managers who have held important unpaid positions in sociopolitical organizations. This is partially an indicator of a manager's willingness to devote time to activities outside his job, but it is also an indicator of the recognition in the community of his extracareer abilities.

Table 14.8 shows the results for all four countries. Positions held may be either current or past; they are in organizations such as the Party, the trade union, and government bodies; all levels of organizations are represented, beginning with enterprise committees (but not those of subunits of enterprises); the positions included are those of head of the enterprise organization and member of the principal elected body of regional organizations.[3] In addition to these elected posts, selection as

[3] In the case of Slovenian enterprises, both workers' councils and managing boards are included.

TABLE 14.8: Known Number of Present and Past Elected Positions of Managers, as Proportion of the Number of All Current Managers (*centrale, Kombinate,* and enterprises combined)

Managerial Level	Hungary	Slovenia	Romania[a]	G.D.R.
All managers				
1. Positions as proportion of managers (percentage)	16	51	27	30
2. Total number of managers in the subsample (number)	77	86	51	20
Top-level managers				
1. Positions as proportion of managers (percentage)	21	125	60	43
2. Total number of managers in the subsample (number)	24	8	15	7
Second-level managers				
1. Positions as proportion of managers (percentage)	15	37	14	23
2. Total number of managers in the subsample (number)	34	41	36	13
Third-level managers				
1. Positions as proportion of managers (percentage)	11	51		
2. Total number of managers in the subsample (number)	19	37		

[a] No information is available as to the large proportion of Romanian managers whose vitae were provided by the Management Development Center. Thus they are not included in the subsamples of this table.

a student at the full-time school run by the Central Committee of the national Party organization is also included as a position.

Table 14.8 must be used with caution, since the personnel managers who offered the underlying data must have had only incomplete knowledge as to this aspect of their colleagues' backgrounds. Furthermore, there is some (but surprisingly limited) doubling in these sociopolitical posts over individual careers.

Two conclusions stand out. First, the proportion of top-level managers who have held such posts is quite high in Romania and Slovenia, as one would expect from the political nature of the job. In contrast, the Hungarian proportion is very low.[4]

The low Hungarian figure of elected positions for general directors is very curious in light of the regime's view, cited in Chapter 8, that en-

---

[4] Those Hungarian top managers who do hold elected positions have much the same distribution of level of position as have the Romanians and East Germans. Thus examination of the level of position introduces no anomaly compensating for the low Hungarian proportion.

terprise general directors should be kept virtually immune from dismissal. It raises a serious question with regard to my hypothesis that this is due to their collective political power. For, if they were indeed politically powerful, one would expect to see them well represented in Party and government elected bodies. However, the problems of data reliability in this table are substantial, and one should not make too much of these figures.

The second conclusion from Table 14.8 is that we do see in Slovenia the working of the self-management principle. Even though the proportion of Slovenian second-level managers who have held such posts is quite low compared to the percentage shown for their superiors and immediate subordinates, this proportion is almost double that found in the three CMEA countries.

A puzzling category in all of the above tables is that of Slovenian second-level managers. Tables 14.6, 14.7, and 14.8 suggest that they have not been chosen for their sociopolitical status; the proportion who were partisans or who have held elected posts is considerably lower than is the case for third-level managers. Table 14.3 shows that their level of education is also relatively low, when compared to that of either their superiors or subordinates. Nor is their age distribution (see Table 14.2) such as to suggest that they have advanced simply by seniority. I have no explanation for this anomaly.

Managerial Careers

In the process of collecting data on individual managers, a major effort was made to trace their careers by organization, job function, and length of time in each job. As expected, the degree and detail to which careers are known differ considerably among individual managers. For some purposes, this problem has been handled by treating the individual job, rather than the manager, as the unit of analysis. For other purposes, the sample has been restricted to managers for whom I have career data extending over at least ten years.

Average number of years in post. Tables 14.9 and 14.10 show the average number of years which managers have spent in the various posts of their careers. The most striking feature of these tables is the relatively long tenure in each post compared with that of their counterparts in large American industrial companies. In this regard, east European managerial careers seem more comparable to those of west European than of American executives.

Problems of sample size prevent us from drawing conclusions as to differences among the four east European countries. However, the partic-

TABLE 14.9: Average Number of Years per Position in Career, All Levels of Management (Sample is restricted to managers whose career is known for at least ten years)

Country	Average Number of Years per Position (years)	Proportion of Managers Averaging more than Three Years in Any One Position (percentage)	Sample Size (number)
Hungary	9.6	95	22
Slovenia	6.8	97	24
Romania[a]			
enterprises and *centrale*	4.9	70	126
ministries	6.6	75	24
United States			
large industrial companies[b]	2.8	15	103

NOTES:

1. The G.D.R. is not covered because only five managers qualify to enter the sample.

2. The American sample includes managers in roughly the same hierarchical positions as do our east European samples. Positions covered are limited to those held within the company. The sample is restricted to managers aged 46 to 55, since relatively few east European managers are older. Positions examined are only those held by the manager after he was 35 years old, but this procedure does not appear to introduce bias relative to the east European samples.

[a] General directors and functional directors of Romanian enterprises who were promoted to the same position in *centrale* are not counted as having changed positions in cases where their *centrala* was formed on the base of their former enterprise.

[b] These data come from three very large American companies of the food, paper, and oil industries, in which full personnel records as of 1967-68 were made available for all executives of the relevant levels. Sample bias here can come only from selection of the companies, not of the individual managers, and there seems no reason to believe that these firms are unrepresentative of very large American industrial firms (D. Granick, *Managerial Comparisons of Four Developed Countries: France, Britain, United States, and Russia*, The M.I.T. Press, Cambridge, Mass.: 1972, p. 214).

ularly long periods in post which are shown for Hungary find substantiation in Table 14.14; Hungary is the only one of the four countries in which a majority of the predecessors of current managers left because of retirement rather than transfer to another position.

Such relatively long tenure in post of the east European managers, compared with their American counterparts, suggests that they are less likely than the Americans to shape their actions closely to their superiors' perceived wishes. This is because the east Europeans seem both to be less at the mercy of their superiors' snap judgments, and to have lesser opportunities for a rapid career rise. However, as was stated in Chapter 5, it is my understanding from interviews that East German managerial careers bear a close similarity to American corporate careers; in

TABLE 14.10: Average Number of Years in Specified Posts

| Post and Country | Average Number of Years during which the Post Was Held Consecutively by a Single Occupant (number) | Post Held for | | | Sample Size[a] (number) |
| | | 2 years or less | 3 years or less | 5 years or less | |
			(percentage)		
Minister or vice-minister					
Romania	4.0	44	59	78	41
Ministerial department director					
Romania	4.5	45	64	77	22
VVB general director or functional director					
G.D.R.	4.9	12	19	50	16
General director of enterprise					
Hungary[b, c]	4.6	35	46	73	26
Slovenia	5.8	22	33	61	18
Romania[d]	5.5	24	33	60	63
G.D.R.	6.4	21	36	71	14
United States[e]					
Divisional general manager	2.6	67	78	89	80
Plant manager	3.7	57	73	89	76
Other directors of enterprise					
Hungary[b]	6.8	25	25	44	16
Slovenia	6.2	20	20	46	41
Romania[d]	5.2	25	40	68	65
G.D.R.	3.4	43	64	86	14
United States[e]					
Posts reporting directly to a divisional general manager	2.4	68	79	97	103

[a] The unit consists of the individual position during the period that it is held consecutively by a single individual.

[b] Hungarian factory directors, as well as enterprise directors, are included here.

[c] The sample for Hungarian general directors seems to be severely biased by the bunched retirements of their predecessors. Of the nine general directors who served two years or less, at least four replaced retirees; of the twelve who served three years or less, at least six replaced retirees.

[d] When general directors or functional directors of Romanian enterprises were promoted to the same position in *centrale*, their *centrala* position is counted as a continuation of their earlier one in cases where their *centrala* was formed on the base of their former enterprise.

[e] These data come from six large American industrial companies. The six include the three described in footnote b of Table 14.9, and three others of the drug, chemical, and large-volume metal-fabricating industries; thus the industry mix covered is very wide (Granick, p. 215, and calculations from the original data).

this regard, East Germany may stand apart from the other three countries of our study.

Functional change. Experience in a number of job functions provides a means for expanding the capacities of individual managers. Furthermore, managers with broader experience are better able to integrate the work of their own function with that of other functions in the organization.

Table 14.11 shows the number of job functions held by that subset of all upper managers whose careers can be traced for more than ten years. The east European proportions working in three or more functions can be juxtaposed to the percentage shown in a comparable sample of American companies.

TABLE 14.11: Total Number of Functions in Which a Given Manager Was Employed during his Career, All Managers (Sample is restricted to those whose career is known for at least ten years)

	Hungary	Slovenia	Romania	G.D.R.	United States[a]
Total number of functions (percentage)					
1	50	42	18	7	20
2	41	42	58	57	30
3	9	12	20	14	27
4	0	3	4	21	17
5 to 7	0	0	0	0	6
Sample size (number)	22	59	149	14	216

NOTES:

1. For the four east European countries, the classification scheme used has eleven job functions: manufacturing, engineering, research and development, planning, finance, sales, purchasing, personnel, teaching, noneconomic functions in a noneconomic organization, and general management and administration.

2. The percentages do not vary greatly between organizational levels within the same east European country. Because of the limitations of sample size, no analysis was made as to differences between levels of management. American data show no differences among the three levels of management examined (Granick, p. 216).

[a] Data from the three large industrial companies described in footnote b of Table 14.9. Only functions occupied while working in the company are included. The classification scheme has fourteen job functions, compared to eleven for the east European countries (Granick, pp. 216-17, and calculations from the original data). The number of functions is slightly exaggerated in the American compared to the east European sample by the difference between the classification schemes used, but it is artificially reduced by the fact that only functions in the manager's current company are included. The direction of bias is unknown; the net amount of bias is believed to be small.

Hungary	9 percent
Slovenia	15 percent
Romania	24 percent
G.D.R.	36 percent
United States	50 percent

While all four countries show less job-function mobility than does the United States, such mobility is particularly low in Hungary and Slovenia. But even the latter two countries probably differ little from large French and British industrial companies.[5]

Average number of organizations in which the manager worked. Table 14.12 shows the average number of different organizations in which managers have worked. Only those managers are covered for whom I have career data for at least ten years. Each separate enterprise, *centrala, Kombinat*, etc. is defined as a separate organization. (In Hungary, each factory is also defined as a separate organization.)

The results are similar to those of Tables 14.9, 14.10, and 14.11 in that, compared to American executives, east European managers have changed organizations relatively seldom. East Germans and Hungarians have changed more than the other nationals, and general directors more frequently than their subordinates.

The American data are biased downward relative to the east European, since the former exclude organizations outside the manager's current company. Despite the results of the American comparison, however, it is clear that east European upper managers are not limited in their career to a single organization. The next question is that of how they move. Is it only upward, from enterprise to *Kombinat* to ministry?

Vertical movement between organizations. One might hypothesize that coordination of the various organizational layers of industry is improved by the movement of upper-managerial personnel in both directions between the various layers. Such moves should provide higher layers with improved understanding of the problems of operating bodies, and should give the latter a broader perspective within which to carry out their own duties. If this function of mobility is to be served, shifts to lower organizational levels cannot be restricted to managers who have failed at the higher levels. The vast majority of the managers in our sample, and particularly the general directors, may be presumed from their current posts to have been considered successful in their former positions.

[5] Compare D. Granick, *Managerial Comparisons of Four Developed Countries: France, Britain, United States, and Russia* (The M.I.T. Press, Cambridge, Mass.: 1972), p. 301.

TABLE 14.12: Average Number of Separate Organizations in Which a Given Manager Was Employed during His Career (Sample is restricted to those whose career is known for at least ten years)

	All Managers		General Directors	
	Average number of organizations	Sample size	Average number of organizations	Sample size
Hungary Enterprises and factories	2.6	22	3.8	5
Slovenia Enterprises	1.8	59	2.6	9
Romania Ministries	2.0	24	2.4	14
Centrale and enterprises[a]	1.6	130	1.6	43
G.D.R. *Kombinate* and enterprises	2.6	11	3.4	5
United States Enterprises[b]	3.3	118	4.1	40

[a] General directors and functional directors of Romanian enterprises who were promoted to the same position in *centrale* are not counted as having changed organizations in cases where their *centrala* was formed on the base of their former enterprise.

[b] These executives are the counterparts to the east European managers. Organizations covered are solely subunits of the company: corporate headquarters, the various divisional headquarters, and all field units (manufacturing, sales, and research locations) combined for each division taken separately. Data are for two of the large industrial companies described in footnote b of Table 14.9 (Granick, p. 219, and calculations from the original data).

Table 14.13 examines the degree of past movement of upper managers among the various layers of industry, and to and from Party and trade union positions. The unit of analysis is a job change which transferred the manager to a different organizational level. All such job changes are characterized as moves upward, downward, or outside of the industrial hierarchy. Thus movement from enterprise to *centrala* management is defined as a move upward (regardless of whether the job level was higher or lower), and movement from a ministry to a *centrala* is defined as a move downward.

In all four countries the amount of movement between the industrial hierarchy and Party or trade union bodies was negligible. Management appears to be a permanent career, rather than one interspersed with positions in the Party or trade union hierarchies. If we had included

TABLE 14.13: Job Changes Accompanied by Movement to a Different Organizational Level, All Managers

	Top Level Managers[a]					All Three Managerial Levels[a]				
	H	S	R[b]	G.D.R.	U.S.[c]	H	S	R[b]	G.D.R.	U.
Organizational moves downward (percentage of upward and downward moves)	52	38	21	28	36	36	54	20	27	4
Moves outside the hierarchy (percentage of upward, downward, and outside-the-hierarchy moves)	4	0	10	6	–	9	0	8	5	
Total organizational moves upward, downward, or outside the hierarchy per manager in the full sample (percentage of number of managers)	69	44	59	124	200	69	20	46	96	1:
Total sample of organizational moves upward, downward, and outside the hierarchy (number)	24	8	69	31	112	69	26	119	43	2:

NOTES:
1. Moves downward and upward: organizations considered are the enterprise (the factory in Hungary), the *centrala* or *Kombinat* (enterprise in Hungary), the VVB, the ministry, and the planning committee.
2. Moves outside the hierarchy: job moves from the Party or trade union bureaucracies to the organizations listed earlier, as well as job moves in the opposite direction.
3. The average number of organizational moves per manager is a minimum figure for the east European countries, and it constitutes a substantial understatement. This is because of the incomplete-

ness of career data for many of the managers; some, I know only their present job.
[a] The level of management is defined in ter of the individual's position at the time of the stu
[b] General directors and functional directors newly created *centrale* are not considered to h changed jobs if their *centrala* was formed on base of an enterprise in which they held the c parable position.
[c] Transfers of 215 upper managers among di ent levels of the corporation in the two la industrial companies of Table 14.12 (Gran pp. 220-21, and calculation from the orig data).

employment in the normal, noneconomic organs of government as a part of "outside employment," the only effect would have been to raise the Slovenian proportion of "moves outside the hierarchy" to the minor level observed in the CMEA countries.

What is perhaps surprising, however, is the degree of downward organizational movement. This varies for all three managerial levels combined from 20 percent in Romania to 36-54 percent in Hungary and Slovenia. Such downward organizational movement was caused partly by the creation of new intermediate organizational forms (*centrale* in Romania, *Kombinate* in the G.D.R., and merged enterprises in Hungary) into which were brought former ministerial personnel, and by the abolition of superenterprise bodies in Slovenia. But this is only a partial explanation of the phenomenon. In Hungary, for example, 43 percent of the career moves of present top-level management at the factory level had been organizationally upward—i.e., to a level higher than the factory.

Similar data, taken from personnel records, exist for a sample of two hundred fifteen executives (at much the same managerial levels as our three levels) in two large American industrial companies. For these executives, the amount of downward organizational movement within the company (from corporate headquarters to divisional headquarters, and from divisional headquarters to factory or sales units) was 42 percent of the combined upward and downward organizational movement. For top executives, all currently employed at corporate headquarters, the downward movement was 36 percent. This is rather greater than in Romania or the G.D.R., but quite similar to that in Hungary and Slovenia.[6]

In regard to vertical movement, the four socialist countries appear to approach the managerial-mobility patterns of large American companies. In this respect, they differ radically from firms of France and the United Kingdom, where organizational movement seems to be much more unidirectional upward. For the three CMEA countries, this pattern should be important in smoothing the relations between the various organizational levels of industry, and in socializing the upper management of production units to the philosophy of the higher, integrating bodies of the economy.

On the other hand, and in sharp contrast to the situation among American top executives working at corporate headquarters, a very high proportion of the top half-dozen officials in each of the Romanian branch ministries and the East German VVBs reached that high organizational level at quite a young age and remained there. In Romania, thirteen of a sample of twenty-four ministers and vice-ministers in industrial branches have worked at the ministerial level continuously since before they were 35 years of age; in the G.D.R., at the VVB level, nine of a sample of twelve general directors and functional directors have worked there since the same age. In Romania, while all of the branch ministers and vice-ministers in my sample who reached the ministerial level after the age of thirty-nine had earlier worked as general directors or functional directors in enterprises, people who had previously held such directorial posts still constituted only one-third of the total sample of branch min-

[6] The figures as to the number of vertical organizational moves per manager are not comparable between the United States and the four east European countries. This noncomparability is due to the fact that career data are fuller for the American sample for the period that managers have worked within their current companies, but exclude career history prior to this.

isters and vice-ministers. In both countries, a large proportion of the top officials of these bodies which administer industry have never held major command positions in operating units of industry.

The next positions of managerial predecessors. The degree of career "punishment" is perhaps the most important single indicator of the pressure placed upon managers to respond quickly and faithfully to signals received from superiors or the market place. Table 14.14 shows this

TABLE 14.14: Next Position of Predecessors of Current Holder of Post (Predecessors who currently hold one of the top three-level managerial posts in the same organization are not included)

	Retirement or death	Promotion	Demotion	Lateral move	Unknown	Other position	Predecessors as Proportion of Current Holders of Posts[a] (percentage)	Sample of Predecessors (number)
				(percentage)				
Total sample of managers								
Hungary	52	9	17	9	13	0	30	23
Slovenia	14	7	16	27	27	9	51	44
Romania	14	14	0	71	0	0	5	7
G.D.R.	0	20	27	33	7	13	42	15
Total sample of managers in *centrale*, *Kombinate*, and enterprises only								
Hungary[b]	52	9	17	9	13	0	30	23
Slovenia	14	7	16	27	27	9	51	44
Romania	0	20	0	80	0	0	10	5
G.D.R.	0	30	10	30	10	20	56	10
Top-level managers in enterprises								
Hungary[b]	73	9	9	9	0	0	46	11
Slovenia	0	0	40	20	30	10	125	10

NOTES:

1. Positions at the same managerial level in a higher organization are defined as promotion. Those at a substantially lower level there are defined as demotion but, for example, movement from an enterprise general director position to that of a *centrala* functional director is defined as a lateral move.

2. Ten of the Hungarian top managers came from factories rather than enterprises. The eleventh was demoted in 1957, more than ten years before the reform period began. In contrast, the Slovenian top managers were all general directors of enterprises.

[a] For Romania, the managers whose vitae were collected through the Management Development Center are excluded from the count of current holders of posts, since no data are available for any of their predecessors.

[b] Factories are also included.

for the four countries, and is one of the most important tables of this chapter. It analyzes where the former holders of managerial positions have gone.

In reading this table, it is significant to note that data are available for a high proportion of such predecessors in three of the countries. (Often predecessors other than the immediate one are included. This compensates for the fact that a number of current managers are the first occupants of their posts.) The exceptional country is Romania, and this is also the nation for which our sample contains the smallest absolute number of predecessors. I would take the Hungarian, Slovenian, and East German data quite seriously, while the Romanian are included only for completeness.

The most striking column in the table is the one showing retirements. Half of all the Hungarian predecessors, and three-quarters of the predecessors of the Hungarian factory general directors,[7] retired from their posts or left through death. Clearly the danger of removal for poor performance has been particularly low in Hungary; the retirement data support the conclusion from Table 14.9 that rotation of posts has been exceedingly slow in that country. (Here, and throughout Table 14.14, predecessors who held an upper-managerial post in the same organization at the time of my interviews are not included as predecessors. This is to eliminate simple rotation of posts which is often due to changes in the organizational chart.)

Known demotions constitute some 16-17 percent of total job changes in Slovenia and Hungary. Given the relatively long tenures in position, this does not seem sufficient to make a managerial post one of high risk. Demotions are perhaps more important in East Germany (particularly at the vvb level). These figures are in line with the impressions I gathered in the different countries.

Slovenian general directors. Since Slovenian general directors are elected by the workers' councils of their enterprises, although their nomination is under the influence of extra-enterprise bodies, it seems particularly

---

[7] There is almost no information as to the predecessors of the general directors of Hungarian enterprises, in contrast to the predecessors of general directors of factories. Of the five current enterprise general directors, two succeeded to their posts from ministerial positions at the time that the enterprise was formed by combining formerly independent factories; thus they had no predecessors. One succeeded a man who was demoted to another enterprise; but this was in 1956. A fourth had held the position since 1954, with two years' intermission for work at the industry's branch ministry; during these intervening two years, the current economic director of the enterprise had headed it. (The current economic director, after stepping down from his two-year stint as general director, was still in a position one managerial notch above that of his post prior to being made general director.) No information is available as to the predecessor who left in 1954. I also have no information as to the fifth enterprise.

important to trace their careers. Table 14.15 does this for predecessors of current general directors, and Table 14.16 shows the previous positions of the current general directors.

TABLE 14.15: Slovenia: Next Position of Both Immediate and Earlier Predecessors of Current General Directors of Enterprises

Next Position of Predecessor	Predecessors (number)
In engineering-consulting enterprise (high paying) Level of functional director	2
In commercial enterprise (high paying) Unknown level	1
In trade association (high paying) Lateral move	1
In foreign firm abroad Lateral move	1
In foreign affiliate of original enterprise Lateral move	1
In other enterprises Demotion	2
Within the same enterprise Demotion[a]	2
Total	10

[a] Both positions were that of "adviser."

Of the ten predecessors for whom information is available, four moved to organizations in other sectors where incomes, on average, were substantially higher than in their old enterprises. Two moved to comparable positions in western Europe, one in a foreign affiliate which he had himself recently established. However, 40 percent of this small sample had to accept demotion—half of them in their old enterprises. Thus, while the horizontal rotation (commented on in Chapter 12) of holders of the politicized post of general director does indeed seem to be realized, the fall-out in this sample was substantial.

Table 14.16 shows the working of horizontal rotation even more sharply. Of the eight current general directors of enterprises, only one had reached this post after a career within the same enterprise. Four of the eight came to their posts from governmental positions, at least three of the four moving laterally at the same managerial level. Of the remaining three who came from outside the enterprise, two had been general directors of their previous enterprises.

TABLE 14.16: Slovenia: Previous Organization and Position of Current General Directors

Previous Organization and Position	General Directors (number)	Years in Present Post (number)
Federal ministry[a] Same level	1	less than 1
Slovenian coordinating agency of the same industry[b] Unknown level	1	1
Municipal government[c] Same level	1	less than 1
Municipal government[d] Same level	1	18
Foreign trade enterprise Same level	1	7
Independent industrial enterprise Functional director	1	18
Affiliated enterprise[e] Same level	1	4
Same enterprise Personnel director	1	6

[a] Immediately before working for five years in a federal ministry, he had worked for eight years in the Slovenian government administration at the same level.

[b] This agency has now been abolished.

[c] Prior to becoming general director, he worked for one year as a plant director in the enterprise he was to head. At the time he joined the enterprise, however, it had already been arranged that he would soon become general director.

[d] This move was not direct. Having worked for seven years in the municipal government, he then became a functional director of the enterprise for two years before becoming general director. The enterprise was tiny when he became general director, and became important only under his leadership.

[e] Prior to being general director of this affiliated enterprise for one year, he had been general director of an unrelated enterprise.

It is clear from these tables that Slovenian workers' councils of large enterprises do not generally choose a new general director from among candidates they know well after long work in the firm. Rather, their choice is such as to suggest room for a good deal of political and personal influence by republic and commune organizations.

TOP MANAGEMENT EDUCATION AND CAREER PLANNING[8]

Both Romania and the German Democratic Republic have taken seriously the task of providing post-university-degree training for existing

---

[8] For a description of formal managerial education in Romania, East Germany, and Hungary, see E. Sidel'nikov in *Planovoe Khoziaistvo*, 1971, 7, pp. 91-95.

managers. Hungary, with United Nations' help, established a managerial training center in 1968; but Hungarian training, at least through 1970, seems to have been much less extensive than that of the other two countries. Yugoslavia appears to have done virtually nothing in this regard, although some Yugoslav managers have attended foreign management courses.

The Romanian effort began in 1967, when a national Management Development Center was founded with United Nations' aid. In the three years through 1970, over seven thousand students (including both professionals and managers) were trained there. It is probably not coincidental that this Center opened in the flush of the top leadership's professed interest in decentralizing some of the powers of the branch ministries. This was also the period when (as was seen in Chapter 2) a major expansion began in the number of economics students entering the universities, and when economics training shifted markedly to business school subjects.

Training of existing top managers, however, began only in 1969—shortly before the *centrale* were created. During 1970, some one hundred eighty managers passed through the Center's course for top management. This was a full-time program of eleven weeks, broken into two periods by an interval in which each student was expected to prepare a project for the better organization of his own unit. The main concentration of the course was upon the training of directors of *centrale*; thirty-two general directors and seventy-three functional directors of *centrale* studied in this course during 1970. The seriousness of the educational effort can be judged from the fact that about 16 percent of the general directors of all *centrale* in the country were taken away from their posts for one-fifth of the first year in which the *centrale* existed. As of the end of 1970, the Center hoped that by the end of 1973 all *centrala* directors would have been required to take this course.

The Center has had the aid of some foreign experts, but they were there primarily to train the Romanian instructors. The pressure for starting the Center quickly once the decision was made virtually precluded any real selection of instructors, and as of late 1970 there had been almost no turnover. From personal observation of some of the sessions, it was clear to me that the students did very little of the required preparation for the classes and seemed to take their attendance at the course as somewhat of a holiday. But these are normal problems in starting a program which is brand new for a country.

On the other hand, the instructors spent half their time doing research in Romanian pilot enterprises so that their teaching might better reflect Romanian conditions. High-level personnel from the ministries lectured to the students and engaged in a surprising degree of give-and-take. The Center's administration thought in 1971 that it was passing over the hump, and that it would soon be in a better position to demand proper study habits from the participants.

For all its weaknesses, this major effort to train all the top management of the country's *centrale* is most impressive. It appears to be a token of the new role which was then intended for the *centrale*, and also to represent a recognition by the top government leadership that different skills are desirable for the management of the *centrale* than had earlier been needed to operate the enterprises when they were directly subordinate to the ministries. Nothing fully comparable has occurred in any of the other east European countries studied.

Managerial training was to be extended to the top level of administration in 1971. The Management Development Center was to present a course in management, meeting about once a month, for ministers, vice-ministers, and regional Party secretaries. This course was to be given at the Higher Party School, whose program up till then had been strictly political and ideological. Thus the concentration on improving the qualifications of existing top managers was continuing and even being extended.[9]

In addition to creating the national Management Development Center, Romania has also made some feeble efforts at providing local management courses for those currently holding positions as lower and middle managers. Some fifty-five regional centers have been established. But the investment here has as yet been minimal: all these centers together had only about eighty full-time employees in late 1970. There is talk of also carrying out managerial training within the branch ministries, but no real start appeared to have been made on this by the end of 1970. Not unwisely, priority has been given to the training of top management; in time, presumably, this will work down.

Although the G.D.R. may not have mounted a top-management training program which covers as high a proportion of top managers as does that of the Romanian Management Development Center, its program predates the Romanian. A fair number of top managers have been sent to short, postdegree courses: some for as long as five months. Advanced education is treated as a continuous process for the leading men of the *Kombinate* and VVBs. For example, the forty-six-year-old general director of an important *Kombinat* had been on three such special courses (each some four to eight weeks) since his university graduation.

[9] In late 1971 or early 1972, the Management Development Center was merged with the Higher Party School in a newly created Academy, established directly under the control of the Central Committee of the Party.

In addition, people intended for top posts have been provided with short tours of training in other, more advanced industrial branches than their own.

While the G.D.R has no official top-management school such as that of Romania, the Higher Communist Party School of the Central Committee fulfills the same function. Its courses are normally limited to people currently holding such positions as *Kombinat* general director or department head in a ministry or in the State Planning Commission; in addition, a limited number of places are reserved for people being trained for such posts. Both of the *Kombinat* general directors whom I interviewed had attended this Central Committee school, as had also the two people to be discussed below who were being groomed for top-management posts.

Courses seem to run between four to eight weeks and five months of full-time study, overlapping the length of time spent in the Romanian Management Development Center. Courses offered are said to be the following: operations research, cybernetics, electronic data processing, Marxist-Leninist organizational science,[10] foreign trade, and pricing policy. It is clear that the function of the courses is much less that of providing ideological training than of offering a technical training for management which is said to be superior to anything available in the G.D.R. at the university level.

People below the top management level may take postdegree courses at universities; I was told that a *Kombinat* functional director (but not a general director) would typically go there. At one university, I was informed that its three priority areas for such postdegree courses are electronic data processing, operations research, and personnel management. It is not engineering as such which is given prime emphasis in the postdegree courses, but rather studies intended to improve both planning and management.

Perhaps of equal or even greater importance than the formal top management program is the careful grooming of at least some East Germans through planned career progression—a practice which I have not encountered in any of the other three countries studied. In one light industry *Kombinat*, two people were being so groomed when I visited it. One was being prepared to assume the post of general director in an unspecified *Kombinat* of his branch by 1975. At the age of twenty-eight, having already received a junior college diploma, he had been sent to a university for four years of full-time studies to earn a doctorate in engineering. He then returned to his old plant where he spent one year

[10] The brief verbal description which I received of this course suggests that it is not so much ideological as similar to an organization course in a major American graduate school of business.

as the assistant to the general director of the enterprise, half a year in accounting, and then one year as commercial director. He was scheduled to next become (in late 1970) the *Kombinat* director of economics and organization.

A second man in this same *Kombinat* was being trained to become a department director in his branch ministry in 1974. This man was thirty-four, and had also earned a doctorate in engineering. At the time I visited the *Kombinat*, the fact that he had had no experience in managing people was considered his major training deficiency. In the four years remaining before his appointment to the ministry, he was to function as the first deputy director of a small enterprise, then as general director of another small enterprise, then as general director of a larger enterprise, and finally as the economic director of the *Kombinat*.

This East German attention to top-management further training and to career progression has doubtless been heavily influenced by the shortage of experienced managers following the exodus of the 1950's. The Romanian effort was motivated by the creation of new institutions (the *centrale*) which were expected to take over some of the responsibilities of the branch ministries. But "need" alone is not a sufficient explanation. One might have expected the far greater decentralization in Hungary and Yugoslavia to have made similar programs appear even more urgent in these countries; yet no similar effort has been made there.

RELATIVE MANAGERIAL EARNINGS

Table 14.17 presents a very crude measure of the material incentives for managerial advancement which exist in the various countries. The table provides available data as to relative gross (net in the case of Slovenia) earnings during 1969-70 within the large production units in which I conducted interviews. No attempt is made to compare absolute earnings between countries; not only would such a comparison require the development of indexes of purchasing-power of different currencies, but it would be irrelevant to the question of material incentives for career advancement within any single country.

The figures of the table should be taken only as rough approximations of money earnings; partly this is because I have had to make estimates of bonus earnings, but even more it is because the various positions (e.g., skilled worker and head of a production department) were not rigorously defined in the interviews, and positions treated in the table as comparable are in fact so to only a limited degree.

Even more significant, however, are two problems involved in interpreting money incomes. The first is that money income ignores all perquisites of managerial positions, both those that are informally granted

TABLE 14.17: Relative Earnings in Industry (indexes)

Position	Average Earnings in the Enterprise's Industrial Branch = 100						Average Earnings of an Engineer in the Enterprise with Three-years' Experience = 100		
	H	S	R	G	USSR[a]	U.S.[b]	H	S	R
General director of *Kombinat, centrala,* or large enterprise	487 to 602	239 to 393	333 to 437	281 to 361	276 to 434	1,891	269 to 528	150 to 224	267 to 315
Top four to eight functional directors below the general director of *Kombinat, centrala,* or large enterprise	387 to 465	186 to 331[d]	302 to 378	204 258	. . .	. . .	213 to 267	124 to 186	273
Head of a production department in a factory	198 to 251	167 to 288	235 to 271	183	179 to 261	. . .	109 to 239	106 to 184	158
Engineer with three years of experience	105 to 181	156 to 193	139 to 163	. . .	. . .	. . .	100	100	100
Sample size[c]	3	7	4	4	5	670	3	5	4

NOTES:

1. H is Hungary; S is Slovenia; R is Romania; G is G.D.R.

2. Data for the four east European countries were collected from the large production units in which I interviewed. Ranges express the average figures collected from the different units in each country. All earnings include average bonuses as well as piece-rate earnings for manual workers.

3. All earnings are gross of personal taxes for countries other than Slovenia. For Slovenia, earnings are net of taxes.

4. Average earnings in the enterprise's industrial branch are official national figures for 1970 for Slovenia, Hungary, and the G.D.R. The Romanian and Soviet figures refer to average figures in the branch for manual workers alone; since no official Romanian figures are available, enterprise figures are used for that country. The American figures refer to all manual workers in manufacturing.

No significant problem of incomparability is introduced by using as a base the average earnings of all employees in some countries, and the average earnings of only manual workers in other countries. This is because the two averages appear to be virtually identical in the CMEA economies (see footnote 14 of this chapter).

5. Although no data are available for East German engineers with three years of experience, other data suggest that their earnings relative to skilled workers' are fairly similar to those of Hungarian and Romanian engineers.

[a] Official Soviet data for five industries during 1959-64, with adjustments. Average industrial worker earnings are for the branch of the specific enterprise (Granick, p. 262).

[b] Median salary plus bonus (but not value of stock options) as of 1967 for an 88 percent sample of the 762 chief executives of the manufacturing companies listed on the New York Stock Exchange. (H. Fox, "Top Executive Compensation," in National Industrial Conference Board, *Studies in Personnel Policy*, 213, New York: 1969, pp. 10-11, as referred to in Granick, p. 284.)

[c] This is the maximum number of production units from which data are available for a single row figure. The sample is often smaller for other rows.

[d] Comparable national sample statistics are available for Yugoslavia for 1969 in all industrial enterprises; however, small enterprises must be excluded, since these would not have such posts. The figure given in the national statistical yearbook is a ratio of 235 (Socijalistička Federativna Republika Jugoslavija, Savezni Zavod za Statistiku, *Statistički Godišnjak Jugoslavije 1971*, Beograd: 1971, pp. 268 and 271).

and those informally taken. This leads to a major understatement of income inequality. The second is that the rate of sales tax is considerably higher on the market basket of goods purchased by upper-income groups in eastern Europe than it is on necessities; this operates to overstate inequality. No attempt will be made to estimate the net effect of these counteracting factors.

Restricting ourselves to comparisons of gross monetary earnings, several conclusions can be drawn from the table and from other data not presented there.

(1) Salary plus bonus of the chief executive bears much the same relationship to average earnings in the industry in Slovenia, the G.D.R., Romania, and the Soviet Union. Within individual industrial units, income inequality is greatest in Hungary; this is a result of the sharp increase in top-management incomes which accompanied the introduction of the 1968 reform.[11] Thus material incentives for managerial advancement are relatively high in this country. The Slovenian data, however, indicate that one should not generalize that a decentralized socialist economy requires greater income differentiation than does the customary CMEA type of economy. Comparison with American manufacturing companies shows the relatively narrow earnings differentiation which exist in all five of the socialist countries.

Moreover, managerial incomes do not appear to rise substantially in industrial organizations above the production unit. Data for two East German VVBS (one of which had under its administration a labor force of fifty thousand) show that functional directors of the VVBS earn only some 6 to 13 percent more than do their counterparts in the *Kombinate* which they supervise. In Romania, functional directors in industrial ministries earn within 10 percent of their counterparts in the *centrale* administered by the ministry. Top executives in the Romanian State Committee for Planning earn an additional 10 percent; but the earnings of the senior managerial layer below the half-dozen or so vice-presidents of the Committee are similar to or slightly lower than that of a general director of a *centrala*. In Hungary in 1967, the heads of the major directorates of ministries averaged only 99 percent of the earnings of all general directors of both enterprises and plants in state industry.[12]

(2) Although income inequality between top managers and average industrial personnel seems to be greater in Hungary than in the other

[11] Compare the Hungarian data in Table 14.17 to that of Központi Statisztikai Hivatal, *Foglalkoztatottság és Kereseti Arányok*, 1969, 1, which reports on national averages for different national posts in all state industry in 1967. Unfortunately, so far as I know, no official averages have been published for a later year.

[12] The East German and Romanian figures come from interviews. The Hungarian figures are national averages from *Foglalkoztatottság és Kereseti Arányok*, 1969, 1.

socialist countries, this inequality applies only to the highest positions. Middle managers—roughly the lowest earners within the top 1 percent of the industrial labor force, and a group that is represented in Table 14.17 by heads of production departments in factories—earn no more compared to manual workers in Hungary than they do in the other socialist countries. Hungarian wage and salary inequality within industry would not appear in conventional statistical analyses which group into a single category at least the upper 1 percent of income recipients.

A comparison of the pretax incomes of the lowest earners within the top 1 percent of wage and salary recipients in large industrial organizations shows that the east European countries, the Soviet Union, and Great Britain constitute a single group in contrast to the United States and France.[13] Such income, as a proportion of the income of average industrial personnel in the same country, seems to be approximately the following:[14]

Four east European countries	One and one-half to two and one-half times the average income of all industry personnel
Soviet Union	Two to three times the income of all manual workers in industry
Britain	Two and one-quarter to three and one-half times the income of all manual workers in industry
United States	Four times the income of all manual workers in industry
France	Four and one-quarter to six and one-half times the income of all manual workers in industry

[13] East European data are for 1970; data for the other countries are for the middle 1960's.

[14] The G.D.R. is the only east European country for which data are available both for all personnel employed in individual industrial branches and for the subgroup of manual workers. The difference there is negligible: between 1 and 3 percent higher incomes for all personnel. The same relationship holds in the Soviet Union for industry as a whole. Thus it would seem that the ratios for eastern and western Europe, the Soviet Union, and the United States are properly comparable.

The Soviet, British, American, and French ratios are taken from Granick, *Managerial Comparisons*, p. 264, the British and French being adjusted to take account of all manual workers rather than only males.

Just as British industry is commonly believed to suffer in efficiency from the low monetary incentives provided to its managers,[15] so too east European industry may suffer from the same defect.

(3) In Chapter 4 we saw that decisions as to economic trade-offs in Romania seem essentially to lie within the sphere of authority of ministerial rather than *centrala* officials. One might expect that this centralization of authority would have its counterpart in much higher incomes for managers in the industrial ministries than for those working in the *centrale* and enterprises subordinate to them. In fact, however, such income differentials are very slight. Perhaps one reason for this is that top management at ministry headquarters is recruited primarily from men who have spent their whole career at headquarters, and thus their movement upward in authority is accompanied by salary increases.[16]

(4) Compared with the other three east European countries, Slovenian engineers earnings are quite high relative both to average industrial earnings and, particularly, to that of the general directors of their organizations. I suggested in Chapter 12 that this phenomenon may be due to the fact that Slovenia, unlike the other countries, allows its citizens free access to foreign labor markets, and that Slovenian engineers' incomes have been more influenced by such wage-pull than have the incomes of either ordinary workers or top managers.

CONCLUSION

Both the patterns of relative earnings and the career patterns suggest that industrial management in all four of the east European countries is a less high-pressure occupation than it is in the United States.

At the level of middle management, and even more so at the level of top management, the material rewards of career success (at least as expressed in gross salary) are slight compared to those in the United States or western Europe. This is true not only in absolute terms, but also in relation to the average earnings of industrial personnel in the same country. One might hypothesize that the meagerness of material reward would have some effect on the intensity of effort to gain and hold top-management posts.

In all countries except possibly Slovenia, higher education is more prevalent among top managers than is the case in the United States. Since it is far less widespread in the population as a whole, the breadth of

[15] But the relatively low level of managerial incomes in Britain does not apply to the incomes of chief executives (see Granick, pp. 284-85).

[16] Of the twenty-four ministers and vice-ministers of industrial branches in our sample, only nine had earlier served as either general directors or assistant general directors of enterprises or trusts or *centrale*.

competition among those who have obtained it is much less in eastern Europe than in America. At least in Romania and among top managers in Slovenia (data are not available for the other two countries, but one would expect them to be closer to Romania than to Slovenia in this regard), political requirements have further thinned out the competitive field.

The G.D.R. is the only one of the four countries in which the bulk of upper managers have received their higher education either through evening school or only after a period of some years of industrial experience. Here one might conceivably regard the attainment of higher education by managers as part of career competition. But even under this interpretation, career advancement in the G.D.R. has been greatly eased by the shortage of skilled managers resulting from the emigration of the 1950's.

When we turn to career paths, we see much greater stability in individual posts in all four of these countries than in the United States. We might have expected the opposite in Romania, whose rapid industrialization has required a sharp expansion in the stock of managers, and in the G.D.R. which has had a similar opening up of management posts for different reasons. Yet in none of the four countries have managers changed positions during their careers with anything like the frequency found in large American companies. The psychological pressure emanating from the fact that job change is to be expected every three years or less, and that the individual must struggle to insure that such change is favorable rather than lateral or sidetracking, is an American but not an east European phenomenon.

While this situation seems to be true in all four of the countries studied, it is probably least so in East Germany. This is also the only country in which the number of job functions held during an average upper-managerial career approaches the figure observed in the United States; in which there are at least suggestions that demotion of less capable managers is viewed as a fairly respectable method of creating openings for the more able; and in which career planning has been mentioned as consciously applied. In these regards, East Germany comes the closest to the American pattern.

Hungary, on the other hand, is outstanding for the number of years in which managers have remained in a single post. It is the only one of the four countries in which more than half of the current upper managers' predecessors had freed their post through retirement or death, rather than through continuation of career moves. Career pressure would appear to be particularly low in this country.

It might seem that Slovenian general directors are exceptions to the generalization that career pressure is weak. After all, four of the ten predecessors of the current general directors in our sample left their posts in what was clearly a demotion. But two cautions are needed here. The first is that careers of Slovenian general directors seem peculiarly heavily determined by political factors rather than by simple managerial competence; how else explain that seven of the eight current general directors came to their posts directly (or within a very brief period) from outside the enterprise, despite the fact that they had to be elected by the workers' council of the enterprise? The second caution is that Slovenian general directors receive peculiarly poor financial remuneration in comparison to what they would earn as simple engineers.

In judging east European managerial career patterns as ones of comparatively low pressure, it must be remembered that the standard of comparison chosen has been the United States. Certainly they would appear much more customary if we had taken as our norm the careers of their managerial counterparts in large west European companies. To a considerable degree, and perhaps entirely, the east European countries are in this regard simply a homogeneous part of the general European business culture.

Yet even if this is the case, it is important to note the relative mildness of the pressures upon east European top managers to act in a fashion defined as successful by their superiors. The combination of this perhaps general European career pattern, of meager salary rewards relative to those of continental western Europe and the United States, and of a fairly small share of income coming from fluctuating bonuses compared to the situation in the USSR, makes the eastern European countries internationally unique. This combination would seem to give their managers a greater degree of material independence in determining the amount of effort to put forth in their jobs, and a greater freedom in choice of response to pressures from their superiors or the environment, than are encountered elsewhere.

CHAPTER 15

Conclusion

Market Socialism and Self-Management

OF the four socialist economies examined in this book, three incorporate significant elements of market socialism. In neither Yugoslavia nor Hungary are any plans at all given to microunits; coordination of the production and sales decisions of the enterprises is in theory carried out in the market place through the enterprises' attempts to approximate some form of profit maximization. In the G.D.R., a major portion of state industry uses profitability criteria in determining its own product mix within rather broad limits, and least-cost considerations are significant in the choice among many forms of inputs. Only in Romania are economic choices all made at the hierarchical level of the ministries; even in this country, there is a desire on the part of central authorities for the *centrale* to exercise some choice on the basis of market considerations.

This substantial role of the market place, as well as the existence of wide national variations in the methods used for controlling and coordinating the enterprises, may be interpreted as demonstrating the considerable changes which have occurred since the original socialist model was evolved during the 1930's in the Soviet Union. Yet in one most critical sense, nothing in the direction and coordination of socialist production units has altered in any of the three CMEA countries—nor, perhaps, could it.

Each of the CMEA economies, even that of Hungary, is still operated as though it were a single, giant corporation. In all three countries, managers of enterprises, *centrale*, and *Kombinate* are appointed, promoted, rewarded through fluctuating bonuses, and dismissed by their hierarchical superiors in central administration (VVBs and ministries). In none of these countries are the managers responsible in more than a token sense to groups internal to their own firm. Since each hierarchical level appoints and removes lower-level managers, it is held directly responsible for the success of the level below it. Given the resultant concentration of responsibility at branch-ministry level, it is inevitable that these ministries should interfere in enterprise decisions when major "incorrect" choices would otherwise be made. The degree of such interference varies significantly as between the three CMEA countries examined, but the principle is the same throughout. The national differences reflect both varying conditions and opposing views as to the most appropriate managerial devices for coordinating each specific economy; however, these are the kinds of differences one also finds among large corporations in capitalist countries.

In short, even in Hungary where the market place is used as a major mechanism in the coordination of the actions of the various enterprises, these latter are not truly independent business organizations. While subsidies and tax advantages are one category of device used to alter what would otherwise be market financial pressure compelling particular enterprise actions, still more important in affecting enterprise behavior is the fact that managements must give major consideration to "social aspects" of their decisions which are not internalized in their own financial results. The market place is used as a coordinating device quite similar to that of the intracorporation market for transfers of goods and services among the various units of individual capitalist firms; but it is falsified and weakened as a coordinating device for the identical reasons.

Thus all of the CMEA countries have in common a total absence of self-management of the enterprise in the Yugoslav sense. Even in Hungary, the problem of inciting enterprise managers to take proper risks is unresolved. Economic successes or failures of individual enterprises have their effect primarily on the welfare of society as a whole rather than on that of the employees of the specific unit. Furthermore, this seems unavoidable so long as managerial decision-making power at the enterprise level is legitimized solely by approval at ministerial level.

The absence of the autonomy aspect of self-management has two major negative economic implications. The first is the reduction in static efficiency which arises inevitably both from the lesser quantity and quality of information available at the points of decision making, and from the blurring of authority and responsibility at each managerial level which reduces the potential degree of initiative taken by enterprise management. The second is the inability of the system to offer sufficient permanent wage incentives for the rank-and-file employees of any individual enterprise to encourage them to increase their labor intensity.

These are problems which Yugoslav self-management, legitimized by the doctrine of workers' management, has resolved in principle and to a considerable degree in fact. But the economic costs of this solution have been high. The critically important autonomy element of self-management became significant in Yugoslavia only in 1961, and has really flowered only since 1965; this is the same period in which central national planning essentially disappeared, and in which the central government proved incapable of adopting even such monetary and fiscal means of handling unemployment, inflation, and balance of payments problems as have become conventional in developed capitalist countries the world over.

Since the triumph of self-management, Yugoslavia has suffered from a combination of high unemployment, high emigration, high inflation, a heavy negative balance of payments on current account, and much duplicative investment. The ability to grapple with factors external to the success of the individual enterprise and small region has disappeared. If we put to one side the ability of the communes and, to a lesser degree, of the individual republics to influence the enterprises to consider factors external to them but internal to the small region, the Yugoslav economy is run along Adam Smith lines to a degree which is quite unusual for Europe as a whole. Judged from the viewpoint of conventional western doctrine as to the proper role of the national government, the system would appear at best to be an unregenerate nineteenth century market economy.[1]

Is this an accident of the peculiar nationality problems of Yugoslavia which have made strong federal actions of any type politically unacceptable? Perhaps. I would suggest, however, that the Yugoslav experience has more general significance for socialist economies. The history of Hungary since the January 1968 reforms has shown the strong temptations which exist for any reforming socialist government to revert to its past traditions of central interference and control. The ideology of planning is a powerful one in all socialist economies (including Yugoslavia), and it seems likely to lead to the falsifying of free market conditions by the central government whenever anything goes wrong. Perhaps only a still more powerful counterideology can restrain such actions.

As we have seen, self-management in Yugoslavia is not simply an institutional fact; it is also an ideology, and its adherents are zealous in singling out all heretical actions. Since the principle of self-management autonomy is most likely to be threatened by the federal government, it is not surprising that any federal initiative in the economic sphere should be interpreted as such an attack. Federal decisions cannot be made pragmatically (difficult as it would be to implement even a purely pragmatic decision-making process in the light of the conflicting interests of the

[1] Viewed from a different perspective, however, the system represents a major step toward communism. As the secretary of the commission for self-management of the council of the Confederation of Yugoslav Trade Unions has stated, "the process of the withering away of the state and that of the realization of self-management are in essence one and the same social process, designated by different terms" (N. Jovanov, "Définition théorique de la notion et de l'essence de l'autogestion en Yougoslavie," in *Participation and Self-Management*, papers presented at the December 1972 first international sociological conference on participation and self-management, Institute for Social Research, University of Zagreb, Zagreb: 1972 and 1973, I, 13).

different republics); federal decisions automatically arouse strong ideological opposition. So long as this opposition stems from the dominant and official ideology, it is difficult to see how effective economic policy can be carried out on the national level.

In one sense, my interpretation of the Yugoslav experience with self-management is quite discouraging for its possible proponents in other socialist countries. It suggests that the immediate effects of its introduction elsewhere would likely be more negative than positive. But the longer-run effects may be quite different. If the self-management ideology continues to dominate Yugoslav political thinking, its proponents are likely to become more secure—and thus more tolerant—over time. There seems no reason why self-management cannot be merged with national macroeconomic policy in the same fashion that in western countries private capitalism has been merged with a major economic role for government. But this is a matter of evolution. Acceptance of such a modification of Yugoslav self-management in the early 1970's would, in my view, most probably lead to an emasculation of a genuine market economy and to a return to federal government control.

WORKERS' MANAGEMENT AND "TRUE SOCIALISM"

Workers' management has aroused considerable enthusiasm both in Yugoslavia and in western leftist circles as a means of providing genuine popular control over the working of the economy, as opposed to the "bureaucratic" (i.e., managerial) control which is believed to characterize the socialism of the CMEA countries. The benefits are described as twofold and interconnected: the creation of genuine industrial democracy, and the formation of the conditions for eliminating much of the "alienation" of workers which is found in both capitalist and CMEA-socialist nations.[2]

The analysis in Chapter 12 of the functioning of workers' management in Yugoslav, and particularly in Slovenian, industry suggests that these virtues have been considerably overdrawn by the ideologues. Mass decision making on issues of major importance to the enterprise is a rare event; such matters are normally decided by the general director, and when he is overruled it is by other members of the permanent full-time management of the firm. Only three democratic accomplishments stand out from the interviews. Most important is providing to elected and

[2] The secretary of the commission for self-management of the council of the Confederation of Yugoslav Trade Unions believes that workers' management should also, at least theoretically, provide economic advantages over other social systems, both capitalist and state socialist. In fact, he goes further; in the Marxist tradition of historical analysis, he states that "it is only insofar as it can do so that it can be historically legitimate" (ibid., pp. 11-12).

rotating members of workers' management bodies considerable access to information about the affairs of the enterprise and the alternatives facing it. This informational and educational role can be realized only to the degree that the freely elected workers' management bodies, with their perennially changing composition of membership, have the genuine impression that the results are worth the effort: i.e., that, if it is necessary for the well-being of the enterprise's labor force, they have the power to overturn basic management policies and to dismiss the general director and his top full-time aides. The granting of such power is the second democratic accomplishment. The third is that enterprise decisions affecting individuals are made or reviewed by organs of elected workers' management. The first two accomplishments seem unique to Yugoslavia among European socialist societies; the third, however, may well be common to the CMEA economies as well.[3] Yugoslav sociological studies suggest that the institution of workers' management has up to now not been a particularly effective device for reducing the alienation of manual workers.

If the contributions of workers' management to industrial democracy have not been as impressive as had been hoped, it must be remembered that workers' management functioned only to a limited degree and under most inappropriate conditions before the 1960's. Without genuine self-management by the individual enterprise, there was little which workers' management bodies could decide; thus one would not expect them to have developed significantly. The five to ten years of experience with workers' management under conditions of self-management is scarcely long enough to provide a historical record by which the institution may be judged. The system of frequent rotation of membership of the elected bodies may end by creating a working force which is truly educated in managerial problems and as to the genuine alternatives which are available. Thus one cannot reject the view that the future development of the system will justify its ideologues; but this is for the future and, in my view, probably the rather distant one if ever.

As of today, however, the principal contribution of workers' management has not been along the lines suggested by its proponents. Instead, it has been that of providing the only possible basis for legitimizing the autonomy element of self-management in a socialist society. Yugoslav market socialism, defined as a market place in which *independent* microeconomic units meet, is conceivable only on this basis. If the ideology of workers' management did not underlie the reality of self-management,

---

[3] See the comparison in Chapter 12 between Yugoslavia and the Soviet Union. The statistical data indicate that the two countries may be on a par with regard to the significance of the role of worker representatives within enterprises in making decisions as to individuals.

it would seem quite impossible for society to accept a situation in which workers' earnings differ substantially between enterprises depending upon their market success.[4] In this regard, workers' management must be given the credit for whatever static efficiency and worker-incentive improvements are shown in Yugoslavia as contrasted with the CMEA economies. It must also be credited with helping to create a society with many relatively independent power centers, a political consequence which may be even more significant than the economic results. Similarly, however, the institution must be debited with the country's reduced ability both to handle successfully, through national planning, problems of economic externalities, or to internalize to the enterprise the social criterion of achieving full employment.[5]

Workers' management, with its concomitant of self-management, must also be debited with effects on income distribution which are now arousing new cries of exploitation. Under both capitalism and CMEA-type socialism, the long-run equilibrium tendency is toward equal wages for all employees who have equal skills and who put forth equal effort, wherever they may work in the economy.[6] This is much less sure in Yugoslavia. Since Yugoslav workers' earnings differ between enterprises according to the firms' net income per workers, and since there is no economic incentive for an enterprise to employ additional labor at an income level equal to the worker's marginal product, there is no tendency toward equalization between enterprises of wages for the same skill unless the forces of competition tend to equalize per capita net income of different firms. Chapter 13 suggested that, although such competitive forces are indeed strong in product markets, they are relatively restrained in the capital markets. As a result, richer firms have greater access to capital accumulation than do poorer ones, and income dif-

---

[4] Note that such enterprise differences are quite unacceptable even in Hungary, despite that country's ideological insistence on the importance of attaching workers' interests to those of their enterprises. As a result, substantial overfulfillment of worknorms by piece workers is quite unacceptable to enterprise management both in Hungary and in the G.D.R., and the intensity of worker effort suffers accordingly.

[5] We have seen in Chapter 12 that Yugoslav enterprises appear to be biased, both in theory and in fact, toward capital-intensive types of investment compared to those which would be expected in either a capitalist or CMEA-type socialist economy at a similar level of real wages. This leads to greater unemployment than would otherwise occur.

[6] Monopolies in the labor market interfere with this under capitalism. For considerable periods (over forty years in the case of the Soviet Union), wage differentials transcending those justified by skill and effort variations have existed between different CMEA industries according to their relative planned rates of labor force growth. These differentials have resulted from imperfections in the labor market and lengthy time lags in adjustment.

ferentiation among workers of the same skill in different enterprises may well increase in the future. Furthermore, there are at present clearly much greater differentials paid for the same skill between different enterprises of the same industry than is the case in individual CMEA economies, and probably such differentials are also greater than those found in individual capitalist countries.

Both in CMEA-socialist and in capitalist economies, the basic rule for determining relative wage and salary incomes is that of "income according to work." Only in Yugoslavia, where the workers of each individual enterprise replace both society as a whole and the shareholders of the capitalist firm as the entrepreneur and risk taker, is the system of wage-and-salary distribution fundamentally different, while yet being no closer to the communist doctrine of "to each according to his needs." It should not be surprising that the Yugoslav income-distribution system gives rise to complaints of exploitation of one enterprise by another through the market place.

Furthermore, for the same reason that central planning is today particularly difficult to reconcile with the Yugoslav self-management system, nationally sponsored direct income redistribution presents greater political difficulties than it does in either capitalist or CMEA-socialist societies. Capitalist countries employ the device of progressive income taxes to alter income distribution; this device would be sharply rejected, as counter to the doctrine of self-management, if it were proposed to extend it in Yugoslavia to any substantial proportion of wage earners in even the most prosperous of the republics. CMEA countries carry out national wage policies to increase the relative incomes of low-wage recipients. Aside from setting a minimum wage which is at such a low level as to have no significance for the entire republic of Slovenia, national wage policies are impossible in present-day Yugoslavia. CMEA countries also redistribute income indirectly by means of sharply differentiated sales taxes which favor goods with low income-elasticities of demand. This method of redistribution is also ruled out on any large scale in Yugoslavia by the view that differentiated sales taxes (except for a few luxuries which traditionally are heavily taxed throughout Europe) would represent a major form of interference with the market economy and therefore with self-management. The elimination of such differentiated sales taxes is regarded as a major accomplishment of the 1965 reform.

Thus, judged from the viewpoint of the radical left of America or western Europe, Yugoslav workers' management and self-management should be regarded as constituting an institution which is even less congenial than the CMEA structure of socialism to "appropriate" income distribution. This is quite apart from the fact that self-management has led to still greater emphasis upon material as opposed to moral incentives than has the CMEA economic system.

THE SIGNIFICANCE OF THE FULL-EMPLOYMENT CONSTRAINT

Discussions of the possible evolution of socialist societies from a command-economy (in which detailed plans are given by the center to enterprises) to market socialism have in the past concentrated upon four issues. The principal two are efficiency and the effective transition from one system to another. A third is whether central planners are compelled under market socialism to restrain their objectives to a considerably less detailed welfare function (particularly as to product mix and its distribution among users) than the one to which they have been accustomed. The fourth issue is whether the development of market socialism will lead to the withering away of the power of regional and local Communist Party organs as many of their most important current functions disappear. The latter two issues are political, involving sacrifices by both central and regional authorities if market socialism is to operate effectively.

There is, however, a fifth major issue: namely, the impact of an attempt to maintain microeconomic full employment. If self-management is one of the key ideological ingredients of Yugoslav society, acting as a major constraint on federal regulation of the economy, the concept of socialism as a "workers' state" plays the same role in the CMEA economies. The most significant meaning given there to the term "workers' state" is that employees should be protected not only against the reality of unemployment, but also against the need to change either occupation or place of work under threat of unemployment. Increases in wages as an incentive for changing jobs are fully acceptable, and the high rate of labor turnover in Hungary shows that they are often all too successful (in the view of Hungarian authorities) in this regard; but the stick of dismissal is regarded as proper only to capitalism.

Of course more is involved than pure ideology. In Yugoslavia, self-management serves as a shield behind which the richer republics protect themselves against pressures for income equalization with the south; to a considerable degree, it is a product of the nationality conflicts which are traditional in this country. In the CMEA lands, employees of all types can find great comfort in the fact that they are virtually immune from pressure to undergo job changes which they personally regard, for whatever reason, as reducing their individual welfare. The political unacceptability of dismissals provides workers with a security which is absent even in those capitalist countries with the lowest rates of unemployment. Thus the self-interest of important groups in society provides a political base for these ideological concepts in all four of the countries we have studied.

The ideological full-employment constraint, by reducing the feasible rate of adaptation to changing conditions, must be a force holding back the growth of national output even in an economy such as that of Romania where market socialism has seen very little development. It is most serious, however, in the case of Hungary, the CMEA country which has gone the furthest in attempting to transform its economy into one guided through the market place. For microeconomic full employment seems incompatible with efficient market socialism.

Chapter 8 developed the argument that, in a socialist system where individual enterprises must pay their own way financially, microeconomic full employment can be attained only under conditions of a general sellers' market. But if this is true, then allocation of production capacities among different products, and distribution of intermediate products among consuming enterprises, cannot be accomplished effectively by use of the market place alone. It is not accidental that interference with the free working of the product market has been omnipresent in Hungary.

This suggests that effective market socialism would require the renunciation of a long-standing ideological principle of CMEA socialism, and the sacrifice of a major accomplishment of socialism in these countries. The sacrifice would not be made solely by leadership groups; rather, employees at all levels of the labor force would perceive themselves as sharing in it. The political difficulties in renouncing microeconomic full employment, and in limiting the employment constraint binding on market socialism to that of macroeconomic full employment, can be easily imagined. As of the early 1970's, there have been no serious efforts in Hungary to wrestle with them.

On the other hand, Yugoslavia—the country with the greatest degree of market socialism, and the only one without sellers' markets in intermediate products and capital goods—has rejected both the microeconomic and the macroeconomic constraints of full employment. Its government does not claim to be able to resolve the capitalist problem of macroeconomic unemployment; in fact, it adapts to it in the same fashion as do the less-developed capitalist countries of Europe, namely, through massive migration of its labor force to central and northwest Europe.

It is true that Yugoslav communes and republics go a long way in trying to protect workers from dismissals. Various devices shield firms from bankruptcy and closing. Even if new entrants into the labor force, as well as former private farmers seeking paid work, are allowed to bear the brunt of unemployment, those currently engaged are offered a fair degree of the protection provided in the CMEA countries. Nevertheless, Yugoslavia is alone among the socialist countries of Europe in opting out of the ideological issue of full employment, having substituted for it the equally powerful ideological issue of self-management.

How can even the Yugoslav degree of protection for currently employed workers be accomplished without the creation of a sellers' market? The answer is that different Yugoslav enterprises pay radically varying incomes to workers of the same skill. The slack which is created in capitalist economies through dismissals of redundant workers is created in Yugoslavia by enterprise reductions in real wages. Only in the CMEA countries are neither of these sources of slack available.

CENTRAL PLANNING TO THE LEVEL OF THE ENTERPRISE

Chapter 4 presented the orthodox model of the enterprise for those socialist economies in which central plans are detailed to the level of the firm. In this model, plans are set at a level of difficulty such that a large proportion of enterprises cannot meet them completely; because rewards (particularly high bonuses) for enterprise managers are linked to only one or a few success indicators, managers concentrate on the fulfillment of these indicators. This leads to serious neglect of the other aspects of performance with which central authorities are also concerned. Since managers are rewarded according to their degree of plan fulfillment, and since even 100 percent fulfillment is so difficult to accomplish, managers tend to misinform higher authorities as to their enterprises' potentials for future increases. Finally, because planned targets are increased each year in correspondence with the attained success of individual enterprises, and because bonus payments constitute a highly kinked function of the percentage of plan fulfillment, enterprise managers are reluctant to overfulfill their plan indicators by a substantial margin even in those cases where this is feasible.

The orthodox model was drawn primarily from the experience of planning and plan execution in the Soviet Union, but also from that of Hungary during the 1950's and of Poland. When we place its conclusions into the context of the analysis of Chapter 1 as to MANAGERIAL EFFECTIVENESS in a CMEA-socialist industrial system, the following positive and negative results appear:

(A) Positive Results

(1) A high degree of concentration of enterprise effort on those aspects of performance which are accorded greatest priority by the central managers of the industrial system.[7]

---

[7] The degree of priority may be measured by the reluctance of central authorities to allow performance to fall below the centrally-expected level of realization. However, since an expected level need not necessarily be that specified in the official plan target, the priority concept is difficult to operationalize.

(2) Probably a high degree of intensity of work effort by managerial personnel in the enterprises, at least so long as the degree of PLAN AMBITION (degree of difficulty in achieving the targets for the key success indicators) does not grossly exceed an optimum level.

(B) Negative Results

(1) A high degree of suboptimization by enterprise managers, who concentrate entirely on achieving SPECIFIC INDICATORS of performance which are quantified in their annual plans, at the expense of neglecting aspects of performance which are nonquantified, are of primarily longer-run significance, or which have their main effects upon other enterprises.

(2) A low level of contribution by enterprise managers to the quality of central planning; enterprise managers are given strong incentives to manipulate the information they provide so as to minimize the degree to which their enterprise plan targets will be raised in future years.

Romania. We saw in Chapter 4 that the Romanian enterprise does not appear to follow the orthodox model. A statistical comparison of enterprise performance with plans yielded results sharply at variance with the predictions of the orthodox model. A study of bonus payments as a proportion of managerial base salaries, and an analysis of the degree and timing of changes in the annual plan targets set for enterprises, indicated that key mechanisms of the orthodox model do not apply to Romania.

In contrast to the orthodox model, "economic choices" (the trade-off of gains in one area of performance against losses in another) in Romanian industry seem to be concentrated entirely at ministerial and higher levels. Enterprises (and *centrale*) engage only in technical decision making. Our study of Romania yielded the surprising result that it is indeed possible for an industrial complex employing 1.6 million people to operate in this fashion, and to do so successfully enough to show very high rates of growth of industrial production over a long period. Of course, this method of operation has been employed in a relatively underdeveloped industrial society, and one which produces a fairly simple product mix in long production runs. Nevertheless, Romania has demonstrated that it is feasible to decentralize to the enterprise and *centrala* level no more power than is customarily given in western capitalist firms to foremen and junior managers.

The advantage of this managerial system compared to that of the orthodox model of the socialist enterprise is that the problems which arise in the latter from the concentration upon fulfillment of SPECIFIC INDICATORS of success disappear (see the analysis of Chapter 1). There is, for example, no reason for enterprise managers to neglect product quality or product-mix objectives; the sharp distinction between MEA-

SURED SUCCESS, and those aspects of performance which are not specified in the enterprise's annual plan but are nevertheless considered important by central authorities, becomes a thin and shifting line. Moreover, enterprise and *centrala* managers are freed from the incentive, and often the virtual need, to distort the information sent upward by them for the formation of future plans by their branch ministry and by the State Committee for Planning; thus the quality of their contribution to planning is not reduced in the fashion described in the orthodox model.

Nor does it seem to be the case, as one might have expected from the elevated hierarchical level at which economic decisions are taken, that individual Romanian branch ministries are motivated to act in the fashion predicted for enterprises in the orthodox model. Managerial bonuses are virtually nonexistent at the ministerial level. So too are dismissals and demotions. Ministerial officials are in a position to take what seem to them to be the best decisions, without great regard for the resulting effects on the performance of the ministry in comparison with the narrow standard of the ministry's own specific success indicators.

Finally, the peculiarly feeble state of development in Romania of SIGNALS RATIONALITY in cost, pricing, and other media used as methods of aggregation must be taken into account. This weakness is recognized by Romanians as injurious to the quality of central decision making at ministerial and higher levels. It would be far more serious, however, if decentralized decision making at the level of the enterprise and *centrala* were actively pursued. Given the existing degree of SIGNALS RATIONALITY, and the impossibility of quickly raising it to a qualitatively higher level even if there were no ideological barriers, significant decentralization might have particularly harmful effects.

But the cost of reaping the advantages of their exceedingly centralized system is high, and Romanian authorities appear to have been increasingly unwilling to pay it. Economic decisions are neither prepared nor taken by the enterprises or *centrale*. Decentralization of economic decision making does not exist below the level of the ministry. Not only are many decisions taken at too high a level for the quality of information to be satisfactory but, even more important, many decisions are simply not made at all. It is the total absence of decision making in a large number of cases which is the most serious fault of the system.

Unfortunately, it does not appear feasible to increase the manpower available at the level of the ministries, and in this way expand the potential of the system to take a substantially increased number of minor economic decisions. Already, as estimated in Chapter 2, some 20 to 35 percent of Romanian industry's stock of fully job-trained personnel with higher education, men who have moved a notch beyond the position of an ordinary engineer, are concentrated above the level of the *centrala* (a body which itself has an average labor force of about eight thousand). The manpower investment involved in maintaining this most centralized of socialist industrial systems is already truly formidable.

Another negative feature of the Romanian environment is that it restrains the training of new managerial cadres; those at the enterprise and *centrala* level receive almost no experience in economic decision making. Careers in enterprises and ministries appear to be more distinct from one another than are those in other socialist countries; perhaps this is because it is only by working in a central organization such as a ministry that a manager can gain experience in making economic choices.

A further problem is that the betterment of SIGNALS RATIONALITY depends primarily upon the improvement of detailed cost and pricing information which can be developed only at the individual enterprise and *centrala* level. Yet personnel working here have little incentive to invest time in such improvement, since they themselves seldom really utilize such data.

Finally, intensity of managerial effort in the enterprises and *centrale* is restrained by the system. Managers in these units cannot truly be held responsible for their results, and they perceive this fact anew each year when the criteria of judgment (the plan indices) are altered during the operating year and even at its very end. Only managers at the ministry levels have the authority which makes possible the assignment to them of genuine responsibility; enterprise and *centrala* managers unquestionably feel this and respond accordingly.[8]

The German Democratic Republic. Enterprises and *Kombinate* in the G.D.R. also differ sharply in their operation from the pattern depicted by the orthodox model of the socialist enterprise, but for reasons radically different from those which apply to Romania. There is considerable decentralization of authority and responsibility to the enterprise and *Kombinat* level, but the way in which they are exercised seems to bear a closer resemblance to that found in American decentralized companies than to that of the orthodox model and of Soviet industry. It should be noted that this is not simply a result of the fact that the G.D.R.

---

[8] An example can be seen in the performance of the directors and general directors of *centrale* and large enterprises at an eleven-week full-time course which they attended at the Romanian national Management Development Center. My observation of some of their sessions in 1970 showed that these students did very little of the required preparation for the classes, and that they seemed to take their attendance at the course as somewhat of a holiday. Yet this was the first exposure that the vast majority of these quite senior men had ever had to formal managerial training; furthermore, national authorities had demonstrated how seriously they regarded these courses by bringing into them about 16 percent of the general directors of all *centrale* in the country during the single year of 1970— absenting them from their posts for one-fifth of the year.

is the most developed of the CMEA countries; the administration of large industrial corporations in Britain and France is typically quite different from that of their counterparts in the United States.[9]

The description of the East German system given here applies particularly to the situation in that country through 1970. As was pointed out in Chapter 7, changes introduced during 1971 and 1972 modify this description. While both the extent and duration of this modification are unclear, it would seem that the most important mutation of the system consists of the reduction of the power of enterprises and *Kombinate*, and the decrease of the influence of financial criteria in general, in determining the output composition of any given branch of industry.

The role of central administration (VVB, ministry, and above) in East Germany must be sharply differentiated according to whether specific enterprise products and tasks are defined as "structure determining." The output of such products and the performance of these tasks are planned in considerable detail from the center, and enterprises and *Kombinate* seem in reality—and not just in theory—to be prohibited from exercising trade-offs on their own responsibility. The quantitative significance of such central planning is shown by the estimate of Chapter 5 that something on the order of twice the Romanian proportion of the industrial labor force is occupied in the G.D.R. with the coordination of the activities of operating units.

However, despite the importance of detailed central planning in the case of structure-determining products, all or virtually all enterprises are directly affected in their work by the less centralized mechanisms of planning. Many and probably most enterprises produce no structure-determining products nor have any structure-determining tasks, and few if any produce only structure-determining products.

For nonstructure-determining items, enterprises and *Kombinate* receive annual plan targets which place great emphasis on aggregative financial indicators, and particularly on that of profit. The planning of product mix, and to a lesser extent, of material inputs, is to a considerable degree left to these operating units. It is true that their recommendations are coordinated by "product groups" located in whichever VVB is the main producer of these items,[10] but the planning initiative and responsibility are taken by the operating units—a situation which differs sharply from that of Romania.

Although the individual enterprise and *Kombinat* receive SPECIFIC

---

[9] D. Granick, *Managerial Comparisons of Four Developed Countries: France, Britain, United States, and Russia* (The M.I.T. Press, Cambridge, Mass. and London: 1972), chapters 2, 3, and 13.

[10] Physically, such product groups often work out of the headquarters of individual *Kombinate* or even of their member enterprises.

INDICATOR targets of success,[11] and although the bonus fund of the enterprise—which is distributed among all its members—depends upon the fulfillment and overfulfillment of these success indicators, this situation is similar in only a formal sense to that depicted in the orthodox model of the socialist enterprise. First of all, the size of bonus award paid to the enterprise depends less upon the indicators[12] to which maximum bonus is attached than upon those whose fulfillment is a precondition of maximum bonus payment, and for which there is no reward at all for overfulfillment.[13] Thus there is little bonus reward to the enterprise as a whole from overfulfillment of plan indicators; the whole emphasis is upon fulfillment rather than overfulfillment of these SPECIFIC INDICATORS.

The experience of those enterprises and *Kombinate* in which I interviewed during 1970 suggests that SPECIFIC INDICATORS are not set at exceedingly ambitious levels, and that even rather mediocre performers can normally fulfill at least the total output target.[14] PLAN AMBITION does not seem to categorize East German planning.[15]

Second and more important, the enterprise bonus fund has only limited significance in motivating the top managers of enterprises and *Kombinate*. Data as to the sources of bonuses paid to three enterprise general directors for 1969 results show that the bulk are paid not from the enterprise bonus fund but rather from the VVB bonus fund. While the size of the enterprise bonus fund has been important to top managers insofar as it allows them to reward, and so retain, ordinary personnel of the enterprise, the force of this consideration must have been greatly diminished in 1972 when the guaranteed bonus fund per employee was raised to 80 percent of the total planned for the enterprise for the year. Thus it is really the bonus distributed by the VVB which is the one of major significance to the directors of enterprises and *Kombinate*.

[11] Profit must be considered as such a specific indicator in the East German context. Since an enterprise's aggregate revenue is a function of the prices it receives for its products, and since these prices reflect only standard costs rather than the equilibrating of supply and demand, profit maximization by the enterprise—whatever may be the set of constraints to which it is subject—cannot be regarded as an optimizing procedure when judged from the viewpoint of central authorities.

[12] One indicator until 1972, and two thereafter.

[13] Such side conditions for planned payments to the enterprise bonus fund were eliminated in 1972. At the same time, however, their influence on above-plan payments to the bonus fund was further strengthened.

[14] Even the garment enterprise of Chapter 6, whose performance in 1969 was so poorly regarded that no managerial bonuses at all were paid there for that year, was able to meet 100 percent of its annual production target.

[15] M. Keren and others take a different view of the subject for the period after 1968. The figures of Chapter 7 as to the extraordinarily high proportion of industrial enterprises which met their sales targets during 1972 and 1973 are counter-evidence to their view.

As we saw in Chapter 6, top-management bonuses are quite high as a proportion of base income; in this sense, they are similar to the bonuses of the orthodox model, to those of the Soviet Union, and to those typically paid to divisional management in large American corporations. But while the orthodox model and the apparent practice in the Soviet Union both link such bonuses to the degree of plan fulfillment of SPECIFIC INDICATORS, East German practice is like the American in that these bonuses are not directly attached to MEASURED SUCCESS. Instead, East German and American corporate bonuses are determined on subjective grounds in terms of the superior's judgment of overall performance.

Thus SPECIFIC INDICATORS are robbed of much of their importance in East Germany, just as they are in the typical American corporation. In neither case is managerial income tied to them, although gross underfulfillment would certainly be punished. There is no reward as such for their overfulfillment, and both East German and American managers tend to avoid this.

Instead, both East German enterprise directors and American divisional managers seem to operate in the same fashion: they appear to "satisfice" in the sense of fulfilling 100 percent of their SPECIFIC INDICATOR targets, and of using their remaining resources to maximize aspects of performance which are not detailed in the plan targets set for them.[16] The contribution of these managers to effective planning by higher officials constitutes an important element of this second type of performance, and one which seems to be recognized as a significant criterion in promotion. In this fashion, both countries' managerial systems seem to reduce to a minimum the suboptimizing behavior which was discussed in Chapter 1 as being induced by MEASURED-SUCCESS REWARD.

The "satisficing" managerial approach appears particularly fitting for the G.D.R. in view of the top leadership's considerable emphasis upon the development of new capital equipment products. Of all the CMEA countries, it is the G.D.R. which has to the greatest extent visualized its role in intrabloc trade as the providing of machinery which, in terms both of its modernity and quality, is unavailable from other CMEA sources. Since the G.D.R. has few "hard goods" (raw materials and foodstuffs) to export, and must import these from other CMEA countries by persuading them to accept precisely those types of goods (machinery) which are least wanted within the bloc market,[17] East Germany has

---

[16] See Granick, chapter 2 for an elaboration of the contrast between American corporate satisficing-planning and Soviet maximizing-planning.

[17] In 1971, 56 percent of the G.D.R.'s total exports, compared to only 33 percent of total imports consisted of machinery and equipment. Net exports (defined as gross exports minus gross imports) of such machinery and equipment constituted 21 percent of the country's total gross exports; net imports of "hard goods" were

every reason to emphasize the modernity of its products. Although the G.D.R. shares with Czechoslovakia the position of the most developed of the socialist countries, it has differed considerably from Czechoslovakia in its emphasis upon the importance of developing new technology. During at least the latter half of the 1960's, the East German central leadership seems to have been much more concerned with attaining such modernity than with achieving maximum rates of production growth. The importance for system structure of the G.D.R.'s modernity goal is that the difficulty of bringing new products into production has been one of the major problems predicted for economies organized along the lines of the orthodox model of the centrally planned socialist enterprise, and that such difficulty has in fact been a major characteristic of civilian industry in the Soviet Union during the postwar period.

Partly, introduction of new models has been accomplished in the G.D.R. through centralized planning of structure-determining tasks. Partly, it has been done by allowing the producing enterprises to share in the cost economies achieved by consuming firms through their use of the more modern equipment—and, more significant than the sharing itself, to retain all of their share of these economies for their bonus funds. Most important of all, enterprises and *Kombinate* are not faced with ambitious targets for SPECIFIC INDICATORS (including profits), nor do they attempt to overfulfill these targets; thus they have resources available for fulfilling such unmeasured-performance objectives as the rapid introduction of new models.

Aside from the realization of plans for structure-determining products and tasks, East German enterprises and *Kombinate* have been permitted considerable flexibility in achieving their principal MEASURED SUCCESS objectives of profit and total sales. Interviews have suggested that significant autonomy has been left to them—certainly in contrast to Romanian enterprises and *centrale*—in the realization of these composite planning targets. The role of the banking system in the G.D.R. appears to be peculiarly great (by the standard of CMEA countries other than Hungary) in the supervision of production units and even in the planning of industrial investments, and the Industry and Trade Bank is strongly biased toward laying primary emphasis upon financial results.

---

more than the 22 percent of total gross imports which are accounted for by the categories of agricultural, mining, and forestry products, plus the semifinished products of basic industry (*Statistisches Jahrbuch der Deutschen Demokratischen Republik 1972*, Staatsverlag der D.D.R., Berlin: 1972, pp. 302 and 306, and *Jahrbuch 1973*, p. 301).

For a discussion of hard-good and soft-good trade within the CMEA bloc, see S. Ausch, *Theory and Practice of CMEA Cooperation* (Akadémiai Kiadó, Budapest: 1972), especially chapter 7.

The system of pricing also seems unusually rational for CMEA countries,[18] yielding a *relatively* high degree of SIGNALS RATIONALITY. Thus, for the major elements of industry which are not defined as structure-determining, decentralization has been a marked feature of East German management. However, it must be said that the changes introduced in 1971 and 1972 seem to have reduced the degree of autonomy of enterprises and *Kombinate*, most particularly in the choice of products.

Just as the bonus system for middle and upper managers is more similar to that of large American corporations than it is to that depicted in the orthodox model of the socialist enterprise or observed in Soviet experience, so too does career progression in East Germany seem to come closest to the American model. Demotions are an accepted part of the managerial milieu. Upper executives, reaching even as high as the VVBS, appear to be unusually young by international standards—and there appears to be considerable justified belief among managers in the possibility of rapid advancement. Career planning for selected industrial executives is done much more carefully in the G.D.R., and with considerably greater attention to providing experience in a variety of functions, than in any other country which I have observed aside from the United States.

The relative similarity of both the managerial bonus systems and the managerial career patterns in the G.D.R. and in large decentralized American corporations helps to reinforce the tendency of industrial managers in both economies to maximize a somewhat vague combination of the unquantified, and often unspecified, objectives of central planners of the organization, subject to constraints as to the fulfillment of SPECIFIED INDICATOR targets. The similarity of this managerial behavior in East German industrial organizations and in component divisions of large American corporations, and its distinction from managerial behavior in other countries of either eastern or western Europe, show that organizational behavior can to a considerable degree be divorced from the total socioeconomic system. The common characteristics of East German and American managerial behavior derive from the linking of the managerial reward system in both countries more to subjective appreciation by superiors than to objective results compared to target. The relatively low degree of MEASURED-SUCCESS REWARD permits them to function in a

[18] Although producers' prices are established on the basis of planned costs, as is primarily the case in the other two CMEA countries studied as well, the G.D.R. is the only one of the three countries which includes in these prices only a charge on capital and not on labor. (See Chapter 9, footnote 3 for a discussion of the two-channel tax.) The G.D.R. is also the only one which has established a system for continual downward revision of these prices as the technology of production improves.

fashion fundamentally different from that postulated in the orthodox model of the socialist enterprise or observed in the Soviet Union.

The materials allocation system. Probably the most surprising result of my interviews in Hungary was discovering the apparent unimportance of the ending of central allocation of materials to individual enterprise. The overnight abandonment in January 1968 of the vast majority of such allocations had none of the disruptive influence on the economy which might have been predicted. Nor, at the end of three years, could I observe any of the expected advantages of such abolition. It is as though the formal materials allocation system in CMEA countries were just an excrescence on the centrally planned system which has no effect other than to waste manpower.

As was pointed out in Chapter 10, it would appear from Hungarian experience that an informal rationing system for intermediate products and capital goods can successfully replace the formal system used in the other CMEA countries. One might well postulate that such a substitution works best where the structure of industry does not change radically, and that it is thus most appropriate for a relatively short period of years; one might also postulate that it would tend to restrain rapidity of adjustment of the product mix of final products to the demands of the internal and export markets. Nevertheless, the fact that this informal system has operated effectively in Hungary under conditions of a sellers' market for a period of at least three years does suggest that formal materials allocation may be a less essential part of centralized planning than has been thought.

THE REWARD SYSTEM FOR MANAGEMENT

As was seen in Chapter 14, all four of the east European countries offer low financial rewards to management (relative to the earnings of the average industrial employee in their own country) when comparison is made with western continental Europe or the United States. In Hungary, where the monetary rewards to top enterprise managers are the highest among the east European countries studied, the effect of this higher reward pattern on managerial behavior is offset by the lower promotional opportunities for managers and by the reduced danger of demotion.

If comparison is made with American industry, east European enterprise managers appear to operate under conditions of peculiarly low pressure. Their career patterns show much greater stability in post than is the case for their American counterparts; their salary rewards for avoiding demotion or receiving promotion are relatively meager compared to those observed in western continental Europe or the United States; their fluctuating bonuses constitute a much smaller proportion of income (except perhaps in the G.D.R.) than they do in the USSR or in the United States. This unique combination would seem to permit managers in eastern Europe to exercise greater personal discretion in responding to pressures from their superiors or from the economic environment than is the case elsewhere.

The ability to use such personal discretion stands out particularly strongly in the response to MEASURED-SUCCESS REWARD, and this fact is highly relevant to the degree of compelling power inherent in SPECIFIC INDICATORS laid down by central authorities. For, as was argued in Chapter 1, the degree of emphasis upon MEASURED-SUCCESS REWARD in an organization depends upon a combination of career patterns, bonuses, and the degree of income differentiation among the different levels of professional and managerial personnel. (Income differentiation is the only one of the three which does not discriminate between behavior which is directed toward achieving quantified measures of performance and that which is aimed at other aspects of performance which are not quantified in plans. Its importance is solely that greater income differentiation increases the significance of promotions, and enhances the importance of career patterns as compared to bonuses.)

What is critical about the criteria for upper management bonuses in eastern Europe is that they do not follow the Soviet Union's pattern of maintaining a regular relationship between the amount of bonus and the fulfillment of specified indicators of performance. Rather, they are financed primarily out of branch ministry (rather than enterprise) bonus funds and they are discretionary. In awarding bonuses to enterprise managers, top ministerial personnel use subjective rather than objective criteria. Thus the distribution of managerial bonuses is much more similar to the pattern found in decentralized American companies than to that of the USSR.

It is, of course, extremely difficult to determine the criteria used for promotion and demotion of managers in different countries. What can be observed, however, is that the length of tenure in post of east European managers is striking by standards of American industry. This is most so in Hungary. Here it is clear that there has been no hasty career reward or punishment for success or failure in meeting designated targets. In the country where the tenure in post is probably shortest (the G.D.R.), the pattern of managerial moves most resembles that of American industrial corporations, where promotions and demotions are determined more by an evaluation of managerial potential than by quantified measures of performance.

MISCELLANEOUS COMPARISONS

The private sector. There is little relationship between the degree of centralization in the economy and the relative importance of the non-state sector.[19] Only in Yugoslavia does agriculture consist primarily of private peasant farms. Only in the G.D.R. was a large proportion (one-fourth) of the industrial labor force employed until 1972 in the private and semiprivate sector. These important variants from the pattern of socialist ownership of the means of production exist for historical and political rather than economic reasons.

Coordination of supply. Similarly, only the G.D.R. and Yugoslavia have been successful in utilizing very small enterprises, socialist or not, to provide the flexibility so important for any industrial system. In both of these countries, small firms play a significant subcontracting role for the larger enterprises.

In contrast, Romanian small firms are under regional jurisdiction, and they devote themselves essentially to producing final goods needed in their own districts. Hungarian subcontracting by small firms (cooperatives in this country) was only poorly developed at the time of the reform; although there has been expansion of their subcontracting role after 1967, this had not even begun to reach the East German level as of the end of 1970.

[19] Recent official data are available for the proportion of the industrial and industrial-handicraft labor force in the CMEA countries employed in cooperative, private, and (in the case of the G.D.R.) semiprivate enterprises. Romania (1970) has 8 percent, Hungary (1971) 17 percent, and the G.D.R. (1971) 27 percent. By the fall of 1972, after the nationalization of the vast majority of private, semi-private, and cooperative firms in East German industry and industrial handicrafts, the G.D.R. figure was reduced to 11 percent. The Romanian figure (as well as the other Romanian one given below in this note) is presumably a minor understatement compared to Hungary and the G.D.R., since only the Romanian excludes small-scale private firms. The above figures lump together industry and industrial handicrafts since these are not separated in the Romanian or Hungarian yearbooks. For industry alone in the G.D.R., the comparable figures are 16 percent (1971) and 2 percent (fall 1972).

There is also no clear relationship between the degree of centralization of management and the extent to which industry is administered by national ministries. In order to calculate the latter, we must add to the above percentages for nonstate industry the proportion of the state-employed industrial labor force which is administered by local councils rather than by national ministries. Unfortunately, estimates for ministerially administered industry as a percentage of total (whether or not state owned) must be based on old data for Hungary and the G.D.R.; the Hungarian data, in particular, substantially antedate the reform. These figures, for what they are worth, are the following: Romania (1970) 82 percent; Hungary (1960) 73 percent; the G.D.R. (1967) 63 percent. (All percentages are computed from the national statistical yearbooks except for the Hungarian 1960 percentage. This last comes from Frederic L. Pryor, *Property and Industrial Organization in Communist and Capitalist Nations*, Indiana University Press, Bloomington and London: 1973, p. 238.)

Subcontracting in Yugoslavia is no more surprising than in any other market economy. But the East German success in developing this important function demonstrates that subcontracting by small firms can be made to operate successfully within the framework of a centrally planned, primarily nonmarket economy. It represents a triumph for the G.D.R.'s system of product groups, in which much of both the product mix of output and the distribution of inputs is planned by other than central authorities.

All three of the CMEA countries rely heavily upon producer ministries or enterprises to determine both the product mix and distribution of intermediate products and capital goods. But here the similarity ends. In Romania and the G.D.R., but not in Hungary, the allocation and product mix of the most important products are determined by central authorities above the level of the producing ministry; this highly centralized system automatically shifts conflicts between consuming and producing organizations to decision by a neutral body which has no stake (in the form of the effect upon its own plan fulfillment) in the outcome.

In Romania, the vast majority of the large number of remaining decisions are made by the producing ministry. The *centrale* and enterprises play no significant role here. Such centralization to the ministry level is viewed as a means of providing the decision-making process with some insulation from the special interests of individual producing units; it is apparently believed that officials at the ministry level will adopt a more objective standpoint in terms of the welfare of the economy as a whole.

The G.D.R. goes much further, entrusting the VVBs—and even many *Kombinate* and enterprises—with this allocative task. The risk of ignoring the interests of consuming branches is much greater in this procedure, although the apparent absence of taut planning, and the concern of the producing units with other than measured aspects of performance, provide some protection. But the gain is substantial in that widespread subcontracting by small firms would be quite impossible without a decentralized allocation system.

Hungary has no formal system of materials allocations, and central state authorities appear to play only a negligible role here. But the existence of a sellers' market implies that product-mix and allocation decisions cannot be ground out automatically by the market system. In fact, the individual producing enterprises constitute the mainstay of the informal allocative system.

Price changes. Both Romania and the G.D.R. use a price system in which the overwhelming mass of prices are set by higher authorities, or at least cannot be changed without their permission. Both Hungary and Yugoslavia share the ideal of prices which are established automatically through the clearing of the relevant product markets; in both cases, a large proportion of prices are in fact subject to change only with permission of a central price office.

Thus, in theory, Romania and the G.D.R. constitute one common group of countries with regard to pricing, while Hungary and Yugoslavia constitute a second. In fact, however, Hungary is much more similar to the first group than to Yugoslavia. The role of the price office in Yugoslavia has been sufficiently formalistic so that this body has constituted only the most minor of obstacles to a galloping open inflation. Even during 1971, when a total price freeze was supposedly in effect, the cost of living rose by 16 percent. In Hungary, the unofficial as well as official pressure of the price office has led to considerable stability of prices.

The monetization of export decisions. Although all four countries have been concerned with improving direct contacts between exporting production units and foreign importers, as well as with giving production units more freedom in their choice of goods to export, only Hungary and Yugoslavia have granted their firms freedom to choose whether and how much to export. Only enterprises in these two latter countries may determine whether exports are worth their opportunity cost in terms of foregone sales on the domestic market.

Surprisingly, true monetization of exports seems to have gone further in Hungary than in Yugoslavia. This is because it is Yugoslavia which has a closer and more comprehensive linkage between the exports and imports of individual enterprises; generally speaking, Yugoslav industrial exports to convertible currency countries are made so as to finance the exporting enterprise's own imports, rather than in terms of a calculation of direct export profits. While this is also to some degree true in Hungary, it is my impression that the element of "barter" on the enterprise level is considerably less widespread there.

However, profit calculations as to the net effect of an individual enterprise's foreign trade transactions on its own total profit-and-loss statement are more likely to be consistent with those for the national economy in the Yugoslav case. Both countries use a single rate of exchange for exports by all sectors to a given foreign currency market, and export subsidies in both are quite differentiated among export branches. Where the countries differ is that export subsidies appear to be much more differentiated to the individual enterprise level in Hungary, in spite of the Hungarian effort in 1971 to reduce such differentiation. As a result, Hungarian profit calculations serve as a weaker guide to the national advantage, with regard to having exports carried out by one enterprise rather than another, than do profit calculations by Yugoslav enterprises.

All in all, I would guess that Yugoslavia does better than Hungary in exporting those goods in which it has a comparative advantage. The relatively narrow mark-up of 25 percent over the official rate of exchange, which one Yugoslav enterprise was paying to another in 1970 for the purchase of convertible currency, is my main basis for this judgment.

Decentralization of investment decisions. Both in Hungary and Yugoslavia, a high proportion of investment decisions are decentralized to the enterprise level. It is true that such decentralization is reduced de facto in Yugoslavia by the predominant role of bank financing, and by the fact that banks give heavy weight in their choice of borrowers to considerations of the economic welfare of the communes in which the specific bank primarily functions. In Hungary, the high weight of self-finance in gross industrial fixed investment—about 55 percent in 1970 as compared with 30 percent in Yugoslavia—is somewhat deceptive; informal controls, and in particular the power of the Hungarian National Bank to determine compulsory allocation of individual enterprises' sources of self-finance to the repayment of bank loans made for working capital purposes, reduce the apparent degree of enterprise autonomy. Nevertheless, the degree of decentralization of investment decision making in both countries is striking when compared with that in other socialist nations.

While decentralization is not surprising in the case of the Yugoslav self-managed enterprise, it is remarkable for Hungary. One might have expected that a centrally planned economy would keep the levers of investment decision making in central hands, since the composition of national investment is the most important factor in determining the future sectoral structure of production. De jure, however, Hungarian central planners have been willing to give up most of this power; even de facto, they have renounced a considerable portion of it.

Neither Hungary nor Yugoslavia has gone far in creating a normal capital market for the transfer of internal investment funds between sectors. But Yugoslavia, which because of the greater independence of its enterprises is much more in need of a capital market, has realized a considerable degree of intersectoral transfer of funds through the expansion of individual enterprises into different sectors of the economy, and after 1968 through mergers. Thus, in fact, a partial substitute for a capital market has developed there. The prime difficulty with it is that it is highly compartmentalized, only quite exceptionally cutting across republics or autonomous regions. This difficulty is particularly limiting in Yugoslavia because of the great differentiation of economic development between the various regions of the country.

DECENTRALIZATION OF AUTHORITY TO THE PRODUCTION UNIT, AND THE CHANGE IN SIZE OF THIS UNIT

During the second half of the 1960's, the G.D.R. and Hungary have seen considerable devolution of authority from central administrative bodies to production units. In Yugoslavia, self-management of the enterprise has flowered during this period. Even in Romania there has been much talk of devolution of authority, although it has not yet been realized.

In Hungary, however, this devolution was preceded by the concentration of existing enterprises into a far smaller number of large ones. In the G.D.R., the devolution of authority was accompanied by the creation of large *Kombinate* which took over the power of those enterprises merged into them. Romania has seen more merger (through the creation of *centrale*) than devolution of centralized authority. Even in Yugoslavia, the flowering of self-management after 1965 was followed in 1969 by what appears to have been a major merger movement, although nothing on the scale of what has occurred in the other three countries.

Thus, while there has been a reduction during the 1960's in the degree of detailed control over the economy by central authorities, these years have also seen a reduction in the responsibility and authority of management at the individual factory level. It is the intermediate bodies— the merged enterprises in Hungary and Yugoslavia, the *Kombinate* in the G.D.R., and the *centrale* in Romania—which are the heirs of authority both from above and below. This is a path also followed in other socialist countries which we have not studied in this book; even the Soviet Union legislated a move along it in 1973.

When one points to the potential efficiency gains from the economic reforms, both in information processing and in improving the initiative and morale of managers at lower hierarchical levels of industrial organization, and to the potential losses from poorer national coordination (particularly so long as prices remain relatively controlled and the market system remains inefficient), one must remember that the CMEA countries have hedged their bets by a process of massive concentration. Within each of the new units created through merger, the "command system" of planning and administration is tighter than had been the case prior to the reforms. In all of these countries, decentralization at one level has been accompanied by centralization at another. Certainly both Hungary and East Germany depend much more than previously upon the market system to coordinate different industries; but within individual industries, the position is ambiguous. Even in terms of coordination between industries, the possibilities of informal central control in the CMEA countries have been considerably enhanced by industrial concentration.

Failure to realize the magnitude and significance of these mergers must inevitably lead to misunderstanding the various national economic reforms, and to considerable overstatement of the degree of growth in the importance of markets in eastern Europe.

EVALUATION OF THE ECONOMIC REFORMS

Our comparison of industrial operations in four east European socialist countries does not point to any firm relationship between national economic efficiency and the degree of decentralization and monetization through the market place. It is true that the country with the highest rate of industrial growth in the 1960's was Romania—the economy with by far the greatest centralization and the least monetization. Yugoslavia, standing far at the other extreme of the institutional continuum, is unique in the degree to which it has suffered during this period from both unemployment and inflation. But no efficiency conclusions should be drawn from these facts; too many elements both of factor inputs and of outputs are ignored in such simple-minded international comparisons. My only analysis of the results of the reforms has been a comparison of the Hungarian record before and after January 1968; here there has been no dramatic effect sufficient to demonstrate unambiguously an improvement or worsening of efficiency.

Nor is this really surprising. Reform-type modifications of a centralized socialist system may be expected to have different results depending upon the total societal and economic environment. Within the CMEA framework, there is not even a unidirectional effect of the reforms on the efficiency of information processing or on the localization of authority to the operating level.

All three of the CMEA countries appear to suffer seriously from a lack of incentive given to the enterprise labor force to increase its work intensity. There is no indication that the Hungarian reform has ameliorated this situation. Only the Yugoslav system appears to provide such an incentive, and the costs of this are very high in terms of the absence of even that degree of national planning which has become commonplace in developed capitalist countries. There has been very little success anywhere in replacing the incentives inherent in a capitalist economy with a new set of socialist incentives.

When we look at the two most market-oriented socialist economies—Hungary and Yugoslavia—it is clear that the real issue as to the efficiency of centralized versus decentralized systems is that of the political-social constraints on the functioning of markets. The Hungarian market system has been hampered by a microeconomic full employment constraint and by an anti-inflation constraint; these have compelled it to function in an environment of disequilibrium sellers' markets, and have prevented it from providing significant incentives for profit improvement either to the workforce or to the managers of individual enterprises. The blossoming of the Yugoslav market system has been made possible only by a rigid interpretation of the doctrine of self-management; this, in turn, has prevented the federal government from dealing successfully with those market results which are externalities to the individual enterprise and commune.

One can make a strong case for the view that, in the short run, it is the most modest of the reform systems—that of the G.D.R.—which has been the most successful. For this is the only one of the three which has established a reform system that is perhaps fully viable within the existing societal constraints.[20]

Of course, this tells us nothing as to the likely efficiency results in the future of either the Hungarian or Yugoslav versions of market socialism. Both systems are quite young in their present form, dating only from 1968 and 1965 respectively. With time, the sociopolitical constraints of the two systems may be either softened or abandoned. If this were to occur, efficiency in the sense of improvement in factor productivity might be expected to increase substantially. But such a development would require major modification of the social welfare functions of these two societies. It is by no means clear that this will occur.

More than two decades ago, von Mises argued that even the most decentralized socialism must be inherently inefficient in the way that it uses factors of production. He based his case on what amounted to the system's constraint of eliminating private ownership of the means of production. In light of this constraint, he held that market socialism offers no solution to the inefficiencies which are found in centralized, command-economy socialism.[21]

East European experience since the middle of the 1960's does not provide us with any real guidance in evaluating von Mises' verdict on

[20] The viability of even the East German reform is denied by Keren, who writes of its at least temporary demise (M. Keren, "The New Economic System in the GDR: an Obituary," *Soviet Studies*, XXIV, 4, 1973, pp. 554-87).

[21] See the excerpt by L. von Mises, "Economic Calculation in Socialism," in M. Bornstein (ed.), *Comparative Economic Systems* (2nd edition, Richard D. Irwin, Homewood, Illinois: 1969), pp. 61-67. This is taken from von Mises' 1951 study, *Socialism: An Economic and Sociological Analysis* (Yale University Press, New Haven: 1951), which in turn is an expanded translation of *Die Gemeinwirtschaft* (1922).

market socialism. The political-social constraints which I have emphasized are sufficient to account for whatever lack of success has been observed. Given these constraints, certainly less intrinsic to socialism than the elimination of private ownership of the means of production, it appears to me that von Mises' verdict—if not his reasoning—was justified. The question we are left with is whether these constraints, or substitutes which end up as equally constricting, will prove to be permanent features of socialism.

Library of Congress Cataloging in Publication Data

Granick, David.
  Enterprise guidance in Eastern Europe.

  Includes index.
  1. Industrial management—Europe, Eastern—Case studies. I. Title.
HD70.E7G68   658.4'00949   75-2992
ISBN 0-691-04209-8